A HISTORY OF MODERN POETRY

From the 1890s to the High Modernist Mode

A HISTORY OF
MODERN POETRY

From the 1890s to
the High Modernist Mode

DAVID PERKINS

THE BELKNAP PRESS OF

HARVARD UNIVERSITY PRESS

Cambridge, Massachusetts, and London, England

Library of Congress Cataloging in Publication Data

Perkins, David.
  A history of modern poetry.

  Includes index.
  1. English poetry—20th century—History and
criticism. 2. American poetry—20th century—History
and criticism. 3. English poetry—19th century—
History and criticism. 4. American poetry—19th century
—History and criticism. I. Title.
PR610.P4   821′.009   76-6874
ISBN 0-674-39941-2 (cloth)
ISBN 0-674-39945-5 (paper)
Acknowledgments begin on page 603

TO
W. JACKSON BATE

PREFACE

THIS is the first of two volumes presenting the history of English and American poetry in the twentieth century. It covers the formative period during which the Romantic traditions of the past were abandoned or transformed and a major new literature created. The second volume, *From the 1920s to the Present,* will complete the history. The volumes divide in the mid-twenties because by this time what I have called the high Modernist mode was established and major works in that mode—*The Waste Land, Harmonium,* Lawrence's *Birds, Beasts, and Flowers,* Williams' *Spring and All,* Pound's *A Draft of XVI Cantos*—had been published; the next generation of poets, including W. H. Auden, Dylan Thomas, and Hart Crane, was about to step forward.

Although the twentieth century is three-quarters over, the history of modern poetry has not thus far been presented with the amplitude and detail it deserves. At least a hundred and thirty poets are distinctly treated in this first volume, and many more are noticed in passing. Opposed and evolving assumptions about poetry are traced, and the book also considers the effects on poetry of its changing audiences, of premises and procedures in literary criticism, of the publishing outlets poets could hope to use, and the interrelations of poetry with developments in the other arts—the novel, painting, film, music—as well as in social, political, and intellectual life. And so far as is possible, the poetry of the British Isles and the United States is seen in interplay rather than separately. The main single influence on both sides of the Atlantic over the last fifty years has, in each case, been the writing of the other country.

To consider literary history on this breadth of scale is to attain a more inclusive, impartial, and complex understanding than can be obtained when we focus, as we usually do, on only a few writers or on particular types of verse. The modern movement as a whole is extraordinarily rich and diverse. Our need now is to gain perspective over the whole field. A broader scale of treatment makes it possible to reconstruct historical contexts in detail.

While looking back from the vantage ground of our own time, I have also tried to present the poetic milieu as it was seen by poets and readers then and, by studying the literary past through the eyes of the writers for whom it was contemporary, to understand better why their work took the directions it did. In short, the effort here is to portray the dramatic diversity and interplay of the different kinds of poetry that make up the modern movement as a whole, as well as to note the accomplishment and distinct contribution, in their time, of individual poets.

One fundamental purpose of this book is to go behind the interpretation of modern literary history that has been current for the last forty years. In this respect it may seem to fit in with the contemporary reaction, both in England and America, against the long hegemony of high Modernist poetry and criticism. But the purpose is not polemical. I have aimed to present each poet and type of poetry sympathetically. To do this compels a partial supression of one's own critical personality. But understanding and sympathy do not preclude evaluation.

This book is written both for the general public and for students. Many of the poets and movements it takes up have been discussed at far greater length in works devoted to them as a special subject; on some there are hundreds of books and monographs. I am enormously indebted to these specialized studies, but it would be idle to hope that the authors of them will be completely satisfied by my synoptic treatment. Nevertheless, there is some consolation in what Goethe had the theater director say in the Introduction to *Faust*, "Wer vieles bringt, wird manchem etwas bringen." Since no one can be a specialist in the whole field covered by this book, I hope that most readers may find some portions of it to be of fresh interest, and that the perspective of the whole context may throw new light even on the most familiar writers.

To know where the main discussion of the poets should be placed is sometimes a puzzle. Usually it is appropriate where their work first began to make its impact. Even when their careers were long, most poets did not change their styles radically, or, if they did, the later styles did not exert much influence. A few major poets, however, produced significant, changing, and influential work throughout the entire modern period. In a historical discussion they present problems of placing to which there is no wholly satisfactory solution. The careers of Hardy, Frost, and Yeats are treated as a whole within this first volume. Although Yeats lived until 1939 and continued to be an active influence on other poets long after his death, his career sums up, in some respects, the general course of poetry from the 1890s into the 1920s, and thus makes a fitting conclusion to the first volume. In the cases of Eliot and Pound, this volume concentrates on only their early careers, tracing the development of their poetry up to the full establishment of the high Modernist mode. These chapters end with a brief look ahead at their later careers, which will be treated in detail in the second volume. The strong influence of Williams and Stevens did not come until the 1940s and 1950s, and is, in the second volume, a major concern in my discussion of those years. Hence this first volume merely describes the forming of their art and notices their first mature works, postponing further discussion of these writers until they can be viewed along with the poets they influenced. A number of other poets who were starting to publish during the years covered by this volume but became prominent only later—for example, to mention only a few, Roy Campbell, Austin Clarke, Hart Crane, Cummings, Day Lewis, Jeffers, Hugh MacDiarmid, Archibald MacLeish, Edwin Muir, E. J. Pratt, John Crowe Ransom, Yvor Winters—are also reserved for the second volume.

Writing this book, I have received much kindly help which it is a pleasure to record. The project was aided by a grant from the Guggenheim Foundation. Mrs. Jane Hatfield and Linda Segal prepared the manuscript. Professors Douglas Bush, W. Jackson Bate, Walton Litz, and Ronald Bush read the manuscript in whole or part and offered long lists of useful suggestions and criticisms. The book is dedicated to Jackson Bate in gratitude for wise counsel and friendship in this and many other projects over the last twenty-five years.

Cambridge, Massachusetts   D.P
May 1976

CONTENTS

Part One. Poetry around the Turn of the Century

Part Two. Poetry in Rapport with a Public

Part Three. Popular Modernism

Part Four. The Beginnings of the High Modernist Mode

POETRY AROUND THE TURN OF THE CENTURY

1

BRITISH POETRY IN THE 1890s
INTRODUCTION

THE reasons for beginning the history of modern poetry with the 1890s lie in facts of literary history. The poets now recognized as the major figures of the whole modern period and the fathers or grandfathers of most present-day writers—Yeats, Frost, Stevens, Pound, Williams, Eliot—were born in the latter part of the nineteenth century. The poetry of this period forms the immediate background and matrix of their own work, so much so that unless one keeps the later nineteenth century in mind, one cannot fully understand how and why modern poetry took the directions it did.

The situation of young poets growing up in the United States at the end of the nineteenth century differed from that of their contemporaries in England. Throughout the 1890s poetry in America continued, on the whole, to follow the norms and premises of the Romantic and Victorian traditions. Moreover, the known and respected American poets of the decade obviously lacked talent of the first order. Thus, the first generation of Modernist poets in America had the special advantage in their own national context that they were coming into a scene of traditional poetry that was also weak, a circumstance which helps account for the boldness, elan, and rapid spread of the Modernist movement. England, on the other hand, had a strong, rebellious avant-garde poetry in the 1890s, and the next generation of English poets, whom we may loosely call Georgian, reacted against this and returned to more traditional modes. But in the 1890s London was still the cultural capital of the United States as well as of England; the theories and poems of the London avant-garde commanded the attention of American literary under-graduates, such as Pound, Stevens, and Eliot. And the high Modernist mode, when it developed in the 1910s and 1920s, was in some respects a revival of the premises and intentions that had also shaped the avant-garde poetry of England in the eighties and nineties, though "revival" does not seem the right word for a poetry that in genius and boldness went so much further. Never-theless, Modernist poets shared with the earlier avant-garde of London a similar perception of their historical place and literary mission: both groups were eager to reject the nineteenth cen-tury mentality and the habits of verse associated with it. And particular tendencies such as Imagism, realism (including the urban and sordid), Symbolism, formalism, and the praise of im-personal craftmanship were all anticipated in the 1890s.

THE ROMANTIC LEGACY

Among the conventions of the more traditional verse in Eng-land and the United States throughout the nineteenth century was, obviously, the use of nature or landscape as subject matter, setting, symbol, or metaphor. Nature is almost omnipresent in this poetry, and, despite the more depressing pronouncements of nineteenth-century science, it is almost always favorably regarded: it is refreshing, aesthetically appealing, sympathetic, wise or a source of wisdom, occasionally even divine. Poetry from the eighteenth century on was assumed to be a source of consolation, whatever else it might be. Even if the poem uttered darkly pessimistic thoughts, the vehicle and setting modified their impact and made the poem agreeable. (The term is bor-rowed from critics of the eighteenth century and the Romantic period; as distinguished from the intellectual perception of the beautiful, the feeling of the "agreeable" arises when poetry presents what is inherently pleasant or has become so through association.) One favorite technique was to put landscape and human emotion side by side so that the landscape became the exponent of the emotion, as in Tennyson's,

> Break, break, break,
> On thy cold gray stones, O Sea!
> And I would that my tongue could utter
> The thoughts that arise in me.

The sea conveys the feeling of empty grayness and repetitive monotony in many aspects and with rich effectiveness, but still agreeably. The subway ride in Eliot's "Burnt Norton" brings similar feelings to a more troubling focus. Picasso's remark, "I am not interested in beauty," comes from a state of mind that sharply differentiates Modernism from the Romantic tradition. What Picasso meant by "beauty" was the Romantically agreeable: in poetry the singing line, the easily intelligible utterance, the ample, unqualified emotion, the imagery and setting that, as Keats put it, "sooth the cares, and lift the thoughts of man."

Poetry in the nineteenth century was generally considered personal utterance. That lyrics voice the emotions of the poet was taken for granted. Even with dramatic monologues and narrative poems, the assumption was still that poetry offered a valued, intimate contact with the poet. Poets knew the assumption was overly simple, but that did not prevent them from accepting and even exploiting it. One result of this convention was that criticism of the poetry tended to become criticism of the character and way of life of the poet, so far as these could be inferred from his writings. "I confess," says Leslie Stephen, "that I at any rate love a book pretty much in proportion as it makes me love the author." The convention of personal utterance has continued to be important in the twentieth century. It operates in Yeats, Frost, and many other poets of their generation, and it later came again to the fore, especially in so-called "confessional" poetry. Nevertheless, both the aesthetes of the eighties and nineties and the Modernist poets of later decades repudiated it. It was, in their eyes, one of the more naive items of the Romantic-Victorian legacy. It assumed the worth of individual experience as opposed to tradition; it tended to confuse literary with moral judgment; and it failed to stress the necessity of professional study and self-conscious laboriousness, thus heartening the amateur in criticism and poetry.

Poetry was essentially the voicing of emotion, the "delineation of states of feeling," as Mill phrased it. It would include other things as well, such as narration and reflection, but what peculiarly distinguished poetry from the other verbal genres was the greater intensity of feeling it presupposed and expressed. Here indeed might be its justification. It was a culture of the feelings; it unified the rational with the emotional side of human nature; it was, according to Wordsworth, "truth . . . carried alive into the heart by passion." Ordinary readers might not trouble themselves with such arguments, but they expected a direct release of strong feeling, for which they were grateful. Hence the adverse emphasis toward the end of the century on formal distance and marmoreal reserve—qualities that might in those days be deemed either French or "classical"—and hence also the anti-Romantic cultivation in the twenties, thirties, and forties of poetic "wit" and cerebration.

Romantic and Victorian poets could view their art as endowed, at least potentially, with the utmost significance. The grounds changed somewhat. For the Romantics it was chiefly the poetic imagination, regarded as a power that could reunite man with nature and with the Divine and so offer salvation—no lesser word can be used—to the individual and to society as a whole. This faith, which was never securely held, waned rapidly in the Victorian age, but the great poet was still thought of as a sage, a thinker who has achieved a comprehensive and important world view. One example was Wordsworth, whose profundities of feeling and reflection solaced many a troubled seeker. Another model was found in a somewhat idealized version of Goethe. In fact, whatever poet one was partial to would be praised for the depth, breadth, and helpfulness of his thoughts. This put pressures of responsibility on Victorian poets and may have hampered imagination and inhibited the uses of their art as play, but it also led them to write a poetry that was directly and intelligibly relevant to the general concerns of mankind. It kept them in touch with an earnest, educated public that generally shared their lofty estimate of the poet's role.

If one asks what happened to the grand view of poetry after the mid-Victorians, the situation is complicated. Modern poets have usually rejected or at least modified the sage's stance. But the major poets did not therefore lose a high estimate of the importance of poetry, and they supported this estimate on grounds of every description except the Victorian. Nevertheless, the general history of poetry in our period shows a recurring tendency to retrench deliberately to the minor. Examples recur from Impressionists in the nineties, through the Georgians and Imagists to the later Auden and the poetry of ordinary urban life in the fifties. The point is not merely that this is a minor poetry; it is valued and defended precisely because it is minor. It is one instance of what Santayana calls the "penitent art" of the modern period, the psychological retrenchment that came with disillusion, when it seemed that poetry in the past had entertained excessively inflated hopes and pretensions.

Finally, this personal, emotional, agreeable, reflective poetry was, like prose fiction, music, and painting in the nineteenth century, essentially a popular art. In due course there was a direct turnabout. English aesthetes in the 1880s and 1890s caught from France the concept of the poet as intrinsically alienated from society. By "society" they meant, of course, the middle class, for which the major Victorians had written. Would not this class prefer plumbing to poems? Had not Matthew Arnold, himself an earnest Victorian, rightly characterized middle-class values and styles as Philistine and utilitarian, "purblind and hideous"? With such persons there could be no rapport, and the poet withdrew to cultivate peculiarities of impression or sensation, or to worship Beauty, or sometimes to study in the library. Modernist poets later mocked both aestheticism and its correlative notion of Beauty, but they shared the aesthete's opinion that the first duty of the poet is to his art. Art was not necessarily communication—that would be "rhetoric," for which few tolerant words have been said in the twentieth century—and they were often willing to be unpopular. But it was not just that. There is some truth in the argument of Ortega y Gasset and others that high Modernist art was not simply unpopular, as any new art may be for a while, but antipopular. This helps explain why some Modernist poets were willing to exploit an idiom that is dry, oblique, learned, and extremely compressed. Like Marianne Moore's hedgehog or "spine-swine" the poetry had all its "edges out"; whoever was put off by it was not wanted anyway. You were not writing for readers of newspapers. If you had any audience in mind, it was an elite of fellow writers and literati.

BRITISH MODES AND POETS OF THE DECADE

The chief poet who came to the fore in the 1890s was William Butler Yeats, who published three collections of lyrics between 1889 and 1899. By the end of the decade he was a respected figure in literary circles. Among the poets of previous generations Tennyson continued to write until his death in 1892, and there were volumes of verse from other such old hands as William Morris, Swinburne, R. W. Dixon, Oscar Wilde, W. E. Henley, Meredith, Christina Rossetti, Francis Palgrave, Austin Dobson, Sir Edwin Arnold, and Sir Lewis Morris. Several younger poets who first began publishing in the nineties became better known after the turn of the century and belong more essentially to the Edwardian-Georgian period: Laurence Binyon, A. E. Housman, Sturge Moore, Sir Henry Newbolt, John Cowper Powys, George Russell (AE), Katherine Tynan. The works of some long-lived writers began to appear in the days of Swinburne and the Pre-Raphaelites and continued relatively unchanged in the season of Eliot and Auden: Hardy, Bridges, Kipling. These writers may also be deferred for later discussion.

The names mentioned so far suggest the quality and kinds of poetry in the 1890s, but the special exponents and representatives of this decade would naturally be those poets who did their chief work and had their greatest impact in it. Of these the most important are Sir William Watson, Alice Meynell, Francis Thompson, Arthur Symons, Ernest Dowson, Lionel Johnson, and John Davidson. They are minor poets, and there is perhaps no poem of the 1890s that is not minor. But they generally preserve a high level of craftsmanship. Moreover, though it is true that the poets of the period did not, on the whole, wish or expect to reach a large public, a few poems from the decade have probably been more widely read and quoted than any poem of the twentieth century. Examples would be "The Lake Isle of Innisfree," "Danny Deever," the lyrics of Housman that begin,

> Loveliest of trees, the cherry now
> Is hung with bloom along the bough . . .

and,

> With rue my heart is laden,
> For golden friends I had . . .

and the unforgettable lyric of Dowson's—

> Last night, ah, yesternight, betwixt her lips and mine
> There fell thy shadow, Cynara!

Of such poetry the secret may be the emphatic, artful rhythms, the interest of setting or event, and the emotions of accessible and popular kinds.

The self-appointed successor to the role and inheritance of the major Victorian poets was Sir William Watson. If hard work and high-minded purpose could suffice, he would rank with Tennyson, just as the eighteenth-century poet Sir Richard Blackmore would with Milton. Other "Victorian" voices include the impressively good-intentioned, long-winded didacticism of Baron Latymer, the "rhetoric" of Stephen Phillips and the two ladies who published under the pseudonym of "Michael Field," the insipidities of F. W. Bourdillon, and the Laureate, Alfred Austin, who, despite some passable lyrics, was an object of ridicule. "A Defence of English Spring," with its decayed Wordsworthianism, shows why:

> Yes, Cuckoo! cuckoo! cuckoo! still!
> Do you not feel an impulse thrill
> Your vernal blood to do the same,
> And, boylike, shout him back his name?

Among these less innovative poets a distinguished, special group is made up of the Roman Catholics, Alice Meynell, Francis Thompson, and Lionel Johnson. Their habits of sensibility and style belong to their age, but through their religion they were also led back to a different tradition, that of the Anglo-Catholic poets of the seventeenth century, and this unites in their work with the more usual procedures of nineteenth-century verse. Alice Meynell, for example, has affinities with Christina Rossetti and also with the "metaphysical revival" of the

1920s and 1930s. The poets of the Celtic Revival should also be noticed. Douglas Hyde, William Sharp in his alter ego as Fiona Macleod, Yeats, and Lionel Johnson may be seen as transitional between poets in the Victorian tradition and the avant-garde. They adopted "Celtic" subject matters and idiom, elegiac emotions, and a peculiarly vague atmosphere that reminds one of Ossian, although Sharp, Yeats, and Johnson were in touch with many other tendencies.

Though the Victorian tradition remained the accepted and prevalent one throughout the nineties, the better poets of the decade reacted against it. These reactions essentially went in two opposed directions. There were the poets of what may be called *Ars Victrix*. The phrase is taken from the title of Austin Dobson's loose translation of Gautier's "L'Art":

> Model thy Satyr's face
>   In bronze of Syracuse;
> In the veined agate trace
>   The profile of thy Muse.
>
> All passes. Art alone
>   Enduring stays to us;
> The Bust outlasts the throne,—
>   The Coin, Tiberius.

From this creed writers such as Yeats, Bridges, Dowson, Housman, and Johnson drew inspiration. They were, for the most part, melancholy stylists in retreat from the modern world, for which they felt a strong aversion. Other poets of the nineties acquired their identity from a reaction against both the Victorians and the poets of *Ars Victrix*. Poets of this tendency usually reflected contemporary life in a more or less realistic way, and thus recaptured rapport with middle-class readers.

The poetry of *Ars Victrix* includes diverse, shifting, and vague groupings, since it refers generally to the aesthetic-decadent-symbolist-formalist poetry of the period. The "Aesthetic" premise of the autonomy and supremacy of art is a shaping factor in all this poetry; the "Decadents," cultivating morally dubious sensations and subject matters, emphasized it more aggressively. Such work may be found in some poems of Arthur Symons and Ernest Dowson, and in ancillary figures such as John Barlas, Lord Alfred Douglas, and Aubrey Beardsley. "Symbolism" was

just beginning to be proclaimed as a movement in poetry. Its notable exponents in England were Yeats and Symons. Other
poets, such as Bridges, Housman, Dowson, and Johnson, carried
on the aesthetic devotion to craftsmanship and perfected form
without accepting associated premises of aestheticism. All felt
that the writing of poetry must be made a more difficult art.
They looked for models to the Latin classics and the recent
poetry of France. Perhaps the most representative single volume
for this group is John Gray's *Silverpoints*.

Impressionist poetry belongs to the same tradition, but with
special premises and techniques. In poetry, "impressionism"
might be described as the presenting of a scene by rapid notation. The scene evokes a mood, but, ideally speaking, the poet
refrains from personal comment or discursive interpretation,
and the poem remains concentrated on the complex of momentary sensations and feelings. This kind of poetry was in many
respects a forerunner of Imagism, and many of the impressionist poems were in free verse. No poet of the nineties was
always "impressionist," but such poems were written by Wilde,
Henley, Sharp, Binyon, and Arthur Symons. The attempt to
express contemporary reality in poetry appears in many Impressionist poems, as well as in other, less classifiable poets. Writers
of prose fiction, for example, incorporated aspects of fictional
technique in poetry. One thinks of Hardy—not the poems of didactic, cosmic accusation, but those that pick out a brief, telling
event or situation in the lives of ordinary, middle- or lower-class
people. Kipling explored the thoughts and feelings of the unpoetic middle class in such dramatic monologues as "The *Mary
Gloster*" or "M'Andrew's Hymn." In the *Barrack-Room Ballads* he
climbed down the social ladder to express the views and experiences of common soldiers, using "Tommy Atkins" as his mouth-
piece. In each of these dramatic monologues he tried to catch
the actual language, the vocabulary, idiom, and pronunciation
of his protagonist. John Davidson also wrote fiction, and in a few
of his poems, such as "Thirty Bob a Week," he went further than
any other poet of the time in depicting the drab and anxious
lives of the urban lower middle class. In other poems, especially
the monstrous dramatic works of his last years, he preached in
the wake of Nietzsche a gospel of joy in amoral existence—joy at
least for the tyrant or superman who is able to work his will.

With Davidson we come to the life-affirmers. They flaunted zesty attitudes in self-conscious repudiation of the aesthetic-decadent sensibility, which to them seemed effete. They were trying to be relevant to modern life, but their sensibility was often boyish and romantic. Henley appointed himself antagonist to Wilde and expounded the heroic power of the individual to will, do, and overcome joyfully. A similarly romantic rejection of romance is voiced by Kipling and Masefield, and such poets as Stevenson, Chesterton, and Noyes affirm not the romance in the real, but rather that romance is real. Other poets with a sensibility close to Henley or Kipling are W. S. Blunt, Sir Owen Seaman (the *Punch* parodist), and Sir Rennell Rodd, whose poems might have had a tendency to recruit adolescents for the Royal Navy.

THE LITERARY MILIEU

Poetry at the start of the modern period had ceased to be the most important literary genre, its traditional place having been taken over by prose fiction. The situation is unique in the history of English literature. (The great development of drama in the Renaissance is not an exception, for drama was still a subdivision of poetry.) The "importance" of a given genre in the total literary culture may be estimated by such criteria as quality and quantity of production, size and diversity of audience, appeal to literary talent, and critical prestige. The decline of poetry in relation to prose fiction began in the eighteenth century, but with the burst of poetry in the Romantic period, it was not until after 1830 that prose fiction finally attained primacy. In the days of George Eliot and Dickens prose fiction was the dominant literary type by every criterion except general critical esteem, which was still given chiefly to poetry. Furthermore, for all its brilliance, even the poetry written in the Romantic period shows something of the retreat into specializations (feeling, personal subjectivity, the lyric) that always occurs when a genre is on the defensive against its own past successes or against a developing new genre.

If Edmund Wilson's question, "Is Verse a Dying Technique?" might have been asked with some propriety at any time in the last hundred and fifty years, it would have been more appropriate in the 1890s than in 1938, at the close of the great modern development. For one thing, the twenties and thirties had seen a sharp rise in the amount of poetry published. By my count there was in the 1890s an average of about fifteen books of poetry of some significance published each year, the number being smaller at the start of the decade and increasing toward the end. A plateau was reached in 1900–1908, after which there was a steady rise. By the late teens over forty books of significant poetry were published each year. The figures are admittedly subjective, but it is plain that the later 1910s and the 1920s saw a large advance both in number and worth of volumes of poetry. Writers such as Frost, Pound, Stevens, Eliot, and Yeats can at least be mentioned in the same breath with Joyce, Lawrence, Woolf, and Forster. In the 1890s, on the other hand, the major novelists were Hardy, Conrad, James, and Meredith and, with the possible exception of Hardy's poetry, no poets of the 1890s were doing work of remotely comparable significance. The diversion of talent into prose fiction at this time appears, moreover, not only in its quality but also in the amount of fiction published, which was enormously greater than poetry.

There was relatively little audience for poetry in the 1890s, not only in comparison with fictional prose but even in comparison with earlier ages. In terms of sales, one of the more successful poets was Stephen Phillips; his publisher, John Lane, says that at one time 10,000 copies of a new volume by Phillips "would be subscribed for before publication." To Lane this seemed so remarkable that he imagined "such a demand was never before experienced by a poet." The figure of 10,000 may be compared, however, with the 100,000 who placed an advance order for a reprint of *Lorna Doone* in 1897, or the 50,000 who purchased Hall Caine's *The Christian* in one month in the same year. It may also be compared with the 20,000 readers who purchased a copy of Scott's *The Lady of the Lake* in 1810, when the population of England was only a third that of 1900, when a much smaller proportion was able to read, and when a book of poetry cost relatively much more. At the end of the nineteenth century 70 percent of the books borrowed from British public libraries were prose fiction; the rest were likely to be other varieties of prose.

Given this taste in the reading public, the publishing trade also took little interest in poetry. An honorable exception was John

Lane, without whose efforts noticeably fewer volumes would have appeared. Otherwise the records and histories of the various publishing houses show that poetry was at best a minor activity for which there was no enthusiasm. It is sometimes claimed that there was substantial support for poetry in periodicals of the time, but the claim is misleading. General periodicals such as *The Cornhill, The Nineteenth Century, Longman's,* and *Murray's Magazine* published a little poetry; but others did not, and where poetry did appear it was as an occasional tailpiece or interlude between the prose fiction and essays that filled these magazines. Periodicals had space and pay for writers of prose fiction but very little for poets. A number of specifically "literary" periodicals were founded in the 1890s and usually included poetry. They were, however, limited in circulation and short-lived: for. example, *The Yellow Book* (1894–1897); *The Savoy* (1896–1897); *The Hobby Horse,* a quarterly (1886–1893); *The Pageant,* two numbers in 1896; and *The Dome* (1897–1900). Poets might be paid a few shillings for a poem published in a journal, and books of poetry sold for about what they now do in terms of relative purchasing power, but of course they sold in fewer numbers. Moreover, poets did not on the whole have the additional sources of income they may now have through public readings, radio and television, university sinecures, and the like. As a result, they could make a living from their poetry even less than at present. William Watson later said he had made £500 a year from his poetry during the 1890s, but most poets either held a job, like Austin Dobson, or had a private income, like Bridges and Johnson, or supported themselves through general literary work, like Arthur Symons, or starved.

Though there was much less general interest in poetry than is usually asserted, there was a very intense interest among poets and hangers-on. A coterie spirit flourished. Here is a fundamental difference in situation between English and American poetry in the modern period. Throughout the nineteenth century, London was the literary center of England, but there were also a succession of provincial centers. By the end of the century, however, virtually the whole literary life of England was concentrated in London. Hence the poets came into contact, and were well aware of each other's work. In the United States, on the other hand, there was no literary center in the same degree, and the better poets tended to form their styles on their own.

2

THE VICTORIAN TRADITION AND THE CELTIC TWILIGHT

IN THE 1890s Queen Victoria still reigned and so did all we vaguely identify as Victorian. Most poets of the decade sound at times like Tennyson, Browning, or Arnold, or like the Romantics of the previous generation. When they react against these figures, they often sound like the Pre-Raphaelites or Swinburne. Those who most approach the twentieth century are backing toward it with timid steps. Among those who deliberately wished to continue the Victorian tradition, the most important was Sir William Watson. Perhaps nothing more strikingly illustrates both the group spirit and the historical awareness of the nineties than that he assumed his role self-consciously and even belligerently, and that he was praised by like-minded, would-be rescuers of poetry and of Old England for doing so.

Watson, who was born in 1858, saw himself as the heir to Tennyson and more generally as the preserver of the central English poetic tradition, which he trusted would be handed on from his work to later poets. According to him, this tradition included Milton, Gray, and Wordsworth, as well as Tennyson. It excluded hardly any major poet, though Shelley, Browning, and Arnold were relegated to lower places respectively for their vagueness, obscurity, and unfortifying, agnostic sadness. If one asks what,

in Watson's view, characterizes the great tradition, the answer is
best given in phrases of Matthew Arnold. For, though Watson
did not view himself as particularly a follower of Arnold, the
ideals he held before himself found their finest, most influential
expression in the high-minded humanism and classicism of
Arnold's criticism. For Watson, as for Arnold, the mark of the
truly great was to be found in the union of reflective depth,
sincerity, and noble plainness of diction and accent. One thinks of
such phrases, echoing through Arnold's critical writings, as "high
seriousness," the "noble and profound application of ideas to
life," and the "grand style" that arises "when a noble nature,
poetically gifted, treats with simplicity or severity a serious subject." Pondering the Arnoldian phrases until they become meaningful and felt, one understands how poets such as Swinburne,
Kipling, Wilde, Dowson, Symons, and Yeats seemed to Watson
unbearably frivolous. (Watson lived until 1935. What he must
have thought of later poets staggers the imagination.) He believed that one explanation for this loss of dignity and strength
was that poets had deserted English for foreign examples. He
did not think of himself as a major poet in the great English tradition, but rather as a lesser follower, faithful in an adverse time.
For Tennyson had died in 1892, and if the "strenuous and virile
temper" of English poetry was not to sink under "emasculate
euphuism" or finally die "surfeited with unwholesome sweet-
meats" and "smothered in artificial rose-leaves," Watson must
save it.

He prepared himself for his role with deliberation. A frail and
quiet boy, Watson had, like Milton, a father who indulged his literary leisure and supported his hopes. The father paid the costs
of publishing his first volume, *The Prince's Quest* (1880), a poem
much influenced by William Morris. It failed to win notice, and
Watson set himself to write a less sensuous, more objective, disciplined, and condensed poetry. The results of this self-correction
appeared in *Epigrams of Art, Life, and Nature* (1884). He now
moved to annex another quality of the great poet—passionate
and patriotic concern for public affairs and the nation—and
wrote a sequence of Miltonic sonnets from the Tory standpoint
on the Sudanese and Afganistani questions. These years of preparation ended with *Wordsworth's Grave and Other Poems* (1890),
which reaped some very good reviews and won the large audience that he held for approximately ten years. The volume was

praised by Hardy, Yeats, Edward Dowden, W. D. Howells, and A. E. Housman. Favorable notice from such diverse writers is another indication of the general uneasiness about the state of poetry. However admirably modern or marmoreal contemporary poetry might have been, a certain breadth and centrality seemed wanting. At least by his ideals or aims, in other words, Watson addressed not only poetic conservatives but the half-suppressed dubieties of the literary world as a whole.

By the end of the decade Watson had begun to lose his audience. The causes were partly the rising popularity of other poets, such as Kipling, and partly the pessimistic agnosticism into which he was drifting (expressed particularly in *The Hope of the World and Other Poems,* 1897). Although nothing was more common in the poetry of the nineties than pessimistic agnosticism, this was not what Watson's readers expected of him. Also, his admirers found it progressively harder to be enthusiastic about high aims that did not lead to high performance. The perception spread that, as Lionel Johnson put it, he was at best only an "understudy" of the "great men . . . capable of deceiving you for a time by his airs of being the true master instead of a very serious and accomplished substitute." As Watson's audience deserted him, so also did his self-confidence. He wrote less, and what he wrote became increasingly embittered. His long decline in the last thirty years of his life is a painful study; he died eclipsed and forgotten.

"Wordsworth's Grave," his best-known poem, gives in forty-seven elegiac quatrains a general history of English poetry from the Augustan age to the present. It characterizes Wordsworth as the poet who brings rest and peace and regrets the contemporary state of poetry. The poem is traditional without being closely imitative of anybody in particular. It is typical of Watson and sounds like this:

> Where is the singer whose large notes and clear
> Can heal, and arm, and plenish, and sustain?
> Lo, one with empty music floods the ear,
> And one, the heart refreshing, tires the brain.
>
> And idly tuneful, the loquacious throng
> Flutter and twitter, prodigal of time,
> And little masters make a toy of song
> Till grave men weary of the sound of rhyme.

The poem is reflective and wistful. Though sometimes allegorical, it proceeds for the most part by articulating logical (at least consecutively articulated) ideas in a diction that is clear, slightly heightened, and restrained. It shows control without compression. One trouble with Watson's poetry is that everything has come from books. Even though he wrote political poems, he seems not much to have noticed actual life or experience in the world, and this lack was not compensated by pressure of subjective experience or imagination from within. His strongest emotion was his desire to be a great poet.

If Watson was one of those writers who please, as Samuel Johnson remarked of similar poets in the eighteenth century, "principally by not offending," this tepid praise is, nevertheless, a great deal more than can be claimed for such other high-aspiring and traditional poets as Stephen Phillips and "Michael Field." Both were primarily dramatists. Phillips (1868–1915) was widely read and admired in the nineties, but the vogue quickly passed and he was ignored thereafter. "Michael Field" was the pseudonym of Katherine Bradley (1846–1913) and Edith Cooper (1862–1914), who was her niece. They aroused some interest in the 1880s, but interest waned with the discovery that the passionate, tragic dramatist, Michael Field, was actually two maiden ladies. The poems of both Phillips and Field have been completely forgotten; to recall them may seem unkind, almost gloating. Nevertheless, since they were once esteemed, they show what, at a level of taste and intelligence below Watson's, the middle class assumed "poetry" to be. One can find in Phillips the plaintive, "simple," mealymouthed style that has been fondly read for at least the last two hundred years:

> It is the time of tender, opening things.
> Above my head the fields murmur and wave,
> And breezes are just moving the clear heat.
> O the mid-noon is trembling on the corn,
> On cattle calm, and trees in perfect sleep.

But his particular forte is rather the enthusiastic effusion, supposedly passionate, usually bombastic. In "Marpessa" the heroine is loved by Idas,

> Because Infinity upon thee broods;
> And thou art full of whispers and of shadows.

> Thou meanest what the sea has striven to say
> So long, and yearned up the cliffs to tell;
> .   .   .   .
> The face remembered is from other worlds,
> It has been died for, though I know not when,
> It has been sung of, though I know not where.
> It has the strangeness of the luring West,
> And of sad sea-horizons.

This kind of poetry did not end with the nineteenth century; we shall find many later avatars. It is not especially "Victorian" or ninetyish. It is, like its plaintive, namby-pamby counterpart, a degenerate Romanticism. There is a distant family resemblance between Phillips' rendition of Marpessa's beauty and Yeats's poems on the Rose, and both are related to a side of Shelley. The work of the Michael Fields illustrates a slightly different, equally stock notion of "poetry," namely, pure passion and spirituality, emotion flying high over the patched and warty realm of actual life. Not that the emotion is insincere. It is what a character in a noble book might feel, and such books, taken with too literal a faith, had formed their sensibility. Theirs is a hothouse high-mindedness, genuine but too simply fervid and ideal:

> I love you with my life—'tis so I love you;
> I give you as a ring
> The cycle of my days till death:
> I worship with the breath
> That keeps me in the world with you and spring;
> And God may dwell behind, but not above you.

Among the remembered poets of the 1890s quite a few were Roman Catholic. Even educated non-Catholic readers were at this time much less familiar with Catholic belief and practice than is now the case. (Sir Arthur Quiller-Couch thought the word "monstrance" was one of Francis Thompson's eccentric inventions.) As a result, the atmosphere of Catholic faith in this poetry struck readers as special and obtrusive, and Catholic poets were seen as a particular, exotic group. Today one may be more impressed by the differences between them. Several were converts who came to the church more by way of Pater than of Paul. They belong to the aesthetic movement. But at least three poets who did their chief work in the nineties—Alice Meynell,

Francis Thompson, and Lionel Johnson—were more deeply imbued with Catholic faith and sensibility. This made them take an interest, relatively unusual at the time, in the English religious poets of the seventeenth century.

Alice Meynell (1847–1922) became a convert to Roman Catholicism in 1872. In her youth she passed through enthusiasms for Wordsworth, Keats, Shelley, and Tennyson; she was acquainted through her family with Aubrey de Vere, Ruskin, Sir Edwin Arnold, and Coventry Patmore. All of these Victorian worthies, including Tennyson, encouraged her poetic efforts. Patmore became, for a while, a close friend. From him she learned, says her daughter and biographer, that "the greatest poetry has a simplicity beyond imagery." Her anthology of English lyrics, *The Flower of the Mind* (1897), shows an independent taste. It is unusual for the late Victorian period in that half of it is given over to poets between Shakespeare and Dryden. (It is more typical of its time in that a mere eight pages are allotted to Dryden and Pope, the latter being represented by only one poem—the slightly romantic "Elegy to the Memory of an Unfortunate Lady.") But except for her co-religionist Richard Crashaw, the anthology does not particularly favor the metaphysical poets. Herrick, for example, gets more space than either Donne or Herbert.

That Mrs. Meynell appreciated the poets of the early seventeenth century more than most of her contemporaries may be the result of her religious sensibility. She was a loving mother; she had many interests and friends; she was busy in the literary world, helping her husband edit a succession of periodicals and writing much sane, animated criticism. But her central emotions related to religion, and her own poetry is largely, though not exclusively, a poetry of Christian devotion. It is not, however, in any way like the usual Victorian or late Victorian religious poetry, which is a poetry of honest seekers, troubled by doubts, full of questions and arguments. With her the faith and the love are possessed, and the poetry creates vehicles or occasions to utter them. Hence her attraction to the poetry of the seventeenth century: it is hard to see where else she could have found a poetry so likely to nourish her own. Because she did not much admire metaphysical "wit" and complexity, she emulated rather such qualities of metaphysical poetry as speed, grace, economy, plainness, concentrated intelligence, direct and homely imagery, dialogue, and the sudden, dramatic start. "Via, et Veritas, et Vita" is typical:

> "You never attained to Him?" "If to attain
> Be to abide, then that may be."
> "Endless the way, followed with how much pain!"
>   "The way was He."

Mrs. Meynell had little or no direct influence on the "metaphysical revival" of the twenties and thirties. This side of her work should not be too much stressed, for in most respects her art and sensibility are unmistakably of her own time. Hers is a distinguished minor poetry, thoughtful, high-minded, disciplined, but without freshness or power of language, and without sufficient exploration of self or the world to go widely or deeply into human experience. The clarity and direct force of the argument, the neatness and condensed strength are, however, always admirable.

Francis Thompson (1859–1907) was rescued from illness, poverty, and obscurity by the Meynells; he remained thereafter a dependent friend of the family. With their protective encouragement he published three volumes of poetry in the 1890s. He did not share Mrs. Meynell's devotion to spare, sinewy thought, a fact of which she often reminded him. For such fantastic and elaborate heaps of language as his "Sister Songs" an appropriate epithet is "baroque." This poem of 1,271 lines celebrates the young Meynell daughters, Sylvia and Monica, as the saving heart of Childhood, the harmony of Woman, the embodiment of Love and Beauty, and so on. Similarly, small precedent outside the baroque can be found for "The Making of Viola," a poem which tells how baby Viola Meynell was made item by item in heaven. In this poem the Father in Heaven first commands Mary to spin Viola's hair ("Spin a tress for Viola"), next orders angels to weave a "Velvet flesh for Viola," and so forth through eyes, soul, and rosy cheeks, after which the angels carry her down to earth. At the start of the "Orient Ode," an intricate and extended conceit compares the sun to the host taken at dawn from the tabernacle, raised in benediction, and set finally "within the flaming monstrance of the West." The germinal idea of "The Hound of Heaven" compares God's grace to a pursuing dog. That these comparisons are so often frigid, external, and uncontrolled does not much distinguish Thompson from many a predecessor in the baroque style.

His revival of this older style was noticed from the start. He is, however, usually incapable of keeping to the impersonal elaboration of the baroque style through a long poem, and lapses into self-expression and autobiography. In these passages, often his more impressive ones, we hear the nineteenth-century poet voicing his terror, frustration, regret, and longing, and struggling toward acceptance and hope. The personal theme is touched at every point by the religious commitment that, through all his suffering, he never lost. This more personal utterance is naturally charged with deeper feeling. The diction, syntax, and rhythm take on rhetorical urgency. The imagery tends to become more romantic and visionary, making a stronger emotional impact and reminding the reader of Shelley, De Quincey, Tennyson, or Rossetti:

> Across the margent of the world I fled,
>   And troubled the gold gateways of the stars;
>   .   .   .   .
> To all swift things for swiftness did I sue;
>   Clung to the whistling mane of every wind;
>   .   .   .   .
> I dimly guess what Time in mists confounds;
> Yet ever and anon a trumpet sounds
> From the hid battlements of Eternity;
> Those shaken mists a space unsettle, then
> Round the half-glimpsed turrets slowly wash again.
>   But not ere him who summoneth
>   I first have seen, enwound
> With glooming robes purpureal, cypress-crowned.

The lines come from "The Hound of Heaven," one of the impressive poems of the nineteenth century. It has all Thompson's literary vices, but our sense of these is mitigated by the emotionally realized immediacy of the central imaginative conception.

At the turn of the century Thompson's reputation was much higher than it now is. Modes and fashions have changed of course, but other contributing causes for his decline have been the discovery of Hopkins and the later poetry of Eliot, in other words, the emergence of directly religious and devotional poets

of greater stature. He had splendid gifts, but tasteless jumble
and garrulousness spoil most of his work. A few pages, however,
seem likely to last—probably "The Hound of Heaven" and certainly a few short lyrics such as "To a Snowflake" and "In No
Strange Land."

THE CELTIC TWILIGHT

   The so-called "Celtic Twilight" makes a hazy border between
the more traditional poetry of the nineteenth century and the
aesthetic-impressionist-symbolist work of the 1880s and 1890s.
It was a movement that briefly attracted a number of poets—
Yeats, George Russell (AE), Lionel Johnson, William Sharp, and
some less-known Irish contributors such as Katherine Tynan,
Nora Hopper, and Seamus O'Sullivan. Even the urban, Franco-
phile Arthur Symons was led by Yeats from London gaslight to
twilight and from the demimonde to the wee people. There are
poems, though not many, where Symons hears the crying of
Sligo waters or walks in the fairy wood of Finvara:

> I have grown tired of sorrow and human tears;
> Life is a dream in the night, a fear among fears,
> A naked runner lost in a storm of spears.
>
>   .   .   .   .
>
> Here, in the fairy wood, between sea and sea,
> I have heard the song of a fairy bird in a tree,
> And the peace that is not in the world has flown to me.

Later on Walter de la Mare dreamed and ruminated in an
English twilight. Naturally these poets handled the Celtic materials in different ways, combining them with other proclivities of
their own. In Yeats the twilight takes on a romantic, aesthetic,
magical, Symbolist tinge; in Fiona Macleod it tends to be Impressionist; in AE it becomes less misty but more mystical. Moreover,
there was no very sharp or delimited criterion of what made a
poem Celtic. With Yeats as recruiter, publicity agent, impre-
sario, and star performer, the poets had a sense of participating
in a literary movement. But the movement remained undefined.
   The Celtic Twilight was the title of a collection of short stories or
sketches by Yeats published in 1893. The collection explores
Irish folklore and shows that imaginative belief in fairies and

supernatural beings of every kind is still found among the peasantry. In an essay on "The Celtic Element in Literature" (1897), Yeats affirms that "the Celtic movement" is principally the opening up for modern poetry of the old Gaelic legends—of Deirdre or Cuchulain, for example—and, after a richly cadenced sentence or two on Symbolism as "the only movement that is saying new things in the arts," he suggests that Gaelic legends will give "the opening century its most memorable symbols." In these instances the Celtic movement is conceived as the use of "Celtic" folklore and myth for subject matter, allusion, or symbol. But this is much too simple. Most "Celtic" poems, including Yeats's (for example, "The Lake Isle of Innisfree"), made no mention of lore and legend. As the phrases "the Celtic twilight" and "the Celtic mist" made clear, the Celtic quality was also a particular landscape and atmosphere, a vaporous and watery, gray, drearily beautiful natural world, whether in Ireland, Wales, or Highland Scotland. Writing in 1969, the Irish poet Austin Clarke still notices this as an achievement in itself: "Much of English poetry," he says, echoing a remark of Yeats, "exists in an ideal sunshine, that of Greece and Rome." The Celtic poets found their way back to "our lowering skies . . . the mists and twilight of the northern latitude. . . . Yeats, in his masterly way, could express in a single line the atmosphere of Connemara, 'the wet winds are blowing out of the clinging air.'"

But then, especially in the wake of influential essays by Matthew Arnold and Ernest Renan, the Celtic element could also be found in a particular mood or set of emotions: "Come away, O human child! / To the waters and the wild . . . For the world's more full of weeping than you can understand"; "Empty your heart of its mortal dream"; "I see my life go drifting like a river / From change to change"; "Men's souls, that waver and give place / Like the pale waters in their wintry race"; "And I am old, and in my heart at your calling / Only the old dead dreams a-fluttering go"; "Come to the Land of Youth: the trees grown heavy there / Drop on the purple wave the starry fruit they bear";

> I have seen all things pass and all men go
> Under the shadow of the drifting leaf:
>   Green leaf, red leaf, brown leaf,
>   Grey leaf blown to and fro.
>   Blown to and fro.

The quotations are from Yeats, O'Sullivan, AE, and Fiona Macleod, but the mood is the same—wan, listless, disillusioned,
world-weary—and the poet dreams of escape into the vague,
infinite, or supernatural. We may think these emotions typical of
the period, indistinguishable from what Yeats, Symons, Johnson,
or Sharp expressed in other poems that are not part of the Celtic
movement. But uttered amid gray stone and heather in Galway
or Inverness, they were taken as Celtic, the genuine emotion of
the race. When also the poem was spoken in the person of a
peasant farmer, fisherman, Gaelic bard, or ancient chief, it
became the voice of the primitive and the folk. The aesthete's
rejection of "Victorian" rhetoric and argument, the penchant of
the nineties for unqualified pessimistic commonplace seemed, in
this case, not the latest mode but the earliest, the melancholy of
ancient men and especially Celts, who were "weighed down," said
Yeats, "by the emptiness of the great forests and by the mystery
of all things." Dowson's famous lines,

> They are not long, the weeping and the laughter,
> Love and desire and hate,

seem on his page vaguely "classical" and fin-de-siècle. But they
might easily have come from some "Lament of Ian the Proud"
or "Chant of Ardan the Pict."

Celtic lore and the landscape of Cornwall had been touched
on by Tennyson in *The Idylls of the King.* Ernest Renan, in *The
Poetry of the Celtic Races* (1854), and Matthew Arnold, in *On the
Study of Celtic Literature* (1867), had attempted to describe the racial traits of the Celts in their literature. These explorations were
typical of the nineteenth-century concern to characterize racial
and national identities, an impulse that had come to the fore in
most European countries during the Napoleonic wars, partly as
a reaction against French neoclassical and revolutionary cosmopolitanism. Intertwining with other Romantic motives, it had
prompted a study of the folklore, the early epics and legends of
every race, for these were taken to be the expression of the *Ur-
volk,* in which the racial identity had been present in its purest
form. Poets in every European country had exploited this material, retelling myths and heroic stories, and it was natural that
the same thing should take place in Ireland. Perhaps even more
so than in other countries, for in Ireland patriotic and national
feeling was raised to special intensity by opposition to English

rule. The poetry of the Celtic Twilight, then, in its attempt to be local in setting and racial in mood, and to revive the imaginative heritage of the people, was a late product of Romanticism in its interplay with nationalism. Yeats especially hoped that the old mythology might once again become familiar to every mind, for this mythology, referring to a still existing countryside, would foster a sentiment of national unity, and "move a whole people and not a few people who have grown up in a leisured class." Thus, in a few generations habits of sensibility would be re-educated; the mind and the language would be cleansed of abstraction; and a large, diverse, imaginative audience would come into being, the sort of audience that must exist before there can be a great age in literature and the arts. In short, literature would create Ireland, but an Ireland that would then itself create a magnificent literature.

Just when or how the Celtic movement began is a matter of dispute. Yeats's *The Wanderings of Oisin* (1889) is sometimes taken as the inaugural production. But in this poem Yeats is dependent on the work of Sir Samuel Ferguson, who in *Lays of the Western Gael* (1865), *Congal* (1872), *Deirdre* (1880), and *Poems* (1880) had gone back to the ancient Irish legends—which Yeats could not read in the original—and had rendered them in English verse. Ferguson also translated and himself composed shorter poems and ballads, some of which possess already much of the Celtic Twilight, for example, this description of the fairy dance around a thorn tree:

> They're glancing through the glimmer of the quiet eve,
> Away in milky wavings of neck and ankle bare;
> The heavy-sliding stream in its sleepy song they leave,
> And the crags in the ghostly air.

The Wanderings of Oisin is a Shelleyan, Pre-Raphaelite, and symbolical narrative, but it uses characters and incidents out of Irish legend. In the ten years after *The Wanderings of Oisin* Yeats continued to publish poems of this type, among others of very different kinds, in successive volumes of lyric—such poems as "The Stolen Child," "To The Rose Upon the Rood of Time," "Fergus and the Druid," "The Hosting of the Sidhe"—and, indeed, he continued occasionally to write them throughout his life. His last poem, written two weeks before he died, was "The Black Tower," in which, though his style has changed greatly from the nineties, he uses once more the atmosphere and setting of pre-Christian Ireland.

A good example of Yeats's poetry of the Celtic Twilight is "The Song of Wandering Aengus." The poem reflects the mingling of influences and motives typical of all his poetry in these years—personal experience, especially his disappointed love for Maud Gonne; studies of magic and the occult; Symbolism; and of course Irish landscape, folklore, and myth. Though the poem was suggested by a Greek folksong, Yeats thought of "the spirits that are in Ireland" when he wrote it. The setting is timeless; it could be then or now:

> I went out to the hazel wood,
> Because a fire was in my head,
> And cut and peeled a hazel wand,
> And hooked a berry to a thread;
> And when white moths were on the wing,
> And moth-like stars were flickering out,
> I dropped a berry in a stream
> And caught a little silver trout.
>
> When I had laid it on the floor
> I went to blow the fire aflame,
> But something rustled on the floor,
> And some one called me by my name:
> It had become a glimmering girl
> With apple blossom in her hair
> Who called me by my name and ran
> And faded through the brightening air.
>
> Though I am old with wandering
> Through hollow lands and hilly lands,
> I will find out where she has gone,
> And kiss her lips and take her hands;
> And walk among long dappled grass,
> And pluck till time and times are done
> The silver apples of the moon,
> The golden apples of the sun.

The poem refers obliquely to Yeats's love for Maud Gonne, whom Yeats associated with apple blossom. She had, he said, "a complexion like the bloom of apples," and when he first saw her she was standing by a great heap of apple blossoms in the window. The hazel wood would especially recall the wood, called the "Hazelwood," on the shore of Lough Gill, near Sligo, where Yeats spent summers in boyhood and youth. Hazel wood has a springy, flexible quality, good for fishing rods but also for magical rites. The "wand" is both a fishing rod and a magic wand; this is both a fishing trip and magical incantation. Accordingly, the rhythm and syntax are natural, colloquial, yet have something of the repetitive structure of incantation: "And cut and peeled . . . And hooked . . . And when." The imagery of nature is presented with concrete simplicity and homeliness, and this suggests, among other things, an attempt to approximate the folk sensibility. At the same time there is something suggestive, symbolical, or magical in this imagery. The "little silver trout," for example: a trout might be silver in the gray light of dawn, yet also it seems unreal, peculiarly glittering, as though made of silver. The final images,

> The silver apples of the moon,
> The golden apples of the sun,

suggest occult lore and Symbolism. The colors are typical of Yeats's Celtic verses—white, glimmering, and silvery colors of dawn, twilight, or night. In general Yeats's poetry of the Celtic Twilight combines the stock diction of the fin de siècle (roses, pale, dim, stars, old, dream, sorrow, passion) with traces of the vocabulary, rhythm, and syntax that Douglas Hyde developed in translating from Irish into English and that Synge, Lady Gregory, and many others exploited to render Irish peasant speech. A typical passage from Hyde's *Love Songs of Connacht* (1893) goes: "If I were to be on the Brow of Nefin and my hundred loves by my side, it is pleasantly we would sleep together like the little bird upon the bough. It is your melodious wordy little mouth that increased my pain, and a quiet sleep I cannot get until I shall die, alas!" Wandering Aengus is a typical figure—melancholy, old, seeking some other realm elsewhere to redress the disappointments of this.

The only other poet of the Celtic movement worth notice is William Sharp (1855–1905), who wrote his Celtic poems under the pseudonym of Fiona Macleod. It was for the sake of this mysterious poetess of the Hebrides that Yeats named the movement Celtic rather than Irish. Some readers in the nineties thought Fiona Macleod and Yeats were the same person. There are affinities. The poems of Fiona Macleod are romantic-mystical celebrations of a face, a love, a vague something that is somewhere beyond. They evoke a Celtic landscape and mood and exploit Gaelic words. The dedication to Yeats of "Foam of the Past" (1901) expresses Fiona Macleod's sense of fellowship: "And I, too, like Befinn, sister of Boinn"—there is a lot of this in the dedication—"am spell-bound in that vision of sorrowful beauty . . . of beauty that comes secretly out of darkness and greyness and the sighing of wind, as the dew upon the grass and the reed by pale water: and is, for so brief a while: and, as the dew is gathered again swiftly and in silence, is become already a dream." Under her name Sharp wrote dramas of the doings of Eochaidh and Etain, Concobar, Duach the Druid, and Cravetheen the Harper. His poetry is given over to mood even more completely than that of Yeats, as in "The Lament of Ian the Proud":

> What is this crying that I hear in the wind?
> Is it the old sorrow and the old grief?
> Or is it a new thing coming, a whirling leaf
> About the grey hair of me who am weary and blind?
> I know not what it is, but on the moor above the shore
> There is a stone which the purple nets of the heather bind,
> And thereon is writ: *She will return no more.*
> O blown whirling leaf,
> And the old grief,
> And wind crying to me who am old and blind!

The poem shows the wish of a sophisticated modern poet to identify with the primitive and bestow on moody commonplaces something age-old, deeply felt, and profound. The diction combines the ninetyish stock (old, sorrow, gray, weary) with the conscious simplicity and would-be Celticness of "new thing coming" or "hair of me." The cadence and assonance are effectively wailing and chantlike. The landscape is highland moor, shore, and heather. The emotion is melancholy. Except for the Impressionism of the last three lines, the poem is as typical of the Celtic Twilight as one could find.

3

ARS VICTRIX
THE LONDON AVANT-GARDE

I F WE usually think of the 1890s as Aesthetic, Decadent, or
fin-de-siècle, one reason is that the late Victorian avant-garde
was unusually colorful and magnetizes attention. With Yeats,
Dowson, Johnson, and Symons, the group included much of the
poetic talent of the time. And the avant-garde poets have the
special interest that, in rejecting the Victorian tradition, they
adopted premises and methods which later characterized the
Modernist poets. In deliberately violating the governing conventions of nineteenth-century poetry, the Aesthetes were repudiating not merely a poetic mode, but even more an ethos and
modus vivendi.

To discuss the leading traits of Victorian culture against which
these multiple reactions occurred would involve another book,
but we can remind ourselves that the mainstream of mid-
Victorian thought assumed the rational character of the human
mind and its capability not only to find out truth but also to govern emotion and behavior. With this basic faith in human nature
there was naturally a tendency to optimism: intellectual, moral,
and social progress had been and would be taking place. This
optimism did not maintain itself without challenge and debate.
Many mid-Victorians, including some of the major literary fig-

ures, held the opposite view. But on the whole trust and optimism prevailed. They underlay the liberal ideal of open, responsible discussion with tolerance for diverse points of view, a tolerance that served, as Mill argued, the further discovery of truth and right. Along with this went ethical idealism and purposefulness, the sense of duty that survived even when religious faith had been shaken or eradicated.

Any man, Keats once remarked, can be torn to pieces if you take him on his weak sides; and so can any cultural milieu. Victorians in the middle of the nineteenth century could easily become hypocritical and smug, deserving the satire directed at them. However, it was not satire that killed the Victorian consensus of ideals, but the joint effects of what might be termed cultural disappointment and the need for novelty. Human life and history are such that ideals to which the heart is strongly committed will, sooner or later, appear inadequate. The way things turn out always violates the ideal hopes, which are then felt to have been out of touch with reality all along. And even were this not the case, men cannot be inspired by the same ideals indefinitely. In the latter part of the century there was a tendency toward more austere and tragic modes of thought: pessimistic interpretations of life and history; an emphasis on the pull of the unconscious as opposed to the control of the conscious mind; skepticism and nihilism or, alternatively, dogmatic belief and authority; a quest for irrational and supernatural modes of knowledge and truth. The mid-Victorian ideals could not simply be abandoned and forgotten: they had to be offended, deliberately. In the later nineteenth century there was a strong tendency toward what, at least since Baudelaire, has often been called Dandyism—behavior dramatizing an aristocratic and contemptuous scorn of the commonly accepted code. This rejection, expressed not by arguing but by posing, required both a mirror and an audience. For fin-de-siècle writers the audience was the reading public that still shared mid-Victorian premises and expected mid-Victorian styles.

The avant-garde derived much of its identity from a negation: it was not so much *post* as *anti*-Victorian. It continued the revolt of Swinburne, of the Pre-Raphaelites and Morris, and of Pater and Wilde. Like Swinburne, Pater, and Wilde, yet even more eagerly, it looked to the recent literature of France for models of how to live and what and how to write. Yet the avant-garde poets were extremely diverse in personality, in literary and cultural background, in opinions and beliefs. One ground on which they more or less united was the assertion of the autonomy and value of art. Victorian writers had been, it now seemed, tamed by middle-class respectability and responsibility. The principle of the autonomy of art therefore meant, at least in one implication, the refusal to make any concessions to the feelings of the middle class. On this issue the Realists or Naturalists of fiction and the Aesthetes and Decadents of poetry could unite: both Wilde and the English translator of Zola had been sent to prison; the Philistine herd had stampeded equally over Rossetti, Swinburne, and Hardy's *Tess*.

It was a question of asserting the integrity of the artist, his right and obligation to follow his own vision of truth and beauty. But some poets were tempted to an even more extreme and rebellious doctrine: art can be art in the purest and highest sense only when it is free of any other ideal commitment, whether to moral good, religious belief, truth to life or nature, or social betterment. "Poetry," as Baudelaire put it, "has no other end than itself." "I say that if the poet has pursued a moral end, he has diminished his poetic force . . . Poetry cannot, under pain of death or decline, assimilate itself to science or morality. It has not truth for its object. It has only itself." In this case one naturally wonders, what is poetry or art? Tolstoy's famous question was not answered in Tolstoy's way; to these poets, whatever else "art" might be, it was especially style and form. Whether Aesthetes, Decadents, Symbolists, or Impressionists, they were always formalists.

The borders between these classifications were unclear and easily crossed. The reason for trying to distinguish them is not to divide the writers into different schools but to indicate the separable though overlapping premises within the avant-garde. An Asethete, in a rough, preliminary summing up, was one who held to the principle not only of the autonomy of art but also of its supremacy over all other goods. Art or beauty could be the object of exclusive and priestly devotion because it was the highest thing. "This love of art for art's sake," Wilde explained, "is the point in which we of the younger school have made a departure from the teaching of Mr. Ruskin . . . The constancy of the artist" can be to the "principle of beauty only." "As for living," Yeats fondly quoted from Villiers de L'Isle Adam, "our servants will do that for us." The Decadent asserted the autonomy of art more aggressively by his choice of subject matter, or, more exactly, by his attitude toward his subject matter. He might dwell on the colors of a corpse, affirming that the greens were fine as meadow grass. He presented without criticism the ugly, morbid, perverse, pathological, neurasthenic, self-destructive, and the like, and he found in them a deeper reality and a strange new beauty, as is suggested in Baudelaire's title, *Les Fleurs du Mal*. The Symbolist of the nineties returned, often by way of German or English Romanticism, to Neoplatonic philosophy, Rosicrucianism, alchemy, Jakob Boehme, Giordano Bruno, and occult lore of every kind. The hope was to find how through symbols the mind may suggest, evoke, or even touch a reality beneath or beyond the routines and ordinary concerns of life—something more essentially real than business, child-rearing, politics, war, and death. Symbolism expressed a religious feeling or hope, and, though the distinction between symbolism and mysticism was well understood, the two modes of quasi-religious experience were often presented in the same writer, so that in practice "symbolic" and "mystical" tended to become interchangeable epithets. Impressionism, on the other hand, presupposed skepticism and relativism. Nothing can be known in itself; one has only the impression of the particular observer from his particular relation to the object. Everything in the outer world and the mind of man is in flux; there is only the fleeting moment. One renders the impression—something briefly observed and the feeling associated with it. In its pure form Impressionist literature goes no further. It does not assign meaning to the impression or relate it to others, for to do so would be to begin building up the coherent world in which the Impressionist writer no longer believes.

L'ART POUR L'ART

The phrase *l'art pour l'art* was first enunciated by Gautier. Before it gained much currency in England the premise had a long, complicated history in France, descending from Gautier,

Baudelaire, Flaubert, and others. Its English source is usually said to be Pater, though traces of the ideology have been discovered at least as far back as Blake and Keats, and have been occasionally noticed as a subordinate element in most English writers of the Victorian period. As the century wears on, the traces become larger and plainer in Swinburne and the Pre-Raphaelites, and by the late 1880s and 1890s the doctrine is openly espoused by Wilde, Symons, and numerous lesser figures

L'art pour l'art was grounded in hostility to the middle class, its way of life and its values. In the internecine wars of literature, however, it was directed against the Realists or Naturalists, against those writers, chiefly novelists, who held that the purpose of art is a faithful and detailed representation of contemporary and ordinary life. Against this, the makers of art for the sake of art argued for the formal, stylized, and conventional. Art, says Wilde, keeps between itself and life "the impenetrable barrier of beautiful style, of decorative or ideal treatment": "that unfortunate aphorism about Art holding the mirror up to Nature, is deliberately said by Hamlet in order to convince the bystanders of his absolute insanity in all art-matters." It follows of course that art is not to describe social realities and problems. It is not even to take a stand concerning them. One may think of Camus' anguished appeal: what of "the miner who is exploited and shot, the slaves in camps and colonies, the legions of persecuted?" Have they not a need that "everyman who can speak should cry out in place of their silence and not separate himself from them?" To this appeal the art-for-art's-sake writer might answer with the aphorism Pound puts in the mouth of Propertius: "We have kept our erasers in order." The loyalty and service of the artist belong to his art and nothing else. Let us, says Wilde, have no more "foolish attempts to draw attention [in literature] to the state of our convict prisons, and the management of our private lunatic asylums." The artist will not march to a social drum. He is indifferent to the cloudy turmoil of his particular spot in history.

The purpose or end of art is beauty, and beauty is style. Style is a supremely difficult achievement, won by knowledge, calculation, and scrupulous toil against the resistances of language. Hence there is in these writers an immense pride in their craft. The poet, according to Gautier, pursues "the profile of Apollo," working "with a delicate hand in a vein of agate"; he writes, says Pound, with an "engraver's tool" in the hardest of all materials. Vigny was honored for having said that "a book, such as I conceive it," must be "composed, sculptured, gilded, cut, finished, filed, and polished, like a statue of Parian marble." The poet was a cutter of jewels, for "in truth," says Pater, "all art does but consist in the removal of surplusage . . . the last finish of the gem-engraver blowing away the last particle of invisible dust." Or if the poet was not compared to an engraver, sculptor, or gem-worker, he might be thought of as a student, applying himself, says Saintsbury, with the "patient energy of sculptors, painters, and musicians" to discover the secrets of his art. Or he might be thought of as an initiate or priest in a sacred order, learning and carrying on the arcane discipline. Whatever the metaphor, the point is that only the fellow workman can appreciate the work. As for the generality of mankind, they may be dismissed, as Eliot dismisses the globe-trotter who stares at a perspective of Canaletto with "lustreless protrusive eye." And only the fellow workman can appreciate also the morality of the artist, which lies in deletion, revision, in patient self-submission to the perfecting of the work. With this devotion the artist both serves and brings into being the only permanence men can attain. "The bust survives the city," in Gautier's haughty words, "the gods themselves die, but the sovereign verses remain stronger than brass." There is the paradox: though art and beauty are the human handiwork of the artist, only in art can one mirror or, perhaps, dwell with the divine. The eternal descends to man not through revelation but through artifice, in Yeats's phrase, "the artifice of eternity."

Art was emphatically not what it was in the Romantic tradition, a cooperation with nature that completes it, an activity grounded in and witnessing to "a bond," says Coleridge, "between nature in the higher sense and the soul of man." Nature could not be the object of art; though by nature the Romantics had not meant merely countryside, the art-for-art writers tended to dwell on the distinctively man-made—the life of the city; the ceremonies and coiffures, so to speak, of civilized fashion; and art itself: paintings, Chinese jars, cameos, the Javanese dance, the carved lapis lazuli, and the bird of hammered gold. Nature could not suggest a process of composition, for organic form and emotional spontaneity were distrusted and abjured. Above all, nature could supply no criterion of the beautiful, and art was the opposite of nature—formal, conventional, traditional, artificial, and studied.

In this assertion of a divorce between nature and art, the art-for-art's-sake writers prepared the way for such later figures as Hulme, Pound, the New Humanists, Eliot, Richards, and the so-called New Critics. These writers also denounced individual emotional expansiveness and urged, though on different grounds, the importance of scrupulous workmanship and of the formal, traditional, and conventional elements in poetry. The art-for-art's-sake writers directly influenced poets such as Yeats and Wallace Stevens, whose ideas about poetry were first formed in the nineties, even though their own finest work came much later. For example, in "The Decay of Lying" Wilde makes a significantly typical remark about oriental art, praising what he takes to be "its frank rejection of imitation, its love of artistic convention, its dislike to the actual representation of any object in Nature." In Yeats's later poetry the art and civilization of the Far East are interpreted in similar terms. He modeled his verse drama partly on the Noh plays of Japan, and wanted the actors to wear masks for a typically ninetyish reason: "a mask will enable me to substitute for the face of some commonplace player . . . the fine invention of a sculptor . . . A mask never seems a mere dirty face." Such attitudes finally play into Yeats's "Sailing to Byzantium" and "Byzantium," two of the greatest lyrics of the century. These poems are inconceivable without the *l'art pour l'art* premise that there is a radical opposition between nature and art or artifice. And the art to which these poems refer is that of Byzantium, which Yeats thinks of as traditional, conventional, and stylized. But the same feeling of a split between nature and art could lead in the opposite direction, not toward tradition and convention but toward an assertion of complete creative freedom. Gautier remarked, "I should like prairies colored red, rivers golden yellow and trees blue. Nature has no imagination." This suggests how much in modern painting may also descend from the ferment of *l'art pour l'art*. The feeling of independence from nature could come as a relief, fostering an enormous zest in the direct expression of the purely human intellect and imagination. Of this tradition Wallace Stevens became, especially in his later poems, the chief poet.

With these ideas of the character and purpose of art, the art-for-art's-sake writer was likely also to insist that great art is impersonal. Its aspiration toward beauty has nothing to do with individual life and opinions; as for passion, it is, Baudelaire explains, "too natural" to be intruded into the realm of beauty. Wilde joins Eliot, who would certainly have endorsed at least half of the statement that "to reveal art and conceal the artist is art's aim." Neither is art formed or influenced by the prevailing attitudes of the age. "Art," to quote Wilde again, "has an independent life, . . . and develops purely on its own lines," a remark that shows some affinities with Northrop Frye's principle that all art comes from previous art. And of course the art-for-art's-sake writers assumed that art is to be judged as art. They were as ready as later generations to repudiate what have been called the "biographical fallacy" and the "intentional fallacy," and to brandish the New Critical principle that the poem is to be viewed in itself, without relation to the writer or his life and purposes.

Turning to Ernest Dowson and Lionel Johnson, I do not mean to suggest that they are followers of *l'art pour l'art*. They cannot be classified with any one premise or group. Nevertheless, they are typical of the formalist workmanship of the avantgarde. Dowson (1867–1900) was personally acquainted through the Rhymers' Club with Wilde, Yeats, Richard Le Gallienne, Johnson, and Arthur Symons. The club was simply a loose association of poets who met occasionally at the Cheshire Cheese in order to read their verses aloud and engage in literary conversation. The group was committed to no ideology, though generally they were much influenced by the Pre-Raphaelites and Pater and also interested in Baudelaire and the *symbolistes*. Dowson himself fits almost too well our stereotype of the fin-de-siècle poet. He was a Roman Catholic convert with an imaginative interest in monasticism. At least in his later years, he was more at home in France than in England. He was prey to an idolatry in love and worshipped from afar his "cold" and inaccessible Adelaide until, some years having lapsed, she married a waiter in her father's restaurant. He was tubercular, and further shortened his life by dissipation. Dowson seems to have thought of poetry not as the articulation of ideas or the release of emotion, but as music and form. In a letter of 1891 he states his aspiration to write "verses in the manner of the French 'symbolists': Verses making for mere sound, and music, with just a suggestion of sense, or hardly that."

Major shaping influences on Dowson's writing include not only Pater and Swinburne, Baudelaire and Verlaine but also such Roman poets as Horace, Catullus, and Propertius. (He liked to give his poems long Latin titles, which are sometimes quotations.) His poems take up themes—the frustration or transitoriness of love, the vanity of life, the allure of the grave—that such reading could easily suggest, though these themes are also natural products of his own experience. There are whiffs of the exotic, morbid, or morally questionable that one associates with the Decadents—for example, his prose piece on absinthe ("Absinthia Taetra"), or the questioning "Why wine-stained lip and languid eye . . . Should move us more" than virginity ("Rondeau"), or, in his famous poem to Cynara, the reference to the "bought red mouth" of the prostitute with whom he spends the night. Classical models in the late nineteenth century rarely resulted in the precision, economy, or weight of meaning of the truly classical, but only in studied and polished form. Dowson's reticent temperament and emulation of the French poets, as he understood their purposes, worked to the same general end. The result is a formal and musical virtuosity that eliminates almost everything else, including interest. It sounds like this:

> When I am old,
>   And every star above
> Be pitiless and cold:
>   My life's one love!
> Forbid me not to go:
> Remember nought of us but long ago,
> And not at last, how love and pity strove
>   When I grew old!

Or it sounds like this adaptation of Elizabethan song:

> Exceeding sorrow
>   Consumeth my sad heart!
> Because to-morrow
>   We must depart,
> Now is exceeding sorrow
>   All my part!

Though undeniably accomplished, such verse lacks the wealth of concrete imagery that has been a unique endowment of

English poetry in the Spenser-Keats tradition. Neither, though classically restrained, does it have the compression and wit of English neoclassicism in the tradition of Jonson or Pope. There is none of the specificity of plot and novelistic detail that works so effectively in Hardy, or, among Dowson's own models, in Baudelaire. One might think of Dowson as writing a poetry of "pure" emotion, but even the emotion is not intense. Dowson's temperament, his intentions as a poet, and his models as he interpreted them combined to produce poetry of which the essence is a thin purification of form achieved by leaving out almost everything else. It is a highly specialized art in which, as with Wilde or Housman, strict versification becomes the vehicle of sentimental feeling. The combination has charm, especially for adolescent moods—self-pity enjoyed under the mask of firmness.

Dowson's style goes beyond most poets even of the fin de siècle in intricacy and subtlety of versification; in other respects he shares in a subdued way many mannerisms of the time. His interest in versification led him, as it led other contemporaries, to some of the more complicated French lyric forms, particularly the *rondeau* and the *villanelle*. He does not usually follow these forms strictly, but preserves the effects gained by repetition of line both in substantive body and as lyric refrain. He was also fond of repeating phrases with slight variations. His stanzaic constructions skillfully evoke nameless emotion through such repetitions, and also through alternating masculine and feminine rhymes, varying line length, cadence, and pause. For example:

> They are not long, the weeping and the laughter,
>> Love and desire and hate:
> I think they have no portion in us after
>> We pass the gate.
>
> They are not long, the days of wine and roses:
>> Out of a misty dream
> Our path emerges for a while, then closes
>> Within a dream.

The effect of this depends more on versification than anything else, though much must be allowed also for the world-weariness conveyed by cataloguing love and laughter in the same tone as weeping and hate. The poem is typical of Dowson's diction and imagery. The diction can have a biblical or classical simplicity and directness (he is the source of the phrase, "gone with the wind"); but it can also be archaic or exotic and is, on the whole, rather Latinate. The general effect is to dissociate his poems from actual life, evoking literary tradition and artifice instead. He has a stock of favorite words and images—pale, cold, passionate, wild, dream, silence, weary, sorrow, wine, roses, lilies, moon, viols, and the like—and these express and create a literary stylization of experience.

Of the famous "Non sum qualis eram bonae sub regno Cynarae" Eliot once remarked, "the lines have always run in my head," and he adapted a phrase from it ("falls thy shadow") for the refrain at the conclusion of "The Hollow Men." Many readers have found it similarly haunting:

> Last night, ah, yesternight, betwixt her lips and mine
> There fell thy shadow, Cynara! thy breath was shed
> Upon my soul between the kisses and the wine;
> And I was desolate and sick of an old passion,
>   Yea, I was desolate and bowed my head:
> I have been faithful to thee, Cynara! in my fashion.

The poem is not quite typical of Dowson, for it conveys relatively more "plot" and more passion than one expects of him. But it is typical in its metrical achievement, the supple handling of the alexandrine, and it exploits repetition with special effect, each stanza having the same fourth line and concluding with the rich melange of irony and self-pity in "faithful . . . in my fashion." The poem, written in a bar, has been called the most complete expression of the fin de siècle in England, doubtless because of its obvious intention to defy middle-class morality, its plush and gaslit classicism, its elaborate and musical artifice, its nostalgia of the libertine for lost innocence, its desperation and hopelessness.

According to Yeats, Lionel Johnson (1867–1902) was a dominating figure in the Rhymers' Club. He intimidated the others by his erudition, by the intellectual precision of his talk, and perhaps even more by his silences—"the only man I know," said Yeats, "whose silence has beak and claw." In the club meetings Johnson enforced a doctrine, Yeats says, whose chief article was "an opposition to all ideas, all generalizations that can be explained and debated." The great Victorian poets had filled their poetry with thoughts about politics, science, history, and religion; the younger Rhymers in reaction felt that "we must create once more the pure work." Yeats (in his *Autobiography*) portrays Johnson as a Pre-Raphaelite and a follower of Pater. In his own critical prose Johnson further and especially shows himself a disciple of Newman and Arnold. Literature, he insists, must be written and judged in the light of the real and permanent classics. "Let us value our age and ourselves, according to the *mind* of the great masters, and in *their* spirit." The writer must possess these great masters as a "conscience." The principle is not inconsistent with those of Pater or the Pre-Raphaelites but it blocks the one further step into aestheticism. Though he was a Rhymer, Johnson is perhaps more essentially related to writers such as Bridges or Housman in whom objectivity or at least personal reticence, studied and polished form, and an emphasis on tradition, consciousness, and criticism as essential elements in the creative process were fostered more by devotion to the classics than by the current excitements. In fact, the classics, Pater, and Arnold all equally encouraged in Johnson a haughty independence of contemporary movements and a special contempt for self-conscious contemporaneity, whether in the form of Kipling's public-spirited journalism or of the private Impressionistic sensitivities of Henley, Wilde, or Symons. Of the latter type he says, "This literature of throbbing nerves and of subtle sensations . . . must lose half its beauty, by losing all its humanity: it ceases to continue the great tradition of polite, of humane letters: it becomes the private toy of its betrayers."

Johnson was a Roman Catholic convert and many of his poems are specifically churchly as well as religious in theme. For this reason he is often mentioned with such dissimilar writers as Hopkins, Patmore, Dowson, Francis Thompson, and Alice Meynell. One would expect a reader of Pater to respond appreciatively to the historical associations and liturgy of the church, and Johnson does, perhaps most memorably in "The Church of a Dream," a synthesis of romantic nostalgia, Arnoldian melancholy, and Pre-Raphaelite color:

> Sadly the dead leaves rustle in the whistling wind,
> Around the weather-worn, gray church, low down the vale:
> The Saints in golden vesture shake before the gale;

The glorious windows shake, where still they dwell enshrined;
Old Saints by long dead, shrivelled hands, long since designed:
There still, although the world autumnal be, and pale,
Still in their golden vesture the old saints prevail;
Alone with Christ, desolate else, left by mankind.

Only one ancient Priest offers the sacrifice,
Murmuring holy Latin immemorial:
Swaying with tremulous hands the old censer full of spice,
In gray, sweet incense clouds; blue, sweet clouds mystical:
To him, in place of men, for he is old, suffice
Melancholy remembrances and vesperal.

But Johnson was not one who, in Eliot's phrase, swallowed the dogma for the sake of the ritual. Like Eliot, he possessed a close and appalled vision of evil; it is unforgettably expressed in "The Dark Angel." He was driven on the same quest for meaning or significance in living: without faith he has "nothing in the world, but death." And both poets were attracted to the church as a source of authority and dogmatic rigor. The inflexibilities of dogma were the more necessary to Johnson as a support in his long, tragically defeated battle against dipsomania. Yeats remarks that "his doctrine, after a certain number of glasses, would become more ascetic, more contemptuous" of human weakness, and Pound says that "the pure mind / Arose toward Newman as the whiskey warmed." But these discrepancies between conduct and doctrine become less amusing when we think how much they reveal Johnson's self-struggle and self-contempt. The conflict between aesthetic and ascetic values or between the world and the church is an occasional theme of his poetry—for example, in "To a Passionist," "Men of Assisi," or "Men of Aquino"—but in his poetry the theme has none of the urgency it must have had in the life of this reticent man who dreamed of being a monk but was only a bookish recluse, losing day after day his private, humiliating battle.

His other main anchor and loyalty, besides the church, was Ireland. Johnson had no family connection with Ireland, but he felt Celtic affinities from his fondness for Wales, he was a liberal in politics and favored Irish independence, he knew and admired Yeats, and he threw himself into the cause, persuading himself somehow that he was an Irishman and becoming a

leading figure in the Irish Literary Revival. The many poems he
wrote in 1893–94 are chiefly of this patriotic kind, in which Ireland is symbolized as a sorrowing mother, and the "host of Inis-
fail" is heartened by promises of bloody victory. Much of his effort went into committee meetings and lectures, and he was the
most important Catholic poet of the movement.

George Santayana, who knew him slightly, saw Johnson as a
romantic with a "passionate need of sinking into . . . dreams,
and defying the false world that pretended to be more real." In
reading him, "you are aware of a great wind of passionate language, but not of what was said or of what it was all about." "To
Morfydd" might be a poem of this kind:

> A voice on the winds,
> A voice by the waters,
> Wanders and cries:
> *Oh! what are the winds?*
> *And what are the waters?*
> *Mine are your eyes!*

But such vague and haunting music is not characteristic. One
finds instead a poetry of clear and definite statement, however
emotional. Yeats tells us that his favorite adjective was "marmoreal," a word appropriate to the studied concision of his verse,
as in "A Burden of Easter Vigil":

> This only can be said:
> He loved us all; is dead;
>   May rise again.
> *But if He rise not?* Over the far main,
> The sun of glory falls indeed: the stars are plain.

The lines are typical in their firm and telling phrases, slowed
movement, weighted pauses, spoken idiom, and relatively complicated, difficult form. They are typical also in their absence or
failure of what might be called imagination; when he reaches for
metaphor at a climactic moment, he can find only the conventional and ineffectively vague.

Johnson's poetry is too limited to have major importance. Reticence, ordered statement, feelings of undeviating noble ardor
and melancholy compel respect, but one regrets the lack of
imagination, concrete incident, personality, and humor. He is at

his best in poems such as "The Dark Angel" or "Mystic and Cavalier," where the tragedy of his personal life is most immediately expressed, though still with profound reserve:

> Go from me: I am one of those, who fall.
> What! hath no cold wind swept your heart at all,
> In my sad company? Before the end,
> Go from me, dear my friend!

THE DECADENCE

That human nature and civilization are in decline has been a perennial theme in literature for as long as there has been any literature. In the later nineteenth century this feeling expressed itself, among other ways, in the literature of the Decadence and in the many attacks upon it. The Decadent writer saw himself as the late product of an overripe civilization, jaded, bored, and no longer capable of natural emotion. Ultrasophisticated, with an insect feeler's sensitivity, he might give himself over in an amoral way to new, monstrous, or perverse emotions and sensations, the sharp spices craved by his dulled palate. In the pathological and self-destructive he might find, he hoped, the Orphean path, descending from the superficial ordinary to the deeper reality. Genius, as Mann later kept suspecting, might be disease. In Baudelaire and Laforgue, Schopenhauer and Nietzsche, Proust and Mann, one finds that on the Continent both a fear and an ambiguous celebration of Decadence were interwoven through a literature of profound and complex power.

In England, however, all that happened in the literary Decadence per se was that a few minor writers made superficial gestures. There was the young George Moore imitating Baudelaire in *Flowers of Passion* (1878) and *Pagan Poems* (1881). *Flowers of Passion* includes an "Ode to a Dead Body," of which one line goes, "Poor Breasts! whose nipples sins alone have fed." Or there was Theodore Wratislaw (1871–1933), whose poems might have been composed expressly to illustrate our stock image of the nineties. In *Love's Memorial* (1892) one sees that he has been reading Baudelaire. In *Caprices* (1893) he switched his imitation to Arthur Symons' *Silhouettes,* which had been published the year before. According to Nietzsche, in his famous attack on Wagner, the three greatest stimulants of an exhausted sensibility are brutality, innocence, and artifice. Wratislaw tells us, however, that even brutality, or at least sadomasochistic emotions, may become a bore. In "Sonnet Macabre" he writes, "I love you . . . because you wear / Corruption with a vague and childish air . . . I love you for . . . The avid poison of your subtle kiss," but in "Satiety" he is,

> weary of the heat of hell,
> The perfumed palace of thy love.

In "Palm Sunday" he turns to the Roman Catholic mass to savor the feeling of purification at the altar. His most amusing poem is "Orchids," a stock subject which permits all the usual things. Orchids are exotic, artificial flowers that grow out of the "rank / Fierce hotbed of corruption." In a "clamorous orchestra" their "hues . . . diffuse / Weird dreams." Inspired by orchids, his poems will be a "temple of coloured sorrows and perfumed sins." John Gray (1866–1934), was said to be the original for Wilde's Dorian Gray. He published two volumes of poems in the 1890s, *Silverpoints* (1893) and *Spiritual Poems* (1896). Some of these are imitations of French poets, including Baudelaire, but Gray was only occasionally a Decadent. His most impressive quality is his perfectionist workmanship whatever his theme or mood. He became a Roman Catholic convert and entered the priesthood in 1901.

Between 1884 and 1893 John Barlas (1860–1914) put forth eight small volumes of verse under the pseudonym "Evelyn Douglas." He was a socialist and praised free love in Shelley-Swinburnian images and rhythms. In other poems he exploited the femme-fatale motif:

> As a cat watches mice, she watches us;
> And I am sure her claws are murderous—

"Terrible Love" sought horror through expressive distortion, much as in Aubrey Beardsley's drawings:

> Oh sweet delicious lips
> From which I fancy all the world's blood drips!
> Oh supple waist, pale cheek, and eyes of fire,
> Hard little breasts and white gigantic hips,
> And blue-black hair with serpent coils that slips
> Out of my hand in hours of red desire.

"A Dream of China" reflects the modish orientalism of the day.
The Chinese ladies, with their "tiny feet" and "wrought elaborate hair," are dressed

> with diamond butterflies, and laced
> With artificial flowers metal-faced,

while their "almond eyes glint amorously." The poem is one of a
number which Barlas said were composed "as deliberate dreamy
reveries while awake." Since it has no plot or order, its effect is
made only by the separate images, each one being required to
outdo the last in order to hold interest. Some of the closing lines
faintly remind one of Yeats,

> There at a great chess-table, rose and white,
> Sits many a grave and blue-robed mandarin,
> Moving the carven pieces, left and right,

and the revery ends with an image of the empress descending
some "snowy marble corridor" at midnight, going perhaps to
her lover. The poem evokes ideas of luxury, refinement, intellect, artifice, sensuality, strangeness, and, above all, of the re-
moteness of these mandarin figures from life.

The most ambitious literary expression of the Decadence in
England was Wilde's play *Salome* (1894), a fact that illustrates
once again what a minor thing the Decadence was. Yet the play
is brilliant in its way. With its exotic, oppressive style, based remotely on the Song of Songs, its repetitive, artificial dialogue, its
concentration on a single event, its climactic summing up and
symbolizing of the whole in Salome's dance, it hypnotizes attention and closes perspectives, so that this elaborate, stylized world
takes on a reality of its own and holds one in a reluctant fascination. One sees how it is being done; one knows that it is prepos-
terous; but one feels that it works. (The technique has some affinities with Yeats's later plays, which also concentrate on a
single action and rely much on mannered style, gesture, and
dance.) The drama has for its setting the luxurious and sensual,
oriental court of King Herod; it is filled with peculiar passions
such as the insatiable lust of Herodias and the erotic fascination
of the king for his daughter. Salome is the archetype of the
femme fatale. Sexually excited by John's religious austerity and
harshness, she is fascinating and cruel. Her passion, like all passion in the play, is gratuitous yet also obsessive and irresistible.

Despite all this, the drama—this is its special grace—does not take its own exhibitionist and mummified Decadence quite seriously. It hovers continuously on the edge of a wit that reminds one of Shaw or of Wilde's own comedies. At one point in the play Herod says to Salome, "come and eat fruits with me," and the traditional symbolism speaks of sensual appetite, lust, and the invitation of the serpent. "I love," he adds, "to see in a fruit the mark of thy little teeth," and if this shows a Decadent odd obsession, it also shows Wilde's sense of fun, the whimsicality of *The Importance of Being Earnest.*

As a final illustration we may take Arthur Symons' "Javanese Dancers." The poem is not typical of Symons, who was only sporadically a Decadent writer, but it draws together many of the themes of the Decadence. It describes oriental dancers, presenting the dance as an art that is sensual and yet also traditional, learned, and arcane.

> Twitched strings, the clang of metal, beaten drums,
> Dull, shrill, continuous, disquieting;
> And now the stealthy dancer comes
> Undulantly with cat-like steps that cling;
>
> Smiling between her painted lids a smile,
> Motionless, unintelligible, she twines
> Her fingers into mazy lines,
> The scarves across her fingers twine the while.
>
> One, two, three, four glide forth, and, to and fro,
> Delicately and imperceptibly,
> Now swaying gently in a row,
> Now interthreading slow and rhythmically,
>
> Still, with fixed eyes, monotonously still,
> Mysteriously, with smiles inanimate,
> With lingering feet that undulate,
> With sinuous fingers, spectral hands that thrill
>
> In measure while the gnats of music whirr,
> The little amber-coloured dancers move,
> Like painted idols seen to stir
> By the idolaters in a magic grove.

In the dancers one sees a version of the famous La Gioconda figure from Pater's *The Renaissance,* the inscrutable and haunting face both of a woman and a work of art, the mysterious beauty

that is age-old and beyond good and evil. One has the femme fatale with suggestions of cruelty and irresistible fascination. One
has human figures taking on the stiffness and artifice of works
of art as they are compared to "painted idols" with "fixed eyes"
and "smiles inanimate." There is the dance itself—an elaborate,
slow, and unnatural rhythm performed to the exotic sounds of
"twitched strings, the clang of metal, beaten drums." The poem
is all stylization, ritual, artifice, exoticism, and dubious eroticism,
and in these respects sums up the interplay of *l'art pour l'art* with
the Decadence.

SYMBOLISM

One may take these images another way—the dance with its
traditional gestures and meanings, the idols that stir to life somewhere in a magic grove. These may be symbols, pointing toward
or evoking ultimate mysteries or truths. The poem then becomes a fascinating example of Symbolism as it was practiced by
Yeats and Symons in the 1890s. Most avant-garde poets of the
time were well aware of Baudelaire, Mallarmé, and other French
writers who were sometimes called *symbolistes*. They did not,
however, usually think of them as *symbolistes;* neither had they
much considered what *symbolisme* might be. Dowson's idea of it is
given in the remark already quoted: "mere sound, and music,
with just a suggestion of sense, or hardly that." For George
Moore, Symbolism was "saying the opposite of what you mean."
Wilde seems to have remarked chiefly its style: "that curious
jewelled style, vivid and obscure at once, full of *argot* and of ar-
chaisms, of technical expressions and of elaborate paraphrases,
that characterizes the work of some of the finest artists of the
French school of Symbolistes." The remarks are typical.

The only really important discussions of either Symbolism or
French *Symbolisme* in the 1890s are by Yeats in the essays collected as *Ideas of Good and Evil* (1903) and by Symons in *The Symbolist Movement in Literature* (1899). Though in literary history
Symons' book had the greater impact, Yeats had a better understanding of symbolism. He develops his ideas in essays on symbolism directly, and also on Blake, Shelley, magic, painting, and
the literary scene. For Yeats an image becomes symbolic within a

tradition. The tradition may be that of literature, religion, occult lore, or the folk imagination. The point is that the traditional symbol, having been used time after time in so many different contexts, calls up a dense nexus of meanings, emotions, and associations. The rose is a traditional symbol of this kind, and he makes central use of it in the group of poems entitled "The Rose" (1895). But for Yeats symbols may be more than traditional. They may be supernatural. They express or, perhaps, they summon a reality beneath or beyond mortal life. Just how this may be he himself wonders. Perhaps as in the ceremonies of magic the symbol is in touch with unknown beings or forces by its own inherent virtue. The power, in other words, lies in the symbol, not in the mage. The mage knows how to invoke the supernatural through the symbol; he himself does not know the supernatural directly. Or possibly the imagination of the artist knows ultimate reality and expresses in symbols what it knows. What matters most is that, whether we think it merely traditional or also supernatural, the symbol is charged with meanings deeper, wider, and more precise than anyone can say. What it conveys cannot be put in other words, for the symbol is "the only possible expression of some invisible essence." What it contains cannot be exhausted. "A hundred generations might write out what seemed" its meaning, "and they would write different meanings, for no symbol tells all its meaning to one generation." And yet, though unanalyzable, the symbol is not vague. "All sounds, all colours, all forms, either because of their preor-dained energies or because of long associations, evoke indefin-able and yet precise emotions." With symbolism, as Yeats states in "The Philosophy of Shelley's Poetry," the literary work takes on depth, mystery, and abundance.

It is only by ancient symbols, by symbols that have numberless meanings beside the one or two the writer lays an emphasis upon, or the half-score he knows of, that any highly subjective art can escape from the barrenness and shallowness of a too conscious arrangement, into the abundance and depth of nature. The poet of essences and pure ideas must seek in the half-lights that glimmer from symbol to symbol as if to the ends of the earth, all that the epic and dramatic poet finds of mystery and shadow in the accidental circumstances of life.

It seemed to Yeats, pondering these matters in the 1890s, that the arts had reached a crisis in their history. From the "first days," he said, man had been descending the stairway toward a mastery of actuality, the mortal world of common experience. Art also had increasingly become "a critic of life and an interpreter of things as they are." But now the direction was reversing itself. Art was turning away from the outward world of things, hence from scientific curiosity, moral responsibility, political passions, from description and argument. "With the wealth he has been so long gathering upon his shoulders," man was starting to ascend the stairway from nature to the supernatural. The coming age of art would dwell on the "invisible life," the "essences of things," delivering "the ever new and ever ancient revelation." To this new art Yeats applied the word "symbolical." But true art had always been symbolical. What was the difference now? The modern symbolical movement, he felt, was more conscious of itself; it was more eclectic in calling upon many and diverse traditions; it was less under the censorship of moral and social opinion, for it had "accepted all the Divine Intellect, its anger and its pity, its waking and its sleep, its love and its lust." Above all, the symbolical movement would be a final movement in the arts: man has "fallen weary" of the world, and "not, I think, for a time, but with a weariness that will not end until the last autumn, when the stars shall be blown away like withered leaves."

Symons was a friend of Yeats and shared lodgings with him in the 1890s. Keenly interested in recent French literature, he published between 1895 and 1898 enthusiastic essays on Huysmans, Mallarmé, Nerval, Rimbaud, Villiers de L'Isle Adam, Verlaine, and Maeterlinck. He did not at first view all his authors as Symbolists, but gradually, talking with Yeats, was persuaded that a new development of the highest significance was taking place in the arts—Yeats's Symbolical Movement. With this in mind, Symons gathered together and somewhat retouched the essays he had already published, wrote a new one on Laforgue, and added a Preface and a Conclusion that embodied, as Richard Ellmann says, "the new insight Yeats had helped him to reach, the perception of a singleness of purpose among these disparate talents." The result was the famous *The Symbolist Movement in Literature* (1899). It is a series of introductory essays on recent French writers, with impressions of their personalities, brief accounts of their theories and styles, and examples of their work.

Though much has little connection with Symbolism in stricter senses of the term, the title seemed to tie it all together. The notion that there was a Symbolist Movement caught on. In fact, the term "Symbolist" no longer necessarily implies what it did for Symons and Yeats, the quest for transcendent reality. It is sometimes used as a name for the whole Modernist movement in twentieth-century literature, especially in poetry. Symons' book was the most important single work in transmitting the ideas and practices of the French poets to the younger writers in English. As T. S. Eliot later testified, but for having read Symons "I should not, in the year 1908, have heard of Laforgue or Rimbaud; I should probably not have begun to read Verlaine; and but for reading Verlaine, I should not have heard of Corbière."

In this book Symons' notions of Symbolism shift a bit from essay to essay. In general, however, Symbolism is an attempt to make "the soul of things visible." Reacting against scientific materialism, the Symbolist poet assumes that reality is ultimately "spirit" or "soul." Seeking to evoke this, he exploits symbols, but also dream, vision, association, suggestion, connotation, and deliberately indefinite reference; he avoids whatever might seem denoted and external, especially plot, logic, and "rhetoric." As a literary mode Symbolism is the opposite not only of fictional realism but also, Symons argues, of Parnassian poetry, with its emphasis on precise description and statement. An Idealist in philosophical premise, the Symbolist writer may affirm the Platonic concept that everything in the actual world of experience presents itself as a reflection of something in the transcendent realm of the real. Or he may believe in an organic cosmos in which one identical Life or Spirit pervades the whole. Symons quotes Nerval: "All things live, all things are in motion, all things correspond . . . Now a captive upon the earth, I hold converse with the starry choir, which is feelingly a part of my joys and sorrows." For Symons, the intuition of organic unity or correspondence provides the ground for a technical procedure which later appears everywhere in Modernist poetry: the juxtaposition or "setting together" of "apparently alien things." Such juxtaposition is possible because all things, however "distant and divergent" they may seem, are really connected by "hidden links." To sum up, "the ideal of lyric poetry . . . is to be this passive, flawless medium for the deeper consciousness of things, the mysterious voice of that mystery which lies about us, out of which we have come, and into which we shall return." And Symons also insinuates, like Yeats, that since the Symbolist Movement is under way, younger writers would do well to climb aboard. He concludes his essay on Mallarmé by saying, "it is on the lines of that spiritualising of the word, that perfecting of form in its capacity for allusion and suggestion, that confidence in the eternal correspondences between the visible and the invisible universe, which Mallarmé taught, and too intermittently practised, that literature must now move, if it is in any sense to move forward."

IMPRESSIONISM AND ARTHUR SYMONS

Though Symons is hardly the best poet of the avant-garde in the 1890s, he is the most representative, at least in the sense that he subsumes the most diverse trends and influences. Briefly surveying his career, I shall notice poetic Impressionism in the 1890s. For Symons' contemporaries viewed him primarily as an Impressionist—"he is a slave to impressionism," Lionel Johnson remarked.

Arthur Symons (1865–1945) published his first book, an *Introduction to the Study of Browning,* when he was twenty-one. For the next two decades he was a central figure in the literary world, active as a poet, critic, essayist, and editor. His first volume of poetry, *Days and Nights* (1889), shows the mingled influence of Browning and Pater, to whom the book is dedicated. The poems tend to be melodramatic exercises on fin-de-siècle topics: "The Opium-Smoker"; "The Abandoned," which describes a suicide; "Satiety," in which the speaker asks, "What joy is left in all I look upon? / I cannot sin, it wearies me." In this same year Symons traveled to Paris in the company of Havelock Ellis, who introduced him to Verlaine, Mallarmé, Huysmans, and other figures of the French literary world. The trip had a crucial importance for Symons, since he became henceforth a main English advocate of the work and theories of these writers. His next volume of verse, *Silhouettes* (1892), shows this influence in a number of Impressionist and Symbolist experiments. One typical and successful poem is "Maquillage," an impression of a prostitute that dwells appreciatively on her fragile charm, especially as it is enhanced by cosmetics. Because it presents a courtesan without moral repudiation, the poem might have seemed a trifle shocking, even though Victorian convention still prompts Symons to hint that her charm will soon fade and wretchedness follow. From another point of view, the poem exemplifies Pater's aesthetic hedonism: the girl's charm becomes "choicer," to use Pater's word, because it is transient. With pathos the impression becomes the more curious and aesthetically interesting. In *Silhouettes* and the next volume, *London Nights* (1895), Symons' poetry reached its finest development, and, though it gradually changed in kind, there is no need to notice it further. In 1908 Symons suffered a mental breakdown; he recovered and continued to write prolifically, but his work no longer held an audience. He took little interest in the literature written after 1908.

Of Symons' critical essays, those that matter for our purpose are the ones that expound his own aims as a poet or those of the avant-garde. These are particularly "The Decadent Movement in Literature," published in *Harper's New Magazine* in 1893; the Preface to the second edition of *Silhouettes* (1896); the Preface to the second edition of *London Nights* (1897); and *The Symbolist Movement in Literature* (1899). The Preface to *London Nights* only repeats former arguments more stridently, and *The Symbolist Movement in Literature* has already been touched on. In "The Decadent Movement in Literature" Symons uses the term "Decadence" as a large, covering label for the new literature in general. By 1899 this literature was termed Symbolist, but in 1893 Symbolism and Impressionism are listed as subordinate terms that designate the "two main branches" of the Decadent movement. This literature may be called "Decadent," Symons argues, because "it has all the qualities that mark the end of great periods," namely, "an intense self-consciousness, a restless curiosity in research, an over-subtilizing refinement upon refinement, a spiritual and moral perversity." It lacks the sanity, simplicity, proportion, health, and energy of the classical, but, after all, sophistication, artificiality, and perversity are typical of present-day civilization. How much do we ourselves possess the classic qualities, "that we should look to find them in our literature?" (The same argument will be used throughout the Modernist period to apologize for modern art. If modern life is multi-farious, complex, and disjunctive, art must follow suit, and so on. The argument betrays itself, however, by its selectivity. You notice only those aspects of modern life that justify the particular poet and his supporters in their procedures. It was absurd for Symons to argue that late Victorian civilization—of which Kipling and Wells are truer exponents than he was—was overly self-conscious and refined, restlessly curious and perverse. These adjectives applied, at most, to a small group of intellectuals.)

Silhouettes had been attacked by reviewers who held that the poems were immoral. In the Preface to the second edition, Symons replied in an essay, "A Word on Behalf of Patchouli," which is a disarming, typical defense of the autonomy of art. It is also, however, a defense of artifice, of Impressionism, and of the diminished stance, the poet presenting himself not as a bard or sage but as a minor cultivator of pleasant, minor feelings. "However you may try to convince yourself to the contrary," says Symons, "a work of art can be judged only from two standpoints: the standpoint from which its art is measured entirely by its morality, and the standpoint from which its morality is measured entirely by its art." Symons goes on as an Impressionist to claim "liberty for the rendering of every mood of that variable and inexplicable creature which we call ourselves, and of every aspect under which we are gifted or condemned to apprehend the beauty and strangeness and curiosity of the visible world." He argues in the tradition of Baudelaire and Wilde on behalf of the artificial, even perhaps of the perverse, not as the necessary or the most promising field for poetry but as an entirely legitimate one. "If you prefer your 'new mown hay' in the hayfield, and I, it may be, in a scent-bottle, why may not my individual caprice be allowed to find expression as well as yours?" And so the argument maintains its uninsistent, urbane, ironic poise. Health and wholesomeness are found in nature; artifice and perversity in the city. But, then, without belittling health, wholesomeness, or nature, Symons asks whether they are charming? And whether they are all that is charming? And why should one not enjoy the charming moment or sensation wherever it may be found? "Why not Patchouli?" "Is there any 'reason in nature' why we should write exclusively about the natural blush, if the delicately acquired blush of rouge has any attraction for us?"

The essay is hedonist, aesthetic, and Impressionist, blandly debonaire in pose and deliberately anti-Victorian. Its tone and style might have been thought Parisian, as Symons intended, and so also might the constellation of values. Yet fully to understand Symons' view of things one must turn not to France but to Oxford, to Walter Pater, who diffused from his quiet study attitudes he never quite intended and slightly deplored. All shades of avant-garde opinion owed much to Pater; Symons may be said to have owed him almost his intellectual being. It is well-known that after he had written the famous Conclusion to *Studies in the History of the Renaissance* (1873), Pater was embarrassed by it and withdrew it for a while; in subsequent works he modified his position. Nevertheless, these were the pages that summed up for the coming generation what Pater had to say, the pages in which some few seemed to find the desperate solace of truth. It is easy to see why the Conclusion is often taken as a document in the history of *l'art pour l'art*. Pater ends with praise of "art for art's sake," since art offers the supreme examples of the intense experience he is looking for. But he does not make art an end in itself; he values it only for what it brings to life. His real affinities are with literary (and critical) Impressionism.

In a series of reductive assertions, he characterizes all that we can know or possess as reality. We suppose, he argues, that we dwell in a world of external objects, but objects are not what we actually experience. As soon as we reflect upon it, "each object is loosed into a group of impressions," into subjective and fleeting nodes of consciousness. "Experience, already reduced to a swarm of impressions, is ringed round for each one of us by that thick wall of personality through which no real voice has ever pierced on its way to us, or from us to that which we can only conjecture to be without"; and, "Analysis goes a step farther still, and assures us that those impressions of the individual mind to which, for each one of us, experience dwindles down, are in perpetual flight." Having come to this point, Pater restates the basic premise of Impressionism in literature:

To such a tremulous wisp constantly re-forming itself on the stream, to a single sharp impression, with a sense in it, a relic more or less fleeting, of such moments gone by, what is real in our life fines itself down.

If this be reality, how can the writer of poetry or fiction be true to it? Pater does not say, but the inference was clear: one can

render the movement of consciousness, "the passage and disso-
lution of impressions," and nothing more. For to relate these
moments to each other except by temporal succession, or to interpret them except conjecturally, would be to assert a coherence and meaning in experience for which there is no warrant.

On these premises Pater rears an Epicurean morality. "Success in life" lies in maintaining the greatest possible intensity in
experience as it passes. The intensity is heightened, our flame of
consciousness becomes more "hard" and "gemlike," to the extent that our faculties of perception and response are sharp-
ened. This, indeed, is the service of philosophy and reflective
culture. Knowledge cannot itself be the end or purpose of living,
for it can never be more than guess or theory, but thought and
analysis have at least this great value, that they awaken the
human spirit into "eager observation." Pater also assumes that
there is a real, objective difference in intensity among possible
experiences. He is obsessed by metaphors of "focus" and "convergence," and urges that we seek out those experiences in
which "the greatest number of vital forces unite in their purest
energy." From this side of Pater the Impressionist writer, especially Symons, could derive further hints toward composition
and treatment. One strives not simply for truth to the impression, but especially for the impression of some "passionate attitude" or "tragic dividing of forces on their ways." The specifically "aesthetic," even decadent element in Pater emerges only
now. He measures all possible experiences by the same criterion—the degree of intensity they afford. "Any exquisite passion" may be valued equally with "any contribution to knowledge," and so also may "any stirring of the senses, strange dyes,
strange colours, and curious odours, or work of the artist's
hands, or the face of one's friend." At the end of the essay Pater
adds that to this "quickened, multiplied consciousness," art
offers the most; for "art comes to you professing frankly to give
nothing but the highest quality to your moments as they pass,
and simply for those moments' sake." The impact of the Conclusion to The Renaissance cannot be understood without also
keeping in mind its style, that "sedulous ritual," as Max Beer-
bohm called it, in which Pater "laid out every sentence as in a
shroud." The cadences are still worth quoting:

Not the fruit of experience, but experience itself is the end. A counted
number of pulses only is given to us of a variegated, dramatic life. . . .

To burn always with this hard, gemlike flame, to maintain this ecstasy, is success in life. . . . Not to discriminate every moment some passionate attitude in those about us, and in the brilliancy of their gifts some tragic dividing of forces on their ways, is, on this short day of frost and sun, to sleep before evening. With this sense of the spendour of our experience and of its awful brevity, gathering all we are into one desperate effort to see and touch, we shall hardly have time to make theories about the things we see and touch.

Though Pater was the essential influence on Symons' Impressionism, other English and French writers also played their roles. From his early admiration for Browning, Symons retained at least the feeling that poetry may deal with actual people in the actual world. From such poems as Henley's *London Voluntaries* or Wilde's "Impression du Matin" came a tendency to associate Impressionist methods and feeling with urban scenes, though he also gathered impressions in the countryside and by the ocean. Like Wilde and Henley, he was well aware of Whistler, whose paintings created purely aesthetic relations among objects, ignoring their moral or anecdotal interest. This was an art of visual impression without comment and of mood without sentiment. Symons himself could rarely achieve it. Meditative thought and point kept breaking in. But to others at the time his poetry seemed relatively free of such things. You get, Lionel Johnson said, "a London fog, the blurred, tawny lamplight, the red omnibus, the dreary rain, the depressing mud, the glaring gin-shops, the slatternly, shivering women: three dexterous stanzas, telling you that and nothing more." We may take "At the Cavour" as one example:

> Wine, the red coals, the flaring gas,
> Bring out a brighter tone in cheeks
> That learn at home before the glass
> The flush that eloquently speaks.
>
> The blue-grey smoke of cigarettes
> Curls from the lessening ends that glow;
> The men are thinking of the bets,
> The women of the debts, they owe.
>
> Then their eyes meet, and in their eyes
> The accustomed smile comes up to call,
> A look half miserably wise,
> Half heedlessly ironical.

Symons also learned from the French poets he studied, especially from Verlaine, who had said "Take eloquence, and wring its neck!" and had showed "that French verse could be written without rhetoric." From such instructions one might derive the relative directness and simplicity of Symons' own syntax and idiom, at least in comparison with the more ornate and stylized work of his associates. Though he, unlike Henley and Sharp, did not use free verse in his Impressionist poems, his rhythms have a colloquial naturalness unusual for the avant-garde of that age. And the reason is the same one that T. E. Hulme stressed in the next generation: sincerity, the "passionate desire," in Hulme's phrase, "for accuracy," for getting "the exact curve," the "individual quality" of the thing, whether it be "an object or an idea in the mind"—a truth to the object which enacts itself as much in rhythm and meter as in the pin-pointings of descriptive epithet. As Symons put it, Verlaine had "learnt the secret of liberty in verse" because of his "endeavour to be absolutely sincere," to render "the impression of the moment followed to the letter."

Symons used to jot down in his notebooks brief descriptions of his own fugitive moods. His poems are not usually the evocation of external sights only; they are pervaded with emotion and with a vague suggestivity, an aura of indefinable significance. For example, "At Dieppe: Grey and Green":

> The grey-green stretch of sandy grass,
> Indefinitely desolate;
> A sea of lead, a sky of slate;
> Already autumn in the air, alas!
>
> One stark monotony of stone,
> The long hotel, acutely white,
> Against the after-sunset light
> Withers grey-green, and takes the grass's tone.
>
> Listless and endless it outlies,
> And means, to you and me, no more
> Than any pebble on the shore,
> Or this indifferent moment as it dies.

Because we should not allow our sense of the potentialities of this type of poem to be governed by the limitations of the poet, it may be mentioned that Eliot's technique in his early poems is strongly influenced by Impressionism:

The winter evening settles down
With smell of steaks in passageways.
Six o'clock.
The burnt-out ends of smoky days.
And now a gusty shower wraps
The grimy scraps
Of withered leaves about your feet
And newspapers from vacant lots;
The showers beat
On broken blinds and chimney-pots,
And at the corner of the street
A lonely cab-horse steams and stamps.
And then the lighting of the lamps.

To mention Eliot is to be reminded that there are strong affinities between Impressionism and Imagism, the movement Ezra
Pound founded and briefly commanded just before World War
I. To Pound, Symons was a personal "god," as he once said, and
he was well aware of Symons' poetry and criticism. The famous
Imagist statements of purpose by Pound in *Poetry* (1913) offer
directions that would, on the whole, apply equally for Impressionist poetry. Both groups of poets strove for direct presentation of the object without discursive reflection ("abstraction,"
"rhetoric"); accuracy, concreteness, and economy in language
without "poetic" heightening or ornament; and rhythms that
contributed functionally to the presentation. Both groups
tended to write free verse. Both groups reacted against those
many readers who valued poetry by the importance of its subject
and the scale of its emotion, though the Imagists were more confident in urging the irrelevance of these factors. The differences
between the two are generally that Imagism—more militant,
self-conscious, craftsmanlike, manifestoed—went further in the
shared directions; it reflected Pound's positivism rather than the
skeptical, relativistic uncertainties of the Impressionist mind; it
typically focused on single objects rather than the Impressionist
scape or scene; it tended to dwell on static things, or on motion
in a phase of stasis, as opposed to the Impressionist sense of flux.
Moreover, there was in the Imagist movement a special emphasis on metaphor as the most effective mode of presentation. This
emphasis, which had momentous importance for Modernist
poetry, was altogether lacking in Impressionism.

4

THE NARRATIVE PROTEST

A S THE poetry of *ars victrix* established itself, counterten-dencies developed. Because the avant-garde was Franco-phile, other poets were the more heartily English and patriotic. Because the avant-garde was indifferent to politics and social causes, other poets were warmly committed. Because the avant-garde idealized the poet in his lonely, contemplative devo-tion, some poets idealized the man of action; they hoped that poetry might be a mode of action, at least a battle-cry. Because the avant-garde was in retreat from modern reality, or content to take impressions of it without commenting or judging, other poets felt a responsibility to it all the more. They sought to be directly relevant to the actual experience of men and women in the modern world.

Some were occasionally "realists." Kipling's was a popular and garish realism, as in *Barrack-Room Ballads,* which are supposed to express the character, speech, experiences, and ideas of common soldiers. John Davidson wrote a few poems depicting lower-middle-class life. Henley's scenes of harsh actuality in "In Hospital" were based on his experience as a patient in the Royal Edinburgh Infirmary. They were written between 1873 and 1875, although they were not published for thirteen years. But, though "realism" was widespread in prose fiction, there was relatively little of it in poetry through the closing years of the nineteenth century. A more widespread impulse was to flout the shrinkers and desponders by affirming the romance and gusto of modern living, as do Kipling, Henley, and, in a more escapist vein, Stevenson. The positive message of Kipling or Henley takes for granted that strife and suffering are fundamental. They are optimists only in the muted sense that they assert the joy of action and the possibility of winning through. They wished, like Davidson, to achieve an ideology that would be grimly honest to modern experience and thought, and yet make place for zest and hope.

There may have been as many of such poets in the 1890s as there were members of the avant-garde. Moreover, there were cross-affinities and overlappings of every kind. Henley, the chief harrier of the aesthetes, wrote in the Impressionist way in *London Voluntaries* (1892) and was an accomplished formalist and technical experimenter. Some of his "In Hospital" poems are early examples of free verse in England. Yet despite their numbers, the poets opposed to the avant-garde did not produce work of first importance during the 1890s. Unless we also include Hardy, the only significant poets of this kind were Henley, Kipling, and John Davidson. In the next decade, however, Yeats also reacted against the manners and attitudes of the fin de siècle, that is, against his earlier self, and as he gradually changed his own style, he exerted an enormous influence on other poets also. In fact, English poetry from 1900 to the First World War was dominated by a massive, many-sided repudiation of the avant-garde of the generation before.

In this continuing reaction a number of poets made their reputations chiefly as narrative poets. The narrative poets may be discussed as a group, however, not so much because they wrote ballads, romances, and other types of tales as because they did so for the same reasons. Kipling, Davidson, Chesterton, Noyes, and Masefield, among others, set forth to restore to poetry all that, in their opinion, the aesthetes had relinquished. They felt that the aesthetes, with their absinthe and library langor, had lacked gusto and wholeness of personality and had shrunk from life to render peripheral feelings caught only from introspection. So doing, they had naturally lost any audience except themselves. The point may be made, in an oversimplified way, if one remarks that while Dowson or Symons turned for parental example to Gautier or Verlaine, Masefield turned to Chaucer.

The general premise with which all these writers proceeded is given by Masefield in his pamphlet *With the Living Voice* (1925): poets must use "the whole of life as their material. . . . Those poets who shrink from the life about them, however skilfully they invent or imagine, will appeal in the main, not to the world, but to those few who . . . cannot or will not face the world." The premise, so stated, seems valid enough, especially as the response of poets to a felt need of their time. One wishes, therefore, one could apply to their poetry Dryden's famous remark about Chaucer: "'Tis sufficient to say, according to the proverb, that here is God's plenty." But the entire development of literature in the twentieth century suggests that such wholeness, variety, and abundance is impossible for any modern writer (and therefore, one supposes, for human beings in the modern world), and that literature must strive to make up in depth for what it lacks in breadth. The narrative attempt was on the whole a quixotic failure and shows that these poets lacked literary tact, an intelligent appraisal of what is now possible. But, as always, to know what these poets aimed for helps one better to appreciate what they achieved.

Their narratives are sometimes more or less romantic in action and setting (Kipling's India; Chesterton's Middle Ages), sometimes realistic, but usually a blend of both. Diverse types of character are introduced, but they are usually familiar and unreflecting types: soldiers, squires, engineers, and ne'er-do-wells rather than artists and intellectuals. Because the psychology of these protagonists is seldom complex and never aberrant, the reader can easily identify with them. Rhythms are emphatic and swinging. Ideas are not compressed but spaced out so that everyone can follow. It is a thoroughly accessible, deliberately popular poetry. Whatever they take up, these poets do with gusto, or at least with sympathy and appreciation. Masefield's *Everlasting Mercy* (1911) dwells on scenes that are quite as contemporary and sordid as anything in *The Waste Land*. The difference is that Eliot feels spiritual anguish and horror; Masefield feels interested. If Eliot's response is hypersensitive and precious from Masefield's point of view, at least it is more intense. In general these poets criticized too little the materials they presented. As a result, their effects are likely to seem broad or even flat. The reputation of most of these poets, at one time very high, now has sunk, perhaps unduly. Among their typical poems are Noyes's "The Highwayman," Kipling's "Mandalay" or "Danny Deever," and Chesterton's "Lepanto." The poems have none of the refinements of reflection, but they sustain, for many readers, a lively interest.

RUDYARD KIPLING

Born in Bombay, India, Kipling (1865–1936) learned Hindustani while he was learning English and acquired a sympathetic sense of Indian life and values. From his father, a painter and designer, and later from two uncles on his mother's side who were artists, the sensitive, nearsighted, and lightly built youth also acquired a lifelong respect for disciplined craftsmanship. At the age of six he was sent from India to England for his education. He was placed in the charge of a stupid, self-righteous relative and treated roughly. (When his mother on a visit to England came to his bed to say good-night, he instinctively raised an arm as if to ward off a blow.) He seethed with inner rebellion against injustice, but in compensation he developed a strong respect for authority, a determination to work for justice within the "system," and an ideal of quiet courage and responsibility. At eighteen he returned to India and started work as a journalist for the Lahore *Civil and Military Gazette*. His writing included some verse, later published as *Departmental Ditties* (1886), and stories collected in *Plain Tales from the Hills* (1888).

Returning to England at the age of twenty-four, Kipling found his work praised by critics for whom it provided a refreshing change in the literary scene. Concurrently with his novel, *The Light that Failed* (1891), the two *Jungle Books* (1894–1895), and *Captains Courageous* (1897), he brought out two books of verse that quickly became famous: *Barrack-Room Ballads* (1892) and *The Seven Seas* (1896). Meanwhile he married an American woman and spent four years (1892–1896) in Brattleboro, Vermont. Emotionally receptive to the United States ("I love this people . . . My heart has gone out to them beyond all other people"), he became involved in an absurd quarrel with his wife's brother, a hotheaded ne'er-do-well who, in a drunken moment, threatened to kill him. This led to an unfortunate lawsuit by the shocked Kipling and later, in embarrassment, to a decision to leave the country.

Disillusioned with America, Kipling maintained an ideal of the British Empire (conservative, protective, uplifting, and firmly legal); he became its most popular spokesman and one of the noblest. He settled near the village of Burwash in Sussex. In his later thirties and early forties he was at the height of his fame; he received the Nobel Prize in 1907. But despite the widespread patriotism of World War I—in which he lost his only son—his work began to be neglected. He was too vividly associated in the public mind with British imperialism of the 1890s, with a past age that seemed remote from the battlefields of western Europe and still more remote from the revulsion, after World War I, against militarism. He continued to publish poetry but never regained the reputation and enormous popularity he had once enjoyed.

In the 1880s and 1890s Kipling's poetry was the most impressive single alternative to the "high" poetic culture of the time. Across this scene of late-Romantic, late-Victorian, Pre-Raphaelite, Parnassian, Aesthetic, Impressionist, Decadent, and Symbolist writers he moved like a locomotive, purposeful, effective, incredibly energetic. He is usually (and correctly) considered a leader in the reaction against the Aesthetes and Decadents. While they aspired to write a "pure" poetry of form, mood, atmosphere, and overtone for a refined and elite audience, Kipling was deliberately obvious, emphatic, interesting, and popular; as for "purity," no writer ever had or wished it less than he. Instead, he put poetry to use—to praise, remind, warn, denounce, in short, to produce action. His disrespects were blatant. He plainly shared, for example, the disgust of his dying ship-owner, Sir Anthony Gloster, at his aesthetic son:

> For you muddled with books and pictures, an' china an'
>   etchin's an' fans,
>   And your rooms at college were beastly—more like a whore's
>   than a man's.

But the heroes of his poetry are not only at a far remove from Des Esseintes or Dorian Gray. They also bear no resemblance to Faust, Alastor, Prometheus, Manfred, Rabbi Ben Ezra, Ulysses, Empedocles, the Scholar Gypsy, or innumerable other heroes of intellectual and spiritual quest in nineteenth-century poetry. Kipling not only challenged the aesthetes; he rejected the Romantic tradition which, throughout the nineteenth century, took the poet, artist, or seer, the man of profound search or vision of ultimate things, as the highest type of human greatness.

His values and purposes have made him unusually difficult for literary criticism to come to terms with. For one thing, his poetry enforces his opinions, so that his opinions still tend to influence our judgment of his work, whether favorably or otherwise. But discussion of Kipling runs into obstacles deeper than whatever one thinks of his views in their historical and biographical context. If one could imagine a critic who was himself conservative, nationalist, imperialist, militarist, and racist—and whether or in what sense Kipling was any of these is disputable—even he might find it almost impossible to sympathize with Kipling's attitudes and emotions. Most critics value qualities of mind that are, or ought to be, their own, or that, at any rate, as is now usually supposed, give their profession its authority and justification: intellectual curiosity and disinterestedness, sensitivity, imagination, breadth of sympathy, a civilized, complexly aware, self-critical intelligence. These, however, are not qualities Kipling much praises. What he did value we shall see, but it may be provisionally suggested in the words of his Scottish engineer, M'Andrew, words that are more hateful than ever to many contemporary ears: "Law, Orrder, Duty an' Restraint, Obedience, Discipline." His heroes are the "sons of Martha" who do the world's necessary work, men of action, responsibility, and fidelity. And while literary criticism may agree that these are useful and admirable persons, it resists the implied corollary, namely, that it is itself less useful. There is thus an inevitable gap between the minds of most critics and the mind of Kipling, and nothing can bridge it. He could be unreservedly praised only by those who do not write criticism. Those who do are likely to experience mixed reactions. They might like to dismiss him as no poet but a journalist, a Philistine boomer, jingling and jingoistic. But an honest critic may find himself responding to Kipling's poetry more than he thinks he ought to. And he finds much to respect. Kipling was undeniably a very skilled writer in some ways. And he has a further significance: he had a grasp of some truths or realities which have a large place in actual life but are often scanted in literature.

Kipling is the most distinguished and widely read practitioner in the mode of narrative verse we are now exploring. Indeed, he did more than anyone else to create it. The chief purpose of this discussion of his work is to explain or at least conjecture why it was so popular and, in doing so, to account also for the popular success of such poets as Chesterton, Noyes, Newbolt, and Masefield, poets who, whatever their ideological differences, practiced a similar mode of verse for the same audience. The audience, it should be remembered, was the middle class, the only class in which a large audience for poetry could conceivably have been found in England at this time.

One reason why Kipling's readers admired him was that he admired them. There was a spiritual rapport. We may begin with the characters he typically created, for example, the Scottish engineer, M'Andrew, or the self-made shipping magnate, Sir Anthony Gloster. In remarkable dramatic monologues, each in a different dialect, these formidable persons reveal their past history, the milieu of their lives, and their tastes, opinions, morality, and aspirations—in short, their souls. They are characters everyone can understand. In addition, they are figures of the commercial or professional middle class, so readers can the more easily identify with them, and they are sympathetically portrayed. The last point should be stressed. Both M'Andrew and Sir Anthony may be presented as slightly comic; to that extent Kipling keeps a distance between their point of view and his. But the virtue of Sir Anthony and M'Andrew, from Kipling's point of view, is that they know life and the world for what they are—scenes of inexorable competition and danger. In this respect Sir Anthony's milieu of cutthroat commercial competition resembles that of Kipling's *Jungle Books,* where unremitting prudence, courage, alertness, and discipline are necessary for survival. The army in the *Barrack-Room Ballads* is similarly a schooling in reality. The moment of danger will always come. The undisciplined will be killed. When the British army defeats the hill tribes, it is not because of any man-for-man or racial superiority but because, thanks to years of drill, the Tommies are steadier under fire, and especially because they have machine guns. The same truths apply through the whole of human life. In "The Secret of the Machines" the machines speak as symbols of all the ruthless circumstances that condition man's existence:

> Remember, please, the Law by which we live,
>   We are not built to comprehend a lie,
> We can neither love nor pity nor forgive,
>   If you make a slip in handling us you die!

"M'Andrew's Hymn" owes some of its power to the convergence of three such symbols of inexorable reality: the sea, the ship's engines, and the Calvinist world-view of the Scottish engineer.

Kipling responded deeply to Romantic individualism and exemplified it in a range of figures from artists to Afghan chiefs. But if he had to choose between this and training, discipline, self-sacrifice, and service—between, if the comparison may be allowed, the Afghan chief and the astronaut—he would choose the latter, if only because these qualities conduce to power and hence to survival. Kipling did not believe that might makes right; his moral principles were not in the least those of a bully, as is sometimes asserted. But he did assume that the first moral duty is to recognize realities; the second, to accept the discipline they impose. It must be stressed that the realities he had in mind are not merely natural; they include equally inexorable psychological, moral, and religious imperatives. Kipling's sense of man's ineluctable human responsibility for the human order must be seen within the larger moral and religious context of "Recessional," with its warning against the

> Heathen heart that puts her trust
>   In reeking tube and iron shard,
> All valiant dust that builds on dust,
>   And guarding, calls not Thee to guard.

These convictions were presented in a style that is sometimes immensely bold and sometimes absurd. (One witness to Kipling's interest in style is *The Muse Among the Motors,* a neglected but lively collection of twenty-five parodies of different poets, including himself.) He had no specific stylistic program, and seems chiefly to have observed the stylistic gods of the copy-book headings: clarity, economy, force. One can sometimes see the influence of particular poets—Byron, Tennyson, especially Browning and Swinburne—as well as popular forms such as hymn and ballad, and he was steeped in the Bible. He practiced, like many nineteenth-century poets after Swinburne, a very diverse versification, though he always employed stanzas and meters. He heightened energy and perspicuity by swinging, drumming rhythms, and the use of assonance, alliteration, and internal rhyme for emphasis. He had a Byronic audacity in phrasing. I am thinking especially of the Byron of *Childe Harold,* with the sweeping panoramas and bold contrasts of that poem, the rapid, positive, emphatic statement. In Kipling too one typically finds the vehement, unqualified assertion:

> East is East, and West is West, and never the twain shall meet;

or the geographical, vast antithesis:

> Beneath whose awful Hand we hold
> Dominion over palm and pine;

or the rhetorical amplification with anaphora:

> Never the lotus closes, never the wild-fowl wake,
> But a soul goes out on the East Wind that died for England's sake;

or the Biblically concrete, vigorous phrasing:

> . . . the Dog returns to his Vomit and the Sow returns to her Mire,
> And the burnt Fool's bandaged finger goes wabbling back to the Fire.

He is at his best in ballad dialogues, such as "Danny Deever" or "A St. Helena Lullaby," where the form especially promotes drama, urgency, and suggestion. He has, like Auden, a reporter's eye for the characteristic, telling detail, and he builds up a milieu by rapidly assembling general images. The milieu is that of the modern world, and he deploys a contemporary and urban imagery—stock dividends, strikers, coal smoke, valves and screws, public houses, cricket matches, local trains—with a casualness, a lack of ostentation, that was extremely rare in nineteenth-century poetry, and is usually associated with the post-Eliot poetry of the 1930s. He has a special talent for low-grade, semiaphoristic, quotable simplifications. Sir Anthony Gloster says:

> For a man he must go with a woman, which women don't understand—
> Or the sort that say they can see it they aren't the marrying brand.

The first line is a sort of remark that keeps recurring through Kipling's poetry and that, under the right conditions, to some readers seems aphoristic. The second line represents a kind of humor that occurs frequently (especially in the utterance of Tommy Atkins) and can evoke a chuckle of knowingness and complicity. Kipling was especially and sometimes ridiculously eager to exploit the authentic diction of a class, group, or profession. A reader of "M'Andrew's Hymn" must leaf through the dictionary (in vain) for such items as "coupler-flange," "spindle-guide," "crosshead-gib," "follower-bolt," and "differential valve-gear." In "The Ballad of the Bolivar" one must hope with the imperiled crew that the Lord will keep His "thumb on the plummer-block." The poems spoken by Tommy Atkins, as George Orwell remarked, would read better if they were not in Cockney. Also, for American readers Tommy's utterance, with its lack of aitches and final g's, recalls such other literary dialects as that of Artemus Ward, Thomas Augustin Daley, or Mr. Dooley. And low as Kipling sometimes sank, this is a company to which he does not belong.

Kipling's imperialism and his celebration of English national character have occasioned much unfavorable criticism. In themselves these sentiments might be no more disturbing than other typical emotions of previous ages, for all past writers expressed feelings that might be thought peculiar and offensive if they were uttered in the present day. The difficulty with Kipling is that he often articulated his sentiments in remarkably unqualified, simpleminded ways, and his too-crude commitment becomes especially obvious and embarrassing when we regret the sentiments themselves. Celebration of England and the English character was typical of most of the more popular English poets from the 1890s until the First World War, but in a different way. Instead of Kipling's theme of Empire, there was a quiet love of English countryside, a confidence in English rural types in their rooted strength and humor, and an imaginative fascination with English history. With the political collapse of imperialism after the Boer War, Kipling's themes also changed, and he gradually became a poet of these typically Edwardian appreciations.

JOHN DAVIDSON

Davidson (1857–1909) was born in Renfrewshire, Scotland. He entered Edinburgh University in 1876 but stayed only a year. About this time he met Swinburne and read him some verses. Swinburne, who later did not answer Davidson's fulsome letters ("the greatest poet since Shakespeare"; "ready . . . to lay my neck beneath your foot and call you king"), is said to have placed both hands on Davidson's head and pronounced the single word "Poet!" Then came twelve years of schoolteaching at various places in Scotland (1877–1899), during which he published three plays, *Bruce* (1886), *Smith* (1888), and *Scaramouch in Naxos* (1889), which remained relatively unnoticed. He married in 1885. Giving up schoolteaching, he went to London at the age of thirty-two, hoping to begin a literary career. In addition to much journalistic work for a variety of periodicals, he wrote poems, novels, and short stories and made some translations from the French. His lyrics appeared in *In a Music-Hall, and Other Poems* (1891), *Fleet Street Eclogues* (1893), *Ballads and Songs* (1894), a second series of *Fleet Street Eclogues* (1895), and *New Ballads* (1897). Davidson was by now a member of the Rhymers' Club. Similar volumes followed: *The Last Ballad, and Other Poems* (1899) and *Holiday and Other Poems* (1906). Meanwhile, his work had begun to enter another and, as it proved, final phase, while at the same time his health became precarious (though this was partly hypochondria—he was obsessed, for example, with the fear of cancer). He published his "testaments"—*The Testament of a Vivesector* (1901), *The Testament of a Man Forbid* (1901), *The Testament of an Empire-Builder* (1902)—and planned a dramatic trilogy to be called *God and Mammon,* of which two parts appeared: *The Triumph of Mammon* (1907) and *Mammon and his Message* (1908). Receiving a small pension, he moved with his family to Penzance in Cornwall, and within a year committed suicide by drowning.

Because Davidson's mature work divides into two parts—the shorter poems and the expression of his "philosophy" in the Testaments and late dramas—we may consider it in that order. His narrative power shows itself most in two blank verse poems, "A Ballad in Blank Verse" and "A Woman and her Son." Both present a theme which must have touched Davidson deeply, the rebellion of a son against the fundamentalist piety of his parents. Both sides—the son in his atheism as well as the parents—manifest a bigoted intensity or fanaticism that was probably familiar to Davidson from his childhood in Scotland and may have been a tendency of his own character. The poems effectively depict persons caught at a pitch of conflict and treading the brink of psychological breakdown. They are also occasionally effective in the rendering of setting through accumulated detail, as in the modified Impressionism of this passage from "A Woman and her Son." The son, having watched his mother die, becomes aware of the sights and sounds of the outside night:

> Outside a city-reveller's tipsy tread
> Severed the silence with a jagged rent;
> The tall lamps flickered through the sombre street,
> With yellow light hiding the stainless stars:
> In the next house a child awoke and cried;
> Far off a clank and clash of shunting trains
> Broke out and ceased, as if the fettered world
> Started and shook its irons in the night;
> Across the dreary common citywards,
> The moon, among the chimneys sunk again,
> Cast on the clouds a shade of smoky pearl.

To portray middle- and lower-class life in the metropolis was relatively new in poetry. Another such poem of Davidson's was the monologue of a poor clerk struggling to make ends meet on a meager salary ("Thirty Bob a Week"). T. S. Eliot later said it had a "terrific impact" on him in his formative years because it was written "in an English such as one would speak."

> And it's often very cold and very wet,
>   And my missis stitches towels for a hunks;
> And the Pillar'd Halls is half of it to let—
>   Three rooms about the size of travelling trunks.
> And we cough, my wife and I, to dislocate a sigh,
>   When the noisy little kids are in their bunks.

Poems similar in subject matter but not in diction are "Holiday at Hampton Court," "The Crystal Palace," "Piper Play," "A Ballad of the Exodus from Houndsditch," and "A Northern Suburb":

> Roused by the fee'd policeman's knock,
>   And sad that day should come again,
> Under the stars the workmen flock
>   In haste to reach the workmen's train.

> For here dwell those who must fulfil
>   Dull tasks in uncongenial spheres,
> Who toil through dread of coming ill,
>   And not with hope of happier years—
>
> The lowly folk who scarcely dare
>   Conceive themselves perhaps misplaced,
> Whose prize for unremitting care
>   Is only not to be disgraced.

Other lyrics were more conventional. Davidson was perhaps best known for his two volumes of *Fleet Street Eclogues,* poems in which the shepherds of the classical eclogue are replaced by journalists pleasantly talking. He wrote descriptive nature lyrics, such as "Epping Forest in November,"

> Woods and coppices by tempest lashed;
>   Pollard shockheads glaring in the rain;
> Jet-black underwood with crimson splashed—
>   Rich November, one wet crimson stain!

or "A Runnable Stag" with its thumping, headlong rhythm:

> When the pods went pop on the broom, green broom,
>   And apples began to be golden skinned,
> We harboured a stag in the Priory coomb,
>   And we feathered his trail up-wind, up-wind,
>   We feathered his trail up-wind—
>   A stag of warrant, a stag, a stag,
>   A runnable stag, a kingly crop,
>   Brow, bay and tray and three on top.
>   A stag, a runnable stag.

Davidson was responsive to many other poets, and could patch his style from Jacobean drama, Blake, Wordsworth, Shelley, Keats, Tennyson, Browning, the Pre-Raphaelites, and especially his contemporaries, for he was open to most of the poetic movements of the time. But urged by poverty, he wrote in haste, and the result was variability and inconstancy of style, not only from poem to poem but within the same poem.

Many of Davidson's lyrics testify to his feeling that in writing trivial pieces for a living, he was daily betraying his own aspiration. In his forties he bravely refused to go on with this and began to voice his message in long blank-verse poems, his Testaments, and in the unfinished *God and Mammon.* The task he shouldered was nothing less than the reconciliation of truth with the imagination. In the middle and latter part of the nineteenth century it seemed to many troubled persons that truth could be known only through scientific rationalism and that shapings of the imagination reflected nothing more than subjective emotion. At the same time, however, there was a fear that the split between truth and imagination, or the awareness that there was such a split, had impoverished life. "Art," as Davidson put it, "knows very well that the world comes to an end when it is purged of Imagination." He held that the Christian conception of the universe, which had been imaginative, could no longer be believed and that scientific rationalism could create for the heart and mind no world, no life, but only an "eviscerated Life-in-Death." Hence Davidson would make "in my Testaments and Tragedies a new form and substance of Imagination; and by poetic power certify the semi-certitudes of science." In practice this meant that he accepted, as he understood them, the conclusions of science, attempted not only to express them in poetry but to imagine a world in their light, and attempted also to show that in such a world men and women could lead richly fulfilled lives.

He urged his message with the utmost vehemence and iteration. All reality, he asserts, is material. From this it follows that the universe is beyond good and evil and that God does not exist. Like everything else, man is only matter, but matter that has become conscious. Man is therefore the greatest object in the universe and is morally free to fulfill himself in every possible way. (Like some of the Decadent writers of the period—and Existentialists in the 1940s and 1950s—Davidson shows a certain interest in torture as a way of dramatizing moral freedom.) At this point contradiction has set in. For although in theory "all men are great," in practice the strong fulfill themselves at the expense of the weak—and have Davidson's enthusiastic sympathy in doing so. Mammon, the young king, takes as his models Napoleon, Mohammed, Caesar, and Alexander. The program of this ruler is to extirpate Christianity, himself replace God, and then,

> I, Mammon, mean to make
> This mighty world a hundredfold itself.
> There shall be deeper depths of poverty,
> A more distressing toil, more warlike war,
> An agony of spirit deadlier

Than that which drenched Gethsemane in blood;
A rapture of dominion hitherto
Unfelt by conquerors, kings or priests; a power,
A beauty and a glory of the world.

Whatever the immediate source of these ideas, they were typical of a time when social Darwinism and Nietzsche were in vogue and many were struggling to throw off Christianity. Davidson was as much a part of this movement as Hardy, Wells, or Shaw. And he shared with Shaw and Wells a contempt for the past that is often astonishing: "there has been no philosophy, no religion, no art, literature, hitherto; . . . there is nothing for [a child] to learn; . . . everyone must make for himself his own philosophy, religion, literature . . . the world is really a virgin world awaking from a bad dream"; "It is a new poetry I bring, a new poetry for the first time in a thousand years."

In his will Davidson stipulated that no writing other than his own should appear in any of his books. This condition effectively prevented the publication of selections until the copyright expired a half-century later. Were it not for this his work would doubtless be better known. But no strong revival of interest can be predicted. His lyrics are not sufficiently stamped with his own individuality, and by the time he came to write his more ambitious works, which he enjoined all men to "study and discuss in private and in public," his personality had become relatively rigid, unbalanced, and even megalomaniac. How much this resulted from the many frustrations of his life one cannot say, but at the end he can remind one of the stock Elizabethan figure of the railing malcontent. "Anarchic and indefinite," as Yeats truly said, he "lacked pose and gesture, and now no verse of his clings to my memory." Nevertheless, aspects of his work were new or significant enough to influence younger writers, particularly his prophetic stance, use of scientific and urban material, and experiments with a natural idiom.

G. K. CHESTERTON AND ALFRED NOYES

A brilliant and prolific man of letters, G. K. Chesterton (1847–1936) was only incidentally a poet, though he produced six volumes of verse. His reputation used to be much higher than it now is. I have found one critic, Theodore Maynard, who thought him the finest of living poets. Maynard's view was given in 1922 in a book called *Our Best Poets;* hence he was exalting Chesterton above Yeats and de la Mare, not to mention others. (Hardy was deliberately excluded from the list because though his verse had "intense intellectual interest," it was not "poetry." Of Eliot, Maynard had apparently not yet heard.) The reasons why he preferred Chesterton are not entirely clear. They seem to be that, starting with his first book, *The Wild Knight* (1900), Chesterton "burst through the evil cowardice of the decadence," and that through all his poetry he expressed the "idea" of a "Christian victory."

If Maynard's specific taste was eccentric, the general premises he vaguely implies were typical of one trend in the Edwardian age, even though he was writing a decade afterward. In this type of literary criticism, form and style, to which the avant-garde had paid sacrificial devotion, might be scarcely noticed, and discussion centered on content, more exactly, on "ideas." It was the flowering time of Wells and Shaw. The Liberal Party ruled for the last time in Parliament (1905–1915), and the Asquith cabinet was carrying forward a program of social reform. The departing ray of liberal faith in reason, or reasonableness, was often mistaken for a dawn, and intellectuals, though they might argue that human nature is essentially irrational, continued to argue hopefully, for in their hearts they trusted that knowledge and free discussion might lead man endlessly forward. What mattered most about people was the ideas they held. Chesterton was one of the leading critics of the day; in his books on Browning, Dickens, Shaw, Blake, Stevenson, and Chaucer he exemplifies this approach to literature. Though he likes such qualities as gusto, what especially interests him is the "ideas" he finds in his authors. These are pounced upon, abstracted from the works in which they are implicit, and debated as general propositions. The worth of the writer is measured very much by the worth of his "ideas." The approach continued to be more or less current until it was put out of fashion by the new formalism after the Second World War. It could be handled in a rather crude way, as in the influential criticism of Irving Babbitt, or it could be sophisticated and sensitive, as in the admirable essays of Charles Williams. At its most literal, it tended to treat poetry as little more than versified prose.

Chesterton wrote topical and political verse (such as "Antichrist, or the Reunion of Christendom: an Ode"), songs of a hearty kind (the drinking songs published as *Wine, Water and Song,* 1915), and incidental poems ("Lepanto," "The Ballad of St. Barbara," *The Ballad of the White Horse*). Except for the narrative poems, most of these strike us as essays versified. "The Rolling English Road," for example, happened to become a poem, but could have been just as adequately expressed in a pleasant newspaper paragraph. Chesterton's poetry exists on one level only. It makes its full effect on first reading; subsequent readings give less pleasure, since one notices more the slipshod technique and phrasing. As challenges to the Decadence, his poems decry pessimism and summon readers to gusto and fight. He is a poet of whoops, either of pleasure or battle. Battle, in fact, makes up the essence of his vision of life, but the battle is essentially related to his Christian faith. (He became a Roman Catholic convert in 1922.) As Charles Williams remarked, his faith and his imagination were centered on the paradoxes of the Incarnation and the Passion of Christ. Just as the figure of paradox, bringing victory out of apparent defeat, characterized his prose, the heroes of his ballads war against seemingly overwhelming power and triumph only at the last extremity. They are prototypes of the Christian soul striving in the world, but they are also prototypes for all the seemingly frail, struggling existences with which Chesterton invariably sympathized. In this context it may seem strange to add that Chesterton took sides too blatantly; but his heroes and villains are, for the most part, billboard figures, lacking depth, detail, and credibility.

His most ambitious poem is *The Ballad of the White Horse* (1911), a hundred-page quasi-epic of Alfred the Great in his struggle with the Danes. But the best is "Lepanto." Here the forlorn hope is represented by Don John of Austria, the overwhelming might is that of the Turkish Sultan, and the battle is the famous naval engagement in which the Christians under Don John broke the Turkish power in the Mediterranean. The strength of the poem lies chiefly in its method of presentation. Chesterton avoids consecutive narration, and with it much potentially tedious business. He relies instead on images in series. One sees the Sultan in his garden, the various European monarchs, the galley slaves, and so forth. By freeing himself from the obligations of narrative sequence, Chesterton can move rapidly, while exploiting all the opportunities for color and romance implicit in his theme. He can roam freely through the whole scene of Europe, setting the battle in a large, historical perspective. The poem ends with an ironic juxtaposition. The victorious Don John, the last crusader, rides homeward while Cervantes on his galley is already envisioning the figure of Don Quixote.

The prolific Alfred Noyes (1880–1958) published nine books of poetry between 1900 and 1910, the latter date being that of the *Collected Poems,* which appeared when he was thirty. Like Kipling, Chesterton, and Masefield, he repudiated the fin de siècle by offering popular entertainment—narratives of action in a spirit of gusto. He altogether lacks the sometimes harsh, contemporary realism of Kipling or Masefield, however. He worked, instead, the Stevensonian vein of boyish romance, profusely bringing forth stock items such as brigantines, buccaneers, Sherwood Forest, and the Spanish Main. His poetry is a tissue of romantic conventions. The verse, imagery, setting, characters, and action of his best-known poem, "The Highwayman," offer an example. It begins:

> The wind was a torrent of darkness among the gusty trees,
> The moon was a ghostly galleon tossed upon cloudy seas,
> The road was a ribbon of moonlight over the purple moor,
> And the highwayman came riding—
>   Riding—riding—
> The highwayman came riding, up to the old inn-door.

This operatic romanticism invites comparison with the equally traditional romanticism of Walter de la Mare—for example, in "The Listeners." De la Mare exploits romantic convention with a full literary knowingness; his is the consummate refinement and subtlety that may come at the end of a tradition. Noyes, on the other hand, writes as if he had no idea that the tradition was dying. His self-confident use of such materials is, at this date, astonishing, almost incredible. His rapid rise to popularity and prestige shows, however, that if he was not in touch with the actual literary situation he certainly was in touch with an audience. Like most poets of his day, he celebrated English landscape, history, and character, which he conceived only in literary conventions. He has an elvish England of twilight witchery, turnstyles, and cottages; a merry England of bowls, beer, roasting crabs, and good Queen Bess; and an eighteenth-century England of country roads and inns, highwaymen and red coats. *Drake,* his blank-verse epic in twelve books (1908), follows the adventures of the seagoing hero up to the Armada, and sees in Drake and in England embodiments of political and spiritual freedom. His patriotism is almost embarrassingly simpleminded and fervent, as may be seen also in his "Tales of the Mermaid Tavern," which deal with the same period of history. Some lines are

> Englande!—Englande!—Englande!—Englande!—
> Glory everlasting and the lordship of the sea!

(The archaic final *e* is typical.) In the well-known "The Barrel-Organ" he finds a romantic beauty in the sights and sounds of London, a perception that was also handled in popular style by Thomas Burke in *London Lamps* (1917).

Like Bridges, Binyon, and Masefield, Noyes also wrote philosophical poems of an uplifting tendency, expressing his conviction that human life and history are related to a Divine Being and purpose. Married to an American, and a professor at Princeton from 1914 to 1923, he knew the United States well (and expressed his pleasure in its landscape in such poems as "The Crags," "Mountain Laurel," and "In Southern California"). He was warmly welcomed everywhere, and the accounts in his autobiography of reading poetry to large, enthusiastic audiences remind one how much Anglophilia there was in America then. He was a critical foe of the Modernist movement, but his own poetry, bereft of sharp focus and freshness, illustrates the acute need, at that time, for a new development.

JOHN MASEFIELD

Masefield (1878–1967) was the author of at least thirty-four books of poetry, not to mention plays, novels, short stories, criticism, and miscellaneous genres. He reflected the modes and feelings common in English verse from the turn of the century to the First World War. He had a literary zest for romantic adventure in the spirit of Chesterton or Noyes; a deep affection for English landscape, ways of life, character, and history; a carefully cadenced, quiet, and agreeable mode found also in Bridges, Sturge Moore, and Laurence Binyon. (In this mode he expounded, like Bridges, the possibility of spiritual consolation based on the experience of beauty.) Finally, he shared the endeavor, which he caught partly from Hardy and Kipling but especially from Yeats and Synge, to energize and enlarge the subject matter and idiom of poetry by turning directly to actual life. The latter aspect of his work was chiefly responsible for his fame.

Like Chesterton, Yeats, Synge, and many other poets at the turn of the century, Masefield was discontented with the established poetic tradition. He was more sweeping, however, in identifying what tradition he had in mind. That the poetry of the fin de siècle was a painted corpse he took for granted. He repudiated with some politeness the "imitators" of Tennyson, who, although "faultless," were unadventurous and merely respectable. But he urged that, however brilliant it was in some respects, the whole development of poetry in modern times, beginning at least with the Romantic period, was regrettable. If poetry was to have a significant role in the civilization of the future, this long historical trend must be reversed.

The overriding necessity was, in his opinion, to recapture the broad, diverse audience for poetry that was lost with the triumph of Romanticism. Gray, Blake, Wordsworth, Coleridge, Keats—"beautiful intelligences" though they were—explored specialized emotions which could be shared by only a small number of persons. Poets ever since have "belonged, surely, to the camp of exclusion." They have written "with a restricted sense of what is poetical" and have used "a language which the multitudes seldom spoke and often could not understand," picking out "sometimes with power, but more usually with labour, the epithet, the right word . . . content if a few people like themselves . . . appreciate their skill and their sensitiveness." The inevitable result was that most people ceased to read poetry. But without a large and miscellaneous audience no major poetry—poetry of the order of Chaucer's or Shakespeare's—can be produced. Such an audience is always potentially available. Poetry is essentially a "heightening" of our "sense of life." The need for it is always felt. The "multitudes" excluded from the enjoyment of poetry have been taking "every substitute that was offered." Poetry's present limited appeal does not arise from historical necessity. It is a situation poets created and can change.

The prescription is contained, more or less, in the diagnosis. If poetry hopes to obtain a wider audience, it must reflect, Masefield argued, not the feelings of a few literary people but those of most men and women in the contemporary world. Moreover, poetry must be written to be heard in public performance. For in public performance there is a direct contact between the poet and his audience, and emotion is deepened because it is shared. And there is the further advantage that if the poet knows his work must be understood immediately when it is heard, he is not tempted into recondite ingenuities.

Masefield's own poetry is designed for performance. And it is written out of a sense of solidarity with the normal feelings and interests of the larger public. Although I have been quoting from a speech given in 1924 (*With the Living Voice*), these were Masefield's opinions from the start of his career. They were instilled by Yeats around the turn of the century, when Masefield, already an admirer, began to attend the older poet's Monday evening *conversaziones*.

Yeats was at this time repudiating much of his own earlier poetry of mood and dream and making a renewed, more strenuous effort to write the poetry of what he called "personal utterance." "Personal utterance" meant, among other things, that he had to teach himself to express a larger range of emotions, particularly those which arise in the ordinary activities of life—friendship, politics, business. Poetry was to be a heightening of actual experience and feeling, but no longer a departure from it. Hence this poetry of "personal utterance" would, Yeats hoped, appeal to a less bookish audience. (At this time he was also more than usually interested in the art of speaking poetry aloud and wished to train speakers for such an art—a project Masefield revived some twenty years later.) To create this new mode Yeats needed, he felt, a new self-image, and he held up before his mind's eye "those careless old writers" whom he liked to imagine "squabbling over a mistress, or riding on a

journey, or drinking round a tavern fire, brisk and active men."
He diffused these ideas, along with innumerable others, wherever he went, and Masefield was one of several poets Yeats swept
up in the advancing eddy of his own development.

However enthusiastic he may have been about it, the ideal of
"personal utterance" was for Yeats continuously opposed and
qualified by others. As is usually the case, his followers took up
not the whole complex of his diverse premises but only one tendency from the churning mass. What the Yeatsian ideas could
mean to some of his hearers is suggested by the Preface to his
own poems that John Millington Synge wrote in 1908. Precisely
because Synge's formulation was definite and relatively unqualified, it was, perhaps, more influential than any single utterance
of Yeats:

The poetry of exaltation will be always the highest, but when men lose
their poetic feeling for ordinary life, and cannot write poetry of ordinary things, their exalted poetry is likely to lose its strength of exaltation. . . . Many of the older poets, such as Villon and Herrick and
Burns, used the whole of their personal life as their material, and the
verse written in this way was read by strong men, and thieves, and
deacons, not by little cliques only. . . . It may also be said that before
verse can be human again it must learn to be brutal.

Since Masefield was a friend of Synge's, having met him in 1903,
the Yeatsian influence may be said to have come to him from a
double source.

Masefield's first book of poems, *Salt-Water Ballads* (1902), was
written under the immediate stimulus of this influence. Like the
subsequent *Ballads* (1903), these poems may now seem soft
tissues of commonplace, derivative from many diverse poets, including Kipling, Dowson, Housman, and Browning. But in intention this was the "manly" poetry of active life, energy, and
directness that Yeats advocated, and it is in this light rather than
as Stevensonian romance that we should view such anthology
pieces as "Sea-Fever" and "Cargoes." "The West Wind," the
other widely known poem in this collection, seems to follow the
"Innisfree" mode which Yeats was trying to rid himself of. In
this poem one even hears echoes of the idiom that Douglas
Hyde, Lady Gregory, and Synge were developing at this time,
a literary idiom modeled on the English spoken by the Irish

peasantry: "It's a warm wind, the west wind, full of birds' cries . . . It's the white road westwards is the road I must tread."

Masefield said it was not until 1911, when he wrote *The Everlasting Mercy* in three weeks, that "I first found what I could do." This long narrative (fifty pages in the collected *Poems*) has a contemporary setting, lively and picturesque action such as a prize fight and a drunken rampage, and a more zesty realism in depicting lower-class life than could be found in modern poetry at that time. The story is about the religious conversion of a ruffian, Saul Kane, who is the narrator. Told in octosyllabic couplets, it ranges in diction from the simple and straightforward to the low colloquial. In one much-cited passage two poachers meet and exchange insults:

> "This field is mine," he says, "by right;
> If you poach here, there'll be a fight.
> Out now," he says, "and leave your wire;
> It's mine."
>   "It ain't."
>   "You put."
>   "You liar."
> "You closhy put."
> "You bloody liar."

Though this heavily censored version of poacher speech now seems tame, it was, in the poetry of 1911, an extreme and arresting verisimilitude. Something similar may be said of Saul Kane, who, though inarticulately responsive to natural beauty, is otherwise the opposite of the literary sensitive or intellectual, being a swaggering man of crude emotions and dim self-awareness. In these respects *The Everlasting Mercy* goes further than most of Masefield's later poems; otherwise its chief ingredients continued to reappear. *The Everlasting Mercy* is set in an English country village, which affords Masefield opportunity to render what he thinks of as traditional varieties of English character. There is the parson, the barmaid, the Quakeress preacher, and there are of course many allusions to "squire." (Seventy such types are presented in the first part of *Reynard the Fox*, which was published in 1919. The poem is one of the few poems of the twentieth century in which the action arouses suspense, but that is only in the second part. The first part unsuccessfully emulates the Prologue to Chaucer's *Canterbury Tales* by introducing and describing the characters.) Masefield also depicts the village way of life, which he sees as traditional and organic, and the country setting provides material for passages of descriptive beauty, dwelling on landscape. The religious conversion with which the poem concludes seems to be motivated not only by an inward communion with conscience and the Lord, but also by an outer communion with the beauty of nature.

To follow Masefield's career after *The Everlasting Mercy* is not necessary. The poem had a very considerable success, both in sales and in literary influence. It reached some part of the wider audience Masefield was seeking, and he continued to hold this audience for some years. Nothing after *The Everlasting Mercy* made the same impact. His poetry was much too loose and slipshod to please the usual appreciator of poetry, yet much too poetic to please the ordinary reader. His reputation was never high in literary circles, and with the triumph of Modernism his purposes were rejected and his work went largely unnoticed. But though the bulk of Masefield's poetry seems likely to lie unread, lyrics such as "Cargoes," "The West Wind," "A Consecration," and "Sea-Fever" will continue to give much pleasure in anthologies.

go to p. 135

5

THE AMERICAN MILIEU, 1890–1912

AROUND the year 1900 literature in America could boast of Howells and Twain, Stephen Crane, Ambrose Bierce, Sarah Orne Jewett, Frank Norris, Theodore Dreiser, and such vigorous essayists as Henry Adams, John Jay Chapman, William James, and George Santayana. Henry James, equivocal in this as in much else, was a large, lustrous ornament of either American or English literature, just as one pleased. But these were writers of prose. In the United States as in England poetry seemed not to be attracting the literary talent of the age. To the American literary nationalist, anxious for the fame of his country even in poetry, the gods had lately departed in the persons of Emerson, Whittier, Lowell, and Whitman—and, as he belatedly found out, Emily Dickinson, whose poems were first posthumously published in 1890. Only minor voices could be heard, in what E. C. Stedman, in the Introduction to his massive and influential *An American Anthology, 1787–1900* (1900), called a "twilight interval."

The contemporary poets who were well known in 1900 are no longer much remembered. Though Edwin Arlington Robinson and George Santayana had each published two volumes, they had few readers. Just after the turn of the century two other Harvard poets, William Vaughn Moody and Trumbull Stickney, produced distinguished work. Their fame—especially

Moody's—was to spread. But the important contemporaries seemed to be Richard Watson Gilder, James Whitcomb Riley, John Bannister Tabb, Lizette Woodworth Reese, Louise Imogen Guiney, Richard Hovey, Stephen Crane, Edwin Markham, Madison Cawein, and others whose names need not be listed for the moment. Yet within a little more than two decades the contemporary American poets included T. S. Eliot, Ezra Pound, Robert Frost, Wallace Stevens, Edwin Arlington Robinson, E. E. Cummings, William Carlos Williams, Conrad Aiken, Vachel Lindsay, Amy Lowell, Edgar Lee Masters, Marianne Moore, and Carl Sandburg.

We are confronting one of the most remarkable developments of a major literature in history, a development comparable in rapidity, at least, to that of English drama in the sixteenth century, or of English poetry from 1790 to 1820. The story of this transformation presents complexly interacting themes, powerful and sometimes gaudy personalities, and an increasingly crowded and thriving bustle of little magazines and manifestos. But more important than the drama of cultural change are the reasons for it. What fostered this sudden achievement in two decades? What determined its particular directions? In answering such questions one must begin with the poetic milieu of America in the 1890s and the early years of the twentieth century, for the poets of this generation were the opportunity which the next generation brilliantly exploited. "The reactions and 'movements' of literature," Ezra Pound said in 1917, "are scarcely if ever, movements against good work and good custom." He was speaking of the development of a more regular versification in English poetry at the end of the seventeenth century. Dryden was not reacting against *Hamlet*. But Pound was also speaking out of his own self-awareness as a leader of a "movement." The truth his remark uncovers is of fundamental importance if we are seeking to explain the rise of Modernist poetry. "Only the mediocrity of a given time," Pound added, "can drive intelligent men of that time to 'break with tradition.'"

THE ISOLATION OF AMERICAN POETS

If we compare the situation of poets in America in the 1890s with that in England, the most striking single fact is their isolation. The northeast seaboard was the literary and publishing center of the country, but it was a diffused center, and its gravitational pull was weakened across continental space. British poets almost invariably sought their fortunes in London, and so became acquainted. Along with critics, publishers, and hangers-on, they made up a sophisticated literary community. American poets, on the other hand, might stay in Kentucky, Indiana, or California, a long way from New York or Boston as well as from each other, and were nourished and guided only by their solitary reading and reflection and by whatever literary culture might be found in their local communities. They were especially likely to spend their formative years, when they were working out their intentions and style, in relative isolation. In contrast to the young poets of the Rhymers' Club in London, meeting to hear each other's verse at the Cheshire Cheese, we have the literary aloneness of Edwin Arlington Robinson in Gardiner, Maine, or Robert Frost on his chicken farm in Derry, New Hampshire, or Edwin Markham teaching school in Coloma, California. Naturally, then, American poetry at the turn of the century does not show the relatively coherent trends and groups that English poetry does. There were a few Decadents, Impressionists, Symbolists, Realists, Henleyesque life-affirmers, and the like, but they were scattered individuals usually taking their cue from England or France. On the whole, American poetry was written by men and women who taught themselves, without being exposed to either the discipline or the intimidation of an aware criticism at the start of their careers.

Since they were not likely to be living in a literary milieu, we should ask how poets acquired their notions and standards of poetry. The first introduction was usually at school, and anthologies were an important formative influence. To read poetry mainly in anthologies had significant effects. Writers from different ages blended together, to some degree, and seemed timelessly present. What mattered about Chaucer, Shakespeare, Milton, Wordsworth, Keats, Tennyson, Whittier, Emerson, and Browning was not when they wrote, but that all spoke directly to the heart and imagination. Collectively, they represented "poetry." To the extent that American poets were isolated from each other, they were left alone with the great poets of the past. This might reinforce in some minds the notion that poetry dwells apart in a region of its own, remote from the life immediately around you, so that one typically finds Edwin Markham in California writing neat, small verses about muses and elves.

Anthology reading wakened no aspiration to be "modern." It even promoted a readiness to try the styles and effects found in Milton or Keats, with results that were sometimes disastrous and sometimes boldly splendid. A too simple-hearted openness to such models could produce unintended comedy, as when Cawein recollects Keats's sensuously weighted ode "To Autumn," makes it a lush and voluptuous August, and adds touches of the diction of Cowper and of Arnold:

> Can freckled August,—drowsing warm and blonde
>   Beside a wheat-shock in the white-topped mead,
>   In her hot hair the oxeyed daisies wound . . .

In "Ode in Time of Hesitation," on the other hand, Moody writes lines that are, perhaps, not less reminiscent, for they blend the Jacobean or even Metaphysical mode with the elegiac sweetness, the melody and cadence of the nineteenth century. (One even hears a distant echo of Omar Khayyam: "I sometimes think that never blows so red / The Rose as where some buried Caesar bled.") But if this verse is, like Cawein's, compounded from reading, it is nonetheless powerful; the subject is the Abolitionist Colonel Shaw buried at Charleston, South Carolina, with his black soldiers:

> Now limb doth mingle with dissolved limb
> In nature's busy old democracy
> To flush the mountain laurel when she blows
> Sweet by the southern sea,
> And heart with crumbled heart climbs in the rose.

There is a certain innocence of approach, which comes as a shock after the English poetry of the 1890s. With Cawein, Markham, Moody, and many other Americans, one encounters what did not exist in England, a poetry that is not on the defensive. These poets were not striving to be different from their predecessors or contemporaries. They were not reacting against anybody. They were merely emulating what they understood to be poetry. In this they were not typical of all American poets. Far from it, as we shall see. But, collectively, they add a note that strongly differentiates American poetry at this time from that of England.

Besides anthologies and of course editions of the established British and American poets, readers gained their notions of poetry from magazines. Those that mattered included the *Century, Harper's, Scribner's,* and *Atlantic,* journals of large circulation designed for middle-class, family reading. They concentrated on fiction and general prose, but included some verse, usually by the older, better-known poets. Only two magazines in the 1890s were devoted mainly to poetry, and their circulation was very small; they had almost no influence on the kind of poetry that was written. Thanks to their circulation and prestige, the *Century* and its fellow magazines set the standard in verse which most poets were content to accept. If an aspirant could write well enough to win publication in one of these large Eastern magazines, he might confidently assume he was a poet. Compared with some of their present-day counterparts, the magazines speak well for the intelligence and taste of the middle class eighty years ago, but their editors were in no position to publish verse that was challenging or adventurous in style or subject. This widely circulated and favorably reviewed "magazine verse" had a powerful contrary effect on the stronger talents of the age. It provided a negative model. The poetry of Crane and Robinson, for example, is much influenced by a wish not to resemble the magazine poets.

When a poet in Chicago, Indianapolis, or Louisville began publishing, he was not likely to lack a receptive audience among his fellow citizens. Most paid no attention, but the hunger for poetry was intense in some circles, and any sizable city was likely to have a literary club or at least a group of readers eager to find and encourage a poet. George Sterling was the boast (to his own embarrassment) of literary San Francisco, and at the San Francisco World's Fair in 1915 he alone among living poets was quoted on the triumphal arches, in company with Confucius, Firdousi, Shakespeare, and Goethe. Madison Cawein (1865–1914), a very minor poet locally known as the "Keats of Kentucky," had during the course of his career at least thirteen extensive notices in the Louisville papers. His admirers gave him a silver loving cup on the twenty-fifth anniversary of his first publication and presented a bronze bust of the poet to the Free

Public Library. Artists painted scenes described in his verse, and his favorite stroll in Iroquois Park was called Cawein Walk. After he died, a memoir was published in which one can read tributes and reminiscences and view photographs—for example, of the poet "in the heart of nature." (The picture is not conventionally romantic. One sees a slight, tidy man, standing in a woodsy spot, dressed in coat and waistcoat, high collar and tie, dark trousers and derby hat. In the heart of nature he preserved middle-class respectabilities.)

Whether the isolation of American poets was or was not good for their poetry is hard to say. Probably it was deleterious to minor talents. Because they lacked contact with each other and with criticism, their consciences as writers did not fully develop and they were satisfied with an easy, conventional achievement. The extent to which this was the case is suggested by the exception, the group of poets at Harvard—Santayana, Moody, Stickney, George Cabot Lodge—who were subjected to the discipline of their fellows and of a relatively alert and sophisticated society. Unquestionably some of them made more out of their gifts than they would have otherwise. The perception of this situation helps explain some of the prescriptions of the next generation. If Pound was, as Gertrude Stein said, a "village explainer," he was what America needed. Pound explained that poetry is not an amateur hobby. It should be practiced professionally, as a craft; one studies it, he said, in several languages; one labors at technique; one weighs and ponders in conscious self-criticism. And yet the amateur atmosphere of American poetry at the turn of the century cannot have been wholly disadvantageous, if only because Robinson, Frost, Pound, Williams, Sandburg, Masters, Eliot, and Stevens grew up in it—better poets than many reared in the more professionally sophisticated and critically watchful milieu of the last forty years.

POETIC INNOCENCE

The stream of verse in America was swollen from a source that was much less noticeable in England—the "handyman" or "do-it-yourselfer." His was a poetry written simply for expression, and he composed in utter innocence, without literary training, sophistication, or standards. He was, in short, a true primitive. (A good example is the man whose wife sent his poems to *Scribner's,* explaining: "My husband has always been a successful blacksmith. Now he is old and his mind is slowly weakening so he has taken to writing poems, several of which I enclose herewith.") Much of this poetry was written for decorative and minor supplementary purposes at public or private occasions—weddings, deaths, groundbreakings. This use of poetry reached an apogee of sorts when Harriet Monroe, who was of course not a primitive poet, read her "Columbian Ode" before 125,000 people, celebrating in 1892 the Dedication of Buildings as part of the preliminaries to the Chicago World's Fair.

Most of this poetry was not published, not even in local newspapers. It is in the vein parodied by Mark Twain in Emmeline Grangerford's "Ode to Stephen Dowling Bots, Dec'd" in *Huckleberry Finn,* and treated with fine sympathy by Mary Wilkins Freeman in her short story, "The Poetess." But work of this kind, usually at a slicker level, also was published in books, of which there are hundreds, most either sentimental or humorous, or both. Perhaps a quarter of the titles published in the United States between 1890 and 1912 show an unashamed frankness of sentiment that is unimaginable in England. James Whitcomb Riley, though a much more aware and contriving poet than those I have in mind, notoriously exploited this hunger for sentiment, even sharing the fashion for the word "old" in titles, as in *An Old Sweetheart of Mine* (1902) and *The Old Swimmin'-Hole* (1912). Also in this vein were Alice Folger's *Songs from the Heart* (1905), Seth Downie's *Heart Helps* (1907), Clara Lindsay's *In Life's Sweet Afternoon* (1909), and David Murphy's *Backlog Ballads . . . Written on Paradise Road Near Oxford, Ohio, 1895 to 1912, and While Near a Backlog Fire on Winter Evenings;* Murphy was also the author of *Pensive Pansies* (1901). To illustrate other types of this unsophisticated poetry, one may pick out Dell Hair's *Echoes from the Beat: A Collection of Poems by Dell Hair, the Policeman Poet* (1908) and John Hall's *Panama Roughneck Ballads* (1912), published in the Canal Zone.

PREOCCUPATION WITH ENGLAND

For the poets of England in the nineties and the Edwardian age, American poetry scarcely existed. If they knew it at all (a few admired Whitman), it had little effect on the way they wrote. In America, however, the poetry of England exerted enormous pressure on critics and aspiring poets. If the isolation of American poets strikes us first, this is our second point of contrast, and it is easily accounted for. The greatest writers of the language were English, not American. Their superiority was impressed upon you not only by your own reading, but by critics, professors, and members of the literary clubs. And, as I pointed out earlier, the imagination, stimulated by the reading of anthologies, brought the past and present poetry of England before the mind in one dazzling, wholly intimidating mass. England had, it seemed, cultural "advantages" that drab America lacked. It had history, visibly embodied in ivied abbeys, castles, manor houses, and half-timbered cottages; it had literary associations everywhere—how inexpressibly significant to live near Stratford-on-Avon, or where the miller in Chaucer's "Reeve's Tale" had cheated his customers at Trumpington; it had wealth, fox hunts, "lords and ladies gay," and the ceremony of Court, Church, and Parliament; above all, it had London, with its literary traditions and knowingness, its famous publishers, journals, and critics. "The U.S. thirty years ago," Ezra Pound reminisced in 1942, "was still a colony of London so far as culture was concerned." No wonder American poets were intimidated! If many of them meekly followed English models, perhaps mere imitation seemed a valuable achievement. Some identified themselves with an image of England elicited from reading. The Irish-American Louise Imogen Guiney, for example, composed marching and drinking songs for the soldiers of the king, so much were her feelings engaged in the English civil war of the seventeenth century. And George Woodberry, who taught Comparative Literature at Columbia, wrote accomplished sonnets of English patriotism.

But these were exceptions. Most poets of the 1890s fall into a style not much distinguished from that of the more traditional English poets, but not closely imitative either, and they were recognizably American in their subject matter. England's impact shows in ways more significant and more difficult to trace than imitation or influence, namely, in the alarmed sensitivities, pricklinesses, aggressions, and submissions that stem from feelings of inferiority. These sometimes led poets to defy whatever they took to be English—generally speaking, the highbrow,

sophisticated, and genteel. On the other hand, feeling themselves alone and disadvantaged, they were frequently ready to
embrace whatever standards and ideals were established in the
literary center, the glamorous, remote seat of learning and
refinement. American poets hungered for approval. The favor
of the literary club and the local newspaper, even if they enjoyed
it, was not enough. They wanted the approval to be authoritative; and the authority was London. At the criticism of a London
journal, literary America could quake. To appreciate just how
wide and deep the attitude went, one must keep in mind that for
writers—and readers—in the middle and far West, the prestige
of England enveloped and haloed what was generally referred
to as "the East," that is, New York, Boston, and their environs. It
was nearer to England in miles and in style of life. Most of the
leading American writers had dwelt there. And the majority of
well-known living writers were still there, along with editors,
publishers, critics, and men of culture, such as Charles Eliot
Norton, who corresponded with English writers and entertained
them when they came to America. The approval of the East was
almost the same as that of England. At least, it was as much
approval as most Americans could hope for.

Some of the poets who rebelled against England and the East
might have been as much motivated by American inferiority
anxieties as those who meekly emulated; writers often exagger-
ated "American" qualities because they were secretly ashamed
or dubious of them. But the use of American materials in poetry
was not always defensive and rebellious. Many poets had a
straightforward pride in America—its landscape, history, life
and values—and articulated what they took to be the American
sensibility without any suggestion that it might be of inferior cultural worth. Some assumed that America would create a new
mode of poetry, one more vital and intelligent than the old and
open to the whole range of human experience. Others studied
the scene in search of a distinctively American identity or character, for this perennial motive of American literature was as
lively in 1900 as it had been in the colonial period.

Whatever their motives, many poets sought to portray American life, character, attitudes, and feelings—often in association
with a particular region—and to do so in a distinctively American style, which usually they took to be plain, colloquial (some-

times in dialect), low-keyed, and humorous. The best of these poets was Edwin Arlington Robinson. Most of the others were popular entertainers and newspaper poets, such as James Whitcomb Riley, Eugene Field, T. A. Daly, and Captain John Wallace Crawford, "the Poet Scout." The protest on behalf of America could involve, at one extreme, nothing more than the description of American landscape in an idiom and form borrowed from British models, as in Joaquin Miller or Madison Cawein, or it could involve radical and thoroughgoing changes in poetic language and sensibility, as in some of Robinson's early poems. It could arise at the highest level of poetic intelligence and purpose or it could be a convention of popular entertainment. A reaction long and deeply present in American feeling and cultural expression, it had recently found magnificent poetic illustration in Whitman.

We have noticed how the isolation of American poets could foster either artistic independence and innovation or docility before accepted models, and how both tendencies were strengthened and complicated by the prestige of England and the East Coast. This dialectic of intimidation and challenge, long characteristic of American literature, continues in the twentieth century. Its effect on modern American poetry cannot be overstated. The opposed tendencies can be variously named, depending on whether one chooses to emphasize the historical and social setting of literature, literary history itself, or the general ideals and values in living that express themselves in what and how people write. The important point is that the conflict was fought out not only between schools of writing but within the minds and hearts of individual writers. As an American, a poet may feel that he should—and should want to—express an American reality, an American identity; probably, he may suspect, he does so willy-nilly. As a writer, however, he may fear that to be American is necessarily to be inferior. As a result, he may defensively cultivate whatever qualities he thinks American and stress those he imagines the "old world" most views askance: democratic vulgarity and bad taste, breeziness, brashness, quirky inventiveness, the fresh and childlike gaze, optimism, the anticultural stance. At the same time he seeks to identify with whatever virtues he supposes Europe has and America lacks—depth of culture, tradition, discipline, learning, artistic sophistication, tragic awareness, and modern sensibility—and he may emulate not so much England as France, partly in order to get ahead of the English by being more European and less provincial than they. These rival inclinations of modern American poetry might be termed the "Genteel" and the "Whitmanic." Or we might say that one is elitist, cosmopolitan (or Europe-oriented), Eastern, formalist, and seeks tradition; while the other is democratic or populist, native (or America-oriented), Western or regional, and realist, and seeks, in Pound's maxim, to "make it new." None of these terms is adequate by itself, and no poet belongs entirely to one camp or the other; for the scene of battle was the psyche of each writer.

THE RECOIL FROM CONTEMPORARY AMERICA

At the end of the nineteenth century, the attraction of the "Eastern" pole was intensified by circumstances special to that time. So far as poetry goes, the bright mist of the Genteel covered the land. One major reason for its prevalence has been suggested: the relative isolation of poets from each other, and, as a consequence, their insecurity and vulnerability to whatever was approved by those supposed to know best. Other reasons may now be explored.

Americans after the Civil War felt that they had broken with their own past. Doubtless the feeling was in part subjective; for the imagination, as it reorganizes the past, is likely to fix on a large, traumatic event as a watershed or divide. But if we ask what at the time impressed the imagination about contemporary America, the sense of a break can easily be understood. These were years of westward expansion, frontier violence, a flood of arriving immigrants, rapid growth of large cities and industry, the huge frauds and cunning of the robber barons, and the garish luxury of the gilded rich. Not that such things were new in American history, but they were taking place on a vastly larger scale and in accelerated tempo and thus made a dramatic impact on the way Americans perceived and interpreted their country. As a result, the United States seemed a newer, rawer land than it had seemed before the Civil War, less stable, less homogeneous, less endowed with traditional values and ways of life.

Poetry was an attempt to compensate. In this raw, materialistic land, it was a refuge. It might even, as poets incorrigibly hope, be a corrective, a formative influence on readers and, through them, on society as a whole. Genteel poetry was only one manifestation of a widely shared state of mind, a state of mind that influenced not only poetry but countless other doings as well. There was a yearning for "culture" in America, the more dedicated and intense precisely because the milieu seemed so unpropitious. We cannot begin to understand the poets of the Genteel Tradition unless we see them as characteristic, as products and exponents of typically American fears and hungers. What was yearned for is hard to say precisely. "Culture" might be something of what it was for Henry James and Ezra Pound in their weaker moments, that is, lots of art objects and an elegantly articulate society of appreciators, their souls formed, nourished, and refined by books, salons, plays, palaces, cathedrals, paintings, sculptures, and ruins. Or it might be what perhaps it was for the many Dante societies, Browning circles, Shakespeare reading clubs, Ruskin chapters, and Goethe associations, that is, what Matthew Arnold—a tremendously influential figure in America at this time—called "criticism," a study of "the best that is known and thought in the world." In any case, many educated Americans at the turn of the century had a remarkably literal faith in culture and culture objects. In this respect, too, the American milieu differed from that of England, where the same faith was seldom held in so simple and direct a way. It contributed, psychologically and socially, to an imprisoning stock conception of what poetry should be (beautiful, elevating, refined, traditional, and ideal), and, still more important, of what it should not be (vulgar, homespun, idiosyncratic, realistic, deflating). The role of poetry was to maintain the "spiritual" side of life. If it was out of touch with American realities, it was in touch, poetry-lovers felt, with what America needed. The same could have been said of the fashionable sermon and the commencement address. The Genteel view tended to make poetry one of the many spiritual, acknowledged irrelevancies on which Americans sometimes bestowed a few moments snatched from business. Hence some of the next generation of poets went to the opposite extreme. They were ready not only to deal boldly with American actualities but to wallow in them. Sandburg's famous "Chicago" is an example—

•

> Hog Butcher for the World,
> Tool Maker, Stacker of Wheat.

Although the poem was no longer so unusual when it was first published in 1914, Sandburg had been composing similar verse since 1904. Whatever one may think of it, it was, in its day, a significant and hopeful development.

Poetry was also confirmed in the Genteel or Ideal mode by the prose fiction against which it reacted. Since at least the early nineteenth century, poets had written with an anxious eye on the rising genre of the novel, which was seducing the audience of poetry and taking over many of its functions. Poetry was pressed to find an identity or role that the novel and short story could not usurp. The effects of this pressure were diverse, depending on the poet and the milieu in which he worked. American fiction from 1890 to 1912 was increasingly dominated by Realism and Naturalism. To poets attached to the Genteel or Ideal premise, it seemed as though novelists such as Norris and Dreiser had become disciples not of the veritable, as they pretended (for Truth was eternal and spiritual), but of the merely external, temporal, and material aspects of existence, of facts of social environment and organization, and, moreover, that they deliberately portrayed the low, vicious, and revolting. Except that usually it seemed critical of what it described, such literature was another illustration of the crass and vulgar state of mind from which poetry hoped to redeem its readers, or, at least, to eloign itself.

In adhering to the Genteel mode, poets affirmed a spiritual allegiance, vague but sincere. They also obtained psychological reassurance. For commitment to the Genteel put a wide distance between poetry, as it was understood, and the increasingly dominant modes of prose fiction. And it afforded an urgent justification for poetry.

THE POETRY MARKET

Poets depend on the publishing trade, if only for the obvious reasons that they need access to an audience and to the work of their contemporaries. They require that books of poetry be published, distributed, promoted, and kept in print. And of course it is desirable that publishers find and further the better poets rather than the mediocre ones. If we judge publishing houses at the turn of the century by these criteria, their record is not always admirable. One cannot know how much good poetry was written but not published, or how much was not even written, the poet having lost hope of breaking into print. But it is possible to think of major poets—for example, Robinson and Frost—whose work publishers rejected and discouraged for a long time.

On the other hand, if we assume that publishing houses exist not to encourage good literature but to make profits, it is much to their credit that they handled as much poetry as they did; for there was usually little profit in it. (About two hundred books of poetry were published in the United States in 1900; in 1925, the heyday of the poetic revival, there were about four hundred.) The poetry that produced substantial profits was invariably second-rate or worse. A major poet might eventually earn something for his publisher, but only after many years and in a small way. None of the major poets of the twentieth century have been best sellers, whether we think of the best sellers year by year or cumulatively over the years.

The attitude of American publishers to poetry was generally similar to what we have noticed in England and reflects the confusion in the trade as a whole as to its proper role or purpose. To the extent that publishers were motivated by a wish to serve literature, they felt they should publish poetry; so far as they were businessmen, they had no enthusiasm for it. Perhaps there was even less enthusiasm in the United States than in England; for books of poetry in England seem at this time to have enjoyed larger sales and to have lost less money; therefore, probably, more were published. If a publisher brought out a book of poems, it was usually because he felt a responsibility either to literature or to the prestige of his firm or to a writer who also turned out profitable prose.

In America as in England magazines often included some poetry, though only as occasional tailpieces or pages inserted between the fiction, essays, and journalism to which they mainly devoted their space. The "quality" magazines were *Harper's, Century, Scribner's* and the *Atlantic*. In the next class were *Lippincott's, Frank Leslie's Popular Monthly*, and *Bedford's Monthly*. Weeklies with large circulation, such as *Collier's* and the *Saturday Evening Post,* also printed some poetry. The extraordinary magazine for children, *St. Nicholas,* was in the 1890s at its highest point, with stories and poems of remarkable quality. Two reviews devoted to poetry had been founded in 1889, *The Magazine of Poetry* and *Poet-Lore.* They merged in 1896 and continued as *Poet-Lore* vigorously until 1930, and intermittently until 1953. When in 1894 *The Yellow Book* arrived from England, it inspired many imitations—avant-garde "little" magazines of which *The Chap-Book* (1894–1898) was the most important. But neither in quantity, quality, or impact was this the flourishing age of the little magazines. Precisely how much poetry was published through these various magazine channels is not known. *The Weekly Review,* which listed the contents of the principal magazines and papers in the United States, cited an average of sixty to seventy poems per week during the 1890s.

Payment for poetry in the quality magazines seems to have compared favorably with English standards. A dollar a line was high, but the rate could go much higher. Kipling was paid nine dollars a line for some poems. The average short poem seems to have been sold for five to twelve dollars. These sums may seem picayune, but they were not despicable. Cawein told the Louisville *Courier-Journal* that his returns from "magazine verse from the year 1900 were about $100 per month," at a time when the salary of university professors was likely to be $1500 to $2000 per year.

I have suggested that because of their literary prestige and their importance as publishing outlets, the magazines strongly influenced the kind and quality of verse written. The editors often denied this. They wished, they said, to publish more and more adventurous verse but could not find it. This must frequently have been the case. Bliss Perry, whose critical work and whose teaching at Harvard attest to his range of taste and his interest in new writing, had especially hoped to keep a place for poetry after he took over the editorship of the *Atlantic Monthly* in 1899. But he told the *Writer* (November 1904) that, in order to maintain the standard of what the *Atlantic* had published in the past, he was forced to "give relatively little space to verse." The truth may be that the magazines contributed to the decline in quality of verse, and then saw themselves forced to publish less of it than they might have wished.

The state of affairs in the poetry market did not conduce to the health of poetry. It was not that an audience was lacking— any more than is usually the case in the modern world—though it was mainly an unsophisticated audience. Will Carleton, author of "Over the Hill to the Poor-house" and similar poems, sold over six hundred thousand volumes during his lifetime; doubtless his follower, James Whitcomb Riley, did still better. "The Man with the Hoe" is said to have earned over $250,000 for Edwin Markham during the course of his life. The trouble was that publishers were relatively few, unenthusiastic, and like-minded in literary taste. It was, therefore, not easy to break into print at this time, especially for the unconventional. The situation may be contrasted with the twenties, when pub- lishing outlets—particularly poetry journals and little maga- zines—abounded, and when a welcome could be found some- where for every originality or eccentricity. This also had liabil- ities, but it is significant that when a greater poetry gradually developed in America after the turn of the century, there were, as both a result and a cause, more and more diverse publishing outlets, and more poems published.

6

THE BEGINNINGS OF THE MODERN
MOVEMENT IN AMERICA

AMERICAN poets at the turn of the century had little traceable influence of a positive kind on the development of modern poetry. When Pound, Eliot, Williams, H. D., Marianne Moore, Stevens, and the other Modernist poets of their generation cast off the late-Victorian styles that were usual in America around 1900 (and in which they had composed their own early work), they turned for psychological support and technical example to poets in foreign languages, to painters and sculptors, and, among American poets, to Whitman.

But as a negative influence, American poetry from roughly 1890 to 1912 played a large part in bringing on the Modernist revolution. The need to repudiate the conventional, usually insipid, see-no-evil verse of this time acted as a motive and spur of the strongest possible kind. In fact, if we ask why the development of the Modernist mode was chiefly by American poets, one reason is that American poets had no strong, innovative, and rebellious avant-garde movement among their immediate predecessors in their own country. After 1900 English poets reacted against the Aesthetic-Decadent-Symbolist-Impressionist poets of the 1890s and returned in some ways to the traditions of English Romantic poetry (for the poetry of the Romantic period is to the modern world what the Roman classics were to Augustan England). American poets, on the other hand, grew up during the predominance of a traditional poetry that was second-rate. Naturally they eloigned themselves from it, and with fewer misgivings and greater boldness because it was visibly weak.

Their rebellion was anticipated, though timidly, in the previous generation. Inevitably the Genteel Tradition engendered countertendencies. American poetry at the turn of the century must, accordingly, be viewed from a double standpoint. With the important exceptions of Crane and Robinson, it seems more or less of one piece to readers now, for most poets cultivated the decorous, elegiac, uplifting, and so forth, using a traditional, carefully worked diction and versification. But to readers seventy years ago, the poetic scene presented an altogether different aspect. The Genteel Tradition was obviously prevalent, but opposition movements were strong. If the former monopolized prestige, the latter aroused more interest and hope. Markham, Hovey, and the Canadian Carman were read far more eagerly than their genteel contemporaries, for they conveyed a greater reality and zest. They illustrate the degree of rebellion for which publishers and an audience could then be found.

At the end of this chapter we shall come to the one great American poet of the 1890s, Edwin Arlington Robinson. He is placed there because his work both includes and goes beyond the two large tendencies explored in it, the Genteel Tradition and its counterpointing oppositions. Robinson was not anti-Genteel. He emerged from within the fold, even from within its home territory of New England. He studied hard, he practiced craftsmanship, he echoed the major Romantic and Victorian poets of England, he had the conscientious moralism of his inheritance. But along with this he assimilated elements of American regional writing—the rendering of local speech, setting, and types of character—not in the theatrical and mannered way of Riley but with a tenacious fidelity to the concrete case. He also took over methods and subjects from prose fiction and created, at his best, a poetry that was subtle, bold, contemporary, and completely original. No one else in the nineties, either in England or the United States, was writing verse remotely akin to "Richard Cory" or "Reuben Bright." He was not quite the founder of modern verse in America, for the first wave of modern poets did not learn their art from him. But modern poetry in America begins with Robinson.

THE GENTEEL TRADITION

The phrase "the Genteel Tradition" owes its currency to George Santayana, who used it in a famous lecture ("The Genteel Tradition in American Philosophy," 1911) and recurred to it on many occasions. To Santayana it suggested much of what made him uncomfortable in American academic and cultural life generally, and especially in the intellectual milieu of Boston and Harvard, where he taught philosophy: vestigial Puritanism in the form of excessive moral anxiousness and timidity; vestigial Transcendentalism in the form of vague idealism, not much related to actual life; earnest pursuit of "culture" and a faith in its spiritual or quasi-religious value, with the assumption also that America lacks "culture," and hence a special deference and attraction to Europe, where "culture" was thought to have its native home. As Santayana conceived it, the Genteel Tradition was without intellectual rigor or vital force; it could not accept natural, robust realities; it could hardly even perceive them. The extent to which he had a point may be illustrated in Madison Cawein. After he graduated from high school, Cawein took a job in Louisville, Kentucky, as a cashier in Waddill's Newmarket poolrooms. It was, in fact, a gambling house, and he saw much that another poet—Whitman, for example—might have exploited, since the place was thronged with gamblers, jockeys, sports, swashbucklers, and sharpers. In the midst of this Cawein wrote, in intervals of cashing bets, such verses as,

> What wood-god, on this water's mossy curb,
>   Lost in reflection of earth's loveliness,
> Did I, just now, unconsciously disturb?

For, as a newspaper interviewer explains, the gambling house would "furnish excellent material for a novelist," but "where is the poet that ever sang, who could suck inspiration from such an olio of humanity?" (This Genteel explanation was probably Cawein's.) Above all, Santayana felt, the Genteel philosophy and values failed to express fully not only the life about them but even the life of those who cherished them. They had stifled many of the promising writers he had known at Harvard. As he told William Lyon Phelps, "All these friends of mine, Stickney especially, of whom I was very fond, were visibly killed by the lack of air to breathe. People individually were kind and appreciative to them . . . but the system was deadly."

But the Genteel tendency had only to be characterized another way, and it became one of the great, valued roads always open to the human spirit. In this prestidigitation no one was more adroit than Santayana, who would argue that there is, after all, no compelling reason why a poetry or a philosophy must express the life either of the author or of whatever time and place it happened to be composed in. If Santayana was in some moods a materialist and naturalist, in other moods he was more a Platonist and pursuer of unchanging essences. And so he could say that one's allegiances are spiritual and ideal and that one should live in eternity. Although he was the most penetrating of the many critics of the Genteel Tradition, Santayana was also, in some respects, its greatest exponent, both as a philosopher and as a poet. In him the Genteel attitude purged itself of most of its timidity and soft-headedness, which he brilliantly satirized, and presented a permanent intellectual challenge to the self-consciously American and Modernist movements that were soon to dominate poetry in the United States.

In style the Genteel type of poetry was earnest and unequivocal, traditional, abstract, well-bred, inspirational, and meticulous. The chief historical service of this style to the development of American poetry may lie in its emphasis on formal craftsmanship. It is at its best in Santayana's sonnets, for example:

> O world, thou choosest not the better part!
> It is not wisdom to be only wise,
> And on the inward vision close the eyes,
> But it is wisdom to believe the heart.
> Columbus found a world, and had no chart
> Save one that faith deciphered in the skies.

The liveliest defense of this style comes, as one would expect, from Santayana in the Preface (1922) to his poems. He notes with ironic apologies that their "language is literary," that they are enveloped in an "aura of literary and religious associations," and that "their prosody is worn and traditional." For, he says, they represent not "the chance experiences of a stray individual" —which might require, or at least justify, a personally distinctive diction, imagery, and versification—but rather the "submission" of the individual to "the truth of nature and the moral heritage of mankind." "Borrowed plumes would not even seem an ornament if they were not in themselves beautiful. To say that what was good once is good no longer is to give too much importance to chronology."

The most important of the other "Harvard poets," as they are usually called, are Trumbull Stickney (1874–1904), George Cabot Lodge (1873–1909), and William Vaughn Moody (1869–1910). As students at Harvard in more or less the same period of time, they were acquainted with each other as well as with other young writers and intellectuals. Trumbull Stickney was one of the many expatriate, late-nineteenth-century Americans of moderate means and fine cultivation who might have stepped from a Henry James novel. He was born in Switzerland, grew up in Wiesbaden, Florence, Nice, and New York, was sent to schools in England, France, and the United States, and, after four years at Harvard, spent eight years studying at the Sorbonne, where he became the first American ever to receive the Doctorat ès Lettres. He then taught Greek at Harvard until his death at the age of thirty. His *Poems* (1905) were published posthumously, edited by his friends George Cabot Lodge, John Ellerton Lodge, and William Vaughn Moody. They made little impression, however, and Stickney was all but forgotten until Conrad Aiken, long an admirer (he had introduced T. S. Eliot to Stickney's poetry in 1908), included some poems of Stickney's in his anthology, *American Poetry, 1671–1928* (1929). Since then his reputation has spread, thanks especially to a eulogistic essay by Edmund Wilson in 1940. Wilson called him "a remarkable American poet whom too few people have read," and added, "this spareness and simplicity of language that carries a charge of meaning is quite unlike the decadent romanticism that reigned at the end of the century." My own reading bears out these observations on the whole, but I do not take the pleasure in Stickney that Wilson did. He was a poet of taste, sensitivity, intelligence, and accomplished craftsmanship in the traditional mode, and easily rates well above Josephine Preston Peabody,

Louise Imogen Guiney, Katherine Lee Bates, or Logan Pearsall Smith, if they represent the "decadent romanticism" Wilson had in mind. But by present-day expectations Stickney's poems are usually abstract, diffuse, and sentimental. He had the typical expertise of the better poets of his age in all aspects of prosody; some lines from "In Ampezzo" recall Hart Crane's "Voyages":

> At sunset, south, by lilac promontories
> Under green skies to Italy, or forth
> By calms of morning beyond Lavinores
> Tyrolward and to North.

His mood, like Santayana's, was frequently joyless, elegiac, and stoic. One of his best lyrics is "In the Past," a powerful, symbolic concentration of depression and despair. The English poets he most resembles are the pessimistic late-Victorian classicists, such as Johnson or Housman, although he is gentler and more wistful, and lacks Housman's sardonic bitterness.

George Cabot Lodge, known as "Bay" Lodge, was also a scholar, whose field was Romance languages. He moved restlessly about in Boston society, thought philosophically, and was warmly liked for his kindness and charm. His verse is highminded, but interest flags, perhaps because Lodge was too attuned to generality. Few poems can be more conventional than the title piece of his first volume, *The Song of the Wave and Other Poems* (1898): the wave gathers, crests, falls on the shore, "And the end is Death!" His second volume, *Poems, 1899–1902* (1902), was dedicated to Walt Whitman, from whom Lodge had indeed much to learn. "A Song for Walking" shows him trying for what he took to be Whitman's spirit and imagery. His philosophical moiling led him to a conception of Will working through Nature: God as Will exists only as creative subject declaring itself and becoming manifest in the object (Nature), which is knowable only as ourselves. This distillation from German philosophy, especially Schopenhauer, was stirred in the pot with Buddhistic flavorings. Whatever one may think of the concoction, it lies inert in his poetry, for Lodge lacked emotional reaction to concrete and specific embodiments of Will. His third book, *The Great Adventure* (1905), consists of sonnets, which are printed in three sections— "Life," "Love," and "Death." He also wrote two blank-verse plays, *Cain* (1904) and *Herakles* (1907).

William Vaughn Moody was probably, after Robinson, the most important poet of the age. He did not rival Santayana or Lizette Reese in perfected short pieces but he wrote with bigger ambition; in the ten years before he died he was viewed with pride as at least potentially a major poet. His poetry descends from the great English Romantics and Victorians, whose breadth of concern he emulated, but it also experiments with new modes. "Jetsam," a long, blank-verse utterance written between 1895 and 1897, shows him mounting elements of *symboliste* technique on traditional narrative and meditative form. The poem moves in an intelligible sequence (psychologically or associatively probable, if not logical) of thoughts and feelings, but, compared with most meditative or dramatic monologues of the nineteenth century, the transitions, like those in Eliot's *Prufrock,* are more abrupt, surprising, and irrational. The poem presents "ideas" or conscious meanings but creates also a nimbus of unsayable or unknowable suggestion around its major images, such as the moon. These symbols are, however, presented more by the methods of Shelley than of Mallarmé. Moody adopts in the poem the sordid urban setting of Baudelaire and, occasionally, of the Impressionists; so far as its topic goes, a line such as "The river lay / Coiled in its factory filth and few lean trees" might have been written by Eliot. "Until the Troubling of the Waters" is a blank-verse dramatic monologue, spoken by a working-class woman, which anticipates Robert Frost in its psychological insight, realism, and colloquial idiom and rhythm.

Moody had also a public voice, and his poems of social and political protest brought much renown. The most ambitious, "An Ode in Time of Hesitation" (1909), attacks the American annexation and brutal pacification of the Philippines. The ode is slow, weighty, and appropriately external, like a parade, with vistas of American landscape, richly cumulative detail, and dramatic shifts from high-minded elegy to satire. It contrasts the idealistic motivations of the Civil War with the sordid commercialism that animates American imperialism forty years later. The poem begins in the Boston Common, the speaker looking at Saint Gaudens' statue of Colonel Shaw and his black regiment, and may be compared with Robert Lowell's poem on Colonel Shaw, "For the Union Dead," which also views the American historical past and present in one perspective. In Moody's poem a morally superior past is brought forward to confront and shame the present. The speaker can express straightforward anger and scorn, for he has no impulse to look within and find in himself the corruption he denounces. Lowell's poem differs strikingly at these points. The contemporary world he presents is almost unbearably sordid and frightened. But the past was not really different, and the speaker recognizes in himself every woeful and vicious impulse that disgusts him in the world about him. Thus, where Moody speaks in lofty indignation, inciting readers to protest and battle, Lowell looks without and within in anguished despair. To the complex self-consciousness of the later poet, the battle, if any can be fought, is not merely against politicians and financiers but against the heart and nature of man, and there is no hope of a victory.

Moody possessed a large imaginative endowment, a full mind, and a readiness to confront the modern social, economic, and political scene. His stylistic control was not constant, but he had a sensitive ear, his phrasing was consistently above the level of the unrefreshed routine, and there were brilliant passages. He had courage for big undertakings. He wrote three works in the traditional, nineteenth-century mode of blank-verse closet drama: *The Masque of Judgment* (1900), *The Firebringer* (1904), and *The Death of Eve,* which he left unfinished. He also wrote two prose plays, *The Great Divide* (1906), which enjoyed a long run, and *The Faith Healer* (1909). In subject and technique he sometimes went far beyond the usual limits of the Genteel Tradition, and he was thought of as a much needed tonic to the poetry of the age. But during the twenties he was more or less lost from sight.

Among the lesser poets of Boston at this time was Thomas Bailey Aldrich (1836–1907), editor of the *Atlantic* and still slightly remembered for his novel *The Story of a Bad Boy* (1870). He began by writing poetry of a Keatsian and oriental sumptuousness, but as he grew older his style became more chaste and finished; he thought of it as "classical." His late, short poems are his best; in them he is a low-key Landor. Louise Imogen Guiney (1861–1930) was a gallant lady, who had, along with diffuseness, vagueness, and clichés, a sense of rhythm (she also wrote free verse) and a loving heart. The poetic object of her love was England, especially the England of the seventeenth century.

After 1901 she lived near Oxford on a small income, skimping on food in order to buy books. Her "The Wild Ride" is lively:

> I hear in my heart, I hear in its ominous pulses
> All day, on the road, the hoofs of invisible horses,
> All night, from their stalls, the importunate pawing and
>   neighing.
>
> . . . .
>
> We spur to a land of no name, out-racing the storm-wind;
> We leap to the infinite dark like sparks from the anvil.
> Thou leadest, O God! All's well with Thy troopers that follow.

Another kind and gracious woman was Josephine Preston Peabody (1874–1922). Her verse drama *The Piper* had a resounding success at Stratford-on-Avon in 1910. She is said to have described poetry as "the richest expression of noblest ideals." Louise Chandler Moulton (1835–1908) may be mentioned for her cautious, unlifelike sonnets. Gently moralistic and reflective, she deployed familiar, rather limp images, and an idiom that is prosaic without being colloquial. Jessie Rittenhouse (1869–1948) was a lecturer, anthologist, and commentator. In prose and poetry her style was thin-spun and archaic, with fluttery nods and curtsies. In 1913 she put together *The Little Book of Modern Verse,* which contains only American poets. By this time the better American verse was no longer Genteel, but Miss Rittenhouse, like most of her fellow critics and readers, was not yet aware of the fact. (She was, however, by 1919, when she brought out *The Second Book of Modern Verse.*) Accordingly, if one wants to see the Genteel poetry of the age in one volume, her anthology may be recommended. It includes sixty-nine poets; the largest number of poems (four each) are from Bliss Carman, Louise Imogen Guiney, Richard Hovey, Richard Le Gallienne, Edwin Markham, Lizette Woodworth Reese, and Arthur Upson.

In New York, Edmund Clarence Stedman (1833–1908), a stockbroker, found time to read verse in immense quantities. His *American Anthology* (1900) includes about six hundred poets, some almost unknown before he called attention to them. Learned, fair, and intelligent, he was probably the most influential critic of poetry in the United States at the turn of the century. The tone and premise of his criticism are indicated, perhaps unfairly, in an anecdote Harriet Monroe gives in her autobiography. During a dinner at Stedman's home she was arguing the merits of Shelley with Henry Harland, who was standing up for Browning. "Just then Mr. Stedman became interested from the other side of the room, and rushed to my assistance. 'That is true—and I respect you for feeling it,' he said; 'Shelley soared higher into the Empyrean.'" Stedman's own verse is flaccid. Richard Watson Gilder (1844–1909) was editor first of *Scribner's* and then of the *Century*. He was a humanitarian interested in social and political causes and a befriender of Whitman, but none of this shows in his poetry, which is committed to Beauty and the Ideal. Robert Underwood Johnson (1853–1937), who succeeded Gilder at the *Century*, was an energetic, honorable man whose main contribution to poetry was not through his own writing. George Woodberry (1855–1930) believed that poetry "softens, refines and ennobles the soul" and illuminates "life from within the consciousness of the reader"—words with which we would like to agree, except that the phrasing seems overly confident and glib. Woodberry's own poetry refines "life" until it evaporates. He wrote much on American literature but had a low opinion of it; the United States had "never yet produced a poet of the rank of Gray," an opinion typical of teachers of literature in America at this time.

Lizette Woodworth Reese (1856–1935) was in Baltimore, teaching English in the Western High School. It was Anna Hempstead Branch (1875–1937) who wrote a much anthologized poem, "The Monk in the Kitchen," in praise of household order; it is, she felt, a reflection of the eternal and divine. But Lizette Reese better exemplified a fine cleanliness of style. Her apparently simple, always lucid poems are traditional, reticent, and firm, with phrases carefully scoured and placed. Her method is illustrated in her portrait of "A Puritan Lady." The poem is clear and reasoned discourse but releases a rapid sequence of concrete, precisely phrased images. The images are handled in a way that anticipates Imagist poetry; at their best—"a white flower on a grave"—they are the "objective correlatives" of complex impressions. The poem concludes:

> What grave long afternoons,
>   What caged airs round her blown,
> Stripped her of humor, left her bare
>   As cloud, or wayside stone?

> Made her as clear a thing,
> In this slack world as plain
> As a white flower on a grave,
> Or sleet sharp at a pane?

Miss Reese was a foe to sloppiness and sentimentality. Her best-known poem, "Tears," deserves its fame, if only because of its fine, elegiac cadence and swift accumulation of suggestive metaphors. But it is slightly sentimental and, to that extent, not quite characteristic:

> When I consider Life and its few years—
> A wisp of fog betwixt us and the sun;
> A call to battle, and the battle done
> Ere the last echo dies within our ears;
> A rose choked in the grass; an hour of fears; . . .

She achieved, on the whole, a more concentrated, concrete, and precise expression than other Genteel poets. Miss Branch, however, was more intellectual, speculative, and mystical, and appealed more to readers such as Alfred Kreymborg who cared less about formal qualities. Her *Nimrod* (1910), a long, narrative poem about the biblical character, was noticed by him with eulogies that are now sobering to read, though even Kreymborg, who thought *Nimrod* much better than *The Waste Land,* admitted that the poem sometimes "flies off into dizzy abstractions the human reader cannot follow."

In Kentucky, Cawein's crown of laurel was contested by Cale Young Rice (1872–1943), who wrote poetic dramas and lyrics, some of which got into magazines. Virginia could boast of Father John Banister Tabb (1845–1909), who, like Lizette Reese, struggled for a more condensed style than was usual at this time. His great fault is insipidity. The anguish he suffered—in a Northern prison camp during the Civil War, in the postwar financial ruin of his family, and in the spiritual turmoil of religious conversion—goes unmentioned. The censorship may have been either clerical or literary, but it makes his verse relatively impersonal. His poems are expressions of literary or religious devotion, and he concentrates to a remarkable extent on flowers. Perhaps his brief lyrics on "Golden-Rod," "Wild Flowers," "Cherry Bloom," "Immortelles," and "Peach Bloom" were remotely connected with a feeling of God's immanence, but the feeling receives no powerful or even direct expression and his fancies are at best delicate. Sometimes they are only coy, as in "Peach Bloom":

> A dream in fragrant silence wrought,
> A blossoming of petaled thought,
> A passion of these April days—
> The blush of nature now betrays.

In California George Sterling (1869–1926), a typical late-Victorian bohemian, was one of the early poets to write of the landscape around Carmel. But for the most part, landscape, like other objects of a relatively solid and definite kind, gets short shrift in his poetry. He was fascinated by the sea and much tempted to vague, cosmic flights of imagination. Short lyrics such as "The Black Vulture" are his best.

The poets of the Genteel Tradition were usually treated with contempt by literary historians of the last generation, and it may be conceded that as writers and thinkers most of them were timid. But they were often persons of learning and integrity and may safely be admired by poets and critics of the present generation, who may be equally shackled by different conventions. The English poets whom the Genteel ones most resembled were the more conservative Edwardians, such as Mary Coleridge, R. C. Trevelyan, Gerald Gould, Laurence Binyon, and Sturge Moore.

REACTIONS AGAINST THE GENTEEL MODE

Poetry of the Genteel Tradition predominated throughout the country. Reactions against it were seldom wholehearted. James Whitcomb Riley is an example. His barn settings and dialect speech thumb their nose at the Genteel schoolmarm and were the more enjoyed for that reason. His vision of midwestern life had additional meaning and impact because it was implicitly contrasted with Eastern urban culture. Against one myth Riley upheld another, for he claimed that the contentment and goodness of Our Town is better than the sophistication of the Old World, or of Boston. On the other hand, if the Genteel Tradition suggests (as it does, on its weaker side) a deliberate cultivation of the more ideal emotions and an unreadiness to look at disagreeable realities, Riley is as blatant an example as can be found. It is not surprising that he detested the poetry of Whitman. Or we may think of Edwin Markham. He wrote the most powerful poems of social protest of his generation, at least in America, and thus departed completely from the usual subject matter of the poets we have been discussing. But he composed these poems in a form and idiom that were not in the least radical, since they were caught directly from the Romantic poets of England and America, especially Bryant, Wordsworth and Shelley; and he wrote a great many other poems that are remarkable only for their total conformity to Genteel conventions, such as "After Reading Shakespeare," "Song of the Followers of Pan," "Fay Song," and "Keats A-Dying." His first book, *The Man with the Hoe and Other Poems* (1899), was dedicated to E. C. Stedman. Its contents show that if he wished to agitate social sympathies, he also wished, perhaps rather more, to win the approval of the usual critics and readers. Except for Stephen Crane and Robinson, every important American poet in the 1890s followed the prevailing mode at least as much as he strayed from it.

This is the way turn-of-the-century America looks from our perspective, after more than seventy years of poetry that has been sedulously un- or anti-genteel. But to readers around 1900 contemporary poetry apparently was alive with conflicting tendencies. Poets such as Markham, Riley, Richard Hovey, Eugene Field, and Stephen Crane seemed to mount strong, direct protests and challenges to the Genteel Tradition.

These poets of the opposition were popular, and they were comparatively bold. At least the homely dialect of Riley, the social protest of Markham, the iconoclasm of Crane, the brashness of Field, and the praise (though not the example) of free, amoral vitality in Hovey departed widely from Genteel conventions. Not one of the poets discussed earlier in this chapter sold as well as any of the five just mentioned. The fact cannot be explained by qualities of style or sentiment shared by the five, for they differed greatly from each other. Riley was the most widely read poet in America; but Crane also enjoyed brisk sales, although he was the antithesis of Riley, blotting out the "old swimmin'-hole" and "old Aunt Mary" with visions and parables of a powerfully satiric and grotesque kind. The greater popularity of these five poets must be explained in part by the comparative lack of appeal of the Genteel Tradition, which, except in Moody, offered no very broad or relevant contact with life. Although most readers of poetry had a genuine faith in the approved mode, they also felt its parlor confinements and fatigues and were ready to applaud rebellion, at least of a limited kind.

THE VAGABOND THEME

In the 1890s two young poets, Richard Hovey (1864–1900) and Bliss Carman (1861–1929), jointly produced three volumes of "vagabond" lyrics (*Songs from Vagabondia*, 1894, *More Songs from Vagabondia*, 1896, and *Last Songs from Vagabondia*, 1900). These lyrics portrayed or cried out for a life of footloose wandering, love, drink, comradeship, battle, and nature. They include such favorites as Hovey's "The Sea Gypsy":

> I am fevered with the sunset,
> I am fretful with the bay,
> For the wander-thirst is on me
> And my soul is in Cathay—

and Carman's "A Vagabond Song":

> There is something in the autumn that is native to my blood—
> Touch of manner, hint of mood;
> And my heart is like a rhyme,
> With the yellow and the purple and the crimson keeping time.

Hovey also wrote "A Stein Song" with its well-known refrain—

> For it's always fair weather
> When good fellows get together,
> With a stein on the table and a good song ringing clear—

and the better, in some ways lovely, "Comrades, pour the wine to-night." The vagabond lyrics occasionally show the influence of Whitman in form and phrasing (as in "Spring"), and perhaps also in some of the attitudes expressed, for example, their protest against moralism and the success ethic. But if Whitman influenced them, it was pouring a gallon into a thimble. Everything was lost in the process, and the poems are quite conventional, often scarcely distinguishable from the boyish and swashbuckling romanticism popular at the time and exemplified in England in the verse of Stevenson, Chesterton, and Noyes. Their message is summed up in Hovey's line (from "The Faun"), "There is only the glory of living, exultant to be."

Toward the end of his life Hovey wrote a number of poetic dramas based on the Arthurian stories; his approach is more down to earth than Tennyson's. He wrote philosophic lyrics, articulating what seems to be a progressive pantheism, the belief that as time goes on the world will become more and more divine. He studied the French *symbolistes*, translated lyrics of Verlaine and Mallarmé, and rather timidly imitated them in some of his poems in *Along the Trail* (1899). Carman, a Canadian who went to Harvard College, also wrote philosophic lyrics. He had been impressed at Harvard by Josiah Royce's lectures on Spinoza and hoped to write a Wordsworthian poetry adapted to the New World. His underlying theme is the valuably formative impact of Nature on Man. But he lacks Wordsworth's profundity and also his meditative form and can voice his theme only as a lyric cry. Perhaps for this reason his verse did not develop and his later work seems monotonously repetitive. Thanks to his spontaneity, breezy cheer, strong rhythms, and direct emotion, he was widely read on both sides of the Atlantic. Even Wallace Stevens went through a brief infatuation with Carman and vagabondia. Carman's standing was such that he was asked to edit *The Oxford Book of American Verse* (1927).

EDWIN MARKHAM: POETRY OF SOCIAL PROTEST

Edwin Markham (1852–1940) grew up in California, teaching himself to write verse and using for models what he found in high-school anthologies. As a young man he found companionship and literary encouragement among radical intellectuals; under their influence he studied Ruskin, Morris, Marx, and such native writers as Laurence Gronlund (*The Co-operative Commonwealth: An Exposition of Modern Socialism*, 1884), and he was moved by the paintings of Millet. He wrote poems of radical sympathies and denunciation; one of them, "The Song of the Workers," was published by William Morris in his Socialist journal, *The Commonwealth*. But such verses would not have been approved by the Eastern custodians of poetry, and for the most part Markham buried them in his notebooks, making no effort to publish them. What he did submit for publication was, for example, "After Reading Shakespeare," a sonnet which appeared in the *Century* in 1886:

> Blithe Fancy lightly builds with airy hands
>   Or on the edges of the darkness peers,
>   Breathless and frightened at the Voice she hears.

At about the same time he mailed a packet of similar verses to E. C. Stedman, who sent back an encouraging letter, saying that they were "truly and exquisitely poetic." At length his famous poem of social anger, "The Man with the Hoe," was printed in the San Francisco *Examiner* in January 1899, the editor having heard Markham recite it at a New Year's Eve party:

> Bowed by the weight of centuries he leans
> Upon his hoe and gazes on the ground,
> The emptiness of ages in his face,
>
> . . . .
> O masters, lords and rulers in all lands,
> Is this the handiwork you give to God,
> This monstrous thing distorted and soul-quenched?
>
> . . . .
> How will it be with kingdoms and with kings—
> With those who shaped him to the thing he is—
> When this dumb Terror shall reply to God,
> After the silence of the centuries?

The poem is effective by its broad, direct rhetoric, its earnestness, outrage, and prophetic threat. It was reprinted in one newspaper after another across the country to a chorus of praise. For Joaquin Miller it had in it "The whole Yosemite—the thunder, the might, the majesty." For William James it was "magnificent and impressive in the highest degree, and reeks with humanity and morality." After this success Markham was approached by publishers. His first book, *The Man with the Hoe and Other Poems* (1899), was followed by many others through a long and distinguished career. In general Markham wrote three kinds of poetry: conventional and namby-pamby songs and sonnets; rhetorical and visionary radicalism; and earnest contemplation, sometimes meditative and sometimes visionary, of

the mysteries of man's fate and the cosmos. The last was probably his natural bent, much more than his books reveal, for many
such moilings never reached publication. An epic to be entitled
Destiny—he called it "Des" in his notebooks—consumed the
greater part of his literary energies for years. His commemo-
ration of Lincoln shows Markham at his best. Thoughtful, idealistic, well-meaning, and decent in feeling, it is written in large
sweeping phrases, impressionistic rather than pin-pointing:

> The color of the ground was in him, the red earth;
> The smell and tang of elemental things:
> The rectitude and patience of the cliff;
> The good-will of the rain that loves all leaves;
> The friendly welcome of the wayside well.

The independence and size of Markham's achievement are
apparent when we reflect that, although radical or Populist feeling was relatively intense and widespread at the turn of the century, he was the only poet before Lindsay and Sandburg who
was able to voice these feelings in an important way.

POPULAR ENTERTAINERS AND NEWSPAPER POETS

The primary aim of some poets was to appeal to as large an
audience as possible. They succeeded brilliantly through genial
humor and sentimental feeling, conveyed in homely or easy language and supported lavishly with stock associations. The most
accomplished and important of these was James Whitcomb Riley
(1849–1916). (The poetry of Paul Lawrence Dunbar, 1872–
1906, who studied Riley's methods, will be discussed in Chapter 18.) Riley took over the large audience that had delight-
edly responded to James Russell Lowell's *Biglow Papers* (first
series, 1848) and, more recently, to Will Carleton's *Farm Ballads,*
which had appeared in the late 1860s and early 1870s—the best-
known of which is "Over the Hill to the Poor-house." Slightly
oversimplifying, one may say that Riley learned from Lowell the
appeal of rustic speakers using dialect, and in Carleton, among
others, he saw that at this time of rapid industrialization and urbanization the widespread nostalgia for village and rural ways of
life might be exploited. As he read his poems before large audiences he studied their reactions and was able, he explains, to

"use the knowledge gained in my writing." The public, he discovered, "demands simple sentiments that come direct from the heart." Poems such as "Out to Old Aunt Mary's"—fond backward glances, smiling through tears—shamelessly gave the audience what it wanted.

Riley's poetry has much pathos but no tragedy; there is no evil caused by passion or will. (The closest he comes is in "A Man by the Name of Bolus," where tragedy is something experienced by a stranger.) And there is no social conflict. Persons in his world are good-hearted, humorous, contented, loving, and innocent. Childhood is the best time of life, and nostalgia the dominant emotion. "Old" is a favorite word of Riley's, as we noted earlier—"The Old Hay-Mow,""The Old, Old Wish," "Old-Fashioned Roses." In "An Old Sweetheart of Mine" he hears "the old school-bell," and in "The Old Swimmin'-Hole" there are "the old sickamore" and "the old dusty lane." His poems in dialect make a homespun impression and his others are more obviously slick, but their style is essentially the same. Given his purpose, he was an extremely capable workman. Rhythms are catchy and swinging; images are thickly clustered; plot moves rapidly and is shaped for dramatic impact; everything is on the surface, without complicating eddies or murky depths. Riley also wrote poems for children—for "children of all ages," in the phrase publishers used to be fond of—and these *Rhymes of Childhood* (1890) contain his two best poems, "The Raggedy Man" and "Little Orphant Annie." From such talents thus applied Riley became one of the most popular poets in American history. Records of sales before 1893 have disappeared, but between 1893 and 1949, when a study was made, close to three million of his books were purchased. He had many imitators, especially in newspapers, but the only one now remembered is Sam Walter Foss (1858–1911), and he is known only for "The House by the Side of the Road."

Riley first made his reputation with poems in newspapers, but he was not a journalist by profession. Other poets were, such as Eugene Field (1850–1896) and Thomas Augustin Daly (1871–1949), and their verses were part of their regular, usually humorous columns for the newspapers that employed them. Daly, who lived in Philadelphia, wrote in Irish and especially in Italian immigrant dialects. His first volume of verse, *Canzoni*

(1906), sold about fifty thousand copies. Field, who spent the latter part of his life in Chicago, had a large appreciative readership in the 1890s. He wrote in dialect occasionally, but many of his poems seem bookish, especially for a newspaper jester. He composed (with his brother) a series of free translations from Horace, *Echoes from a Sabine Farm* (1892), and it was typical of this complicated, sensitive, puckish man that, while some of them are humorously colloquial and seem to slap Horace on the back, the greater part are carried out with straightforward taste and affection. Field also wrote verses for children, of which favorites include the "Dutch Lullaby" ("Wynken, Blynken, and Nod"), "Little Boy Blue," and "The Sugar-Plum Tree." Some of these share with Riley's poems an unabashed sentimentalism of which no English poet would have been capable. "Little Boy Blue," for example, would have embarrassed even Robert Louis Stevenson.

Among these newspaper entertainers was Guy Wetmore Carryl (1873–1904), perhaps the leading writer of light verse at this time. Until he retired (to a cottage that Carryl, a bachelor, named "Shingle Blessedness") he was also a journalist and magazine editor. He showed sparkling wit, skill, and charm in parodies of Aesop (*Fables for the Frivolous,* 1898), Mother Goose (*Mother Goose for Grown-Ups,* 1900), and Grimm's fairy tales (*Grimm Tales Made Gay,* 1902), and wrote for a more knowing taste than did Riley or Field.

Poetry in the vein of Riley or Field overlaps in a significant way with the unsophisticated "handyman" verse. In the one case we have poetry for the people; in the other case it is by the people. The distinction is not always easy to make, for, generally speaking, the same sentiments appear in both kinds of poetry; the difference lies in the degree of technical expertise and imagination that are brought to bear. Among the many poets who stand on the borderline—for this kind of poetry was extremely common—John Wallace Crawford (1847–1917), "The Poet Scout," is the most interesting. He was born in Ireland. Wounded in the Civil War, he learned to read and write in a Northern military hospital. After the war he moved to the Western frontier, becoming one of the original seven settlers of the Black Hills. He served intermittently as an army scout (he was also a rancher, miner, and Indian agent), and succeeded "Buffalo Bill" Cody as chief of scouts during the campaign against Sitting Bull in 1876. He subsequently took part in the Apache wars in the 1880s. Meanwhile, he was acting as correspondent for several news-papers and also publishing stories and poems. At the end of these adventures Crawford cashed in on his reputation, making frequent lecture and reading tours. He explains that his poems were "the crude, unpolished offspring of my idle hours . . . spontaneous bubblings from a heart whose springs of poetry and poetic thought were opened by the hand of Nature amid her roughest scenes." Be that as it may, his verses have a sleek journalistic effectiveness that is not quite artless or primitive. Many are in dialect. They are humorous or sentimental ballads and songs; the sentimental ones dwell on mother, home, and death, as in "Dreaming of Mother," "Farewell, Old Cabin Home" (adapted from a popular song), and "Death of Little Kit," written "on hearing from Mr. Cody (Buffalo Bill) of the death of his little boy, Kit Carson Cody." Obviously, Crawford's experiences were vivid and novel, but they served him only for incidental details of plot and setting. His forms, phrases, feelings, and stories had been the stock property of poets at least since Sir Walter Scott, as one sees in the opening of "The Dying Scout":

> Comrades, raise me, I am dying,
>   Hark the story I will tell;
> Break it gently to my mother,
>   You were near me when I fell.
> Tell her how I fought with Custer,
>   How I rode to tell the news:
> Now I'm dying, comrades, dying—
>   Tell me, did we whip the Sioux?

EARLY MODERN POETRY: CRANE AND ROBINSON

The poems contained in the two volumes Stephen Crane (1871–1900) published in the nineties, *The Black Riders* (1895) and *War is Kind* (1899), differed diametrically from the pre-vailing mode. They were in free verse; instead of discursive statement, they were suggestive metaphors and parables; in-stead of expressing the more ideal and uplifting emotions, they attacked religious faith and cosmic optimism with bitter ingenuity. Nothing in history is unprecedented, and Crane was aware of Emily Dickinson and Whitman, of Ambrose Bierce, and of English Victorian pessimists such as Edward FitzGerald. Yet he does not really resemble them or any previous or contemporary writers. In their precision and spareness, their paradox, violence, visionary satire, and grotesquerie, his poems, more than any others of the time, anticipate the Modernist mode:

> I walked in a desert.
> And I cried,
> "Ah, God, take me from this place!"
> A voice said, "It is no desert."
> I cried, "Well, but—
> The sand, the heat, the vacant horizon."
> A voice said, "It is no desert."

Crane has suffered a frequent fate of anticipators and forerunners. What seemed shocking iconoclasm became common in the next generation, and when many poets were doing more or less what he had done, his weaknesses were more readily noticed. His protest is certainly more strident than profound. His inventions, though tersely and concretely phrased, are without density or manifold interaction in the phrasing; they arrest attention, but do not hold it. And there are many passages in which Crane did not work hard enough. The first sentence of "To the maiden" might almost have been written by Wallace Stevens, but not, one imagines, the conclusion of the second:

> To the maiden
> The sea was blue meadow,
> Alive with little froth-people
> Singing.

> To the sailor, wrecked,
> The sea was dead grey walls
> Superlative in vacancy,
> Upon which nevertheless at fateful time
> Was written
> The grim hatred of nature.

Edwin Arlington Robinson was born December 22, 1869, in the village of Head Tide, Maine. He was the youngest of three sons of Edward Robinson, a former shipwright who kept the local general store. The background is relevant, for this wind-swept area of Maine combined the simplicity, even poverty, of village and rural America with the New England respect for books and the cosmopolitanism often found in seafaring places. When he was six months old, his family moved to the nearby town of Gardiner, the "Tilbury Town" of his poems. A quiet, conscientious boy, he excelled at school in Latin and English and began to write poetry in his early teens, composing or reading in a rocking chair (a habit that lasted throughout his life). He went to Harvard (1891), but during his second year his father died and Robinson returned to Gardiner.

Meanwhile the family fortune had been collapsing because of unwise investments made by a kindly older brother, Herman, who was now drinking too much. His even more gifted brother Dean was becoming a morphine addict and also turning to al-cohol. Both appear, years later, as disguised characters in some of the longer poems. Robinson himself had been suffering from chronic mastoiditis, often with severe pain (it finally left him deaf in one ear), and lived in fear that the growing damage of the inner ear would reach the brain and cause insanity. At home he did the chores and continued to write. Finding the magazines closed to his work (a familiar experience until his middle forties), he brought out at his own expense (it cost fifty-two dollars) a small volume, *The Torrent and the Night Before* (1896). Already we see in these poems the plain honesty and patient craftsmanship he shared with his shipbuilding ancestors. Just as the book was about to appear, Robinson's mother died, and he decided to move to New York, hoping it would be easier to find publishers for his work. Here he lived in destitution for the next ten years, except for a six-month period when, at the age of thirty, he returned to Harvard as a sort of office boy to President Eliot—a job he detested. He never married. Thin, reticent, with dark searching eyes behind the glint of his spectacles, partially deaf, he could often talk freely with one person but became quieter with two and almost tongue-tied in a group.

Robinson's next two volumes, *Children of the Night* (1897) and *Captain Craig and Other Poems* (1902), attracted little attention. Refusing to turn to hack writing, he took what positions he could find, serving for a while as a timekeeper for the subway con-struction. When out of work, he was able to stay alive by eating in the cheapest restaurants or at free-lunch counters in saloons; occasionally he had to content himself with a meal consisting of a roll from a bakery. He began to drink heavily and for seven years was a near-alcoholic. President Theodore Roosevelt became interested in his work, reviewed a second edition of *Children of the Night* in *Outlook* magazine (1905), and secured him a job in the New York Custom House, which Robinson kept until 1909. Despite Roosevelt's review, magazines remained uninterested in Robinson's verse, and the rejection slips continued to mount. Meanwhile he worked on his next volume, *The Town Down the River* (1910), dedicated to Roosevelt.

In 1911, when he was forty-one, he began spending his summers at the MacDowell Colony in Peterborough, New Hampshire, and continued to do so until his death. This gave him increased freedom and marked a turn in his life. Here in his cabin he would sit and rock for days on end, patiently composing. Winters were spent at the home of New York friends and, after 1922, at the home of the sculptor James Fraser. A growing range as well as increasing public recognition came with the writing of this decade and a half (1911–1927): the notable volume *The Man Against the Sky* (1916); *Merlin* (1917), the first of his three long Arthurian poems; *Lancelot* (1920); *Collected Poems* (1921); *The Man Who Died Twice* (1924); *Dionysius in Doubt* (1925); and *Tristram* (1927)—after the last of which his financial struggles were ended. In 1923 (by then fifty-three) he fulfilled a lifelong dream of visiting England, where he was warmly received by writers. Though he had planned an extended visit, in a few weeks he found himself missing the stone walls and forests of New England and returned to Peterborough. Meanwhile he had tried playwriting, but without success, though two of the plays—*Van Zorn* (1914) and *The Porcupine* (1915)—were published. He also wrote several long poems of a psychological character: *Avon's Harvest* (1921), *Roman Bartholow* (1923), *Cavender's House* (1929), *The Glory of the Nightingales* (1930), *Mathias at the Door* (1931), *Talifer* (1933), and *Amaranth* (1934). He was determined, as he grew older, to bring out a volume almost every year. In January 1935 he was found to have cancer; he continued to work in the hospital on his last poem, *King Jasper,* and died on April 6, 1935, at the age of sixty-five.

Although literary historians are tempted to classify Robinson as a Realist, the label is misleading. His verse could be described as classical or Romantic with almost equal plausibility. As the name of a literary school "Realism" may suggest ideas of style and subject not fully appropriate to Robinson; his art (in contrast to his life) never descended into what Tennyson called the troughs of Zolaism. As with Frost, his reversion to reality was more in the Wordsworthian tradition and could be described in phrases from Wordsworth's Preface to the *Lyrical Ballads*: subject matter taken from common life and presented in a language really used by men. A closer statement of Robinson's intention and success might be that he moved poetry in the direction of the novelistic.

He formed his methods in relative isolation, and it is hard to say just what models or influences counted most. He studied the Latin classics; he read the major poets and novelists of England; he acquired some knowledge of French poetry through a friend; and he put all this to use in his own verse. George Crabbe, Emerson, W. M. Praed, Whitman, Meredith, and a few others are often mentioned, but these may be affinities rather than sources. The fact is that among earlier writers no particular figure or group seems to have swayed his course very much. As for contemporaries, he seems to have emulated none. But distaste can motivate as strongly as admiration, and Robinson, scorning the magazine verse of the day, worked to be as unlike it as possible. His achievement can be estimated in different ways. There is the impressive size and variety of the effort—1,488 pages in small print, written throughout with intelligence and integrity. There is the much smaller number of poems—about forty pages by my estimate—that are likely to last. A few, such as "Richard Cory," "Reuben Bright," and "Miniver Cheevy," miniature the whole. They do not reflect his entire range but they exhibit in flawless performance what was innovative in his art.

If one compares these poems with the typical verses in American magazines in the nineties, they stand out in the respects major poetry always does—more individuality and more mind. But there are also differences in kind that sharply illuminate how independent and new Robinson was. Poetry in the prevailing mode was usually an expression of personal feeling, earnest in tone, general in subject, "beautiful" or "poetic" in diction, image, and setting. In contrast, "Richard Cory" concentrates on a particular character. The poem is no lyric self-expression, but an impersonal, objective report. The setting is an American town of the time, the provincial imagination engrossed and dazzled by a figure of consummate gentlemanly elegance (of royalty, as the townsfolk take it, if one regards a counterpoint in the images—"crown," "imperially slim"). The idiom, though cultured, is colloquial, not in the least "poetic." Except at the end, the poem selects the most ordinary incidents as points of focus and plays down emotion.

Above all there are the irony and humor from which the poem chiefly derives its effectiveness. The surprise ending may be a little easy, and the implied moral—something like "how little we really know about the lives of others!"—may be trite. (The "idea" of the poem, Douglas Bush suggests to me, may have been taken from a bit in *Bleak House,* chapter 22.) But what matters is the attitude of the speaker toward himself and especially toward the other townspeople: his self-awareness, ironic distance, and detached amusement with the human comedy. The poem is subtle, however, and it is easier to sense this attitude than indicate its source. It depends very much on the characterization of the speaker through language, syntax, and metrical form. The idiom ("clean favored," "in fine") is itself "admirably schooled," the syntax controlled and orderly, and the neatness of the quatrains further contributes to the impression. One infers that the speaker is an educated man and hence that his self-identification with the too-admiring townsfolk is half ironic, a circumstance that becomes especially clear in the exaggeration of the lines,

> So on we worked, and waited for the light,
> And went without the meat, and cursed the bread.

The speaker has a self-conscious, fastidious awareness of his language. In the phrase, "yes, richer than a king," the "yes" means, "yes, we even used the stock cliché," and one thus understands that the phrasing throughout is adjusted in irony to convey the sayings and feelings of the townsfolk more than his own—for example, the subtly telling cliché, "from sole to crown," or the excessive enthusiasm (and bathetic fall) in the phrase, "imperially slim." A speaker so aware must also be aware of the discrepancy between the commonplace actions of Cory (going down town, saying "good-morning," or simply walking) and the reactions of the townspeople (staring from the pavement, "fluttered pulses," their feeling that Cory "glittered when he walked"). Even the initial metrical inversion of the third line ("He was") counts by glancing invidiously at "we" others. The result is a reflective, shrewdly humorous portrait by implication of the town and townsfolk. Low-keyed, cerebral, ironic, impersonal, mingling humor and seriousness and implicating a whole social milieu, the poem was without precedent or even parallel in the 1890s.

> Whenever Richard Cory went down town,
> We people on the pavement looked at him:
> He was a gentleman from sole to crown,
> Clean favored, and imperially slim.
>
> And he was always quietly arrayed,
> And he was always human when he talked;
> But still he fluttered pulses when he said,
> "Good-morning," and he glittered when he walked.
>
> And he was rich—yes, richer than a king—
> And admirably schooled in every grace:
> In fine, we thought that he was everything
> To make us wish that we were in his place.
>
> So on we worked, and waited for the light,
> And went without the meat, and cursed the bread;
> And Richard Cory, one calm summer night,
> Went home and put a bullet through his head.

Robinson worked in many different modes. There are poems of direct meditative reflection, such as "Credo," "Hillcrest," or "The Man Against the Sky"; poems of characterization, such as "The Poor Relation" or "Miniver Cheevy"; poems in which narrative interest predominates, such as "The Mill"; symbolist lyrics, such as the villanelle "The House on the Hill" or "Luke Havergal"; and ballad-dialogues, such as "John Gorham." But what more typifies him is the convergence of these modes in his poems that are at the same time character study, narrative (usually indirect or implied), and meditative utterance. In "Eros Turannos," for example, a story is allusively and obscurely referred to and characters are sketched in some traits as well as in their local and social setting. The poem—and this is also typical—is spoken by an onlooker (one of the townspeople), whose character also plays a role and who only partly knows and partly conjectures the circumstances he tells. He reflects upon them, but his interpretations remain inconclusive, and we are left with a sense of the complexity of this human relationship and the difficulty of deciding anything about it. "Captain Craig," to take a very different example, is a ruminative poem; but the ruminations are quoted by the narrator as part of the characterization of the Captain, who is further characterized in other ways; also there are indications of personal tensions between the narrator and the Captain. In the dramatic monologue "Ben Jonson Entertains a Man from Stratford," the interest centers in the characterization of Shakespeare as the subject of the monologue, but it also includes the characterization of Jonson as the speaker of it, general reflections on genius and life of which Shakespeare becomes the occasion, and the mode of discourse itself, creating a dramatic interest by its colloquial idiom, syntax, and movement—its seemingly casual, eddying, and spontaneous flow. Robinson is often compared to Frost, and this interfusion of narrative, character, reflective, inconclusive wisdom, and low-keyed, colloquial talk gives point to the comparison. Robinson worked at times, though infrequently, in Frost's chosen region of the New England countryside, producing at least two masterpieces—"Isaac and Archibald" and "Mr. Flood's Party"—that are perhaps funnier, and more loving in their fun, than anything in Frost.

If a formula could be given for a typical poem of Robinson, it would include the following elements: characterization; indirect and allusive narration; contemporary setting and recognition of the impingement of setting on individual lives; psychological realism and interest in exploring the tangles of human feelings and relationships; an onlooker or observer as speaker, making the poems impersonal and objective with respect to Robinson himself; a penchant for the humorous point of view combined with an awareness that life is more essentially tragic; a language that is colloquial, sinewy, and subtle as it conveys twists of implication in continually active thinking; a mindfulness of the difficulty of moral judgment but also a concern for it. Feeling that all this can justly be said, one wonders why Robinson's reputation is not higher. For one thing, readers are doubtless intimidated by the volume of his productivity. It is discouraging to face so fat a book, and, like most poets, he is more enjoyably read in selections than in toto. A less trivial cause is that, amid so much writing, a great deal seems bad, or more exactly put, it practices skills that seem less important at the cost of liabilities that now seem glaring.

I am referring to the nineteenth-century pursuit of strict metrical form. Robinson, however innovative with respect to syntax and diction (the first four lines of "The Clerks" contain 38 words, of which 36 are monosyllables and 2 are dissyllables), was a traditionalist in stanzaic form and meter. Of this traditional versification he was also a master, exploiting it in different ways and in countless skillful touches. But since poetry is or should be a too-demanding art, a certain slackness (or "license") in the medium must be allowed, and from time to time conventions change as to where the slackness will be tolerated. Anyone who pays attention to the verse of the middle and later nineteenth century will find that for the sake of filling their metrical boxes poets would permit themselves writing that was turgid, clotted, needlessly involved, padded, eked out, imprecise—bad by the standards of any age. This kind of thing gives point to Pound's remark that poetry should be at least as well written as prose, and it is this that spoils, at least for present-day taste, a great many of Robinson's poems.

During the last eighteen years of his life Robinson devoted himself mainly to long narrative poems. They illustrate at large the qualities already noticed in the shorter poems. *The Glory of the Nightingales,* for example, is a study of egoism. The circumstances are that Nightingale, a man of inherited wealth in the New England town of Sharon, undergoes his first serious rebuff in life when he fails to win Agatha, she preferring Malory, a poor, idealistic physician. Nightingale takes his revenge when, learning that the stock of a mine in which Malory had invested will be worthless, he does not tell Malory, who loses all his money. Agatha dies of the shock and Nightingale rejoices vindictively. As the poem opens Malory is on his way to kill Nightingale and then himself. He finds Nightingale in a wheelchair, however, and sees that he is mortally ill. A long conversation follows in which Nightingale confesses his self-centeredness and vanity and talks of all that Malory can still do for mankind. He makes a will leaving his fortune to Malory for a hospital, and, when Malory goes, shoots himself with Malory's pistol. The story is more indirectly told than this summary indicates, but my sketch may suggest the contemporary, novelistic, psychological, reflective mode of this and the other tales. *Merlin, Lancelot,* and *Tristram,* which deal with Arthurian material, reveal Robinson's general intentions, the tales being divested of magic and romance. In *Merlin* the wizard becomes instead an intelligent, middle-aged man whose powers of prophecy stem from reflectiveness and experience. Much of the poem is given over to the love affair between Merlin and Vivian, which is treated not as medieval romance but as "modern love" more or less in the style of Meredith.

These long narratives go on mostly for between eighty and a hundred pages and make up about two-thirds of Robinson's total output. They appear to have been admired mainly on principle and to have been more praised than read. Neither can one challenge this consensus of inattention. It is impossible to read them with more than languid interest. To ask why this is so, however, is to raise fundamental questions about the limitations and the evolution of poetry in the modern world. Robinson, to be sure, was not a storyteller of Chaucerian genius. But since the Romantic period no poet has scored a major success in narrative poems of this length, though a good many have tried. One thinks of Browning's *The Ring and the Book,* Arnold's *Sohrab and Rustum,* the tales of Morris, and Yeats's *Wanderings of Oisin.* The short short story of a few hundred lines, such as Frost's "The Witch of Coos," or a series of linked lyrics making up a story, such as Meredith's *Modern Love,* seem to exhaust the possibilities open to poetry on this line. Why? Answers can only be speculative, and while we are speculating, we should keep in mind that the question of the long narrative poem overlaps the question of the long poem generally. Here again there have been few successes that cannot be reduced to the general form of a long poem made up out of linked short ones: for example, *In Memoriam, The House of Life, The Waste Land, Four Quartets, The Bridge, Paterson.* The few exceptions that spring to mind—the longer epistles of Auden or Ginsberg's *Kaddish*—are especially revealing: they succeed precisely because they avoid the more condensed uses of language that have been the norm of poetry for the last fifty years.

Two large, historical facts explain the present state of affairs. In the eighteenth century there was a rapid disappearance of the kind of thinking that judges a poem by expectations derived from the genre to which it belongs. For practical purposes—guiding the procedures of the writer and the expectations of the reader—the traditional genres of epic and mock-epic, epistle and satire vanished, leaving the poetic scene to the lyric or to the indefinite and amorphous genre of the descriptive-meditative poem, such as Thomson's *Seasons* or Cowper's *Task*. The disappearance of definite genres for the long poem meant that every long poem had to be a more or less original and ad hoc invention and, once developed, it could not be adopted by another poet without the stigma (in the modern world) of being an imitator. Thus, there can be no second *Don Juan* simply because there is the first, no second *Four Quartets* because there is the first. The poet must not only invent an original form, he must do it, as W. J. Bate has argued, in a milieu where the possibility of new invention may seem to the poet all but exhausted.

A much more important fact is that since the eighteenth century poetry has existed in competition with imaginative prose, and that prose has increasingly devoured the possibilities open to verse. Though this applies especially to prose fiction, one should not forget the essay and the descriptive vignette. Why prose has been able to do this so triumphantly is a question that can ultimately be answered only by referring to the intrinsic potentialities of the medium; for many purposes prose is a more flexible instrument. Whatever the explanation, the process has become a vicious circle or spiral. As prose has taken over steadily more, poetry has increasingly come to mean the lyric—the short, intense utterance. This shift of expectation was complete by the middle of the nineteenth century, and one result was that the reading of poetry was relegated to rare, particular moods. But at this time poetry still retained a "popular" or at least an easily accessible idiom. A further step was taken with the development of the Modernist idiom in the 1920s. This made poetry more difficult and therefore intellectually more challenging and thus created a different audience for it. But this audience was more specialized and limited than ever before, and it was an audience for exceptionally condensed uses of language. Readers capable of reading the current, serious prose fiction often could not read the poetry that corresponded to it, so, to some extent, a different audience developed for the two arts. Moreover, the audience for poetry—which includes poets themselves—was looking for condensed and heightened uses of language that absolutely prohibited the long poem, for the simple, practical reason that attention cannot be kept at such a pitch for long. The audience for a long poem no longer exists; and, to return to Robinson, there is particularly no audience for an attempt to write novels in verse. The reader of fiction is put off because it is poetry; the reader of poetry, because it lacks the intensity he seeks. And because these pressures of expectation are felt most of all by poets themselves as they write, their intentions are divided and they fail to accomplish either. It is extremely doubtful that, had Robinson been writing prose, he would have allowed himself the fatal excess of reflection that clogs his plots or the too-easy melodrama of the plots themselves.

I have said little about the didactic and "philosophical" poems of Robinson, for I think they present his weakest side. They are, however, large in quantity and aim and have figured prominently in criticism devoted to him. Robinson felt it was part of the duty of a would-be major poet to have a "philosophy," and in "Octaves," "Captain Craig," "Credo," "The Man Against the Sky," and a great many other poems he set forth to expound one in a more or less direct way. Yet it is hard to know just what his "Credo" was. The tendency of his mind was more to questions than to convictions, which may be more "philosophical" in the true sense but impedes didactic ambitions. Also, he was no more practiced than most poets in the rigors of philosophical expression, and his meanings blur in vague abstraction and vague metaphor. Finally, his "philosophy" in didactic poems seems to be contradicted by the sense of life that emerges more concretely in character portrait and narrative. He is often described as a Transcendentalist, which he sometimes is. At other times he simply asserts an ungrounded hopefulness:

> No, there is not a glimmer, nor a call,
> For one that welcomes, welcomes when he fears,
> The black and awful chaos of the night;

> For through it all—above, beyond it all—
> I know the far-sent message of the years,
> I feel the coming glory of the Light.

In the more concrete and memorable poems, however, things usually turn out badly; many of them are starkly tragic. His characters learn wisdom, if at all, through failure and suffering, and there is little happiness that is not an overcoming of sorrow. But to these generalizations there are many exceptions, and perhaps the poems are more accurately described as the play of a shrewd, reflective, and uncommitted intelligence. There is the moral and metaphysical concern of the New England mind, but also the wariness of judgment. What Robinson sees more clearly than anything else is ambiguity, complexity, open possibility— how little we can know we know.

Between 1890 and 1912 Robinson was America's most important poet, though he was not so recognized at the time. He was an encouraging example to Amy Lowell, Pound, Frost, and a few others; but he was too isolated, too incapable of self-advertisement and pushiness, and too unlucky to have much influence on later writers. What they might have learned from him, they mostly learned elsewhere. Though Robinson was briefly a favorite of Auden's at Oxford, the objectivity, impersonality, reticence, wit, and ironic poise of poetry in the thirties, the offhand, colloquial, low-keyed and glancingly humorous manner, did not come particularly from Robinson. Yet they had one of their beginnings in his lonely, obstinate experiments in Gardiner, Maine, in the early 1890s.

PART TWO

POETRY IN RAPPORT
WITH A PUBLIC

7

TRANSITIONS AND PREMISES

I N THE first quarter of the twentieth century new types of poetry emerged in both England and America. They were many and diverse, yet similar in two fundamental respects: they were viewed by poets and readers as distinctively "modern"; and though "modern," they could be read with pleasure by a relatively large public. These facts are reflected in the titles of parts Two and Three of this book, and the titles are almost interchangeable. "Poetry in Rapport with a Public" deals chiefly with Britain. But America's early modern poetry was generally not the compressed, disjunctive, oblique, allusive, and sardonic writing for an elite that we now usually associate with Modernism. In Lindsay, Sandburg, Masters, Frost, and Amy Lowell it was accessible, sympathetic, and sometimes deliberately popular. Even Imagism had, as it turned out, a broad, intrinsic appeal; although it began as an avant-garde defiance and corrective to the "conservatives," it ended in the 1930s as a leading style of verse in high school yearbooks. Hence Part Three, which mainly takes up the new poetry of America, is entitled "Popular Modernism," the purpose being to distinguish this first phase of the modern movement from that which developed subsequently. But in Hardy, Lawrence, the Georgians, and the poets of the First

World War, British poetry also seemed modern, and although it was a different modernity from that of the United States, it was equally open and accessible.

These generalizations are made with exceptions; the most important are the works of Ezra Pound after 1919 and of T. S. Eliot. Whoever writes literary history finds that the greatest figures present problems to which there are no perfect solutions. The doings and influence of Pound and Eliot loom large in the period we are now taking up, the first quarter of the century, yet discussion of them is mostly deferred for the fourth part of the book, where we concentrate on the creation of the high Modernist mode. Eliot and Pound were the chief inaugurators of an essentially different, anti-popular poetry, the poetry that in the thirties and forties gradually, partially, and temporarily displaced the sorts that had prevailed in the 1910s and 1920s. As for Yeats, his work from roughly 1900 to 1922 was not untypical of the period, except in its excellence. He was probably the single most important contemporary influence on other poets as well, yet lengthy discussion of his career is also postponed. In the great poems of his last period Yeats participated in the high Modernist mode, at least in some respects, but he is the subject of the final chapter of this volume because his development was so representative that it allows us to hold in one final perspective much of the general history of poetry in his time.

THE DOMINANT MODE

Aside from Pound and Eliot, the major poets of the opening twenty-five years of the century were Hardy, Yeats, and Frost. In these poets and in many ancillary figures we recognize a prevailing mode of the period. It may be provisionally characterized as a quietly reflective, colloquial poetry of actual life. As modal poems one might think of Hardy's "Afterwards," Frost's "After Apple-Picking," or Yeats's "The Wild Swans at Coole." A few lines illustrate that, despite individual differences, the poems are essentially similar in kind and unlike anything in the British or American poetry noticed up to now. Here is Hardy:

When the Present has latched its postern behind my tremulous
    stay,
And the May month flaps its glad green leaves like wings,
Delicate-filmed as new-spun silk, will the neighbours say,
    "He was a man who used to notice such things"?

Frost:

My long two-pointed ladder's sticking through a tree
Toward heaven still,
And there's a barrel that I didn't fill
Beside it, and there may be two or three
Apples I didn't pick upon some bough.
But I am done with apple-picking now.

and Yeats:

The trees are in their autumn beauty,
The woodland paths are dry,
Under the October twilight the water
Mirrors a still sky;
Upon the brimming water among the stones
Are nine-and-fifty swans.

These poems were published between 1914 and 1917. They
represent at its most accomplished the dominant kind of poetry
in the decade before *The Waste Land,* of which some representative lines are:

A rat crept softly through the vegetation
Dragging its slimy belly on the bank
While I was fishing in the dull canal
On a winter evening round behind the gashouse
Musing upon the king my brother's wreck
And on the king my father's death before him.

The passage from Hardy exhibits his strengths of honest accuracy and control. The peculiar activity of the word "tremulous"
in the first line may be noticed, and the uncouth, original exactness of "flaps" in the second. The passage from Yeats loses in
quotation, partly because much of the effect of the poem lies in
the shapeliness of the whole. But even in excerpt, the limpid
beauty is felt. The teasing skill of Frost's meditative evasion may
be focused in our uncertainty how to take the word "heaven," or
what, if anything, may be meant—more than what is said—by
the finality of "I am done with apple-picking now."

Attempting to describe the mode, we may begin by remarking that it gives the effect of talk—a leisurely, reflective, slightly heightened talk which is entirely individual with each writer. Such talk is a more difficult art than the poets of the nineties achieved, though it pretends to be no art at all. The idiom is colloquial and fresh, though also controlled and deliberated. The versification is traditional, but a little roughened and irregular. For theme or occasion the poems go to actual and familiar experience. Story elements are present: if there is no narrative, at least there is incident, character, and locality. In such respects the poems might be called "realistic," but their realism combines with the associatively pleasant or "agreeable." In what may have been an implicit protest against urbanization, mechanization, and deracination, this poetry tends especially to refer to the countryside and its traditional yet still contemporary objects and ways of life. Toward these the writer feels a quiet respect, a *pietas,* and whatever the more particular emotions of particular poems, this is a basic attitude conveyed by the poetry. (It contrasts sharply with the satire of *The Waste Land.*) It is a reflective poetry, but it wages no argument and reaches no conclusions.

The intention and balanced appeal of the mode also reveal themselves in what it avoids. It is as far as possible both from *l'art pour l'art* and from Impressionist notation of fugitive moments, and equally far, on the other hand, from a poetry of opinions and emotional generalities. It does not "soar into the Empyrean," neither does it strike rhetorical blows on behalf of some party or policy. It reminds us neither of Dowson, Symons, Tennyson, Browning, Kipling or of any of the Genteel poets of America. Symbolism, if there is any, comes without traditional emblems, portentous emotions, or airs of mystery, but is present only as an elusive suggestion, a glimpse of possible further vistas of meaning. *Symboliste* technique, with its deliberate concentration and obscurity, is utterly rejected. There are narrative elements, but rarely narrative poems. In poems typical of this mode, form is carefully studied and controlled, but the purpose is to repudiate formalism, if by that we mean the prizing of form for its own sake. Adhering to the traditionally familiar and ordinary, this poetry shuns whatever might seem either Decadent or Romantic—for example, the aberrant, the exotic, the remote, the wonderful—and it equally refuses ostentation of modernity.

There are no Impressionist vignettes of city life, neither is there the bleak, accusing realism occasionally found in Davidson. To sum up, this poetry makes a quiet, somewhat cautious approach to actual experience, feeling, and reflection, and in doing so preserves poetic pleasantness. Though an American, Robert Frost, was one of the masters in this style, the style itself was based on a traditional, typically English way of writing. It has its nearest precedents and affinities in the quiet lyric or short meditative poem of the Romantic period—Coleridge's "Frost at Midnight," or Wordworth's "There Was a Boy" and "The Solitary Reaper."

POETS AND SCHOOLS

From the 1910s on Thomas Hardy was an important influence on younger poets, an influence that has never ceased to be felt. Yet to the present day the scope and power of his vision, at once tender, homely, grotesque, and terrifying, has not been generally appreciated. Already a well-established novelist, he published his first volume of verse in 1898. It might be chosen to inaugurate the modern period in poetry.

Aside from Hardy and Yeats, the first ten years of the century were dominated in England by two groups of poets: Edwardian entertainers, such as Kipling, Chesterton, Belloc, Noyes, Newbolt, and Masefield; and studious workmen in traditional veins, such as Bridges, de la Mare, Sturge Moore, Laurence Binyon, James Elroy Flecker, and Lascelles Abercrombie. The term "entertainers" might have been welcomed by the poets to whom it refers, but does not imply that they lacked a serious and intelligent purpose. The other main trend in Edwardian verse might be characterized as a use of poetry for solace through beauty. To poets of this school the entertaining versifiers appeared intolerably journalistic and slapdash. They themselves had a touch of the academic, if by "academic" one means an art that is learned, intelligent, controlled, and possibly quite admirable but that lacks strong individuality and freshness.

In order to judge these poets rightly, one must keep in mind their premises. To them the function and justification of poetry was its rich presentation of "beauty." The beauty they had in mind was not, however, the austere perfection of form that the term had suggested to the Aesthetes. It was, instead, a vaguer derivative of the Romantic tradition, and might be briefly characterized as the idealistic in theme or sentiment combined with the associatively pleasant in imagery. A well-known sonnet of Masefield's illustrates this conventional, widespread type of poetry:

> Be with me, Beauty, for the fire is dying,
> My dog and I are old, too old for roving.

The Beauty here addressed is companionable and can be invoked along with cozy images of dog and fireside (the "fire" here is literal as well as metaphorical). The idea of poetry presupposed is one that descends, to repeat, from the later eighteenth century. As Keats put it in the line quoted earlier, the "great end" of poetry is "To sooth the cares, and lift the thoughts of man." Unless one grasps how generally in the opening years of this century it was assumed that poetry is uplifting, solacing beauty, one cannot fully appreciate the countertendencies. Yeats, Brooke, Owen, Eliot, and many other poets trained themselves not to write in this way only by effort. It may be added that the partisans of poetic beauty were entrenched in the leading journals; if a poet offended their sense of values, their reviews could be gruesome. In the middle phase of his career Yeats was abused for the lowness and coarseness of many of his poems, and even to Yeats the work of Eliot hardly seemed poetry. No wonder Marianne Moore later reproached a rose for its blooms: "You do not seem to realize that beauty is a liability rather than an asset."

The poetry of Ireland forms a third distinct strain. These were the formative years of the Irish literary Renaissance, when the Abbey Theatre was entering upon its fame, and Joyce in exile was writing *Ulysses*. Throughout the teens and twenties Irish poets continued the national impulse that had quickened at the end of the last century. Poems were often patriotic celebrations, as in Yeats's "Easter, 1916" (which voiced, however, more doubts and qualifications than pleased Ireland at this glorious hour) and in a great many by Dora (Sigerson) Shorter, who is said to have died of heartbreak and overwork after the failure of the Easter Rebellion. Or, like Padraic Colum in his early volumes, poets took their subjects from Irish legend, folklore, and popular story. Or, as in the poems of James Joyce, they repudiated the patriotic milieu by aspiring only to excellence.

With the year 1911 a number of circumstances tended to create a wider public for poetry. Masefield's *The Everlasting Mercy* was published in that year. The poem had enough narrative speed to hold interest and enough lower-class realism in setting and dialogue to arouse controversy; it was a bold challenge, going further even than Kipling to overthrow poetic proprieties. It caused much discussion and encouraged other poets to dare in other ways. In 1912 the first of Edward Marsh's anthologies, *Georgian Poetry, 1911–1912*, appeared. The name, chosen in reference to the new king, George V, was intended to suggest that a new age of major poetry had arrived. The dawn could be seen bursting in Marsh's anthology, which, however, exhibited not merely poets who were just becoming known but such veterans as de la Mare, Chesterton, and Gordon Bottomley. What Marsh printed in his anthologies was adventurous enough to provoke discussion, but his taste was representative of middle-class readers and the Georgian anthologies enjoyed booming sales. This commercial success called forth a number of other anthologies, all of which tended to win new readers for poetry. A third factor was the outbreak of war in 1914, which England entered with a high-minded, emotional idealism, for which poetry seemed the especially appropriate vehicle. Any number of ardent civilians wrote poems for the first time, and any number of others read almost the first contemporary poetry of their lives. The mood of that hour was caught memorably in Brooke's five patriotic sonnets. They are the poems, as has been remarked, of a civilian in uniform; the poems of experience were to come two years after Brooke's death and to express a harshly disillusioned view of the war.

"Georgian" poetry continued to be written and read throughout the 1920s; it has in fact never ceased, though it has gone through many mutations. But Robert Frost had been writing a poetry that was essentially of the Georgian type before the Georgians were recognized as a school. It is partly because his work so finely answered to the taste of the Georgian poets and their readers that he first made his reputation in England rather than in America. Generally speaking, the English poets of the First World War began as Georgians, and their poetry gradually changed as they underwent the appalling conditions and experiences of combat in the trenches. The intention of some of these poets is symbolized by the fact that Owen carried with him, on leave in England, photographs of casualties; the home patriots must see what war is like. They wrote under the shock and moral outrage of immediate experience as soldiers, and their purpose was to show the blundering slaughter for what it was and to stop it. To this end they summoned violence in shockingly vivid description, bitter irony, satire, and invective—modes of utterance that had been explored only occasionally before the war in a few poems of Rupert Brooke, and, more cautiously, in Yeats, Hardy, Wilfrid Gibson, and a few others. The War Poets were perhaps too close to their subject, but they widened the possible tones and subjects of poetry, and it has never been the same since.

8

THOMAS HARDY

EVEN when they are dull, Hardy's poems are characteristic and, therefore, fetching. We like the personality they reflect—the compassion, reflectiveness, wistfulness, interest in character and story, elegiac and commemorative respect for human fates. Above all, there is the appeal of the firsthand, of experience and feeling that seem caught from life rather than literature. That we should have this impression is an achievement of Hardy's art. His style was an instrument for integrity, though in speaking of "integrity" one has in mind, in his case, not wholeness or unity but honesty, fidelity to his own self-divided, complex responses.

Born in Dorset, near Dorchester, in 1840, the son of a prosperous stonemason, Hardy was apprenticed at sixteen to a local church architect and went on to study in London (1862–1867) under the noted architect Arthur Blomfield. He continued to practice this profession for another six years. On a visit to Cornwall he met Emma Lavinia Gifford, who encouraged his growing interest in writing, and they were married in 1874. It was his lifelong conviction that "in verse was concentrated the essence of all imaginative and emotional literature." But his own poems were rejected by editors whose stock conceptions of poetry they offended. For thirty years Hardy wrote mainly prose fiction. Almost a dozen of his novels are still being read and reinterpreted, and at least half—*Far from the Madding Crowd* (1874), *The Return of the Native* (1878), *The Mayor of Casterbridge* (1886), *The Woodlanders* (1887), *Tess of the D'Urbervilles* (1891), and *Jude the Obscure* (1895)—are among the masterpieces of English literature. It is often said that the attacks on his last two novels, especially *Jude the Obscure,* induced Hardy to abandon prose fiction for poetry. But he had never valued his novels as highly as his verse, and the reception of *Jude* simply jelled a decision he had long been making. A note written on Christmas Day 1890 expresses his growing mood: "While thinking of resuming 'the viewless wings of poesy' before dawn this morning, new horizons seemed to open, and worrying pettinesses to disappear." In 1898 he assembled his first volume of verse, *Wessex Poems,* which included many written during his years as a novelist. This was followed by *Poems of the Past and Present* (1902), his powerful *The Dynasts: An Epic-Drama of the War with Napoleon* (published in three parts, 1904–1908), and *Time's Laughing-Stocks* (1909).

Mrs. Hardy died in 1912. The later years of the marriage had not been happy. She had become difficult to live with and at times almost unbalanced, though Hardy endured the situation with patience and gentleness. Shortly after her death the seventy-three-year old poet composed the deeply personal group of poems he colorlessly entitled "Poems of 1912–13," a series of lyrics about his wife and their life together that, with their vivid memories, passion, tenderness, bitterness, grief, resentment, and remorse, present a complicated, authentic human situation and make up the most remarkable elegy written in the modern period. Beginning with *Satires of Circumstance* (1914), another six volumes were published, the last, *Winter Words,* just after his death in 1928 at the age of eighty-seven. In his last years Hardy was generally recognized as the greatest of England's living writers, but his essential humility was untouched. When he was seventeen a friend had given him a copy of *The Golden Treasury of English Poetry,* and he always kept it. Not long before he died, he told his second wife, Florence Dugdale, that if he had a genuine ambition, it was that "some poem or poems" he had written might be included "in a good anthology like *The Golden Treasury.*"

Hardy might be described as a belated and very rebellious Victorian or perhaps as a transitional figure, showing both "Victorian" and "modern" habits of sensibility and technique. His writings are, among other things, one long questioning of ideas and codes of behavior—religious, sexual, social, familial—which for many Victorians seemed dictated by nature and God. In this respect he joins the company of Swinburne, Symons, Butler, and Shaw, or, at a lesser rank, Havelock Ellis, Edmund Gosse, and Norman Douglas. If he has outlasted these fellow protesters, one reason is the profundity and grandeur of his imagination. A second reason is the greater complexity of his responses. Opinions date, and so with Hardy's if expounded abstractly. But usually his poems involve opinions as only one element in a drama of opposed values; it is this drama of the divided mind seeking truth and wholeness that is moving and perennially relevant. Hard-won convictions of reason are maintained with fidelity and yet massively countered by allegiances of feeling—and perhaps by a remembrance that reason, like everything else, evolves historically and must remain open to further consideration and data.

Hardy's self-division was not along one axis only but was an interaction of manifold, opposed commitments. It is not just the split between his "modern" or "philosophical" ideas and the yearnings of his heart. His ideas were themselves held in a more uncertain and provisional way than critics have usually admitted, despite Hardy's own statements to this effect. One obvious illustration comes at the end of *The Dynasts,* where the Pities suggest that the Immanent Will may evolve into conscious and kindly Deity, thus ending the vast drama on a note of hope that violates the mood and argument of everything that went before. Hardy was subject also to opposed, fundamental tendencies of imagination: the human and the vast impersonality of nature; temporal event and the eternal; the modern spirit—racked and weary—and the primitive; "realism" and the archetypal; irony and pathos. Caught amid such tensions, his general views and his particular, concrete responses were hesitant and complexly qualified.

This tentativeness suggests a possible further explanation for his stronger satisfaction in writing poetry than prose fiction. However complex and ironic its method, a novel must maintain

a reasonably consistent tone of feeling and some overall interpretation of reality—at least, this was Hardy's opinion; otherwise there could be no aesthetic unity or form. If, however, the
writer's own perception of reality is radically self-divided and
unfixed, such imposed consistency may trouble his conscience.
Hardy, as if in compensation, alternated the writing of his tragic
novels with others of a lighter and happier kind, which unluckily
were less successful. A poem must also be consistent, but since it
is short, whatever point of view it embodies can be challenged
by the next poem, and a volume of lyrics, offering, Hardy explains, "unadjusted impressions," "contrasting moods and circumstances," may seem incomparably more honest to the writer's
whole state of mind than any novel could be. Obviously this becomes a pressing consideration to the extent that the writer approaches literature as the sincere articulation of meanings.

Hardy's formal procedures have been repeatedly analyzed
and need be only summarized here. There is not much to be
learned on the subject from noting the various "influences" that
show in his poetry: the classics, Wordsworth, Browning, William
Barnes, Swinburne, the hymnal, ballads. Neither is there much
point in tracing the evolution of his style through his long
career, for once he had formed his methods (and his ideas) in
the 1860s and 1870s, they changed relatively little. His diction,
considered as the stock or vocabulary on which he draws, is
extremely heterogeneous. It includes, in the inventory of F. R.
Leavis, "the romantic poetical, the prosaic banal, the archaistic,
the erudite, the technical, the dialect word, the brand-new
Hardy coinage." Sample verbs are *to onflee, to unbloom* (meaning,
not to bloom), and *to outskeleton* (meaning, to be more skeletal
than); some nouns are a *Powerfuller,* a *hope-hour,* and a *roomage.*
They reveal that Hardy was not committed to the conventional
idea of the poetic and have elicited much, mostly deprecating
comment. Devoted Hardyans usually view them as lovable
lapses. But it can at least be said that this vocabulary is ample
and expressive. Moveover, the juxtaposition of words and
phrases from different realms of discourse demands of us a constant readjustment or "note-catching," as Hardy called it,
making it difficult for a sensitive reader to doze through his
poetry. The juxtaposition also permits innumerable more particular effects. A line of "Hap," for example—

Crass Casualty obstructs the sun and rain—

opens with Latinate plangency and grandeur, as if with a sound of cymbals crashing, and crosses by the bold bridge of "obstructs" to a phrase of utmost simplicity.

Hardy always wrote in metrical and stanzaic forms; there is no free verse. But the versification is calculated and manipulated for expressive function rather than for smoothness and harmony. Though many of his poems adopt stanzas from ballads or hymns, or modify these forms, many others exhibit complicated frames of his own devising. Hardy himself once accounted for these structures by referring to the "Gothic art-principle in which he had been trained as an architect," which taught him to value an appearance of spontaneity—the unpredictable or even "freakish." He also admired visible performance, craft showing itself in difficulties overcome. The profound vision of his novels must emerge through or despite forced ingenuities of plot; in his poems the intricate stanzas are another self-imposed arabesque. But the difficulties are not always surmounted happily. The stanza becomes a torture box in which he stretches, squeezes, and contorts, filling it out as best he can, and the writing falls into blank filler, pointless involution, gnomic knot, and the like:

> Things were not lastly as firstly well
> With us twain, you tell?

The variety in stanzaic patterns shows an effort for ad hoc adjustment of form to content. (It is astonishing that of the more than 900 poems in his collected volumes, only 141 duplicate stanzaic patterns.) In addition to the frequent intricacy of the stanzaic form, Hardy makes much use of run-ons and medial pauses. Complication of stanzaic form, interplaying with grammatical pause and sweep, gives him an unusually rich punctuation, so to speak, which he uses to bring out the dramatic development and fluctuation of feeling. In the closing stanza of "The Going" Hardy, confronting the death of his wife, first attempts to dismiss with stoic, weary finality the remorse he has felt, then breaks out into stark bereavement, and ends with an odd, crooning, reproachful forgiveness. The steps of feeling are embodied in rhyme, line break, and pause:

> Well, well! All's past amend,
>   Unchangeable. It must go.
> I seem but a dead man held on end
> To sink down soon. . . . O you could not know
>   That such swift fleeing
>   No soul foreseeing—
> Not even I—would undo me so!

Hardy's meters work to similar purposes. His favorite line mingles anapests and iambs, manipulating them for emphasis, as in "Neutral Tones":

> And a few leaves lay on the starving sod;
>   —They had fallen from an ash, and were gray.

He makes use of frequent irregularities of every kind. Though his remarks about his own poetry were almost uniquely few, general, vague, and defensive, a few phrases already cited above from *The Life of Thomas Hardy* (a memoir by his second wife, but mostly compiled from dictations by Hardy) may be quoted in fuller form. He "decided that too regular a beat was bad art. . . . He knew that in architecture cunning irregularity is of enormous worth, and it is obvious that he carried on into his verse, perhaps in part unconsciously, the Gothic art-principle in which he had been trained . . . that of stress rather than of syllable, poetic texture rather than poetic veneer."

It is an art that places expressive function before "beauty." It directs, ideally speaking, distinct, particular attention to each word and phrase. Without this heightened attention, a great many of Hardy's poems will not be much enjoyed, for they will seem dull, prosy, eccentric, and lame—sketchy incidents of a predictable kind, diction that is odd without purpose or appeal, jolting meters, awkward metaphors, an inert, flattening tone of voice. But with attention, the real "plot" and interest of many a poem takes hold. One follows the suspense, hesitation, and fluctuation of feeling and interpretation, the deeply pondered play of meaning.

This can be seen in his well-known poem, "The Convergence of the Twain," on the sinking of the luxury liner *Titanic* in the North Atlantic, after collision with an iceberg. The poem is an august memorializing of the event. Each of the three-line stanzas is numbered, and in the first part of the poem each stanza is one sentence; it is as though each sentence were engraved on a tablet. It begins:

I

In a solitude of the sea
Deep from human vanity,
And the Pride of Life that planned her, stilly couches she.

II

Steel chambers, late the pyres
Of her salamandrine fires,
Cold currents thrid, and turn to rhythmic tidal lyres.

III

Over the mirrors meant
To glass the opulent
The sea-worm crawls—grotesque, slimed, dumb, indifferent.

IV

Jewels in joy designed
To ravish the sensuous mind
Lie lightless, all their sparkles bleared and black and blind.

With what Auden calls his "hawks's vision," Hardy focuses on two things—the ship being fitted out for her maiden voyage, and the iceberg simultaneously forming far away—from their origins to their collision, which he calls, with fine ironic and imaginative appropriateness, a "convergence." The poem dwells on the incalculableness, yet also sees from the start the finality of the far-off event, so that it releases an irony like that of Greek tragedy. We—and Hardy—know what was fated; the protagonists do not. He enhances the feeling of doom by reference to a mythological being, the Immanent Will, which he invented and expounded especially in *The Dynasts*. Here it is also called the Spinner of the Years. The collision is the doing, he implies, of this power.

The poem moves us by its awe before fate, its thoughtful solemnity at human woe. But having noted that the disaster took place and was in some sense preordained, the poem has nothing more to add, however much it may convey to the emotions. My point—to which I shall return—is Hardy's muteness before fact, his reserve of interpretation and judgment. When in the final stanza the collision takes place, he says only that it happened; there is no comment:

> Till the Spinner of the Years
> Said "Now!" And each one hears,
> And consummation comes, and jars two hemispheres.

Nevertheless, the tragedy is presented in terms that are completely Hardy's. The first stanza sets up a contrast: feelings and associations clustered around such phrases as "human vanity," "Pride of Life," "planned," and the opposed order of "solitude," "sea," "deep," stillness. Of these opposed realms, the ship and the iceberg are the particular embodiments, and, after they "converge," the ship becomes part of that silent, black, alien world, characterized as "grotesque, slimed, dumb, indifferent." Given this contrast, we might suppose that Hardy would interpret the sinking of the *Titanic* as a rebuke to "human vanity." He might take his stand in eternity, so to speak, like many a biblical prophet and Romantic poet, and mark as a judgment on human pride how all the ornate gear of the luxury liner now lies bleared and lost. Or we might expect the more typically Hardyesque sense that man finds himself in a universe that is always and terribly threatening and is here manifested in the sea, mythologized as the Immanent Will. Faced with such a universe, Hardy elsewhere repeatedly condemns and yet stands fascinated before man's recklessness and self-assertion.

But if Hardy implies such attitudes here, he does so only in the most tentative way, and he quickly cancels them, keeping judgment in suspense. The fluctuation of attitude is caught primarily in the diction. "Human vanity," for example, seems a faintly pejorative term, but "Pride of Life" seems to correct it, at least until one thinks of its biblical source (1 John 2: 16,17), where "pride of life" is condemned as of the world that "passeth away, and the lust thereof." Hardyesque fishes muse, "What does this vaingloriousness down here," and if "vaingloriousness" suggests gentle condemnation, it has already been countered by Hardy's obvious sympathy with all this vitality and splendor. He feels himself the fascination of

> Jewels in joy designed
> To ravish the sensuous mind.

Later he speaks of the "smart ship," and "smart" may be pejorative, but he also calls it a "creature of cleaving wing," responding positively to this adventurous swiftness. Throughout the poem his attitude is never settled, but wavers and hovers, balancing one phrase against the next. Many phrases are of the kind readers find "trite" and "awkward," but they are not less effective for that reason. Triteness and awkwardness are here felt as a reassuring human ordinariness, a plain honesty of utterance as Hardy records an almost mute depth of feeling and a groping uncertainty what to think. In rapid reading the last line may seem an anticlimax. When the disaster takes place, all that Hardy can say, after so much build-up, is, it "jars two hemispheres." Many a reader must feel that a poem that begins so weightily ought to end in something more impressive and less homely than "jars." But then, one reflects, it is an exact word. The two hemispheres have an impressive bulk, and even to jar them implies a strong impact. Nothing follows from the sinking of the *Titanic;* no moral is drawn. "Jars" is all Hardy could claim—some reverberations, and then everything settles down as before. The word has an unadorned, dogged truthfulness. It is "poetic texture rather than poetic veneer."

Whether or not they may be called "realistic," Hardy's poems deal with ordinary life, rather than the romantically wonderful or remote. His approach is often dramatic or novelistic—he presents character, incident, or story—at the same time that it is also reflective. In many poems, however, there is no articulate reflection. He suggests no judgments or interpretations, not even qualified and uncertain ones. His silence in such cases has, I think, the same source as his hesitation between points of view: his own complex and divided responses. It is as though he found, after musing attention, nothing he could say—or too much. We are left with the fact, and it sets the mind in motion. Hardy has a mute sense of the strangeness of everything. One of his poems is called "Nobody Comes," and that is what happens. He stands by the entrance to his house; cars go by; none stops. He doesn't seem to regret it. He doesn't react in any way. He just notices it. So also, though much more powerfully, with the larger strangenesses of life. "Drummer Hodge" tells how a rustic from Wessex lies buried in South Africa as a result of the Boer

War. Part of the effect lies in Hardy's silence before the situation, except for his emphasis that it is "strange."

I

They throw in Drummer Hodge, to rest
　　Uncoffined—just as found:
His landmark is a kopje-crest
　　That breaks the veldt around;
And foreign constellations west
　　Each night above his mound.

II

Young Hodge the Drummer never knew—
　　Fresh from his Wessex home—
The meaning of the broad Karoo,
　　The Bush, the dusty loam,
And why uprose to nightly view
　　Strange stars amid the gloam.

III

Yet portion of that unknown plain
　　Will Hodge for ever be;
His homely Northern breast and brain
　　Grow to some Southern tree,
And strange-eyed constellations reign
　　His stars eternally.

Such happenings are indeed "strange," but they occur so commonly that few of us waste thought on them. Hardy never gets used to things; he continues to notice, possessing in his uninsistent way that fresh, almost philosophical wonderment and questioning found in many great artists.

"The Man He Killed" is typical of many poems in which Hardy creates a character and refuses to go beyond the point of view of the created character. Here the speaker is a rustic ex-soldier of limited perceptions and ordinary vocabulary, so that the poem has neither intellectual concentration, passion, beauty, nor grandeur of imaginative conception. It has a rather simple irony as the speaker reflects that he shot a man in the opposing army, although he had no quarrel with him and felt no enmity. The poem traces the stops and turns of thought as the speaker contemplates this fact:

> I shot him dead because—
> Because he was my foe.

Having achieved this justifying classification ("foe"), he feels comforted:

> Just so: my foe of course he was.

But doubts continue to nag:

> . . . my foe of course he was:
> That's clear enough; although
>
> He thought he'd 'list, perhaps,
> Off-hand like—just as I—
> Was out of work—had sold his traps—
> No other reason why.

At the end of the poem the ex-soldier abandons the problem as too knotty:

> Yes; quaint and curious war is!
> You shoot a fellow down
> You'd treat if met where any bar is,
> Or help to half-a-crown.

Hardy's attitude toward war is obvious; but if we wonder what he thinks of the speaker, the poem casts no light. We approach Hardy's rustic persons with a prejudice in their favor. They are usually colorful, likable, and often wise. But can this be said of a man who, having shot another, can pronounce that the fact is "quaint and curious"? The words are so far below the mark that they tease and trouble in a peculiar way. Hardy once wrote that "if way to the Better there be, it exacts a full look at the Worst." Perhaps this shallow, cheery stupidity is not the Worst, but it is a mighty obstacle to the Better. But is this our inference or Hardy's?

I have been describing Hardy as divided and uncertain in his responses, so that he rarely knew what to make of things. In an influential book, *The Pattern of Hardy's Poetry* (1961), Samuel Hynes argued that Hardy's poetry is "antinomial," that is, he was confronted by antinomies he could not resolve, and these, in the absence of a firm structure of belief, provided the structural basis for his poetry. He placed opposed premises, emotions, or values side by side and allowed them to play against each other.

His vision is thus essentially ironical. Very often Hardy proceeds by ironic juxtaposition of images, the images embodying counterperceptions and commenting on each other, with no overt comment from the author. The technique affords surprise, shock, and speed; it was much favored by Modernist poets in the 1920s and later.

But ironic structure and style should not be emphasized to the point that they are held to be omnipresent in Hardy's poetry or a main source of its power. Many of his finer poems, such as "Afterwards," are largely without them. In others they are present but are not what makes the poems memorable. "The Oxen," for example, contrasts the religious belief of his childhood with the modern enlightenment of his adult years. The past is pictured in a genre scene, and the scene expresses positive values of a potent kind—living tradition, imaginativeness, human community, simple trust, kindness. Toward this past Hardy feels such loving tenderness and nostalgia that by the end of the poem he figures, typically, as a man vitally wounded by modern lore. Here indeed is "antithesis" and "irony," but the terms seem too simple for the complex wistfulness of feeling. We are closer to the true sources of Hardy's greatness if we use less technical terms, speaking rather of perplexity, tentativeness, many-sided sympathies, self-division, and honesty; of a gentle, thoughtful, powerfully imaginative man confronting life directly and seeking truth and unity of being. The human interest of this state of mind is what gives Hardy's poetry its lasting appeal.

If, however, this characterization of Hardy is accurate, it is not the one that used to be accepted. What of Hardy the philosophical "pessimist"? He wrote, after all, many poems in which he took firm positions on religious and cosmological questions, poems such as "Hap," "God-Forgotten," "Before Life and After," and "New Year's Eve." In them he explains that life is ruled not by Providence but by chance; God has forgotten all about the suffering earth, or, more scientifically stated, God is nothing but a mindless productive source working "by rote"; consciousness is, in metaphysical terms, an inexplicable anomaly, but it is also the capacity for pain, and "nescience" is preferable; life and the cosmos have no purpose. *The Dynasts* attempts to integrate these opinions through the concept of the

Immanent Will. Since Hardy committed himself on such momentous questions, how can his mind be thought tentative and
uncertain? Of course he insisted that poems such as "Hap" or
"God-Forgotten" should be interpreted as expressing impressions of the moment, not settled opinions. He was not a "pessimist" but a "meliorist," though perhaps, he admitted, he became
"vocal" as a poet especially at the thought of pain. Despite such
pleadings, the critic argues, Hardy's poetry inculcates gloom.
Certainly he writes no verses of philosophical "optimism." The
stories he tells mostly illustrate his "philosophy" or "pessimism."
Things turn out badly, and with a regularity that seems improb-
able to most readers even in their hours of midnight depression.
If ever, the argument goes, there was a poet with opinions, it was
Hardy, opinions that were forthrightly announced and that controlled his poetry.

   This was once the usual view of Hardy. Within its own frame
of reference, it was accurate. If it seems less persuasive now, the
reasons are partly a different relation to the religious problems
Hardy was concerned with, and partly a different criterion of
"pessimism" in approaching any writer. For an older generation
of admirers—John Crowe Ransom is an example—the religious
questionings or accusations of the cosmos were among the most
stirring of Hardy's poems. These readers were struggling with
the same problems. But in the terms in which Hardy posed and
answered them, these issues are now less actual for most readers.
As a result, when Hardy deserts concrete experience for abstraction and controversy, he is read with diminished sympathy and
interest. Because they are noticed less, the cosmological poems
less influence our response to others, and if Hardy's lyrics are
really the "unadjusted impressions" he said they were, we are
more likely to appreciate the fact. They cannot, in any case, now
seem as pessimistic as they once did. Readers who have found
their own spiritual landscape in *The Waste Land* or Sartre cannot
be much impressed by Hardy's bitterness. What strikes them is
his tenderness, passion, attachment to things, piety before
life—qualities that now seem not only positive but almost hopeful by comparison. And if we think his mind was made up, we
need only consult our own. That there is no cosmic purpose,
that change and chancefulness prevail in human affairs, that
man's free will—if it exists at all—is severely conditioned, and

that life disappoints hopes and runs steadily down are opinions that do nothing to free us from divided emotions and perplexed states of mind.

But Hardy's cosmological utterances cannot be so easily dismissed. They may not be the poems in which his genius most fulfilled itself. They may mislead us about his "pessimism," making it appear more fixed than it was. They may suggest that his melancholy was caused by his beliefs, when the opposite is just as likely. Not that one questions the integrity and objectivity of his thought. But the tone of any man's reflection is far more influenced by temperament and personal circumstances than we usually keep in mind. Not enough is known about Hardy's private life to trace this in detail. But about the time he wrote "Hap" (1867), with its grand rhetoric assailing a universe ruled by "purblind" doom, he was suffering acutely from editorial rejection of his poems and probably also from a love affair that "unbloomed." His powerful poems "In Tenebris," written in 1895–96, affirm that the world is a "welter of futile doing," and that he "waits in unhope." One may, if one likes, relate these sentiments to his perusals of Herbert Spencer, Schopenhauer, and von Hartmann, but he was then forty-five years old, often an age of depression. His marriage, begun twenty years before in ardent romance and hope, had drifted into hostility; it was a trouble he could neither expect would pass nor remedy. The long work on which he had lavished his most ambitious reflection was being smeared as "Jude the Obscene." Amid such "satires of circumstance" it is not surprising if he interpreted human life pessimistically. Nevertheless, the habit of mind that led him to seek a completed explanation of experience by relating it to an overworld is of utmost importance to his poetry and part of its greatness. His overworld—which was for his reason utterly abstract, but on which he bestowed an imaginative concreteness—was only the final stage in his habitual, imaginative recession from the focused point of experience to the infinite context about it.

He was a religious man deprived of belief, but with religious sensibility unimpaired. He needed perhaps not only to seek an ultimate cause for things but also to feel religious emotions. Whether this be true or not, he possessed a quasi-religious awareness of vast background. His sense of this was imaginative and reflective as well as "philosophical," and resulted in what may be called distancing effects. Present-day writers often seek to produce an emotional shock as immediate and violent as possible. Hardy, in contrast, puts the human stories he tells at a distance, and so evokes an attitude that is both sympathizing and reflective. He creates distance by seeing the individual human fate within an immeasurably larger context. Among such contexts are time, space, nature, multiplicity, and recurrence. He beheld things in relation to endless vistas of the past, or to limitless space, or to the huge backdrop of nature, or to the numberless multiplicity of goings-on in any moment of time, or to the archetypal recurrence of the same event throughout time and space. When human life is played on these vast stages, its suffering cannot completely fill attention. We—and Hardy—participate, but with a half-absence, the mind being directed in brooding contemplativeness to the background at the same time. At the end of "Channel Firing," for example, the noise of naval guns in 1914 roars inland from the sea. The recession takes us far back in history also, and the present war dwindles before ideas of immemorial time, recurrence, stillness, and vast space:

> Again the guns disturbed the hour,
> Roaring their readiness to avenge,
> As far inland as Stourton Tower,
> And Camelot, and starlit Stonehenge.

"In Time of 'the Breaking of Nations'" gives only the background, the foreground of the First World War being suggested in the title. (The title refers to Jeremiah 51:20, "I will break in pieces the nations.") The poem pictures human life in a few timeless and elemental scenes, which are themselves beheld from a distance in a wide landscape. Human beings disturb the landscape in a way so minimal that, for the imagination, they are assimilated to it and take on its reassuring qualities of silence and perduring being.

I

> Only a man harrowing clods
>   In a slow silent walk
> With an old horse that stumbles and nods
>   Half asleep as they stalk.

II

Only thin smoke without flame
  From the heaps of couch-grass;
Yet this will go onward the same
  Though Dynasties pass.

III

Yonder a maid and her wight
  Come whispering by:
War's annals will fade into night
  Ere their story die.

Hardy is one of the great poets of nature. If, as W. P. Ker once remarked, description is the poet's act of love, probably nowhere else has an alien and indifferent natural world been loved so attentively. In his own way Hardy belongs to the Wordsworthian tradition. He did not believe that nature could ever be a quasi-divine, ministering Presence, but neither could he simply accept the situation and let nature alone. It is, again, a case of divided sensibility: he shares Wordsworth's primitivism to some degree; he finds in nature sources of beauty, resigned wisdom, and sympathy; but at the same time he rejects the Wordsworthian hopes and writes to expose them. The result is a natural world completely Hardy's own, composed of grays, bleakness, emptiness, chilling winds and rain, yellowing leaves, and mutely suffering creatures, with signs everywhere of dreariness, ominous threat, and blight, yet all—this is the paradox—observed with close fidelity and rendered with an etched austerity of language:

I travel on by barren farms,
And gulls glint out like silver flecks
Against a cloud that speaks of wrecks,
And bellies down with black alarms.

Another example is the image of the black yew-tree boughs against the sky:

The yew-tree arms, glued hard to the stiff stark air.

Or the grim, visionary metaphor of "The Darkling Thrush," where the features of a winter landscape become the outline of a corpse stretched out, the dark sky its overarching tomb:

The land's sharp features seemed to be
The Century's corpse outleant,
His crypt the cloudy canopy,
The wind his death-lament.

Nature is, however, almost never the subject of a Hardy poem. It is present only as context and background. As such it may harmonize or contrast with the human event in the foreground, but in either case it tends to foster the catharsis of which I have been speaking, the almost philosophic contemplation that distinguishes tragedy from mere pathos.

Among Hardy's shorter poems the interplay of landscape, human event, and cosmological overtone can be best studied in "Neutral Tones." "Tones" here means colors, for the scene is sketched in grays and whites. But the word might secondarily suggest tones of voice in this meeting at love's end. There is also the narrator's tone of mind, inert before the occasion he remembers:

We stood by a pond that winter day,
And the sun was white, as though chidden of God,
And a few leaves lay on the starving sod;
   —They had fallen from an ash, and were gray.

Your eyes on me were as eyes that rove
Over tedious riddles of years ago;
And some words played between us to and fro
   On which lost the more by our love.

The smile on your mouth was the deadest thing
Alive enough to have strength to die;
And a grin of bitterness swept thereby
   Like an ominous bird a-wing. . . .

Since then, keen lessons that love deceives,
And wrings with wrong, have shaped to me
Your face, and the God-curst sun, and a tree,
   And a pond edged with grayish leaves.

One notices that the story is not told. Why or how the love affair came to this moment seem questions that no longer matter. The persons are not characterized, nor is their conversation related. We have a sense of numbed energies in the speaker, as though he were hardly able to recall more than these few, seemingly random details. Of course they are not random, for they convey the mood with extreme vividness, the mutual, weary disillusion. Some are unusual in a poem written in 1867—for example, the reproaches exchanged by the lovers, the unexpected "grin of bitterness"—but they are felt to be psychologically right, and the typically odd metaphors further support our impression of a real happening. Lyric verse would not usually compare a smile to a dead "thing," much less to "the deadest thing / Alive enough to have strength to die," but Hardy's eccentricity and awkwardness seem natural by-products of exact rendering. The poem illustrates his realism and human interest, his power to convey complex human situations and feelings.

The description of the natural scene has some of the same specific detail—"few leaves . . . They had fallen from an ash, and were gray"—that creates the illusion of actuality. It is, moreover, Hardy's pinched nature, wan and wintry—the sun "white" through cloud or mist, the leaves few, gray, and fallen, their motion past. (The tree is, typically, an ash, with a pun on the color.) It is a sparse, unified, rather beautiful pencil drawing on gray paper, and it portrays faded energies and lifeless inertia. Even the sod is "starving," suggesting something vaguely blighting or scanting in nature or the universe. In this poem nature is not present as vast, overarching context, but in another, equally Hardyesque role as fellow-sufferer. The poem exploits the common technique in nineteenth-century poetry, in which nature and human feeling are placed side by side and the natural scene becomes the exponent or expression of the feeling. Both the human event and the landscape evoke one mood of dead energies and hopelessness. Going beyond the scene, Hardy seeks the source or cause of this failed relationship (for which no cause is suggested in external circumstance or in the psychology of the lovers) and of this dreary landscape, and posits some ultimate meanness or, possibly, anger in the universe, in God. (There is a strengthening of this feeling from the first stanza to the last; in the first Hardy exploits the hypothetical "as though" and the weaker verb, "chidden"; in the last he uses the phrase "God-curst.") But this religious speculation, momentous as it may be, does not seem to be the object of the poem. It is characteristic of Hardy to extend his speculation to an ultimate source, but here the ultimate source enters for purposes that are mainly aesthetic. It further defines, expresses, and intensifies the mood. It raises the poem—which otherwise would present only one of life's moments—into a symbol of universal truth. Thus it enormously weights the impact. But one is not asked to consider whether the theological assertions may be true or false. They serve the work of imagination, not of inquiring theology.

The problems and effects we have been analyzing have their largest field in *The Dynasts,* Hardy's long epic-drama of the Napoleonic wars. Taken lyric by lyric, chorus by chorus, there is not much major poetry in *The Dynasts.* Taken scene by scene, only a few are really effective in a dramatic way. But taken as a whole, many readers have been unforgettably impressed by the imaginative sense of context. Nature or landscape plays its role once again. In his stage directions Hardy withdraws to an immense height, and sees the individual figures and even armies diminished in the panorama of Europe:

A view of the country from mid-air, at a point south of the River Inn, which is seen as a silver thread . . . The Danube shows itself as a crinkled satin riband, stretching from left to right in the far background of the picture, the Inn discharging its waters into the larger river. . . . A vast Austrian army creeps dully along the mid-distance, in the form of detached masses and columns of a whitish cast. . . . The silent insect-creep of the Austrian columns towards the banks of the Inn continues to be seen till the view fades to nebulousness and dissolves.

The sense of context is also expressed through the plot, for Hardy shows each episode as part of a huge historical web of cause and effect, so that a naval battle off Spain sends its reverberations through every capital of Europe and hundreds of thousands of men marching eastward into Russia. But it is not only of episodes that we should think. The strands of the web are people, and Hardy moves up and down the social scale, from common soldiers and camp followers to generals, parliamentarians, and princes, his purpose being to suggest what myriad diverse lives are caught up and interact in this uncoiling of history. Here especially in *The Dynasts* his philosophical overworld comes into play, his need to confront the ultimate cause of all these events. The philosophical or religious problem is discussed by a mythology of spirits—the Spirit of the Years, of the Pities, the Ironies, and the like—who comment on the action and on its ultimate source, toward which they articulate differing emotional responses.

Hardy's search for an ultimate cause finds its solution in an ultimate myth or mythical identity called the Immanent Will, which is said to pervade and determine all existence. If we ask what the Immanent Will may be, one answer is, it is almost nothing—hardly more than a name for what happens. The term posits that human will, in the proper sense, is an illusion, since all thoughts and actions are manifestations of the cosmic Will. (The Will lacks consciousness and purpose, however, so that whatever happens may be merely accidental in the course of its blind moiling. All things, one might say, are determined, but chance is what determines them.) But Hardy cannot make the Will a convincing cause of anything. That, writing poetry, he is precluded from step-by-step exposition and argument does not matter in the least. What does matter is that he cannot secure dramatic belief, for he is unable to show the Will as a cause by dramatically effective means. He asserts that the Will determines all; he even concocts a lurid and grotesque vision of the Will pulsing, jellying, and tendrilizing everywhere, but there was no way he could bring the Will on stage as an agent. As soon as we return from the assembly of Spirits to the scenes of human action we forget about the Will. His characters have no notion of it (except for a few broody speeches by Napoleon). They think and behave as if they were responsible for their own actions. This is Hardy's irony, but it is an irony he cannot make felt.

Although it cannot be made convincing, the Immanent Will, with the Spirit commentators on it, plays an all-important role in our response to *The Dynasts*, simply because it embodies Hardy's sense that human life must be related to something ultimate, even if that something is only a tautology or a nothing. The Immanent Will is a modern version of Zeus or Fate or Fortuna, the difference—and the advantage—being that, as Hardy put it, these older myths "will not bear stretching further in epic or dramatic art . . . one must make an independent plunge, embodying the real, if only temporary, thought of the age." The Immanent Will sounds, or sounded, modern and credible; the imagination requires no more. As with other religious beliefs, it creates a cosmos that is one vast whole. We see human life flick-

ering against something incomparably vast and all-pervading.
Our sense of man's helplessness in an alien, overwhelming
cosmos is magnified and combined with a quasi-religious awe.

Hardy's influence on later poets has been large but is difficult
to trace. If only because of the sometimes quirky individuality of
his style, he has seldom been imitated closely. Throughout our
century he has appealed to each generation of poets in succession. Pound affirmed, with typical brashness, that "no one
taught me anything about writing since Thomas Hardy died."
Younger contemporaries such as Blunden and Graves were
admirers. Auden said he was his first object of poetic devotion as
a schoolboy, and throughout his life he spoke of Hardy with
appreciative affection. Dylan Thomas knew long swatches of
Hardy by heart, and is said to have remarked that "Hardy was
his favourite poet of the century," even though he knew he
ought to prefer Yeats. It is unlikely that these diverse poets were
reacting to the same qualities. The Georgian poets relished especially his contemplativeness, tenderness, and piety, his country
setting, rustic characters, sense of local tradition, realism, colloquial speech, and large, authentic personality. Many a poem in
his *Collected Poems* might have slipped easily into the Georgian
anthologies—for example, "A Church Romance," "An August
Midnight" (which is close to de la Mare), or the lovely "Afterwards." Poets who reacted against the Georgians had, however,
no need to repudiate Hardy; they welcomed his austerity, concentration, roughness of texture, and gargoyle satire. If they did
not learn from Hardy such habits of style as swift, ironic, often
shocking juxtaposition, or fluctuation of tone and mood in a
speaking voice, they could respect these virtues. Above all, they
shared and propagated his premise that poetry is subtle, functional writing, demanding from the reader not the unbuttoning
of moods, but active attention.

What Hardy may mean to poets at the present time I cannot
undertake to say. His reputation as a writer is less than it was
when he died. He has, however, admirers of the kind a poet
would wish to have. But he can no longer have the directly formative impact of a contemporary or immediate predecessor.
Poetry in the modern world has become so self-conscious and
specialized that it is in danger of sealing itself off from life. It is

so on the defensive against larger genres that it feels the temptation to abandon the field, retreating into acknowledged littleness. Perhaps all the more because he often failed, Hardy will remain an emboldening example of a poet who took great risks, going out to experience directly and reflecting upon it with the largest concern. If other qualities are absent, human interest and significant meaning may not always appeal, but nothing can long appeal without them.

9

CRAFTSMEN OF THE BEAUTIFUL
AND THE AGREEABLE

THE major poets of the Edwardian age were Yeats and
Hardy, the popular ones were Kipling, Chesterton,
Noyes, and Masefield. But these poets did not represent
the orthodox taste of the poetry reading public. Their works
stirred up protest and controversy. If we ask who was read with
general, if not always enthusiastic approbation, the answer is
Robert Bridges, Laurence Binyon, Walter de la Mare, and poets
of similar description. Some of these were subtly skilled writers;
others were less so. But what they wrote corresponded to the
usual idea of poetry among educated people in England seventy
years ago.

They were cultivated traditionalists. Many had begun to publish in the 1890s or earlier, and in some respects their work resembles the traditionalist poetry of the nineties—that of William
Watson, Stephen Phillips, "Michael Field," Alice Meynell,
Francis Thompson, and Lionel Johnson, many of whom went
on writing into the Edwardian period. One difference is that the
Edwardian traditionalists could not continue past modes with
quite the same unquestioning confidence. They reflected more
deeply upon their purposes, means, and place in tradition,
acquiring a more sensitive poetic sophistication and developing
a more exacting craftsmanship.

For these poets the zeitgeist was only a spook. They agreed with Santayana that all roads are open always. Greek lyric and drama, Lucretius, Horace, and Catullus, medieval aubade and Elizabethan song, Blake, Shelley, Keats, Goethe, or Heine were not possible at one time only in the history of the human spirit. They were perennially available. The modern poet could always write in their way. When they reviewed contemporaries, these poets and critics usually oriented themselves by relating the book to some past exemplar. Thus, the poems of Mary Coleridge remind Bridges sometimes of medieval song and sometimes of Heine. If the feelings she voices are not identical with those articulated in her prototypes, the reasons are personal rather than historical. A modern poet might easily feel just what they had felt and might express himself in the same style, maybe more finely. So far as these writers were concerned, modern poetry required neither a new form nor a new vision.

These remarks are simplifications for the sake of making a point. Poetry was also expected to reflect the modern spirit. This, it was assumed, would appear not so much in the diction, form, or subject as in the "ideas" the poet is aware of. Good poetry would be only tinged with modernity. It would not break with the past but incorporate the past with the present in a poetic form and content of timeless validity. In general, Binyon tells us, "the spirit of art is against the spirit of the age. . . . We express our own age by resisting it, by creating something which will outlast its fevers and its disillusions." The right proportion in blending the past with the present was perhaps indicated by a review of Sturge Moore's *Poems* that appeared in *The Times Literary Supplement* in 1904: his manner recalls the "Greek way" and yet the "romantic way too"; but it is also "his own manner, and one that has the right touch of our day about it."

Eternity, timelessness, the realm of the spirit—this was the realm of the poetic imagination. Moore's poetry, a later review explains, "springs from a serene state remote from squalor and noise, where all fair things inhabit." The largest, most sensitive articulation of this point of view—a central one for understanding the time—was that of George Santayana (see Chapter 6), though his voice descended from eternity with subtler tones in his philosophic essays than in his poetry. He had an intelligence, hence an irony, that gave him an importance more than merely historical. But if one imagines a closely similar knot of ideas in a headpiece of far less acuteness, and with simple but earnest devotion to ideals as contrasted with ideals espoused with irony, one has a general mental portrait of Bridges, Binyon, Moore, R. C. Trevelyan, and many another pursuer of the Beautiful and the Good in the Edwardian age. They had taken to the cultural world of Arnoldian "high seriousness" with utmost commitment. They had fed their minds on the "noblest monuments" of literature and art. They were dedicated and aspiring in traditional senses and ways. Compared to many other writers of their own generation, more especially of the First World War and the twenties—Kipling, Owen, Lawrence—they appear not only higher minded but also better educated and more civilized.

But one remembers that Santayana, while thinking and speaking of the life of the spirit in eternity, might in the same moment have been softening his dessert cake by pouring wine over it. No one would have appreciated the irony more than he; nevertheless it symbolizes a weak side of genteel idealism. Thinking of these poets, one is tempted to suggest that there was something insufficiently real about their poetry. Or perhaps, since the real can mean the ultimate, one should say that they rose into the "real" too easily, being too little tied to concrete fact. They had—or expressed—no adequate sense of the complexity of human feelings and the contradictory many-sidedness of human experience.

But this was not the purpose of their poetry, which was devoted to a higher object. The essence of poetry was "Beauty"— that at least was the usual term. "Beauty is the end and law of poetry," Yeats wrote Russell in a typical statement of 1900. Poetry "exists to find the beauty in all things, philosophy, nature, passion,—in what you will, and in so far as it rejects beauty it destroys its own right to exist." The artist and the poet, Bridges said, "is the man who is possessed by the idea of Beauty." "For Flaubert, as for all great masters," said Sturge Moore, the functions of art were "the evocation, development, and perpetuation of beauty." The same thing would have been said by the Aesthetes, and if one asks how Edwardian poets of Beauty differ, one answer is that for the Aesthetes the Beautiful had no necessary relation to the Ethical. It followed that whatever the poet could behold or create as Beauty was a subject for poetry. But the poets we now have in mind were of the opposite opinion. As with the Aesthetes, their tradition of Beauty had its ultimate source in Plato and descended also from innumerable feeding rills in the Renaissance, the Romantic period, and more lately in Rossetti and the Pre-Raphaelites. But unlike the Aesthetes, these Edwardians retained the ethical idealism of Renaissance and Romantic Platonism. The Beautiful and the Good could not be opposed to each other, for they were one and the same. "Pure Ethics," Bridges said, "is man's moral beauty, and can no more be dissociated from Art than any other kind of Beauty." But to the question, "What is Beauty?" their answer significantly was that one could not say. Beauty was unknowable, hence undefinable, though you were aware of its presence, perhaps because you felt the "vague exaltation" Sturge Moore cited as its effect on Flaubert. Housman affirmed that he recognized poetry only by the bristling of his hairs. The premise was debilitating to criticism. Faced with the unanalyzable, a critic could offer description and scholarly background; beyond that he could only wax enthusiastic, hoping that his emotion might waft the reader toward the mysterious feeling. Hence Stopford Brooke, writing on Keats in 1907:

The best examples of the Odes need neither praise nor blame. They are above criticism, pure gold of poetry—virgin gold. Of them it may be said—with all reverence yet with justice, for these high things of poetry come forth from the spiritual depths of man—The wind bloweth where it listeth, and thou canst not tell whence it cometh or whither it goeth—so is every poem that is born of the spirit.

In due course this type of criticism helped instigate its opposite: criticism by close analysis. Meanwhile, if all one could say about Beauty was what Bridges affirmed in *The Testament of Beauty*—it is

> the quality of appearances that thru' the sense
> wakeneth spiritual emotion in the mind of man—

nevertheless, how all important it is! How conducive and intrinsic to all man's higher life! This awakening and uplifting, this calling upon the soul, this brief and partial intuition of the ultimate—this is the object of poetry. It is, one might say, the Poetry in poetry, giving it a significance and value far transcending whatever mere wisdom or life it may also contain.

How did the artist invoke Beauty? That, too, was a mystery. Beauty was not achieved through form, thoughts, emotions, or images, though all these should be beautiful and tributary to Beauty. Perhaps, Sturge Moore suggested, Beauty is the "harmony" of these aspects, but even this thought might be one of those speculations on Beauty which, according to Bridges, always appear "fanciful and unsound" to the artist. At least, however, one knew what would disturb the feeling of Beauty. A basic premise was that no aspect of the poem should call distinct attention to itself, distracting from the deeper communion. "Harmony," said Moore, "is more explicit than any language; it alone informs the soul, begetting the temper which welcomes knowledge and achieves peace." Ideas, for example, should not be interesting. Moore tells us that Flaubert liked poetry to be "without a single striking idea," and adds that "there is weight enough in a legendary tale or pure invention enveloping a few chosen circumstances or a fascinating situation, such as from age to age may be endlessly transformed,—not burdened by any definite problem or weighty conviction." So also with emotions. If they are too intense, Moore remarks, they may usurp "more than due attention." Even individual words should not stand out in their context, for, as Marguerite Wilkinson explains in a primer on contemporary poetry for college students (*New Voices,* 1922), "a loud, noisy word in a bit of quiet blank verse will sometimes create such a disturbance that the beauty of the other words will pass unnoticed." The effect sought was what Binyon called "divine limpidity," a streamy accord achieved not by reconciled tensions but by restraint, by keeping everything down. In addition you avoided anything that could seem ugly. Hence there was a world of difference between mere skill in expression, however excellent, and the creation of Beauty. A "portrait of a man suffering from confluent smallpox" may be accurate and vivid to the last degree. But, to quote Bridges again, if anyone asserts that it is a fit subject for poetry, "to this I reply that we live in a free country where every one may think and say what he pleases." Beauty fled from drab settings, sordid images, vulgar characters, cynical and depressing ideas, emotions such as anger, guilt, lust, or despair, many forms of irony and wit, conflict and dramatic shift of mood, and versification that was jolting, cacophonous, or dissonant. When *The Waste Land* was

published in 1922, it was interpreted by this taste as sullen and
aggressive ugliness in many modes, betraying a wish to destroy
poetry. But these traditionalist poets were themselves filtering
and narrowing poetry in ways not in the least characteristic of
the traditions they emulated.

In practice the poetry of the Beautiful was seldom distinguishable from what may be called the "Agreeable." The term,
as we noted, is borrowed from the critical writing of the eighteenth century and the Romantic period and refers to the exploitation in poetry of whatever is naturally pleasant to us or has
been made pleasant through association. This had been an element in the appeal of most poetry since at least the middle of the
eighteenth century; with the deliberately disagreeable poetry
of the Decadents, Impressionists, and Realists on the scene, conservative poets stressed the Agreeable perhaps more strongly
than they otherwise would have. Though distinct from the
Beautiful, the Agreeable might contribute to beauty and certainly would not detract. And so in form you got such qualities as
euphony, regularity, anticipation and fulfillment, and gentle
surprise; in diction, the choice, cultivated, perhaps slightly
poetic or archaic; in setting, landscape, classical mythology,
medieval or Eastern romance, and the like, though the rendering was not particular enough to concentrate attention and
make an eddy in the stream of spiritual feeling; and of course
you got also solacing thoughts and the gentler or loftier emotions—nature appreciation, noble patriotism, ideal love. To the
extent that the grimmer sides of human experience were admitted, they were kept at a distance and tamed into meditative
pathos and consolation.

Aside from individual poems and poetic careers, the chief literary monument of this taste is the second part of Binyon's *The
Golden Treasury of Modern Lyrics* (1925). This continuation of Palgrave's famous anthology was designed to represent English
poetry from 1850 to the present, part two being devoted to
poetry from 1892 to 1925. The selections illustrate what, as late
as 1925, still seemed to many the best in modern poetry. Yeats,
for example, is present in relative abundance, but only his earlier, more plaintive writing, nothing published after 1904. From
Kipling there are only a few conventional lyrics, none of the
more famous studies in realism. Hardy is presented in five

poems in which one encounters mainly his pathos, tenderness, and charm; as much as possible his novelistic treatment and philosophic questioning are dropped from view. From "Georgians" such as Rupert Brooke and Wilfrid Gibson we have nobility and narrative, but none of their attempts to explore life's harsher facts. Binyon excluded what he lumped together as the poetry of the Overseas Dominions, India, and America. One would like to know what he would have selected. A good many poems of Ezra Pound, such as the lovely "Envoi," are typical of the school of Beauty at its best, though by including "Envoi" within *Hugh Selwyn Mauberley,* Pound indicated an ironic or ambiguous attitude toward this type of lyric. That poetry in this mode was written by a leader of the Modernist revolution illustrates that the currents of tendency in this period were much more confused than literary history usually suggests. A reader of Binyon's *Golden Treasury* would infer that by 1925 the most important "modern" poets were Bridges, Yeats, Hardy, de la Mare, and Mary Coleridge. Bridges is represented more amply than anyone else, and to this gruff chieftain of the tribe of Beauty we may now turn.

BRIDGES, BINYON, AND MOORE

Robert Bridges (1844–1930) attended Eton and Oxford (where he met Gerard Manley Hopkins). Extensive travels in Egypt, Syria, Germany, France, and Italy were followed by the practice of medicine (1875–1882), though Bridges, having an independent income, seems to have gone into medicine to acquire broader experience in preparation for a literary career. His first volume of poems appeared in 1873 and was followed by three anonymous publications: the sonnet sequence entitled *The Growth of Love* (1876; much revised and expanded in subsequent editions), and two collections of lyrics in 1879 and 1880. In 1882 he abandoned medical practice and settled in Yattendon, Berkshire, marrying two years later. His biography henceforth is a record of publications: lyrics, dramas or dramatic poems, a long narrative poem (*Eros and Psyche,* 1885), *The Yattendon Hymnal* (1895–1899), critical essays on Milton's versification (beginning in 1887 and culminating in *Milton's Prosody,* revised final edition,

1921), Keats (1895), and, more briefly, on many other writers. In 1907 he moved to Chilswell House, near Oxford, and in 1913 was appointed poet laureate. In his later years Bridges was much interested in phonetic spelling, and his works are printed according to his theories. His famous edition of Hopkins, introducing his friend to the literary world, appeared in 1918. The crowning achievement, and the only work to find any popular success, was *The Testament of Beauty,* which he began in 1926, at the age of eighty-two, and published three years later.

The *Shorter Poems,* a famous volume of lyrics which appeared in 1890, was, A. E. Housman said, the most perfect book of verse ever written. It opens with a limpid and flowing lyric, "Clear and gentle stream," a phrase that briefly describes most of Bridges' work. The form of the poem enacts the subject and, one might almost say, is the subject:

> Clear and gentle stream!
> Known and loved so long,
> That hast heard the song
> And the idle dream
> Of my boyish day;
> While I once again
> Down thy margin stray,
> In the selfsame strain
> Still my voice is spent.

The forty-eight lines of the poem float by, smoothed, lulled, easily slipping from one line to the next. Such verse is curiously empty, but the emptiness is a kind of purity, as Yeats noticed in quoting

> I heard a linnet courting
>   His lady in the spring:
> His mates were idly sporting,
>   Nor stayed to hear him sing
>   His song of love.—
> I fear my speech distorting
>   His tender love.

"Every metaphor, every thought a commonplace," comments Yeats, "emptiness everywhere, the whole magnificent."

The *Shorter Poems* are traditional poetry, though never merely derivative, and the traditions are those of Spenser, of "L'Allegro" and "Il Penseroso," of the meditative poets of the eighteenth century, of Wordsworth, Shelley, Keats especially, and, though Bridges would have bristled at the suggestion, of Tennyson and Arnold. "I heard a linnet courting" perhaps owes something to Wordsworth's "The Green Linnet"; "London Snow," except for the versification, might have been written by Cowper; "Elegy Among the Tombs" disinters the "sweet Melancholy" of eighteenth-century graveyard verse:

> Sad, sombre place, beneath whose antique yews
> I come, unquiet sorrows to control.

The themes are as traditional as the modes. There are lyrics of love and nature, love in various moods ranging from disappointment to ecstasy, and nature faithfully observed with a quiet pleasure. There is no reason to doubt that Bridges had these emotions, but one notices the poet's formal artistry rather than his personality.

The reticence and control were temperamental, but they might also be called "classical," at least as the term might have been understood in the latter part of the nineteenth century. Living until 1930, Bridges must have been one of the last English poets to work equally within the double traditions of classical and English verse. Particular influences from Latin poets are numerous, but the most important result of his classical learning was to reinforce a studious attitude toward poetry and poetic composition. Detachment, self-discipline, conscious intention, and scrupulous respect for the medium—these are the scholar's virtues that Bridges brought to poetry.

Poetic craftsmanship meant for Bridges especially versification. It was a subject he studied closely and practiced experimentally; through it, though unadventurous in other ways, he takes his place in the ferment of innovation that characterizes modern art. In the *Shorter Poems* his prosody is usually of a traditional kind. But even here he employs a great variety of lines and stanzaic forms, and the variety itself suggests an interest in research. That he does not repeat metrical forms may indicate that to work out the form was a reason for writing the poem. He had the same attitude toward the achievements of the past; once a form has been fully exploited it cannot be used again: "Anyone may see that serious rhyme is now exhausted in English verse, or that Milton's blank verse practically ended as an original form with Milton." When, in 1877, Bridges encountered Hopkins' sprung rhythm he was shocked. But, given these interests and opinions, the temptation proved irresistible, and he soon tried his own variations of the new meter. The results may be seen in "A Passer-by," "The Downs," "I would be a bird," "London Snow," "The Voice of Nature," and "On a Dead Child." These poems differ considerably from each other. "On a Dead Child" makes its effects by cadenced statement:

> Ah! little at best can all our hopes avail us
>   To lift this sorrow, or cheer us, when in the dark,
>   Unwilling, alone we embark
> And the things we have seen and have known and have
>   heard of, fail us.

In "A Passer-by," on the other hand—

> Whither, O splendid ship, thy white sails crowding,
>   Leaning across the bosom of the urgent West,
> That fearest nor sea rising, nor sky clouding,
>   Whither away, fair rover, and what thy quest?—

the complex assonance and alliteration, the varied handling of the caesura, the energy of the participial rhymes, and the suspended syntax make up a structure of baroque artifice which is, in its way, magnificent. Whoever has heard it read aloud can testify to the effect.

Bridges' sprung rhythm does not leave the same impression as that of Hopkins, who was not always pleased with it. ("A Passer-by," he said, "reads not so much like sprung rhythm as the logaoedic dignified doggerel one Tennyson has employed in Maud.") The differences are temperamental, with Hopkins using the meter in a more dramatic and freely expressive way. His line

> Look at the stars! look, look up at the skies!

contrasts in this sense with Bridges' quieter and more cautious imitation in "London Snow":

> "O look at the trees!" they cried, "O look at the trees."

But the difference is also that Bridges did not accept—or, perhaps, understand—Hopkins' complex superstructure of scholastic explanation, and treated sprung rhythm, as Hopkins complained, "in theory and practice as something informal and variable without any limit but ear and taste."

Perhaps because it seemed merely "informal and variable" Bridges did not continue with sprung rhythm. The next stage was classical, quantitative scansion. If readers may be said to express a judgment by not reading, these experiments have been found unsuccessful, though they are sometimes pleasing. "The Ruin" is a brief example:

> These grey stones have rung with mirth and lordly carousel;
> Here proud kings mingled poetry and ruddy wine.
> All hath pass'd long ago; nought but this ruin abideth,
> Sadly in eyeless trance gazing upon the river.
> Wouldst thou know who here visiteth, dwelleth and singeth
>   also,
> Ask the swallows flying from sunny-wall'd Italy.

Bridges abandoned classical prosody and the final stage was his "neo-Miltonics" or "loose Alexandrines," a measure which he employed in his most ambitious effort, *The Testament of Beauty* (1929). All his previous experimentation lies behind this new meter, but the most important single influence was his study of Milton's prosody. Describing the meter of *Samson Agonistes,* he notices that in the occasional twelve-syllable lines Milton avoided the sixth-syllable caesura that usually divides the Alexandrine into hemistichs. The examples he cites also show that Milton introduces frequent variations from the iambic meter. Bridges' "neo-Miltonics" adopt as a norm a twelve-syllable line with six rather irregularly spaced stresses (frequently a stress is divided between two half-stresses). He departs freely even from this loose pattern. The verse sounds like this:

> As some perfected flower, Iris or Lily, is born
> patterning heav'nly beauty, a pictur'd idea
> that hath no other expression for us, nor coud hav:
> for thatt which Lily or Iris tell cannot be told
> by poetry or by music in their secret tongues,
> nor is discerptible in logic, but is itself
> an absolute piece of Being . . .

The meter, Bridges felt, was "the freest of free verse." Its "beauty," as he said of Milton's prosody, is "its perpetual freedom to obey the sense and diction." If in this obedience it cannot always be distinguished from prose, that is perhaps not much amiss in a long, argumentative poem.

The argument moves in a leisurely way, keeping within the genteel ranges of thought and avoiding intense emotion. (Bridges "is a . . . chaste old bird," Sir Walter Raleigh said, "Just a shade too little of a blackguard.") The phrasing is choice, if often archaic, the tone diversified, the descriptive and musical set pieces generously frequent. Bridges' learned art makes pleasant reading. As for doctrine, he maintains that man's spiritual life (in art, love, ethics, or religion) is continuous with the whole of nature, from which it develops and of which it is as much a part as everything else. The standpoint may be characterized as an evolutionary Platonism. Beauty is the mediator or awakener. It is, to repeat the lines quoted earlier,

> the quality of appearances that thru' the sense
> wakeneth spiritual emotion in the mind of man.

As such, Beauty is the "prime motiv of all [man's] excellence." The formulation, it may be noticed again, differs sharply from art for art's sake. Beauty is not itself the highest good, but rather the motive, the principle of transition toward.

Considered as doctrine, the poem has afforded easy victories to many critics. But in the long run the style proves more damaging. For instance, one may well agree with Bridges that Freud presented a too simple view of the mind and its development. But to speak as he does—some

> impute precocious puberty
> to new-born babes, and all their after trouble in life
> to shamefast thwarting of inveterat lust—

is to lose contact with the fact of infant sexuality. It is a too-decorous elegance.

Bridges has considerable significance in literary history but as a representative of his time rather than as a powerfully creative influence. His philosophical celebration of aesthetic experience or Beauty—turning away from "the vivacity of common life" to serve "a lonely and distinguished ideal," as Yeats put it—was typical of many poets, the greatest being Rilke. The pleasant melodies of his versification, the familiar beauty of landscape, the happy or gently plaintive tones of feeling created that poetry of frankly offered refreshment which was and still is a loved English mode. On another side, Bridges had more austere affinities with those poets who sought to make the writing of poetry more difficult, seeking a stricter formal order, a more objective craftsmanship; for this, as Yeats said, "all who write with deliberation are his debtors." It is especially revealing that where he had most completely pondered and mastered his art, in versification, even this traditionalist poet felt the strong need of a new departure.

Laurence Binyon (1869–1943) had a full-time professional life in the department of prints and drawings of the British Museum. In addition, he lectured and wrote on the fine arts, acquiring a considerable reputation. Nevertheless, he found time to produce at least thirty-five books of poetry, poetic drama, and translation. His version of Dante (1933–1943) is especially notable. In *London Visions* (1896) he recorded the life of the city in impressionist vignettes, and was one of the earlier workmen in this vein. This was, however, an exception, for Binyon was among the poets who wrote, said Yeats (numbering himself in the company), "as men had always written." More precisely, he wrote as the English Romantics had, though he assimilated other current modes to this main tradition. "Flame and Snow" shows his impressionist interest in evoking subtle, strange, and fugitive emotion. He speaks of the flames,

> Trembling aloft to the wild music that Fire sings
> Dancing alive from nothing, lovely and mad. And still
> The snow, pale as a dream, slept on the old hill,
> Softly fallen and strange.

"Snow, pale as a dream," may be an effective phrase, but the intended contrast between the dithyrambic and the mysteriously quiet does not come off. *Wild, lovely, pale, dream, old hill,* and *strange* are items of a stock diction that muffles and sentimentalizes. Such diction comes from two closely related sources: the Celtic Twilight of Yeats and the Agreeable England of the Edwardians. What the latter could furnish in the way of pleasant items is illustrated by a few lines of "Goblin," where Binyon collects *night, moon, English meadow, old farm, dewy grass, bean-blossom,* and *rose*. This is the stock that Walter de la Mare deployed with conscious sophistication and haunting effect. Binyon was equally aware that he was exploiting stock responses, and the awareness is thematically active in the poem. But unlike de la Mare, he could not manipulate stock responses to release imagination rather than deaden it.

The defect of imagination is something Binyon shares with Bridges and Moore. In fact, these writers tended to confuse imaginative poverty with restraint. Binyon wrote poems of versified eloquence. "Thunder on the Downs" is a descriptive-meditative effusion of high-minded patriotism, so dull one can hardly pay attention while reading it. "For the Fallen" was a war effusion, first published in *The Times* in 1914. It is a poem of stately, reflective mourning for the dead soldiers and finds consolation in the thought that they are not dead in their noble influence. It had much success and, though it has only twenty-eight lines, was subsequently published as a separate book. Binyon also wrote long, narrative poems, such as "The Death of Adam" or "The Death of Tristram." He is, in his verse, an admirable figure, possessed of sincerity, intelligence, sensitivity, and culture. Even the names of Italian cities—Assisi, Spoleto—are so exciting to him that they flush "the heart like wine." But nothing he wrote seems likely to last.

T. Sturge Moore (1870–1944) learned from Ricketts and Shannon, whom he met in the 1880s, to think of art as traditional and impersonal beauty. He wrote lyrics, narrative poems, poetic dramas, criticism, and aesthetics. At their best his poems are distinguished by the union of three qualities: richly concrete and consciously beautiful detail; imagination of a romantically alien world or state of mind; a search for moral relevance or meaning. For Moore, however, relevance and meaning are many-sided and elusive. His poems are not escapist daydreams but neither are they contrived allegories. They are symbols for meditation. With a few exceptions his finest work recreates the traditional literary image of classical Greece, rehandling the Arcadian and mythological materials with freshness and conviction. His other chief source of story is the Bible. *The Vinedresser,* the title poem of his first and most successful volume of nondramatic poetry (1899), is a georgic composed as a letter to an ancient Sicilian vintner, giving directions how the choicest of wines may be produced. Its dense and lustrous images compose a world of idyllic beauty, but it also teaches by inference what elaborate care and knowledge are necessary to the making of any fine thing, such as the poem itself. *The Rout of the Amazons* (1903) tells of the invasion of Attica by an army of Amazons and their defeat in battle. A few lines describing the coming of the Amazons illustrate Moore's style:

> A thousand rode together, poising darts,
> Behind them those with other arms came on;
> All flaunting down a green-sward valley came
> Between Arcadia's gentle holted hills.
> It was for beauty like a fleet at sea,
> Or like an hundred swans
> Sailing before the breeze across a lake!
> Their vests of daffodil, or pallid pink
> Or milky violet! their saffron caps
> . . . .
> the rich green sward,
> The morning light, the blossoming hawthorn trees!

The purpose of this is to present the densest possible sensation of beauty. It is, however, a beauty that reminds one more of the poetry of Flecker, H. D., or Pound in early *Cantos* than of Bridges or Binyon, for it is invoked in an alien, pitiless Arcadia. It altogether lacks the reassuring familiarity, kindliness, and solace of the English landscape tradition. In largeness and integrity of aspiration, as well as in some qualities of imagination, Moore was a poet of more than modest potential. But he lacked control of language and rhythm, and one is continually jarred by infelicities. Also he suffers by competition. What he could do well was done better by Shelley and Keats.

WALTER DE LA MARE

Of the poets discussed in this chapter, the finest and most original was Walter de la Mare (1873–1956). His full stature has not been generally recognized. Educated at St. Paul's Cathedral Choir School, where he founded and edited the school magazine, he went to work at the age of seventeen as a bookkeeper in the London office of the Anglo-American Standard Oil Company. His first publication was a short story, "Kismet," and his first book of poems, *Songs of Childhood,* appeared in 1902 under the pseudonym of "Walter Ramal." In 1908, when he was thirty-five, the Asquith government awarded him an annual pension of £ 100, the grant being made on the advice of Sir Henry Newbolt, who had published his poems in the *Monthly Review.* With the pension and what he could earn through reviewing and freelance writing, he was able to quit office work and devote himself to full-time authorship. Within a few years he retired to the country with his wife and four children, living at Taplow, Buckinghamshire. His outward life was uneventful. He wrote poems and fiction, producing over fifty books, though some of them are anthologies and others collect previous publications. Among the more significant are *The Listeners and Other Poems* (1912), *Peacock Pie* (1913), *The Riddle and Other Stories* (1923), *The Winged Chariot* (1951), and two anthologies, *Come Hither* (1923) and *Behold, this Dreamer!* (1939), the latter with an extended introduction, "Dream and Imagination," which is a prose exposition of his views on lifelong topics of his meditation: poetry, dream, the unconscious, time, death.

Of all the "last Romantics," as Yeats characterized himself and his fellow poets, none seems at first glance more naively a Romantic than de la Mare. Yet the more one studies him, the more ambiguous one finds his relation to the tradition of the great English Romantic poets. Nevertheless, the first impression is of themes, images, and feelings that are familiar from the poetry of a hundred years before. His sources, moreover, include not only the English Romantics and their followers down through the Pre-Raphaelites, but sources from which they had themselves drawn, such as Spenser, Shakespeare, Elizabethan song, and ballad. De la Mare also drew from the folk literature for children, especially fairy tale and Mother Goose. His feelings, too, are of the gentler Romantic kind; they are nostalgia, tenderness, mystery, melancholy, loneliness, exile, yearning, crossed and complicated by whimsy, modesty, and reserve. He resembles, one might say, Charles Lamb rather than William Blake, and poems such as "Miss Loo," "Old Susan," or "The Tailor" might almost have been written by a Lamb more gifted in poetry. His style is formed out of the deliberate witchery of rhythm, sound, and phrase, the suggestiveness, the accessible and sought beauty familiar in Romantic poetry. Here in his poetry is the "O Lovely England"—the title of a late volume—in which the Romantics are sometimes thought to have dwelt and to which the Edwardians looked back with nostalgia, an England gentled, however, by de la Mare, who delights less in mountain grandeur and storm than in twilit roads, turnstyles, sheep, shepherds, conies, quiet towns, rose-covered cottages, guttering candles, and slow streams. What aligns him more deeply with the Romantic ethos, however, is his feeling that nature may be "a veil over some further reality," which, perhaps, "the imagination intuits." Like Yeats he repudiated late-Victorian scientific materialism, which seemed to him a bustling shallowness. But the age could supply no convincing, at least no fully respectable intellectual support for such repudiation, and, unlike Yeats, de la Mare did not lend much ear to astrologers, cabalists, and Rosicrucians. Like many modern poets, he returned for support to the Romantic protest on behalf of imaginative insight and wholeness, as opposed to scientific reason; in fact he used much the same terms the Romantics had. He did not redeploy precisely the same arguments—how could he a hundred years later?—but he exploited the same or closely similar images and gestures to dramatize his conviction that "reality" is made up of intersecting planes or interwoven aspects, only some of which can be known to reason and the senses.

Hence the central importance in de la Mare's poetry of states or moments when the common day of adult routine falls away or has not yet imposed itself. Childhood, for example. He wrote the finest poetry of the twentieth century for children. It is playful, imaginative, and unsentimental. (His children are innocent only in the sense that their conscience has not yet developed.) But the best of these poems are not merely for or about children. As with Romantic literature generally, they take the child as the symbol of a state of mind, possibly to be briefly recaptured by contemplating the symbol. Childhood is the lost "Eden of the heart"; it knows a wonder and joy that are deeper and truer than our adult "jaded, sated sense of fact," which actually is "all a fallacy." By re-entering the mind of the child, one can possess again the eerie, unknowable, beautiful world that truly is. Many of his children's poems are riddles, and the riddle is another way of achieving a perspective from which the familiar reveals itself as the strange. The answer to "John Mouldy" is "mould." De la Mare doubtless conceived the poem by asking himself the question, what would it be like to be mould in a cellar? But as he describes John Mouldy in the dusk, "smiling there alone," he conjures up something enigmatic, weird, and vaguely frightening. "Old Shellover" is a dialogue between a snail and a slug. They are about to enter a moonlit garden, and imaginative identification with these beings transforms the garden into an alien place of menace and beauty, where the "horny old Gardener" is the archetypal ogre:

> "Come!" said Old Shellover.
> "What?" says Creep.
> "The horny old Gardener's fast asleep;
> The fat cock Thrush
> To his nest has gone;
> And the dew shines bright
> In the rising Moon;
> Old Sallie Worm from her hole doth peep:
> "Come!" said Old Shellover.
> "Ay!" said Creep.

Some of his children's poems are not riddles but verbal puzzles and nonsense. The beautiful "The Song of the Mad Prince" is a poem of this kind. Most Modernist poets sought to break through logical and chronological expression. De la Mare achieved this through the irrational conventions of children's verse as well as through allied forms such as folk and fairy rhyme and tale.

He is a poet of dream and of analogous times when the ordinary world may seem to be dissolving into another: twilight, when the boundaries of things begin to blur; night, when the familiar is veiled in darkness or transformed in moonlight; falling asleep, the rational mind releasing its hold; memory, creating the light that never was in the past. And he is a poet of the quest, the knight or traveler on a heroic, possibly self-destructive, and mad journey to find the "reality" behind actuality.

But he also edges away from the Romantic tradition. Romantic evil and terror are likely to be thrilling or sublime; in de la Mare they are not. One finds rather a mindfulness of the perversities of the heart and the possible horror of life. The short dramatic monologue "Napoleon" is no Romantic idealization of aspiring, if flawed greatness, but rather a portrait of egoism:

> "What is the world, O soldiers?
> It is I:
> I, this incessant snow,
>   This northern sky;
> Soldiers, this solitude
>   Through which we go
>   Is I."

The poems of his middle years contain traces of satire. Even—perhaps especially—in the verse for children, if de la Mare seems a Mother Goose flying by twilight, one is reminded that Mother Goose includes some of the cruelest, most frightening poems in English.

De la Mare most shows himself a poet of the twentieth century precisely in his way of using the Romantic mode, which he handles with the self-conscious knowingness that may come at the end of a tradition. On the one hand, the themes and images of Romantic poetry are what he has to say and the means he has for saying it, both the vocabulary of his imagination and the world it shapes. On the other hand, to this cunning artist they were also a body of conventions and could be exploited with conviction because they were known for conventions. (One dare not say, *only* conventions, for at what point, de la Mare would ask, do conventions leave off and "realities" begin? Yeats wanted to believe in the fairies literally, but could not, despite heroic efforts. De la Mare, whose thoughts all ended in speculation, neither believed nor disbelieved, but used fairies and elves as expressive means.)

To put it another way, de la Mare is, in some ways, a Symbolist poet. His words do not summon substantial things, but, instead, memories and associations, from Romantic literature particularly. As in Symbolist poetry, they create their suggestion as much by sound and color as by sense. At the start of "Andy's Love Song," for example, subtle handling of sound, pace, placing, and emphasis unites with a memory of Coleridge's Ancient Mariner to stir some powerful, though cryptic emotion:

> Me who have sailèd
> Leagues across
> Foam haunted
> By the albatross.

Making the point still a third way, one might say his is an art that depends essentially on stock response. The term, popularized by I. A. Richards (himself an admirer of de la Mare), refers to a mental reaction that has become set or stereotyped and proceeds automatically as soon as the usual signal is given. Such routines of intellect and emotion originally were not fixed or stock but became so through repetition, which is one reason why poetic styles have to change. Since Richards' brilliant discussion, critics have usually deplored the sort of poetry that evokes stock responses, arguing that the stock response is out of touch with the complexity of reality. But this is prejudice. Stock responses should be thought of as resources of poetry, not criteria. A great poet knows how to use them without creating a merely stock poem.

Stock response and archetype are concepts that closely interpret our experience of much of de la Mare's poetry. "Nod" is an example:

> Softly along the road of evening,
>   In a twilight dim with rose,
> Wrinkled with age, and drenched with dew,
>   Old Nod, the shepherd, goes.
>
> His drowsy flock streams on before him,
>   Their fleeces charged with gold,
> To where the sun's last beam leans low
>   On Nod the shepherd's fold.
>
> The hedge is quick and green with brier,
>   From their sand the conies creep;
> And all the birds that fly in heaven
>   Flock singing home to sleep.
>
> His lambs outnumber a noon's roses,
>   Yet, when night's shadows fall,
> His blind old sheep-dog, Slumber-soon,
>   Misses not one of all.
>
> His are the quiet steeps of dreamland,
>   The waters of no-more-pain;

His ram's bell rings 'neath an arch of stars
"Rest, rest, and rest again."

The words, collected for lulling effects, present a dense cluster of m's, n's, l's, s's, and long, echoing vowels, and of sleepy suggestions, such as "softly," "dim," "evening," "shadow," "slumber," and "dreamland." The rhythm is appropriately steady, though slowed by end-stops, medial caesuras, spondees, and long vowels. The images—the road at evening, the journey home to the fold, the old shepherd, the blind old sheep dog—activate ideas of letting go in peace and of gentle, all enfolding protection. Every stanza except the last enacts the transition toward home, night, and sleep. In the last stanza there is no more motion, We are now in dreamland. The beautiful landscape of the poem, in which the sheep along the road are like a golden stream, has become the landscape of a dream, with quiet steeps and waters. Suddenly, in the last two lines, the scene shifts again, or the same scene is beheld as though from far away, framed by the "arch of stars." The poem ends with quiet insistence and finality on the three-times repeated "rest." Stock responses are exploited throughout to evoke and connect archetypal feelings about rest and security, returning home, going to sleep, and dying.

Just as de la Mare exploits the Romantic tradition with a self-consciousness more "modern" than Romantic, he also notes with a disturbing insistence the ambiguities and ironies that have always been part of the Romantic tradition. Many of his finest poems and stories—"The Song of the Mad Prince," "Maerchen," or "The Riddle"—produce not so much Romantic suggestion as suggestive indeterminacy (not vagueness). The famous "The Listeners" may be another poem of the quest motif in which the quester receives no answer, though there are "listeners." Yet this is only one possible view of a poem in which everything is suggestive, but nothing can be interpreted with confidence. And in most such poems there is the possibility that de la Mare is also having his joke; perhaps no "serious" meanings were intended. Just because they may mean much or nothing, these poems may present in miniature the whole human situation. Since we can know nothing for certain, a quiet, unemphatic, faintly humorous, reflective awareness of open possibilities is the only appropriate stance. The irony is a gentle type of what is often called Romantic irony, in which the sense of infinite possible points of view prevents the writer's full commitment to any one in particular. This should not be much emphasized, however, for it is in the background and seldom comes to the fore.

When de la Mare talked theoretically about poetry, he was likely to emphasize a connection between poetry and dream. The conscious mind must "supervise," but "it cannot of itself originate poetry." Poetry has its source in what he variously calls the imagination, the unconscious, and the world of dream; it is read by our "dream-self."

Every imaginative poem, as we allow it to use us, itself resembles in its onset and in its effect the experience of dreaming. . . . What order of listener lies in wait for incantations such as these? A dream-self, surely; as well as a waking self. Just as it was a dream-self that kept the poet company in the conception and in the actual composition of his poem.

Through his lore of dreams and the unconscious de la Mare restates the Romantic and Symbolist doctrine that the poetic imagination is in touch with realities deeper than reason or consciousness and that these realities are presented or evoked in symbols. In the reveries of the night, "we find ourselves straying into far less familiar regions than usual of the mind. An 'emanation far within,' of the 'fathomless and boundless deep,' may awake." But "every dream . . . is and must always remain the secret possession solely of the dreamer." As soon as he awakes, the dream is gone. What fragments survive are "difficult to translate into those obstinate and artificial symbols, words." The same thing is true of those moments when "waking consciousness" is submerged for an instant during the course of the day. The imagery retrieved from the unconscious in such experiences "may have an aptness and a hint of profound significance," but such moments also afford merely "isolated peephole glimpses." To the extent that the dream bits can be rendered, the meanings they suggest can never be pinned down. "Even the most fragmentary of dreams . . . may hint at a variety of meanings," and no "more or less plausible interpretation of a dream" can be "finally refuted." To sum up, the poem is at best a far, faint, and distorted echo of a dream experience, which may or may not have been of "profound significance." De la Mare did not of course suppose that poetry was all or only dream. Neither is there a close resemblance between dream and most of his poems. But his assumption that poetry owes its origin "to a graft of the waking mind on the wild and ancient stock of dream" had important results in his own creative work and helps us orient ourselves to it. If a poem might essentially be the undecipherable fragments of an enigma, of which nothing certain or final could be said—he would leave it at that. No wonder he sometimes explored a daring discontinuity or irrationality, being willing even to verge on acknowledged silliness or nonsense.

The finest poem of this kind, "The Song of the Mad Prince," exploits at least two separate conventions of irrational speech. On the one hand, it pretends to be a poem for children. (It appeared in his second volume of poems for children, *Peacock Pie*, 1913, to which it supplied the title.) One could not call the poem a verbal game, but it has features which bring this type of verse to mind. Six of the sixteen short lines start with the question, "Who said," creating an atmosphere of quizzing challenge. The poem begins,

> Who said, "Peacock Pie"?
> The old King to the sparrow:
> Who said, "Crops are ripe"?
> Rust to the harrow.

That rust tells the harrow crops are ripe may be logical enough. But who is the old King? Why did he say a crazy thing like "Peacock Pie"? Why did he say it to the sparrow? And what have the old King and the sparrow to do with harrow and crops? The parts cannot be fitted together logically, but there are enough hints of logical or intelligibly associative connection to keep one from taking the poem as mere nonsense. The structure of the poem is simple, definite, and shapely, giving pleasure in itself and also implying purposeful utterance; the parallel questions and answers irresistibly suggest a corresponding logical parallelism, which, however, does not exist. In these aspects the poem resembles a teaser or puzzle. It tempts us to try to piece the images together and find their logical relation, maybe even the story they tell, but at the same time, it makes it impossible to do this. To the extent that it is like a game, the poem is playful, but the playfulness is indescribably wistful and pathetic. The effect arises from counterpointing a form for the amusement of children with feelings of loss and grief.

The other convention of irrational discourse invoked in the poem is that of madness, as one finds it portrayed in Elizabethan drama and a few lyrics since (for example, Blake's "Mad Song"). The poem partly suggests the stream of disconnected, irrelevant, uncanny fragments, interspersed with deepest wisdom, that make up mad speech in this convention. If the Mad Prince is Hamlet, as I. A. Richards suggests, he may be mad only north-northwest; but whether or not, the convention assumes that madness attains truths inaccessible to reason. Thus, at the end of the poem the Prince voices an insight or conviction the sane mind could never know. The poem combines nonsense and riddle with the reflective voice of a Prospero. It is deeply moving, complex, and poised.

> Who said, "Peacock Pie"?
>   The old King to the sparrow:
> Who said, "Crops are ripe"?
>   Rust to the harrow:
> Who said, "Where sleeps she now?
>   Where rests she now her head,
> Bathed in eve's loveliness"?—
>   That's what I said.
>
> Who said, "Ay, mum's the word";
>   Sexton to willow:
> Who said, "Green dusk for dreams,
>   Moss for a pillow"?
> Who said, "All Time's delight
>   Hath she for narrow bed;
> Life's troubled bubble broken"?—
>   That's what I said.

De la Mare's first volume, *Songs of Childhood*, contained some poems that became anthology pieces, such as "Bunches of Grapes," "John Mouldy," "The Lamplighter," and "I met at eve the Prince of Sleep." This collection of children's poems was followed by lyrics for adults, *Poems* (1906), though in de la Mare the distinction between poems for children and for adults is not always possible to make. In these publications he is already a master of rhythm and versification. He controls mood through pace, pause, slight metrical variation, and echoing or partially echoing vowels and consonants:

> I met at eve the Prince of Sleep,
> His was a still and lovely face,
> He wandered through a valley steep,
> Lovely in a lonely place.

The immense stride forward that is taken in the next following volumes, *The Listeners* (1912) and *Peacock Pie* (1913), is primarily due to an intensified imaginative concreteness. Where previously there had been relatively abstract conceptions, one now finds character, plot, particularity. One need only compare "Age" in the *Poems* of 1906 with "Alone" in *The Listeners*, or "I met at eve the Prince of Sleep" with "Nod." With more particular characters and incidents to serve as focal centers, images draw together more thickly and the atmosphere concentrates into richer and stranger essences. Among the many famous poems in *The Listeners* are "Old Susan," "Miss Loo," "The Tailor," "All That's Past," "Never More, Sailor," "The Listeners," and "An Epitaph." Aside from its other merits, *Peacock Pie* is the finest volume of verse for children written in this century.

In succeeding volumes from *Motley* (1918) to *Memory* (1938), de la Mare widened his themes and stylistic resources and participated at a distance in some of the poetic tendencies of those years. Such poems as "The Marionettes," "The Wreck," "Drugged," and "The Fat Woman," show an interest in harsher, more realistic themes. He also pruned his dreamy, evocative diction and imagery, becoming somewhat more colloquial and worldly, and there may be fewer of his favorite words—strange, heart, haunt, alone, star, silent, dream, transient, tranquil, beauty, lovely, and so on. He tends more to proceed by the juxtaposition of images alone, or is, in poems of abstract reflection, more concise, even aphoristic. But the versification is still traditional, though with much variation; euphony is everywhere; and the poems especially evoke mood or atmosphere. Although de la Mare gradually modifies his way of writing, it does not change essentially. In these middle years there are perhaps no finer poems than some he had written earlier, but the level of accomplishment remains very high. Any selected edition would be filled largely by the poems published in this period. At the same time, there is a growing tendency to abstract reflectiveness, and imaginative impact is occasionally weakened.

This tendency reached a surprising and impressive culmination in two long poems of his old age, *The Traveller* (1946) and *Winged Chariot* (1951). *The Traveller* is not discursive in form, for it is a last narrative handling of the quest motif, but it is de la Mare's most ambitious attempt to say what could be said about what he considered the ultimate questions. The diction and rhythm are in the Spenserian-Keatsian tradition, but the final vision, in which the traveler beholds, or may behold ("It seemed to him"), the "source of all," preserves a chilling sense of the infinitely remote and alien character of this source. *Winged Chariot*, published when de la Mare was seventy-eight, takes its title from Marvell's

> But at my back I always hear
> Time's winged chariot hurrying near.

Altogether different from *The Traveller*, it is a long, meditative poem touching on such topics as imagination, actuality as opposed to reality, childhood, dread, and, above all, the mystery of time. There are passages of abstract discourse, descriptions, reminiscences, interpolated stories, and quotations from other writers. The iambic pentameter verse is cast into stanzas of three to five or even more lines, all having the same rhyme. In no poem of de la Mare's are the stylistic effects more brilliantly varied. Partly because of the stanzaic form, the poem has a discontinuous, epigrammatic quality that reminds one of FitzGerald's *Rubaiyat of Omar Khayyam* (though it is more continuous than the *Rubaiyat*). It sounds like this:

> Yet, when, a child, I was content to rove
> The shingled beach that I was Crusoe of,
> All that I learned there was akin to love.
>
> The glass-clear billow toppling on the sand,
> Sweet, salt-tanged air, birds, rock-drift, eyes, ear, hand:
> All was a language love could understand.

Or it sounds like this:

> Three score and ten . . . Like leaves our lives unfold;
> Hid in the telling moves the tale untold.
> It is not wishing makes the heart grow cold.

The meditation follows no logical path and seeks no conclusions; it feels over, highlights, and moves to something else. It is a poem to be read in the rather relaxed, speculative frame of mind that it expresses.

It can be argued that de la Mare, like all the poets who belonged essentially to the school of Beauty, was limited by the idea of poetry he accepted. Certainly he does not take firm hold of contemporary life, least of all in its grimmer settings and shabbier states of mind. Neither does he try for vivid drama, conflict, or even the highest intensity of feeling or thought, for such things, if admitted, would crowd out the contemplative feeling for mystery, and this was his deepest feeling as a poet. (Some of these are present in his short stories, however. The fact suggests that his use of poetry was also guided by general assumptions about the nature and purpose of the art.) "Geron-tion," for example, with its intellectuality, self-disgust, and sordid hopelessness, was altogether outside his range. Even de la Mare's best poems are in a sense slight, but they are far from being merely conventional or traditional. They will survive not only because of their stylistic mastery, charm, and speculative openness, but because a very personal imagination expresses itself in them.

A SELECTION OF MINOR POETS

Robert Trevelyan, Maurice Hewlett, Maurice Baring, Hilaire Belloc, "Laurence Hope," James Elroy Flecker, Lascelles Abercrombie, and Gordon Bottomley once enjoyed either the respect of critics or large sales. They deserve more attention than can be given here, where they are mentioned only to illustrate the variety of modes or styles that the Edwardians inherited from the recent past and continued to exploit. Except that they were all "traditional" poets (though not necessarily in the same tradition), they have little in common.

Robert C. Trevelyan (1872–1951) received very little recognition in his life and is now mostly forgotten. He came from a distinguished family, being a grandnephew of Macaulay and a brother of the historian G. M. Trevelyan. He wrote poetic dramas, blank-verse narratives, and lyrics, and was a prolific and accomplished translator, chiefly from Greek and Latin. His poetry is quiet, sensitive, thoughtful, and rather sad. He was strongly influenced by his study of the classics, and is said to have learned from the prosodic experiments of Bridges and the Chinese translations of Arthur Waley. His writing is direct, unadorned, and restrained, without, however, sufficient intellectual force to lift the bareness into intensity. Emotion is stated and slightly enacted in the rhythm, but not otherwise made real. There is hardly a memorable phrase. Nevertheless, one cannot see why he made so little stir and reputation, since he is certainly better than William Watson or Stephen Phillips, to mention only two once-famous names. Like any significant communication from a likable, intelligent person, his poetry can be read with interest and pleasure.

Maurice Hewlett (1861–1923) was one of many poets who wrote what Douglas Bush neatly pinpoints as "well-bred, flowing verse with a due measure of archaism." Another was Maurice Baring (1874–1945). Hewlett had a prolific career as an essayist and novelist as well as poet. His strongest gift was his historical imagination, through which he could sometimes create the sense of mystery and the shock of violence. His best poem is *The Song of the Plough* (1916), an epic in six thousand lines of the English rustic through history. Baring was a scion of the banker family, a diplomat, and a writer in several genres who brought forth almost fifty books. The best of these are novels dealing with upper-class life. He had a more original vein and more mind than most poets, but these appear in his prose fiction. In poetry his depth of feeling and keenness of insight could not lift their heads above his conventional modes of expression. His best poem is "In Memoriam, A. H.," an elegiac tribute in a loose and flowing form, rather impressive in its versified, generalizing eloquence.

Hilaire Belloc (1870–1953) was a man of general letters who included poetry in his prolific authorship, though for the most part he wrote history, travel books, and essays. (He produced over one hundred and fifty books, for he lived by his pen.) In the wars of ideas he was so close an ally of Chesterton's that the two were sometimes known as Chesterbelloc. But he was a very different poet. His taste in reading ran to the Greek and Latin classics, to French literature, and to the Augustan period in England, that is, to the classic or neoclassic mode. His verse, which makes up one small volume, is carefully worked in traditional forms, terse, and intelligent. In poems such as "The South Country" or "West Sussex Drinking Song" he joins the Edwardian celebration of England, its landscape and customs. Others are religious (he was a Roman Catholic). In still others, he lets loose his talent for comic and satiric verse, and everyone knows the rollicking invective that begins,

> Remote and ineffectual Don
> That dared attack my Chesterton,

and the epigram that goes,

> When I am dead, I hope it may be said:
> "His sins were scarlet, but his books were read."

He also wrote books of comic poetry for children, such as *The Bad Child's Book of Beasts* (1896) and *More Beasts (for Worse Children)* (1897). Some of these remotely anticipate the sick humor of the 1960s. One, for example, tells how George's balloon exploded and killed eight people, not to mention other damages;

> While George, who was in part to blame,
> Received, you will regret to hear,
> A nasty lump behind the ear.

MORAL

> The moral is that little Boys
> Should not be given dangerous Toys.

These books were delightfully illustrated and make pleasant browsing.

"Laurence Hope" was the pen-name of Mrs. Adela Nicolson (1865–1904). In view of her date, she might have been discussed in an earlier chapter, but because her books were published after the turn of the century, they are noticed here. Hers are lyrics of intense erotic passion, set in India and supposedly spoken by Indian characters. One hears much of peacocks, temples, monkeys, sword fights, palm trees, and especially of slaves, for the females are usually either literally or figuratively slaves to the males, whom they await with pale yearning. There is also much philosophizing: except for its few, red moments of passion, life is all sandy desert. The atmosphere—exotic, oppressive, and sadistic—recalls the Decadence, while the setting and popular style remind one of Kipling, so that Mrs. Nicolson might be described as a decadent, female Kipling. Her books had many readers—perhaps the same audience that was later to pine at Rudolph Valentino in *The Sheik*. They were sometimes read with an almost pornographic interest. Her best-known lyric is "Kashmiri Song"—"Pale hands I loved beside the Shalimar."

Besides his play, *Hassan* (1922) James Elroy Flecker (1884–1915) wrote a few memorable poems, such as "The Old Ships" or the proto-Imagist "A Ship, an Isle, a Sickle Moon." His undergraduate poetry is said to have followed the Decadent fashion. He was, however, one of those facile writers who never achieve an individual identity. In search of it he borrowed from different models, especially Tennyson, and he exploited the Near East for poetic trappings and atmosphere. He also attempted to form an identity with the aid of ideology. His mature views on poetry, though they are not less borrowed than the poetry itself, amount to a more coherent response to the literary situation. They are put forward especially in the Preface to *The Golden Journey to Samarkand* (1913). The Romantic poetry of the nineteenth century (including Tennyson and Browning) was, he says, too often windy, didactic, egoistic, and formless. As a corrective he prescribes the Parnassian poetry of France:

The French Parnassian has a tendency to use traditional forms and even to employ classical subjects. His desire in writing poetry is to create beauty: his inclination is toward a beauty somewhat statuesque. He is apt to be dramatic and objective rather than intimate.

And the French Parnassian is, Flecker says, a conscious and careful artist. His own poetry sometimes exemplifies this doctrine. He was a somewhat belated, halfhearted disciple of *l'art-pour-l'art,* and his career illustrates the affinities between that movement and both the poetry of Bridges and Moore and also of Pound and the Imagists.

Lascelles Abercrombie (1881–1938) had considerable reputation as a critic. His idea of poetry was formed in partial opposition to the Pre-Raphaelites, Aesthetes, and the more insipid among his contemporaries. He revived the Romantic premise, articulated in England especially by Hazlitt, that the governing purpose of poetry is expression—not self-expression, but the presentation of significant human experience, through which poetry allows us to "possess the world." He argues that anything, beautiful or not, can be the subject of poetry, and that if poetry ignores the painful and evil in life, it becomes trivial. But, while protesting strongly against the tendency of post-Romantic poetry to take "beauty" as its object and justification, he was not ready to surrender the main premise of this point of view. Poetry, he said, embodies the poet's intuition of the ultimate truth or meaning of the cosmos. To "possess the world" is not only to take it up into the imagination with concrete vividness but also to behold even the "evil of things" as a necessary element in the "final harmony." His own work swung between passages of "expression" and passages of "meaning"—or, rather, meanings, for he was more intent on exploring different ideas and points of view than in reconciling them. He wrote a few lyrics and several poetic dramas, but most of his poems were long, quasi-dramatic dialogues, interspersed in some cases with narrative. So described, the form was not essentially different from the Book of Job, or, to descend into the modern world, Frost's "The Death of the Hired Man," and Abercrombie was justified in claiming that it need be no "bastard sort of composition." Yet, as he handled it, that is what it became. A usual criticism of his work was that the dramatic and narrative effects were overweighted and slowed by the exposition of ideas, and this certainly happens. (In "Blind," for example, even the half-witted son makes long, reflective speeches.) But the reverse also took place. The characters and actions he imagined were often too sketchily presented to be interesting in themselves, but, nevertheless, compelled Abercrombie to divert his stream of thoughts. *Emblems of Love* (1912) is a series of dramatic poems tracing the origin, progress, and diverse varieties of love. It is a reflective, quasi-philosophical work for whoever may be interested in the play of ideas. The first poem in the series shows two persons, Brys and Gast, standing guard in the primitive forest against wolves. They discuss love, but the situation forced Abercrombie to discuss wolves as well, though of wolves he could make nothing to his purpose. To sum up, in his poems the reflective and dramatic elements tend to dilute each other reciprocally, and, despite his undeniable intelligence, imagination, and high intention, the poems remain inert and wordy.

Of the poems of Gordon Bottomley (1874–1948) at least one, "The End of the World," ought to be—but is not—in every modern anthology. The greater part of his production was verse drama, and he was much concerned, as were Moore and Yeats, with the theoretical justification of this form as opposed to the use of prose for dramatic writing. Poetic drama, he argued, shapes a vision more exalted, elemental, concentrated, and powerful than can be achieved in the realism or naturalism from which the prose theater can never completely disengage itself. Under the impact of Rossetti he learned to "look for the essentials of life, the part that does not change . . . art is a distillation of life and nature—not a recording or a commenting, and only incidentally an interpretation." The position had close affinities with that of poets who conceived that the purpose of their art was beauty. Bottomley went on to say that the arts "are the language" of an "immortal state" which is temporarily ours as we read. As for poetic drama specifically, its purpose is "not so much a representation of a theme as a meditation upon it or a distillation from it . . . the evocation and isolation for our delight of the elements of beauty and spiritual illumination in the perhaps terrible and always serious theme chosen."

Bottomley's earlier plays continued the Shakespearean and Jacobean conventions traditional in verse drama, though his plays were much briefer than their prototypes and he sought not so much imaginative complexity as intensity through simplification. In later years he came, like Yeats, to realize that if poetic drama were to remain viable in the modern world, new conventions had to be developed. (A Stage for Poetry, 1948, gives his suggestions.) His shorter poems were distinguished by adult intelligence and independent sensibility. A few were irregular odal hymns on topics usually reserved for aesthetics ("A Hymn of Imagination," "A Hymn of Form"). These were weighted with felt meaning and achieved an odd, difficult, and powerful grandeur. A completely different kind of verse appeared in the many dedications to plays and other occasional pieces. Here decorum required a relaxed and colloquial style, and these verses had a talky charm; they were in the vein of poetic talk that Yeats developed during the Edwardian period. In quiet, factual lines "The End of the World" describes snow falling unceasingly on and about a farmhouse. Despite some fumbling at the start, the poem gradually builds up, through careful selection of seemingly casual detail, a powerful illusion of reality and a feeling of the archetypal horror of the situation.

Even though he published no volumes of poetry in the Edwardian period, John Cowper Powys (1872–1963) may also be mentioned with the Edwardian poets. He has closer affinities with Abercrombie or Bottomley than with poets of earlier or later decades. He composed six volumes of poetry between 1896 and 1922, although one of these, *Lucifer,* was not published until 1956. His work as a poet thus antedates his more important achievements as a novelist and autobiographer. His verse is of a distinguished, minor kind. It is firmly articulated, intelligent, and genuinely felt, but its form and phrasing lack freshness.

A. E. HOUSMAN

Housman (1859–1936) published his first book of poems, *A Shropshire Lad,* in 1896. He is often numbered among the poets of the fin de siècle. Although I discuss him with Edwardian craftsmen of the beautiful and agreeable, I do not think his poetry has strong affinities with either that of the Aesthetes of the nineties or that of the Edwardians. He must be taken up at this point, however, because his work influenced the Georgian poets, who are discussed in the next chapter. *A Shropshire Lad* originally was published in five hundred copies at Housman's own expense. A second edition appeared in 1898, and sold steadily. In 1915 Sir Walter Raleigh included some lyrics from *A Shropshire Lad* in an anthology of poems for soldiers (but purchased of course by civilians). With this event Housman's rise to fame accelerated. It was not just that he appealed to a mood of the hour. Thanks to the new hunger for poetry in the middle class at the start of the war, he reached a large, unspecialized public, whose appreciation was immediate. An edition of *A Shropshire Lad* in 1918 sold five thousand copies, and when his second volume, *Last Poems,* appeared in 1922, the year of *The Waste Land,* it sold twenty-one thousand copies in three months. His poetry tells much about middle-class taste in the Georgian period and since, for *A Shropshire Lad* has remained one of the familiar favorites and gift-books, its place in the public heart unshaken despite fifty years of highbrow demolition.

Housman entered St. John's College, Oxford, as a promising scholar. His Christian faith, shaken after the death of his mother on his twelfth birthday, was soon completely abandoned. In 1881 he failed his final examinations at the university, the reason being that he had not prepared subjects he knew would be tested. Why he acted in this self-destructive way cannot be known. Several biographers find indications of a severe emotional crisis arising out of his feeling for a friend, M. J. Jackson, in his last year at college; the crisis may have been one that caused him to turn violently against himself and from which he never really recovered. Certainly there was something self-thwarting about his life from now on, despite the fame he eventually achieved. He worked for a few years in the Government Patent Office. But he also published scholarly articles, and on the strength of these he was appointed Professor of Latin at the University of London, and, later, at Cambridge (1911). Despite his intense love of poetry, most of his mature poems—including those later published in *Last Poems* and posthumously in *More Poems* (1936), as well as those in *A Shropshire Lad*—were written at intervals during a ten-year period, 1895–1905, when, Housman said, composition almost forced itself upon him. Otherwise this highly emotional professor spent his life in writing lectures, articles, and notoriously savage reviews, and in the dryest kind of editorial scholarship. He preferred Greek to Latin, but concentrated on the latter because he "could not attain to eminence in both." Among the Latin poets he loved Propertius, whom he could easily have made the object of his editorial labor, but he chose Manilius, a poetic expounder of astronomical lore whom Housman himself thought tedious and third-rate. He lived as a recluse, shrinking from any approach to intimacy. His edition of Manilius was completed in 1930.

The popularity of *A Shropshire Lad* has been so wide and lasting that a history of modern poetry must try to account for it. One source of appeal is the local and country setting, rendered with affection and nostalgia. Housman's Shropshire has cherry trees, rose-lipped maidens, morning mist on the river, blue hills, market fairs, daffodil-picking, football, and beer. The imagery has its sources both in observed scenes and also in literature; it is familiar and general, and serves less as description than as a system of stimuli through which readers imaginatively enter a sweeter, simpler land of forceful and artless feelings, authentic human relationships, unspoiled natural beauty, and traditional and unchanging ways of life. With this England, whether it ever existed or not, the Georgians had a love affair. Americans responded to it no less nostalgically, for it answered to their stock notions, formed out of the sparkling, rivery landscapes, thatched cottages, and hedgerows that used to be pictured in grammar school reading-books. Had *A Shropshire Lad* been called *A Liverpool Lad,* with setting and actions to match, it might have remained unknown.

Housman's themes are familiar in popular ballads from the Middle Ages to the present day. J. B. Priestley says that in Edwardian music halls much of the entertainment centered upon "those time-old themes that labouring men and soldiers like to sing about when they are half-drunk—lost wonderful mothers, the death of pure young girls, faithless sweethearts, and 'the Boys of the Old Brigade.'" These are, on the whole, what Housman wrote about also, except that, like many poets in the Wordsworthian tradition, he substituted landscape for the maternal figure. As is traditional in ballads, his brief narratives leave a great deal to the imagination. Sometimes they leave almost everything to the imagination, as in "When I was one and twenty," which tells only that a story could be told were the speaker not so reticent. (Yet one knows well enough what sort of story it would be; the sense that we have all gone through it is part of the appeal.) He can indicate both the stories and the themes rapidly and generally because of a heavy reliance on stock responses, though in saying this, one hastens to disown the unthinking prejudice of much criticism against such effects. Examples of his use of the stock or ready-to-hand include, besides the "plots" themselves, such gestures as,

> Leave your home behind, lad,
>   And reach your friends your hand,

and there are images of "golden friends," "calling bugles," wan looks of lovers, and white roads in moonlight. The reaction evoked is one that was to some extent conditioned or built-in before we came to the poem.

His diction and versification are simple and artful, and appeal in both respects. We find the plainest words, often monosyllables, in natural spoken order:

> The time you won your town the race
> We chaired you through the market place.

In the same poem ("To an Athlete Dying Young"), we also finds rhetorical figures—

> Runners whom renown outran
> And the name died before the man—

and stock classicism:

> And round that early-laurelled head
> Will flock to gaze the strengthless dead.

A merely plain diction might have become insipid, as it often does in Georgian poetry, and a continually artificial one might have seemed to divest the emotion of reality; in interplay with a straightforward, direct style, Housman's artifices afford intellectual pleasure, surprise, and elegance. His meters and stanzas are easily recognized and regular, and, in combination with other effects, the strictness of the form suggests that strong emotion is being firmly controlled.

Many a poet might have exhibited similar qualities and virtues without achieving or meriting Housman's fame. More important is his combination of clarity with intensity. Of clarity in the fullest sense, Housman is not always an example, for in individual phrases there is vagueness and loss of focus. But there is no difficulty or obscurity, and the "plot" of his lyrics is always communicated. Intensity is promoted by suggestive brevity (including the suggestion of the speaker's self-disciplined reticence, which leads him to understate his emotion). There are also sudden contrasts ("lovely lads and dead and rotten"), and a constant, blunt vigor with shapeliness, which rises occasionally into aphorism ("Malt does more than Milton can / To justify God's ways to man"). Housman's irony, moreover, is a way of clarifying rather than qualifying a feeling or a meaning; however much they may vary from poem to poem, the feeling and meaning in each poem are simple and emphatic.

A special source of intensity in Housman lies in his effects of finality. We may notice, for example, the brief lyric that goes,

> Now hollow fires burn out to black,
>   And lights are guttering low:
> Square your shoulders, lift your pack,
>   And leave your friends and go.
>
> Oh never fear, man, nought's to dread,
>   Look not left nor right;
> In all the endless road you tread
>   There's nothing but the night.

Much of the power of this comes from the absence of qualification. If it were an utterance of reflective thought rather than emotion, positiveness on such a point would do little credit to the intelligence. (There is a story that Housman's friend Dr. Withers tried once to draw him out on metaphysical questions, and received for reply the angry snort, "That is a subject I will not discuss.") The sense of finality is effectively reinforced by the emphatic, regular rhythm, the end-stopped lines, the short, closed stanzas, the declarative mode, the symmetrical construction, and the clichés.

I have not dwelt on Housman's bleak and sometimes savage "pessimism." This is important in the total effect of Housman's poetry but it is not clear that it contributes to his popularity. Hardy's "pessimism" has, if anything, hindered his reception, and the poets one usually thinks of as "popular," such as James Whitcomb Riley, are determined dispensers of cheer. On the other hand, there is FitzGerald's *Rubaiyat*. Perhaps in winning a large audience such qualities as accessibility, vigorous emphasis, and lack of qualification or complexity in meanings and feelings are more important than the content or attitude expressed. But it may be pointed out that, although the events and emotions of Housman's world are of the painful kind, the fact that they are not strongly individualized or particularized keeps them at a distance, where they can be reflectively contemplated without necessarily being strongly shared. Actually to feel that "high heaven and earth ail from their prime foundation" affords nothing but horror; to read it in a brief lyric does not. What, perhaps, we are enjoying in such poetry is, along with everything else, the pleasure of self-pity.

Finally, the reaction to Housman's verse is influenced by the knowledge that he was a scholar of Latin. Little in his poems is necessarily classical in inspiration, but much can be thought of as classical if we have the idea in our heads—for example, the restraint, studied control, marmoreal phrasing, and generality. To this may be added the conspicuous absence of Christian feeling and the presence of stoicism. There are frequent references to soldiers and warfare, and the opening poem of *A Shropshire Lad* speaks of the far-flung empire. *A Shropshire Lad* taps the identification of England with imperial Rome that had been a persistent subtheme in English culture since at least the end of the seventeenth century. It did so at a time when imperialism was approaching its climax in popular sentiment and political triumph. In its own way *A Shropshire Lad* takes part in the patriotic celebration of England and Empire that was common in Edwardian poetry.

10

THE GEORGIAN POETS

W E OWE the term "Georgian" to Edward Marsh, who, between 1912 and 1922, edited five anthologies of contemporary verse, calling them *Georgian Poetry*. As now used, the term may refer to the poets published in these anthologies, to the poets of the decade in general, to a particular group among them, or, by loose extension, to poets active roughly from 1900 to 1922. Unfortunately, the label is not only indefinite; it is often used pejoratively. The main reason for this lies in the prestige Marsh's anthologies once enjoyed. They were taken as accurately representing contemporary poetry in England. When in their last five years they published verse of poorer quality, they received some justifiably harsh reviews. Usually the reviewers were careful to point out that their charges applied only to some of the anthologized poets. As time passed, however, and the literary history of the modern age was written more and more from a Modernist point of view, the charges once specified against such poets as Drinkwater, Squire, Shanks, Freeman, and Turner, were splashed over the Georgian anthologies as a whole, and, sometimes, over pre-Modernist poetry in general. The conventional statement among critical sheep thus came to be: the Modernists had displaced a school of Georgian poets; these poets had been unoriginal and slack in technique, shallow in feeling, slight in intellect; their poetry specialized in insipid appreciativeness, false simplicity, and weekend escapism.

These things can be found in Georgian verse—whatever we mean by the term—for they are a weak side of much verse in the Romantic tradition, from William Lisle Bowles and Samuel Rogers to the present day. But Edward Thomas and Wilfred Owen are also to be reckoned among the Georgian poets, not to mention Robert Frost, who, though an American, represents the mode—so far as there was a typical mode—at its finest. In other words, Georgian poetry can also be sinewy and subtle. That some of the Modernists, notably T. S. Eliot and Edith Sitwell, felt a need to attack rival kinds of poetry wholesale is understandable. They were out to shame and frighten readers who might otherwise have sympathized with Georgian perspicuity and enjoyment of life. Moreover, they were not kicking helpless victims, but jostling their way into a hostile literary crowd, where they received as much abuse as they gave. But the thorough blackening of the Georgian name was the work of critics writing at a time when Modernism was becoming an academic orthodoxy and Georgian poetry was temporarily dead. (A version of it revived in the fifties.) They were kicking a corpse. If only because it has figured prominently in literary history, the term "Georgian" cannot now be dropped. But it may be used without disparaging implications. It here indicates the non-Modernist English poets who became known just before, during, and after the First World War or who did their best work during this period—Rupert Brooke, Wilfrid Gibson, W. H. Davies, Ralph Hodgson, Edward Thomas, Edmund Blunden, W. J. Turner, John Freeman, J. C. Squire, Edmund Shanks, and also, as war poets, Robert Nichols, Siegfried Sassoon, Isaac Rosenberg, and Wilfred Owen.

Edward (later Sir Edward) Marsh's Georgian anthology was one of the most remarkable publishing ventures in the history of modern poetry. Marsh was a prominent Civil Servant and socialite and a friend of Rupert Brooke and other poets. He and Brooke had the idea that an anthology of recent verse might help win attention for younger poets, especially Brooke. As Marsh pointed out in the Prefatory Note to his first anthology, "few readers have the leisure or the zeal to investigate each volume [of new poetry] as it appears; and the process of recognition is often slow." Marsh was an enthusiast for some contemporary poets, notably Brooke and Masefield, and sincerely believed that "English poetry is now once again putting on a new strength and beauty." Accordingly, he put together a collection of poems, "drawn entirely from the publications of the past two years," and named it after the new king, George V, whose reign had begun in 1910. *Georgian Poetry, 1911–1912* was published by Harold Monro from the Poetry Bookshop in 1912. With the title Marsh meant to suggest "that we are at the beginning of another 'Georgian period' which may take rank in due time with the several great poetic ages of the past." The anthology was the first important example of its kind in the modern period, the first, that is, to collect very recent verse for the sake of directing attention to the poets included.

The plan was quickly imitated, and every year now sees the publication of a book of contemporary poets who, finding it difficult to make an impression individually, group themselves in an anthology and describe themselves as a phase in literary history. But no later anthology has come near the success of *Georgian Poetry, 1911–1912*, which critics respected for a while and which continued to sell well for many years. A number of factors entered into its success. The general public was taking a greater interest in poetry and continued to do so throughout the First World War. Marsh's taste was only slightly in advance of the general public; he favored the bold, but rejected the shocking, and his anthology had no space for obscurity or free verse. In an age of brilliant literary generalship—one thinks of Yeats, Pound, and Amy Lowell—Marsh proved energetic and resourceful. Using both social and literary contacts to place or influence reviews, he organized the favorable reception of his poets. The anthology was fairly representative of British verse at the time. It included such veterans as Chesterton, de la Mare, Moore, and Masefield and newer poets such as Brooke, Gibson, and Lawrence, and it belonged to no clique or party. And, finally, it partially justified its praise of contemporary poetry by offering some memorable poems, of which the best were Bottomley's "The End of the World," Brooke's "The Old Vicarage, Grantchester," and de la Mare's "The Listeners."

The success of the anthology led to subsequent ones, until five books of Georgian Poetry appeared, covering respectively the years 1911–1912, 1913–1915, 1916–1917, 1918–1919, and 1920–1922. The first two were similar in character and quality. They show a tendency toward realism, at least toward a certain harshness and violence, in the work of Abercrombie, Gibson, Lawrence, and Bottomley. Poems of Brooke, Davies, and Masefield offered much physical high spirits and relishing notice of English countryside. When the second anthology was put together, the war had begun, but it made no appearance in the anthology except for two of Brooke's patriotic sonnets. The anthology for 1916–1917 continued to fulfill its purpose and justify its fame. Of the eighteen poets included, half appeared for the first time and were represented generously. In retrospect they divide into two groups: those writing of the war out of direct experience—Siegfried Sassoon, Isaac Rosenberg, Robert Nichols, and Robert Graves—and those who especially fell into the insipid, slack, and escapist verse for which "Georgian" subsequently became a byword—J. C. Squire and John Freeman.

The savagery of the Modernist criticism of the Georgians can only be understood if we keep in mind that the Georgians were widely assumed to be the important new poets of the age. Moreover, they controlled some positions of editorial influence. They could sometimes sink to an extraordinary depth. John Drinkwater (1882–1937), for example, was at one time respected for his plays, especially *Abraham Lincoln* (1918), and his poems were included in the Georgian anthologies. They are verses of reflection, love, country life, and nature, and frankly seek to highlight the amiable aspect of things. In one poem he prayed to be "immoderately wise," but at best his verse is moderate in all things, including interest. He could be silly without knowing it—

> I do not think that skies and meadows are
> Moral—

for he lacked self-critical intelligence. But he did not lack this so completely as John Freeman, who reached the extreme of insipidity:

> It was the lovely moon that lovelike
> Hovered over the wandering, tired
> Earth, her bosom gray and dovelike,
> Hovering beautiful as a dove.

These lines were included in the third Georgian anthology.

In the two final anthologies Marsh's taste was even less catholic and bold. The new poets introduced for 1918–1919 were nonentities—Thomas Moult, J. D. C. Pellow, and Edward Shanks—and the new poets of 1920–1922 were, except for Edmund Blunden, almost as undistinguished. Meanwhile, reaction grew. T. S. Eliot (in *The Egoist* of March 1918) had already attacked the anthology for 1916–1917 (though praising, of all poets, Squire): "Georgian poetry . . . is inbred. It has developed a technique and a set of emotions all of its own." The humor of James Stephens' "A Visit" is "unintelligible to any one who has not substituted Georgian emotions for human ones. . . . What nearly all the writers have in common is the quality of pleasantness . . . the Georgians caress everything they touch . . . Mr. Graves has a hale and hearty daintiness. . . . Messrs. Baring and Asquith, in war poems, both employ the word 'oriflamme.' Mr. Drinkwater says, 'Hist!'" But only with the two final anthologies did many critics become hostile. The bloodiest havoc was wrought by Middleton Murry in the *Athenaeum* for December 5, 1919, and he specifically reserved eight poets from his damnation. The others—Monro, Drinkwater, Squire, Shanks, Turner, and Freeman—are characterized by "false simplicity." There is "nothing disturbing" about their poetry. They worship "trees and birds and contemporary poets . . . If they have an idea it leaves you with the queer feeling that it is not an idea at all, that it has been defaced, worn smooth by the rippling of innumerable minds. . . . They are fond of lists of names which never suggest things." After 1922 no more Georgian anthologies were published, though they continued to be attacked.

RUPERT BROOKE

The most popular of the Georgian poets was Rupert Brooke (1887–1915), who was also the most representative; at least he wrote the poems routinely cited as typically "Georgian." With his death in 1915 he became a half-legendary figure. A promising poet, a high-minded and brave soldier, handsome and vital, he

symbolized to his contemporaries the brilliant youth of England
sacrificed in the war.

There is some irony that, of all his generation, Brooke should
have emerged as the national hero of the middle class. He was
not the son every English mother might have wished. Provocation was a leitmotiv of his career. In his teens at Rugby he struck
the aesthetic-decadent pose, and kept it up until he went on to
Cambridge and found it was out of fashion. Fabian socialism was
popular among the sophisticated, and he eventually became
president of the Cambridge Fabian Society. (About this time he
told his mother that "the chief end of life was Pleasure," and she
burst into tears.) What literary aestheticism and Fabian socialism
had in common was, obviously, rebellion. With either pose he
flouted the Victorian and middle-class (and maternal) army of
unalterable law. His first volume of *Poems* (1911) was chided by
reviewers for the sordid realism—more exactly, the emphasis on
what was considered the disgusting—of a few of its items (for
example, "Wagner," or "A Channel Passage," which dwells on
seasickness and vomiting), and the "realistic" point of view was
exhibited also in a few poems that followed Browning in exploring the more unpleasant passions ("Jealousy"). Other poems
in the volume showed he had been studying the "metaphysical"
lyrics of the seventeenth century. At the start of "Dust," for example, he emulates the shock effects of Donne, seeing beauty
and love in one view with the physical horror of death:

> When your swift hair is quiet in death,
>   And through the lips corruption thrust
> Has stilled the labour of my breath . . .

His purpose was to leave the downy nest of false prettiness
and triviality in which, he felt, poetry was dozing and to move
toward reality and significance. He insisted, against the wishes of
his publisher, that the poem "Lust" be included in the volume
(though he was willing to dress its theme in the fig leaf title of a
dead language; it was finally called "Libido"): "to remove it
would be to overbalance the book still more in the direction of
unimportant prettiness. . . . It seemed to have qualities of reality and novelty that made up for the clumsiness. . . . I should
like it to stand as a representative in the book of abortive poetry
against literary verse." A year or so later Brooke's dissertation on

the Elizabethan dramatist John Webster pronounced a whole-sale historical generalization of the kind usually associated with T. S. Eliot. After the Metaphysical poets, Eliot proclaimed in a famous phrase in 1921, "a dissociation of sensibility set in, from which we have never recovered." Webster, said Brooke, "is the last of earth, looking out over a sea of saccharine"; after him came "an enfeebling malaise of 'sweetness,' a falsification of truth, from which our literature has never fully recovered." In Brooke the same yeast fermented as in Yeats and Synge, Pound, Eliot, and Williams, Abercrombie, Bottomley, Masefield, and Gibson, all of whom took up arms against "unimportant pret-tiness." But in Brooke the sordid or brutal moments were also unimportant, for they had no resonance, were parts of no large, coherent vision. He was out to flutter the dovecotes of the genteel tradition, but himself belonged to the same way of thinking, in which the sick and the sordid were perceived not as intrinsic reality, but at most as aspects only, almost as anomalies.

In a general way this was true of all the writers in the Blooms-bury set, with whom Brooke for a while associated. Though mili-tantly anti-Victorian, they did not therefore resemble in spirit the postwar Modernists but belonged instead to the liberal gen-eration that formed its faith just before the war. Under the influence of G. E. Moore, they believed in fearless honesty to individual truth, in beauty and personal relations. With these ideals for his personal ethic, and Fabian socialism for his social ethic, Brooke could feel—as his biographer, Christopher Has-sall, explains—"he had put his house of life in order." "Dining-Room Tea" reflects this happiness. It begins in the quiet, sensu-ous appreciation of the ordinary—"lamplight . . . On plate and flowers and pouring tea"—that lends charm to poems such as "The Old Vicarage, Grantchester" and "The Great Lover." But it goes on to describe a "perfect" state of mind or "timeless" moment. According to G. E. Moore, such moments constituted the highest good. At least, that is what the young people under-stood Moore to say.

After taking his degree in 1909, Brooke spent the next couple of years in Europe and at Grantchester, near Cambridge, reading and writing poetry and working at his dissertation on John Webster, with which he earned a fellowship at King's Col-lege. In Germany he wrote "The Old Vicarage, Grantchester," a poem of homesickness in which one both shares and laughs at the emotion. So did Brooke, who first took it seriously enough to name it "Home," and then detached himself in embarrassment from the poem by calling it "Fragments of a Poem to be entitled The Sentimental Exile." Despite the good humor of this utterance, Brooke at the time was suffering a wretched and protracted love affair, which released all the potential instability of his character. He collapsed into infantile regression, hysteria, and obsession, and he also had severe physical symptoms. As he gradually recovered, his personality seemed slightly altered. At least he repudiated aspects of his past which he held responsible for his suffering. In particular he broke with those of his friends who were to be known as the Bloomsbury group, partly because he imagined, quite irrationally, that Lytton Strachey had schemed to thwart his love affair with Ka Cox, partly because he was recoiling emotionally from their unconventional views and life-styles. In short, he began to sympathize with the traditional attitudes of the Victorian middle class. This personal development lies behind the patriotic sonnets which, at the start of the war, seemed to voice the feelings of much of the nation.

In 1913 Brooke toured the United States, Canada, Hawaii, and the South Seas, staying three months in Tahiti. On this trip he seems temporarily to have regained emotional balance, and in Tahiti he wrote some slight but pleasant poems, the best being "Heaven," "Tiare Tahiti," and "The Great Lover." They are in the seemingly relaxed and casual, chatty mode of "Dining-Room Tea" and "The Old Vicarage, Grantchester." No better examples than these five poems could be found of what is commonly and misleadingly suggested by "Georgian." They are composed in flowing, easy lines and sentences, without concentration or intensity. There is a sensuous warmth directed toward the ordinary appurtenances of life, an alert gratitude that does not take the commonplace for granted (though it takes for granted the agreeableness of the commonplace; we hear nothing about sooty streets, gasworks, and blown, soggy newspapers):

> White plates and cups, clean-gleaming,
> Ringed with blue lines; and feathery, faery dust;
> Wet roofs, beneath the lamplight; the strong crust
> Of friendly bread.

"The Old Vicarage, Grantchester," weaves a web of images, memories, and literary allusions around this one dear spot, until it becomes a symbol of England, its kindly countryside, history, customs, peace, above all, its unchanging perpetuity. Modernist critics later pounced on this disarming poem, and its closing verses—

> Say, is there Beauty yet to find?
> And Certainty? and Quiet kind?
> Deep meadows yet, for to forget
> The lies, and truths, and pain? . . . oh! yet
> Stands the Church clock at ten to three?
> And is there honey still for tea?—

were repeatedly mocked as representative Georgianism, the critics reading with less humor than Brooke wrote. All these poems contain something of what T. S. Eliot, trying to pinpoint the virtuous quality of the Metaphysical poets, was presently to describe as an "alliance of levity with seriousness (by which the seriousness is intensified)." Seriousness is not intensified in Brooke, but it is combined with play and joke, perhaps permitted by them. As applied to a style of poetry the term "metaphysical" is no more precise and helpful than such terms usually are. But it is worth remarking that the epithet, which became honorific in the wake of Eliot's poetry and criticism, has been claimed for the period preceding World War I, when in such poets as de la Mare, Brooke, or Hodgson there could be a civilized poise and charm that were lost in the war, when physical violence and moral shock brought in a poetry that was more direct, forceful, and actual, but usually also simpler in feeling. And there was less charm in the literature of the postwar period.

When the First World War broke out, Brooke enlisted. "Well, if Armageddon's *on*," was his much-quoted remark, "I suppose one should be there." He served briefly in Belgium, and what he saw there reawakened his capacities for emotional fervor. To his mind the war now became a supreme cause, one to which all personal relations and purposes must be subordinated. He composed gradually the five war sonnets that were soon to give him a popular fame unmatched by any poet since. They express the high-minded idealism, now so difficult to understand, with which much of the educated youth of England, France, Germany, and Austria marched away. At the same time they are intensely personal sonnets, in which war figures as a mode of redemption. He characterizes the old life before the war as psychological illness, moral purposelessness and shame; with the war Holiness, Love, Pain, Honour, and Nobleness have returned. Life has been simplified. Of the crippling of bodies and minds, the erosion of decent feelings, the spreading cynicism and nihilism, which are part of the cost of war, we hear nothing. The worst that war can bring are only pain and death; and death is not terrible to this poet who has made, he feels, a mess of life:

> Nothing to shake the laughing heart's long peace there
> But only agony, and that has ending;
> And the worst friend and enemy is but Death.

What strikes us is that these sonnets, even in what seems their most personal and morally dubious meaning, articulated the feelings of a large number of people. But the most popular of these sonnets is also the least problematic. Here the Brooke of the Old Vicarage returns in war uniform, loving England for the gentle hearts, peace, and country beauty he has known there. He strikes the consoling theme of immortality: the soldier who dies for England is not really dead. The form and rhythm suggest urgent, yet firmly deliberate feeling, and the traditional mode answers to Brooke's rapport with traditional England in this national hour. In one respect it is not a war poem, since the war is present only as the possibility of dying, and so far as the words go, it might have been written by anyone who thought he might be buried away from home. But the date was 1914 and the title, "The Soldier":

> If I should die, think only this of me:
> That there's some corner of a foreign field
> That is for ever England. There shall be
> In that rich earth a richer dust concealed;
> A dust whom England bore, shaped, made aware,
> Gave, once, her flowers to love, her ways to roam,
> A body of England's, breathing English air,
> Washed by the rivers, blest by suns of home.
> And think, this heart, all evil shed away,
> A pulse in the eternal mind, no less
> Gives somewhere back the thoughts by England given;

Her sights and sounds; dreams happy as her day;
And laughter, learnt of friends; and gentleness,
In hearts at peace, under an English heaven.

When Brooke died of fever in the Aegean in 1915, England mourned all her soldiers in him. Men of such opposite sensibility as Winston Churchill and Henry James felt alike, and pronounced their eulogy. "During the last few months of his life," said Churchill, "the poet-soldier told with all the simple force of genius the sorrow of youth about to die, and the sure triumphant consolations of a sincere and valiant spirit." For James, the death of Brooke was war's supreme "disfigurement of life and outrage to beauty. . . . What a price and a refinement of beauty and poetry it gives those splendid sonnets—which will enrich our whole collective consciousness." Persons who had never read poetry before purchased and read the poems of Brooke, and persons who never before wrote verse tried their hand. Perhaps 8,000 copies of a sixpenny-edition containing just these five war sonnets were sold; by 1926 the total sale of Brooke's *Poems* had reached the astonishing figure of 291,998. But the legend is now dead and, without it, neither the man nor the poetry is likely to sustain interest.

GEORGIAN REALISM

In 1912 it seemed to many people that the coming poetry would be characterized by a greater realism. This could be seen in the careers of Yeats and of Synge, Abercrombie, Bottomley, and Masefield and in some younger poets such as Brooke and Wilfrid Gibson. When, however, one spoke of realism, one did not mean the documentation of social reality or the study of the life of man as conditioned by social institutions. This theme had long since been surrendered to the novel. Neither did one much have in mind the psychological exploration of character in the way of Browning and Kipling, unabashed by genteel conventions. This was not much pursued at the time.

Prewar poetic "realism" interwove three distinguishable tendencies. There was anti-aesthetic activism, the praise of "manly" vigor and engagement in the life of the world. This theme regrettably connected Yeats with such figures as Henley,

Chesterton, and Masefield. "Life," however, was usually imagined in escapist terms. It seemed to belong more to sailors, soldiers, fishermen, fox-hunters, and the like than to commercial travelers or typists, persons who did not exist for prewar poetry. Second, there was rebellious provocation, the desire to shock by dwelling on the disagreeable. Historically and psychologically this was often a continuation of the Aesthetic and Decadent revolt of the nineties, as one sees in the life of Rupert Brooke. But the Decadents had been the reverse of realistic. Realism based on a desire to shock reached its apotheosis of violent effect in the poetry of the war, where it was grounded in a moral passion of utmost intensity and seriousness. But the "realism" most strongly recommended to the prewar generation was Romantic essentialism. It descended from Wordsworth and was present with renewed power in Hardy and Synge. It is a poetry that concentrates on elemental human feeling and experience, with the lingering, primitivist assumption that this may be found especially among the poor. The Georgian representative of this type of realism is Wilfrid Gibson (1878–1962). And the tradition he invokes lends worth to his poetry, which is in itself rather plodding.

Gibson wrote personal lyrics, narrative verse, dramatic or lyrical monologues (sometimes in series that make up a composite portrait of a neighborhood), and verse drama ranging in length from brief vignettes to full-scale plays. He began as a poet of the Tennysonian and Pre-Raphaelite kind. Treading the same road as British poetry in general, he gradually developed his more colloquial and realistic verse after the turn of the century. The new style and subject matter were fully achieved in *Stonefolds* (1907), a collection of playlets that deal with northern shepherds and fells-dwellers. Somber, brooding, and intense, these dramatic episodes were perhaps modeled on the plays in verse of Bottomley and on Synge. *Daily Bread* (1910) was similar, except that it also treated of persons in urban slums and mining towns. These and other volumes of the same period won Gibson as much attention as he was ever to enjoy. Known as a grave, sympathetic portrayer of the lives of the rural or industrial poor in Northumberland, he was included in each of the Georgian anthologies.

THE GEORGIAN COUNTRYSIDE

Many Georgian poets expressed themselves primarily through images and scenes of landscape and of the natural or rural world. If we ask why nature poetry was so prevalent at this time, one answer usually suggested is that it provided an escape from the modern milieu. It was, the argument goes, a clinging to tradition because the tradition was felt to be rapidly crumbling. Or it was a flight from the grimness of modern reality into bird-watching. Both statements have their point, but they are not the important explanation. There were no such urgent motives or self-conscious awareness behind this nature poetry. One of the striking things about Georgian verse is the extent to which Wordsworth, Shelley, Keats, and the other English Romantics are taken as the "classic" norm. The English Romantic writers, as we remarked earlier, have assumed the role filled by the Roman poets in Augustan England. They are the tradition to which one automatically refers for model and standard. Accordingly, the Georgians received from Romantic poetry and accepted without question an attitude in which poetry and nature were inextricably associated. They were nature poets by inheritance.

If, however, it is argued that the weakness of Georgian poetry is its irrelevance to modern reality, the position is basically correct, but not for the simple reasons usually given. "Modern reality" is a variable and imprecise concept. The Georgians, with some exceptions, ignored "the great national events which are daily taking place," and the "increasing accumulation of men in cities"—the phrasing is Wordsworth's—but so had their predecessors in the later eighteenth century and the Romantic period. Yet to write of landscape near Tintern Abbey or of a nightingale instead of war and industrial revolution had proved no fatal irrelevance a hundred years before.

For the immense difference in achievement between the original and the Georgian Romantics, genius may be the main explanation, but a contributing one lies in the differing relations of the poets to their own age. A great poet senses where opportunities lie open. Nature in the Romantic period was an opportunity, but the opportunity had shrunk by the time the

Georgians came along. In the early nineteenth century nature had been the center of what Ezra Pound would have called a cultural vortex; it was a node in which innumerable different ideas and feelings came together. The upper middle class enjoyed the countryside as a refuge from urban crowding and noise; aesthetes and modish youth contemplated nature for its picturesqueness; writers such as Scott dwelt on its remote, wild vistas, such as the Scottish Highlands; almost all writers felt awe before its sublime mountain peaks and precipices, its oceans and storms, which overwhelmed and yet somehow elevated the human spirit with their dreadful grandeur; Deists and rationalizing Christians studied nature scientifically, finding evidences of God's existence and benevolence; sentimental Deists, such as Rousseau, felt a tearful gratitude before it; primitivists fled to it as the origin and standard of good, the home of still uncorrupted innocence; pantheists and panentheists argued that it is or participates in the Divine; and anybody might be led to hypostatize nature and feel, like Wordsworth, that it was the "guide, the guardian of my heart, and soul / Of all my moral being." The point is, to repeat, how many fundamental themes of Romantic culture were related to nature or landscape. And so, when poets described nature, the orchestrated culture of the age was summoned to mind. Because this was no longer true, Georgian nature poetry was doomed to be minor. However sincerely the Georgians might share aspects of the Romantic faith, they were not sustained by the large cultural nexus that had energized and given profundity to nature poetry in the Romantic period, making it a major mode for the first time in history. When Wordsworth wrote about daffodils, he was invoking a hundred years of religious thought and feeling that had increasingly nourished intuitions of God in nature. He was also invoking a hundred years of psychological speculation, the premise of John Locke that knowledge begins in sensations. But when a Georgian poet wrote about daffodils, he was invoking only Romantic poetry.

Poetry since the Romantic period suggests that landscape is now likely to divide the sensibility of the poet and to make his utterance seem "poetic." Just as no one can write blank-verse drama without recalling Shakespeare, nature poetry brings to mind the great Romantics, their attitudes and feelings. Obviously, a modern poet cannot share these completely; his own vision is especially apt to conflict with his inherited Romantic response to nature as beautiful and consoling. When this happens, either his own vision is suppressed to some degree, as is the case with Davies and Blunden, or else the conflict emerges in the poem. In Hardy, for example, the description or imagery of nature may summon feelings not in all respects integrated with other aspects of the poem. The only modern poet of nature who manages to overcome this conflict consistently is Robert Frost, who makes it a plot of his poetry. He writes poems that deliberately evoke Romantic feelings and attitudes in order to deny them. He expresses himself by unsaying Romanticism. He is anti-Romantic, but from within the Romantic tradition. But in contriving poetry out of this particular self-division, he is not typical. If, however, we compare the nature poets, such as Frost, with those who exploited a less traditional imagery, such as Eliot, we find that nature now sets poetry at a certain distance. Orchard and barnyard, ironically enough, now put the poem in the realm of convention—of art, of variation on the expected—rather than in the realm of actual experience. It is not because more readers have sat in a pub (Eliot) than have picked apples (Frost). That may be the case, but it makes little difference to poetic effect. The point is that apple-picking is more familiar in poetry. In a poem the pub is (or was) unexpected, and precisely for that reason it is capable of producing an immediate, strong emotional effect—much more so in fact than it could in a novel.

The Georgian nature poets still of some interest are Edward Thomas, W. H. Davies, Edmund Blunden, and Ralph Hodgson. The best of these was Edward Thomas (1878–1917). He lived by writing, and published more than thirty books of biography, travel, and criticism. Yet up to the last two years of his life he had written no verse. But he made friends with Robert Frost—then living in England—and it was with Frost's encouragement that the breakthrough took place. Frost, who was not always modest, minimized his role: "I referred him to [prose] paragraphs in his book *The Pursuit of Spring* and told him to write it in verse form in exactly the same cadence. That's all there was to it. His poetry declared itself in verse form." However much or little Thomas' poetry may have depended on Frost's for its methods, it is remarkably like Frost's. Thomas typically begins with a natural scene or country encounter, rendered in a leisurely and detailed way. The poems then present a ruminative progression of the mind, set off by the objects before it and continuously responsive to them. Like Frost, Thomas is direct, plain, and natural in idiom, and elusive in meaning. At their best his poems are interwoven fabrics of sights, gestures, and meditative acts of mind, on which we in turn may meditate, coming to no final interpretation. Often he presents himself as seeking to clarify some feeling or insight, some recognition diffused through the poem but not to be precipitated into plain conception. He thus dramatizes a speculative, probing honesty, as of a man refusing to say more or other than he knows, yet knowing there is more to be said if only he could put his finger on it. In this respect his art creates and depends on an illusion of sincerity. We are made to feel that the poem presents sights or experiences actually had, and that the steps of mind and feeling in the poem enact a spontaneous search amid experience for its meaning. In fact, the seemingly casual, almost random movement has been purposefully, often intricately designed.

As compared with Frost, however, Thomas was not repudiating Romantic values and feelings. Instead, he was voicing them, like de la Mare or Blunden. But as compared with most other Georgians, his special strength is that he creates the illusion of the first-hand. "Swedes," for example, evokes Romantic mystery and wonder and even includes a stock Romantic allusion to "Pharaoh's tomb," but the traditional feelings and images arise in observing a pile of turnips. "Lights Out" voices the Romantic wish fought out both in Keats's "Ode to a Nightingale" and Frost's "Come In"; and Thomas adopts the intertwined Romantic symbols of entering the realm of sleep and losing one's way in a dark forest. Unlike Keats and Frost, he yields to the yearning to "fade far away, dissolve, and quite forget"—in Keats's flowing volume of phrase—but, like Frost, he diminishes the tone of utterance. Against the Romantic life-weariness and the fascination with the dark of non-personal being, the title opposes a familiar phrase that makes the occasion seem more commonplace and homely. Similarly, the last stanza counterpoints a certain Romantic volume and splendor of diction ("towers," "cloudy," "lowers") with the plain and ordinary ("shelf above shelf"), and the emotion is kept from becoming hypnotic by a constantly varying rhythm:

> The tall forest towers;
> Its cloudy foliage lowers
> Ahead, shelf above shelf;
> Its silence I hear and obey
> That I may lose my way
> And myself.

One particularly illuminating example of Thomas' art is "At the Team's Head-Brass." Like "Lights Out," though more directly, it is about the war. In major images, theme, and implication it closely resembles Hardy's lyric "In Time of 'the Breaking of Nations'"—so much so that Thomas may well have derived his poem from Hardy's. But the method of presentation is altogether different. Hardy makes his effect with the biblical title and three brief images of rural life: the man harrowing with his horse, the couch grass burning, the lovers going by. He points the moral directly:

> this will go onward the same
> Though Dynasties pass.

In Thomas' poem the speaker sits on a fallen elm, chatting with the plowman. At the start of the poem a pair of lovers disappear into the wood; they come out at the end. All between is taken up with description of the fields, the fallen tree, the plowman, and the conversation with him. The conversation alludes casually to the elm; it would have been removed had so many of the farm workers not been off to war:

> "Have many gone
> From here?" "Yes." "Many lost?" "Yes: good few."

The speaker remarks that, without the war, "Everything would have been different," but the poem is also saying that despite the war life goes "onward the same": the fields are plowed; the acquaintances have their casual chat; the lovers come from the wood. The war can be noticed only in the elm still lying where it fell. Even the slightly dialectal idiom of the plowman contributes to the impression of an unchanging way of life. In this instance Hardy shapes the theme more powerfully, but Thomas' leisurely narrative development, richness of detail, and seeming cas-

ualness or lack of insistence give it a fine actuality and root-
edness. Of the poets who died in the war, he was, with Owen
and Rosenberg, one of the great losses to literature.

In the early part of his life W. H. Davies (1871–1940) spent
more than ten years as an itinerant worker and tramp. In 1899,
trying to jump aboard a moving train, he fell under the wheels
and his leg had to be amputated. Unable to continue his former
life, he resolved to make his way in literature. He began to write
poems, teaching himself and living in cheap lodging houses,
sometimes begging on the roads. The story of his six-year
struggle to write, to find a publisher, and to be recognized by the
literary world and the reading public is a heroic one. His first
book, *The Soul's Destroyer,* appeared in 1905 and won for Davies
the befriending attention of G. B. Shaw, Arthur Symons, and a
few other writers and editors of journals. Within the next year
Edward Thomas, though poor himself, provided Davies with a
two-room cottage in the country and introduced him to many
other literary figures. *The Autobiography of a Super-Tramp* (1908)
told his earlier experiences, and the book, substantiating the
image of the poet, gave his verse a further romantic appeal.
With the *Autobiography* and with *Nature Poems* in the same year
his popularity was established. Here, it seemed, were authentic
glimpses of the simple life and feelings of an uneducated man
who had lived on the fringe of civilized society. He contributed
regularly to the Georgian anthologies and was treated respectfully in reviews and critical studies.

Davies' poems are mostly lyrics, and the lyrics short, for he
soon realized he could not integrate longer works. His diction
and forms are simple, direct, and conventional. Though his taste
is uncertain, there are innumerable minor felicities of observation and feeling. Especially he finds the expressive detail. He
tells of his joy at finding bird tracks at his door—

> But what gives me most joy is when I see
> Snow on my doorstep, printed by their feet—

and the words have freshness and reach of suggestion, evoking a
life of shyness, loneliness, delicate sympathies, and intense responsiveness.

Davies' art is usually pastoral. He writes much about animals and flowers, and his poetic world has a simple wholesomeness. He cultivates the sunnier emotions: pleasure, wonder, sympathy, humor, gratitude, joy, love. And the person speaking these lyrics is naive. He may be called Davies, but he is only a version of the author, Davies exploiting his own ingenuousness for literary effect. What seems particularly ingenuous is the absence of sentimental or intellectual comment where one would ordinarily expect it. Not that Davies omits entirely to think about what he observes, but his thoughts go a remarkably little way only, so we are more struck by what he does not reflect than by what he does. In "Sheep" he tells how he received "fifty shillings down" to sail from Baltimore to Glasgow with "eighteen hundred sheep."

> The first night we were out at sea
>   Those sheep were quiet in their mind;
> The second night they cried with fear—
>   They smelt no pastures in the wind.
>
> They sniffed, poor things, for their green fields,
>   They cried so loud I could not sleep:
> For fifty thousand shillings down
>   I would not sail again with sheep.

Though the poem does not explicitly say so, the sheep presumably are being transported to the slaughterhouse. That they were distressed because they smelt no pastures is the sort of realizing detail we learn to expect from Davies. It brings the animals and his sympathy vividly to mind. But if he is thinking of the slaughterhouse, he keeps it to himself. The same quality is found in *The Autobiography of a Super-Tramp,* where encounters with physical suffering and moral aberration are told in a completely factual way with little expression of feeling and almost no concern to explore their wider significance—whether sociological, economic, psychological, or metaphysical. The same quality informs lyrics in which Davies stares at human woe in shapes of sickness, poverty, idiocy, old age, or death. Though infrequent, such glimpses are impressive, and there is some reason to suppose that they correspond to a vivid, abiding awareness. Perhaps at the bottom of Davies' mind there was a ground of horror, a recognition he seldom or never expressed in verse.

For, indeed, there was nothing he could "say" about it. But it would probably supply a further, urgent motive for his pastoral pleasantness.

Edmund Blunden, who was born in 1896, started publishing in 1914. His early poems are in the pastoral mode, descending from the later eighteenth century, for which he was to be noted. (His war poetry is discussed in Chapter 13.) He felt that poetry must be part of a tradition; if there is no tradition behind it, it is not poetry. Much of his own poetry is descriptive and impersonal and presents with loving attention the sights, incidents, and human types encountered in rural life. It dwells in the world of Cowper, Wordsworth, or John Clare. Objects are closely observed and rendered in detail. Clustered images embody attitudes and evoke moods; any deeper meanings must be inferred, for they are not stated. "Mole Catcher," for example, describes the man and his work, explaining how moles are caught. It seems cruel, but the poem insists that the mole-catcher is actually tender toward all living things. Moles are in a different category, for they are his business:

> And moles to him are only moles; but hares
> See him afield and scarcely cease to nip
> Their dinners, for he harms not them; he spares
> The drowning fly that of his ale would sip.

We may be inclined to draw a moral, but Blunden leaves that to us. His technique is typically objective. In later years he wrote fewer poems of this kind, turning to lyrics of a discursive sort. He had also a career as a teacher and scholar; and his many books and editions dealing with John Clare, Shelley, Keats, Lamb, and other figures of the Romantic period are a notable contribution. He is said to have been a favorite poet of Hardy's at the end of Hardy's life.

The *Collected Poems* of Ralph Hodgson (1871–1962) make up a slim volume. He did not start publishing until he was thirty-four. His first volume, *The Last Blackbird and Other Lines* (1907), was followed after ten years by *Poems* (1917) and, many years later, by *The Skylark and Other Poems* (privately printed, 1958). The reasons for this relatively late start, small production, and twenty-year silence between 1921 and 1941, when he published nothing even in magazines, are not known. One of them was probably his fastidious perfectionism.

None of the Georgian poets of nature was better informed about the animals and plants he described, and none was more tenderly sympathetic. None, moreover, took greater pains to find the exact epithet picturing their looks and doings. Yet Hodgson's poetry does not seem naturalistic, as does that of Thomas, Frost, or Blunden. The strengths of his art are imaginative vision and artifice. By "vision" I mean partly that he creates a world of fantasy ("Saint Athelstan," "The Royal Mails"), but much more that objects in his poetry are too artfully presented to seem quite real:

> Eve, with her basket, was
> Deep in the bells and grass,
> Wading in bells and grass
> Up to her knees.

This is a pastoral art, like Blunden's, but where Blunden resembles Cowper or John Clare, Hodgson is closer to the Blake of *Songs of Innocence*. He also resembles a fumigated, bird-watching Dowson, for his visionary simplicity is achieved by means of artistic self-consciousness and manipulation in an extreme degree.

In Hodgson's first volume the artifice is more obvious. We see firmly corseted quatrains, with compressed and inverted syntax, studied epithets, and a judicious intermixture of poetic and archaic vocabulary. One suspects that Hodgson at times was desperate for a subject. Hence, when he found one, he might work it up at excessive length or with excessive emotion. "An Elegy Upon a Poem Ruined by a Clumsy Metre" prolongs humorous slightness into tedium. "The Missel Thrush" describes a bird in a thunderstorm with feelings that remind one of "The Wreck of the Deutschland." The trouble in both instances was probably the same: he had nothing to say, but wanted to write.

The *Poems* of 1917 are just as artificial, but the artifice forces itself less on our attention. Here Hodgson achieves a flowing grace and lightness of touch, a stylistic ease that harmonizes with his seeming simplicity of attitude and feeling. It is a completely self-aware simplicity, however, and evokes relatively complex states of mind. "Time, You Old Gipsy Man," for example, speaks of unresting time and evokes lapsed civilizations in long perspective. The theme usually weights and sobers poetry, but Hodgson handles it with swift, good-humored strokes and achieves a slight, blithe pathos:

> Time, you old gipsy man,
>   Will you not stay,
> Put up your caravan
>   Just for one day?
>
>   .   .   .   .   .   .
>
> Last week in Babylon,
> Last night in Rome,
> Morning, and in the crush
> Under Paul's dome.

As with the art of de la Mare, such a poem depends on the knowing manipulation of poetic tradition and stock response. The finest example of this is "Eve," from which the first lines have already been quoted. Here Hodgson tells the biblical and Miltonic story of the fall of man as though it were a local village seduction. Eve is the innocent, "motherless" girl of melodrama and Satan the lewd "pretender." The charm of the poem lies partly in transposing the grand theme into locally familiar and miniature terms and partly in the naive speaker, who tells the story with open and full-hearted sympathy for the victim, as though he were watching a stage melodrama. By doing so, he keeps the reader at an emotional distance, following and responding to the story and yet appreciating the artist's control. The poem is deliberately minor and playful, yet with pathos and horror. It is witty, poised, controlled, artificial, and evasive— evasive in that it would be impossible to say what Hodgson personally feels.

Though he is no poet of nature, W. J. Turner (1889–1946) may also be mentioned here. He is, like Hodgson, a poet of vision, but in him vision is more completely emancipated from nature. In the exoticism of his decor and the rapidity of his imaginative transformations—for example, he sees models at a fashion show as

> Curved tropical flowers
> As bright as thunderbolts—

Turner resembles Stevens, but he resembles no one very much.
He was known at first for poems of blithe dreaminess and wan-
derlust, such as "Romance" or "The Hunter":

> The land, the land of Yucatan,
> The low coast breaking into foam,
> The dim hills where my thoughts shall roam
> The forests of my boyhood's home,
> The splendid dream of Yucatan!

In these lines the most active word is "Yucatan," and it is active
not so much as a place-name as a collocation of exotic sounds
and associations. Even in this early and simple poem the object
of Turner's enthusiasm is not so much a place as a dreamy state,
one might almost say, a word. The high spirits and charm of
these lines are not typical, for his dreamlike scenes are often
touched with uneasiness and vague horror. His poetry suggests
that moods of depression or melancholy became more frequent
as he grew older. A later volume, *The Seven Days of the Sun*
(1925), voices bitter satire and rage, adopting, incidentally, a
"modern" mode of the twenties:

> For the last time
> I looked upon my beloved.
>
> Her face was a basket of withered flowers!

It was a long stylistic and spiritual journey for the poet who had
made his fame with "Romance" nine years before:

> When I was but thirteen or so
> I went into a golden land,
> Chimborazo, Cotopaxi
> Took me by the hand.

THE GEORGIAN COMPROMISE

Although the Georgians were a diverse group, a brief, collective portrait may be attempted. Like most poets from the 1880s
through the 1930s, they felt themselves in rebellion against the
great Victorians. Unlike the poets of the nineties, they did not
borrow formulas from foreign literatures to exorcise the impres-

sive specters. Like the Edwardians, they reacted against the fin de siècle. The poets they loked to for paternal example were the English Romantics, and, among writers nearer in time, Housman, Hardy, Masefield, Yeats, and Synge. They repudiated the noisier side of Edwardian verse—that, for example, of Chesterton, Kipling, and Noyes—but they continued the Edwardian cultivation of the "agreeable," especially the appreciative treatment of countryside. Their technique avoided Victorian "rhetoric" and the lapidary perfectionism of the nineties, though they were intent on tightening and grooming the slipshod verse of the Edwardian narrative poets. The result was a traditional and popular style, easy, smooth, and perspicuous, usually impersonal and cautiously colloquial, with none of the dissonance, dislocation, and shock effects of the Modernists.

Nietzsche and Schopenhauer had long been modish in some quarters and Marx, Freud, and Kierkegaard were beginning to make an impression in the Anglo-Saxon literary world, but none of these Teutonic lights had dawned for the Georgians. They were "disinherited" of religious faith, but that was not for them a reason for anguish or despair. So far as beliefs can be inferred from poetry, they generally shared a cautiously optimistic naturalism—optimistic because in this merely natural cosmos it was possible for a human being to be reasonable and, with luck, happy. As individuals many of them lived through extreme suffering and horror, but such experience did not take hold of their minds and alter their sense of life and the universe. Their poetic feelings were wholesome, kindly, and compassionate. Their set of mind was, in a sense, compromising and deliberately minor, unable or unwilling to take major psychological, intellectual, or even technical risks. Compared with the great Modernist writers who followed they were of lesser stature, but they were capable of a civilized, complex balance and charm that has been rare since.

11

ROBERT FROST

THE poetry of Robert Frost begins with a radical self-restriction. As Goethe remarked, "In der Beschränkung zeigt sich erst der Meister"—it is above all in the act of limitation that the master shows himself. The limits Frost worked within are a locality and an idiom. Rural New England, its farms, woods, weathers, and typical inhabitants, is the smaller world with which he chose to mirror the world. His idiom is educated but talked American, with a slight wash of country vocabulary and often a Yankee intonation. Traditional grand airs of poetry—volume of sound, for example, or density of metaphor—are not absent, but because they do not belong to the life of the New England countryside, decorum requires that they be kept from notice. Whatever happens to Frost's protagonists, no "aethereal rumours" (to compare Eliot) are going to

Revive for a moment a broken Coriolanus;

for literary allusion has no place in his rural world. Neither could Frost hope for such a swirl of vowels and consonants in the spoken language north of Boston. But if, compared with Yeats or Eliot (for one can compare Frost only with the best), his chosen limits reduce the variety and intensity of poetic effects open to him, there is a compensating gain: the diminishment in "poetry" is felt as an augmentation in "reality." Frost's verse implies at large a typical dramatic gesture of early twentieth-century poetry in which the poet rejects the "poetic"—usually identified as the Romantic—in favor of the actual. His poetry belongs essentially to the Romantic tradition, but as a critique. He invokes Romantic convention in order to correct it.

The greatest poet of New England was born in San Francisco in 1874 and spent the first eleven years of his life there. He was named Robert Lee Frost in tribute to the Confederate general, his Yankee father thus asserting an aggressive independence of mind, a trait for which his son was also remarkable. His mother, a native of Scotland, was a woman of deep poetic and religious feeling. Frost, who went to school only sporadically until he was twelve, had most of his early education from her. His father died in 1885, and the widow returned with Robert and his older sister, Jeannie, to her husband's parents in Lawrence, Massachusetts. After graduating from Lawrence High School, where he studied Latin, Greek, and other subjects required in the college preparatory program, Frost entered Dartmouth College with a scholarship grant. He found himself unhappy, left after a few months, and spent the next four years in various employment, mainly teaching. In 1895, after a courtship marked by dramatic vicissitudes, he married Elinor White, whom he had known since high school. He attended Harvard University for two years as a special student, and in 1900, having been advised by a doctor that the state of his health required fresh air and exercise, he bought a farm in Derry, New Hampshire, and set himself up as a chicken-farmer.

The public image of Frost as a Yankee farmer-poet is accurate but may be qualified. It is true that he had, throughout his life, a succession of New England farms, on which he mended walls, split wood, went blueberrying, and the like, and he knew intimately the way of life and speech of his rural neighbors. But he was never quite a farmer. For one thing, a small legacy from his grandfather meant that he did not completely depend on his farm for a living. He was free to neglect the needs of his fields in favor of long botanical walks or day-long "sprawls" in conversation with a friend. Moreover, whenever he felt the pinch of money or a hankering to practice his ideas of education—an art in which he took much interest—he became a teacher, first in nearby schools and later in colleges, especially Amherst. Above all he thought of himself as a poet.

He composed his first poem, a ballad based on an incident in Prescott's *Conquest of Mexico,* at the age of fourteen and read and wrote poetry ever after. But, living in Derry, he knew no other writers of significance, and he did not read the magazines of the sophisticated. He formed his poetic theories and aims in independent dialogues with his own mind. The poets most impressed on his consciousness were not Baudelaire, Verlaine, Laforgue, Mallarmé, the Pre-Raphaelites, or Dante, but the Latin classics, Shakespeare, the English Romantic and Victorian poets, and Americans such as Whittier, Bryant, Emily Dickinson, and Emerson. The poetry he wrote resembled the Georgian poetry emerging in England in reaction against the fin de siècle, though Frost was not motivated by that antagonism. So far as his verse was shaped by dislike, it was, as with Robinson, dislike of the conventional and insipid Romanticism of most magazine verse in America at that time. He was an anti-Romantic within the Romantic tradition.

In 1912, at the age of thirty-eight, Frost had sold some poems to magazines, but more had been rejected and he had not yet published a book of his verse. He decided to give up the teaching he had been doing for the last six years and settle for a while in England. The move transformed his literary fortunes. From manuscripts he had brought with him he put together *A Boy's Will.* To his delight, this first volume of lyrics was accepted by an English publisher and appeared in April 1913. Reviews were brief and not enthusiastic, but Frost's confidence was now in stride. *North of Boston,* which contained such poems as "The Death of the Hired Man," "Mending Wall," "The Wood-pile," and "After Apple-picking," came out in London the next year. Meanwhile he had been making acquaintances in literary circles. He never could get "Yates"—to use his aggressively mock-ignorant spelling—to pay him much attention, but Pound, then in London, showered peremptory helpfulness, and Frost also became friendly with Harold Monro, F. S. Flint, Walter de la Mare, Lascelles Abercrombie, Wilfrid Gibson, and most of the other Georgians. His midwifery to the poetry of Edward Thomas has already been mentioned; their friendship was so close that Thomas thought of emigrating to America. That Frost had this success in the Georgian poetic world was not accidental, for in many respects his verse shared the Georgian sensibility and realized its poetic ideal.

Returning home in 1915 he arranged for the American publication of *North of Boston*. When it became a best seller, Frost was recognized as one of the "new" or "modern" American poets. Years of fame followed. He supported himself and his family by college teaching (though rarely full-time), public readings, lectures, royalties, and, in later years, by selling the manuscripts of his poems to collectors. (He said he had to watch nervously over his wastebasket.) His middle and later years were saddened by family crises—the insanity of his sister, the death of a daughter and, in 1938, of his wife, and the suicide of his son two years later. His reputation as a poet was assailed from several quarters in the late 1920s and 1930s. Critics such as Granville Hicks, Newton Arvin, Horace Gregory, and Rolfe Humphries complained that Frost did not deal with modern reality, the impact, in Hicks's inventory, of industrialism, science, and Freud. Whether valid or not, these criticisms were unquestionably influenced by antipathy to Frost's politics. In these years of the Great Depression and the New Deal, when most intellectuals went left, he reacted against the modish and went aggressively right, sneering at "bellyachers" and praising free individualism. At the same time he also poked fun at the Modernist movement in poetry. This may have been a reason why the formalist or so-called "New Critics" generally ignored one of the supreme formalists among twentieth-century poets. As late as 1940 the leftist F. O. Matthiessen supplied Harvard undergraduates with a reading list for modern poetry on which Frost figured not at all. To this day the small critic *à la mode* is still likely to be troubled by at least two considerations: Frost was a popular success; and he was regrettably at home in the universe.

But despite the opinions of little magazines, until his death in 1963, Frost remained one of America's more widely read and admired poets. In the 1940s some critics, notably Randall Jarrell, began to enjoy him for the obvious reasons. Meanwhile, public honors were heaped upon him. A Resolution of the United States Senate recognized his seventy-fifth birthday; honorary degrees fell like autumn leaves; he was made Consultant in Poetry to the Library of Congress. In 1961 he received the greatest public recognition yet paid any American poet when, at the age of eighty-seven, he was asked to read at the inauguration of President Kennedy. Subsequently he toured Russia and was able to boast of a conversation with Chairman Kruschev. He hoped the honors he obtained might help win more place for poetry in America. He always felt there should be more public support for poetry; as he said in another connection, though poetry "must remain a theft to retain its savour . . . it does seem as if it could be a little more connived at than it is."

FROST AND THE AGE

Frost belongs to a moment in the literary history of our century that is now largely forgotten. In England in 1912 the Georgian poets had just made their first impact. Repudiating the swashbuckling of Edwardian versifiers and the lapidary sterility (as they saw it) of the fin de siècle, they rendered and took pleasure in familiar sights and happenings. From these they elicited reflection or speculation, which, however, was usually handled with a light touch and often only implied. They valued an accurate and detailed presentation of the object and an easy, direct, and colloquial way of speaking. Most of the time they went, like the Edwardians, to country life and nature for subject and setting, and in their weaker moments the rural slipped over into the merely pastoral, and thoughtful if gentle realism into mere pleasantness. Nevertheless, they believed, and with much justice, that they were bringing a renewed truth and energy into English poetry, while also setting higher technical standards after such loose and rattling Edwardians as Chesterton and Noyes. They had meditative grace, kindliness, humor, and personal charm. Meanwhile in the United States what was recognized as a new and "modern" poetry had also been developing in the hands of E. A. Robinson, Edgar Lee Masters, Vachel Lindsay, and Amy Lowell, with further example and exhortation from Ezra Pound in London. Just how large a step this "new" poetry was taking may be seen by comparing these writers with their conventionally "genteel" and "Romantic" predecessors and contemporaries—for example, Richard Watson Gilder, Louise Imogen Guiney, Richard Hovey, and Bliss

Carman. The new poetry of America combined a greater realism in subject and treatment with a more direct, vigorous, and colloquial idiom.

As compared with the English Georgians, much of this American poetry was more strongly influenced by prose fiction. It sought not only to portray character and local setting but also to trace the impact of social conventions and institutions on individual life, as well as the deeper psychological tensions within and between individuals. And the innovations of the "new" Americans against the inherited poetic forms and language were more radical and explosive. The point of this resumé is to recall to what extent Frost must be seen in relation to both the new English and new American poetry of his day. It is not simply that, having lived in England, he was acquainted with poets on both sides of the Atlantic. What matters more is that to a very considerable degree his own work fulfilled (while it also transcended) the poetic aims of his American and his English contemporaries. When in the twenties and thirties the Modernist tide came in, Frost remained prominent. The excellence of his performance insured that. But most of the contemporaries with whom he had been and should be associated were lost from view. As a result, when we look back on twentieth-century poetry, Frost seems a relatively isolated and inexplicable figure. This was not actually the case. He was the finest representative of a distinct phase in the history of twentieth-century poetry.

THE SPOKEN LANGUAGE

When in 1913 and 1914 Frost first won the attention of critics and other poets, the aspect of his poetry that seemed most admirable was his use of the spoken language—for example, in the first version of the start of "Birches":

> When I see birches bend to left and right
> Across the lines of straighter darker trees,
> I like to think some boy's been swinging them.
> But swinging doesn't bend them down to stay.
> Ice-storms do that.

In basing his idiom on the spoken language, Frost was participating in a main development of twentieth-century poetry, one already touched on in discussing Hardy, Kipling, Yeats, Synge,

Masefield, Robinson, and the Georgians and that continues in most important poets henceforth—the Imagists, Eliot, Williams, Auden, Robert Lowell. To notice what pushed Frost in this direction is to suggest some sources and motivations for this twentieth-century effort as a whole.

A prime motive was aversion, the desire of twentieth-century poets to get rid of the ornate and poetically conventional idiom found often in the weaker poets of the Victorian age, and sometimes in the major ones. (Not to mention inversions, Latinisms, pleonasms, and the like, Tennyson calls grass "the herb," a horse a "charger," poetry a "lyre"; Swinburne speaks of weary wings of love, says "I am fain," and writes "guerdon" instead of reward.) If one asks, why such adornments gradually came to seem blots and why even genuine elegance and sonority ("the deep / Moans round with many voices" in Tennyson's "Ulysses") might also give offense, the answer is partly that such phrasing seemed to seal the poem off from reality, to make of it a splendid indoor space in which the vital "fury and mire" of human life sounded dimly from far away. Twentieth-century poets have typically wanted, to cite Yeats again, "unpurged images" of actuality, confrontations. Such, at least, was the rationalization. But since it could have occurred to Tennyson and Swinburne (and did occur to Browning) as easily as to Yeats or to Frost, it does not explain why the massive reaction came when it did. Perhaps a more immediate motivation lay in what W. J. Bate aptly calls "the burden of the past," the poet's sense that the achievement of recent poets on one line compels him to choose another. Frost was quite clear about this: poetic diction and verbal melody had been carried as far as they could, and spoken language was the only possible source of a new poetic music. "The great successes," he wrote John Bartlett in 1913, "in recent poetry have been made on the assumption that the music of words was a matter of harmonized vowels and consonants. Both Swinburne and Tennyson arrived largely at effects in assonation. . . . Any one else who goes that way must go after them."

The uneasiness of poets before prose fiction has also been a source of creative self-renewal. From the moment the novel was established as a literary form it began to exert pressure on poets, forcing them to concentrate on subjects and uses of language that the novel could not easily appropriate. As the nineteenth century wore on, the novel upgraded its identity. No longer mere entertainment and escape, it was increasingly a literary genre at least as prestigious as poetry and drama. Meanwhile novelists were widening their repertoire of verbal and technical resources and handling them with a more self-conscious sophistication. Naturally, when poets sought to revitalize their own art, they looked to the novel for hints and procedures. The situation is suggested by Ezra Pound's insistence, completely justified in its time, that poetry should be at least as well written as prose. We have seen that Robinson learned his poetic methods partly from reading and writing prose fiction. Some of T. S. Eliot's early poems probably owe much to Henry James; *The Waste Land* is deeply indebted to Joyce's *Ulysses*. In the effort of poets to write a less "poetic" language, the novel played its role. It exemplified (with aid from the drama) the perfections possible in the prosaic or the colloquial. But if the novel was as important to Frost as it was to most modern poets, little record of the fact has survived. Once, however, he asserted an indebtedness to Howells. "I learned from him . . . that the loveliest theme of poetry was the voices of the people. No one ever had a more observing ear or clearer imagination for the tones of those voices. No one ever brought them more freshly to book."

But poets learn chiefly from their own predecessors. Those from whom one or another twentieth-century poet learned a colloquial voice would include perhaps a third of the world's memorable poets. Frost's most important predecessor was Wordsworth. In his Preface to the *Lyrical Ballads* Wordsworth had attacked "poetic diction" and insisted that poetry must use the language actually spoken, the language of conversation, as he specified, in the middle and lower classes of society. In some other respects his views on poetry were shared by Frost—for example, Wordsworth's praise of spontaneous composition and his preference for subjects taken from "humble and rustic life." Frost often cited these principles and would compare his own plain idiom with that of his Romantic predecessor: for example, in *North of Boston*, "I dropped to an everyday level of diction that even Wordsworth kept above." Whether Wordsworth was important to Frost as a source and example or was merely a support in expounding his own views, I do not know. In either case, plain and colloquial language was an ideal strongly advocated within the Romantic tradition which formed his poetry. If radically applied, it promised to correct the idiom of the immediate past with a new way of writing, at least a way not yet exhausted. And then, there was Frost's own extraordinary relish for conversation. He was ready to talk all day and night if he had genial company. His speech, which he practiced as an art, was richly pithy, idiosyncratic, and concrete. He paid loving notice to any fresh, racy element in the speech he heard about him. Frost's talk in poetry expressed a natural trait of his personality.

At its best, Frost's poetic idiom is a unified achievement on three lines, all deliberately pursued. It is colloquially simple; it is dramatic; and it is racy of a locality, a region. Not that these qualities are always present. Frost had more than one style, and, encountered out of context, some of his poems would not be easily recognized. He enjoyed playing the colloquial and the regional against higher-flying modes of speech, usually for humor and parody. Nevertheless, the colloquial, dramatic, and racy especially characterize his idiom, and were noticed and praised by other poets of his generation.

The impression of colloquial speech comes partly from his vocabulary and syntax. Except for particular effects, he was careful to avoid words that would seem out of the way, especially those that would seem literary. "I would never use a word or combination of words that I hadn't *heard* used in running speech." Frost was also careful to adopt locutions that, though not unbecoming, would be unexpected in poetry precisely because they belonged so much more to the spoken than the written language—for example, the elision of "is" and the word "sticking" in the first line of "After Apple-picking":

> My long two-pointed ladder's sticking through a tree.

A special feature of his poetic talk is his use of monosyllables. They are usually numerous in his verse and they come in clumps. Sometimes a whole line (or even successive lines) will be built out of them: "And to do that to birds was why she came." In composing such lines Frost violated one of the persisting taboos of English versification. It had been thought difficult to please the ear when, as Pope put it, "ten low words oft creep in one dull line." Successful control of such lines is one of the most obvious signs of Frost's formal mastery.

The construction of his sentences tends to be coordinate

rather than subordinate, and the clauses are relatively short.

> My long two-pointed ladder's sticking through a tree
> Toward heaven still,
> And there's a barrel that I didn't fill
> Beside it, and there may be two or three
> Apples I didn't pick upon some bough.
> But I am done with apple-picking now.

Lingering over these lines, one notices the effectively patterned variation of shorter and longer clauses, the rhymes handled sometimes for emphasis ("now"), and sometimes muted at the end of run-on lines ("fill / Beside it"), and the play of alliteration on "l" and "t" and of assonance on the short "i." The fresh substantive "apple-picking" is itself a distinct pleasure. The iteration of the verb "is" expresses a flat, objective finality. The declarative, coordinate clauses—"And there's a barrel . . . and there may be . . . But I am done"—permit an easy glide from image to image, thought to thought. The effect of this artistry is colloquial ease and simplicity and depends on the syntax as well as the vocabulary. Frost's syntax can be more radically colloquial. When we talk, this is what our talk often sounds like, rambling on with many whats, whiches, thats, and thises. Frost can sound just as loose and shapeless. The difference is that he is actually moving fast and toward a climax, as in "An Old Man's Winter Night":

> What kept him from remembering the need
> That brought him to that creaking room was age.

With nothing was Frost more concerned than that his idiom and syntax be dramatic, expressive of the character and mood of the speaker to the fullest possible degree. "A dramatic necessity," he said, "goes deep into the nature of the sentence. Sentences are not different enough to hold the attention unless they are dramatic. . . . All that can save them is the speaking tone of voice somehow entangled in the words and fastened to the page for the ear of the imagination." This was the basic meaning of his theory of "intonation," the aspect of poetry he claimed as his own particular discovery and forte. He also called it "the sound of sense" or "tone of meaning." In every living language meaning is conveyed not only by words but also by the sound of the voice in speaking them. One instance comes in some forms of irony, where the tone of voice asserts a meaning that qualifies or undercuts what the words literally say. "Fine weather!" "What a shame you have to *go* now!" When one hears the tones but not the words of a conversation in the next room, one may still catch meanings. Frost wished to exploit intonation deliberately and to the fullest possible degree. He said that every sentence could be regarded as a sound, a vocal pattern or form, that itself expresses meaning. We recognize such sounds in the sentences we read because we have heard them in conversation. "Sentence-sounds . . . are gathered by the ear from the vernacular and brought into books. . . . I think no writer invents them. The most original author only catches them fresh from talk, where they grow spontaneously." No writer, he argued, should set down a sentence that lacks a distinct sound, a sentence in which the reader might not know what tone of voice to use. If this happens, the writer has failed to particularize his meaning fully. In calling it the "sound of sense" Frost distinguished this appeal to the ear from less dramatic and expressive uses of sound in poetry—for example, assonance for its own sake. His phrase the "tones of meaning" calls attention to meanings more nuanced than those stated in the words alone, the wealth of implication given in speaking by pitch, stress, and juncture. Frost knew that writers had always made use of this resource but he felt he had made it peculiarly his own, for no one before had talked about it and no one had worked it with such conscious attention.

In connection with his use of "intonation," Frost also took hold of the principle of counterpoint. The term counterpoint comes into the vocabulary of twentieth-century poetic criticism from Hopkins, who meant by it a "mounting" of one rhythm or sense on another, so that two are going at the same time. Frost did not use the word, but he talked especially about the interplay of the sentence intonation with the meter. The art lies in "skillfully breaking the sounds of sense with all their irregularity of accent across the regular beat of the metre"; "there are the very regular preestablished accent and measure of blank verse; and there are the very irregular accent and measure of speaking intonation. I am never more pleased than when I can get these into strained relations."

Frost's speech has the flavor of rural New England. In producing this impression, vocabulary and syntax play a relatively minor role. He occasionally uses a regionalism, at least a countryism—"*boughten* friendship"—but what especially creates the effect of New England speech is the intonation, the "sounds" of the sentences as the ear hears them. In order to hear the intonation we must first imagine the type of person speaking and what he or she would be feeling. We catch the intonation from the dramatic characterization, to which it then further contributes. Frost says that we recognize intonation on the page only because we have first heard it in "running speech." Presumably he would be appreciated more fully by readers familiar with the tones of voice of country New England seventy years ago. This is not so much an impediment as it might seem. The rural Yankee is a stock figure in American folklore, often exploited in literature and film. We all think we know the type—hard, wary, prudent, independent, fact-minded, with a dry, ironic humor. And we all suppose we know his tones of voice.

In the last stanza of "Come In," Frost activates these recognitions. I pick it as an example because Auden once remarked that only an American could have written it, though he did not say why. The poem is one of Frost's typically anti-Romantic utterances. As it opens, the speaker, standing at twilight at the edge of a wood, hears a thrush singing within—"Far in the pillared dark / Thrush music went." It seems a call to come into the dark woods "and lament." To this point the poem deploys stock Romantic images and feelings. Keats's "Ode to a Nightingale" offers a parallel, though a remote one. But Frost has set up the poem for the sake of the anti-Romantic, tough-minded gesture of the last stanza:

> But no, I was out for stars:
> I would not come in.
> I meant not even if asked,
> And I hadn't been.

The refusal to come in, as he voices it, characterizes the New Englander, and wins a certain humor from the characterization. If we ask just what in these lines seems racy of New England, we may notice that there are four short, declarative clauses, made up mostly of monosyllables. Each is flat, final, and unqualified, expressing a stubborn Yankee downrightness. ("I do not choose to run," said Calvin Coolidge, when asked if he would stand for a second term as President. And that was all he said.) There is also the effect of some phrases: "out for stars," "come in"—the Romantic allure of the dark woods and the singing bird is put with a certain homeliness in the common phrase of friendly invitation. Above all, there are the negatives: four in four lines. They bespeak the Yankee refusal to go along, a refusal rooted in practical awareness. But though the type of person speaking is familiar, what he says comes upon the reader unexpectedly and with a slight effect of wit. The wit depends on the speed of the saying and on our recognition of truth to character and also of truth (of a limited kind) in what is said. At the end the speaker is talking with a self-aware, slightly ironic humor. Even if the thrush has not been singing to him, he has almost been speaking to it ("I meant"). The last line shows him regaining his balance.

This type of humor—for Frost's humor is of many types and omnipresent—is an undernote in many of his finest sayings. It is dry and slightly reductionistic. When, in "The Death of the Hired Man," Warren says,

> "Home is the place where, when you have to go there,
> They have to take you in,"

the remark has something of what Samuel Johnson (in his discussion of the metaphysical poets) described as one of the highest forms of wit, that "which is at once natural and new, that which, though not obvious, is, upon its first production, acknowledged to be just." At the same time, the saying is completely in character. It has the grip on fact, the down-to-earthness deflating sentimental wish, that belong to our notion of the country New Englander. When, in "Birches," the speaker remarks,

> . . . Earth's the right place for love:
> I don't know where it's likely to go better.

the wry understatement expresses, again, a Yankee sense of practical reality. Humor of this kind comes to a grim crescendo in "Provide, Provide." Here Frost pretends to be the prudent, practical Yankee, mindful that one must provide for the future; with what seems a grotesque exaggeration of the attitude, he urges us to "provide" against old age and death. Since that is impossible, the attitude, thus carried to an extreme, is mocked. The basis of this mockery, however, is a view of life even more hard and practical than that of the provider: whatever you do, you are likely to end up miserably. But in making us see this, the poem forces us to concede—this is what appalls—that the advice, though terrible, cannot be simply rejected.

> No memory of having starred
> Atones for later disregard,
> Or keeps the end from being hard.
>
> Better to go down dignified
> With boughten friendship at your side
> Than none at all. Provide, provide!

To take this advice straight would be a silly misreading. But wholly to deny its possible relevance would also be insensitive. The poem, as is often the case in Frost, drives us to a shocked recollection of the minimal lives, the limited and dismaying choices, men and women may be brought to. If it comes to a choice between "boughten" friendship and "none at all," the first must be preferred. A truth of this kind is so shocking and bitter that it is not usually told in poetry—or even in novels and plays. One doubts if Frost would have been willing to say it in earnest as from himself. Said in dramatic character, however, it can be both presented and self-protectively repudiated; it becomes "play" in several senses of the word, including enjoyment of the characteristically Yankee attitude and speech intonation.

Dramatic characterization is one element of Frost's potent appeal in what he called the "market place." But there is much else, including the milieu and the objects that make it up. To find poetry in the familiar was one of his intentions. "Love, the moon, and murder have poetry in them by common consent. But it's in other places. It's in the axe-handle of a French Canadian woodchopper." American poetry should "drop the eternal sublime and see that all life is a fit subject for poetic treatment." When Frost first came to the attention of critics, he was often described as a poetic Realist, a label he partly connived at. But whatever it may have been in 1914, the "axe-handle of a French Canadian woodchopper" is now a relatively exotic item. Similarly with his characters and stories; they now attract more by their Romantic strangeness than by their familiarity. Readers are now drawn to Frost for the same reason—as one reason—that they once went to James Whitcomb Riley. Not of course that Frost is at the level of Riley. He is enormously more authentic, subtle, and complex and lacks Riley's sunny sentimentalism. Nevertheless, whatever else it does, his poetry pleases like a Currier and Ives print. It engages the nostalgic interest of readers in a lost way of life, enjoyed in imagination and thought of as quintessentially American. He rarely composes set pieces of description. Instead, he suggests farm and landscape with a few, usually general references that come without ostentation in the seemingly natural flow of speech. We hear in "After Apple-picking" about a "long two-pointed ladder"—Frost typically describes his tools with loving exactness—"a barrel," apples on a bough, a drinking trough and its water iced over in the morning, frosty grass, the cellar bin, the cider apple heap. From such mentions no one could draw a picture of this farm, but the milieu becomes fixed and vivid in the imagination. In "An Old Man's Winter Night" we pick up images of empty rooms with frosted windows, an old man holding a lantern, the barrels of a storeroom, a stove, snow, icicles, the sound of trees cracking in the cold. Out of this we shape in imagination a New England farm, snowed in on a winter night.

Character, then, and setting, and there is also story, or story elements. Frost wrote the finest short narrative poems yet written in the twentieth century. In poems such as "The Death of the Hired Man," "Home Burial," and "The Witch of Coös" he resembles Chekhov in his ability to reflect nuances of changing emotion in dialogue. He has a shrewd understanding of psychological states, for example, the precarious, slightly self-deceiving self-respect of Silas, the hired man, so terribly on the defensive against his own sense of the worthlessness of his existence. He knows the workings of neurotic elements in personality and the complicated, unhappy knots people get tied into together, as in "Home Burial." He can show the state of affairs between his men and women with uncanny power of brief suggestion. He has an ability to manipulate plot for suspense. "The Witch of Coös" holds attention if it is read simply as a ghost story, though it is so much more than that: it is Frost's largest single revelation of the bleak emptiness of life and of the heart. Years ago her husband murdered her lover. She helped bury him in the cellar. Perhaps she felt there was nothing else to be done. We do not know. In any case, she has lived with that memory "all these years," trying to keep it down and telling no one. When, finally, she tells, we see what it has done to her:

> But tonight I don't care enough to lie—
> I don't remember why I ever cared.
> Toffile, if he were here, I don't believe
> Could tell you why he ever cared himself.

The same dramatic and fictive interests appear in Frost's lyric and meditative verse. "Putting in the Seed" begins almost as a short story. "The Hill Wife" is a short story told in five brief lyrics. Even poems where there is no story as such have an action that catches attention: picking apples, swinging on birches, looking down into a well, grinding a scythe, watching a white spider, stopping by woods on a snowy evening, coming to a crossroad in a wood, two neighbors mending a stone wall. Frost is primarily a lyric and meditative poet, but the lyric and meditative utterance arises from some concrete, particular event and is related to it. The events are also metaphors; if a poem has no action as such, it usually takes hold of an ongoing metaphor, as in "Fire and Ice" or "Nothing Gold Can Stay." One may compare Frost, in this respect, with more disembodied poets such as Bridges or, later, Wallace Stevens. We do not read poems out of curiosity about facts and doings, but a poet who forfeits concrete presentation has a harder time lodging his poem in the reader's imagination. Similarly, a chain of metaphors and illustrations is not usually as effective as a central, continuing action, and a meditative action in the mind is not the same thing as a story. Moreover, when concrete plot or circumstance are not given in the poem, language will be used in a more "poetic" way—that is, with whatever type of verbal heightening or concentration may be the poetic practice of the age.

As in much Georgian poetry, the charm of the speaker's personality exerts a strong appeal. He is not always the same man; "Provide, Provide" is not spoken in quite the same persona as "After Apple-picking." But for the most part he seems humorous and shrewd, sensitive, speculative, poised, and tender. He has a basic decency of feeling. Perhaps it shows especially in his attitude to the characters he depicts. He is neither sentimental, cynical, nor melodramatic. He has a penetrating understanding, combined with half-humorous sympathy and detachment. In the play of moral judgment most people have a case to be made for them, and, as far as possible, he respects the person for what he is. So also with his attitude to natural things. He keeps his distance, though with interest, imaginative response, and intensely noting love. He immensely admires integrity in work, above all when the workman also keeps form and style. At decaying houses, burnt farms, abandoned fields, he feels the *lacrimae rerum*, a pious respect and regret for the labor that made them and the life played out in them. To say that a book or a writer is wholesome is not, to this generation, always a recommendation, but in his poetic persona Frost is, amid all the complexity of his attitudes, wholesome, and that is a large part of his appeal.

UNSAYING THE ROMANTICS

In the course of his career Frost found himself classified as a Realist, a Romantic, a Humanist, and a writer of classical, especially Horatian tendency. Perhaps he would have preferred the label he was never given, a Formalist, though he would have defined the term his own way. He particularly disliked being called a Romantic, for, as used by reviewers in the teens and twenties, the term associated him with one of the weaker types of contemporary poetry. Nevertheless, if we think of the first Romantics, such as Wordsworth, Shelley, and Keats, Frost was clearly one of their followers, though in a peculiar way. He wrote against the background of English and American Romantic poetry. Against. He expressed his own attitudes by repudiating, correcting, or sometimes just refusing to go along with typical Romantic ones. Sometimes he even alluded to a particular Romantic poem. In "Birches" the description of the ice fallen from the trees—

> Such heaps of broken glass to sweep away
> You'd think the inner dome of heaven had fallen—

recalls the famous lines in Shelley's "Adonais" that compare life to a dome of glass:

> Life, like a dome of many-coloured glass,
> Stains the white radiance of Eternity,
> Until Death tramples it to fragments.

Such allusion is a teasing joke, but it is also functional wit, expressing an attitude simply by the lowered tone of voice. An implicit criticism of Shelleyan afflatus, it takes on further point at the end of Frost's poem:

> I'd like to go by climbing a birch tree,
> And climb black branches up a snow-white trunk
> *Toward* heaven, till the tree could bear no more,
> But dipped its top and set me down again.

Perhaps there is even an underthought of comparison here with the last lines of "Adonais," where, symbolically speaking, the poet "goes" up and off *to* Heaven forever.

> The massy earth and sphered skies are riven!
> I am borne darkly, fearfully, afar;
> Whilst, burning through the inmost veil of Heaven,
> The soul of Adonais, like a star,
> Beacons from the abode where the Eternal are.

Since Frost invokes Romantic poems, metaphors, and general attitudes in order to deny them, the more one keeps Romantic poetry in mind, the more subtly one appreciates Frost. To show this in detail we would have to take tedious note of allusion and parody in poem after poem. The same point can be made more generally by drawing attention to his rejection of typically Romantic attitudes and metaphors. There is, for example, the Romantic assertion of a sympathy from nature to man. Frost comes back to it in many poems, but comes back to unsay it, as we have seen in "Come In." In "The Most of It" the speaker "thought he kept the universe alone," and cried out for "counter-love." Nothing came of the cry except, one day, a buck swam across the water and disappeared in the underbrush—the animal living its own life in its own world. In "The Need of Being Versed in Country Things" the speaker describes a burnt-down farmhouse, the barn still standing across the way. In the fourth stanza he speaks of the birds that come to the now deserted barn:

> The birds that came to it through the air
> At broken windows flew out and in,
> Their murmur more like the sigh we sigh
> From too much dwelling on what has been.

Yet for them the lilac renewed its leaf,
And the aged elm, though touched with fire;
And the dry pump flung up an awkward arm;
And the fence post carried a strand of wire.

For them there was really nothing sad.
But though they rejoiced in the nest they kept,
One had to be versed in country things
Not to believe the phoebes wept.

These poems embody gestures of refusal. Frost—in his poetic persona—will not go along with Wordsworth. He would like to believe that sympathy flows from nature to man, he almost feels it may be so, but he rejects the feeling as sentimental self-deception. In pointing to this typical gesture I do not wish to reduce poems to arguments, much less to arguments on a single issue or theme. In his better poems Frost weaves a rich and subtle counterpoint, cross-patterns of imagery and metaphor. In "The Need of Being Versed in Country Things" the main drama—in which the speaker, though tempted, holds to the factual truth of things—is mounted on a multiplicity of other meanings and suggestions. One might notice the play on ideas of dwelling and dwelling on (too much on what has been), of renewing and not renewing; more generally, the poem opposes the natural process of change and renewal to the human wish that things should stay, and even makes an irrational but subtle connection between the thought of things staying and of their being left behind and functionless, as though the one entailed the other. The chimney appears to be untouched by change and process, but there is no longer a house. It is compared in the first stanza to a pistil without petals. Or the pump, now dry. Or the hanging strand of wire.

Unable to believe that any sympathy flows from nature to man, Frost also rejected the Romantic premise of a benevolent, even ministering nature. Against this he distilled his draught of poison in "Design." Because the poem illustrates the "darker" side of Frost, it has been overpraised. In it the speaker sees a white spider holding a moth on a white heal-all flower. The scene, briefly presented, elicits horror and repulsion, and the speaker then questions:

What had that flower to do with being white,
The wayside blue and innocent heal-all?
What brought the kindred spider to that height,
Then steered the white moth thither in the night?
What but design of darkness to appall?—
If design govern in a thing so small.

The title and the last two lines emphasize that the poem is
written with reference to the theological argument from "design." This famous argument had strongly influenced thought
and feeling in the eighteenth century and the Romantic period.
It "proved" the existence, intelligence, and benevolence of God
from evidences of design in the natural world. For, it was
argued, no living thing could sustain itself apart from a natural
order into which it was integrated, and how could the organization and inter-organization of living things be explained except
through the existence of an intelligent organizer or designer?
Frost's evidences of design would presuppose a demonic designer; thus he gives the religious optimist a teasing poke in the
ribs. But if this poem shows that Frost is "a terrifying poet," as
Lionel Trilling claimed, it puts him on the terrifying side of
debate in the Romantic period. The argument from design had
long since been exploded (and parodied) by the time Frost wrote
his poem.

The Romantic poets often expressed a boldly confident humanism, idealizing man's boundless aspiration and potential
greatness. For Frost's anti-Romantic challenge, we may consider
"The Bear." Or there is the Romantic quest of ultimate truth,
the hope, in Shelleyan metaphor, to pass beyond the colored,
manifold veils of illusion and achieve a final knowledge. Frost's
"For Once, Then, Something" gently mocks this hope. Or there
are the Romantic metaphors of ascent to the transcendent, as in
Shelley's soaring skylark. Frost too has metaphors of ascent; you
climb on a birch trunk, or you go up on a ladder sticking
through a tree "toward heaven." You do not get very far and
you come down soon. A voyage is a recurrent Romantic metaphor. The questing mind of genius is "forever voyaging,"
Wordsworth says, "through strange seas of thought alone"; it is
"driven," Shelley says,

Far from the shore, far from the trembling throng
Whose sails were never to the tempest given.

But in Frost you do not voyage. You merely stand on the shore and look out to sea, like the people in "Neither Out Far Nor In Deep":

> They cannot look out far.
> They cannot look in deep.
> But when was that ever a bar
> To any watch they keep?

FROSTIAN IRONY

I have argued that Frost belongs essentially to the Romantic tradition in poetry, not only for the more obvious reasons—he is a "nature" poet, writing lyric and meditative verse on country sights and happenings; he emulates Wordsworth in taking the language actually spoken as his medium and the "ordinary" as his subject matter; he shares the Romantic ideal of spontaneous and "organic" composition—but also because his poetry elicits recollections of English and American poetry of the Romantic period. The comparisons thus activated indicate his own attitudes with enhanced nuance and subtlety, and the attitudes are anti-Romantic; that is, Frost takes his central concerns from the Romantic poets, but what they assert, he denies. In one all-important respect, however, Frost departs from Romantic precedent: in what we may loosely and provisionally call his irony.

Not that irony is absent from the poetry of the great Romantics. In one form or another it is omnipresent. The poetic theory of the Romantic age reinterpreted it profoundly, so that irony, heretofore thought of as one of the figures of speech in rhetoric, was viewed as a spiritual state, a way of relating to the world. But it was not for the Romantics an ultimate state. Yeats, for example, seems sometimes to have believed that all truth is polar or antithetical, hence ironical, but for Shelley or Blake such antitheses as body and soul, time and eternity, rise out of a deeper unity, and irony is an expression of man's limitation. At moments, the Romantics held, man may attain ultimate truth through his imagination. At such moments of highest insight, he is not ironical.

The lack of this faith lies at the heart of Frost's irony. Poetry is not for him what Wordsworth said it was, "Truth . . . carried alive into the heart by passion." Frost does not hold with Shelley that poets commune with "the eternal, the infinite, and the one." A poem is, he says, a "figure"—a shape or form—though a figure that may end in a limited and provisional "clarification of life." It is "play," though for "mortal stakes." It is "metaphor, saying one thing and meaning another . . . the pleasure of ulteriority." It is "performance," and "My whole anxiety is for myself as a performer. Am I any good?" With an ironic echo of Keats's "Ode on a Grecian Urn," Frost adds, "That's what I'd like to know and all I need to know." Such answers are not necessarily anti-Romantic, for mere difference is not necessarily contradiction. But the difference is considerable. Where the Romantic thinks of poetry as essentially a way of knowing (vision, imagination), Frost thinks of it as an aesthetic act with a possible, though limited, cognitive significance. But if poetry is figure, play, metaphor, or performance, so equally for Frost are other modes of thought and creative effort. Their value is practical, psychological, ethical, and aesthetic; they cannot produce ultimate knowledge.

Although Frost doubted the possibility of final truth, that did not prevent him from having opinions. He took sides in what he called the "standing argument," but, like most people, he could not feel certain. On this middle ground of perhaps and probably, irony is self-protectiveness. You may be wrong, so you do not commit yourself all the way. A poet may protect himself in other ways. He may write his poems not from himself personally but in dramatic character. Or, as Genevieve Taggard put it in a review of Frost, a poet may merely spread his metaphors, letting them take responsibility for whatever meanings are caught. But if he protects himself ironically, he is essentially taking both sides of the argument at the same time. He need not argue on both sides equally, and his appearance of concessiveness or even-handedness may itself be ironic, something we are intended to see through. Frost characteristically interprets this in a social context. It disarms criticism. It may even win the reader for your side because you acknowledge his side. Speaking ironically, Frost calls it "cowardice."

Irony is simply a kind of guardedness. So is a twinkle. It keeps the reader from criticism. Whittier, when he shows any style at all, is probably a greater person than Longfellow as he is lifted priestlike above consideration of the scornful. Belief is better than anything else, and it is best when rapt, above paying its respects to anybody's doubt whatsoever. At bottom the world isn't a joke. We only joke about it to avoid an issue with someone; to let someone know that we know he's there with his questions: to disarm him by seeming to have heard and done justice to his side of the standing argument.

Frost's irony might be described as a social poise. "To be at all charming or even bearable," he says, "the way is almost rigidly prescribed. If it is with outer seriousness, it must be with inner humor. If it is with outer humor, it must be with inner seriousness." In poetry, grief must go no further than it can "in play . . . Taste may set the limit. Humor is a surer dependence." But, to repeat, "belief is better than anything else." Social poise and "play" become the more valued as ideals precisely to the extent that they acknowledge and substitute for a lack of belief, at least of "rapt" belief or certitude. At bottom, Frost's irony is not a social performance but an evasion, though one with which most of us can sympathize. It is a means of speaking without affirming or denying, or at least of avoiding full commitment to whatever his words may imply. There is, he says, a kind of reader "who stands at the end of a poem ready . . . to drag you off your balance over the last punctuation mark into more than you meant to say. . . . Such presumption needs to be twinkled at and baffled." As we read his poems, what baffles is how seriously he means what he says and how much more than he literally says he may mean to imply. If one admires this, one may call it balance—as Frost did. If one has no taste for it, one may call Frost a "spiritual drifter"—as Yvor Winters did. But whatever we think of it, it is undeniably important in the chemistry of his effects.

His evasion is likely to be most baffling at the conclusions of his poems. The last line of "Design"—"If design govern in a thing so small"—comes with a sudden change in mood from horror to malicious humor. It pretends to offer an "out" to the religious believer in a designing Providence, an "out" which he cannot logically accept. It is said with a sly, mock tentativeness, a feigned courteous reluctance to insist on his opinion. It is a "twinkle," to use Frost's word, and it makes the poem less "terrifying" and more teasing. In "For Once, Then, Something," the speaker has looked down many a well and never seen to the bottom, but one day he saw something white there:

> What was that whiteness?
> Truth? A pebble of quartz? For once, then, something.

The major theme has been the Romantic quest for ultimate reality, which the poem treats both seriously and humorously, both enacts and parodies. The last line brings both points of view into plainer articulation and collision—"Truth? A pebble of quartz?"—and the final phrase half-humorously dismisses the problem. This typical return from speculation to Yankee wariness pokes gentle fun at whoever takes the question earnestly—the question whether transcendent truth can be known.

In the more recent critiques of Frost, even admirers rarely achieve the full-throated enthusiasm they may have for Yeats or Eliot. There seems to be a difficulty about conceding that Frost is a major poet. His ironic playfulness is one cause of this dubiety. To many minds it is simply not an adequate way of taking life. Those who feel this articulate their sense of Frost's inadequacy in different ways, but what generally they find lacking is seriousness, profundity, and commitment. They have a point. At his best Frost is never unqualified, final, and merely in earnest. As a result, some poetic or imaginative effects are not open to him. At the mysterious ethical and religious commands that conclude *The Waste Land* (doubly mysterious because they are in Sanskrit), we feel a certain awe, a piety in the presence of something ultimate. We never feel this in reading Frost. However irrational the effect may be, we feel for a moment that with Eliot's Sanskrit—DATTA, DAYADHVAN, DAMYATA—we have been given a basis for ordering our existence. The simplicity, directness, and unlimited implication of the words, their emotional weight and authority in their context, produce quasi-moral, quasi-religious satisfactions for the imagination. Such satisfactions may be had from Frost, but they are of a much less immediately powerful kind.

Whether these or any other observations and arguments necessarily mean that Frost was a minor poet, could be debated endlessly. Looking at it from Frost's point of view, I think he might have said, perhaps with only a slight trace of irony, that the wisdom of his poetry lies not so much in what he says as in the way he says it. The form is the major content. He keeps his balance, not coming down on one side or the other of arguments that cannot be settled. He moves forward, and momentary clarifications of an attitude or point of view rise to the surface, shimmer, and are submerged in the ongoing flow. He gives order and unity not to existence, but to an episode, a figure, and the figure has some "ulteriority" about it, a meaning beyond what is said. But even the poet cannot know how far the figure carries. There is no conclusion, merely a bowing out at the end of the performance. If Frost did not take his ideas "seriously," he took seriously what he had to teach about the way we should take ideas. Whether or not this deserves such terms as "profound" and "commitment," each reader may decide. This much can be said. Other major writers of the twentieth century—Eliot, Joyce, Yeats, Lawrence—were committed to beliefs, but the beliefs to which they were committed do not always give one much confidence in the balance of their minds. If Frost was skeptical, or at least remarkably provisional and wary, he is also one of the few significant writers of the twentieth century whose work seems consistently to preserve poise and sanity of mind.

12

THE IRISH SCENE

IN THE first twenty years of this century the situation of writers in Ireland differed fundamentally from those of England. Irish nationalism was the turbulent center of cultural life, and works of literature, like everything else, were informed by it and viewed in relation to it. Poetry like the young Joyce's *Chamber Music* (1907), which pursued art rather than Irishness, was for this reason a defiance, though in England these reticent, formally meticulous lyrics were unremarkable except for their excellence, and Joyce seemed merely a belated disciple of Dowson. Though nationalist feeling exposed writers to more than ordinarily ignorant criticism (the riots at Synge's *The Playboy of the Western World* are an extreme instance), it probably helped literature on the whole. It fostered an extra rapport between writer and audience and led writers to new, distinctive materials in the mythology and literature of ancient Ireland, and in the lore, life, and poetry of the folk. And the common use of these materials by so many different writers gave the appearance of a relatively unified movement to their diverse literary production.

There was in Ireland no immediate literary past to be reckoned with. Where England in the nineteenth century had its formidable Keats, Tennyson, Browning, Ruskin, Dickens, and so many others, Ireland had Mangan, Ferguson, and Carleton. The result was that by the end of the nineteenth century writers in England were on the defensive against the recent literary past and on the lookout for new premises and methods, seeking to establish a distinct identity of their own. Irish writers of the nineteenth century, however, could be regarded as only precursors or scouts. They had blazed trails into the immense, fertile territory to be occupied, but the husbandry remained to be done. So far as writers in Ireland could regard themselves as essentially Irish, rather than English—since they wrote in English their sense of identity was split to some extent—they had an exhilarating feeling of opportunity. Thomas Mann remarked in his journal, on reading Hesse's *Glasperlenspiel,* that it is "always disagreeable to be reminded that one is not alone in the world." This unpleasantness the Irish writers were to some degree spared.

These were the years of the Irish Renaissance, as it is usually called, when Synge, Yeats, and Lady Gregory were turning out plays for the Abbey Theatre, when Joyce was at work on *Dubliners, A Portrait of the Artist as a Young Man,* and *Ulysses,* and when a number of lesser figures were busy in prose and verse. The literary world in Ireland was dominated by the many-sided activity of Yeats as a poet, playwright, essayist, autobiographer, and theater manager. To the younger Irish poets, Austin Clarke recollects, "his renown was a visible legend. He had patrons, a theatre of his own, a private press and publishers ready to reprint the everchanging versions of his plays and poems. . . . In the art shops his best known lyrics . . . hand-printed, illustrated and framed, were on sale," and they were hung in "every house with any pretensions to good taste." The chief volumes of poetry from the Irish Renaissance during these years are Yeats's *In the Seven Woods* (1904), *The Green Helmet and Other Poems* (1910), *Responsibilities* (1914), *The Wild Swans at Coole* (1919), and *Michael Robartes and the Dancer* (1921). But aside from Yeats, whose career must be deferred until Chapter 23, poetry was not the strong point of the Irish movement, a fact which the existence of Yeats may partially explain. Among Irish poets are the famous names of Joyce and Synge, but each produced only one small volume of verse, and their poems are the least significant part of their work. Otherwise, one thinks of George Russell

(Æ), James Stephens, Padraic Colum, Joseph Campbell, Seumas O'Sullivan, Susan Mitchell, Dora Sigerson, Alice Milligan, Thomas MacDonagh, Joseph Plunkett, James Cousins, Francis Ledwidge, and a good many other figures at least equally minor.

Popular, patriotic verse in the nineteenth-century tradition of Young Ireland was continued after the turn of the century especially by two poets, Dora Sigerson (Mrs. Clement Shorter, 1866-1917), who was said to have died of grief and overwork caused by the failure of the Easter Rebellion, and Alice Milligan (1866-1953), whose *Hero Lays* (1908), as Ernest Boyd remarked, "confound in an identical enthusiasm the heroes" of ancient Irish legend and "the leaders of modern Irish" politics. In this imaginative act Miss Milligan was not alone. The writings, including a few poems, of Patrick Pearse, leader of the Easter Rebellion, show that far more distinguished heads made the same identification. In fact, that the heroism of epic Ireland had come again was one implication of Yeats's great poem "Easter 1916," though since the poem makes a qualified judgment on the Irish martyrs, it gave little pleasure in Ireland. The appeal of Miss Milligan, who utterly lacked invention, technique, and phrasing, was through sentiment alone. If one shared her cause, one responded to her emotion. Thomas MacDonagh, who was executed for his part in the Easter uprising, found *Hero Lays* "the best book of national Irish poems by a single author" and urged "all Irish people to buy it." Besides voicing her patriotic ardor right out, Dora Sigerson also wrote poems based on Irish legend and folklore. She was known especially for her ballads, which she composed with brisk management and directness. A more imaginative and expert poet of this description was Emily Lawless (1845-1913). Primarily a writer of fiction and no nationalist, she recreated in ballads times and moments of Irish history. Her other lyrics express an imaginative feeling for nature, especially the western coast of Ireland. The best of these is "A Bog-Filled Valley."

Among more sophisticated poets, the most influential single figure, after Yeats, was George Russell (1867–1935), who wrote under the pseudonym of Æ (derived from "Aeon"). A contemporary and friend of Yeats, Russell was a painter, poet, mystic, editor of *The Irish Statesman,* and noted personality. He contributed to the development of Irish poetry partly through his own lyrics, and even more perhaps through his benevolent editorial labors. Whatever Yeats's writings and example may have meant to younger poets, few of them received from him much direct, personal encouragement or help. (Yeats did, however, recognize and actively aid the best—Joyce, Synge, and F. R. Higgins.) Russell was generously ready to read unknown poets and publish and praise their work in his weekly. In *New Songs* (1904) he collected and brought to public attention the work of a number of young poets, all of whom thus owed their important literary introduction to him: Padraic Colum, Eva Gore-Booth, Thomas Keohler, Alice Milligan, Susan Mitchell, Seumas O'Sullivan, George Roberts, and Ella Young. A little later he discovered James Stephens. The sweet idealism of his nature reveals itself in his conception of a national literature as one "created by a number of men who have a common aim in holding up an overwhelming ideal—who create, in a sense, a soul for their country, and who have a common pride in the achievement of all."

Russell's poems are traditional in form and monotonous in theme. They speak of his mystic aspiration and of fleeting moments of finding and communion. And they speak of almost nothing else. He creates no people or actions, no passions except longing or ecstasy, and no concrete world except some pleasant landscape from which the eye at once lifts. His realm is the heavens, where in poem after poem one swims in radiant light or gazes down infinite starry vistas, symbols of Divine Being. One recurrent theme is the invidious comparison of earthly life or love to the mystic rapture. Some of his poems are in the style of the Celtic Twilight, for instance, "Prayer," "A Summer Night," and "Carrowmore." After 1903 he developed in some poems a more rhetorical eloquence, but essentially his style changed no more than his theme. A typical poem is "Dawn," from his first volume, *Homeward: Songs by the Way* (1894):

Still as the holy of holies breathes the vast,
Within its crystal depths the stars grow dim;
Fire on the altar of the hills at last
    Burns on the shadowy rim.

Moment that holds all moments; white upon
The verge it trembles; then like mists of flowers

> Break from the fairy fountain of the dawn
> The hues of many hours.
>
> . . . .
> Thrown downward from that high companionship
> Of dreaming inmost heart with inmost heart,
> Into the common daily ways I slip,
> My fire from theirs apart.

The relatively direct voicing of mystical feelings poses an utmost challenge to poetry, simply because of the weight and delicacy of the feelings to be expressed. For at least the last two hundred years most poetry of this kind is crudely insensitive, sometimes unbelievably so. Usually the trouble lies, I believe, in the poet's experience as well as in his language. There are more poets writing about mystical experience than having it, and there is considerable eagerness, in our post-Romantic literary culture, to mistake any queer, often self-induced state of mind for mystical communion. The poetry of Russell is inadequate to its theme, but in his case the trouble is not his experience, which was surely genuine, but his lack of technical and imaginative labor and skill. He had not the means powerfully to embody his experience, so the reader's relation to it remains external. He may be compared to Yeats in this respect. Russell's mystical experience was doubtless more authentic, and in this sense his poetry is more sincere. But such experience seems more authentic in Yeats, who was much more devoted as a craftsman to the art of writing poetry and, partly for that reason, was a master of artistic illusion.

Were it not that as poets they are too inept for criticism, something similar might be said of three younger versifiers of mystical tendency, Susan Mitchell (1866–1926), Joseph Plunkett (1887–1916), and Thomas MacDonagh (1878–1916). Susan Mitchell, a follower of Russell, shared his mystical nostalgia in *The Living Chalice* (1908). That same year she published a collection of satires and parodies directed against contemporary Irish personages, *Aids to the Immortality of Certain Persons in Ireland*. Plunkett and MacDonagh hoped to create a poetry of Roman Catholic mysticism, for most poets in Ireland at this time were Protestant and, if mystical, theosophical. Plunkett's sister says he "did not consider the versifying, but the thought expressed, to be of importance," and I fear she is right. In "Easter 1916" Yeats said that MacDonagh was "coming into his force" and "might have won fame in the end," but MacDonagh's poetry does not confirm the opinion. Plunkett and MacDonagh were executed for taking part in the Easter Rebellion. The national state of mind is indicated by the fact that collected editions of both were at once published and sold well.

Meanwhile, the Genteel Tradition was represented in Ireland by James H. Cousins (1873–1956), a poet of post-Tennysonian, cautiously Pre-Raphaelite, and ninetyish style, who specialized in sonnets and mythological tales using Irish mythology. Francis Ledwidge (1891–1917), a more interesting figure, grew up in the countryside, with little schooling and almost no contacts with other writers. Lord Dunsany discovered and introduced him, calling him a "peasant poet, comparable in some ways to Burns or Clare." His mild verse follows the insipid fashion of much English poetry of the later eighteenth century and the Romantic period—refreshment and escape in descriptions of peaceful countryside. It harmonized with Georgian taste in England, the more so since Ledwidge himself—the "peasant" lover of idyllic nature, the gifted young poet killed in the war—evoked a sentimental interest. He has some fresh images and a certain small wit. He is still mentioned respectfully in Ireland, but, though he described Irish landscape, his literary traditions were entirely English and he had no effect on what or how subsequent poets in Ireland wrote. James Starkey (1880–1958), who wrote under the pseudonym of Seumas O'Sullivan, was one of the young poets anthologized by Russell in *New Songs*. He was a lover of books whose inspiration came chiefly from other poets. His early verses mooned in the Celtic Twilight ("The Twilight People," "The Sheep," "The Poplars," "The Others"). He later composed a series of Dublin scenes, and these include his best poem, "In Phoenix Park," which has an actuality and humor he usually lacked. There are also love poems and elegies on Irish figures, including the heroes of the Easter Rebellion. Compared with Alice Milligan or Dora Sigerson—even, perhaps, with Æ—Starkey is a careful technician and cosmopolitan sophisticate. In a wider comparison he is unremarkable.

Apart from Russell, none of the poets noticed hitherto contributed much to the main development of Irish poetry. This had a twofold aspect. On the one hand, there was a spreading boredom with the languors and wearinesses of the Celtic Twilight, and, in reaction, a craving for strong passions and vigorous, coarse life. On the other hand, there was a folk movement, an interest in depicting the life and sensibility of the peasantry and in emulating their poetry. Although the two tendencies often intertwined, as in the poetry of Synge, they were different in motivation. Each corresponded to a phase in the poetry of England. The mode of the Celtic Twilight was in many ways a parallel to the Impressionist-Aesthetic poetry of England, and rejection of it corresponded to the similar English repudiation of Aestheticism in favor of full-blooded zest, as in Chesterton and Masefield. In Ireland the repudiation was more gradual and less decided, for the Celtic Twilight was enforced by nationalism, and even Yeats was berated for emerging into real day. The folk movement in Irish poetry had affinities with the milder type of Edwardian and Georgian verse in England: its affection for countryside, its nostalgia for the immemorial customs of village and farm, its feeling for history, its appreciativeness and benignity. In both countries there was a mellow documenting of a way of life felt to be passing.

The growing reaction against the poetry of the Celtic Twilight may be seen in Russell's review of Yeats as "A Poet of Shadows" (1902). He does not yet mean to object to the Twilight side of Yeats, only to the Symbolist. When he recommends "substance" and "life" he has something supernatural in mind, but his words go beyond his meaning, suggesting the more complete dissatisfaction he was to voice a few years later. "I confess I have feared to enter or linger too long in the many-coloured land of Druid twilights and tunes. . . . We, all of us, poets, artists, and musicians, who work in shadows, must some time begin to work in substance . . . I am interested more in life than in the shadows of life." When Russell, however, brought forward his young poets—Russell's canaries, they were called—in *New Songs* (1904), Yeats deplored his own poetic past in them: he heard "the sweet insinuating feminine voice" of those who dwell in a "country of shadows and hollow images. I have dwelt there too long not to dread all that comes out of it." He adds, in this letter of 1904 to Russell, that a "mysterious command" has gone out in the "invisible world of inner energies," and poets are henceforth to have "no emotions, however abstract, in which there is not an athletic joy." In his lyric, "A Coat" (1914), he heaped public scorn on those who had followed him into the Celtic Twilight and, abjuring the poetic trappings of "old mythologies," declared that there was "more enterprise / In walking naked." Earlier, in "The Passing of the Shee" (1907), Synge also composed a raucous farewell to the Celtic mode:

> Adieu, sweet Angus, Maeve and Fand,
> Ye plumed yet skinny Shee,
> That poets played with hand in hand
> To learn their ecstasy.
>
> We'll search in Red Dan Sally's ditch,
> And drink in Tubber fair,
> Or poach with Red Dan Philly's bitch
> The badger and the hare.

Aside from the poetry of Yeats, what the repudiators of the Celtic mist were looking for did not decisively appear in Ireland until 1909, the year when James Stephens (1880–1950) published his first volume, _Insurrections,_ and when Synge's _Poems_ came out posthumously. A protégé of George Russell, who is said to have been seeking a discovery to rival Yeats's lucky find of Synge in Paris, Stephens presented in this first volume a number of realistic Dublin scenes and portraits, interspersed with other poems of a more conventional kind. Russell acclaimed them as marking a new, needed departure in Irish verse. "For a generation," he said, "Irish bards have endeavoured to live . . . in chambers hung with the embroidered cloths and made dim with pale lights and Druid twilights. . . . It was a great relief" to hear "a sturdy voice blaspheming against all the formulae, and violating the tenuous atmosphere with its _Insurrections._" What Russell had in mind can be seen in "The Dancer," with its portrayal of a bitter anger in direct, colloquial speech. Poems of this kind, of which Stephens wrote several, were modeled partly on Browning. A different realism appears in more external descriptions of Dublin slums ("The Street behind Yours") and the Dublin poor ("To the Four Courts, Please"). That readers were startled and arrested by this imagery and diction is easily understood. For those who admired it, Stephens' later career was a disappointment. He gradually forgot not merely the urban and realistic, but picture and dramatic invention also, pursuing an increasingly bare poetry of ideas. The ideas lie inert, for the phrasing is not memorable and terseness has eliminated any other possible source of interest. Between *Insurrections* and his late abstractions, however, many pleasant poems may be found, such as "The Goat Paths" or "The Rivals." These poems are slight, but they show living rhythms, fresh, simple speech, agreeable fantasy, and a personality of much wistful-humorous charm. When Stephens ventures on large themes, his air of artlessness often gets him into trouble, the verses seeming more birdbrained than birdlike. In "Dance" the theme is caught from Blake—whom Stephens often imitated—but it loses Blake's deep, dramatic tension so that Blakean (perhaps also Nietzschean) innocence becomes mere silliness:

> Good and bad and right and wrong!
> Wave the silly words away!
> This is wisdom—to be strong!
> This is virtue—to be gay!

"A Woman Is a Branchy Tree" is typical of Stephens at his best:

> A woman is a branchy tree
> And man a singing wind;
> And from her branches carelessly
> He takes what he can find:
>
> Then wind and man go far away,
> While winter comes with loneliness;
> With cold, and rain, and slow decay,
> On woman and on tree, till they
>
> Droop to the earth again, and be
> A withered woman, a withered tree;
> While wind and man woo in the glade
> Another tree, another maid.

His finest single volume is *Reincarnations* (1918). These are based on Stephens' study of poems in Irish, and the presence of the Irish poets in these free adaptations gives him a depth as well as a bounce he could not achieve on his own.

Of the lyrics of Synge, many were atypical and had no influence, for they had been written in an earlier period, when he was practicing the Aesthetic-Decadent mode in Paris. None of them had the impact of his plays, where he wrote with greater freedom and color. But because he was famous as a playwright, and because he had composed for his poems a memorable, one-page Preface (see Chapter 4), they also had their effect. In many of his poems he portrayed the life and imagination of the folk, and in doing so, Synge achieved a powerful coarsening of image, diction, and rhythm, as in "Danny." Here, against his own fragile health and earlier aestheticism, Synge spoke in the person of a rural brawler:

> Then Danny smashed the nose on Byrne,
> He split the lips on three,
> And bit across the right hand thumb
> Of one Red Shawn Magee.

The folk movement in verse arose in the search for Irish identity. The poetry of the Celtic Twilight had the same object, but undertook to find it in ancient literature and mythology or distill it from moods of landscape. The folk movement sometimes included the same poets, but was inspired by a different thought: that one need only look at the class that had least assimilated the habits of the English conquerors, the Catholic peasantry. If anything was distinctively Irish, it was their life and thought, traditions, sensibility, and imagination. The folk movement received an especially strong impulse from the work of Douglas Hyde. In *The Love Songs of Connacht* (1893) Hyde had collected native poems in Irish and translated them into English prose. The prose retained much of the Irish idiom and rhythm and in fact approximated the English actually spoken by the peasantry in Ireland. The idiom Hyde created was adopted and developed by Lady Gregory and Synge in their plays. But Hyde's translations from folk songs and folk poets such as Raftery had also a direct impact on poetry, for they made available a native store of themes, feelings, forms, and diction. Moreover, they stimulated poets to learn Irish so they could read folk poetry in the original. Poets of the folk movement attempted to portray the life of the peasantry, using a simpler, more direct and colloquial style than that of the Celtic Twilight. They wrote lyrics in English similar in form and theme to the native Irish folksongs.

Yeats, Synge, and Lady Gregory wrote powerfully in the folk vein, but they did not belong to the Catholic peasantry and their identification with this class was crossed by other identifications and complicated by condescension. Padraic Colum (1881–1972) appreciated the Catholic rural class for the same nationalistic and literary reasons, but he also came from it and hence portrayed it without ironic distance. As a child in the workhouse, where his father was schoolmaster, he met, he says, "waifs, strays and tramps . . . and was entertained by the gossip and history of old men and old women who were survivals from an Ireland that had disappeared." When, a little later, he went to live on his grandmother's farm, he further experienced the traditional way of life; he also learned Irish history and legend from the talk before the peat fire. His early writings came directly out of this background. "The Plougher," "The Drover," and "The Poor Scholar" are sympathetic portraits of the rural poor. Colum was at this time writing plays, and his method in the poems is also "dramatic," as he later said: the poems arise "out of the character and situations" and the invented character is usually the speaker. The poems are informed also by his sense of Irish history; his "poor scholar," for example, is no contemporary figure but a voice from the 1840s, and his words vividly portray the poverty of rural life then and the political turmoil of the nation as it impinged on the life of one man. Other poems are translations or versions of the native folk songs, and still more were suggested by them. Even poems completely original with Colum may be almost indistinguishable from traditional ones. His words and stanzas invite singing so strongly that one improvises tunes while reading.

Oh I wish the sun was bright in the sky,
And the fox was back in his den O!
For always I'm hearing the passing by
Of the terrible robber men O!
    Of the terrible robber men.

Oh what does the fox carry over the rye,
When it's bright in the morn again O!
And what is it making the lonesome cry
With the terrible robber men O!
    With the terrible robber men.

Oh I wish the sun was bright in the sky,
And the fox was back in his den O!
For always I'm hearing the passing by
Of the terrible robber men O!
Of the terrible robber men.

Especially after he emigrated to America in 1914, Colum wrote many poems on animals, flowers, and places such as Carolina or Hawaii. But his best work dwells on Ireland. It should be read in *The Poet's Circuits* (1960), a late volume in which the poems of Ireland written at different times were collected and arranged for unified imaginative impact. It is a very pleasant book of verse, for Colum had simple language, clear images and form, and sympathy with his subject. He had a capable technique, usually unadventurous, though he practiced free verse at times and could also use a quiet, vernacular blank verse, which he may have learned from Robinson and Frost after he moved to New York. There are much humor and pathos in his writing, and moments of sharp anger, as in his poem on the hanging of Sir Roger Casement. But there is not much more, and particularly he lacks intellectual excitement. In addition to drama and poetry, Colum wrote children's books and other fiction, essays, and biographies; in later life he was also known as a folklorist. Through his vast, reminiscent knowledge of things Irish—ways of life, literature, history, legends—he did much to interpret Ireland, and his writings have a special interest for Irish readers.

So far as Joseph Campbell (1879–1944) is a regional poet, his work refers to the north of Ireland, where his early years were spent. As a young man he composed words for the music of traditional songs of Donegal, and the experience shaped his style henceforth. His best poems have the speed, simplicity, and economy of folksong and ballad. Unlike Colum, he also rendered or imitated the religious imagination of the peasantry ("The Gilly of Christ," "Every Shuiler is Christ," "I Met a Walking-Man"). He too composed—especially in *Irishry* (1913)—portraits of rural Irish types ("The Ploughman," "The Gombeen," "The Unfrocked Priest," "The Old Age Pensioner"). Based on firsthand knowledge, these are still fresh. Some have a rough, tragic power, such as "Scare-the-crows," the monologue of a crazed boy set to scare crows from the field. In "The Dwarf," one hears the words of a neighbor looking at a deformed child of the village, the voice conveying hatred born of superstitious fear and rumor. Campbell was the first poet in Ireland to write free verse, but otherwise his technique was traditional. He was an unsophisticated poet, whose strength lay in authenticity. "I Am the Mountainy Singer" is his true note:

> I am the mountainy singer—
> The voice of the peasant's dream,
> The cry of the wind on the wooded hill,
> The leap of the fish in the stream.
>
> . . . .
>
> No other life I sing,
> For I am sprung of the stock
> That broke the hilly land for bread,
> And built the nest in the rock!

Though F. R. Higgins (1896–1941) belongs to the next generation, he is the finest workman in the folk mode. Like Colum and Campbell, he composed portraits of rural types ("A Tinker's Woman," "The Past Generation"), and his historical imagination recreated the life of the past ("Hermits," "The Island Dead of Inchiglill," "Sword-Makers"). He also wrote personal lyrics, elegies, and drinking songs. Mostly his poems take for their themes the ones traditional in folk songs and ballads: the girl deserted by her lover; lovers kept apart by poverty, with the girl driven perhaps into a wealthy marriage; the woman whose lover is dead, in prison, or overseas; the priest tempted by the beauty of a girl ("The Three-Cornered Field," "The Victim," "A Poor Girl"). To these impersonal themes Higgins brought a new intensity. His characters have a more dramatic, individual presence and a greater passionate force than was common in folk speakers in the modern Irish lyric. Colum's "Old Woman of the Roads," for example, is an insipid sketch beside Higgins' "A Tinker's Woman." The randy speaker of "Glory O!," though an old woman, is no "dry nettle," but still juicy and hot for a young lover:

> Before the black hunger I'd husbands in plenty,
> And maybe your grand-dad was one of the many,
> Now was he that red-coat, who swigged more than any,
> Glory O, glory O! swigged a tin can of wine?

Such verse suggests that Higgins had taken to heart Synge's suggestion, that "before verse can be human again it must learn

to be brutal." Synge himself had called attention to the poetry of
Villon as an example. Perhaps one sees in Higgins how the influence of both Synge and Villon could converge, leading the poet
to direct language and elemental themes. In "The Victim," for
instance, a girl, pledged to marry a wealthy man, speaks to her
lover:

>Last fair-day I was decked
>Up in silks to the neck,
>The fair stood hushed to let me by,
>But there they made my match
>To an old man with a crutch,
>Whose green lands run to the sky.
>
>Ah, what of his crescent coach,
>His wine cups, his couch—
>The pride of my poor kith and kin—
>Beside your heart of wealth
>And mouth so sweetly felt
>This night beneath the creaky whin;
>Without shawl, shift or shoe,
>Crushed to sweetness by you,
>I close my eyes in my first bloom·
>Praying this tint of love
>May for a lifetime prove
>The fragrance in my living tomb.

Higgins has a systematic and crowded assonance and alliteration and his rhythms are freely varying and original. A note at
the end of his second volume of verse, *The Dark Breed* (1927),
tells that these—which he calls the "secret harmonies and the
sweet twists" and "the rhythm of a gapped music"—were
learned from the songs still sung in Gaelic, which keep alive the
"rigorous technique" of ancient Irish poetry. The technique
may be seen in the linking of lines through sound in "The Inn of
the Dead Men":

>As the grey air grows darker on grass-hidden water
>And black otters bark at the talking of starlings,
>We've walked, O my darling, so far through the valley
>That shadows are quenching each star.

He has a gift for the unexpected word that brings the object vividly before the eye—"the windy fidgets of September grasses,"

"It's down by hazy pale slabs of water, / Through bushy towns we'll quietly go"—and he heaps up images with a relishing gusto: "a squat hairy stevedore, / Bred on the south butt" of Mount Nephin, "With eyes in his black head like bits of the sun."

In *The Dark Breed* Higgins intended to break with the still lingering poetry of the Celtic Twilight. Gaelic poetry, he said, "is sun-bred": "Not with dreams but with fire in the mind, the eyes of Gaelic poetry reflect a richness of life and the intensity of a dark people, still part of our landscape." But many of the poems in *The Dark Breed* succumbed to the old, dreamy conventions, or only half escaped. His poetry ripened in concreteness, however, as he grew older, and his next and final volume, *The Gap of Brightness* (1940), dwells on this earth. In terms of literary history Higgins' achievement was to combine in a unified mode the two main influences on Irish poets after the turn of the century: folk poems in Gaelic, with their rich music and impersonal themes; and the direct, powerful actuality of Synge and Yeats. But in his later verse Higgins brought into these native traditions some aspects at least of the "modern" mode of the twenties and thirties in England and America. "To My Blackthorn Stick" is a sustained, witty comparison of the poet and his walking stick. The thought is carried in the images, and the poem plays against each other different tones of voice and realms of reference; except for some local allusions, it might have been written in any English-speaking country at this time:

> Lonesome, like me, and song-bred on Mount Nephin,
> You, also, found that in your might
> You broke in bloom before the time of leafing
> And shocked a world with light.
>
> . . . .
>
> I took that strength: my axe blow was your trumpet,
> You rose from earth, god-cleaned and strong;
> And here, as in green days you were the perch,
> You're now the prop of song.

13

POETRY OF WORLD WAR I

THE English poets who saw combat in the First World War were, with unimportant exceptions, Georgian poets. They were either already established within the Georgian literary world, like Brooke, or else they were younger writers developing in the same tradition, like Blunden and Owen. In the poetic milieu of that time it was possible to doubt whether modern war was a fit subject for poetry. In 1936 Yeats was still sure it was not: "passive suffering is not a theme for poetry . . . some blunderer has driven his car on the wrong side of the road—that is all." Moreover, given some of the traits of Georgian poetry—its commitment to nature, to charm, to the agreeable—it especially might seem unprepared to confront the mechanized horror. But in articulating their feelings and experiences during the war, the Georgian poets had in their immediate predecessors and contemporaries models that could be adapted: the novelistic incident and irony of Hardy, the bitterness and cynicism of Housman, the realism and would-be "brutality" of Synge, Masefield, and a few poems of Brooke's.

When the poetry of World War I is now read, it is usually because the emotions of men are part of their history. "Emotion" is an inadequate word; I am thinking of the extent to which poetry allows us intimately to know individuals as they are perceiving and seeking to integrate their experiences. Through poetry, the argument goes, the total response of persons in their time, place, and circumstances is vividly presented to the imagination. This access of historical understanding comes in the reading of all poetry, but when poetry is deliberately used for this purpose, it must be used with caution. What poets express depends not only on personal experience and feeling but also on literary tradition and convention; the personally experienced that cannot be articulated within the current poetic mode may not be articulated at all. Again, it is not a question of what a poet articulates only. Experience—what happens within or without the person—may not be experienced, may not be noticed or take on meaning unless it can be assimilated to prior habits of response built up by cultural tradition.

For at least two years the war had no important effect on poetry. Poets described the sights and incidents of war, but with methods and sensibilities carried over from peacetime. Only toward the end of the war do ideas of the nature and function of poetry begin to change—at least to expand—under the pressure of war emotions. Yet poets in the war were undergoing experiences that were prototypical for the next fifty years of literature. What they actually lived through was to become literary convention in the next two generations. Experiences they had undergone were often to be taken as the modal facts that reveal the essence of the human condition; extreme physical horror; violence; omnipresent death; the meaninglessness and futility of individual effort; the feeling that man is subject to an invisible, apparently insane bureaucracy; the blind turmoil of history shattering the private life. And whatever might be said for individual soldiers and civilians, the corporate behavior of the nations involved was a lesson in human limitation and evil. It was characterized from beginning to end by greed, deceit, false pride, blind unimaginativeness, selfish indifference to the sufferings of others, and stupid slowness to learn from the past. To the war poets themselves, however, these facts were not modal: they were deviations; and the poets responded with shock and protest, not with the helpless moral anguish of, for example, *The Waste Land*. To the end of the war and afterward the Georgians retained essentially that prewar state of mind in which the worst horrors that people do and suffer are viewed as anomalies. The War's deeper impact on literature came in the Modernist writing of the postwar years. But in this writing the impact, though it must have been profound, is practically invisible; it merged with many other intellectual and cultural influences, all leading in a similar direction.

AMERICAN POETS AND THE WAR

The audience for poetry increased in the United States during the war. Books such as Robert Service's *Rhymes of a Red Cross Man,* John McCrae's *In Flanders Fields,* Alan Seeger's *Collected Poems,* and Edgar Guest's *Over Here* enjoyed brisk sales (of these popular poets McCrae and Service were Canadian and Guest was born in England). Most of the better and also the better-known American poets wrote occasionally on themes inspired by the war. Possibly the finest "war" poem by an American was Frost's "Not to Keep." Or possibly some of the loose translations of ancient Chinese poems in Pound's *Cathay* (1915), which can be viewed as oblique expressions of feelings the war occasioned or intensified. And there were also Stevens' "Lettres d'un Soldat."

But neither in quantity nor significance does the American poetry of the First World War begin to compare with that of England. Until the United States entered the war in 1917, there was nothing remotely resembling the popular, patriotic enthusiasm that swept through England when the war began. Sympathies were divided between the Allies and Germany. England—George III—was still assumed to be the traditional enemy in some quarters; moreover, a substantial number of Americans were of German background. The main desire of most Americans was to stay out of "foreign" wars. So far as poetry was concerned, the sole important exception to this national sentiment was found among the exemplars of the Genteel Tradition on the Eastern seaboard. These Anglophiles hurled poetry against the Germans from 1914 on. Helen Gray Cone, who taught English at Hunter College, celebrated Anglo-American brotherhood in *A Chant of Love for England, and Other Poems* (1915). George Woodbury proliferated sonnets of anti-German idealism; his poems of patriotic devotion embraced not only England but other allied countries as well: "Rise, rise, Roumania, yet thy soul is whole!" Poems of tribute to France, with much reference to Joan of Arc, also showered from the Genteel sphere. A recurrent theme for lamentation and wordy vengeance was the German destruction of monuments of French culture—for example, "Rheims Cathedral—1914" by Grace Hazard Conkling. Among the Genteel poets of the war was T. S. Eliot's mother, Charlotte C. Eliot, who published "Crusaders—A War Song" in the Boston *Herald* in 1917.

Because the United States entered the war late, and relatively few poets volunteered or were conscripted, American poets generally lacked the direct experience of combat that gradually altered the style and poetic purpose of their English contemporaries. The most important exception was Alan Seeger (1888–1916). Seeger was living as a student and writer in Paris when the war broke out. He enlisted in the French Foreign Legion and was killed under a crossfire of machine guns. Of some twenty poems that reflected his war experiences and emotions, the best-known is the moving lyric that begins,

> I have a rendezvous with Death
> At some disputed barricade,
> When Spring comes back with rustling shade
> And apple-blossoms fill the air.

"Champagne, 1914–15" is also memorable. Seeger is the only American poet of significant promise who was killed in the war.

To sum up, the First World War was not a transforming emotional experience for most American poets, and in this respect they were representative of their country. Once the United States entered the war there was much popular enthusiasm, which reflected itself in patriotic verse. But the spirit of it was, on the whole, expressed in such songs as "Over There," "When the Boys Come Home," and "Keep the Home Fires Burning." The war was entered reluctantly, the chief desire was to end it as quickly as possible, and the imagination of Americans was fixed fondly on the return of peace, when, it was assumed, life would go on as though the war had never happened.

ENGLISH POETS: THE FIRST PHASE

When war came to England in 1914, poetry was among the first volunteers. The verse of the past was mobilized in anthologies such as *The Flag of England* and *The Country's Call*. New poets sprang up, and the established poets of the day, young and old, united in noble eloquence. Binyon, Kipling, Watson, Freeman, Noyes, Chesterton, Hardy, Newbolt, Flecker, Brooke, and the Bishop of Lincoln, among others, wrote patriotic or martial verses in 1914. They voiced the simple, intense, and ideal emotion that swept England at the start of the war, as it did all the combatant countries. England was not fighting for itself alone, and not only for "ravished" Belgium and France also, but for Freedom, Truth, Justice, Peace, Civilization, and a Better World Tomorrow. As Kipling put it,

> There is but one task for all—
> One life for each to give.
> Who stands if Freedom fall?
> Who dies if England live?

"Happy is England now," thought John Freeman, for

> There is not anything more wonderful
> Than a great people moving towards the deep
> Of an unguessed and unfeared future.

And in "The Stars in Their Courses," where he characterizes war as "all ungentle wantonness," he feels "the heart of England throbbing everywhere" as "her courage rises clean again." High-minded grief and faith were voiced by Binyon in "For the Fallen," an elegy of twenty-eight lines that was published as an expensive, illustrated book:

> With proud thanksgiving, a mother for her children,
> England mourns for her dead across the sea.

The war's first effects on poetry were to promote a feeling of solidarity between poets and their readers and to attract more readers, since more persons than is commonly the case could find their emotions articulated in poetry. And the noble generalizations and national pieties the war fostered in its opening phase presented no challenge to the Romantic poetic tradition. If anything, the war at first heightened the authority of this tradition, felt to be the native one in poetry. The sonnets of Brooke, discussed in Chapter 10, are the memorable product of this state of mind.

Before long, however, a split developed between the poets who merely read about the fighting and those who actually did it. Those who stayed at home perforce continued the generalizing vein. Those who saw combat had unfamiliar, sometimes shattering experience, which they tried to convey. But though they had a new subject, neither as a group nor as individuals did they yet have an attitude toward the war. At least they had no attitude that essentially distinguished them from the stay-at-home poets or from their own peacetime selves. They wrote of their thoughts of home and fear of death, of marching, machine guns, bombardments, assaults, shelled towns, of friendships and conviviality, and of moments of peace, beauty, or religious feeling in landscape—in short, whatever made up their experience of war. Imagists such as Richard Aldington or Herbert Read treated scenes of battle in Imagist style—for example, Aldington's "Machine Guns":

> Gold flashes in the dark,
> And on the road
> Each side, behind, in front of us,
> Gold sparks
> Where the fierce bullets strike the stones.

As Sir Herbert Read put it, looking back in 1939: "The War came, but that did not make any essential difference to our poetry. . . . If War was to be expressed in poetry the imagist technique was as adequate as any other."

Poetry essentially unchanged by war experience appears in Robert Graves (*Fairies and Fusiliers,* 1917), Robert Nichols (*Invocation: War Poems and Others,* 1915; *Ardours and Endurances,* 1917), and in most of the poems Ivor Gurney, Edmund Blunden, and Isaac Rosenberg wrote during the war. Before the war broke out Ivor Gurney (1890–1937) showed startling promise as both a poet and a musician. He fought in the war, was wounded, gassed, suffered a mental breakdown in 1918, recovered sufficiently to study under Vaughan Williams in 1919, had a final mental collapse in 1922, and spent the rest of his life in asylums. He published two books of poetry, *Severn and Somme* (1917) and *War's Embers* (1919), and continued to compose verse until he died. (A selection from his manuscripts was brought out by Edmund Blunden in 1954.) The general theme of his war poems is the recollection of peaceful English countryside, or the sight of unravaged nature in France amid the havoc of war, and they reflect the depth and sincerity of his love for country things:

> Tall elms, greedy of light,
>   Stand tip-toe. See
> The last light linger in
>   Their tracery.
>
> The guns are dumb.

The poems written after his final breakdown are repetitious and usually not quite coherent. Nevertheless, they deserve attention, for his technique matured, and his phrasing gained in intensity:

> What evil coil of Fate has fastened me
> Who cannot move to sight, whose bread is sight,
> And in nothing has more bare delight
> Than dawn or the violet or the winter tree.
> Stuck in the mud—Blinkered up, roped for the Fair.
> What use to vessel breath that lengthens pain?
> O but the empty joys of wasted air
> That blow on Crickley and whimper wanting me!

The war poems of Edmund Blunden also illustrate an exceptionally tough persistence of peacetime habits of sensibility. Blunden was in the army from 1914 to 1919 and saw much of the more terrible fighting. We know from *Undertones of War* (1928) and other retrospective prose essays not only what he went through but its traumatic impact on him. The war seems to have preoccupied the depths of his mind for years afterward. And yet in the poetry he wrote between 1914 and 1919 the war is not usually the main focus of his feeling. It is present in images of devastated fields or farms or in emotions of relief at some sight of unspoiled country things, brief reminders of peace and beauty. But the rural world is still the center of attention. Amid and despite the war, nature is felt to offer sufficient spiritual consolation.

At least three explanations suggest themselves. Trauma does not usually induce an immediate change in habits of feeling. The tendency is much rather for the old patterns to assert themselves all the more. Secondly, the Georgian mode of nature poetry could not easily assimilate war and the responses it awakened. And Blunden probably had little wish to express in poetry either the war or his feelings about it. He was committed to landscape poetry, not only by habit but by belief and love. (He even carried into the trenches a copy of Young's *Night Thoughts*.) Poetry, to his mind, had nothing to do with the war and everything to do with the survival during war of the heart and spirit of man.

Aside from Blunden and a few others, the poetry of 1914–1916 did not avoid or soften the physical horror of war. Neither did it attempt to emphasize it or suggest that war is all horror. It presented war thoughts and happenings, but with no intention to end the war by denouncing and exposing what it was "really" like. That was to come in the poetry of Sassoon and Owen. Poems such as Graves's "A Dead Boche" were presumably written to shock civilians; and its grisly details make one uncomfortable. But if such poems were motivated by a political purpose, it was only an occasional motive in the first two years of the war. The poems of Charles Sorley (1895–1915) are remarkably free from the widespread illusions of 1914 and 1915. With the examples of Hardy and Housman to help him, he articulated an ironic bitterness in envisioning the waste of war, but Sorley was killed too young to become the important poet he might have been. On the whole, the first two years of combat forced poets to articulate new experiences, but this did not essentially change their poetry.

SIEGFRIED SASSOON

In a later stage of the war there was sometimes the feeling of a radical separation between the soldier poets and their audience, though not for the same reasons as subsequently with Modernist poetry. By 1917 the illusions of the first months had faded—more completely in the trenches than at home. The war poets, who were mostly officers, identified with the soldiers they led, felt compassion for them, and admired their endurance, courage, and self-sacrifice. They also felt that with respect to the war soldiers had the moral authority that accrues to firsthand experience and personal suffering. No civilian had the same right to speak of the war, for he could not fully know what he was talking about; neither was his patriotism dangerous to himself. Some of the poets were by this time totally in revolt against the war, which had come to seem an insane slaughter. Out of these feelings came a new use for poetry. It would bear witness to the truth of the war, speaking on behalf of the soldiers and making the civilians see and feel what war actually is. It would attack the emotions and the illusions that permitted the war to go on. This poetry, of which Sassoon and Owen are the chief exemplars, combined a closely detailed presentation of violence and horror with pity for the soldiers and denunciation and ridicule directed toward the implied audience.

At this point the war had brought about some important changes in poetry. It had called forth a gruesome and shocking imagery, which, while not unprecedented before the war, was far from the usual idea of "poetry." It had extended the range of expectable moods, especially in the directions of anger and ridicule, though here also there was much prewar precedent. And in Sassoon it had encouraged an effectively direct colloquial speech. Both he and his soldier protagonists learned their breezy talk from Masefield, but it was more casual and authentic in Sassoon. Moreover, the war led Sassoon, and to some degree Owen, to a poetry of realistic documentation in the service of a political cause. All these tendencies might be summed up under the label "realism," a realism that continued from that developing before the war in Hardy, Masefield, or Synge, but was also different. The difference was between realism as an attempt to reflect life (not to mention realism as literary experiment and provocation) and realism with a further, more particular moral purpose. The purpose unites the realism of Sassoon and Owen with satire and sometimes lifts it into apocalyptic grandeur.

Siegfried Sassoon (1886–1967) produced several volumes of poetry before and after the war, but he owed his fame mainly to the fifty or sixty pages of verse he wrote between 1916 and 1918. Before 1916 his poetry was typically Georgian. When the war came, Sassoon felt the spreading, uplifting fervor, as in "To My Brother":

> Give me your hand, my brother, search my face;
> Look in these eyes lest I should think of shame;
> For we have made an end of all things base.
> We are returning by the road we came.

He was a dedicated, sometimes heroic officer. In the early months of 1915 he was still writing poetry that reminds one of the glossy, illustrated *Country Life,* as in "The Old Huntsman." The poem is a reminiscent monologue lightly sprinkled with dialect. The old fox-hunter recalls the fine chases he has had, the weathers and landscapes, and puzzles about religion. Masefield presides over the poem; so it is not surprising that the old man finds God in nature:

> It's God that speaks to us when we're bewitched,
> Smelling the hay in June and smiling quiet;
> Or when there's been a spell of summer drought,
> Lying awake and listening to the rain.

On leave in 1916, Sassoon met Lady Ottoline Morrell, and through her was introduced to a circle of pacifists and conscientious objectors. In this circle he heard informed criticism of the war, its justification and its motives. This intellectual shock coalesced with the feelings of horror and futility the war was impressing on so many soldiers (the British had 420,000 casualties in the Somme offensive alone) and with his disgust at the contrast between comfortable civilian militancy and the suffering in the trenches. He had already composed a few narrative poems intended to picture front-line conditions ("The Redeemer," "In the Pink," "A Working Party"), and, though these do not question that the war is right and necessary, they dwell on the pathos and self-sacrifice of the soldiers. Now (September 1916) he began to write poems "deliberately devised," as he later said, "to disturb [civilian] complacency." These poems were published in *The Old Huntsman* (1917). "They" is typical. The Bishop mouths the views of stay-at-homes about war, still thinking of it as both justified and redemptive. The soldiers, misunderstanding the vapory clichés, are disconcertingly literal in their reply:

> The Bishop tells us: "When the boys come back
> "They will not be the same; for they'll have fought
> "In a just cause: they lead the last attack
> "On Anti-Christ; their comrades' blood has bought
> "New right to breed an honourable race,
> "They have challenged Death and dared him face to face."
>
> "We're none of us the same!" the boys reply.
> "For George lost both his legs; and Bill's stone blind;

"Poor Jim's shot through the lungs and like to die;
"And Bert's gone syphilitic: you'll not find
"A chap who's served that hasn't found *some* change."
And the Bishop said: "The ways of God are strange!"

In autumn of 1917 Sassoon composed the poems that made up *Counter-Attack* (1918). The title is that of one of the grisly narratives included, but the whole collection may be regarded as Sassoon's counterattack on the war. When he wrote these poems, he was under treatment in a hospital for shell shock, having written and mailed his commanding officer an antiwar declaration. Whether he was in the hospital for his own sake or for the army's, I do not know; his protest was extreme and potentially embarrassing to the military, which may have been glad to dismiss it as neurasthenia. The poems of *Counter-Attack* assail civilian complacency, journalists, parliamentarians, staff officers, and generals. They are mostly anecdotes with satiric points, as in "The General":

"Good-morning; good-morning!" the General said
When we met him last week on our way to the line.
Now the soldiers he smiled at are most of 'em dead,
And we're cursing his staff for incompetent swine.
"He's a cheery old card," grunted Harry to Jack
As they slogged up to Arras with rifle and pack.
. . . .
But he did for them both by his plan of attack.

In a few poems Sassoon creates scenes of lurid, visionary power—

Sad, smoking, flat horizons, reeking woods,
And foundered trench-lines volleying doom for doom—

or of sickening detail closely observed, for example, corpses in a captured trench:

face downward, in the sucking mud,
Wallowed like trodden sand-bags loosely filled;
And naked sodden buttocks, mats of hair,
Bulged, clotted heads . . .

None of his poems can compare with the best of Wilfred Owen, whom Sassoon influenced, and some of them are hardly more than journalism, but his book still impresses by its bitterness, anguish, and despair. There is no doubt that Sassoon was expressing the genuine alienation and disillusion of men in the trenches, and it is equally certain that the targets of his attack too often deserved it. To anyone informed about the Great War, *Counter-Attack* affords a relief to the feelings. But pity and indignation, however justified, do not usually promote balance, resonance, and perspective. Sassoon's poetry of war protest makes a stronger, more immediate impact, but it is not necessarily better in kind than the Georgian poetry of war experience. Wilfred Owen became a memorable poet not by the simplicity of his responses, but by their complexity.

After the war Sassoon continued writing satires for a few years. These were gathered together in *Satirical Poems* (1926). Church and army brass remain targets, but more often he doodles malicious impressions of the bloated rich, of the aristocracy, or of affected appreciators at concert and art gallery. In most poems he is more amused than indignant; accordingly, his style takes its ease, becoming less purposefully focused and effectively unrestrained. In the best of these satires he deflates his own person also, seeing himself as, for example, the cultivated, globe-trotting poet at the Villa d'Este, where he remembers Byron, Landor, Liszt, and Browning, and diligently jots phrases in his notebook. The chief virtue of these poems is the complex and unsettled attitude, the play of one point of view against another; they tend to be more ironic than satiric. He is, in short, a minor Auden—pleasant, witty, and casual.

After 1926 Sassoon's main literary activity for the next twenty years was prose autobiography, first in slightly fictionalized form as the life story of "George Sherston" (*Memoirs of a Fox-Hunting Man*, 1928; *Memoirs of an Infantry Officer*, 1930; and *Sherston's Progress*, 1936), and then directly (*The Old Century and Seven More Years*, 1938; *The Weald of Youth*, 1942; and *Siegfried's Journey*, 1945). These memoirs had considerable success, especially the first, which, idyllic and nostalgic, portrayed a life of fox-hunting and cricket in wealthy country houses before the war. Meanwhile the Georgian sensibility returned to his poetry. One sees the conscientious unbeliever or God-wishing soul, longing for the "day" it cannot find (until in 1957 he joined the Roman Catholic Church); the imagination intuiting immemorial time and history in a particular spot of England; the love of fields, rooks, clouds, bleakly beautiful landscape, and, indoors, fireside solitude and quiet. The social, almost the external world has now vanished from his poetry; all is personal feeling and ruminant mind. The style is direct, simple, grave, and quiet, reflecting his liking for Herbert and Vaughan. It reflects especially his spiritual affinity with Hardy, his "main admiration," as he once said, and his poetic journey after *Counter-Attack* might be described as a retreat (or advance) from anticipation of Auden to remembrance of Hardy. In 1939, in a lecture *On Poetry,* he articulated once again the Georgian view of poetry, long since on the defensive. He praised personality and the "language of the heart" as opposed to logical dehumanization, directness and simplicity as against Modernist complex obliquity, and affirmed with Housman (and Wordsworth) that the function of poetry is to convey emotion. He was against mere undisciplined spontaneity, for, although "sincerity and inspiration" were naturally indispensable, so also were tradition and formal control. The bitterly polemical poet of World War I now deplored poetry with a political purpose, telling the students of Bristol University that it was too likely to be local, transient, and propagandistic, hardly more than tub-thumping.

WILFRED OWEN

Wilfred Owen (1893–1918) was born at Oswestry, Shropshire, and was educated at the Birkenhead Institute in Liverpool. He matriculated at the University of London when he was seventeen, but there is no record that he ever actually studied there. Of delicate health, he had been a dreamy, bookish boy. From childhood he had loved poetry and was particularly fond of Keats. He was already writing verse in the manner of the early Keats and planned a volume with the diffident title, "Minor Poems, in a Minor Key, by a Minor." After a serious illness, he spent two years in France (1913–1915) in order to avoid English winters. He first taught in the Berlitz School of Languages, then served as a tutor in a private family near Bordeaux, continuing to work on "Minor Poems." When the war began he felt it his duty to enlist, despite his health, and was accepted for service in the Artist's Rifles (1915). In a letter to his mother (March 5,

1915) he spoke of his ambitions as a poet: "*To be able* to write as I *know how to,* study is necessary: a period of study, then of intercourse with kindred spirits, then of isolation. My heart is ready, but my brain unprepared, and my hand untrained. And all,—untested. I quite envisage possibility of non-success." The following year he was commissioned in the 5th Reserve Battalion. The experience of trench warfare, vividly described in his letters home, quickly deepened him emotionally as a poet. A friend later wrote of his "intense pity for suffering humanity—a need to alleviate it, wherever possible, and an inability to shirk the sharing of it, even when this was useless. This was the keynote of Wilfred's character; indeed it was, simply, Wilfred. His sensitiveness, his sympathy were so acute, so profound, that direct personal experience . . . can hardly be said to have existed for him. He could only suffer, or rejoice, vicariously." Invalided home in June 1917, he met Siegfried Sassoon, and the older writer encouraged and helped give direction to Owen's poetry. Despite the efforts of his friends to find him a staff position in England, he was sent back to France (August 1918) as a company commander and put in the front lines. He received the Military Cross for gallantry under fire (October 1) and was killed a week before the Armistice.

If Owen at his best wrote more powerfully than the other war poets discussed, it is not through a greater realism but through an ampler gift in traditional and "Romantic" qualities of style and imagination, which unite with the realism and qualify it. His earlier poems show the influence not only of contemporaries and immediate predecessors but also, as I said, of Shelley and especially Keats. When he sought later to make readers feel the war as he felt it, he did not lose these earlier sources nor did he cease to be interested in technique. "I am a poet's poet," he wrote in a letter of 1917. One finds in his greater poetry a combination of qualities that often appear only in separation—traditional Romanticism with realism, moral and political passion and purpose with technical elaboration and control. Though there is only one theme—"My subject is War, and the pity of War"—there is a great variety of treatment—parable and vision, narrative, subjective lyric, dramatic monologue, case history—and a wide range of feeling.

The realism appears most nakedly in such poems as "The

Sentry" (based on an actual experience) or "Dulce Et Decorum Est":

> Bent double, like old beggars under sacks,
> Knock-kneed, coughing like hags, we cursed through sludge,
> Till on the haunting flares we turned our backs
> And towards our distant rest began to trudge.
> Men marched asleep. Many had lost their boots
> But limped on, blood-shod. All went lame; all blind;
> Drunk with fatigue; deaf even to the hoots
> Of tired, outstripped Five-Nines that dropped behind.
>
> Gas! Gas! Quick, boys!—An ecstasy of fumbling,
> Fitting the clumsy helmets just in time;
> But someone still was yelling out and stumbling
> And flound'ring like a man in fire or lime . . .
> Dim, through the misty panes and thick green light,
> As under a green sea, I saw him drowning.
>
> In all my dreams, before my helpless sight,
> He plunges at me, guttering, choking, drowning.

The effect of reality is achieved primarily through the action itself, the shock and terror of a gas attack. It is sustained through unpoetic, observed detail ("Bent double," "Knock-kneed," "Many had lost their boots") and through Owen's care to find the word that accurately corresponds to the sensation, as in the "hoots" of the shells, or the "misty panes" of the gas mask, or the "thick green" of the gas. It further determines the deliberately disagreeable metaphors out of Synge or Yeats ("old beggars under sacks"), and the diction of brutal, unqualifying directness ("hags," "cursed," "sludge," "yelling out") and colloquial casualness ("turned our backs," "just in time"). There is also the rhythm, manipulated through many caesuras to break poetic swing and emphasize or dramatize the action. With its realism and horror, bitterness and irony, force and directness, the poem seems far from the traditionally "poetic," but there is, even here, something of a "Romantic" heightening. It appears in the phrases "All went lame; all blind," where the repeated "all" lends something sublime and visionary to the scene. It appears also in the controlled use of assonance and alliteration to bind the lines together, so that even in a poem that seems an immediate report of actual experience, one finds the complex pattern of "l" and "b" alliteration in,

> But limped on, blood-shod. All went lame; all blind.

This use of vowel and consonant pattern Owen had caught from
Keats. It is as obvious an example as could be found of Owen's
combination of romantic tradition with realism. The start of
"Strange Meeting," for example, goes:

> It seemed that out of battle I escaped
> Down some profound dull tunnel, long since scooped
> Through granite which titanic wars had groined;

or there are the echoing "w's," "r's," and "s's" in,

> But wound with war's hard wire whose stakes are strong,

or the "l's," "d's," and short "u's" of,

> Treading blood from lungs that had loved laughter.

This lingering Romanticism is often mentioned reproachfully,
as though it were a survival of earlier bad habits from which
Owen, dying young, had not yet freed himself. It may be so, but
I view it more as a strength in the poetry. Because Owen's style
was more traditional, it was more accessible than most of the
modern poetry that commands the respect of critics. Poem after
poem illustrates the transition from the romantic tradition to the
realistic;—for example, the often-quoted "Anthem for Doomed
Youth":

> What passing-bells for these who die as cattle?
>   Only the monstrous anger of the guns.
>   Only the stuttering rifles' rapid rattle
> Can patter out their hasty orisons.
> No mockeries now for them; no prayers nor bells,
>   Nor any voice of mourning save the choirs,—
> The shrill, demented choirs of wailing shells;
>   And bugles calling for them from sad shires.

The last line is a fine instance of Romantic suggestion, and
doubtless many readers are also haunted by literary reminiscence in the two previous lines. But if one remembers Keats's
ode "To Autumn,"

> Then in a *wailful choir* the small gnats *mourn*,

the lines become a striking example of literary transplantation, or rather transformation. Despite the bitterness in which it begins, the sonnet gives the kind of pleasure to which readers of poetry were accustomed. Only from a doctrinaire Modernist point of view, now itself outdated, could it be condemned for this reason.

Owen's diction has also been attacked for its Romantic elements. Yeats, having never been able to exclude such items from his own poetry, excluded Owen from his *Oxford Book of Modern Verse* on the ground that "He is all blood, dirt, and sucked sugar stick . . . he calls poets 'bards,' a girl a 'maid' & talks about 'Titanic wars.'" "Titanic wars" comes from Owen's "Strange Meeting," which also has such phrases as "made moan," "grieves richlier," and the Yeatsian "hunting wild / After the wildest beauty of the world." The poem also contains Romantic props such as "sullen hall," "tigress," "citadels," and "chariot wheels." Whether these are appropriate to the context may be argued, but what seems more important is that the poem, which Sassoon calls Owen's "passport to immortality," achieves a greater aesthetic distance, and with this a more complex resonance, through the Romantic mode of visionary poetry. This is a further contribution of the more traditional and Romantic elements in Owen's style—a certain distance from the subject.

The Romanticism of Owen's temperament also reveals itself in an intense and emotional idealization of the common soldier, and this gives his attitudes toward the war a greater complexity. He once described himself as a "conscientious objector with a very seared conscience." With a moral loathing of the war and a huge anger at the civilians who tolerated, supported, or profited from it, he thought of himself as a voice through which the sufferings of the soldiers could be pleaded. And he believed that only if he shared their sufferings had he the right to speak for them. He also felt guilty about the soldiers whom he, as an officer, was leading like cattle to the slaughterhouse. Something of this conflict appears in a letter of 1918:

For 14 hours yesterday I was at work—teaching Christ to lift his cross by numbers, and how to adjust his crown; and not to imagine he thirst till after the last halt. I attended his Supper to see that there were not complaints; and inspected his feet that they should be worthy of the

nails. I see to it that he is dumb, and stands to attention before his ac-
cusers. With a piece of silver I buy him every day, and with maps I make
him familiar with the topography of Golgotha.

To see the soldiers as Christ implied that they were innocent and
crucified; but Owen also felt their suffering released or created
in them a spiritual worth. Among his better-known poems,
"Apologia Pro Poemate Meo" and "Greater Love" are built on
the paradox of the spiritual emerging out of the foulness of war:

> I, too, saw God through mud,—
>   The mud that cracked on cheeks when wretches smiled.
> . . . .
> And witnessed exultation—
>   Faces that used to curse me, scowl for scowl,
>   Shine and lift up with passion of oblation.
> . . . .
> I have perceived much beauty
>   In the hoarse oaths that kept our courage straight;
>   Heard music in the silentness of duty . . .

and,

> Red lips are not so red
>   As the stained stones kissed by the English dead.
> Kindness of wooed and wooer
> Seems shame to their love pure.
> O Love, your eyes lose lure
>   When I behold eyes blinded in my stead!

In these verses the invidious comparison of the lesser love, faith,
and sacrifice of the civilian is plain; it is underlined at the end of
"Apologia Pro Poemate Meo":

>   These men are worth
> Your tears. You are not worth their merriment.

A word should also be said about his important technical innovation: consonant rhyme (escaped/scooped; groined/groaned).
Owen used this in a rather strict way, preserving the same consonants with a different vowel. Later poets employed the device
more loosely (winter/ladder). It was not unknown in English and
Welsh poetry before Owen, or he may have picked it up from
French sources, but it is equally or more probable that he devel-

oped it on his own. Later poets learned it from him. He adopted it in about a third of his mature poems.

Only four of Owen's poems were published in his lifetime. In 1919 Edith Sitwell published some of his poems in *Wheels*, and in 1920 she and Siegfried Sassoon brought out a volume of poems from manuscripts. This was reprinted in 1921 and there was no further printing until the edition of Edmund Blunden in 1931. Then, however, Owen had his impact on the younger English poets, notably Auden, Spender, MacNeice, and Day Lewis. Leftist or Communist in sympathy at that time, they were attracted to his use of poetry for a political purpose, his idealization and celebration of common men, and his wrathful indignation against those who were exploiting them. They also picked up some features of his style, especially his consonant rhyme. In 1935 Spender remarked that Owen was "the most useful influence in modern verse." Most of these poets gave similar testimonials, but what they could not learn were Owen's personal qualities of emotional intensity, directness, boldness, and imaginative grandeur. Lines such as

> Heart, you were never hot
> Nor large, nor full like hearts made great with shot,

— weird —

or, in prophecy of the postwar world,

> None will break ranks, though nations trek from progress,

or

> Was it for this the clay grew tall?

show how much that might have been magnificent was lost through his death.

ISAAC ROSENBERG

Isaac Rosenberg (1890–1918) was one of the finest of the war poets, but the war had no important effect on his methods or sensibility. From the point of view of literary history, he is a transitional figure, having affinities with both Georgian and Modernist poetry. Among the poets of 1916–1918, his attitudes are exceptional, for the war did not confront him with essential truths he could not assimilate. It did not strongly violate his imaginative sense of man's nature and condition. Where Owen's "Strange Meeting" dwells on the tragic waste of this war in particular, Rosenberg's "Dead Man's Dump" articulates the tragedy of man, doomed and helplessly alone:

> None saw their spirits' shadow shake the grass,
> Or stood aside for the half used life to pass
> Out of those doomed nostrils and the doomed mouth,
> When the swift iron burning bee
> Drained the wild honey of their youth.

Though completely "modern," the lines seem almost Homeric also; their effect is, among other things, to set the deaths of these soldiers at an imaginative distance.

Rosenberg's background and early life differed widely from those of other Georgians. He was born to Jewish immigrant parents and grew up in poverty. At the age of fourteen or so he began to write poetry, and he was also gifted as an artist. He read and admired poets as diverse as Rossetti, Francis Thompson, Whitman, and Donne, but the Bible was the chief imaginative influence on him. He gradually attracted encouraging attention from Laurence Binyon, Edward Marsh, R. C. Trevelyan, and Gordon Bottomley. Threatened with tuberculosis, he went to South Africa. A year later he returned to England, joined the army, served as a private, and was killed in France.

The best of his poems are "Dead Man's Dump" and "Break of Day in the Trenches," followed by "Returning, We Hear the Larks," "In War," and "August 1914." His promise is also shown in his letters and essays or jottings on art and literature. No one can read them without being struck by the depth and sensitivity of his reflection and by the naturalness and seriousness with which he assumed the artist's role. They show a mind more professional, in the best sense of that word, than any other Georgian poet's. Moreover, there is Rosenberg's genius for admiration. Not that his judgments were necessarily favorable; he shrewdly noticed, for example, secondhand phrases and undistinguished emotion in Rupert Brooke's "begloried" war sonnets. But habitually he approached the work of others with the readiness and warmth of appreciation that is a frequent trait of masters in the arts. Thomas Mann often affirmed that he could have achieved little without "the gift for admiration"; in saying that, he perhaps remembered Goethe's once remarking that he had actually not much to offer except his large capacity for enthusiasm.

What Rosenberg especially valued and sought to achieve in his own poetry seems to have been definition in form and detail and an inexhaustible total effect. His phrasing of this ideal is frequently Romantic: "an infinite idea expressed coherently in a definite texture . . . a limitless idea, responsive to the emotion but ungraspable by the intellect." He can articulate the same aim in dryer, more "modern" voice: "an interesting complexity of thought . . . kept in tone and right value to the dominating idea so that it is understandable and still ungraspable."

Viewed in relation to the Georgian milieu, Rosenberg's poetry is innovative. He often achieves complexity and spread of implication through a rapid succession or juxtaposition of images, and such passages may seem closer to the Modernist than the Georgian mode. "August 1914" develops the metaphor that the lives of the soldiers, having lost "honey" and "gold," are now only "hard and cold" iron:

> Iron are our lives
> Molten right through our youth.
> A burnt space through ripe fields
> A fair mouth's broken tooth.

He also unrolls a cloudily splendid "rhetoric," one that most Georgian and Modernist poets no longer dared to use, as at the close of "In War":

> What are the great sceptred dooms
> To us, caught
> In the wild wave?
> We break ourselves on them,
> My brother, our hearts and years.

The phrase "great sceptred dooms," though completely Rosenberg's own, is of the type found in Thompson's "The Hound of Heaven"; the passage belongs in the Romantic tradition of powerfully direct emotional statement.

One of Rosenberg's characteristic poems, exhibiting many of

his technical resources, is "Break of Day in the Trenches." Here he presents himself plucking a poppy and sticking it behind his ear. A rat leaps over his hand, and the rat becomes a complex image against which the feelings and behavior of men at war can be evaluated. The "cosmopolitan" reasonableness of the rat emphasizes by contrast the madness of the war:

> Droll rat, they would shoot you if they knew
> Your cosmopolitan sympathies.
> Now you have touched this English hand
> You will do the same to a German.

But the rat also has a sardonic, Mephistophelean aspect:

> It seems you inwardly grin as you pass
> Strong eyes, fine limbs, haughty athletes
> Less chanced than you for life,
> Bonds to the whims of murder,
> Sprawled in the bowels of the earth.

The feeling of these lines is complex in each moment and constantly changing, so that analysis is more than usually challenged. The end of the poem comes back to the image of the poppy, first in a vague but magnificent metaphor, and then in an ironically comforting allusion to the particular flower plucked at the start. Again there is the typical mingling of full-voiced, Romantic power with gentleness and self-mocking charm:

> Poppies whose roots are in man's veins
> Drop, and are ever dropping;
> But mine in my ear is safe,
> Just a little white with the dust.

In all that he writes Rosenberg feels his theme fully. To this impression the rhythm especially contributes; it perpetually varies in minute responsiveness to transitions of feeling.

If Owen and Rosenberg had survived the war, poetry in the twenties would have been different. America would not have enjoyed the same predominance, for these were the English contemporaries most likely to have challenged Eliot, Pound, Williams, and Stevens. As it was, the prestige of British poetry was maintained by the surviving Georgians, the Sitwells, Robert

Graves, and D. H. Lawrence, and especially by the older generation, by the aging Hardy and the Anglo-Irish Yeats.

There was no significant connection between the important
poetry of the war and that of the first Modernists. Eliot, Pound,
and their fellow poets adopted traditions completely different
from those of the war poets. They were advancing on their own
lines before the war began. Sassoon, Owen, and the other
Georgians at war had no influence on their work. Nevertheless,
some of the emotions and effects the Modernists made their own
were similar to those called forth by the war—disgust and
horror, realism and satire. The war poetry undoubtedly helped
prepare an audience for the Modernist poetry of the 1920s. But
the audience for the Modernists, so far as they had an audience,
was formed not so much by the poetry of the war as by the war
itself. More than any other event, the war engendered the spiritual atmosphere of literature in the postwar period.

PART THREE

POPULAR MODERNISM

14

THE NEW POETRY OF AMERICA

THE transition from Romantic and Victorian to "modern" modes of poetry is one of the fundamental shifts in the history of the art. If we look to English verse of the past for instances of comparable transition, only three suggest themselves: the emergence of the poetry of the Renaissance in the sixteenth century, of neoclassic verse toward the end of the seventeenth century, and of Romantic poetry in the early years of the nineteenth century. Because historical changes of this magnitude take place gradually over a long period of time it is difficult, and to some extent arbitrary, to say precisely when the new mode first appears. The avant-garde of the nineties, Hardy, Frost, Robinson, the Georgians, and the poets of the First World War are important figures or groups in the development of "modern" poetry; some are major poets in their own right. Yet with them we are still in the realm of transition. If "modern" poetry had any clear, dramatic beginning, breaking sharply with the past, it was with poets in the second decade of the century in America.

Because literary history must set up artificial delimitations precisely in order to overcome them, we may date the new era from 1912. It was then that Harriet Monroe sent out from Chicago the famous circular in which she announced the founding of *Poetry* magazine and promised poets "a chance to be heard in their own place, without the limitations imposed by the popular magazine" and by an audience "primarily interested in poetry as an art." An alternative inception might be found in the first Imagist anthology, *Des Imagistes,* put together in London by Pound and obscurely published in New York by Alfred Kreymborg, himself in those days a young, impecunious, utterly unknown writer. The year was 1914. The age abounded in significant beginnings: within five years, 1912 to 1917, Frost, Amy Lowell, Sandburg, Williams, and Eliot all published their first important books. At whatever point we choose to inaugurate the "new" poetry, its initial development ended in 1922 with the publication of *The Waste Land.*

The achievement of the "new" poets during these ten years must be presented through a sequence of overlapping portraits of major and minor figures, for only so can one be true to the diversities of impulse within the movement as a whole and to the changes of direction individual poets took.

PHASES OF THE MODERN MOVEMENT

With the publication of *The Waste Land* in 1922 modern poetry in England and America moved into a different phase. With respect to the technique or style of poetry and, more important, to the vision of things that poets tend to share, we gradually find ourselves under another sky. The poetry of the 1910s had a period character of its own, which must not be lost in what developed later. The chief poets of the second phase of the modern movement incontestably were Yeats and Eliot, but Eliot was the main influence on other poets. So much so that if the first twenty years of the century might be called the age of Yeats, the next two decades, from 1922 to the end of the Second World War, frame that of Eliot. *The Waste Land* was the paramount example of the "modern" in poetry and preoccupied the attention of poets. They might cry it up or down, emulate it or not, but they could not put it out of mind easily. With the prestige of his poetry, of the journal (*Criterion*) he edited, and of his criticism, he formed the tastes and opinions of any number of young literary men and women. He argued that poetry must be objective and impersonal, that it must be written with a mindfulness of the poetry of the past and with critical and self-critical intelligence, and that it must, in the modern age, become more and more learned, allusive, and indirect "in order to force, to dislocate if* necessary, language" into the poet's meaning. He praised an un-illusioned, "classical" sophistication combined with firm structure and phrasing, as these qualities may be found, for example, in Dryden. He particularly esteemed the intellectual wit and irony of the Metaphysical poets. He repeatedly said or implied that the criticism or merely the proper reading of poetry required knowledge, training, concentrated intelligence, and a capacity for complex states of mind and feeling—in short, a sensibility and type or degree of attention that few persons could bring to bear; the rest of mankind, if they concerned themselves with poetry at all, could only use it for emotional self-indulgence. In other words, the higher kinds of poetry are accessible only to an elite.

In his poetry and his criticism Eliot communicated with impressive power an austerely pessimistic vision of human life and history. In the presence of the brooding depth, penetration, and dignity of this representation, poets whose note was less somber were thrown on the defensive. It was not Eliot alone who dwelt on the manifold evil, the helpless and abandoned condition of man. The 1920s built up one of the great pessimistic literatures of all time—in 1922 *The Waste Land* and *Ulysses;* in 1923 the *Duino Elegies;* in 1924 *The Magic Mountain* (if this complex immense novel is finally pessimistic); *The Trial* (1925); *The Castle* (1926); *The Tower* (1928); and from 1920 to 1927 the last four of the six volumes of Proust's *Remembrance of Things Past* (1913–1927). To what extent the mood of the age was actually reflected in its major literature is a question, but there is no doubt about the impact of this literature on writers and critics. Critics tended increasingly, and usually unthinkingly, to assume that the darker the vision of life, the greater its profundity and relevance. Humor, shrewdness, even common sense—as one finds them qualifying the pessimism of Hardy, Frost, Williams, Sandburg, and many other poets of the time—often harmed a writer's reputation more than they helped. The preferred tone was that of Eliot, who affirmed with breathtaking bleakness that "the possibility of damnation . . . is an immediate form of salvation—of salvation from the ennui of modern life, because it at last gives some significance to living."

The poetry of the first "modern" phase for the most part might be included in Part Two of this book for it was "in rapport with a public." Sandburg, Masters, Robinson, Lindsay, Frost, Williams, Amy Lowell, Hilda Doolittle, and Pound (in his early years) were writing a poetry that, however innovative and even shocking to some readers, was still essentially a popular poetry. By "popular poetry" I do not mean "people's poetry," though Sandburg and Lindsay were heading in that direction. The "new" poetry was, on the whole, direct and accessible; it was often agreeable or interesting in setting and in the stories it told or implied; the personality of the speaker was likely to be attractive. It had potential appeal to a large public. As for its vision of things, that varied with each poet. The better poets were not sentimental; neither did they go in for the uplift of the Genteel Tradition. If one had to label the attitude many of them shared, one might call it a stoic pessimism. Yet in these years that poets were already comparing to the Renaissance—"our American Risorgimento . . . will make the Italian Renaissance look like a tempest in a teapot," Pound told Harriet Monroe in 1912—there was so much confidence and zest in the renovation of poetry, in throwing off conventions and making new explorations, that this attitude was communicated to readers. The elan of poets, in other words, often had its chief source in their relation to their own art, but it was felt by them and conveyed to readers as a general attitude toward life. Some of these poets claimed moments of mystical communion. Others, notably Lindsay and Sandburg, voiced a huge, unfocused faith in American democracy. And most took an interest in life—in types of character, scenes, experiences, sensations, imaginations—which was, relatively speaking, itself affirmative. There was little of the brilliant distaste of "Sweeney Among the Nightingales," the trapped futility of Prufrock, the acedia of "Gerontion," the hysteria, apathy, and degradation of *The Waste Land*.

In the years immediately following *The Waste Land*, the modern movement split. Poets such as Cummings, Williams, Sandburg or Marianne Moore essentially continued in the way of the 1910s; younger poets generally responded to the influence of Eliot. By the end of the 1930s the "modern" in poetry was iden-

tified in university circles with the poetry of Eliot as its prototype.

For the general public it was not so. The "new" poetry continued not only to be appreciatively read but to form the stock
idea of "modern" verse. In American high schools, colleges, and
reading clubs in the thirties the notion of contemporary poetry
was likely to be the short, free-verse poem of tender impressionism, such as Sandburg's "Fog" or "Cool Tombs" or Amy
Lowell's "Meeting-House Hill." Poems in meter, such as
Lindsay's "The Flower-Fed Buffaloes," or the cinquains of Adelaide Crapsey, or Frost's "Stopping by Woods on a Snowy Evening" are, apart from the versification, of the same kind. If we
had to select what one might call the "modal" poems of the first
wave of the modern development, these might be chosen. Poems
of this kind were brief, and the Imagist influence made for
short, carefully wrought lines. They were sensitive, appreciative,
often slightly wry or humorous, and usually unpretentious.
They evoked fugitive, complex moods by simple means. Class
after class of schoolchildren were set to memorize such poems
(from which, probably, they had more pleasure than similar
adolescents now find in Eliot or Robert Lowell or Sylvia Plath),
and it seems likely that in some minds such poems came to represent the stock idea not only of "modern poetry" but of poetry
per se, displacing the Romantic nature lyric.

THE REACTION AGAINST THE GENTEEL MODE

Different as they were from each other, all the avant-garde
poets were responding to the same historical circumstances.
They were reacting against the poetry of the Genteel Tradition.
Only if we keep this in mind can we understand why the Modernist revolution came when it did and why it developed along
the diverse lines we shall be tracing. By 1900 the poetry of the
Genteel Tradition was easily perceived to be formally and morally timid, conventional, and derivative from past poetry. For
this reason it was relatively easy to write, despite its careful and
polished diction and versification. For subject matter Genteel
poetry articulated generalized attitudes, and in its Romantic
spiritual elevation it did not grapple with experience, that is,

with characters and actions, with society and politics, least of all
with the contemporary milieu. These facts shaped the Modernist effort in its broadest, most general features. Robinson, Frost,
Pound, Eliot, Williams, Stevens, Sandburg, Masters, H.D.,
Fletcher, Marianne Moore, Amy Lowell, Maxwell Bodenheim,
Lola Ridge, Alfred Kreymborg, Mina Loy, and many others
sought to create a new art; in most cases they sought an art that
would be more difficult for the poet to master. They hoped to
write for the same audience that read serious, contemporary fiction. "I have always wanted," Pound said in 1917, "to write
'poetry' that a grown man could read without groans of ennui,
or without having to have it cooed into his ear by a flapper."
They reached out for concrete subject matter. Poetry would
present character, events, or objects, and these would be realisti-
cally treated, closely particularized, and contemporary. Some
poets added that they would be American. The exploration of
the contemporary and the American also governed style. For, in
reaction against the timeless spiritual truth to which Genteel
poetry aspired, the "new" poets wrote with a militant awareness
of their time and place, of history. Some, such as Williams, Sandburg, and Kreymborg, talked as though the European, especially the English past were irrelevant. They sought to start
afresh, with new forms and idioms appropriate to the present
age. Others, such as Pound and Eliot, felt that poetry must be
written with a deep, abiding consciousness of past masterwork
and of "tradition"; but they too assumed that the "modern" era
would call forth distinctively "modern" awareness and style. The
assumption that because one is living in a specific historical age
one has at the least an irresistible tendency, perhaps also a duty,
to express it links avant-garde poets of whatever description at
this time and sharply differentiates them from the American
poets of the Genteel Tradition as well as from Edwardian poets
such as Bridges, Moore, and Binyon. But then the question
arose, what actually is the "modern" character in poetry? There
was much experiment as poets cast about for answers. In their
uncertainty they were peculiarly vulnerable to example or to
plausible argument. For some poets a similar line of reasoning
indicated also that one should express American life and feeling,
using the rhythms and idioms of the American spoken language. This precluded much traditionally associated with

verse—"rhetoric," "poetic diction," or classical allusion. But as a positive guide it led down diverse paths. Williams was ostentatiously faithful to his own natural voice; Frost listened to New England intonations; Sandburg cultivated the low colloquial and slangy. But most poets assumed that the English language in the United States was not the same as that in England—it was based, as Williams put it, on the speech "of our Polish mothers"—and poets strove to highlight the difference.

Modernist poetry was being written in the first decade of the century, but the Genteel Tradition was still dominant. "Realistic" and "experimental" poets had no hope of appearing in literary magazines such as the *Century* or *Atlantic*. Neither could they publish books of their poems unless they paid the costs themselves. Thus, there was a vicious circle. Their poems were rejected, so they resented and reacted still more against the tastes and values of the literary establishment and more eagerly identified with literary rebels of the past. Meanwhile, they might be friendly with painters, sculptors, photographers, and musicians who stood in a similar relation to the "conservative" or "academic" taste that prevailed in their own arts. They sympathized in the struggle of novelists such as Dreiser, who were asserting a right to treat, with naturalistic objectivity and detail, subjects that American fiction had hitherto veiled. Their state of mind was enthusiastic, frustrated, and militant, and at times their poetry was strongly influenced by a deliberate wish to offend the establishment. Whatever flew in the face of poetic or moral convention might be defended as "modern" and acquire a wholly adventitious cachet. "I give you your chance to be modern," said Pound in 1913, sending some of his poems to *Poetry* magazine: "your chance . . . to produce as many green bilious attacks throughout the length and breadth of the U.S.A. as there are fungoid members of the American academy. I announce the demise of R. U. Johnson [editor of *Century* magazine] and all his foetid generation."

After approximately 1912 the situation of the avant-garde gradually changed. Most of them had been working in relative isolation; they now became aware of each other. Their poems were published, taken seriously, criticized. They possessed— and hugely enjoyed—an audience; it was small at first, but eager and alert. They believed America was enjoying a poetic

Renaissance. The excitement of this can be recaptured in autobiographies by Williams, Fletcher, Kreymborg, and Harriet
Monroe. And in this atmosphere of bold and confident revolution they were even more hungry for new forms and subjects,
and borrowed suggestions from wherever they could—notably
from prose fiction, Whitman, French *symbolistes,* oriental poetry,
psychological theory, painters, sculptors, composers, jazz, films,
and vaudeville.

THE WIDENING OF SUBJECT MATTER

With respect to what, admitting the inadequacy of the term,
we may call the subject matter of poetry, the great achievement
of the decade was an immense widening of the range of experience that could be presented. A similar tendency had been at
work in England since the 1890s—in the poetry of the Aesthetic
movement and, more important, in the reaction against it.
Although on the whole the Aesthetes had enormously restricted
the subject matter of their poetry, they had also claimed and indulged a right to explore whatever mood or experience might
intrigue them, however odd or minor it might be. They had
brought into English poetry urban impressions and moral ob-
liquities not much recorded before. In reaction against them,
poets such as Kipling, Synge, Masefield, and Yeats (after the
turn of the century) tried in their different ways to reflect actual
life boldly and concretely, further broadening the scope of poetry. The anger and contempt Yeats might voice in these years
(in "September, 1913," for example) were quite unusual emotions in poetry at the time. Nevertheless, the "new" poetry of
America went much further. By 1922 it was possible to treat almost any subject from almost any point of view. There has been
some slight, additional opening up of new subject matter since,
particularly in the confessional and Beat verse of the 1950s, but
the significant freeing of poetry took place at the outset of the
modern movement.

Despite the views of many commentators, the immediate
cause of this development lies in the reaction of poets to their
late-Victorian predecessors, not in the new experiences and
perceptions modern poets may be supposed to have acquired.

Profound alterations in the conditions of human life were oc-
curring; industrialization, urbanization, and technological
innovations such as the motor car are usually mentioned. New
facts and theories were taking possession of the intellectual
world; Darwin, Freud, Marx, Nietzsche, and Frazer are commonly cited as pillars of cloud and fire that went before the
modern mind in its wandering. And the outcome of all this, the
argument goes, was the building up of a new, specifically modern awareness—new topics and ways of thinking, new emotions,
in short, a new "reality"—which had to be expressed in poetry. In
a general way this is undeniable. But these changes took place
gradually over a long period of time. They do not explain why
the "renaissance" in poetry came when it did; neither do they
explain why it came more as a revolution than as a slow, continuous transition. To account for these facts one must keep in mind
the extent to which poetic conventions control how and what a
poet writes.

The conventions that dominated English and American
poetry at the turn of the century had developed in the Romantic
period. At that time they had expressed, or at least been in
keeping with, what thinking men and women conceived of as
"reality." But as the sense of reality changed, the conventions of
poetry did not, or not to the same extent. The discrepancy was
not usually noticed. After all, there were enormously gifted
poets, such as Tennyson and Arnold. But to poetry the discrepancy was cumulatively deleterious. It helps explain why toward
the end of the century major literary talent went into prose fiction much more than into poetry. And it contributed to a gradual transformation of the "idea" of poetry, so that the essence of
"poetry" was increasingly located in its power to give release, refreshment, uplift; it was, in other words, no longer expected to
reflect the felt realities that, outside of poetry, were themes of
serious awareness, but a "higher" reality instead. At this point
poetry had fallen into the hands of relatively weak writers, in
whose work the gap between convention and realities was especially visible. The gap was perceived by a good many poets at
more or less the same time. From this perception, much more
than from Freud, Marx, and the motor car, the modern revolution in poetry may be traced. Backed by precedents in fiction,
journalism, and a few earlier poets, the "new" poets made the

morally impressive resolve to throw off conventions that had been out of touch with "reality" for seventy-five years. They now wrote on themes—the city rather than landscape, sexuality rather than romantic love, political corruption rather than patriotism—which had been familiar in prose fiction right along but had seldom been mentioned in the poetry of the previous generation.

Having stressed that there was a revolution in the subject matter of poetry, we must immediately qualify. The legacy from nineteenth-century English and American poets included some effective treatments of contemporary materials. The most influential examples were Whitman and Browning. Moreover, the "new" poets were not able to break with Romantic conventions as completely as they wished.

As the nineteenth-century tradition was carried by weaker poets into the twentieth century, the dominant tendency was to write lyrics of personal feeling and reflection. Any more objective subject matter would be either of a conventionally "poetic" kind (classical myth, Arthurian legend) or it would be "poeticized," that is, the poem would highlight the beauty, romance, mystery, sublimity, strangeness, tenderness, charm, magic, or whatever to be found in the stuff one wrote about. All this the "new" poets of America hoped to reject. Against the late-Victorian lyric of personal sentiment and generalization they sought concrete instances, as one sees in Robinson, Lindsay, Frost, Masters, Sandburg, the Imagists, and the early work of Eliot in *Prufrock and Other Observations* (1917) and *Poems* (1920). Instead of classical and medieval subjects they turned to the contemporary American scene. Often they portrayed a particular region: the rural New England of Frost and Robinson (not to mention occasional poems in their vein by Amy Lowell and Witter Bynner); the sketches of prairie life in Sandburg's *Cornhuskers* (1918); the depiction of a Midwestern town in Masters' *Spoon River Anthology* (1915). Often they fixed on the industrial and urban environment of modern life, as Sandburg did in his *Chicago Poems* (1916), Lola Ridge in *The Ghetto and Other Poems* (1919), and T. S. Eliot in his early volumes. The use of such materials afforded not only a break with the recent past (although there was Hardy's rural region of Wessex as well as the urban scenes of impressionist poets in the 1890s), but a genuine advantage. It gave them a relatively unexploited setting and fund of imagery, a source of appeal to a larger audience, and a means of commenting more directly on politics and the social order.

The "new" poets also reacted strongly against the convention of "poeticized" treatment. But at the same time, most of them continued it in their own ways. Though their subjects were often un- or anti-Romantic, their imaginations were less so. Vachel Lindsay presents a Chinese laundryman in an American city, but typically wings back in imagination to a palace in ancient China, where Chang the laundryman was a prince loved by a beautiful princess. Or he takes a look at crapshooters in a gambling hall and thinks of the Congo River, "cutting through the jungle" amid the primitive boom of drums. This mounting of romantic treatment on contemporary material appears in less obvious ways in Robinson, Frost, Sandburg, Masters, and Amy Lowell, even though these poets too were trying to rid poetry of it.

The persistence of the habit was inevitable. The question for literary history is, by what steps did poetry travel the long way from Amy Lowell to Robert Lowell, from a poetry in which a Romanticized handling is still present to a poetry in which contemporary materials are used as expressive images without Romantic feeling and also without any particular thought of being anti-Romantic. How, so far as subject matter and treatment are concerned, was poetry purged of the habitual orientation to Romantic tradition?

Here again we must advert to the powerful influence of prose fiction. Some of Robinson's famous poems, "Richard Cory," for example, might be described as American, lyric sketches in the mode of De Maupassant. Masters achieved some novelistic effects in *Spoon River Anthology*. The impact of Henry James is found in some of Eliot's early poems, and Pound described "Hugh Selwyn Mauberley" as "an attempt to condense the Jamesian novel." (Joyce's *Ulysses* was an important influence on *The Waste Land*. But *Ulysses* and *The Waste Land* belong to a later phase of literature.) The point is that several poets, from Robinson on, began to explore human character and psychology in depth and to explore also the impact of social setting on character, adapting approaches and techniques not only from the poetry of the past but from the serious prose fiction of the nineteenth and twentieth centuries. One thing they learned from prose fiction was to present contemporary life without romanticizing it.

The single most powerful purgative was the poetry of Eliot through *The Waste Land*. Here the contemporary world was seen in vivid detail and with imaginative power. Far from being romanticized, it was viewed with disgust and fear, and, to the extent that these emotions were kept at a distance, the defense was irony, sometimes even satiric contempt for the persons and scenes presented. If, after this, one treated the modern milieu, it might be in Eliot's way or it might be with the more objective and neutral attitude of Auden, to whom motor cars and bars are not repellent; they are simply familiar, casually noticed items of the environment. But Romantic enhancement was henceforth less likely.

THE PROLIFERATION OF FORMAL EXPERIMENT

A second characteristic of the "new" poetry is the proliferation of formal experiment. The point is not merely that the decade was eager in adopting or creating new poetic modes and methods, though of course it was: we may think of Symbolism, Impressionism, Futurism, and Surrealism, of quantitative, syllabic, and stress meters, of haiku, cinquain, polyphonic prose, prose poem, and free verse, of the color symphonies of Fletcher, the syncopated rhythms of Lindsay, the chants of James Oppenheim, and the extreme ellipsis or fragmented utterance of Mina Loy. But, furthermore, literary experiment enjoyed in this age an unprecedented prestige. Never before had experiment been so generally pursued and valued in and for itself, quite apart from whatever worth the experimental poem might have as literature. The reasons for this might be made the subject of a separate book. They have to do, for example, with the special orientation of modern poetry—or at least that part of it for which Pound is a spokesman—to painting and sculpture. From the succession of styles in modern painting (or from French poets who had been influenced by painters) Pound caught and disseminated the idea that there is "research" to be done among poetic forms also and that each formal development should become the cause of a following one. "I said nothing against these poets," Pound remarked in 1917 of his original associates in the 1914 Imagist anthology, "save that they haven't opened up anything new during the past three years. . . . I set my period at three years (definitely and deliberately)." The reasons include also the fact that poets were now divided into two camps, the "conservatives" and the avant-garde. Because formal experiment was part of the definition of the avant-garde and particular experiments ceased to be experimental as soon as enough poets had tried them, one had always to find new experiments simply to keep an avant-garde identity. Further reasons include the extreme development of Romantic psychology and literary theory which holds that since every individual—in fact, every mood of an individual—is unique, his self-expression requires its unique form; the eagerness, often quite conscious and explicit, of many modern artists to "kill" the past or to "kill" habit, logic, grammar, language, and even consciousness itself; and not least the feeling of poets that they were competing for notice amid a crowd of rivals and had somehow to attract attention. Another motivation resulted from the massive, cumulative effect of the Romantic glorification of the poet and artist. As the artist-hero was contrasted with the conventional, money-getting bourgeois, readers were eager to identify with the artist so conceived and to sympathize with his social rebellion. Gradually an unearned moral glamour enveloped the avant-garde, for it was in this group that the artist's rejection of bourgeois convention was most visible. Whatever its merits, an obviously new and experimental poetry such as Mina Loy's "Love Songs" (1915),

> Spawn of fantasies
> Sitting the appraisable
> Pig Cupid   his rosy snout
> Rooting erotic garbage,

did wonders for the the self-esteem of readers (not to mention poets). By appreciating it, or trying to, readers could show themselves on the side of the artist against the Philistines. Whether or not the poetry was of an intrinsically popular kind made no difference; the motive described could predispose readers in favor of Mina Loy and also raise a prejudice in favor of Sandburg or

Lindsay, whose methods also seemed unconventional in their day.

The 1910s in America may be said to have brought in three large changes in poetic style, changes that continue strongly to influence poets to the present day. The "new" poets strove for concrete, economical, exact, and—usually—colloquial phrasing. These ideals received special publicity in connection with the Imagist movement, with which they are still usually associated. But in advocating these ideals the Imagists were participating in a general trend of poetry. Yeats was no Imagist, but his turn after 1900 toward a more embodied, physical presentation in a language of rich concreteness was a development in a similar direction, quite as important as the Imagist influence on modern poetry. Again, the impact of the serious novel on poetry made not only for a more concrete subject matter but, paradoxically, for a more concentrated way of speaking, as poets attempted in their briefer utterance to achieve effects that could be created at greater length in prose fiction.

THE SPOKEN LANGUAGE

In both England and the United States the effort to devise a more colloquial way of speaking was part of the general drift of poetry toward "realism," the impulse to come closer to actual life. Poetry was to adopt the vocabulary, syntax, and rhythm of contemporary speech; it should sound almost like talk. But British and American poets were not reacting against the same "poetic diction." In England the styles to be abjured were relatively definite and individual. One struggled to cast off the idiom of Tennyson, Swinburne, Rossetti, and the nineties, the latter including the Aesthetes, Impressionists, Decadents, and poets of the Celtic Twilight. American poets were eager to reject all this, but particularly they were out to purge poetry of the diction of the Genteel Tradition, which was essentially Romantic and Victorian but included a sprinkling of whatever language might be found in the poetry of any past age. Perhaps for this reason the reaction of American poets against whatever might smack of "poetry" was more violent and extreme. Furthermore, they were often intent on imitating not just speech, but American speech.

So we find Frost writing,

> And having scared the cellar under him
> In clomping there, he scared it once again
> In clomping off;

or Sandburg,

> Go to it, O jazzmen!

or Williams, describing how a hearse should be built,

> Let there be no glass—
> and no upholstery! phew!
> and no little brass rollers
> and small easy wheels on the bottom—
> my townspeople what are you thinking of!

To adopt American speech involved an assertion that poetry could be written just as well out of the American language as the English. Also the American idiom offered itself at this time as a relatively fresh one for poetry, one not yet fully exploited, one that would sound new in the ear. These may have been the primary motivations of poets such as Robinson and Frost. For poets who listened to the call of Whitman, the use of American idiom was motivated also by a democratic faith. The phrasing heard on back porches or streetcorners embodied the American sensibility, the strength and humor of the people. The "new" poets occasionally rendered not only American speech but sounds familiar in American life. In "The Santa Fe Trail" Vachel Lindsay listed the cars driving west:

> Cars from Concord, Niagara, Boston,
> Cars from Topeka, Emporia, and Austin,

and when he recited the poem, he cried out the towns like an announcer in a railroad station. It was, in poetry, a bold, liberating thing, and it was for touches such as this that Lindsay, now so little esteemed, meant so much as an example and inspiration to his own generation of poets. When in *Four Quartets* Eliot incorporates in his own verse the stops of the London subway—

> Hampstead and Clerkenwell, Campden and Putney,
> Highgate, Primrose, and Ludgate—

the novelty was not in making a chant out of such material but in its more integrated and imaginative use.

DISCONTINUOUS COMPOSITION

By discontinuous composition we mean essentially a new mode of transition from one phrase, line, image, allusion, emotion, topic, speaker, or whatever part of the poem we discriminate, to the next. More exactly put, it is the absence of transition, for the discontinuous poem does not evolve gradually from part to part, but places separate, often disparate units of meaning one immediately after the other. The units of meaning are often presented in an elliptical way, as one sees, for example, in Pound's "Hugh Selwyn Mauberley," where the speaker, wondering whether this belated aesthete had been "wrong from the start," explains:

> No, hardly, but seeing he had been born
> In a half savage country, out of date;
> Bent resolutely on wringing lilies from the acorn;
> Capaneus; trout for factitious bait.

This method of composition by juxtaposition can be described and accounted for in different ways, depending on what we relate it to. It is the direct opposite of what is generally found in English and American poetry of the nineteenth century, where the same state of mind and mode of speech is maintained from the start of a poem to the end or else transition is gradual and continuous, not sudden and disorienting. As T. E. Hulme put it, "one of the main achievements of the nineteenth century was the elaboration and universal application of the principle of continuity. The destruction of this conception is, on the contrary, an urgent necessity of the present." If we ask why this destruction was necessary, the general answer is that "continuity" was suspected to be an illusion. It could not be found in the modes and processes of the human mind, and discontinuous structure in poetry was sometimes based on recent psychological theory; it rendered the stream-of-consciousness or it rendered the eruption into one level of the mind of material from a deeper level. Discontinuity was said to be characteristic of modern experience, with its accelerated rate of change and the constant, rapid shifts of attention it requires. The future would be even more so, according to the Futurist Marinetti, when in 1913 he hailed the "wireless imagination" with its "entire freedom of images and analogies expressed by disjointed words and without the con-

necting wires of syntax. . . . Poetry must be an interrupted sequence of new images." His own verse was an example

> Sun gold billets dishes lead sky
> Silk heat bed quilting purple blue.

If we notice the orientation in much modern literature to the
arts of painting and sculpture, we can describe discontinuous
structure as an outcome of the attempt to create "spatial form"
in poetry. The poem, in other words, is not to be regarded as an
utterance—or imitation of an utterance—taking place through
time. Instead, all the parts of the poem are conceived to be
present at the same moment, coexisting as if in space. There is
no transition from one unit of meaning to the next, but between
the discrete units of meaning there are multiple interrelations.
Perceiving these, the reader obtains a complex total impression.
Above all, discontinuous form was sometimes felt to be mimetic
of the ultimate character of reality itself, as, perhaps, in Eliot's
The Waste Land.

If we seek to discover where, apart from their own native
ingenuity, poets learned to write this way, we find that novels
again played a role. So also did previous poetries from English
Metaphysical and Jacobean verse to Browning and the French
symbolistes. One should also stress the importance for poetry of
similar developments in painting and music. Discontinuous
structure promotes effects and states of mind, such as surprise,
wit, nimble intellection, and irony, which differ characteristically
from those achieved through continuous transition. Fully to
explore the provenance, cultural and intellectual implications,
various types, and rhetorical resources of this method of
composition would require a book-length study. It is not
surprising that many assume that it is the basic technique of
modern poetry. But discontinuous composition was not characteristic of the "new" poetry as a whole. The utterance of
Lindsay and Sandburg has sudden transitions and discontinuities
one does not find in Tennyson or William Morris. But they are
still writing a poetry of continuous transition as contrasted with
the Pound lines quoted; and in this respect Robinson, Frost, and
Masters belong well within the nineteenth-century tradition. On
the other hand, after it was first powerfully exploited in the
poems Eliot and Pound wrote around 1920—that is, in "Hugh
Selwyn Mauberley," and in Eliot's poems in quatrains, in

"Gerontion," and *The Waste Land*—discontinuous composition remained a recurrent, though by no means a universal characteristic of modern American poetry.

FREE VERSE

If, as Pound kept insisting, poetry needed to recapture the inveterate virtues of directness, economy, and force, free verse offered itself as a useful discipline. It would redirect—more exactly, it would totalize—the attention of poets. As Pound put it, rhyme "tends to draw away the artist's attention from forty to ninety per cent of his syllables and concentrate it on the admittedly more prominent remainder. It tends to draw him into prolixity and pull him away from the thing." In other words, using free verse poets could no longer give first priority to stuffing stanzaic boxes and, still worse, assume that when the box was full, the poem was made. Instead, they would have to scrutinize their utterance at all points, in theory with the result that, Pound hoped, poetry might be at least "as well written as prose." Free verse might also promote better habits in reading. In traditional verse readers tended to glide from rhyme to rhyme, hardly noticing effects of a less obvious kind.

It was not a wholly new form. At one time or another free-verse poets cited as predecessors the lyric and elegiac poets of classical Greece, *Beowulf,* Langland, Milton (in *Samson Agonistes*), Gray, Blake, Ossian, Hölderlin, Novalis, Wordsworth, Coleridge, Rimbaud, Mallarmé, Heine, Arnold, Nietzsche, Whitman, Laforgue, Henley, Gustave Kahn, Vielé-Griffin, Henri de Régnier, Jean Moréas, and Emile Verhaeren. The list indicates that in the confused dawn of this revolution "free" verse did not always mean nonmetrical verse. *Beowulf,* for example, is in the Anglo-Saxon stress meter rather than the syllabic-stress meter of most poetry since Chaucer; the meter may be comparatively "free," but it would not now be called free verse. And the irregular or "false Pindaric" odes from Cowley to Wordsworth are "free" only in their varying line lengths and disposition of rhymes; the feet are iambic. But for a genuinely nonmetrical verse there was also precedent; the innovation was not, literally speaking, in the form as such, but in the fact that it was now widely adopted for the first time in history. Approximately half of the important American poets of the decade wrote nonmetrical verse either exclusively or in a significant amount of their poetry. And, after the reaction against it from the 1920s to the 1950s, free verse again became a prevalent form.

Among the first English and American poets to write free verse in the twentieth century were Hulme, Fletcher, Pound, Sandburg, Hilda Doolittle, Richard Aldington, and D. H. Lawrence—and Amy Lowell, who learned it mainly from Fletcher and Pound, and Edgar Lee Masters, who took it from Sandburg. Sandburg and Masters were a somewhat isolated development out of Whitman. Fletcher, Pound, H.D., Aldington, and Lowell were acquainted and learned from each other their methods and arguments for the new form. Its first important introduction to readers came in 1912 and 1913, when it appeared in *Poetry* magazine, in Pound's *Ripostes* (1912), and in *The New Freewoman* (subsequently *The Egoist*), of which Pound became literary editor in 1913. From the moment it appeared in *Poetry* it aroused interest and controversy and was soon adopted by other poets.

The free-verse poets were convinced that rhythm has an expressive function, that it articulates emotion. They believed that emotional states are particular and unique, and that, accordingly, for every emotional state there is the one particular rhythm that expresses it. From this they argued that meters, fixed rhythmic patterns, cannot embody the individuality of an emotion. Of course metrical verse varies constantly and with expressive effect from the pattern it sets up; but if one is strongly enough impressed with the uniqueness of the object to be presented, any formal convention will impose a distortion, an insincerity. We are not considering whether these arguments are valid. They were disseminated—for example by Hulme, by French *vers librists*, and by Pound; they were widely current; and they had considerable influence in motivating the writers of free verse. "I believe," explained Pound in 1912, "in an 'absolute rhythm,' a rhythm, that is, in poetry which corresponds exactly to the emotion to be expressed. . . . I believe in technique as the test of a man's sincerity . . . in the trampling down of every convention that impedes or obscures . . . the precise rendering of the impulse." "Form," said Sir Herbert Read six years later, "is determined by the emotion which requires expression. *Corollary:* Form is not an unchanging mould into which any emotion can be poured." Thus the Romantic principle that poetic form should be "organic" rather than imposed—that it should shape itself as it develops, evolving its own essence—was applied to justify free verse. As the Preface to the Imagist anthology for 1915 explained it, the Imagist poets sought "to create new rhythms—as the expression of new moods . . . In poetry, a new cadence means a new idea."

The free-verse poets wanted a prosody that would break decisively with the past, "a new prosody," Williams said, "based on a present-day world." It was not that the traditional meters were exhausted, in other words, that no unexplored variations of an important kind were now possible. Some, indeed, alleged this as an argument for free verse. T. E. Hulme, for example, urged that "we shall not get any new efflorescence of verse until we get a new technique, a new convention, to turn ourselves loose in." But the opinion was opposed by counterarguments and powerful examples, notably that of Eliot. Moreover, the avant-garde was possessed, as we noted, by the sense of modernity. Free verse, to repeat, was not wholly unheard of in past centuries; poets on the defensive could always cite predecessors. But in the past it had been a very minor and occasional experiment. For the emotions, if not quite literally in fact, it was a new form; as such, it was a symbol with potent appeal to poets. It conveyed their sense of a split with the past and suggested that they were articulating the distinctive, new consciousness of "modern" man.

These feelings worked with special force in American poets, for their need was double. They wished to feel that they had a meter "consonant with our day," to quote Williams, but it had to be "consonant" also with America. Traditional prosody, Williams argued, was a product of "the English character." Hence for American poetry its rules were "more or less arbitrary in their delimitations"; the iamb, for example, "is not the normal measure of American speech." Other American poets did not put it so simply, but many of them felt that with free verse they had developed their own poetic form, of equal status with traditional forms and yet specifically adapted to express both the modern and the American character. To the poets of democratic ideology, such as Lindsay and Sandburg, free verse also recommended itself as a mode of direct utterance that put no formal pretensions between itself and the people.

Free verse flows into twentieth-century poetry from two sources. One was Whitman, who to his admirers exemplified a bold, spontaneous way of working. Here was a poet wholly responsive to his urge of the moment, disregarding conventions of meter, coming in like a tide. Among Whitman's descendants were Sandburg and, much more important, Lawrence, who attacked most of his fellow free versifiers because they merely broke metrical verse into fragments. They "do not know" that free verse "is, or should be, direct utterance from the instant whole man . . . the insurgent naked throb of the instant moment . . . instantaneous life plasm." The other source was the example of *vers libre* in such French poets as Rimbaud, Gustave Kahn, Jules Laforgue, Jean Moréas, Henri de Régnier, and Vielé-Griffin. Some of these poets may have been influenced by Whitman, but *vers libre* also developed independently as a reaction against the strict rules of versification imposed by French poetic tradition. These conventions closely governed expectations of readers to a degree that had no parallel in England or America. Hence defiance of them was especially rebellious in a French context, and the dispute over free verse in the United States imported some of its emotion from France.

Compared with free verse in the tradition of Whitman, the *vers libre* of France was written with greater deliberation. This more painstaking and self-critical use of the form was transmitted by Pound to most free-verse writers of the age. Hence in the flowering of free verse in the 1910s the form did not always imply a freeing of impulse. In the second wave of free verse, however, which began in the 1950s, the tradition of Whitman and Lawrence on the whole dominated, and free verse was part of a reaction against formalism in the name of spontaneity and wholeness of being, the unplanned, the poem as act of discovery. Both schools of free-verse poets were seeking to overcome the distinction between art and life. They aimed to make the completed poetic form identical with the natural perception or impulse, but one school hoped to achieve this through a psychic wholeness in the immediate act of composition and the other through deliberation and revision.

From the moment it was introduced, free verse aroused controversy. There is no point in resurrecting these arguments; the majority of them on both sides were superficial and confused. The main charge lodged against free verse was that the rhythm of free verse does not differ from that of prose. This was denied of course, but not validly. Free verse is of innumerable kinds; some is very close to metrical verse but, so far as the rhythm goes, most unrhymed free verse would be prose if it were printed as prose. This being the case, defenders of free verse could argue that there was or should be no essential difference between poetry and prose, or they could argue that lineation makes free verse poetry, even if it would otherwise be prose—because lineation compels reading habits quite different from those brought to prose. Whatever the merits of the arguments pro and con, they are now academic, since for over half a century most readers, poets, and critics have agreed to call free verse a form of poetry. The original controversy was the more intense because free verse was associated with Imagism, which was debatable in other points besides its lack of meter, and because Amy Lowell waged the newspaper and lecture-hall battle for Imagism and free verse with magnificent vigor and aggressiveness. Thanks mainly to Miss Lowell, free verse and Imagism made up the notion of modern poetry in the public mind. Controversy spread the news of free verse and enhanced its allure, so that more and more poets were tempted to try it.

Familiar though free verse now is, readers and critics often assume that its formal effects cannot be analyzed, or, at least, that they are not worth analyzing, since the success of a free-verse poem depends much more on other factors. For this reason, it seems worthwhile briefly to look at examples of free verse. The first is taken from Whitman, since he is one of the begetters of the form. It is impossible to give an adequate impression of Whitman in a short quotation, but we may examine the opening lines of his great elegy on Lincoln:

> When lilacs last in the dooryard bloom'd,
> And the great star early droop'd in the western sky in the
> night,
> I mourn'd, and yet shall mourn with ever-returning spring.
>
> Ever-returning spring, trinity sure to me you bring,
> Lilac blooming perennial and drooping star in the west,
> And thought of him I love.

This is a relatively regular free verse. If it were metered verse, one would observe that the poetic feet are either iambs or anapests. As it is, we notice that rhythms are recurrent:

When lí   lăcs lást
in the dóor yărd blóom'd;

or

         Lí   lăc blóom ĭng pĕr én   ni al
and droóp ĭng stár   ĭn   thĕ wést;

or

Év ĕr- rĕ túrn ĭng spríng,
trín ĭ   tў   súre tŏ   mé   you bring,

The last phrase falls outside the rhythmic pattern (more exactly, it changes the rhythm, mounting a second rhythm on the first), but it also supplies both the verb and a rhyme, thus fulfilling syntactical and aural patterns and creating a strong sense of finality. The basic rhythmic pattern of this verse is the half-line, containing from two to four stressed syllables (though half-lines with up to five stresses are found elsewhere in the poem and some lines are made up of three such units). Besides the recurrent rhythm there are other kinds of recurrence, equally obvious, such as assonance, alliteration, and repetition of phrases. Elsewhere in the poem Whitman also falls into his typical anaphora ("amid cities . . . amid lanes . . . amid the grass . . . passing the endless grass . . . passing the yellow-spear'd wheat . . . passing the apple-tree blows of white and pink in the orchards"). Recurrent images (lilacs, star, spring), as they return in different contexts throughout the poem, gather steadily more feeling and significance about them, becoming dense and moving symbols. In fact, the general procedure of this poetry might be described as incremental repetition, the slow, gradual accumulation and progression of emotion and meaning as the same or parallel elements recur with increasing weight. As additional points of artistry in these lines we may notice how effectively the same phrase, "ever-returning spring," concludes one strophe and begins the next, with the sense of building from a point that had seemed final. And we may notice how powerfully conclusive the last line is ("And thought of him I love"), partly because, as a half-line, it both breaks and fits in with the established pattern and partly because it introduces a new thematic element, though an element that had been foreshadowed in the last line of the first strophe.

William Carlos Williams is also important to a good many poets of free verse at present. Like Whitman, he writes rather different kinds of free verse. "Canthara" was an early poem:

> The old black-man showed me
> how he had been shocked
> in his youth
> by six women, dancing
> a set-dance, stark naked below
> the skirts raised round
> their breasts:
> > bellies flung forward
> knees flying!
> > > —while
> his gestures, against the
> tiled wall of the dingy bath-room,
> swished with ecstasy to
> the familiar music of
> > his old emotion.

In contrast to Whitman, the lines are short, and the shortness of the line forces a distinct emphasis on the words individually. Rather than a recurrence of rhythmic pattern there is constant variation. Mainly, though not always, the lines are arranged to enact the movement of the voice speaking: they reinforce the natural rhythm by linear notation. The enjambment makes for a continuing momentum or "thrust," as Williams would have called it, from the beginning of the poem to the end, yet individual lines are bound together as integral units by assonance and alliteration ("his gestures, against the"). A sense of conclusion is obtained by modulating at the end into a regular iambic rhythm and by echoing in the last line the long "o's" from the first line of the poem. Having noticed these details, however, one should add that the chief use made of the verse form is to avoid clutter, to write with directness and economy.

In the 1920s and 1930s free verse was less generally employed by sophisticated poets, though it continued to be a favorite form of amateurs. In part, this was a reaction against the widespread advocacy of it in the 1910s, which had soon become common-place. In part, it was brought about by the flaccid dullness to which the form lent itself in the hands of minor artists. In part, it was a result of the association of free verse with Imagism, so that when the latter fell into disfavor, so did the former. In part, it was a result of the influence of *The Waste Land,* since this first great poem of the Modernist movement had not adopted free verse but had used traditional meters in a quite irregular way. Pound and Eliot had already reacted strongly against the form in 1917, and the authority of Eliot as a critic also told against free verse in the 1920s and 1930s. Assimilating and adapting the technique of Eliot, the next generation of British poets—Auden, Spender, Thomas, MacNeice, Day Lewis, Empson, Vernon Watkins—tended to avoid free verse, as did Marianne Moore, Hart Crane, Wallace Stevens, John Crowe Ransom, and Allen Tate in America. But against this reaction there was a counter-reaction, as we noted, and free verse is now a form generally used by poets in English.

THE NEW AUDIENCE AND PUBLISHERS

The years from 1912 to 1922 brought not only a "renais-sance" of poetry in America but also in significant attendant circumstances—the size and character of the audience and the ease with which poets could get their work published. By the end of the decade from two to three times as many volumes of some significance were appearing as at the beginning. This means that more good poetry was being written but, unless we indulge the assumption that good work will always find a publisher, it also indicates changes in the publishing trade. New houses were founded by young men and women who caught the spreading élan, the feeling that a new literature was emerging, and wished to contribute to the movement. Some of these publishers were avant-garde and ephemeral. Others, such as Boni and Liveright (*The Waste Land,* 1922; Pound's *Instigations,* 1920) and Alfred Knopf (Pound's *Lustra,* 1917, and *Pavannes and Divisions,* 1918; Eliot's *Poems,* 1920; Stevens' *Harmonium,* 1923), grew into well-established firms. A variety of circumstances—the little maga-zines, the controversies and hopes swirling about the "modern" styles, Harriet Monroe's anthology of *The New Poetry* (1917), the entry of the United States into the First World War, Louis Untermeyer's successive anthologies of *Modern American Poetry* that began to appear in 1919, and, possibly, the quality of the poetry—resulted in an increased public for poetry and in larger sales. As a consequence the older publishing houses showed a diminished reluctance to take a plunge into poetry. One evidence of the changed air was reported to Miss Monroe by a friend. Brentano's bookstore in New York had been keeping its poetry "on a little table away back in a dark corner under the stairs"; it now moved the display to a favored location in the front of the shop.

None of this means that poets could live by their art. Then as now only the triter sort of verse had large sales. Joyce Kilmer's "Trees," for which *Poetry* magazine originally paid $6.00, later produced royalties of $1,500 per year from a motto-card publisher. The war poems of Alan Seeger, Robert W. Service (*Rhymes of a Red Cross Man*), and Edgar Guest (*Over Here*) were best sellers. (And in the whole modern period the largest total sales in America of any contemporary poet have probably been accumulated by the Canadian Robert Service and by Edgar Guest.) But none of the better poets could hope to earn much from royalties. Furthermore, as Harriet Monroe frequently pointed out, for painters, sculptors, and composers (not that these were or are well off) there were prizes, patrons, and lucrative commissions; but no one commissioned a poem and there were before 1912 few patrons or prizes for poetry. Though in the years after 1912 one notes the beginnings of the contemporary support for poets, such as it is, through grants, public readings, college posts, sales of manuscripts, and prizes, it was not yet large enough to make much difference. Miss Monroe pointed out that around 1912 the poet who made $200 per year through his art was "fortunate." Pound's statement in a letter of 1934, looking back on this period, was accurate: "As for 'expatriated' . . . You know damn well the country wouldn't feed me. The simple economic fact that if I had returned to America I shd. have starved, and that to maintain anything like the standard of living, or indeed to live, *in* America from 1918 onwards I shd. have had to quadruple my earnings, i.e. it wd. have been impossible for me to devote *any* time to my REAL work."

But though changes in the audience and in the publishing support for poetry contributed and testified to a "renaissance" in the 1910s, the all-important change was the arrival of the little magazines. Gradually they transformed the milieu of poetry. Today, more than a half-century later, the little magazines are often viewed sourly, as any institution is when it has lasted long enough to show its disadvantages. They create, it is said, a frenetic, self-enclosed environment in which poets write only for each other, losing touch with a larger, more general audience as well as with just standards, proportion, and common sense. Insecure, alienated, and identity-seeking, they issue manifestoes, trumpet eddies as "movements," and whirl in step with fashion. They are subject to extreme pressures to cultivate novelty for its own sake and to bestow excessive watchfulness and instant emulation on the coming writer or phase—while the larger world goes by oblivious of the tempest in this teapot. Of all this the effects are naturally deleterious. But we may again cast our thoughts back to the time when there were almost no little magazines and recollect how difficult poets found it to break into print unless either they paid for it themselves or else conformed to the standards of Richard Watson Gilder and similar arbiters of magazines and books. It may be, as Keats once speculated, that when a society mistreats its poets it forces upon them a broader experience of life and so enriches their work, but no one to my knowledge has argued that poets are helped in their art by struggles and frustrations in trying to publish it.

The founding of *Poetry* magazine, for example, did not for most poets make an absolute difference between being published or not published. Many of the new poets, including Pound, Lindsay, Williams, and Masters, had already brought out books of verse, and some, such as Kreymborg, could not get their work accepted even in *Poetry*. So far as I know John Reed, Carl Sandburg, and Maxwell Bodenheim are the only "discoveries" *Poetry* could claim in its early years, and Sandburg is a doubtful case. But the magazine was publishing thirty pages of contemporary verse each month, possibly more than all the well-established literary journals together. The existence of such a magazine made it enormously easier to be printed. And especially the magazine provided a home for the less traditional kinds of poetry. By the end of its first four years *Poetry* had printed work by, among others, Eliot, Pound, Frost, Stevens, Lindsay, Sandburg, Masters, Amy Lowell, John Gould Fletcher,

H.D., Lawrence, and Marianne Moore—a good many of the poets who were to be important in twentieth-century poetry as a whole. One may well ask whether without little magazines and avant-garde publishers there would have been the same continued production from Eliot, Pound, Williams, and many other experimental poets.

To make it easier for such poets to publish was no slight service but was only a small part of *Poetry*'s impact. We may now ask how poets reacted when they read this varied mass of contemporary verse, much of it daringly avant-garde; certainly they had experienced nothing similar up till then. Two things are important: they obtained a greater sense of community and they saw new styles and methods. The first is probably more important, for it enormously strengthened self-confidence and created the sense of a relatively coherent movement. Before the little magazines came along, the established poets—those published in *The Century, Harpers, Atlantic,* and so forth—had regular opportunity to read each other's work. But if the more experimental poets managed to get published at all, it was likely to be under such obscure circumstances that their work remained unknown. Before 1912 Sandburg had not heard of Pound, nor Pound of Frost, nor Frost of Lindsay, and so forth. These were determined men, capable of working out their methods on their own; but the same isolation could stifle others. Or if that puts it too strongly, we may simply remark that the feeling that one is not alone but belongs to a group or "movement" builds confidence and energizes the psyche. Alfred Kreymborg, for example, was twenty-nine years old when *Poetry* appeared. A struggling, unpublished writer, he was in rebellion against commercial fiction and genteel verse and groping for alternatives. He was acquainted with painters, sculptors, and photographers and found psychological support in these friends, but he knew few writers. Unsure of the value of his own work, he felt the need of "definite contact," a sense that his writing expressed "something beyond mere ego-diagnosis"; that what he was "attempting in the dark" had in it the "power of communication." He suspected that a writer who lacked this would eventually be forced to conclude that he "was nothing but a valueless entity dabbling with solitaire" and that he would either stop writing or capitulate to "the commercial regime." Speaking of himself in the third person, he tells us in his autobiography, *Troubadour,* that when *Poetry* was published, it filled him with an "overpowering" emotion.

The early poems of Pound, Sandburg, H.D., Lindsay and others, in the pages of the Chicago journal, thrilled him to an ecstasy he had never known before, mainly because they were being discovered in his generation and indicated endless possibilities across the vast continent. These men and women, unconscious of one another and unconscious of him in his silent hole, were helping to set him free. He no longer saw masks, but faces; no longer felt himself a hermit, but a related being; his loneliness disappeared.

That poets could borrow methods and aims from the contemporaries they read in *Poetry* needs no elaboration. It was from the free verse published there, especially Sandburg's, that Masters caught the form. He used it in *The Spoon River Anthology* and thus introduced it to a great many readers. When Amy Lowell read the Imagist verse in *Poetry,* she said to herself, "Why I, too, am an Imagiste," and when two months later she read the Pound-Flint account of the new London movement, she decided to go there and learn about it at the fount. Even poets of the old school, such as George Sterling, felt the new stress. Though he never compacted Imagist pellets, he sought to make his work harder and dryer than it had been. "I have," he told Harriet Monroe, "been dropping little things from my style ever since *Poetry* began."

Subsequent little magazines could not hope to have the same impact as *Poetry,* but they have continued to fill the same roles: to publish and encourage young poets; to provide a home for experimental poets; to foster a sense of community among groups of poets or even among poets as a group; to import the works and thoughts of foreign contemporaries; and to make war on middle-class values, provincialism, censorship, and, generally, what Mencken called the "boobocracy." The little magazines, collectively considered, have long since had in their keeping one other function of immense importance: they decide literary reputations. On them depends whether the literary world (writers, publishers, critics, readers) will identify the best, that is, see to it that the best gets out—gets written and recognized.

If we ask how literary reputations have been established in the twentieth century, we find over and over again that the little magazines are the root of the process. A writer is discovered in the world of little magazines, acquires a following there, and the new name spreads gradually to the larger book reviews, commercial publishers, academic departments of literature, and so forth, until eventually the obscure writer may find his face on the cover of *Time* magazine. In 1914 T. S. Eliot, till then unable to publish his verse, showed his poetry to Ezra Pound, a bearded bohemian living in a London garret. Pound was enthusiastic and persuaded Harriet Monroe to print "Prufrock" in *Poetry*. He also placed Eliot's verse in other little magazines—*Blast, The Little Review,* and *Others*—and in 1917 made Eliot assistant editor of *The Egoist,* so that Eliot himself now had a place of some influence in the little magazine–avant-garde milieu. Eliot's verse did not always delight little magazine readers. In her autobiography Harriet Monroe says that when she first read "Prufrock," its "modern sophistication" nearly took her breath away; actually, Pound had to browbeat her for six months before she would print the poem. Louis Untermeyer, who in his anthology was soon to describe "Prufrock" as a "minor masterpiece," found on first reading that it "utterly stumped me . . . the muse in a psychopathic ward." His verdict was that the poem could interest only psychoanalysts. But gradually one admirer persuaded another, and he or she persuaded others still, until when *Prufrock and Other Observations* (1917) appeared in England, and *Poems* (1920) in America, they caused eddies of disgust and praise and were imitated by other poets, particularly the young. By the time *The Waste Land* was published in 1922 and won a prize of $2,000 from *The Dial,* Eliot was well known in avant-garde circles, and the controversy over *The Waste Land* erupted into a wider sphere, making his name familiar to anyone interested in literature. The story is typical. Only rarely now does a commercial publisher bring out a collection of poems by a poet who has not made a name through little magazines.

   This is not the place to tell the history of the little magazines, for we are concerned only with their impact on poetry. Most of the little magazines have been, *mutatis mutandis,* what Pound said of *Others* in 1916: "a harum scarum vers libre American product," which "keeps 'Arriet' (edtr. *Poetry*) from relapsing into the nineties." Some have been long-lived, but usually they last one to three years. New journals always spring up, however, often by cannibalizing the dying. After the founding of *Poetry*, the number of little magazines in America increased steadily; by the mid-1930s perhaps eighty were active (and perhaps two hundred and seventy five had already published and perished since 1912).

The editors of little magazines are commonly young. The first issue usually sets forth their purpose—to introduce new writers, to pursue "beauty," to voice the thoughts and traditions of a particular region, to liberate art from chains of moral hypocrisy, and so forth. The limit in loud intentions was reached early by *Blast*, which Wyndham Lewis and Pound got out in 1914–1915 in London. The preliminary advertisement in *The Egoist* announced "NO Pornography," "NO Old Pulp," "END OF THE CHRISTIAN ERA," and the first issue listed several pages of items to be blasted.

Financially speaking, the life of little magazines is a struggle. Circulation rarely exceeds 3,000 and is usually far less. Kreymborg's *Others* (1915–1919) sold about 500 copies of each issue; Pound supposed that *The Egoist* had about 185 subscribers when it folded—and of course no newsstand sales. The largest little magazine circulation up to the 1940s was probably the 18,000 achieved by *The Dial* (1920–1929) in its first four years. But even with this many readers the magazine could not break even, and circulation was allowed to drop to between 2,000 and 4,000 to reduce costs. Contributors have usually been unpaid, though in its opening years *Poetry* could afford ten dollars and *The Dial* twenty dollars per page. Marianne Moore tells that submitters of manuscripts to *The Dial* sometimes "hid salt between the pages to test the intensiveness" of editorial reading. Obviously little magazines could exist only through the support of patrons; now that they are accepted institutions they have an easier time than they used to. Not only are private patrons more numerous but some editors can hope for foundation grants and even government funds. In earlier days one might bring out a magazine without knowing how one would pay for it or with only enough money for the first issue. *The Little Review*, which printed Joyce's *Ulysses*, cost over $10,000 per year. To pay for it the editors made their own clothes, cut their own hair, and sometimes starved. Usually a little magazine is kept alive by the gallantry and devotion of a few people.

Little magazines are a new feature in the twentieth century,

the only important precedents in England or America being a
few late-Victorian journals, such as the Pre-Raphaelite *The Germ*
(1850), the aesthetic *Yellow Book* and *The Savoy* in the 1890s in
London, and *The Chap Book* (1894–1898), which imitated them
in Chicago. There were also chapbooks and pamphlets, often
arty productions from private presses, through which poets
could reach a smaller, more specialized audience. But collectively
these had less impact than present-day little magazines, and,
though the omens are never favorable for individual journals,
the institution seems likely to persist indefinitely. They are intrinsically connected with the idea of the avant-garde, so much so
that they may almost be said to constitute it, for without them the
avant-garde would have less means of talking to itself and so of
forming and articulating its frame of mind. Instead, there would
be only scattered individuals and groups, mostly unaware of
each other, voiceless and lost in the surrounding mass. There
are actually a great many different avant-gardes in the United
States, each with its own journal from which it bombards the
others. But if from a closer view the avant-garde splits into factions, from a more general perspective the factions make a
coherent impulse and power within American culture. To estimate the importance of little magazines, we need only note how
much intellectual life in America would have been impoverished
had we lacked, to name only a few, *Poetry, The Little Review, The
Sewanee Review, The Kenyon Review, The Dial, The Fugitive, Hound
and Horn, The Partisan Review, Furioso,* and *New Directions.*

THE CONTEMPORARY PERCEPTION
OF GROUPS AND MOVEMENTS

To this point I have spoken of the "new" poets as though they
made up a relatively coherent tendency. So, in fact, they did if
we see them, as we should, as a massive, general reaction against
the Genteel Tradition. But they did not think of themselves as a
tendency. To them the "renaissance" seemed an explosion,
bursting in all directions. More exactly, each thought of himself
as individually unique but perceived his contemporaries as
members of loosely associated groups.

In attempting to identify separate groups or movements

among the new poets, we are confronted by conflicting criteria. Intrinsic affinities must be brought out. But since one wishes also to recapture the sense of things that obtained at the time, one must pay attention to the sometimes accidental groupings made by chronology and geography and to the differing perceptions of poets, each interpreting the scene from his own point of view. One general distinction was between those who thought they were following in the path of Whitman and those who, while admiring Whitman, sought a more perfected artistry. "The 'Yawp,'" said Pound, "is respected from Denmark to Bengal, but we can't stop with the 'Yawp.' We have no longer any excuse for not taking up the complete art." Among the followers of Whitman were Sandburg, Masters, Lindsay, and James Oppenheim. The opposite pole was occupied by Pound and the Imagists; they stressed formal qualities and their influence contributed to a stylistic disciplining of American poetry.

For Pound the only important distinction to be made among American poets was that between those who labored for original and perfected technique—himself, Eliot (who "has thought of things I had not thought of"), Williams, Marianne Moore, H.D. (for a while), and Mina Loy—and those who did not struggle to produce "master-work" but were "content with publicity and the praise of reviewers." The first knew that "poetry *is* an *art* . . . with a technique" and that technique "must be in constant flux . . . if it is to live." They wrote "the sort of American stuff that I can show here [in London] and in Paris without its being ridiculed. Objective—no slither; direct—no excessive use of adjectives, no metaphors that won't permit examination." As for the rest, they were goops; their poems were slush.

Meanwhile, William Carlos Williams spoke for many in his obscure, weltering argument that Pound and Eliot were hindering the development of American poetry. His charge against them, in his Prologue (1918) to *Kora in Hell* (1920), appears to be threefold. First, their poetry derives from that of Europe: Eliot "is rehash, repetition in another way of Verlaine, Baudelaire, Maeterlinck . . . just as there were Pound's early paraphrases from Yeats and his constant later cribbing from the renaissance, Provence and the modern French." Both Pound and Eliot were "men content with the connotations of their masters." Secondly, though Pound and Eliot are marvelously expert, their work lacks value as art, for "nothing is good save the new." (Because of remarks such as this, Pound classified Williams as a Futurist, a category in which he also included Lindsay.) Thirdly, because it derives from Europe their poetry does not express American experience, character, and feeling. Against Pound's insistence that American poets must learn to produce work he can show "in Paris without its being ridiculed," Williams replies that "Paris will be more than slightly abashed to find parodies of the middle ages, Dante, and Lange D'Oc foisted upon it as the best in United States poetry." In his *Autobiography* (1948) Williams tells movingly of his sense of defeat when he first read Eliot's *The Waste Land:*

It wiped out our world as if an atom bomb had been dropped upon it . . . Eliot returned us to the classroom just at the moment when I felt that we were on the point of an escape to matters much closer to the essence of a new art form itself—rooted in the locality which should give it fruit. I knew at once that in certain ways I was most defeated.

If we organize our poets by chronology, Masters, Lowell, Frost, Sandburg, and Lindsay were roughly five to fifteen years older than Williams, Pound, Fletcher, Marianne Moore, and Eliot. The fact reflects itself in the more radical experiments of the younger poets. A still younger group is made up of such poets as E. E. Cummings, Hart Crane, Allen Tate, and Yvor Winters. These poets assimilated the innovations of the "new" poets. They also reacted against them, and achieved individual styles. But the Modernist revolution was essentially accomplished by the mid-1920s, and the role of these poets, who were born six to twelve years later, was to explore and develop what had already been so powerfully opened up. For this reason the younger poets who were just starting to publish in the 1920s are not noticed except incidentally in the present volume. Some contemporaries of Eliot, such as Archibald MacLeish, Robinson Jeffers, and John Crowe Ransom, are also deferred for discussion in the second volume, which covers the history of poetry from the mid-twenties to now. For although these poets were publishing in the 1910s and 1920s, they did their best work or had their important influence in a later period.

If we differentiate by geography, Masters, Sandburg, and Lindsay belonged to the Midwest. That a Midwestern group could be discerned was significant; it meant the rise of another region to challenge the hegemony of the East. The fact that *Poetry* was published in Chicago also contributed to the impression. The new status of Chicago was symbolized in 1914, when W. B. Yeats spoke under the auspices of *Poetry* at a dinner there and Vachel Lindsay, from nearby Springfield, recited "The Congo" to the commendations of the distinguished visitor. In New England the work of Robinson, Frost, and Amy Lowell (in poems where she imitated Frost) made another regional grouping. And in New York City several experimenters were publishing in *Others* magazine—Kreymborg, Marianne Moore, Wallace Stevens, Mina Loy, W. C. Williams, Maxwell Bodenheim, and Lola Ridge. The journal had been started, Kreymborg says, so that America might have "a poetry magazine, not like *Poetry* in Chicago, which admitted too many compromises, but . . . dedicating its energies to experiment throughout." It was to the left of *Poetry*. And in London there were the cosmopolitans, Pound, H.D., and Eliot, whose work seemed rooted in literature of the past and of Europe.

Meanwhile, the perceptions of the public were strongly influenced by Amy Lowell, the "demon saleswoman," Eliot called her, who campaigned to and fro for the new poetry. ("Dear Amy Lowell's talents and temperament," Pound said, "will always be political rather than literary or artistic.") She persuaded, bullied, and paid her publisher to bring out verse (the Imagist anthologies for 1915, 1916, and 1917; Fletcher's *Irradiations,* 1915) She wooed critics and editors, lectured, wrote criticism, and attracted newspaper publicity—all on behalf of the cause. She explained that the new poets in England and America were Frost, Masters, Pound, Lindsay, Fletcher, Aldington, H.D., Flint, Lawrence, Sandburg, and herself. The most important general characteristics of the new poetry were "externality" (by which she meant objectivity, the rendering of outward events rather than impressions and subjective states) and a refusal to draw moral generalizations. The new poets stressed "the poetry in unpoetic things," were sometimes witty, humorous, or playful, and wrote simply and directly "in the syntax of prose," with "clean edges" and a "sparing use of adjectives." Also, they adopted freer rhythms, a fact Miss Lowell did not always expound tactfully. The morning after she lectured to the Contemporary Club

in Philadelphia, the local newspaper headlined, "Tears Punctu-
ate Stormy Spots in Vers Libre Debate." If she had let tears fall,
which she denied, they were from rage at her opponents, but
she had provoked them. Her reward was that her books sold out
in Philadelphia. Her account of the new poetry was the clearest,
most comprehensive then available; although loosely phrased, it
was accurate. From it one learned that there was a new or modern poetry and informed oneself about its antecedents, general
traits, and representative figures. In *Tendencies in Modern American Poetry* (1917) she treated six poets, grouping them to represent three successive phases in the development of the new poetry: Robinson and Frost, Sandburg and Masters, and H.D. and
Fletcher, exemplifying the Imagists. In the Imagists, she said,
the modern impulse reached its fully purified and developed
form, though she did not necessarily mean that the Imagists
wrote better poetry than the others. Gallant, indomitable, and
reasonably fair-minded, in her day Amy Lowell did more than
anyone else to win from the general public an understanding reception for the new poetry.

15

IMAGISM

IMAGISM has been described as the grammar school of modern poetry, the instruction and drill in basic principles. The metaphor greatly exaggerates—neither Yeats nor Eliot were ever Imagists, for example, though both were occasionally claimed for the group—but among the several modern movements in English and American poetry just before World War I, the Imagists probably had a more distinct impact than any other group on the style of American poets. The reasons for this were partly the shrewdness with which first Pound and then Amy Lowell promoted the movement, partly the clear doctrine and practical tips offered by the Imagist manifestos and other bulletins, and partly because the Imagist program merged with other, already influential tendencies: Impressionist exact notation; interest in Chinese and Japanese poetry, in which poets now remarked a spare, suggestive, visual imagery in terse forms such as haiku; the orientation of poetry in the 1890s to painting, sculpture, and other "spatial" arts; the special attention symbolist poetry directed to imagery; Hulme's plea that poetry must be precisely phrased and that the essential means to precision is metaphor; the development of free verse; the rejection of poetic diction and "rhetoric"; the cultivation of the idiomatic and the colloquial. Imagist poems were not difficult to read, and after

1914, when Pound could no longer impose his standards on the movement, they were not very difficult to write. Like Georgian poetry in England or the "realism" of Masters and Sandburg in America, Imagism became a relatively accessible way to be in on the "new" and the "modern."

THE IMAGIST MOVEMENT

Imagism was conceived in the spring of 1912 in a tea shop in Kensington, where, over buns, Pound informed two young poets, H.D. and Richard Aldington, that they were *Imagistes*. What the term then meant to him can only be guessed, but by October he was spreading the news—half-seriously and half as a publicity stunt—of a school of *Imagisme*. "Isms" were in the air. The August 1912 *Poetry Review* included an article by F. S. Flint on "Contemporary French Poetry," in which one could read up on Unanisme, Impulsionnisme, Paroxysme, and so forth. Marinetti had long since caused a stir with Futurism, and before Marinetti there had been the "symbolist movement" of Yeats and Symons. England had its home-grown movement in the Georgian poets.

In October, Pound's *Ripostes* appeared, including as an appendix "The Complete Poetical Works of T. E. Hulme," five short poems. There was also a prefatory note by Pound. *"Les Imagistes,"* he said (typically he used French for literary movements), have the future "in their keeping." They descended from the forgotten "School of Images" of 1909. (He was thinking of the small group of poets who used to meet with T. E. Hulme at The Eiffel Tower restaurant in Soho.) At about the same time Pound used the new term in letters to Harriet Monroe, who mentioned the new school in her November 1912 issue of *Poetry*. The January 1913 issue printed five poems by H.D., which were signed (at Pound's insistence) "H.D. Imagiste." There was also a note by Pound: "The youngest school" in London "is that of the Imagistes . . . one of their watchwords is Precision." In March 1913 *Poetry* printed the famous brief statement of Imagiste principles and the list of tips Pound had originally composed as a rejection slip for *Poetry*.

With these statements, and with Imagiste poems by H.D. and Aldington to serve as examples, the "movement" was successfully planted in America.

Pound decided to put together an Imagiste anthology. By the summer of 1913 he had selected poems by Aldington, H.D., Flint, and himself to make up the bulk of the book and had also accepted for it one poem each from Skipwith Cannell, Amy Lowell, William Carlos Williams, Joyce, Hueffer, Allen Upward, and John Cournos. This collection was sent to Alfred Kreymborg in New York and published as *Des Imagistes: An Anthology* (1914).

Meanwhile, in Boston, Amy Lowell was intrigued. As Harriet Monroe tells it, Miss Lowell read in the January 1913 issue of *Poetry*, "some poems signed 'H.D. Imagiste'; and suddenly it came over her: 'Why, I too am an Imagiste!'" She sailed for London that June armed with a letter of introduction from Miss Monroe. Pound corrected her poetry ("He could *make* you write," she later conceded), and found her "ALL RIGHT." The next summer she returned to London, but her state of mind was less docile and more self-confident. For the April issue of *Poetry* had started off with eight of her poems (mostly in free verse) and her second volume, *Sword Blades and Poppy Seed,* was in proof. She thought the success of the Georgian anthologies might be emulated and proposed to the Imagistes that their anthology be brought out annually for five years. She promised to pay for publication if that proved necessary. But she was miffed that the first anthology had included only one of her poems. Subsequent anthologies, she said, should be "democratic": they should allow each contributor approximately the same amount of space. To Pound the notion was absurd. The arts were not a "democratic beer-garden." Miss Lowell's suggestion was very welcome to the other Imagistes, however, and in 1915 *Some Imagist Poets* (the term now Anglicized—or Americanized) appeared, containing poems of Aldington, H.D., Flint, Amy Lowell, John Gould Fletcher, and D. H. Lawrence. (Pound had formally seceded from the movement.)

Even though Miss Lowell had gone ahead with her "democratic" anthology, she and Pound had managed to part cordially at the end of the summer. But poisons were working. She knew

Pound thought her lacking in standards and she was critical of
him. During the fall Macmillan's advertised her *Sword Blades and
Poppy Seed* by explaining that, "Of the poets who to-day are
doing the interesting and original work, there is no more
striking and unique figure than Amy Lowell. The foremost
member of the 'Imagists'—a group of poets that includes William Butler Yeats, Ezra Pound, Ford Maddox Hueffer. . . ."
Such "charlatanism" was too much for Pound. His letter of protest was firm; he advised her to "cease referring to yourself as an
Imagiste." Miss Lowell made light of the advertisement: "The
names," she replied, "were simply put in to boom the book, a
thing that is constantly done over here." ("Your knowledge of
how to 'get yourself over,'" she later wrote him, "is *nil*.") As time
passed, Pound felt that the poetry of the Imagists (he now called
them "Amygists") was becoming undisciplined, sloppy, and di-
luted. In Miss Lowell's opinion there were now "bitterest en-
mities" between herself and Pound. As for Pound, he thought
her verse "putrid" but liked her personally—at least until 1922,
when she refused to contribute to his scheme of financial support for Eliot. "Aw shucks! dearie," he then wrote her, "ain't
you the hell-roarer, ain't you the kuss." In 1928, in a letter to
Taupin, he summed up the Imagists as a "bunch of goups."

After 1914 the Imagist movement was captained by Miss
Lowell. Richard Aldington, as editor of *The Egoist,* provided auxiliary aid in the form of an Imagist number (May 1, 1915). In the
same year Miss Lowell praised the new school at a meeting of the
conservative Poetry Society in New York, and was henceforth
embattled. She held readings, gave lectures, and cultivated editors, reviewers, and anthologists. Hostile articles on Imagism in
the *New Republic,* Chicago *Evening Post, Nation,* and *Atlantic
Monthly* raised her blood pressure, but were not otherwise un-
welcome. "Well?—Clap or hiss," Miss Lowell used to tell audiences at her readings, "I don't care which; but do something!"
Critical attack provoked defense, and the Imagists were more
widely heard of than any movement since. Imagist anthologies
were issued in 1916 and 1917; thereafter there were no more.
But whenever critics discussed modern poetry, the school continued to be noticed as an important phase or tendency. Poems
of the Imagist kind continued to be written, though it became
increasingly difficult to say precisely what this kind was.

THE IMAGIST DOCTRINE

The first public statement of Imagist principles was that printed by *Poetry* in March 1913. Written by Pound, the statement was signed by Flint, who said he had obtained the three-fold program by interviewing an Imagiste:

1. Direct treatment of the "thing," whether subjective or objective.
2. To use absolutely no word that did not contribute to the presentation.
3. As regarding rhythm: to compose in sequence of the musical phrase, not in sequence of a metronome.

The list illustrates that so far as doctrine was concerned, Imagisme, as Pound conceived it, was not so much a special type of poetry as a name for whatever he had learned (from Hulme, Hueffer, Yeats, and others; see Chapter 20) about "HOW TO WRITE" since coming to London in 1908. He was in the habit of scribbling such recipes. In 1916, for example, "the whole art" of poetry was divided (with no reference to Imagisme) into:

a. concision, or style, or saying what you mean in the fewest and clearest words.
b. the actual necessity for creating or constructing something; of presenting an image, or enough images of concrete things arranged to stir the reader.

The historical importance of Imagism, in other words, does not lie in the formulation of a poetic doctrine, for Pound had developed his ideas with no reference to Imagism and continued to hold them after he disowned the movement. The importance was, rather, the extent to which the name, movement, and attendant controversies caused these values to be effectively disseminated.

So far as Pound endowed Imagism with a program distinct from his principles of effective writing in general, it must be sought in the special role assigned to the "image." Pound defined his key term only vaguely. An image is, he said in the same issue of *Poetry*, "that which presents an intellectual and emotional complex in an instant of time. . . . It is better to present one Image in a lifetime than to produce voluminous works." Whatever else the "doctrine of the image" might include was not to be published, readers were told, for "it does not concern the public and would provoke useless discussion."

The March 1913 issue contained further admonishments from Pound, "A Few Don'ts by an Imagiste," which helped interpret the program: for example, "Use no superfluous word, no adjective, which does not reveal something"; "Go in fear of abstractions"; "Let the candidate fill his mind with the finest cadences he can discover, preferably in a foreign language so that the meaning of the words may be less likely to divert his attention from the movement"; "Don't be 'viewy'—leave that to the writers of pretty little philosophic essays"; "Don't chop your stuff into separate *iambs*." Such tips were admirably practical, and the offhand phrasing enhanced their authority.

In June 1914 in *The Egoist* Aldington again explained what Imagism was, but the most influential single statement produced in the whole course of the movement was his Preface to the Imagist anthology for 1915. It listed six points, "the essentials of all great poetry, indeed of all great literature":

1. To use the language of common speech, but to employ always the *exact* word, not the nearly exact, nor the merely decorative word.
2. To create new rhythms—as the expression of new moods—and not to copy old rhythms, which merely echo old moods. We do not insist upon "free-verse" as the only method of writing poetry. We fight for it as a principle of liberty. We believe that the individuality of a poet may often be better expressed in free-verse than in conventional forms. In poetry, a new cadence means a new idea.
3. To allow absolute freedom in the choice of subject. It is not good art to write badly about aeroplanes and automobiles; nor is it necessarily bad art to write about the past. We believe passionately in the artistic value of modern life, but we wish to point out that there is nothing so uninspiring nor so old-fashioned as an aeroplane of the year 1911.
4. To present an image (hence the name: "Imagist"). We are not a school of painters, but we believe that poetry should render particulars exactly and not deal in vague generalities, however magnificent and sonorous. It is for this reason that we oppose the cosmic poet, who seems to us to shirk the real difficulties of his art.
5. To produce poetry that is hard and clear, never blurred nor indefinite.
6. Finally, most of us believe that concentration is of the very essence of poetry.

The statement was directed against undemanding techniques and against conventional, though not necessarily conservative attitudes. Instead of many adjectives and statements, there would be an image rendered in concentrated, exact, idiomatic speech. Instead, for example, of the looseness of Masefield's "The West Wind"—

> It's a warm wind, the west wind, full of bird's cries;
> I never hear the west wind but tears are in my eyes.
> For it comes from the west lands, the old brown hills,
> And April's in the west wind, and daffodils—

there would be Aldington's "New Love":

> She has new leaves
> After her dead flowers,
> Like the little almond-tree
> Which the frost hurt.

As opposed to frequent demands at this time for a specifically contemporary subject matter, Aldington implicitly defended the "Hellenism" of himself and H.D. by invoking the poet's right to "absolute freedom in the choice of subject," a principle to which all would-be Modernists subscribed. Against the expectation that poetry would be metrical, he adopted a point of view that legitimized free verse without decrying meters. Whether verse was traditional or free, there should be "new rhythms" as the expression of "new" and individual moods.

Against the poets and poetic habits Aldington implicitly criticized, his points were effectively made. On the other hand, though this Preface was so strongly influenced by Pound that it seemed mainly a restatement of his views, one finds, if one compares it with Pound's earlier statement, that a vulgarization has set in. "Concentration," the "*exact* word," and "hard and clear" style do not impose quite so severe a standard as Pound's second article, "To use absolutely no word that did not contribute to the presentation" (and this was the essential article in Pound's opinion). Moreover, although Pound was probably not quite sure what he meant by an "Image," he thought of it as a "complex" concretely presented. In Aldington's Preface the concept of the Image is wavering toward a much simpler notion, that of a clear, quick rendering of particulars without commentary.

Imagist poems of this kind would of course be much easier to write.

The attacks on Imagism that followed in 1915 raised only two important issues. The controversy over free verse—is it poetry?—was discussed in Chapter 14. Secondly, it was immediately pointed out that Imagist successes could only be small-scale. As Conrad Aiken put it, the Imagists

give us frail pictures—whiffs of windy beaches, marshes, meadows, city streets, disheveled leaves; pictures pleasant and suggestive enough. But seldom is any of them more than a nice description, coolly sensuous, a rustle to the ear, a ripple to the eye. Of organic movement there is practically none.

One could not write a long Imagist poem. Quite apart from particular issues, however, controversy gradually caused the doctrine of Imagism to become less definite. For the battle on behalf of Imagism was fought by Amy Lowell. Since her temperament was not ideological but political, she compromised doctrine, like many another politician, in order to prevail in the field. In *Tendencies in Modern American Poetry* she characterized the Imagist principles as "Simplicity and directness of speech; subtlety and beauty of rhythms; individualistic freedom of idea; clearness and vividness of presentation; and concentration." With such generalities no one could quarrel, but neither could anyone be arrested by them, as poets had been by Pound's statement in *Poetry* four years before.

THE IMAGIST POEM

Once the Imagist poem was established as a type, it was written occasionally by many poets who were not members of the original Imagist group. Familiar instances are Sandburg's "Fog" and Williams' "El Hombre." Many other poets, such as Marianne Moore, E. E. Cummings, and Archibald MacLeish, were strongly influenced by Imagist principles and style, even though they did not write specifically Imagist poems. Because the poems of T. E. Hulme were the first examples of Imagism offered to the world (by Pound in October 1912), his "Autumn" may be used to exemplify the mode:

A touch of cold in the Autumn night—
I walked abroad,
And saw the ruddy moon lean over a hedge
Like a red-faced farmer.
I did not stop to speak, but nodded,
And round about were the wistful stars
With white faces like town children.

The poem was probably written in conscious contrast with Shelley's famous "To the Moon," for Shelley's poem also contrasts the moon to the stars and thinks about companionability or the lack of it:

Art thou pale for weariness
Of climbing heaven, and gazing on the earth,
Wandering companionless
Among the stars that have a different birth,—
And ever-changing, like a joyless eye
That finds no object worth its constancy?

Whether or not Hulme recalled Shelley, his verses are anti-Romantic. Within the Romantic tradition to view the cold and starry heavens in autumn would predictably evoke feelings of melancholy, loneliness, and death. If such feelings are present here, it is only in a complex, indirect, and controlled way. Hulme's "red-faced farmer," unlike Shelley's pale moon, seems well fed, healthy, comfortable, and neighborly, and is humorously regarded. What is conveyed by the poem is not, as with Shelley, a comparison that projects the poet's "moan" (as Hulme would have put it) into the moon but a comparison in altogether unexpected terms. If we ask what is communicated in Shelley's poem, "the poet's feeling of loneliness" would be an inadequate, though not incorrect generalization. In the case of Hulme's poem, the "meaning" cannot be conveyed by a generalization.
    Another modal poem, often cited, was H.D.'s "Oread":

Whirl up, sea—
Whirl your pointed pines,
Splash your great pines
On our rocks,
Hurl your green over us,
Cover us with your pools of fir.

The perception of the sea as a pine and fir forest is fresh and apt; the cadenced lines enact an emotional transition; the effect is complex, immediate, and made wholly by concrete means; the poet avoids discursive or generalizing comment. As a final example we may turn to MacLeish's "Ars Poetica," which illustrates much that the Imagist movement taught other poets. A poem, MacLeish writes, should be "palpable and mute"; it should not tell a "history of grief" at length but should evoke it through concrete particulars:

> For all the history of grief
> An empty doorway and a maple leaf
>
> For love
> The leaning grasses and two lights above the sea—
>
> A poem should not mean
> But be.

SOME IMAGIST POETS

None of the poets published in the Imagist anthologies remained an Imagist in later life, and some from the outset were Imagists only occasionally. We may here touch on the careers of five poets—Aldington, H.D., Fletcher, Amy Lowell, and Herbert Read—who were closely identified with the Imagist movement. Pound was, of course, the most important of the Imagists, but his Imagist phase is described in Chapter 20. D. H. Lawrence was included in the anthologies mainly for reasons of good fellowship; he wrote no poems of the Imagist kind, and is discussed in Chapter 19. Of the poets to be taken up here, Aldington, H.D., Fletcher, and Lowell were prominent in the Imagist anthologies; Herbert Read came to the movement slightly later, was strongly influenced by it, and continued thereafter to be a spokesman for the Imagist ideals. In fact, after the mid-1920s he was their most important contemporary spokesman.

Poems by Richard Aldington (1892–1962) were first published in 1909. Labeled "Imagiste" and trumpeted by Pound, the eighteen-year-old Aldington attended Yeats's Monday evenings, knew Hulme, Ford, Lawrence, Amy Lowell, married H.D., became literary editor of *Egoist,* and was in the thick of literary goings-on in avant-garde London. The poems he wrote at this time were often mythopoeic, evoking a Mediterranean landscape. They were composed in free verse and presented "images"—mostly sensuously appealing ones. Aldington's poems were often said to be "hellenic," though their attitudes and scenery descended more immediately from Swinburne and the Pre-Raphaelites. During and after World War I he departed steadily further from the Imagist style; in *Exile and Other Poems* (1923) he wrote the directly personal and talky type of poem that in the nineteenth century was often called an "effusion." "I abandon, cast off, utterly deny the virtue of 'extreme compression and essential significance of every word,'" he wrote Herbert Read in 1924. "I say that is the narrow path that leadeth to sterility. . . . Pound, Flint, both went down on that; I saw them go; and I shall live to see you and Tom [Eliot] go the same way." After *A Fool i' the Forest* (1925) he published mostly prose. His chief success was with his novel of the war, *Death of a Hero* (1929).

According to his occasional private explanations, Pound invented the Imagist movement to obtain attention for the work of Hilda Doolittle (1886–1961), who published under her initials "H.D." She grew up in Philadelphia, where she was acquainted with Pound and William Carlos Williams. She went to Europe in 1911 and spent the rest of her life there. She and Richard Aldington were married in 1912; they separated after the war. Pound, Amy Lowell, Louis Untermeyer, and others frequently mentioned her poems as the purest examples of Imagism. Her phrasing was usually idiomatic and economical. The units of syntax were short and there were few subordinate clauses. Abstract generalizations were infrequent. The poems were made of simple statements juxtaposed, as in "The Pool":

> Are you alive?
> I touch you.
> You quiver like a sea-fish.
> I cover you with my net.
> What are you—banded one?

Such writing struck many readers as clear, swift, and uncluttered.

H.D. translated from classical Greek—Euripides, Sappho, Homer, the Greek anthology. Her original verses also brought Greece to mind, for the light, color, and landscape might be Mediterranean and she usually alluded to Greek myth or recreated it in the poem. Because her landscape, subject, and sensibility seemed "Greek," so did her style. Richard Eberhart summarized a common opinion when he said in 1958, she "gives us the best glimpse we have today of classic poetry, an English poetry . . . nearly Greek in concept and execution . . . crystalbright, hard and pure, clean and fine." Those more deeply versed in English and Greek poetry recognized that her "Greece" was typically Romantic and literary, a Hellenic world distilled from Shelley, Keats, Byron, Arnold, Swinburne, and many another English poet of the nineteenth century. To such readers her Imagist "hardness" of style was not impressively "Greek," neither was it especially "modern," for except that the diction was idiosyncratic and the verse was free, it recalled the familiar "sculpture of rhyme" of the 1890s. It was obvious that her art, like that of the aesthetes, had limited itself by retreating from the world of actual experience. Moreover, the feelings it expressed were often strained and unreal, as when the speaker in the much-admired "Orchard" falls prostrate before a pear,

> crying:
> you have flayed us
> with your blossoms,
> spare us the beauty
> of fruit-trees.

Like other Imagists, H.D. gradually abandoned the mode. *The Walls Do Not Fall* (1944) inaugurated a remarkable poetic self-renewal. This sequence of poems is meditative and also mythical and archetypal, showing the influence of both Freud (whose patient she was) and Jung. The symbols are taken from diverse traditions—Christian, Egyptian, cabalistic, astrological—for she assumed that these different symbolisms evoked the same underlying realities. The poem was written in London during World War II and was followed by two long sequences of a similar kind, *Tribute to the Angels* (1945) and *The Flowering of the Rod* (1946).

John Gould Fletcher (1886–1950) was only occasionally an Imagist, but because he was one of the six poets in Miss Lowell's Imagist anthologies, he was, throughout most of his life, presumed to be an Imagist by a literary public that could hardly have been paying close attention to his works. In fact, he began as an aggressively experimentalist, Modernist poet and ended as a regional one. In 1908 (one year later than Pound) he sailed for Italy, for, as he later explained, he was disgusted with the "mediocrity, the optimism, the worldliness" of the United States, and regarded Europe as the place to "acquire an education." Again like Pound, in 1909 he moved to London. He studied Impressionist and post-Impressionist painting, oriental poetry (in translation), and the French symbolist poets (he claimed to have introduced Pound to them). He read, it was said, a book of French poetry every day.

In 1913 he was briefly at the center of avant-garde affairs. He published five books of poetry at his own expense. He agreed to back Pound financially (Fletcher had inherited money) in taking over the suffragette *New Freewoman*, which eventually became *The Egoist*. When Amy Lowell came to London that summer he told her his plan to write a poem on a modern city by objectively recording just what one sees. Quarreling with Pound, he refused to appear in *Des Imagistes*, and proposed to Miss Lowell that they jointly edit and finance a rival anthology. He was determined "to risk everything in order to become a modern artist." His notions of what constituted modernism were strangely external and confused but for this very reason they were typical of many writers at the beginning of what Pound called "le mouvement." To be a modern artist, as Fletcher saw it, involved "a determination to make and accept every kind of experiment." If one "aroused the hatred of the mob," so had Cezanne, Gauguin, Van Gogh, and Stravinski. There was "but one lesson the modern artist must learn," which was (quoting Synge) that "to be human again, we must learn first to be brutal." Having just seen Stravinski's *Rite of Spring*, he felt that artists everywhere "were turning back to the primitively ugly, knowing that in primitiveness alone lay strength."

Fletcher's verse of this period may be illustrated by his "Irradiations" and Color Symphonies. His purpose in these poems was to evoke and orchestrate moods, while excluding any more

definite content. Some of the "Irradiations" were recognizably
symbolist:

> Far trumpets like a vague rout of faded roses
> Burst 'gainst the wet green silence of distant forests:
> A clash of cymbals—then the swift swaying footsteps
> Of the wind that undulates along the languid terraces.

Some however, were Imagist:

> Flickering of incessant rain
> On flashing pavements:
> Sudden scurry of umbrellas:
> Bending, recurved blossoms of the storm.

And in other instances the mood he sought to evoke required an
emulation of Whitman, whom Fletcher had also been reading:

> I saw that all the women—although their bodies
>   were dexterously concealed—
> Were thinking with all their might what the men were like.

The Color Symphonies, he later explained, attempted to render
"certain predominant moods in the terms of things happening.
Thus one gets expectancy described as a traveler looking at blue
mountains in the distance." The "prevailing mood" was indicated by a color, as in the "Blue Symphony," in which images of
blue objects recur. In this symphony the setting, decor, and
suggestive spareness in description produce a vaguely "oriental"
feeling, as in the lines evoking an autumnal garden:

> Sombre wreck—autumnal leaves;
> Shadowy roofs
> In the blue mist,
> And a willow-branch that is broken.

> Oh, old pagodas of my soul, how you glittered
>   across green trees.

Becoming dissatisfied with these shimmerings, Fletcher
wished to articulate ideas. In the 1920s and 1930s he composed
meditative, often religiously questing lyrics and effusions of a
kind that used frequently to be called "cosmic." Gradually, he

became a regional poet of his native Arkansas, where he was now living, for he felt the poetic appeal of American landscape and regional life. He sympathized with the social values of Allen Tate, John Crowe Ransom, and other Fugitive writers, for he shared their idealization of Southern agrarian traditionalism as opposed to urban, industrialized rootlessness in the North. The most important product of this late, regional phase was *South Star* (1941). The volume includes a poetic history of the state of Arkansas, more impressive as regional piety than as poetry, as well as shorter lyrics which effectively combine his Imagist-Impressionist methods of presentation, his search for general, ultimate meanings, and his imaginative response to local objects and scenes.

Amy Lowell (1874–1925) was one of the distinguished and wealthy Lowells of Boston. The family tree included generals, judges, historians, and the poet, James Russell Lowell; Robert Lowell is of the same family. Her brother Abbott Lawrence Lowell, who became President of Harvard, made no public comment on the avant-garde writings and other eccentricities of his sister. She was enormously overweight because of a glandular disturbance, smoked cigars, slept with sixteen pillows, and worked from midnight to dawn, sleeping by day. These and other oddities contributed to her reputation, but what contributed more were her energy, shrewdness, determination, and pluck. By these virtues she thrust herself into prominence among the poets of the time, but her position was precarious. Her poetry, though often written with sensitivity and intelligence, could not justify the importance that seemed to be hers—that was hers if we think only of her leadership in promoting the new art.

Her first volume, *A Dome of Many-Coloured Glass* (1912), was conventionally derivative from the English Romantic tradition. Her next one, *Sword Blades and Poppy Seed* (1914), showed the impact of her contact with the Imagist and experimentalist avant-garde in London in the summer of 1913. Along with its ballads, dramatic monologues, and rhymed, stanzaic lyrics, it included poems in free verse. There were also three examples of what she called "polyphonic prose," a way of writing, she explained, that uses cadence, assonance, alliteration, rhyme, echo effects, and even "perhaps true metre for a few minutes," but handles them in a more varying and flexible way than is possible in traditional verse:

The inkstand is full of ink, and the paper lies white and unspotted, in the round of light thrown by a candle. Puffs of darkness sweep into the corners, and keep rolling through the room behind his chair. The air is silver and pearl, for the night is liquid with moonlight.

Men, Women and Ghosts (1916) was a collection of narratives in meters, free verse, and polyphonic prose. Among them was the much-anthologized dramatic monologue, "Patterns" and a block ("The Overgrown Pasture") of four dramatic monologues by rural New England speakers. In these she was deliberately challenging Robert Frost and wrote in dialect, as she considered he ought to have done. *Can Grande's Castle* (1918) was a volume of polyphonic prose, and in *Pictures of a Floating World* (1919) Miss Lowell, who felt that volumes of poetry should have a unified character and effect, published the short lyrics she had written and stored up since 1914.

These free-verse lyrics display the qualities for which her work was exemplary at this time. Her diction and syntax are relatively simple, straightforward, and idiomatic. She renders sensations with exact impression. The poems adhere closely to the concrete, avoiding generalization and "rhetoric." "November" is an example:

> The vine leaves against the brick walls of my house
> Are rusty and broken.
> Dead leaves gather under the pine-trees,
> The brittle boughs of lilac-bushes
> Sweep against the stars.
> And I sit under a lamp
> Trying to write down the emptiness of my heart.
> Even the cat will not stay with me,
> But prefers the rain
> Under the meagre shelter of a cellar window.

Despite its virtues the poem illustrates how Miss Lowell, like Sandburg, H.D., Aldington, and many other "new" poets, was "modern" only in some aspects of form and style. In sensibility and imagination she was safely within the fold of familiar Romantic convention.

In 1921 she published *Fir-Flower Tablets,* a volume of translations from ancient Chinese poetry. She knew no Chinese and used English versions supplied by Florence Ayscough, a friend who lived in Shanghai. "The great poets of the T'ang Dynasty," she felt, "are without doubt among the finest poets that the world has ever seen". (Such a judgment on poets she could not read tells much about Miss Lowell.) Her translations would "knock a hole" in Pound's *Cathay.* In 1922 her *A Critical Fable* appeared. Imitating a poem of the same name by James Russell Lowell, it contained doggerel criticisms of contemporary poets, including herself (her authorship was concealed at first), excited much interest, and shows how the poetic scene was viewed from one influential and representative perspective in the year of *The Waste Land.* By this time Miss Lowell was heavily engaged in her massive biography of Keats. She was ill and unused to close and detailed scholarship ("Keats is killing me"); but she was indomitable, and the work was published in 1925, four months before she died. The three volumes of poetry published posthumously show no change in the direction of her talent, and include two of her better-known poems, "Lilacs" and "Meeting-House Hill."

A distinguished essayist, novelist, lecturer, and critic of art and literature, Sir Herbert Read (1893–1968) was also an autobiographer. His account of his early poetic career (*The Innocent Eye,* 1933) reveals much about the feelings and aspirations of the first young writers formed by the Modernist revolution. Read's situation differed from that of Hulme, Pound, Eliot, or Lawrence in the crucial respect that he did not participate in creating an avant-garde poetry but adopted one created by others. His interest in poetry was awakened by a schoolteacher, but for a long time the only audience, patron, and encourager of his verse was a Quaker tailor in Leeds, where Read was working as a bank clerk. The seventeen-year-old poet delighted in Tennyson; Blake descended on him "like an apocalypse"; he was entranced with Yeats and Ralph Hodgson, Donne and Browning. It was apparently in the Imagist anthology for 1915 that Read first encountered Imagist verse and doctrine. Now twenty-two or twenty-three, he had found, he felt, the essence of the avant-garde or modern movement in poetry. As an officer in the trenches he composed Imagist poems of war experience; for example, "Movement of Troops":

> We entrain in open trucks
> and soon glide away
> from the plains of Artois.
>
> With a wake of white smoke
> we plunge
> down dark avenues of silent trees.
>
> A watcher sees
> our red light gleam
> occasionally.

To the end of his life Read was likely to identify the "new poetic awareness" of the twentieth century as Imagism and to restate some of the leading premises of the Imagist manifestos as his own poetic creed: "A poem is not a statement, but a . . . manifestation of *being*"; "The rhythmical pattern corresponds . . . with the inner feeling."

War experience caused him to question his Imagist procedures, for he was trying, he later said, "to maintain an abstract aesthetic ideal in the midst of terrorful and inhuman events." He wished to achieve a more direct expression of what he was feeling and undergoing; he therefore composed longer narrative and meditative poems, which turned out to be diffuse and uncontrolled. Toward the end of the war, on leave in London, he became acquainted with Flint, Aldington, Pound, and Eliot (who became a lifelong friend), and learned, he said, to write in a more self-disciplined way: "Poetry was reduced to an instrument of precision"; "Criticism had become innate.")

If we mean by Imagism only the sort of poem exemplified in "Movement of Troops," Read rarely wrote Imagist poems after 1919. He sometimes emulated the Metaphysical Poets in the 1920s and Auden in the 1930s, and practiced diverse styles through his long career. He called himself a Romantic, wrote several books on the English Romantic poets, and turned for inspiration to their work as much as to that of his twentieth-century contemporaries. His lacks of intensity and control were usually less apparent in his lyrics than in his longer meditative or "philosophic" utterances. But in a general sense of the term Imagist, Read may be said to have remained true to his first phase, for images are the especially striking and valuable element of his poetry. He had a gift for seeing freshly and for imaginatively transforming what he saw.

To represent the many, minor American poets who, though not among the original Imagist or "Amygist" groups, adopted the mode as a consequence of the publicity it received, we may mention Henry Bellamann (1882–1945). Although known mainly for his novel *King's Row* (1940), he published poetry in the 1920s. Applied to poets such as Bellamann, the term Imagist suggests short, free-verse impressions of objects, places, or human encounters, with a reticent evocation of emotion and deeper significance. Such poems are more concrete and succinct than the conventional poems of the previous generation. Their subjects are less likely to be beauty, death, love, and God, but, instead, such poems focus on "Hedges," "Goose Creek," "Leaf Prints," or "Wind in the Sycamores"—often with a touch of humor. Bellamann tried the notes of many poets, including Adelaide Crapsey and H.D., but the general model for all this poetry in America was Amy Lowell.

16

POETRY FOR A DEMOCRACY

CARL Sandburg, Vachel Lindsay, and Edgar Lee Masters are usually discussed as a group because they all came from the Midwest, portrayed that region, and emerged in approximately the same years (1913–1916). With Robert Frost and Amy Lowell they were among the first of the new poets to catch the attention of the public, and their work had much effect in disseminating and winning acceptance for the stylistic innovations of that time. They were also bearers of a tradition that persists throughout the history of American poetry and had found flamboyant expression in Whitman. It is that of a poetry strongly influenced in style and content by an ideal of American democracy. Democracy is an imprecise term, and the poets discussed in this chapter leaned variously toward Socialism, Populism, or Liberalism. But to them the "isms" were much less important than sympathy with the common man. They differed in many ways from later poets who might also be characterized as descendants of Whitman—the poets of radical protest in the 1930s and the Beat Poets of the 1950s and 1960s—and particularly in feeling confident that they spoke for a majority of Americans. They criticized American society, but on the basis of what they believed had always been and still was the central political faith of the American people. The radical poets of the thirties and the fifties and sixties possessed this element of Whitman's legacy in a much lesser degree.

The poetry of Sandburg, Lindsay, and Masters had other precedents besides that of Whitman—Edwin Markham's "The Man with the Hoe," for example. A less obvious influence was American regional poetry in the latter part of the nineteenth century. The region presented was usually considered quintessentially American. Farm or frontier society was usually depicted and portrayed as virtually classless. Even Riley's small town was happily without class distinctions. The persons characterized in regional poetry were conceived as representative of common men and women; their virtues of self-respect, shrewdness, humor, and rooted strength were stressed.

To dwell on precedent and tradition alone would be misleading. One must emphasize that Lindsay, Masters, and Sandburg were poets whose work sent an awakening shock. The Genteel Tradition still prevailed in American poetry when they started to write. In fact, throughout their careers Lindsay and Masters continued to write poems of the Genteel kind. And yet the works that made them famous were altogether different. Here, suddenly, amid the firm Victorian meters and polite diction of Genteel poetry came the boom of Lindsay's poem celebrating the founder of the Salvation Army, "General William Booth Enters into Heaven." The poem pounded out the rhythm of a Salvation Army parade and quoted revivalist hymns:

> Booth led boldly with his big bass drum—
> (Are you washed in the blood of the Lamb?).

Master's *Spoon River Anthology* (1915) was written with an unilluded, almost muckraking realism, though this was combined with a more traditional, elegiac feeling. A year before there was Sandburg, chanting his myth of Chicago: "here is a tall bold slugger set vivid against the little soft cities,"

> Bragging and laughing that under his wrist is the pulse,
>   and under his ribs the heart of the people,
>   Laughing!
> Laughing the stormy, husky, brawling laughter of Youth,
>   half-naked, sweating, proud to be Hog Butcher,
>   Tool Maker, Stacker of Wheat, Player with Railroads
>   and Freight Handler to the Nation.

At the time all this seemed vulgar to most readers of poetry, but
it was also exhilarating.

VACHEL LINDSAY

Before 1913, when *Poetry* printed "General William Booth
Enters into Heaven," Vachel Lindsay (1879–1931) was unknown. He was born in Springfield, Illinois. His parents were
Campbellites, and lasting traits of his mind derived from his
upbringing in this fundamentalist religious sect: his unworld-
liness and millennial hope; his habit of belief rather than analysis or questioning; above all, his sense of life as warfare in the
spirit. He also absorbed Populist democracy and learned from
his mother a profound respect for art. In Springfield he campaigned in speeches and pamphlets (which he called *War Bulletins*) for beauty, democracy, temperance, and chastity. He took
long walking tours across the country, sometimes paying for his
food and shelter by reciting his "Rhymes to be Traded for
Bread." Sometimes he begged. Wherever he went, he preached
his gospel of "democratic beauty." The triple themes of his
upbringing—Christian warfare, Populism, and art—had fused
in his mind and his New Jerusalem was the United States as it
would be: a country in which art and beauty would pervade the
lives of everybody, not only in the cities but also in each rural village. He called it "The New Localism":

We should make our own home and neighborhood the most democratic, the most beautiful and holiest in the world. The children now
growing up should become devout gardeners or architects or park architects or teachers of dancing in the Greek spirit or musicians or novelists or poets. . . . They should believe in every possible application to
art-theory of the thoughts of the Declaration of Independence and Lincoln's Gettysburg Address.

Though "The New Localism" was derived from the social
theories of Ruskin and Morris, Lindsay's democratic zeal led
him to conclusions of which these mentors would not have approved. His idea of art became, furthermore, a polar opposite of
art for art's sake and Modernist elitism. In a poem celebrating
Willian Jennings Bryan he called the famous orator "Homer
Bryan" and praised him as "the one American poet who could

sing outdoors," for Lindsay's notion of "song" or "poetry" was broad. In a footnote to "Old, Old, Old, Old Andrew Jackson" he directed that the poem was "to be read aloud, in the way one would read a political speech from the newspaper at election time, when such issues are really before the people." In poetry the idea was radical. Lindsay did not intend his poem as a political speech, but he wished to echo a familiar, distinctively American use of language, one that would remove his utterance from the ambience of "poetry" and associate it with a form the people were accustomed to listen to with interest. In other poems he mimicked or adopted ways of speaking or types of sound that were common in American life, though novel in poetry: revivalist preaching, folk or popular song, vaudeville patter, railroad announcements, jazz, and brass bands. The "Homeric" quality in all these sounds was, to repeat, that they were paid attention to by multitudes. He wanted poetry to be heard just as much. But Lindsay desired that appreciation of poetry be not only universal but a genuine appreciation of the best. He wished to raise popular taste, not lower poetry to it. The first step, nevertheless, was to catch the ear of the common man. Although the ultimate object was to lift and refine standards, the poet must begin by taking his standards and his technique from the people.

With this in mind, Lindsay invented his "Higher Vaudeville," poems that used methods adapted from vaudeville and were intended to appeal to the same audience that enjoyed it. These were the poems that made him famous—for example, "General William Booth Enters into Heaven," "The Congo," "The Chinese Nightingale," "The Santa-Fé Trail," and "Bryan, Bryan, Bryan, Bryan." He wrote a great many poems of more conventional kinds. Some are admirable, such as "The Flower-Fed Buffaloes," "Abraham Lincoln Walks at Midnight," or "The Eagle that is Forgotten," his elegy on the liberal Governor of Illinois, John P. Altgeld. Others are insipid, such as his many lyrics to the moon. But the "Higher Vaudeville" was the bold experiment from which other poets could borrow suggestions. It cannot be fully appreciated unless one keeps in mind that it was meant for performance—specifically, for Lindsay's performance, which was remarkable. He sang, chanted, shouted, vibrated, accelerated, stopped, started again in a whisper; in short, he used widely varying volumes, pitches, and tempos, changing with dramatic suddenness. Meanwhile, he gestured, paced, cake-walked, mimed, and stamped out the rhythm of his accumulative catalogues. The audience was delighted.

Lindsay was an authentic primitive. More exactly, his imagination absorbed and recreated religious and historical myths, which he rendered in clear, naive pictures. Sometimes these were literally pictures, for Lindsay was an artist as well as a poet. "General William Booth Enters into Heaven," for example, "goes all the way back to a 1902 Chicago drawing I made . . . a picture with crowned and robed saints climbing a ladder to the sky." As the blind hero-general of the Salvation Army leads his followers into heaven, Lindsay, with the confident directness of the primitive, sees heaven as a Midwestern city, Springfield:

> Jesus came from out the court-house door,
> Stretched his hands above the passing poor.
> Booth saw not, but led his queer ones there
> Round and round the mighty court-house square.

When he wrote of political figures, the same imaginative conviction and simplicity characterized his work. Those he disliked, such as Mark Hanna, became poster-painted monsters and demons. Democrats and Populists—"Old, Old, Old, Old Andrew Jackson," John P. Altgeld, Williams Jennings Bryan—became mythological heroes:

> Prairie avenger, mountain lion,
> Bryan, Bryan, Bryan, Bryan,
> Gigantic troubadour, speaking like a siege gun,
> Smashing Plymouth Rock with his boulders from the West.

Lindsay's vision was always concrete. Interpreting "In Praise of Johnny Appleseed," one might be tempted to say that this hero symbolizes many processes of American history and many sensitive hopes about America, but Lindsay did not present him that way. He saw what Johnny Appleseed was doing, and told what he saw. His animals also became mythical, as in "The Broncho That Would Not Be Broken" and "The Ghost of the Buffaloes." In concrete, myth-making imagination he resembled Blake.

Had this been united with other gifts in equal degree, he might have been one of the greatest American writers. As it was, Lindsay's gifts were largely wasted, and his life became increasingly sad and defeated. Psychologically speaking, he had been battling against heavy odds from the start, as may be indicated by the fact that he suffered a total collapse, at the age of forty-three, when his mother died. He could never bring himself wholly to credit either the value or the rationale of "Higher Vaudeville." As he went about the country reciting these poems between 1915 and 1920, he attracted large audiences. Thereafter, he could not stop the performances, partly because he still half-believed in them, partly because he needed the money, and, eventually, because he was worn out and could do nothing else. Critics sank their teeth into him—after hearing him in London, Eliot said he was "impossible"—and Lindsay was helplessly vulnerable to such attacks, which confirmed his inner doubts. Meanwhile, this spiritual crusader felt that he was turning into a mere showman. In shame and guilt, he looked back to the high-minded mental fight of his youth, when he had tramped across the country, or issued *War Bulletins*. In 1920 he published his supreme effort, *The Golden Book of Springfield,* a prose volume with visions and revelations describing what would take place in that city in 2018. He thought the book would begin the regeneration of Springfield from the moment it appeared; its failure was a deep discouragement. In 1924 he was found to be epileptic. In 1925, being desperately lonely, he married, but thereafter felt complexly guilty toward his wife. Meanwhile, he was losing his audience. Gradually his mind gave way to despair and paranoia, and in 1931 he killed himself horribly by swallowing a bottle of Lysol. Yet, as Edgar Lee Masters pointed out, if in viewing his career we give full weight to the handicaps and "defective mentality" with which he began, the wonder is not that he despaired in the end, but that he achieved so much, and not only in literature but in resolution and discipline of character, a resolution and discipline maintained over many years of disappointment and in spite of the powerful imagination that threatened his sanity.

EDGAR LEE MASTERS

Edgar Lee Masters (1869–1950) owed his fame to *The Spoon River Anthology* (1915), which in its day was more widely read than any other book of serious American verse by a contemporary poet. It was also immensely exciting to the avant-garde. In his autobiography John Gould Fletcher recalled how the "fierce sincerity" of these poems, "the detailed power of character drawing, the knowledge of American types" stirred "literary circles to their depths." By "sincerity" he meant Masters' willingness to expose the seamier workings of individual psychology and of social institutions, for such moral uglinesses had been passed over in the poetry of the Genteel Tradition. Only if we keep in mind the eagerness of poets to throw off late-Victorian conventions can we understand why Masters was praised so extravagantly.

The Spoon River Anthology comprises two hundred and fifteen short poems, each spoken by a different character, all of whom lived or at least were born in the Illinois town of Spoon River. The characters, now dead, sum up their lives. The volume relates to the elegiac tradition in poetry. Wordsworth, for example, had given in the Excursion a sequence of similarly elegiac, brief life histories of the persons buried in a village graveyard. The Anthology is also related to the poetry from Crabbe to Hardy, Robinson, and Frost, in which a region and its typical inhabitants are portrayed. Just what suggested the idea to Masters is not completely clear. W. M. Reedy, editor of Reedy's Mirror, urged him to read the Greek anthology and seems to have pointed out to him the lack of contemporary reality in his poetry before the Anthology. Harriet Monroe adds that the example and friendship of Sandburg helped jolt him out of his "ineffectual early period." One critic speculates that the poems that eventually made up the Anthology were begun as a parody of free verse, and that when the first ones to appear attracted serious praise, Masters also decided to take them seriously.

Wherever it came from, the collection of short, elegiac summings-up of lives has obvious advantages as a literary form. The utterances are not, strictly speaking, epitaphs, though the circumstances in which they are spoken lend a weight and finality similar to that of the epitaph. The wealth of characters and life histories provides variety. The work is unified by the setting within the town of Spoon River, by the obituary mode, and by persisting themes, which are the author's own concerns diversely voiced by different persons. The order in which the characters are presented allows contrast and cumulative progression. "The fools, the drunkards, and the failures" appear first, Masters explained, and "the heroes and the enlightened spirits come last, a sort of Divine Comedy."

The Spoon River Anthology is closer to Sherwood Anderson than to Dante. It was a conspicuous success in the effort, which so many poets were making, to transform poetry by incorporating some of the subject matter and narrative interest of fictional prose. Masters was more powerful in invention than in rhythm and phrasing, but though his poems might be called prosaic, they were not merely short passages of prose arranged in lines. His line breaks were functional; he kept to the spoken vocabulary, but with more figures and more devices of sound than are normal in speech; he followed prose word-order, but, like Sandburg, repeated rhythms and syntactical structures, so that his utterance has a greater formal shapeliness than is usual in prose. The total effect of these voices from the grave yielded a "philosophic" pathos characteristic of nineteenth-century poetry. Nevertheless, his book also reads like a novel. Each character tells the story of his life, but since lives are interwoven in the town of Spoon River, continuing stories are set going (there are nineteen by Masters' count). One speaker knows part of the tale, and another contributes additional information or a different point of view. The characters are themselves ordinary, representative men and women. There are instances of heroic idealism and self-sacrifice, and of greed, envy, malice, and obscure cruelties in domestic life. (Masters has much to tell about what Mrs. Pantier in the *Anthology* calls the "marital relation." He resembles Hardy in the irony and ingenuity of the sufferings he inflicts on his characters.) Whatever happens is presented without comment from the author.

The chief creative achievement of Masters is the town itself. We come to know Spoon River intimately. We hear of the early settlers—their origins, way of life, religious faith—and of the later history of the town in the Civil War and other crises. We learn the social strata that now exist—the judge and the bank president; the clergy, journalists, schoolteachers, and clerks; the farmers and workers; the n'er-do-wells. We see the harsh and venal operation of political and social institutions. Politicians are bribed; the poor are neglected; injured workmen are defrauded of compensation; big businessmen buy judges. We see also church-going narrowness, timid conformity, hypocrisy, and the revenges of gossip and petty persecution against whoever violates the local mores. A pervading impression is of lives stunted by the poverty of the cultural soil. This is especially suggested by the lives of the sympathetic characters. They encounter little that can enlarge ideas or formatively guide spiritual aspiration. On the whole, Spoon River is the antithesis of Riley's small town and the forerunner of *Winesburg, Ohio*. It supports the diatribes of Mencken against American provincial ignorance and petty moralism.

Perhaps no book of poems more dramatically illustrates how much a formal conception can do for a poet. Before *The Spoon River Anthology* Masters, a Chicago lawyer, had published several books of conventional and plodding verse. Afterward, the now-famous poet reverted to his former modes and level of performance. According to Harriet Monroe, he planned to begin the next volume after the *Anthology* with an Arthurian narrative on Launcelot and Elaine. His later career disappointed his admirers, and Masters was embittered by the adverse criticism. But he could not have been expected to write a second anthology on another town; the idea was valid only once.

CARL SANDBURG

Lindsay once said that "the people of America walk through me, all the people walk through my veins, as though they were in the streets of a city, and clamor for voice." But it was Carl Sandburg (1878–1967), even more than Lindsay, who wrote the poetry whose underlying intention is suggested by these words. His legacies to later poets were his "report of the people," as William Carlos Williams called it, and his flexible, inventive, and scrapbook methods of presentation. His work provoked bitter controversy. To admirers he seemed to give poetry purpose and relevance and to liberate its technique.

He was born in Galesburg, Illinois, the son of Swedish immigrants. His father worked in the railroad yards. The poverty of his family compelled Sandburg to quit school at the age of thirteen; he delivered milk, cut ice, vended on streetcorners, labored on farms, washed dishes, and held other odd jobs, until, at the age of twenty, be became a soldier in the Spanish-American

War. Thereafter he worked his way through four years at Lombard College in Illinois, where a gifted teacher, Philip Green Wright, recognized his talent and encouraged his efforts at self-expression. "I don't know where I'm going," Sandburg wrote, "but I'm on my way."

Meanwhile, he had enthusiastically committed himself to Populist ideals in Illinois in the 1890s. At fifteen he had made the reformist Governor Altgeld his hero; he had been swept along by the oratory of William Jennings Bryan; he had read and discussed *Das Kapital* with Wright. In Chicago in 1908 he became a district organizer and propagandist for the Social-Democratic Party and he also worked as a journalist, voicing his political convictions in newspaper stories. In 1914 Harriet Monroe published "Chicago" and eight other poems in *Poetry*. He was now known locally. *Chicago Poems,* his first volume, was published in 1916.

The *Chicago Poems* were a shock to most readers. The title poem created a myth of the city as a strong man, a sweating worker, and rejoiced in his brutal strength. Other poems pictured the urban and industrial milieu. Sandburg underscored the contrast of the slums with the wealthy homes along the lakeshore; he pictured such sights as the skyscrapers looming in the smoke and the working girls going to their jobs, their "little brick-shaped lunches wrapped in newspapers under their arms." He tended especially to give portraits or brief accounts of typical characters: the "stockyard hunky," whose "job is sweeping blood off the floor"; the "fish crier down on Maxwell Street," who "dangles herring before prospective customers evincing a joy identical with that of Pavlowa dancing."

Here was a directly phrased poetry of the contemporary world. It gave sights and sounds. It showed people at work. It had something to say about the character and quality of their lives. It dwelt on the romance in the familiar and it enforced a political and social message by concrete contrasts. "The Shovel Man," for example, contrasted the economic or capitalist measure of a man's worth with a truer one. The "dago" works for

> a dollar six bits a day
> And a dark-eyed woman in the old country dreams of him
>   for one of the world's ready men with a pair of fresh
>   lips and a kiss better than all the wild grapes that ever grew
>   in Tuscany.

Sandburg did not merely describe the people; he glorified them. He was the opposite of Eliot, who was repelled by "Apeneck Sweeney" and the "damp souls of housemaids." To Sandburg the picnicking Hungarians, the prostitutes, the shovel man, and the working girls were so many jewels, which his poetry exhibited. He hunted out their virtues like a mother. The working girls have "beauty" like "peach bloom"; if, growing older, they lose beauty, they will then have "wisdom." The Hungarians know "happiness," which professors and executives do not.

The theme of his next volume, *Cornhuskers* (1918), was the prairie. Here he pictured farm people and their work. He also dwelled on the beauty and fatness, the mellow scents and sounds of the land. Social protest was not present in all his *Chicago Poems* nor was it absent from *Cornhuskers,* but most of the pieces in the latter, such as "Grass" and "Cool Tombs," were lyrics of a more traditional type, contemplating time, vastness, change, perenniality, and death. Sandburg did not wrestle very strenuously with these mysteries; neither did he find them very chilling. It is poetry of the agreeable kind, bland, relaxed, simply direct, and very fond of its subject.

Henceforth Sandburg's poetry tended to fall into one or the other of these loosely separate kinds: he either dwelled on the lives and qualities of the people or felt a "philosophic" pathos—he often did both in the same poem. There are also pleasant poetic impressions, such as "Fog." The effect of the 771 pages of his poetry is no test of his worth, but it may be remarked that his "philosophic" pathos becomes wearisome because it lacks energy. He recites fact with an absence or inarticulateness of feeling and with comparatively few thoughts in his head. The effect is of a quizzicalness or a slight wonder or a vague, momentary disturbance of mind, soon settling into calm:

> The buffaloes are gone.
> And those who saw the buffaloes are gone.
> Those who saw the buffaloes by thousands and how
> they pawed the prairie sod into dust with their
> hoofs, their great heads down pawing on in a
> great pageant of dusk,
> Those who saw the buffaloes are gone.
> And the buffaloes are gone.

Similarly, his poems of social protest are often no more than sketchy outlines in black and white. "Jack" tells of a "swarthy, swaggering son-of-a-gun," who worked on the railroad "ten hours a day," was tough, had a "tough woman" for a wife, and eight children. The wife died, the children moved away, and Jack spent his last years in the poorhouse. But he had "joy on his face" his life long. Though short, the poem is tedious. Jack is no more than a peg for Sandburg's stock attitudes, which in this poem are automatic and sentimental projections, not responses to the concrete case.

Better than any other poet, Sandburg represents the new style of the 1910s—the "modern" style before Eliot. Poets who wrote finer poems were less typical. They had stronger personal twists of their own or firmer commitments to a particular school or theory. In Sandburg one sees what the age had to teach about writing. "Chicago" is an imitation of Whitman; some of the *Chicago Poems* might be one-dimensional versions of the Robinsonian portrait; some are Impressionist; some combine Impressionism with the sparer imagery of Japanese verse. As for Imagism, Sandburg said he had no connection with it. But his poems seek the concreteness and objectivity which the Imagists communicated to American poetry in general. He is not always simple or easy to understand, but the materials of his poetry—the facts, images, allusions—are never recondite.

The most striking thing about Sandburg's style is its flexibility and inventiveness, its freedom to use whatever means or methods seem appropriate. When his subject is Pocahontas, he pursues "beauty," packing his verse with agreeable images and melodiously echoing sounds:

> Pocahontas' body, lovely as a poplar, sweet as a red haw
> in November or a pawpaw in May, did she wonder? does
> she remember? . . . in the dust, in the cool tombs?

When his theme is a whore and her troubles, his manner varies accordingly:

> "A woman what hustles
> Never keeps nothin'
> For all her hustlin'."

His vocabulary is simple and seldom "poetic" or abstract but, with these limitations, it is flexibly ready to adapt to the subject.

He exploits the diction of common speech when it suits him, and one finds slang and vigorous folk metaphors ("And two of them croaked on the same day at a 'necktie party' "). Usually, however, his diction has a precision that mitigates the impression of vernacular speech. His syntax can have the shapelessness of talk:

> And I saw a crowd of Hungarians under the trees with their
> women and children and a keg of beer and an accordion.

But he also makes much use of parallel syntax and repetition, and his effects can be decidedly rhetorical. He never uses meters. That is the only general remark that can be made about his versification, for everything depends on the effect he seeks, which may require a drumming, recurrent rhythm or a rhythmless sprawl. The principles of form that govern his poetry are simply the principles of effective thinking and presentation in general—relevance, economy, contrast, conclusion, and the like.

He was more gifted in sympathy than in synthesis. He enters, though not deeply, into characters, feelings, and objects over a broad range but takes them one at a time. One sees a farm, and later a river with birds; still further on comes a field of corn. The objects accumulated or contrasted make a meaningful pattern, but they do not interpenetrate. "Nocturne in a Deserted Brickyard"—

> Fluxions of yellow and dusk on the waters
> Make a wide dreaming pansy of an old pond in the night—

illustrates what is usually lacking. The list of associations is one of his main poetic forms. He picks a large, vague subject—"Prairie," "River Roads," "Band Concert," "Smoke and Steel," "Pennsylvania," "Hazardous Occupations"—and accumulates facts, thoughts, images, and poetic feelings about it. The effect is of a scrapbook. Its items convey the same general attitude of appreciation, social protest, or whatever. *The People, Yes* (1936), a heap of sayings, anecdotes, character sketches, dialogues, and the like, shows the method at book length; the subject is "the people" and the attitude is "yes." Sandburg's greatest weakness as a poet was the minimal demand he made of a poem. It was enough to render the sound of the wind ("Wind Song") or contrast the bustle of a street by day with its stillness by night

("Blue Island Intersection"). Or it was enough merely to make some bland observation, or evoke some pleasant object or feeling, or accumulate images without tension or wit. His example helped poets surrender to what Yeats called the greatest temptation of the artist, creation without toil.

He was much read and admired. In 1926 the first volume of his ambitious biography of Lincoln appeared. Presenting massed, concrete details, it built up a vivid, romantic picture of the United States in Lincoln's time. Lincoln himself was slightly mythologized. The huge effort was completed in 1939. Because of it, Sandburg was widely regarded as an authoritative interpreter, almost an embodiment of America. In 1940 he was suggested as a candidate for President (he declined, preferring Roosevelt). He also collected folksongs, which he published in *The American Songbag* (1927). He developed a fetching platform performance: he would recite some poems, sing folksongs, which he accompanied with a guitar, and intersperse poems and songs with homely philosophy and anecdotes. In 1946 his birthplace was dedicated as a museum. In 1956 the University of Illinois paid $50,000 for four tons of his papers.

JOHN V. A. WEAVER AND LOLA RIDGE

John V. A. Weaver (1893–1938) wrote poems in urban dialect, depicting the lives and feelings of the people. He shared the democratic ideals of Sandburg and his experiment in using the vernacular was suggested by the example of Sandburg. He was also influenced by the argument of Mencken, in the conclusion of the first edition of *The American Language* (1919), that "Given the poet, there may suddenly come a day when our *theirns* and *woulda hads* will take on the barbaric stateliness of the peasant locution of old Maurya in [Synge's] 'Riders to the Sea.'" The characters who speak in his poems were, however, conceived in flat, conventional terms, and his attitudes toward them were humorous and sentimental, so that his poems remind one of the lyrics in immigrant dialect of T. A. Daly. In setting and type of character they also recall the O. Henry stories. His volumes sold very well until he abandoned dialect in the latter part of his career, and wrote in a straightforward, conversational idiom.

Lola Ridge (1871–1941) in her first and best book resembles Sandburg. In political sympathies she was farther left than the other poets discussed in this chapter. Her enthusiasm was directed less to the ideal of American democracy than to the re-making of society through the triumph of the working class. She was born in Dublin, Ireland, spent her childhood and youth in Australia and New Zealand, and settled in New York City in the 1910s. She supported herself by writing fiction and advertising copy, modeling for artists, and working in a factory and had personal experience of tenement life. In her first volume, *The Ghetto and Other Poems* (1918), the title poem dwells on sights, sounds, types of character, and ways of life among the Jewish poor in Manhattan. The treatment is realistic, but the realism, like Sandburg's, is tempered by affection and by a romanticizing imagination. Her mind wings back, for example, from the city streets to the Israelite slaves in Egypt. The merit of the poem lies in Miss Ridge's vivid, sympathetic interest in her subject more than in the formal qualities of her expression. *Sun-Up and Other Poems* (1920) contains short lyrics, more or less in the style of Sandburg or Amy Lowell; the title poem recreates childhood experiences. *Red Flag* (1927) celebrates the Russian Revolution. There are also tributes to fellow artists and writers. *Firehead* (1929) is said to have been inspired by the Sacco-Vanzetti case, but it is a book-length narrative of the crucifixion of Christ. *Dance of Fire* (1935) is a collection of lyrics, including a sonnet sequence in three parts. An obscure symbolism of fire runs through the volume. Miss Ridge had never written in a wholly natural and limpid syntax and diction, and by this time her style had become highly "poetic":

> The dawn is pearling through the locust tree
> Adrip, and all the feathered air achoir
> With multi-voice. O high antiphony!

To develop from "The Ghetto" to a difficult, mannered, symbolic style of writing with a traditional versification was not untypical of the evolution of American poetry between 1918 and 1935. The dedication and selflessness of Miss Ridge greatly impressed those who knew her, and her influence as a person may have been greater than that of her poetry.

17

CONSERVATIVE AND REGIONAL
POETS OF AMERICA

W̲HEN reviewers referred in the 1910s and 1920s to "conservative" or "traditional" poets, they had in mind poets who continued to write in a Romantic-Victorian or Genteel way. The adjectives acquired their reso-nances—defensive, condescending, or dismissive—from the emergence and spread of "new" or "modern" ways of writing, which increasingly called into question hitherto accepted styles and uses of poetry. Regional poets were those who sought, as one of their primary aims, to exhibit the typical ways of life, traits of character, imaginative lore, and speech of a particular section of the country. Except in dwelling on such materials, however, the minor regionalists taken up in this chapter— figures such as Robinson, Frost, Sandburg, Masters, and the Fugitives are more appropriately discussed elsewhere—were not innovative. Many of them were college professors who took a quasi-scholarly interest in local history and customs and usually adopted in their poetry the received idiom. Other regional poets were hardly aware of the styles developing in the little magazines. Still others, wishing to be read by the people, were eager to continue the "open," accessible poetry that had been one of the triumphs of Romanticism. Unfortunately, as they saw the spread of an involved or oblique idiom in the writings of the avant-garde, these more democratic poets tended to feel defensive. Some, asserting all the more their alliance with the folk, adopted the kind of colloquialism (that of Riley, for instance) that had been accepted—and in the process domesticated—by the Genteel Tradition as an ally against fundamental changes. In short, the motives and circumstances of the minor regionalists usually kept them within traditional styles, and for most of them an additional motive was that they wrote for a regional audience, not for New York sophisticates. As a group the regional poets contrasted in some ways with the "conservatives," not only in subject matter but also in procedure, for they usually worked in a more popular style and with a more realistic treatment (although their realism was often that of calendar art), and they tended more to narrative verse. But if they are contrasted with the "new" poets, the regionalists resemble the conservatives much more than they differ from them and can be viewed with them in one perspective. Of regional and conservative poets we shall notice about thirty-five, all minor, but some extremely competent.

The general theme of this chapter is the traditional mode of poetry in the age of Modernism. For although the poems of Sara Teasdale, for example, or Elinor Wylie, Adelaide Crapsey, or Edna St. Vincent Millay somewhat resembled those written by Genteel poets twenty to forty years before, these twentieth-century poems could not be confused with earlier ones; the new tendencies influenced the traditional mode also. At least this was generally true, although such poets as John Erskine, Thomas S. Jones, and Percy Mackaye show that it was possible to ignore the new developments altogether. Most conservative poets were well aware of the Imagist movement and of the controversies surrounding it. They rejected free verse but strove for concision, concreteness of imagery, and spoken (rather than poetic or rhetorical) syntax and diction, at least, they strove more for these qualities than had been usual with Stedman, Moody, Santayana, or most other Genteel poets. Moreover, in the age of Robinson and Frost, of the Imagists and the Georgians, most poets who used the traditional modes also returned from the empyrean. They continued to associate poetry with the ideal, the beautiful, the emotionally intense, and the agreeable, but their poetic emotions and spiritual exaltations were registered in *vox humana;* they no longer pulled all the organ stops. Finally, some of them addressed a wider range of experience and feeling than the Genteel poets had thought appropriate.

POETS IN TRADITIONAL MODES

Sara Teasdale (1884–1933) was born in St. Louis, and grew up a sensitive, dreamy girl with delicate health. Her early productions included sonnets on poetry, nature, art, and beauty, as well as blank-verse monologues by Guinevere, Helen of Troy, and other passionate women of the past. She was also writing a different, though equally familiar kind of poetry, the brief, lyric utterance of elemental emotion. This became her chief mode. She loves, she loves no more, she longs to be loved, she is not loved in return, or not so much as before; but who, when, how, and why are all omitted, for she wished to avoid anything that might complicate and so lessen her immediate emotional impact. For the same reason her idiom, which was genteel at the start of her career ("beauty—brighter thro' the veil"), evolved toward plainness. "The poet," she said, "must put far from him the amazing word, the learned allusion, the facile inversion, the clever twist of thought, for all of these things will blur his poem and distract his reader. He must not overcrowd his lines with figures of speech, because, in piling these one upon another, he defeats his own purpose. . . . The poet should try to give his poem the quiet swiftness of flame, so that the reader will feel and not think while he is reading."

Christina Rossetti and A. E. Housman were among her favorite poets, and she emulated their restraint of style. As she approached middle age, her traditional skills became steadily more charged with expressive suggestion. The phrasing in her better poems is sometimes almost aphoristic. The "plot" is carefully structured, often with a surprise or paradox at the end of the poem. Her lines master the late-Victorian, elegiac cadence. Her prosody is formal and disciplined. A run-on line says much. Toward the end of her life, her moods seem to have changed or, more exactly, to have narrowed into melancholy. It is a distinguished melancholy—if the phrase does not seem precious—deeply felt, fairly faced and uttered, yet expressed with tact and austerity.

Sara Teasdale was one of the more popular poets of her day. Her businessman husband, Ernst Filsinger, is said to have known most of her poems by heart before he met her in 1914; doubtless many other readers were almost equally devoted. The first lines of some of her better-known poems are,

> When I am dead and over me bright April
> Shakes out her rain-drenched hair;

and,

> Let it be forgotten, as a flower is forgotten,
> Forgotten as a fire that once was singing gold;

and,

> When, in the gold October dusk, I saw you near to setting,
> Arcturus, bringer of spring,
> Lord of the summer nights, leaving us now in autumn . . . ;

and the finely wistful "The Long Hill,"

> I must have passed the crest a while ago
> And now I am going down—
> Strange to have crossed the crest and not to know,
> But the brambles were always catching the hem of my gown.

Her best-known collection, *Love Songs* (1917), won two prizes and went through five editions in one year. In 1943 a Liberty Ship was named the Sara Teasdale.

Ridgeley Torrence (1875–1950) was poetry editor of *The New Republic*. The few poems he published are carefully phrased and cadenced and of remarkably different kinds. The best are "The Bird and the Tree," a ballad about a lynching, and "The Son," an effectively contrived poem in which the thoughts of a farm-wife move back and forth between crops, prices, weather, and her dead son. The last stanza of "The Son" is,

> "It feels like frost was near—
> His hair was curly.
> The spring was late that year,
> But the harvest early."

"Three O'Clock" is a cityscape. There are also poems in the vein of Housman, of Yeats, and of other poets, but Torrence's usual type of poem—so far as he had one—was the dreamy, cosmic allegory, promising "light" and "beauty" somewhere beyond or within. These might often be called Pre-Raphaelite.

Arthur Davison Ficke (1883–1945) wrote lyrics, sonnets, and sonnet sequences, the most ambitious being "Sonnets of a Portrait-Painter." He did not shrink from clichés:

> Dear fellow-actor of this little stage,
> We play the hackneyed parts right merrily.

In 1915–1916, just after publishing these lines, Ficke joined with Witter Bynner in perpetrating the "Spectra" hoax. Poking fun at Imagism, Futurism, and the like, the two poets pretended to invent another modern movement. They issued a book of Spectrist poems, with a Preface to explain their principles. The literary world obliged by taking the movement seriously. *Others* magazine even devoted its January 1917 issue to *Spectra*. Ficke also wrote a "Guide to China" in sonnet sequence. Some of his poems were slightly tinged with the Decadence. He was first a mentor and then a lover of Edna St. Vincent Millay. Their affair prompted numerous sonnets on both sides.

Joyce Kilmer (1886–1918), an editor of *The Literary Digest,* is remembered for "Trees," which begins, as everyone knows:

> I think that I shall never see
> A poem lovely as a tree.

Grace Conkling (1878–1958) taught at Smith College; her ballads and nature lyrics have much charm. Rudolph Valentino, the matinee idol, published his *Day Dreams* in 1923. The protected child of wealthy parents, Gladys Cromwell (1885–1919) handled the traditional forms sensitively, but her poetry took no hold of experience. She and her twin sister served with the Red Cross in France during the last year of the war. Shattered by what they had seen, they committed suicide on the boat going home. Leonora Speyer (1872–1956) did not begin to write until 1915. Her *Fiddler's Farewell* (1926) won the Pulitzer Prize. John Hall Wheelock (1886–1978) was a friend of Sara Teasdale, to whom he and his work represented an ideal of sensitivity and spiritual height. He wrote love poems of a rather abstract kind, nature poems, and poems in which, always maintaining euphony and dignity, he sought the meaning of the cosmos. His moods tended to plaintiveness, nostalgia, yearning, and melancholy. His poems were diligent and thoughtful, but tired.

The poets mentioned so far were influenced to some degree by the contemporary avant-garde achievement. But there was also a rear guard on whose work the new tendencies had no impact at all. These poets, most of whom were cultivated and informed about literature, remind us again how wide the gap between the Modernist modes and the general, cultivated taste of the age could be. John Erskine (1879–1951), a famous teacher of the Humanities at Columbia, initiated the Great Books program, which had immense influence on American higher education during the next generation, especially at the University of Chicago and at St. John's College. He wrote criticism, novels, and three volumes of poetry: *Actaeon* (1906), *Collected Poems* (1922), and *Sonata and Other Poems* (1925). His earlier verses were mournful, mythological, and Tennysonian. Later he also sporadically emulated Browning and Robinson. In everything except chronology, he belonged to the Genteel Tradition. Amelia Burr (b. 1878) was a less sophisticated writer. Her poems appeared in the magazines of large circulation for middle-class, family reading. So far as I have perused the several volumes she brought out between 1912 and 1923, she declaimed high-minded emotions. The verses of Thomas S. Jones (1882–1932) were of the openly sentimental and heart-warming type that was extremely popular in America. Two of his poems, "As in a Rose-Jar" and "An Old Song"—

> Low blowing winds from out a midnight sky,
>   The falling embers and a kettle's croon—
> These three, but oh what sweeter lullaby
>   Ever awoke beneath the winter's moon—

used to appear in old-fashioned anthologies of "modern" poetry. His idiom and versification were carefully worked in the Genteel way, and he had the command of musical cadence that one learns to expect even of minor poets in the Victorian tradition. Among his several volumes is *Sonnets of the Cross* (1922), a sequence that traces the progress of Christianity in the British Isles. Jones typically took pains to make these sonnets historically accurate. Percy Mackaye (1875–1956) wrote voluminously in an open-idiomed, low-pressured way. He was known chiefly for his poetic dramas. His first volume of lyrics appeared in 1909. One of his last works, *The Mystery of Hamlet King of Denmark*

(1950), consists of four dramas (more than 650 pages) in blank verse and deals with events at the court of Denmark antecedent to Shakespeare's play. Its challenge to Shakespeare was even more open and venturesome than Gordon Bottomley's dramatization of the earlier life of King Lear, for Mackaye not only used Shakespeare's story but also took over his dramatic form and even, to some degree, his Elizabethan English. The attempt obviously could not succeed, but it was a remarkable feat for a poet over seventy years old, living in a lonely cottage in Massachusetts after the death of his wife. One is glad that it was performed in 1949 at the Pasadena playhouse—the longest presentation in the theater since the productions of ancient Athens.

MILLAY, WYLIE, AIKEN, AND OTHERS

Elinor Wylie, Edna St. Vincent Millay, Harriet Monroe, Louis Untermeyer, Witter Bynner, Donald Evans, Adelaide Crapsey, and Robert Hillyer were the most important of the many poets who were essentially traditionalist, but at the time were usually numbered among the "new" poets. Either they had personal associations with the avant-garde or they adopted some more modern content or style. Many of these poets were self-divided. Like Harriet Monroe and Louis Untermeyer, they hungered for the old, opulent emotional idealism, but bravely tried to relish the spare, small, and dry accuracies of the new age. Or, like Edna St. Vincent Millay and William Ellery Leonard, they used the idiom and poses of the Victorian and Genteel tradition to voice modern sexual emancipation. Or, like Orrick Johns, they wavered amid styles; Johns sometimes imitated Housman, Kipling, or Whitman, and sometimes Kreymborg or Eliot.

The debt of poetry readers to Harriet Monroe (1860–1936) and Louis Untermeyer (1885–1977) is immense, but it is less for their verse than for their work as editors and promoters. The importance of *Poetry* magazine, which Miss Monroe founded and edited, was discussed in Chapter 14. She also prepared, with Alice Corbin, an influential anthology of *The New Poetry* (1917), which included both British and American poets and went through several editions. This anthology was gradually eclipsed by the deservedly famous ones of Louis Untermeyer. *Modern*

American Poetry appeared in 1919, *Modern British Poetry* in 1920; both are still in print, having gone through many revisions; over the years they introduced hundreds of thousands, perhaps millions of readers to contemporary poetry. Untermeyer included between one and two hundred poets, each successive edition dropping some names and adding others. His taste was formed in the first decade of the century, and he had favorites (Frost, Sandburg, James Oppenheim) and suffered from imperfect sympathies (with Pound and Stevens), but he was catholic and fair. Certainly he was not out to undermine or build up any movement or party. For each poet he wrote a Preface, telling something about the poet's life and briefly reviewing the work. These Prefaces might ideally have been more sensitive to the poetry they discussed, but Untermeyer's style was vigorous and rapid (though sometimes spotted with meretricious antitheses and paradoxes). He made his poets interesting and mustered as much enthusiasm for each as he could. Though he did not neglect formal qualities, he dwelt on the emotion and vision of his poets—and he especially liked strong emotion and hopeful vision. Besides these anthologies of modern poetry, Untermeyer edited at least eighteen others of poetry of various descriptions. He also wrote prose fiction.

Untermeyer translated poetry and published twenty volumes of original compositions; they place him among "conservative" poets of the period, where he might not enjoy finding himself. Some poems pleaded for social justice and many had a light, half-humorous touch in handling serious themes; in both respects his work might have seemed slightly new or modern when it was published. In retrospect, however, he can be seen as one of many poets who participated in modern movements only cautiously and from a distance. His poetry was fluent, accessible, and facile; his parodies can still be read with pleasure.

Harriet Monroe was forty years old at the turn of the century. In her early verse she had accepted with full faith the Romantic and Victorian conventions (see *Valeria and Other Poems*, 1891). After 1900 she experimented with more modern subjects and forms—free verse, contemporary spoken idiom (she made a special point of avoiding mythological allusions), urban and industrial subject matters. She boasted that "The Hotel," a survey of the objects and goings-on in the Waldorf-Astoria, was "a pioneer in free verse." But in her work the new themes and forms seem hardly less conventional than the old, and the poetry they led her to write was even more willed and external.

Alice Corbin (Henderson) (1881–1949), who helped Miss Monroe edit *Poetry* during its first years (1912–1916), was a better poet and emulated several contemporary styles with distinction. "Echoes of Childhood" drew on folksongs for swinging rhythms similar to the vein of Lindsay; "Love Me at Last" was worthy of Sara Teasdale in her better moments; "One City Only" was free-verse declamation (such poems were legion at the time); "Music" shows she had been reading Richard Aldington, and "In the Desert," Lawrence. After 1916 she lived in New Mexico, and the landscape, primitive life, and folklore of this region lent a new impulse to her verse. She had gifts for musical phrasing, for a careful and suggestive juxtaposition of images, and for conveying emotion.

Both Donald Evans (1884–1921) and Adelaide Crapsey (1878–1914) died before their remarkable gifts had fully matured. They were very different, however. Evans made a laborious living in newspaper work but cultivated a Dandyish pose unusual in the United States at the time. He probably influenced Wallace Stevens. His café sophistication seemed beguilingly European. His mild eroticism and exotic, luxuriant phrasing were doubtless meant to seem decadent. He composed realistic and satiric portraits of human failure, which remind us slightly of Robinson's. They are mostly ephemeral, but there are brilliant touches, as when he writes (of Mabel Dodge), "Her hidden smile was full of hidden breasts." "Dinner at the Hotel de la Tigresse Verte" is a splendidly comic, mordant poem: the lovers

> were certain that they had forever
> Imprisoned fickleness in the vodka.

Adelaide Crapsey is best-known for having invented a new form, the cinquain, a five-line poem in which the number of syllables in each line are two, four, six, eight, and two successively. The form imposes strict economy, and Miss Crapsey used it mainly for effects of emotional suggestion of an impressionistic kind, as in "The Warning":

> Just now,
> Out of the strange
> Still dusk . . . as strange, as still . . .
> A white moth flew. Why am I grown
> So cold?

There has been some dispute as to whether she knew haiku, but on both external and internal evidence it seems probable that she did. The cinquains are similar in brevity, in concentration on an image or impression, in sensitive feeling and suggestion, and in their mood of quiet sadness. She also wrote more conventional poems which show the same disciplined manipulation of form. It is not form achieved for its own sake, but an expert use of formal means to direct distinct attention to each word or phrase. Her poems are severely impersonal, save for one written at the tuberculosis sanitarium at Saranac, "To the Dead in the Grave-yard Underneath my Window." It voices the awareness of her early death and the protest against it that had been unexpressed but implicit in many of her other poems.

For approximately fifteen years, 1917–1932, Edna St. Vincent Millay (1892–1950) had a wide, enthusiastic following. Some critics ranked her among the best living American poets, and a great many readers formed their idea of the contemporary or modern poet from her example. The poem that made her famous was "Renascence," which she wrote at the age of nineteen. This archetypal effusion describes a mystic moment in which she finds herself buried and then brought back to life. Before she sinks into the grave, she beholds and feels herself crushed under the sorrows and sins of the cosmos; when she is reborn, she acclaims the world, life, and God. Her phrasing is inadequate to the experience it is supposed to present—

> Ah, awful weight! Infinity
> Pressed down upon the finite Me!—

but "Renascence" is partially redeemed by its directness, boldness, and naiveté. In contrast to this and similarly "cosmic" poems in which the Everlasting Yea strives against the Everlasting No, she made saucy pokes at bourgeois convention in *A few Figs from Thistles* (1920). Her "First Fig" was widely quoted—

> My candle burns at both ends;
>   It will not last the night;
> But ah, my foes, and oh, my friends—
>   It gives a lovely light!—

and her "Second Fig" was equally high-spirited:

> Safe upon the solid rock the ugly houses stand:
> Come and see my shining palace built upon the sand!

She also composed verses of radical political protest, and she wrote a great many sonnets, mostly love sonnets; admirers were reminded of such exemplars as Shakespeare and Elizabeth Browning, except that Miss Millay, the "female Byron," was sometimes more sensational:

> What lips my lips have kissed, and where, and why,
> I have forgotten . . .

Her sonneteering reached its ambitious climax in *Fatal Interview* (1931), a sequence of fifty-two Shakespearean sonnets marking the course of a love affair. Along with these more frequently discussed poems, she wrote a great many simply planned and phrased lyrics of traditional kinds.

The poems Miss Millay wrote as a schoolgirl in Camden, Maine, were typical of the provincial, self-taught, boldly naive American style that we observed, for example, in Edwin Markham. It is as though the young poet, reading anthologies, had compounded a style out of whatever might be found in them. This style divorced poetry from contemporary speech and ordinary reality, and was valued because it did so. Miss Millay employed and was probably delighted by poetic diction ("stretcheth," "I would fain pluck"), including expletives ("I do fear") and poetic interjections ("nay!" "prithee"). "Renascence" awakens recollections of English Romantic and seventeenth-century poets. In short, Miss Millay offered with full sincerity the highflying style and content that most Americans had expected of poetry before the Modernist revolution came along.

The response she evoked may testify to a hunger for this at a time when so much contemporary poetry seemed to many readers restricted and drab. From their point of view Frost and Robinson were prosaic, however skillful. The Imagists worked up minute visual glimpses, with perhaps a Japanese suggestiveness. The *Others* poets, such as Kreymborg, Stevens, and Mina Loy, were often viewed by such readers as slight and silly. Feminine lyricists, such as Sara Teasdale and Lizette Reese, were minor, Eliot satiric and exhausted. Miss Millay's rhetorical fine feathers, her huge hyperboles, apostrophes, and poses—

> Sweet sounds, oh, beautiful music, do not cease!
> Reject me not into the world again—

at least gave readers a strong sensation.

Her themes were sometimes sensational—and so was the gossip about her. She lived in Greenwich Village, and became—or was reputed to be—a bohemian, politically radical and sexually emancipated. She had, one heard, a succession of lovers, and her poems seemed to confirm the fact; they were praised or condemned for telling of love and sex frankly and from a feminine point of view. She was a rebel in ways that were typical of the twenties and that made her seem a peculiarly "modern" figure. Her appeal lay in this combination of the conventionally "poetic" high style and theme with a more contemporary intimacy or frankness that seemed adventurous and liberating at the time. But of course the poet-as-rebel was itself a conventional Romantic role.

When Miss Millay's reputation began to decline the reason usually assigned by reviewers for rejecting where they had once praised was either that she had changed for the worse or, at least, had made no progress toward the better—the "better" being usually conceived as a more mature attitude to life. Both assertions were questionable, though her *Conversation at Midnight* (1937) certainly revealed that philosophic reflection was not her forte. In general, the evolution of her own poetry affected her reputation much less than the evolution of poetry at large. She lost ground because of the gradual acceptance in the late 1920s and 1930s of what I have called the "high Modernist mode," that is, because of the spread of critical expectations and criteria of which Eliot was the chief symbol and exponent.

With Miss Millay we may mention William Ellery Leonard (1876–1944), for he also combined traditional form and diction with a new, autobiographical intimacy. *Two Lives* (privately printed in 1922; published in 1925) told the painful story of his marriage in a sequence of sonnets. It had a brief success, but his less personal poems are better. Although weakened by Romantic clichés, they impress one by their intelligence and weight. He is remembered primarily for his *The Locomotive God* (1927), a prose autobiographical work of psychological interest.

Those who found Miss Millay excessively vehement and even blowzy often admired the elegant Elinor Wylie (1885–1928). She, too, lived among the bohemians in Greenwich Village, but she was not of them. She was wealthy, beautiful, and cultivated and the impression she made by her presence favorably influenced the reception of her work. She sought to master a "small, clean technique," as she put it, to turn out "brilliant and compact" stanzas comparable to "enamelled snuffboxes."

Her phrasing was usually direct and vigorous, her verse firmly molded, her rhythms varied and controlled. She wrote epitaphs in Roman and songs in Elizabethan style. She read lyrics of the seventeenth century and emulated their grace, or paradox, or elaborate conceits. She adored Shelley. She wrote sonnets of personal emotion in the style of Elizabeth Barrett Browning or of Edna St. Vincent Millay. She could sound like Blake or Keats, Walter de la Mare or Housman. "Let No Charitable Hope" concluded with Henley's "Invictus" note which was so widely imitated:

> In masks outrageous and austere
> The years go by in single file;
> But none has merited my fear,
> And none has quite escaped my smile.

As the metaphor of "enamelled snuffboxes" suggests, the strongest influence on her poetry was probably the aesthetic avant garde of England in the 1890s. In her last years, however, she wrote some poems of a length and "philosophic" ambition she would not have attempted earlier; these involved something of a departure from her former ideal of polished technique.

In "The Eagle and the Mole," which Yeats thought "a lovely heroic song," Miss Wylie voiced contempt for the "polluted" and "reeking herd" and praised the inviolate "eagle of the rock." The attitude was typical of her, and had obvious literary sources in British poetry of the 1890s. In other poems she voiced a Shelleyan longing for the Eternal and the One. Along with such admirations and longings went a recoil from what seemed to her the crass, equivocal, and vaguely monstrous character of human nature and the world. Hence her heroic contempt and Shelleyan mysticism shaded over into fantasies of escape and hiding; in other poems, recoiling from this impulse, she embraced or resolved to embrace the monster, life. The presence of these opposed impulses frequently made her utterance tense and ambiguous, and the persistence and permutation of this conflict gave her work added interest.

Other poets whose work was modified by one or another of the contending modernisms of the age included Witter Bynner (1881–1968), Orrick Johns (1887–1946), Hermann Hagedorn (1882–1964), Hervey Allen (1889–1949), and Robert Hillyer (1895–1961). Bynner wrote poems of many kinds—sonnets and lyrics, free verse effusions, translations, meditations, monologues—and underwent diverse influences in successive phases. He took part with Ficke in the *Spectra* hoax and cultivated enthusiams for Whitman, Housman, Chinese verse, Mexico, and the myths and dances of the American Indians. His spiritual autobiography veiled in allegory, *Eden Tree* (1931), was followed by *Guest Book* (1935), a collection of sonnets characterizing, sometimes satirically, persons he knew. Orrick Johns once seemed promising to both the "conservative" poets and to the avant-garde. *Asphalt and Other Poems* (1917) contained a series of trite poems in New York City dialect and a section of "Country Rhymes"; these were lyrics of a traditional kind:

> So I took her where she spoke,
> Breasts of snow and burning mouth . . .
> Crying cranes and drifting smoke
> And the blackbirds wheeling south.

In his next volume, *Black Branches* (1920), this slight, appreciative lyrist became an experimentalist, an unnatural phase that probably indicates a wish to keep up and in with the avant-garde. He practiced, however, the experiments of other poets and even tried his hand in the latest style of Eliot:

> The daedal queen edulcorate
> strove with her sleepiness at tea;
> Theos, attending lounged and ate
> the crumbs of social apathy.

Johns returned to the style of his "Country Rhymes" in *Wild Plum* (1926), and after that he published no more volumes, though he continued to write. He ended his life by taking poison. The lyrics of Hermann Hagedorn were slight but sensitive. He also wrote novels and an important biography of Edwin Arlington Robinson (1938). Hervey Allen published eight volumes of poetry in the 1920s. His forte was narrative verse, and his most successful efforts were "The Blindman," a ballad, and "Children of Earth," a long poem that slightly recalls Robert

Frost. *Earth Moods* (1925) was an epic history of the earth in free verse. He was best known for his biography of Poe, *Israfel* (1927), and his novel *Anthony Adverse* (1933).

Robert Hillyer's poetic lineage may be traced through Santayana and Bridges, on the one hand, and through Robinson and Frost, on the other. In him the "genteel" ideal of poetry as reflection, consolation, and beauty combined with something a little harder, shrewder, more contemporary, and closer to actual speech. He was impeccably skillful within his self-chosen limits. If poetry were only the management of rhythm and syntax, smooth (or delicately roughened) diction, stanzaic form, assonance, and alliteration, Hillyer would have been one of the finest poets of his generation. Here he is in his Bridges vein:

> There is always the sound of falling water here;
> By day, blended with birdsong and windy leaves;

and here in a slightly more colloquial rhythm:

> For forty years and more my hand has shown
> The scar where once a fishhook tore the flesh.
> The body bears these grudges of its own.

The self projected in his poetry was kindly, humorous, and nostalgic, resolved to be hopeful, and grateful for beauty and country calm. His feelings were rarely intense. Intellectually he resembled, as he said, Samuel Johnson's old college friend Mr. Edwards, who had tried to be a philosopher but found that "cheerfulness was always breaking in." His poetic "Letters" ("A Letter to a Teacher of English," "A Letter to Robert Frost"), which he wrote in the 1930s, display the most skillful satiric use of Pope's closed heroic couplet that has been achieved in this century, though Hillyer is much less concentrated and biting than Pope:

> Taste changes. Candid Louis Untermeyer
> Consigns his past editions to the fire;
> His new anthology, resigned and thrifty,
> Builds up some poets and dismisses fifty.
> And every poet spared, as is but human,
> Remarks upon his critical acumen.

Loyal to the poets and methods he loved, Hillyer found himself on the defensive as the Modernists became a highbrow vogue in the 1930s, and his life was troubled by feuds with their critical disciples, feuds for which he lacked aptitude.

CONRAD AIKEN

If Conrad Aiken (1889–1973) was a conservative or traditional poet, his work did not much resemble that of other poets noticed in this chapter. He is discussed here mainly because to place him anywhere else would be even less appropriate. He belonged to the generation of Pound, Eliot, Stevens, and Williams, but, except for his college friendship with Eliot at Harvard, he was not associated with any of them. He was living in Boston in 1915, when Boston became, thanks to Amy Lowell, the American center of the Imagist movement. He was friendly with John Gould Fletcher at this time and intrigued by his "symphonies," but Aiken was no Imagist. In fact, he attacked the movement in reviews and essays. He had no sympathy with the "democratic" and "Whitmanesque" tendencies in American poetry, nor, at the other extreme, had he a good word for the "word-jugglers and sensation-balancers," as he called them—Maxwell Bodenheim, Wallace Stevens, Mina Loy, William Carlos Williams, and the other poets associated in the 1910s with Alfred Kreymborg and *Others*.

Because he wrote his finest poems in the 1930s he might be taken up in connection with a later period. But Aiken had no important influence on poets from the thirties to the present, neither did he reflect the tendencies of those years. He is a product of the ferment in American poetry of the 1910s; and once he had formed his own voice, method, and theme in the "symphonies" he began to compose in 1916, his development proceeded organically and independently. But to notice him with the conservatives has the advantage of recalling a label often applied to him in the 1910s and 1920s. He was called a conservative because he used traditional prosody, still more because he criticized all brands of Modernism with shrewd common sense. As Marianne Moore remarked, he was a reviewer who feared to displease no one—except himself.

His first volume, *Earth Triumphant and Other Tales in Verse* (1914), was in a traditionally Romantic vein and showed that he had been reading Masefield. In the next couple of years he sometimes emulated Masters and sometimes Eliot. His "symphonies," composed between 1916 and 1925 (such as *Senlin: A Biography,* 1918), attempted to adapt principles of structure from music. Aiken hoped to obtain "contrapuntal effects in poetry" through "contrasting and conflicting tones and themes." "One employs what one might term emotion-mass with just as deliberate a regard for its position in the total design as one would employ a variation of form." In theory, the intended "musical" form or effect would determine what ideas or emotions were presented as well as the method used to present them; "symphonic" poetry, as Aiken conceived it, would not even convey emotions so much as it would evoke their "shimmering overtones." In fact, however, the "symphonies" enacted a strenuous, intellectual questioning. The general theme of *Senlin,* as he explained in *Poetry* (1919), "is the problem of personal identity, the struggle of the individual for an awareness of what it is that constitutes his consciousness; an attempt to place himself, to relate himself to the world of which he feels himself to be at once an observer and an integral part." As he later summed up his lifelong article of faith: "Consciousness is our supreme gift. . . . To see, to remember, to know, to feel, to understand, as much as possible—isn't this perhaps the most obviously indicated of motives or beliefs, the noblest and most all-comprehending of ideas which it is relatively possible for us to realize."

In his subsequent poetry Aiken continued to pursue this "theme" and experimented with different formal means for embodying it. In *The Coming Forth by Day of Osiris Jones* (1931) he drew his procedure from Egyptian religious ritual. The dead Osiris must give to the judge, Memnon, a complete accounting of all that he has done in life. *Landscape West of Eden* (1935) expressed developing consciousness in changing landscapes. *The Kid* (1947) treated the westward expansion of America as a symbol of widening awareness. His finest volumes are the two sequences of *Preludes for Memnon* (1931) and *Time in the Rock* (1936). Aiken also wrote fiction, autobiography, and criticism and edited five successful anthologies. His work of more than sixty years in literature displayed intelligence, integrity, ambition, and power of growth. He was belauded by critics, such as R. P. Blackmur and Dudley Fitts, whose opinions can be re-

spected; he won important prizes; and he is included in many
anthologies. But he remains a "neglected" writer. Hence his
work attracts the sort of reader who is eager to make a "discovery." Having invested hope and effort, such readers are tempted
to proclaim that the neglect is unjust.

Though Aiken was gifted in many forms of poetry, most of his
more important poems can be described as "meditative." And to
suggest the meaning of the term, as it applies to his work, the
later poetry of Wallace Stevens can be mentioned as a better-
known example. Not that Aiken much resembles Stevens in
theme or style, but both sought to represent in poetry the "del-
uging onwardness," as Stevens put it, of the mind in its dialogue
with "reality." And both assumed that the "onwardness" ceases
only with death. As long as we are alive, new aspects of "reality"
continually emerge in consciousness. From Aiken's Romantic
point of view, the moving on to include new awareness is more
essentially valuable, more in touch with the character and
process of reality, than the structuring of awareness into an
intellectual synthesis; the synthesis at best can only be provisional.

This continual transition of awareness is enacted in his poetry
and may explain a weakness in it. There are passages of "symphonic" return-with-variation to previous formulations; but otherwise individual moments of awareness (or phases of his utterance) receive more or less the same emphasis. It is not simply
that there is little qualitative discrimination among different moments of awareness but also that one moment is hardly exhibited
more than another. Imagination is diffused through the whole
poem but not coagulated in nodes. The result is that attention
quickly flags. Aldous Huxley, voicing a common complaint, remarked in 1920 that Aiken "runs along like Wordsworth's hare
in 'The Leech-Gatherer,' in a rainbow mist of his own making."
This mist was of Huxley's making; the rainbow vapors are what
one sees when one reads Aiken inattentively. Aiken is quite clear
when one reads him attentively; but it is difficult to read him attentively for long.

THE BENÉTS

Stephen Vincent Benét (1898–1943) was a frail boy, read
widely and counted Browning, William Morris, and Chesterton

among his favorite poets. He published his first book of poems at the age of seventeen and, after college, made his living as a free-lance writer. His works included novels, short stories, book reviews, radio scripts, and the libretto for an operetta version of his short story, "The Devil and Daniel Webster." In 1926 and 1927 he put other projects aside and, supported by the Guggenheim Foundation, settled in Paris, where he could live more cheaply while concentrating on the long poem for which he is best known, *John Brown's Body* (1928). In his last years he was working on a second long poem, *Western Star,* which was to tell the changing story of life on the American frontier as it moved westward. Only one book of the poem was finished when he died of a heart attack.

Although he wrote lyrics of many kinds, his ballads are his best. Many of them present romantic adventure in picturesque historical settings. His ballads do not always deal with American subjects, but these seem to have tapped in him a richer fund of association and nostalgia ("The Ballad of William Sycamore," "The Mountain Whippoorwill"). He used emphatic rhythms and clear, simple images of a relatively expectable kind. Describing the frontier cabin of his childhood, William Sycamore recalls:

> The cabin logs, with the bark still rough,
> And my mother who laughed at trifles,
> And the tall, lank visitors, brown as snuff,
> With their long, straight squirrel-rifles.

In "American Names," which was composed in France, Benét exploited the impressionistic values of place names:

> I have fallen in love with American names,
> The sharp names that never get fat,
> The snakeskin-titles of mining-claims,
> The plumed war-bonnet of Medicine Hat,
> Tucson and Deadwood and Lost Mule Flat.

John Brown's Body takes for its subject the Civil War from Brown's raid at Harpers Ferry to Lee's surrender at Appomattox Courthouse. One of Benét's motives for writing this narrative poem of more than three hundred pages was that he wished to highlight the diverse strength of the American heritage, from which present-day Americans might draw inspiration. "I am tired, not of criticism of America, for no country can be healthy without criticism, but of the small railers, conventional rebels. We also have a heritage—and not all of it wooden money." The poem is sometimes described as an epic, and if "epic" implies only a narrative work of unusual scope that deals with significant events in the life of a nation, the term may be appropriate. Benét presents Lincoln and Jefferson Davis, cabinet members, generals, officers, plantation owners, farmers, backwoodsmen, and slaves, and typical landscapes and ways of life in the major American regions at the time of the Civil War. Scenes of battle are counterpointed by episodes of civilian life behind the lines.

For his poem Benét read widely in the literature of the war, and his view of its causes, course, and outcome is relatively nonpartisan and complex. So far as he achieves an interpretation of it, he presents the war as tragic and ironic in its course and meaning. A scene on a slave ship makes the Prelude to the whole poem; the human suffering and moral wrong of slavery are ominous for the future, though the protagonists in the scene sense this only vaguely or not at all. Benét does not present John Brown as a heroic, old-testament prophet but underscores his limitations and possibly twisted psychology. Whatever his personal character, in the development of history Brown was a "stone" which some underlying, impersonal force or fate used because of its hardness. What resulted from the Civil War was remote from any ideal for which the antagonists fought. It was simply modern, industrial America, and Benét does not celebrate the "great, metallic beast."

Benét follows several characters, including Jack Ellyat, a Yankee from Connecticut; Clay Wingate from a Georgian plantation; Luke Breckinridge, a Tennessee mountaineer; Jake Diefer, a Pennsylvania farmer; and Spade, a runaway slave. Their stories are intertwined with and throughout the historical action. These original inventions are the least successful part of Benét's poem. The characterizations, though occasionally vivid, are somewhat predictable. The plots are mostly romantic—for example, the lovers are reunited at the end—and in this respect the lives of the individual characters usually do not substantiate Benét's unsentimental historical vision.

In descriptive and narrative passages Benét's style is clear, rapid, and uncompressed. He has a gift for images and metaphors that bring a scene vividly before the mind. As in motionpictures, attention is sustained by cutting quickly from scene to scene. He also shifts from mode to mode, as passages of narrative, reflective commentary, and character portrayal succeed each other, often with a change of meter. If such a poem was to be written at all, his stylistic aims seem generally appropriate.

W. R. Benét (1886–1950) was the brother of Stephen Vincent Benét. He became an assistant editor of *Century* magazine and subsequently a co-founder of *The Saturday Review of Literature.* He remained with this journal as an associate editor for the rest of his life, and wrote for it a weekly column, "The Phoenix Nest." He was a remarkably facile versifier. His earlier volumes include poems of historical pageantry and swashbuckling, quasi-mystical religious utterances, ballads such as the often praised "Jesse James: American Myth," and miscellaneous shorter lyrics. Some of the latter reflect his admiration for the poetry of his second wife, Elinor Wylie, whose example led him to strive for a more economical and reserved expression ("The Faun in the Snow"). In others, however, he seems to have been influenced by Robert Frost and tried for a more naturally flowing, colloquial speech ("The Woodcutter's Wife"). *Man Possessed* (1927), a collection of poems from earlier volumes, has a Preface that speaks of his likings in poetry and aims as a poet, but it is airy and affected and tells very little. From the general character of Benét's poetry up to this point it is clear that he sought beauty and romance and that he found romance especially in such places as the Wild West, Cathay, the Arabia of Scheherazade, ancient Rome, or Alfred's England rather than in the familiar and contemporary. He might have been characterized as an American Alfred Noyes. Hence *Rip Tide* (1932) was somewhat unexpected. It treated contemporary love and marriage in three interconnected short stories in verse. This was followed eventually by *The Dust Which Is God* (1941), a book-length, quasi-autobiographical novel in verse, which won the Pulitzer Prize for poetry in 1942. He continued to publish collections of lyrics, of which the best may be *The Stairway of Surprise* (1947). Writing *The Dust Which Is God* seems to have taught him a defter, swifter presentation than he had previously mastered. One may also mention as a curiosity *With Wings as Eagles* (1940), a lyric history of aviation; it describes notable pilots and flights in ballads, sonnets, and other short forms of verse.

REGIONAL POETRY

Regional poetry has been written in America with diverse motives. Among them are local piety and patriotism, fascination with the history, ways of life, types of character, folk lore, and speech of a geographical section, the wish to exploit in poetry a relatively unfamiliar subject matter and idiom, and sometimes a more commerical wish to cash in on popular nostalgia for the days of dory-fishing, or stovewood splitting, or sod-breaking, or bronco-busting, or turkey-in-the-straw. Regional poetry has been written in the twentieth century at every level of poetic ability and sophistication, from the complex artistry of Robert Frost to the knowing slickness of MacKinlay Kantor or to the warm naiveté of Jesse Stuart of Kentucky.

In the latter part of the nineteenth century and the early part of this one, regional poetry was often taken up as a means of rebelling against the poetry of the Genteel Tradition. Yet most regional poets of the 1910s and 1920s were far from being rebels; many of them sought only to express the subjects they loved in what they understood to be the approved style of poetry. Madison Cawein presented Kentucky haunts in the language of Keats and Shelley; Edwin Ford Piper described a wagon train in the idiom and rhythm of English descriptive verse of the later eighteenth century. As conventions of poetic style changed, regionalists began to write in the newer ways; by 1927 Piper was adopting free verse, just as, a little later, Robert P. Tristram Coffin and August William Derleth picked up the style of Frost. But in these poets the modern styles were no less derivative than the Genteel one had been.

No just estimate of the strength of the regional impulse can be formed without keeping in mind the poets we treat elsewhere, such as Riley, Robinson, Frost, and the many who, though not primarily regionalist, nevertheless composed regional poems at times—for example, Sandburg in *Cornhuskers*, John Gould Fletcher in his poems on Arkansas life and history, Witter Bynner on rural New York, and Amy Lowell on New England. We here notice most of the other regionalists who are worth mentioning from the start of the century to the present. The early period was the important one for regional poetry; few poets of the younger and middle generations are now writing in this vein.

Who should be included as a "regional" poet is not always easy to decide, for many poets reflect the life and speech of whatever milieu is familiar to them. Followers of William Carlos Williams believe as a matter of principle that poetry ought to be rooted in the local scene. Yet Frost is a regional poet, whatever else he is, and Williams is not. The essential difference is that Frost viewed rural New England as having a distinctive character of its own and valued it as a setting and subject of poetry. Williams, on the other hand, wrote about Rutherford and Paterson, not because these cities were regionally distinctive but because they were, he felt, representatively American. Turning to the local environment he knew intimately, he sought to find and express not a regional but an American sensibility. Both points of view derive from the Romantic period, when the feeling spread among educated persons that the distinctive life of a class, such as the peasantry, or of a historic period, or of a region, or of a nation might embody special values that were worth cherishing. The Scotch novels of Sir Walter Scott or Wordsworth's loving portrait of the Westmorland peasantry in "Michael" are examples. In the later nineteenth century the regional impulse was reflected in the local-color school of American fiction and with imaginative profundity in novelists such as Hardy, who combined the regional with the elemental and universal. Although regional poetry was already a well-established tradition, both types of fiction have something to do with the vogue of it in America in the early part of this century.

We may begin with Kentucky, where an indigenous culture survived among the hill people. Elizabeth Madox Roberts (1886–1941) was primarily a novelist and made her reputation with *The Time of Man* (1926), a moving study of the rural poor. The poems she wrote occasionally were collected in *Song in the Meadow* (1940). About half of these expert and sensitive lyrics might be called regional. "Stranger," for example, imitated a folk ballad sung with a banjo accompaniment, "A Ballet Song of Mary" used the archaic English that was still heard among the hills, and "Woodcock of the Ivory Beak" drew on local folklore. Her poems deserve to be better known.

Roy Helton (b. 1886) also exploited the idiom and imaginative lore of Kentucky in the first part of *Lonesome Water* (1930). His "Old Christmas Morning" is a fine ballad of feuds and ghosts:

> "What should I see there, Sally Anne Barton?"
>
> "Well, sperits do walk last night."
>
> "There were an elder bush a-blooming
> While the moon still give some light."

Helton was a less gifted poet than Miss Roberts, however, and the regional vein somewhat disguised the conventionality of his imagination, which appeared undisguised in the other parts of *Lonesome Water* and in *Come Back to Earth* (1946). James Still was born in 1906, became a librarian in rural Kentucky between 1932 and 1939, and then a college teacher. The poems of *Hound on the Mountain* (1937) have the hill country for their setting. Their imagery is vivid and concrete, their phrasing vigorous, and their incremental rhythms and syntax generate powerful emotion.

Jesse Stuart is a more ingenuous describer of the Kentucky hill country, where he was born in 1907. He believes that poetry should "communicate," that it should speak immediately and clearly to anyone. "I have never," he says, "tried to develop a style. I just feel the compulsion to write, and I write." No sophisticated modern poet could come forth with:

> I'll stand beneath the gray-marked sycamore
> And with soft hands I'll feel its scaly bark,
> Not any man will ever love life more;

but a great many sophisticated writers at times have uneasy consciences because they feel they cannot feel, or would not care to express, such simple, wholesome emotions, and Stuart has received favorable attention in and around New York, where reviewers have compared him to Robert Burns. Kentuckians have given the prideful encouragement that local poets usually receive in the United States if they celebrate their region and also become known outside it. The special interest of many Southern writers in the literature of their own region has also contributed to Stuart's reputation. He is Poet Laureate of Kentucky; there is a Stuart room at Murray State College; and several university dissertations have been written on him, of which one has been published. He has also written short stories, novels, and other types of prose.

DuBose Heyward (1885–1940) came from an aristocratic family in Charleston, South Carolina, but grew up poor. He met Hervey Allen in 1918, and in *Carolina Chansons: Legends of the Low Country* (1922) the two writers celebrated the region in traditional meters. Heyward's novel *Porgy* (1925) was intended as a study of black American character. He and his wife turned it into a play (1927), and Gershwin's celebrated musical *Porgy and Bess* (1925) was based on it. *Skylines and Horizons* (1924) included a group of poems depicting life in the Great Smoky mountains ("Skylines") and a number of lyrical and meditative utterances ("Horizons") suggested by the landscape and history of the South Carolina low country. In "The Negro," the only new section in his *Jasbo Brown and Selected Poems* (1931), two short narrative poems are "Jasbo Brown" and "Gamesters All." Although their subjects are a jazz musician and a group of crap-shooters, their idiom is genteel.

In the state of Maine a consciously homespun regionalist was Holman Francis Day (1865–1935), who was a newspaper editor and novelist as well as a poet. His first book, *Up in Maine: Stories of Yankee Life Told in Verse* (1900), follows the example of J. W. Riley in its uses of rural dialect, though the characters typify traditional Yankee virtues—integrity, independence, stoic endurance, and single-mindedness. *Pine Tree Ballads* (1902) and *Kin o' Ktaadn* (1904)—which takes its name from a mountain—also exploit the dialect and demonstrate a growing range and skill in realistic portraiture, which Day was better able to pursue, he felt, in the novels of Maine life to which he increasingly turned. Wilbert Snow (b. 1884) wrote poems that convincingly express his love for the country along Maine's Penobscot Bay. Since he was not only a professor at Wesleyan, but also Governor of Connecticut in 1946–1947, he may have felt a special need for the solace and refreshment his poetry dwells on. James Whaler (b. 1889) was also a professor, and published several studies of the poetry of Milton. In *Hale's Pond* (1927) he pictured life in the Maine woods in a sequence of eerily imaginative narrative poems. His subsequent *Green River* (1931) is not a regional work, but a poem about the naturalist Constantine Rafinesque.

Robert P. Tristram Coffin (1892–1955), who taught at Bowdoin College, was a prolific writer of essays, biographies, novels, and poems. In the early part of his career he turned out a great many ballads; later he tended to present familiar scenes and types of character of coastal and rural Maine. Robert Frost was, he said, an influence in "opening my eyes to the poetry in common speech and people and in usual sights." His pictures and comments were slightly sentimental, nostalgic, often humorous, and competently executed in traditional meters and simple words. Like Riley, toward whom he descended as much as he rose toward Frost, he felt that the success or failure of a poem could be gauged by the response of an audience when he read it aloud, and he somewhat modified his style as experience taught him what would stir his hearers.

August William Derleth (1909–1971) also absorbed the poetry of Frost. His region was Wisconsin, and he claimed to be the "most versatile and voluminous writer in quality writing fields," but his poems are better than this boast might suggest. His rural setting is roughly similar to Frost's, and he shared some of Frost's virtues, such as sly humor and reflective point.

Going west across the Missouri, we come to *Barbed Wire and Other Poems* (1919) by Edwin Ford Piper (1871–1939). This volume depicts the lives of homesteaders in the early 1880s. Piper knew his subject thoroughly and worked with historical and stylistic diligence. At his best he mastered a fairly direct and pithy style, not far from the spoken idiom. *Paintrock Road* (1927) presented similar material in a similar style, except that Piper now occasionally experimented with free verse, and some of these poems are Imagist. John Neihardt (1881–1973) lived among the Omaha Indians for six years. His later poems, composed in a forthright style, depicted frontier life. He wrote an epic of the West and was made Poet Laureate of Nebraska in 1921. Lew Sarrett (1888–1954) also wrote of the Indians and the wilderness.

Harold L. Davis (1896–1960) was primarily a novelist and did not publish a book of poems until 1942. He had a wide experience of life in the Western states as a shepherd, sheriff, and rancher. *Proud Riders and Other Poems* has two sections, "Far Western Pastorals" and "Narrative Poems." The pastorals are short poems of a loose-limbed, mildly thoughtful or cud-chewing description. The narratives exploit colloquial dialogue in the manner of Frost. Davis, who knew several European languages, was a sophisticated poet, and his poems in both sections are "pastoral" in the same sense as the better Western movies; they present Western scenery, characters, and ways of life with considerable authenticity but still with a consciousness that they are simplifying in accordance with conventions.

The verses of MacKinley Kantor (b. 1904), a newspaper poet, were collected in *Turkey in the Straw* (1935). They are mostly ballads, recalling the life and history of frontier America. One section deals with the Civil War, in which Kantor is keenly interested. Although the volume was subtitled *A Book of American Ballads and Primitive Verse,* and some of the ballads are in dialect, they are anything but primitive, for they have a journalistic effectiveness in exploiting stock sentiment. The most obvious literary influence is that of Vachel Lindsay in poems such as "The Black Bison" and "When the Angels Came for Bryan." *Glory for Me* (1945) is a novel in verse. Poetry is only a sideline for this successful novelist and writer of screenplays.

18

BLACK POETS OF AMERICA
THE FIRST PHASE

IN almost all our chapters on American poetry we could have dwelt also on the work of black poets. Paul Lawrence Dunbar could be discussed along with James Whitcomb Riley. Claude McKay, Countee Cullen, W. S. Braithwaite, and Georgia Johnson were among the poets who in the Modernist era continued to use traditional forms and idioms. Fenton Johnson was among the "new" poets in Chicago in the 1910s, and Langston Hughes and Sterling Brown were creative and original figures in the style of poetry, descending from Whitman, Lindsay, and Sandburg, that reflected a commitment to democratic, Populist, and later sometimes to Marxist ideals. Black poets seldom exploited the oblique, elliptical styles of Pound and Eliot—not at least until after the 1920s,—but they figured in every other important tendency of twentieth-century American poetry.

There are good reasons for devoting a separate chapter to their work. There is wide interest today in the history of the literary expression of black Americans. Also, within the general evolution of modern American poetry, that written by black Americans constitutes a distinct vein to a degree that the poetry in English of other minorities, racial or religious, does not. The following pages survey black poets from the 1890s through the 1920s, from Dunbar to the publication of Sterling Brown's *Southern Road* in 1932. This first phase anticipated in some respects the more radical phase of black poetry that began in the 1960s, although leading poets of this later period, such as Imamu Baraka (LeRoi Jones), have often been savagely critical of black poets of the twenties.

Inquiring why or in what ways the poetry of black Americans is distinctive, we may begin by noting the obvious fact that black poets look with different eyes on the American past, seeing contours, points of emphasis, and meanings less perceived by most whites. For socioeconomic and psychological reasons the classical world of ancient Greece and Rome has meant less to black intellectuals as a source of values, ideals, historical precedent, or literary allusion. The content of black poetry responds to the sorts of personal experience that blacks in America are likely to have. Religious faith provides an example of the more subtle kinds of qualitative difference in the experience of black poets. They have been as likely as any others to break with Christianity in this century—perhaps more likely because of the association of Christianity with white dominance. But to repudiate Christianity was to break with the faith from which the community had historically derived much of its culture and social cohesiveness; it meant separating oneself from the majority of blacks. Yet the black intellectual might wish to feel his solidarity with the common people. Thus, for black writers the problem of Christian faith typically presented itself in dimensions and ramifications that were not quite the same for writers who were not black. These examples are mentioned only as representative of the many that might also be cited to illustrate why the themes, subject matters, feelings, and concerns of black poets have differed to some degree from those of American poets in general.

Similarly with the form and style of black poetry. But at this point one must distinguish between poets such as W. S. Braithwaite and Countee Cullen, on the one hand, and Langston Hughes and Sterling Brown, on the other. The former were concerned to be recognized as poets, not as black poets, and their style was shaped accordingly. But poets such as Hughes and Brown drew forms and techniques from, for example, the spirituals and field songs of rural Southern blacks or from blues and jazz. In exploiting this material they resembled other modern poets who widened the resources of poetry by incorporating elements of popular culture. One might think of Lindsay's uses of jazz syncopation in "The Congo" or his incorporation of a revivalist hymn in "General William Booth Enters Heaven" or of Eliot's adaptation of the music-hall skit at the end of part two of *The Waste Land*. Also, because the modes of expression they adopted were associated with one group of Americans particularly, Hughes and Brown might be compared to regional poets such as Frost. Their motives, however, were closer to Lindsay's or Sandburg's than to Frost's or Eliot's. They sought not so much to renew the poetic tradition by mingling it with something else as to express the black people, their attitudes, experiences, ways of life, and imaginative styles, in forms that would speak to them because they were theirs.

We are better able to appreciate their poems if we know the prototypes on which they are based. These are sometimes esoteric; for example, a poem may be modeled on a particular folksong. Moreover, the prototypes may be invoked only allusively. Also the prototypical element usually includes not just a form and idiom but also the tempo, pitch, emphasis, and modulation that would be used in speaking or singing. Nevertheless, even if one is not adverted to these things, the poems still communicate. Few readers of Sterling Brown's "Southern Road" have actually heard the singing of the chain gangs as they work on the road, but it is easy to imagine the prisoners swinging their sledgehammers to the rhythm of a song:

> Swing dat hammer—hunh—
> Steady, bo';
> Swing dat hammer—hunh—
> Steady, bo';
> Ain't no rush, bebby,
> Long ways to go.

The only frequently invoked prototype that could cause serious confusion if one were not familiar with it is the blues song. In Langston Hughes's "Bound No'th Blues" one must be able to interpret the emotion by hearing the intonation and the rhythm. This can only be done by readers who have heard such songs sung. The last stanza, for example, goes:

> Road, road, road, O!
> Road, road, . . . road . . . road, road!
> Road, road, road, O!
> On the no'thern road.
> These Mississippi towns ain't
> Fit fer a hoppin' toad.

Many black poets composed in dialect, but the dialects were not the same, neither were they adopted for the same motives. The important distinction is between the dialect poetry of Dunbar and his followers around the turn of the century and that of poets such as Hughes and Sterling Brown in the next generation. Dunbar's dialect was a literary device modeled chiefly on the speech attributed for comic purposes to the "darkies" of minstrel shows, although he avoided the more demeaning characteristics of this speech, such as malapropisms and grotesque mispronunciations. The dialects used by Hughes and Brown, on the other hand, were authentic. They transcribed or at least adapted the linguistic individualities of actual groups of speakers, whether in the rural South or in Harlem. The passages quoted from Brown and Hughes may serve as illustrations and may be contrasted with typical lines from Dunbar's "When de Co'n Pone's Hot":

> An' you want to jump an' hollah,
>   Dough you know you'd bettah not,
> When yo' mammy says de blessin'
>   An' de co'n pone's hot.

As these lines illustrate, in his use of dialect, though not in the particular dialect he used, Dunbar was emulating Riley. The extent to which his motives for exploiting dialect were not racial is suggested by the fact that he also wrote poems in German, Irish, Scottish and Riley's own Hoosier dialects. To say that his motives were commercial would be an unkind simplification, but it should be stressed that the dialect he adopted was associated, through the minstrel tradition, with stereotyped interpretations of black life and character—the black as happy-go-lucky primitive—that had been created by white authors and confirmed the premises about racial differences that prevailed in America eighty years ago.

There were of course poets in the age of Dunbar who attempted to write in an authentic dialect which would not invoke sentimental and condescending stereotypes. James Edwin Campbell was one. But on the whole their effort failed, and black poets of Dunbar's time had only two literary idioms available to them. They could use the standard language or they could use a dialect that was racial but which, because of its literary and minstrel associations, imprisoned the characterization of blacks within falsifying conventions. With this in mind, one appreciates the significance of the breakthrough that dissociated dialect from these conventions.

TYPES AND HISTORY OF BLACK POETRY

The classifications made in literary history are always unsatisfactory and must be continuously qualified. If black poets are treated separately as a group, the extent to which their work reflects the development of poetry in general must also be emphasized. With black as with white poets the differences between those of the turn of the century and those of the next generation were fundamental. They show not only in the handling of dialect but in the franker, bolder speech of the modern generation, in their technical inventiveness—in almost all the respects, including the sheer quantity of memorable poets, that I have emphasized in distinguishing the generation of Pound from that of Stedman and Santayana. But with black poets of the 1910s and 1920s, the distinction of "conservative" and "new" poets, hitherto stressed in discussing this period, is less significant. Certainly the distinction can be made. W. S. Braithwaite, Georgia Johnson, Claude McKay, and Countee Cullen were among the conservative poets of the age, and Fenton Johnson, Jean Toomer, and Langston Hughes were "new" poets—though not in the same way. But black poets were not battling each other over new or old forms and styles. On the whole, one accomplished black poet was ready to welcome another, whatever his style, for the accomplishment was what mattered for racial pride.

In the 1920s there was, however, a running dispute as to whether poetry by blacks should or should not deal with specifically racial experience. Should it adopt distinctive idioms and forms? Should it address itself especially to a black audience? Or should it reject such demands as restrictive? Although such questions were important to the writers concerned, virtually all black poets wrote their best poems when they spoke out of a racial feeling or identification, race being, as James Weldon Johnson put it, "perforce the thing that the American Negro poet knows best."

Black poetry of this period is usually discussed in connection with the Harlem Renaissance. The phrase refers to the heightened vitality and achievement of black cultural life in Harlem in the 1920s. The causes of this flowering are not completely explicable. Doubtless the migration of Southern blacks into Northern cities was important, especially since blacks were also emigrating from the West Indies and Africa, and in Harlem, which had the largest population of black people of any city in the world, widely diverse traditions and cultures encountered each other. By the 1920s, moreover, new institutions, furthering the political, social, economic, and intellectual needs of black people, were beginning to have a noticeable impact on feelings and perceptions. The National Association for the Advancement of Colored People had been founded in 1909, the National Urban League in 1911, and in 1915 Carter G. Woodson had set up the Association for the Study of Negro Life and History, with the influential journals it published. On a more popular level Marcus Garvey had a large following. He preached that all American blacks should emigrate to Africa and found a new nation there. No one went, but Garvey intensified feelings of racial solidarity. This was the age of blues and of jazz—an age in which music created by blacks first acquired a worldwide following. In Harlem itself whites and blacks mingled at every cultural level, from the audiences in nightclubs to the cafe conversations of intellectuals. The advent of little magazines and of more liberal or adventurous book publishers made it easier for black writers to handle racial themes honestly; blacks also edited little magazines of their own. All this made a more fertile milieu for poetry, if only because it quickened intellectual life and enhanced self-confidence. We should also keep in mind that the years of the Harlem Renaissance were the heady years of the spread of the "new" poetry in the United States and also of a more skilled accomplishment within the conservative tradition as these poets responded to the challenge of the new styles. The heightened creative achievement of black poets at this time was part of the same ferment and undoubtedly shared in the same general causes, whatever special circumstances were also influential.

The poets now usually associated with the Harlem Renaissance were not participants in an organized movement analogous to the Imagists. Neither did they possess a common tendency that justifies thinking of them as a group. If they are discussed together, it is because their first important volumes came out at more or less the same time: Claude McKay's *Spring in New Hampshire* in 1920 and *Harlem Shadows* in 1922, Jean Toomer's *Cain* in 1923, Countee Cullen's *Color* in 1925, and Langston Hughes's *The Weary Blues* in 1926. It was a sudden, unprecedented emergence of talented black poets. The momentum was kept up by new volumes from these poets and by James Weldon Johnson's *God's Trombones* in 1929 and Sterling Brown's *Southern Road* in 1932; there were also less important works by other poets who established themselves in the twenties. Moveover, these poets illustrated, though in very diverse ways, the growing self-confidence and racial pride of black intellectuals. We have already noticed the use in poetry of the culture and idiom of the folk. There was also a tendency to identify with racial origins and history in Africa and the South, and, more significant, to find in this identification a source of self-respect. Protest against racial injustice was more defiantly voiced. And for the first time in American poetry the presentation of ordinary black people and experience was liberated from comic or sentimental stereotypes. None of these generalizations apply to all the poets of the Harlem Renaissance, however, and where they do apply to a poet, it may be to some of his poems only. In fact the differences between these poets are more obvious than the similarities. Although the "Harlem Renaissance" may be a useful term if it reminds us that there was a significant cultural development in this period, it can also be misleading if it suggests that there was a relatively coherent literary movement.

Around the turn of the century most black poets wrote in the traditional and conventional styles of the age. They declaimed noble emotions or they murmured melodiously in the wake of Tennyson or Swinburne of "Long nights, long nights and the whisperings of new ones" or they fondly remembered Sewanee Hills in neat verses:

> Sewanee Hills of dear delight
> Prompting my dreams that used to be . . .

No poets of this kind were unusually gifted, though Roscoe Jamison, J. D. Corrothers, W. H. A. Moore, and G. M. McClellan may be mentioned. Interpreting their work with emphasis on

the fact that they were black, Sterling Brown points out that
their refusal to write in dialect meant also a rejection of

stereotypes of Negro life and character. Too often, however, their reaction . . . seemed to mean something else. References to race were
avoided or else couched in abstract, idealistic diction. Valuably insisting
that Negro poets should not be confined to problems of race or pictures
of Negro life, these poets often committed a costlier error out of timidity at being Negroes: they refused to look into their own hearts and
write.

He adds that "the lives of many of these poets were exciting; the
difficulties met and surmounted would have been fine material
for poetry," but "they chose to write conventionally about the
peace of nature. . . . Among their adventures, that which
meant most to them, apparently, was their obtaining an education. . . But worship of education meant a worship of the traditional and bookish." These are important insights, but one must
stress that the "timidity" of these poets was typical also of most
white poets of the time, who similarly turned from their own
experience to "write conventionally about the peace of nature."

The dialect poets of the turn of the century wrote of the
simple joys and sorrows of (usually) rural life. They posed no
threat to genteel premises. They wrote of the poor, but showed
that they were happy. Their speakers were black, but voiced no
racial protest. Their style was conventional in everything save
diction, and this was humorously intended. Their work, especially that of Dunbar, was welcomed in family magazines such as
the *Century*. Among Dunbar's numerous imitators were C. B.
Johnson, R. G. Dandridge, W. T. Carmichael, J. D. Corrothers,
J. W. Holloway, and D. W. Davis.

Dunbar did not live to see the revitalizing of American poetry
that began after 1910, though before the Harlem Renaissance.
The most important black poets of the 1910s were Fenton
Johnson, W. S. Braithwaite, and Georgia Johnson. Mention
should also be made of Benjamin Brawley and Edward Smith
Jones, though their poems are now little read. Brawley's *The
Negro in Literature and Art* (1910) was one of the early, extended
studies of this subject; Jones is remembered for the moving story
of his walk of hundreds of miles from his home in the South to
Harvard University. Having arrived in Harvard Square, he was
arrested for vagrancy. In jail he wrote a poem entitled "Harvard

Square." This was published in the newspapers and caused so much favorable publicity that he was able to bring out a volume of his poems in the following year (1911). Unfortunately, the poems are wooden.

In the 1920s there was a burst of new talent—Claude McKay, Jean Toomer, Countee Cullen, Langston Hughes, Arna Bontemps, and Gwendolyn Bennett. James Weldon Johnson accomplished his finest work in this decade, and Sterling Brown emerged in the early 1930s. On the whole, the most significant developments in this period were: the participation of black poets such as Toomer and Hughes in avant-garde movements and methods; the use of folk idioms and forms by Hughes, Brown, J. W. Johnson, and others in a poetry written with full seriousness and integrity; and the increasing influence on poetry of political and racial ideologies and purposes. In the last respect, the work of black poets was again typical of a more general development.

PAUL LAWRENCE DUNBAR AND THE MINSTREL AND PLANTATION TRADITIONS

Paul Lawrence Dunbar (1872–1906) was the first widely known American black poet. He achieved this by catering to popular sentiment and humor, and his verse showed remarkable skill in these ways. He also had more earnest aspirations. The depiction of black people in his dialect poems was influenced by three sources: the representation of small-town and rural life in James Whitcomb Riley, minstrel shows, and the South's post-Civil War "plantation" literature. Riley and the minstrel shows are still somewhat familiar. The songs of Stephen Foster, for example, were composed for the minstrels. These performances in blackface included dances and dramatic skits as well as songs, and the depiction of blacks could be grotesquely comic and degrading as well as sentimental.

The "plantation" tradition in literature developed before the Civil War, partly in response to abolitionist works like *Uncle Tom's Cabin*. It was not till after the war, however, that it achieved its greatest victory over fact and the feelings of readers. These many stories and poems portrayed life on antebellum plantations as having been idyllic. "Mahsr" and his lady were benevolent and protective. Black slaves were devoted and child-like, though guileful in stealing watermelons; they spent much of their time singing, dancing, and eating. Nowadays black people were far less happy—a point often made by attributing such sentiments to former slaves. *Befo' de War* (1888), a collection of poems by Thomas Nelson Page and Armistead C. Gordon, is one example. Dunbar did not push this theme as far as Page and Gordon did, but "Chrismus on the Plantation" shows how far he could go. In the poem the bankrupt master after the war calls his ex-slaves together. He is forced to sell the plantation. Tears are shed, and then one of the blacks voices the feeling of all. Whether master can pay them or not, the former slaves will not desert him:

> Er in othah wo'ds, you wants us to fu'git dat you's been kin',
> An 'ez soon ez you is he'pless, we's to leave you heah behin'.
> Well, ef dat's de way dis freedom ac's on people, white or
>   black,
> You kin jes' tell Mistah Lincum fu' to tek his freedom back.
> We gwine wo'k dis ol' plantation fu' whatevah we kin git,
> Fu' I know hit did suppo't us, an' de place kin do it yit.

The minstrel shows and the "plantation" literature were very popular. Their representation of black men and women was widely assumed to be authentic. Had Dunbar seriously chal-lenged these stereotypes, he would have violated the doctrine of compromise and accommodation rather than confrontation, which was preached by leading blacks in his time; moreover, a more realistic description of black people would have been neither credited nor published. The extent to which conventions were accepted as realities is illustrated by W. D. Howells. Re-viewing Dunbar's *Majors and Minors* (1895), Howells compared him with Robert Burns, seeing Dunbar as a peasant poet voicing the actual feelings and experience of his race.

The facts were remote from this interpretation. Dunbar was born in Dayton, Ohio, the son of freed slaves. In high school he wrote poems that received local recognition. At the age of nine-teen he took a job as an elevator boy. In the elevator he spent much time reading the English poets of the past and even more time studying the poems published in *The Century* magazine. In such early efforts as "The Ol' Tunes," "The Old Apple Tree,"

"The Old Homestead," and "An Old Memory" he brilliantly imitated the manner of Riley, sometimes using Riley's Hoosier dialect. His reputation quickly spread, and by the age of twenty-five he was well-known. Success brought no happiness, for he was found to be tubercular, and his marriage was embittered by incompatibilities and, finally, separation. During his short life he produced stories, novels, minstrel shows, and six volumes of verse.

Dunbar's poems in dialect give much pleasure from their shrewd, kindly humor, their skill in portraying character through dialogue or monologue, their deft handling of "plot," their unscrupulous appeal to sentimental self-indulgences, and their strong, lively rhythms. Reading them, one should keep in mind that Dunbar was a talented showman, who composed for public performance. "A Negro Love Song," for example, was written in 1893, when he held a job as a cook in a Chicago restaurant. In free moments the kitchen help would get together and talk about their amours. Waiters passing through the group would clear a path by calling, "Jump back, honey, jump back." The poem Dunbar fashioned out of this circumstance has obvious potentialities for effective recitation in the repetitive emphases and counterpoint of the refrain. The last stanza goes:

> Put my ahm aroun' huh wais',
>   Jump back, honey, jump back.
> Raised huh lips an' took a tase,
>   Jump back, honey, jump back.
> Love me, honey, love me true?
> Love me well ez I love you?
>   An' she answered, "Cose I do"—
>   Jump back, honey, jump back.

Though Dunbar was known for his poems in dialect, he wrote more frequently in ordinary, literate English. One finds poems of love and nature, moral declamation, celebrations of such heroes as Robert Gould Shaw and Booker T. Washington, and poems for schoolboys such as "The Colored Soldiers" and "Black Sampson of Brandywine." It seems likely that his use of dialect and the stereotypes that went with it troubled his conscience. He told James Weldon Johnson, "I've got to write dialect poetry; it's the only way I can get them to listen to me." The remark was accurate—his audience wanted only his poems in dialect—yet since his death readers have gone carefully through his other poems, and the ones in dialect continue to be more frequently reprinted. Although some of his poems in literate English are fine—"We Wear the Mask," for example—they are not better than many other poems composed more or less in the same forms and styles by other poets in the same period. His poems in dialect, on the other hand, are unique achievements.

POETS OF THE 1910S AND 1920S

William Stanley Braithwaite (1878–1962) was born in Boston of West Indian parents and made his living in the editorial room of the Boston *Transcript*. He was well-known in the 1910s and 1920s as a reviewer and as the editor of numerous poetry anthologies; the most important of the latter were the annual anthologies of magazine verse he brought out between 1913 and 1929. He was ready to praise and print all schools, but his personal ideas about poetry were genteelly conventional to a remarkable degree, as were his own lyrics. These were often whimsical, sometimes vaguely mystical, and usually insipid. Whether for reasons of poetic decorum, as he understood it, or for more personal or psychological reasons, his poetry did not handle racial themes. The feelings he voiced came from poetic tradition:

> Mind free, step free,
>   Days to follow after,
> Joys of life sold to me
>   For the price of laughter.
> Girl's love, man's love,
>   Love of work and duty,
> Just a will of God's to prove
>   Beauty, beauty, beauty!

Fenton Johnson (1888–1958), who was born in Chicago and lived there most of his life, brought out at his own expense three volumes of poetry in the 1910s: *A Little Dreaming* (1913), *Visions of the Dusk* (1915), and *Songs of the Soul* (1916). These volumes contain genteel verses ("The Awakening of Poesy," "Eulogy of the Fairies") and dialect poems in the vein of Dunbar; they do not include the poems for which Johnson is remembered. In 1916 he sponsored and edited a little magazine, *The Champion*

Magazine, followed by *The Favorite Magazine,* which, according to its title page, was "The World's Greatest Monthly." In both he published short stories, essays, and poems. He also placed some spirituals in Harriet Monroe's *Poetry.* In the late teens he seems to have been working on a fourth book of verse, to be called *African Nights.* Although this volume was never published, eight short pieces from it were included in Alfred Kreymborg's annual anthology of avant-garde poems, *Others,* in 1919.

In the *African Nights* Johnson departed from his earlier styles and depicted the life of black city dwellers in free verse similar to Sandburg's. "Tired," which articulated the hopelessness and apathy of the impoverished blacks, clearly belonged to the age of *The Waste Land:*

> Let us take a rest, M'Lissey Jane.
> I will go down to the Last Chance Saloon, drink a gallon or two
> of gin, shoot a game or two of dice and sleep the rest of the
> night on one of Mike's barrels.
> You will let the old shanty go to rot.

Such poems troubled black writers of the older generation in somewhat the same way that the "sordidness" and "defeatism" of Eliot's poem was shortly to cause protest in 1922, since most readers still expected poetry to express a more liberal, optimistic, and high-minded vision. To a writer like James Weldon Johnson, whose emotions were deeply engaged in the racial struggle, such a poem seemed to despair of the battle, and he read it almost as if it were a betrayal. Today the bitterness of Fenton Johnson appears as much and as effectively a revolutionary stance as the noble hope of James Weldon Johnson ("Fifty Years") or the indomitable defiance in despair of Claude McKay ("If We Must Die"), but it is significant for the history of attitudes toward poetry and racial struggle that the older generation might not sympathize with a revolutionary gesture of this type.

In the 1920s the Johnson family, which had been comfortably off, encountered hard times. Fenton Johnson was no longer able to publish his books and edit his magazines and sank into obscurity. In the 1930s he worked in a writer's project of the W.P.A. He continued to compose poetry; some of these later poems have been published since his death but most were destroyed in the flooding of a cellar where they had been stored.

Neither by her family nor by her art was Georgia Johnson (1886–1966) related to Fenton Johnson. She resembled Sara Teasdale or Elinor Wylie in that she was a writer of short, musical lyrics in traditional forms, who flourished amid the ferment of Modernism and profited from the emphasis on concise, vigorous language within the modernist milieu. She published three books of verse between 1918 and 1928, and a fourth in 1962.

As a boy in Jamaica, Claude McKay (1889–1948) explored the world of books in the library of his older brother, a freethinking schoolteacher. At nineteen he became a policeman, but he was also writing verse. *Songs of Jamaica* and *Constab Ballads* (both published in 1912) contained fluent expressions of local black experience. Many of these poems were in the island dialect, and McKay was praised as a Robert Burns of Jamaica. He went to the United States, ostensibly to continue his education but actually because he was fascinated and appalled by its size and turbulent energies. He also hoped to develop as a poet and to reach a wider audience. In 1914 or 1915 he moved to Harlem, where, having used up his money, he worked as a porter, bartender, waiter, longshoreman, and houseman. Throughout this period he was publishing poems in magazines. His next book, *Spring in New Hampshire* (1920), was published in London; it was followed by *Harlem Shadows* (1922). By this time he was interested in Communism and went with Max Eastman to Russia, where the two writers spent a year. He then settled in France, turning out four books of prose fiction during the next ten years. After 1932, disillusioned with the development of the Communist state in Russia and increasingly depressed, he wrote little. In 1942, again living in the United States, he became a Roman Catholic convert. He spent his last years in poverty and obscurity as a teacher in Catholic schools in Chicago.

In mode and style McKay was confidently old-fashioned. Most of his poems voiced personal feelings directly, with many "oh's!," "ah's!," and even an occasional "alas!" He deployed rhetoric boldly and adopted such traditionally poetic phrasing as the "sable sheet" of night and "Peace, O my rebel heart." In rhythm, diction, and construction his many sonnets have their closest prototypes in those of Wordsworth, Keats, and Shelley. He most approached a modern style in renderings of black life in Harlem, but he wrote no more than eight of them. In sentiment and method some of these poems recall the Impressionism of the 1890s. In theme or content, however, McKay's work had a liberating impact on younger black poets. In many poems—for example, in his poems of love and sexual passion— he spoke out of a full, rich humanity that was not informed primarily with a racial self-consciousness. He was able to voice freely and directly his ambivalent feelings about America and about white culture. He cried resounding defiance, especially in "If We Must Die," a poem written in response to the race riots of 1919, which were terrifying to the black community. The poem was reprinted in an English anthology during the Second World War and maybe stirred the Edwardian heart of Winston Churchill, who is said to have read it in the House of Commons. The sestet goes:

> Oh, Kinsmen! We must meet the common foe;
> Though far outnumbered, let us show us brave,
> And for their thousand blows deal one death-blow!
> What though before us lies the open grave?
> Like men we'll face the murderous, cowardly pack,
> Pressed to the wall, dying, but fighting back!

Jean Toomer (1894–1967), who came from a New Orleans creole family that had moved to Washington, D.C., was light-skinned, and sometimes thought of himself as white rather than black. As he later put it, "My position in America has been a curious one. I have lived equally amid the two race groups. Now white, now colored. From my point of view I am naturally and inevitably an American." He studied law at the University of Wisconsin and at City College in New York, but abandoned law for literature. Making friends among the literary avant garde, he was able to publish short stories, poems, and critical pieces in little magazines. In 1923 *Cane* appeared, his first and, as it turned out, his only important work. A brilliantly promising book, it was typical of the experimental milieu of the early twenties. It mingled short stories, dramatic sketches, and poems to build up an imaginative impression of the rural South. In the materials it presented it sought the symbolic and the mythical, like other contemporary works in the high Modernist modes. It also shared their tragic vision of human life. It highlighted the ambiguity and self-conflict of human feelings, the violence and degradation of human nature, and the extent to which actions and emotions are formed by history, in this case by the psychic and social structures grounded in the history of the South. Although the protagonists cannot control their own destiny nor even know the deep forces that shape it, they take on a kind of splendor in their helplessness, for they are perceived with lyric intensity and endowed with mythical significance. Faulkner was not to begin to publish his major novels for another six years. Toomer's achievement was perhaps all the more unusual in that he had no firsthand experience of the rural South except for a brief period when he taught school in Sparta, Georgia. That an urban sophisticate who could pass for white should have written such a book, confronting a racial and historical past he could easily have ignored, was obviously a fact of much personal significance.

After publishing *Cane*, Toomer fell under the spell of George Gurdjieff, who taught the way to attain world or even cosmic consciousness. Toomer studied with this master in France, then expounded his system in various American cities. His marriage to a white Gurdjieffian disciple caused a certain amount of scandal; and the novels Toomer now wrote defended his system and his marriage and were rejected by publishers. In fact, after *Cane* hardly anything was published for the rest of his life, though he continued to write. He devoted himself in his later years to the study of psychiatry, mysticism, and the religious teachings of the Quakers.

Some of Toomer's later poems have now been published, but since they are likely to interest few readers, we may here notice only the fifteen lyrics included in *Cane*. They are uneven in quality and dissimilar in kind. They show that Toomer had sensitively read the Imagists and Frost and that he had heard or read the folk- and worksongs of Southern blacks. The poems were scrupulously planned: symbols and their interrelations were closely thought out and the course of emotion was carefully plotted. But Toomer's sensuous and imaginative fecundity sometimes got out of hand, obscuring his intentions. His most moving lyric is the "Song of the Son," which articulates, so far as

any single poem does, the personal and imaginative impulses
that led Toomer to write his book:

> Pour O pour that parting soul in song,
> O pour it in the sawdust glow of night,
> Into the velvet pine-smoke air to-night,
> And let the valley carry it along.
> And let the valley carry it along.
>
> O land and soil, red soil and sweet-gum tree,
> So scant of grass, so profligate of pines,
> Now just before an epoch's sun declines
> Thy son, in time, I have returned to thee,
> Thy son, I have in time returned to thee.
>
> In time, for though the sun is setting on
> A song-lit race of slaves, it has not set;
> Though late, O soil, it is not too late yet
> To catch thy plaintive soul, leaving, soon gone,
> Leaving, to catch thy plaintive soul soon gone.

Countee Cullen (1903–1946) was the adopted son of a Meth-
odist minister in Harlem. He took his surname from his adop-
tive father, having been born Countee Leroy Porter. Just when
and in what circumstances he was adopted is uncertain. One
story goes that he came as a child with his mother, or possibly
with his grandmother, to New York, where he lived in poverty
until his mother (or grandmother) died. At this point the
fifteen-year-old was placed with the Cullens by the National
Urban League. But his widow said that he was born in Louisville
and adopted as a baby, his mother being unwilling or unable to
keep him. In any case, the Reverend Cullen was a central figure
in his life, and Cullen's career owes much to the fond encouragement he received.

He was writing verse in high school and at New York University, accomplished verse in traditional forms, and recognition
came early and easily. His poems were accepted by *The Crisis* and
Opportunity, the prominent magazines of the day for blacks, and
by *Harper's*, *The Century*, *The Bookman*, and *Poetry*. In 1925 Witter
Bynner, Carl Sandburg, and Alice Corbin awarded him a prize
for poetry by college undergraduates; in the same year Harper
published his first book, *Color*. That a young black poet had been
accepted by a well-established publisher was a significant augury
of hope and opening opportunity for black writers. Within two

years more than six thousand copies of the book had been sold.

At the age of twenty-four or five Cullen became an assistant editor of *Opportunity*, with responsibility for literary criticism. *Copper Sun*, his second book of verse, came out in 1927, and in the same year he also edited *Caroling Dusk*, an admirable anthology of poetry by black contemporaries. But his star, now at its zenith, fell swiftly. His argument in the Preface to *Caroling Dusk* that black poets should not accept the restrictions of racial themes and forms offended some persons, especially since he warned against the too-indulgent standards that may debilitate a poet who writes for a particular group. Others, though agreeing with him on these points, felt that his talent was failing. Troubles increased when he married the daughter of W. E. B. DuBois. The marriage took place within the Reverend Cullen's church, with most of the notable figures in the black community attending the ceremony. After a few months it ended in divorce and whispered scandal.

In 1929 his final volume of poems, *The Black Christ*, appeared. He still continued to write—a novel in 1932, translations, two books for children, a play—but he seems to have felt that his literary career, which had opened with such promise only five years before, was essentially over. In 1934, the Depression having dried up his sources of income, he became a high-school teacher of French in Harlem, and this work increasingly absorbed his interest and energy. He died at the age of forty-three.

Cullen formed his poetry on the example of the established poets of the English language. He emulated many but especially loved and identified with Keats, whom he viewed as an apostle of beauty. His use of traditional procedures was further confirmed by study at Harvard with Robert Hillyer, who assigned exercises in different traditional stanzas and meters. Many of his poems might have been written by a somewhat blander Housman, by a Keats with less imaginative and verbal intensity, or by a Shelley with less fantasy:

> Silver snakes that once a year
> Doff the lovely coats you wear,
> Seek no covert in your fear.

Cullen was not merely derivative; what he took over, he made his own. But too often the effect of his lyrics was diminished because they could not support the comparisons with other poets that they brought to mind. His best poems are generally those in which he expressed with moving directness his feelings as a black in America.

Langston Hughes (1902–1967) was born in Joplin, Missouri, to educated and ambitious parents. They separated while he was a child, and his father went to Mexico, where he became a successful businessman. His mother moved from job to job, and the young Hughes lived sometimes with her and sometimes with his maternal grandmother, whose first husband had followed John Brown at Harpers Ferry. He was a bookish child and started writing verse in grammar school. In high school he was introduced to the poetry of Masters, Lindsay, Sandburg, and Amy Lowell, and his writing was much influenced by these new poets, especially Sandburg. When he graduated from high school, he visited his father in Mexico. There was little sympathy between them because, Hughes said, his father "had a great contempt for all poor people," holding that "it was their own fault that they were poor." On this trip he wrote one of his better-known poems, "The Negro Speaks of Rivers." His father decided that Hughes should study engineering, and Hughes chose Columbia in order to see Harlem. He had no interest in engineering, however, and quit college after one year, thus forfeiting the financial support of his father, with whom there was a complete break. After holding a number of jobs, he embarked for Africa as a mess boy. On a subsequent voyage he jumped ship in Rotterdam and made his way to Paris, arriving with seven dollars in his pocket. He found jobs as a doorman and a dishwasher and then traveled to Italy with two Italian friends. His passport and money were stolen in Genoa, leaving him stranded for a while, but eventually he worked his way back to New York on a ship.

Hughes had already published poems in *Crisis,* and he now met Countee Cullen, James Weldon Johnson, and other figures prominent in the black community. He went to Washington, D.C., where his mother was living, and, failing in his effort to obtain a scholarship to Howard, took a job as a busboy at the Wardman Park Hotel. Vachel Lindsay stayed at the hotel one day, and Hughes copied out three of his poems and laid them on Lindsay's table beside his plate. The next morning he read in the newspapers that Lindsay had discovered a busboy poet. Helped by this publicity, he was able to publish his first volume, *The*

Weary Blues, in 1926. He now received a scholarship to Lincoln University, in Pennsylvania, and his second volume of poetry, *Fine Clothes to the Jew* (1927), came out while he was a college student.

Hughes was fully embarked on an astonishingly productive literary career. In the course of his life he wrote fifteen volumes of poetry, six novels, three books of short stories, eleven plays, children's books, autobiographies, biographies, histories, opera librettos, essays, articles, radio scripts, and songs for musicals; he also translated from Spanish and French and edited several anthologies. He gave public lectures and readings, taught in Mexico and in universities in the United States, and served as war correspondent during the Spanish Civil War.

The excellence of his poetry lies in its directness, vitality, inventiveness, actuality, humor, and sanity. He did not seek compression of phrase; "Dig and Be Dug / in Return" was his motto. Reading Hughes's verse, one should keep in mind that he was, like Dunbar, an effective reciter of his poems, and that they were conceived more or less for public performance. In many of his poems he caught the rhythms of jazz or the blues:

> Thump, thump, thump, went his foot on the floor.
> He played a few chords then he sang some more—
> "I got the Weary Blues
> And I can't be satisfied.
> Got the Weary Blues
> And can't be satisfied—
> I ain't happy no mo'
> And I wish that I had died."

He boldly exploited the modern freedom of poetic content and form in order to render the life, feelings, and speech of people in Harlem. Though his presentation was naturalistic, it was in some ways a sentimental naturalism. Remarkably many of the characters in his poems are whores, gamblers, drug addicts, gangsters, drunks, and the like, so that Hughes's Harlem becomes a lurid place remote from the actual city. The feelings of his protagonists were those implicit in the music on which he based his poetic forms. In jazz pieces they tended to be vital and insouciant and in blues they tended to be despondent, but in either case they reflected conventions. Nevertheless, Hughes's rendering of contemporary black experience was more realistic and vivid than that of any other poet before or during the 1920s. He looked further into the heart than any black poet except Toomer, sensitively noting the ambivalences and psychic harms to which blacks are vulnerable in America.

In the 1930s Hughes, along with many other intellectuals, was impressed by Communist teachings and began to coalesce racial themes with ideological ones. Blacks were oppressed not only as a race but as members of the working masses, and Hughes spoke both for them and for the proletariat generally, including the white proletariat which was envisioned as brother to the black. *Scottsboro Limited* (1932) is a one-act play on the celebrated case in which eight blacks, convicted on flimsy evidence of raping two white girls, were sentenced to death in Scottsboro, Alabama, in 1931. At the end of the play the eight condemned youths clasp hands with eight Communist workers, and the two groups utter in antiphony and chorus their united promise of a utopia that will end both "greed" and the "color line's blight." In the 1940s and 1950s he was one of several poets—one thinks especially of Rexroth and Patchen—who gave public readings of their poetry to the accompaniment of a jazz band, hoping thereby to develop a new popular art. Portions of *Montage of a Dream Deferred* (1951), a seventy-five-page impression of Harlem, easily lend themselves to such performance. The first section is a "Dream Boogie" and concludes:

> *What did I say?*
> Sure,
> I'm happy!
> Take it away!
>
> *Hey, pop!*
> *Re-bop!*
> *Mop!*
>
> *Y-e-a-h!*

(Hughes's technical inventiveness was at its far-out freest in this poem. One section even consists of a sequence of "Neon Signs.") His next volume of poetry, *Ask Your Mama* (1961), was explicitly written for a musical accompaniment. "The traditional folk melody of 'The Hesitation Blues'" is the leitmotif, he pointed out, and "in and around it, along with the other recognizable melodies employed, there is room for spontaneous jazz improvisation." The margins contain further directions for the musicians. A final volume of verse, *Black Misery,* was published posthumously in 1969. Hughes was sometimes ready to call an utterance a poem on easier terms than he should have, but the whole oeuvre makes a remarkably broad, rich, forceful, appealing impression. Though his poems already are widely read and admired, his reputation and his readership seem likely to increase in the future.

Arna Bontemps (1902–1973) wrote novels and other prose as well as poetry. He also edited several anthologies of poetry by blacks. Of his own verse he said with typical modesty that it was all composed in the early 1920s, during and just after his years in college, at a time when he knew nothing "of new criticism or a new look in poetry." The statement should not to be taken literally; Bontemps was one of many poets who usually composed in traditional idioms and measures and yet learned from the "new" poetry to articulate a wider range of experience and feeling and to write in a tauter, more economical way. Waring Cuney (b. 1906) is known for "No Images," which he wrote as a college student. Like his other poems, this is a brief, free-verse lyric, sensitive in feeling but with no marked power of phrase. Of the lyrics of Gwendolyn Bennett (b. 1902), "Heritage" is the most frequently quoted because of its theme, though it is not her best poem. It begins,

> I want to see the slim palm-trees,
> Pulling at the clouds
> With little pointed fingers. . . .
>
> I want to see lithe Negro girls,
> Etched dark against the sky
> While sunset lingers.

Anne Spencer (b. 1882) was librarian of the Dunbar High School in Lynchburg, Virginia. She published no book of poems until *African Panorama* (1970), but her work was familiar from the poems included in anthologies. She was a meditative poet, articulating conventionally poetic responses in elaborate imagery and phrase.

James Weldon Johnson (1871–1938) became principal of the black grammar school he had attended in Jacksonville, Florida, and transformed it into the first black high school there. He then moved to New York City, where he collaborated with his brother in writing songs and musicals. From 1906 to 1913 he was in the United States consular service in Venezuela and Nicaragua. During this period he wrote *The Autobiography of an Ex-Colored Man* (1912), an anonymously published novel that deals with the subject of "passing." He became a field secretary of the NAACP and then its general secretary, resigning his post in 1930 to take a professorship at Fisk University. He was killed in an automobile accident.

Some of Johnson's early poems were in Dunbar's minstrel dialect, but he soon rejected this, recognizing that dialect imposed comic or sentimental conventions through which the black writer was tempted to falsify his subject. His memorable lyrics are in standard English. "O Black and Unknown Bards" is an eloquent tribute to the unknown creators of the spirituals. "Fifty Years" asserts, on the fiftieth anniversary of the Emancipation Proclamation, the equal right of black Americans to freedom. "Brothers" describes a black burned to death by a white mob. The black, brutalized by fifteen generations of oppression and the stored-up hate within his people, has committed a crime; the whites torture him with ferocious cruelty. In the perspective of the poem the black criminal and the white mob are "brothers," for both show human nature degraded by the tragic history of black and white relations in the United States. In the power of its grisly detail and in the charitable profundity of its insight the poem reminds one of Faulkner, though in style it recalls Markham's "The Man with the Hoe," especially in its declamatory opening.

Johnson was intent on conveying, as one leading theme, the pride that blacks should take in the historical and cultural achievements of their race in America. The same intention prompted him to compile the first anthology of poetry by blacks in America, *The Book of American Negro Poetry* (1922), which was prefaced with "An Essay on the Negro's Creative Genius." He edited with his brother, J. R. Johnson, *The Book of American Negro Spirituals* (1925) and *The Second Book of American Negro Spirituals* (1926). The work for which Johnson is most remembered is *God's Trombones,* which caused a sensation when it was published in 1927. Impressed with the power and dignity of Synge's rendering of the imagination and speech of the Irish peasantry, Johnson wished to create a similar monument—and literary movement—for his own race. *God's Trombones* consists of seven sermons by a black preacher. Though Johnson did not use dialect, his free-verse paragraphs are in the rhythms of this indigenous oratory and his imagery caught the simplicity and grandeur of the preacher's imagination, nurtured on the Bible:

> And now, O Lord—
> When I've done drunk my last cup of sorrow—
> When I've been called everything but a child of God—
> When I'm done travelling up the rough side of the moun-
>   tain—
> O—Mary's Baby—
> When I start down the steep and slippery steps of death—
> When this old world begins to rock beneath my feet—
> Lower me to my dusty grave in peace
> To wait for that great gittin' up morning.

The use of the redundant auxiliary ("done"), the biblical, concrete imagery ("cup of sorrow"), the anaphora ("When I've . . . When this . . ."), and the allusion to well-known spirituals ("Mary Had a Baby, Yes, Lord" and "In Dat Great Gittin' up Mornin'") are typical of Johnson's style in this work. In an actual church sermon the last line would be a signal to the congregation to break into singing the spiritual.

Sterling Brown (b. 1901) attended Williams College, received an M.A. from Harvard, and taught literature, mainly at Howard. *Southern Road* (1932) was perhaps the most moving volume of poems published up to that point by a black American. Since then he has brought out pithy critical studies and anthologies of literature by black writers, but no subsequent books of poetry. The power of Brown's writing in *Southern Road* comes from his sympathy with the folk imagination as it is embodied in songs and ballads; he uses the folk speech as the basis of his own poetic idiom. These poems are in dialect, but the dialect is authentic and evokes none of Dunbar's minstrel associations. Hardy must have been a favorite of Brown's, for although there is no obvious influence from Hardy in his poems, the two poets invite comparison. Both make effective use of story or story elements, both are fascinated by the folk imagination, and both feel a warm sympathy with the humor, shrewdness, and stoic endurance they observe in the folk. Both invest their rural laborers with tragic grandeur and feel the mute, hopeless pain of existence. Both invidiously contrast the urban and the contemporary with the rural life of the past. A major difference between Brown and Hardy is that Brown remains closely dependent on his sources of inspiration in the songs and ballads of the people. He wonderfully recreates and potentiates these forms, so that, for example, in the lines we quoted at the start of the chapter he raises the type of song sung by chain gangs into a moving work of art. When he deserts these models altogether, as in his poems in standard English, he becomes less imaginative.

"Odyssey of Big Boy" is based on folk songs of the John Henry type; the speaker tells the jobs and women of his life and becomes a half-mythical, heroic image of the black laborer. "Long Gone" is spoken by a railroad man who is leaving his woman because the pull of the rails on his imagination is making him restless. The Slim Greer ballads present a rogue who is too quick and shrewd to be caught. He tells his exploits with a typically American, comic hyperbole. Brown was also interested in the blues as a type of folk expression; "Memphis Blues" and "Tin Roof Blues" adapt their form and content from such music. The feelings expressed in these poems are often bitter and satiric, as is appropriate to the blues style. They deal with urban blacks, and Brown seems to have regarded this group as deracinated and lacking in the strong, traditional values of the black rural South. Among his pieces in standard English, "Strong Men," an elaboration of a line of Sandburg's, is perhaps the most impressive in its urgent, cumulative eloquence.

With the publication of *Southern Road* in 1932 the first creative phase of black poetry reached its climax. Poetry by black people had achieved not only a new level of interest and excellence but also a tradition and an identity on which succeeding generations of poets could build, or against which they could react. During the next twenty to thirty years there was not the same sudden emergence of a wealth of new talent. Generally speaking, the younger poets who established themselves, Melvin Tolson or Gwendolyn Brooks, for instance, were skilled, sophisticated wordsmiths, completely aware—to refer back to Bontemps modest disclaimer—of the "new" poetry in all its aspects and of the New Criticism. In the sixties, however, still another type of verse emerged, composed by young men and women who allied themselves with the personalities, and adopted the conventions of the "beat" poets. They were reacting against the formal, cerebral poetry that had to be created in slow, deliberate touches, and that seemed reprehensibly disengaged from the crying need, as these poets felt it, for political, social, and ideological revolution.

19

BRITISH POETRY AFTER THE WAR
1918–1928

THE main drama of these years in the history of English poetry was the clash between Modernist and traditional modes. Had one inquired in England or America in 1925, most readers and critics would have agreed that the greatest living poets of the English language were Yeats, Hardy, and Bridges. In the second rank English readers might have mentioned Housman, de la Mare, Hodgson, Frost, Masefield, and Davies. Pressed to name additional American poets, perhaps they would have recollected Lindsay, Amy Lowell, Sandburg, and Robinson. The controversial poetry of T. S. Eliot was widely heard of, but not much read as yet. He certainly would not have been ranked with Yeats or Hardy. In fact, many critics still doubted whether Eliot's intellectual verse, so deficient in melody and beauty, could be considered poetry at all. Disillusionment, as Edward Shanks added in 1926, is at best "an infertile source" of poetic emotion, "and, in practice, the poetry which issues from it is thin and lacking in heat." Sir George Sitwell, father of Edith, Osbert, and Sacheverell, complained that "Edith's poems make *me* look ridiculous." (Actually this was not true, for Miss Sitwell had few readers, though her name was frequently mentioned.) Pound was known only in avant-garde circles. The names of Williams, Marianne Moore, and Stevens were still obscure to most American devotees of poetry; they hardly existed for Englishmen. London remained the poetic center of the English-speaking world, just as it had twenty years before. And in England poets still generally derived their technique, subject matter, and sensibility from nineteenth-century precedents. The tradition a young poet would be expected to assimilate and carry forward included the Romantics, Tennyson, Hardy, Yeats, and the Georgians.

The modern or contemporary movement in English poetry was still usually identified as the Georgian. Georgian anthologies continued to be published until 1922, and the years from 1918 to 1928 also saw one or more volumes from Davies, Gibson, John Drinkwater, John Freeman, Edward Shanks, J. C. Squire, and W. J. Turner. Perhaps the Georgians seemed the more "modern" because poets of earlier generations were still active, among them Bridges, Binyon, Sturge Moore, de la Mare, Chesterton, and Kipling. Had one wished in the early 1920s to predict the future course of taste, it would have seemed especially significant that so many of the most recent poets, those who emerged during the war or immediately after it, seemed to share the Georgian sensibility: Edmund Blunden, Edward Thomas, Robert Graves, Richard Church, A. E. Coppard, and Victoria Sackville-West.

By the end of the decade, however, most of the young poets were writing in styles altogether different from those of the Georgians. They had assimilated a more radical Modernism, which Richard Church characterized as the "American-Montparnasse" influence and viewed, typically, as a threat to "our native English literature." The Modernist idiom of young poets at the end of the twenties was created out of more sources than Church indicated. Eliot was a powerful influence, and so were French symboliste poets from Rimbaud and Baudelaire to Valéry. But the need to be unlike these predecessors was at least equally influential as a factor. The younger poets at the end of the decade learned from the immensely vigorous, densely symbolic style of talk that Yeats evolved in his poetry of the twenties. They responded to the shock effects of the war poets and also picked up Owen's consonant rhyme as a technique. In 1918 Bridges had edited and published the poems of his friend G. M. Hopkins. They had been almost unknown hitherto, and young poets in the 1920s were impressed by the novelty and vigor of his densely concrete imagery and sprung rhythm. The style of Lawrence is less traceable in English poets at the end of the 1920s, but his stark, uncensored directness and mythopoeic perception made their impact, as did his feeling of the depth and significance of sexuality.

Nevertheless, after one has noted the diversity of models and influences that formed the Modernist style in English poetry, one must add that three were especially important. Eliot, Edith Sitwell, Aldous Huxley, and Edgell Rickword are among the many poets who at a relatively early age studied the avant-garde French poets of the nineteenth century. Their own work reflected attitudes and methods of these poets, which thus became a part of their legacy to the younger poets at the end of the decade. At this time, however, the Metaphysical poets of the seventeenth century were a greater influence. Interest in their work had been growing since the late Victorian years. During the 1920s Metaphysical "wit" was emulated by, for example, Rickword, Graves, and Andrew Young. At the start of the 1930s it was cultivated by many young poets; Auden and Thomas are examples. The French Symbolistes and the Metaphysical poets were powerfully advocated during the 1920s in the criticism of Eliot, whose poetry illustrated how effectively their techniques could be combined or "crossed," to use his word, with other elements to produce a contemporary idiom. It should be added that admiration for both schools of poets had been growing in England before Eliot made his impact. Eliot was the third major influence on younger poets. It was a diverse, complexly working influence, for Eliot's style varied considerably in "The Love Song of J. Alfred Prufrock," the poems in quatrains such as "Sweeney Among the Nightingales," "Gerontion," *The Waste Land,* and *The Hollow Men.* Although younger poets assimilated what they could from him, they naturally sought to establish their own identity. By the end of the 1920s the most significant single feature in the situation of younger poets was, from their point of view, that they were coming after Eliot. They were writing for an audience he had done much to create or educate and they could not relinquish the dense, taut idiom that was established and expected. Yet they felt that Eliot's brilliant style had renounced some possibilities of poetry, such as discursive statement and personal emotion, which they felt it was vital to recapture, and they hoped to write in ways that would be more immediately accessible to the intellect or to the emotions. Because their dilemma was many-sided it is not surprizing that their early poems could not resolve it.

The development of Modernist style in England was accompanied during the 1920s by sophisticated criticism of a kind that hardly existed in the United States. The most important of these critics, Eliot, was an American, but most of his essays appeared in British journals. Among the notable moments in the evolution of this criticism were the attacks of Eliot and Middleton Murry on the Georgian poets. Though crude and unjust, these polemics are important as early expressions of Modernist taste. Eliot's *The Sacred Wood* (1920) gathered together essays of his that had been previously published in periodicals. The book was immensely influential, as was his *Homage to John Dryden* (1924), which contained three essays on seventeenth-century poets. In 1924 the notes and essays of T. E. Hulme were edited by Herbert Read and published as *Speculations*. About this time I. A. Richards' *Principles of Literary Criticism* (1924) was widely read in literary and academic circles. In 1928 *A Survey of Modernist Poetry* by Robert Graves and Laura Riding attempted to offer a description and explanation of Modernist ways of writing. Exploring one aspect of poetic language, William Empson's *Seven Types of Ambiguity* (1930) implicitly defended the Modernist complex idiom. Two volumes of *Scrutinies*, edited by Edgell Rickword in 1928 and 1931, contained critical essays by himself and others. The purpose of the first *Scrutinies* was to puncture the overblown reputations of such older authors as Galsworthy, Bennett, Masefield, Chesterton, and Shaw. As the title suggests, the example and opinions of Rickword had a strong influence on F. R. Leavis. The list may be closed with Leavis' *New Bearings in English Poetry* (1932). In this volume the new premises and tastes had hardened into a militant orthodoxy.

Taken as a whole, this critical movement denied the central and normative role of the Romantic tradition in English poetry and called favorable attention to other types of poetry in English and in foreign languages. It inculcated new criteria of critical judgment and advocated new reading habits, especially a closer attention to the text. From the autobiographical recollections of

British poets who were in school and college during the twenties one sees how important this criticism was in shaping their style.

Most of the poets reviewed in this chapter were not of the first rank. Hardy, Yeats, and Eliot are discussed in separate chapters devoted to their work. Some of the younger poets who began publishing in the 1920s did their important work or had their important influence in a later period; they include the South African Roy Campbell, the Scot Edwin Muir and his compatriot Christopher Grieve (writing under the pseudonym of Hugh McDiarmid), the Welsh Dylan Thomas, and W. H. Auden, C. Day Lewis, and Louis MacNeice. Discussion of all these writers is deferred until the second volume of this history where they can be treated in the context of poetry in the 1930s.

D. H. Lawrence, who is discussed at the end of the chapter, seemed at first to be a poet of the Georgian kind. Others who were or seemed to be in the Georgian vein were Martin Armstrong, Richard Church, and A. E. Coppard. The early poems of Andrew Young and Robert Graves were significant enough to warrant notice in this connection. John Galsworthy and Eden Phillpotts were poets of an older generation, and two younger poets, Hugh I'Anson Faussett and L. A. G. Strong, wrote as though they belonged to an older generation. The verse of John Middleton Murry supplies a transition from traditional to Modernist styles, and varieties of Modernism are sampled in the poetry of the Sitwells, Aldous Huxley, Harold Monro, and Edgell Rickword. No survey of British poetry in the 1920s should fail to mention the light verse of A. P. Herbert and Humbert Wolfe. There are also the two books of verse A. A. Milne wrote ostensibly for his son, of which *When We Were Very Young* (1924) was the first. *Winnie-the-Pooh* (1926) was in prose, but *Now We Are Six* (1927) gave a delighted world more poems about Christopher Robin.

CHURCH, COPPARD, AND YOUNG

Richard Church (1893–1972) wrote novels, prose, and some eighteen books of verse. Though he was friendly with Herbert Read, Bonamy Dobrée, F. S. Flint, Richard Aldington, and T. S. Eliot and took part in the discussions that led to the founding of

The Criterion in 1921, he remained unsympathetic to the Modernist movement. His poetry in the 1920s included descriptions of rural scenes, narratives, visionary allegories, and love lyrics. Some of the love poems were of a psychologizing, Hardyesque kind. His poems are often plainer in diction and more prosaic in word order than they might have been if written fifty years earlier, but in sensibility and style they are still closer to Tennyson than to Eliot or Pound. After the 1920s he devoted himself increasingly to writing novels, and his poetry went downhill. He was guilty of melodrama, coyness, and bathos. Martin Armstrong was distantly related to William Wordsworth, fought in the First World War, and made his career in literature as a novelist and poet. He was included in the Georgian anthology for 1920–1922. His poems are short ambles down beaten paths of description and reflection; in "On the Salt Marsh," for example, a storm at sea becomes a metaphor of "Passion."

A. E. Coppard (1878–1957) came of impoverished parents. He left school at nine, worked at various jobs, and finally became an accountant in an engineering firm in Oxford. A gifted athlete, he bought books with the money he received in prizes. He started writing short stories and poetry in 1907, but had little success in publishing his work. In 1919, with £50 saved up, he quit his job in order to devote his time to writing. His fame rests on his short stories. His first volume of lyrics, *Hips and Haws*, published in 1922, was followed by six more.

Like Church, Coppard found "the new mode of verse" unattractive; it "merely rumbled with cerebral bumptiousness." He wrote in free verse and in traditional forms, being as devoted to Whitman as to Bridges. In both forms he had his own voice—kindly, whimsical, humorous, and quietly melancholy. His poems in longer lines are likely to have an elaborately musical assonance. He created memorable rural characters in ballad poems such as "Betty Perrin" and "The Unfortunate Miller." He had gifts for unexpected, original metaphor and mythopoeic vision. Like Brooke and Hodgson, he combined the Romantic tradition in poetry with something of the formal grace, lightness, and wit of the seventeenth-century lyric.

Andrew Young (b. 1885) wrote in the tradition of Wordsworth's shorter nature lyrics, presenting natural things as exponents of human feeling or in interrelation with it. Davies and

Blunden were the contemporaries he most resembled. His descriptions cannot quite compare with Davies' in morning freshness of response or with Blunden's in close particularity, though Young is not lacking in these qualities. But Young, a clergyman, had studied the lyricists of the seventeenth century, and a quiet but pervasive wit, irony, and paradox gave his writing a denser, more active texture. His image of a decaying tree-trunk illustrates that he could convey intense emotions through impersonal description:

> Riddled by worms' small shot,
>   Empty of all desire,
> It smoulders in its rot,
>   A pillar of damp fire.

ROBERT GRAVES

Robert Graves (b. 1895) has been writing for sixty years in many genres—poetry, fiction, autobiography, criticism, translation, and studies in myth. His Irish father was a poet and figured in a minor way in the Celtic movement in Irish literature. His mother was German, a niece of the historian Leopold von Ranke. He started writing poetry in school. In 1914 he enlisted in the Royal Welsh Fusiliers, was seriously wounded in France, hospitalized, returned to duty, and eventually was sent back to England for treatment for shell shock. Near the end of the war he married. After the war he studied at Oxford, but soon withdrew to make his way as a writer. In 1926 he became acquainted with the American poet Laura Riding; a close professional and personal relationship with her lasted for the next thirteen years. The two poets went to live on Majorca, where Graves still makes his home. His career as a poet may be divided into three phases. The conclusion of the first is marked by the publication of a collected edition, *Poems, 1914–1926* (1927). The second phase is that of his association with Miss Riding. She exerted a strong influence on his writing and on his ideas about poetry. In the third phase Graves has elaborated a myth of the White Goddess (more lately it is a somewhat different myth of the Black Goddess of wisdom). These myths organize his presentation of his central theme of love.

He began as a typical poet of the generation of Brooke, Blunden, Sorley, Gurney, Owen, Sassoon, and Rosenberg. During the war he published three small books of verse. The first, *Fairies and Fusiliers* (1917), was typical. Though some poems were exceptions, this particular soldier poet did not usually represent pain, horror, fear, exhaustion, disgust, anger, and the like, but dwelt on humorous incidents or celebrated how war knits bonds of friendship or remembered or anticipated peacetime pleasures. In *The Treasure Box* (1919) and *Country Sentiment* (1920) Georgian lightness, charm, and artful unpretentiousness filled the blithe pages. There were folksongs, ballads, lullabies, nonsense poems, nursery rhymes, and other types that are less quickly classified but not much less traditional, impersonal, and closely governed by conventions. We are in the poetic milieu of Hodgson and de la Mare, although Graves was more intellectual than Hodgson and lacked de la Mare's glimmering, elvish qualities. Several of these poems contain suggestions of the ominous, cruel, and grotesque, of a lurking horror in the background or below the surface of consciousness, but such suggestions were present in other Georgians, including Hodgson and de la Mare, and were characteristic of the folk forms that Graves exploited for models. In short, the war seemed forgotten. In this accomplished but somewhat unadventurous poet no one could have predicted the future devotee of the White Goddess.

Yet we know from Graves's autobiography, *Good-Bye to All That* (1929), that in the years when he was writing these poems he was suffering severe psychological symptoms in the aftermath of his war experience—grisly nightmares, hallucinations, neurasthenia, and a deep, unfocused sense of guilt. Knowing his state of mind, one can find generalized or allegorized references to it in his poems ("The Haunted House," "Outlaws"). But the poetic traditions he could draw on gave him no way of conveying such mental states adequately. Furthermore, he had no wish to convey them. In 1923 he said that the poems in *Country Sentiment* reflected a "desire to escape from a painful war-neurosis into an Arcadia of amatory feeling." In fact, he continued for several years to escape occasionally into this region. He even developed what may be called the amatory nursery rhyme, love poems with nursery-rhyme characters and technique ("One Hard Look," "Henry and Mary").

Between *Country Sentiment* and the collected *Poems, 1914–1926*
however, the main evolution of his art was toward an anti-Romantic, disillusioned, lightly ironic, actively thinking type of
poetry, with formal elegance and economical, perspicuous
phrasing. The overall effect sometimes resembled the mature
verse of John Crowe Ransom, with whom Graves was corresponding. "Richard Roe and John Doe," for example, tells how
Richard Roe was cuckolded and robbed by John Doe, and how
poor Roe successively wished he were Solomon, Alexander the
Great, and Job:

> He wished himself Job, Solomon, Alexander,
> For patience, wisdom, power to overthrow
> Misfortune; but with spirit so unmanned
> That most of all he wished himself John Doe.

At other times Graves emulated the Metaphysical poets of the
seventeenth century. "Pure Death" has something of the surprise, ingeniously sustained metaphor, and subtle analysis of
feeling associated with Donne. The opening lines are memorable:

> We looked, we loved, and therewith instantly
> Death became terrible to you and me.

In other poems of interior monologue or narrated interior
monologue he represented states of psychological disturbance
directly ("The Pier-Glass," "Down"). One of his finest poems,
"Rocky Acres," had appeared as an anomaly in *Country Sentiment*. It expressed an identification with the buzzard's cruely and
violence:

> He soars and he hovers, rocking on his wings,
> He scans his wide parish with a sharp eye,
> He catches the trembling of small hidden things,
> He tears them in pieces, dropping from the sky.

The sort of poem that was now especially typical of Graves
conveyed moral or psychological insight indirectly by briefly embodying it in a symbolical or allegorical action. Often the poem
might better be described as a sustained metaphor. His diction
was that of contemporary educated speech, though many
phrases recalled earlier poets. His stanzas and meters were traditional, though he often returned to traditions that had been little

exploited since the Renaissance, such as Mother Goose, Skeltonics, and scansion based solely on the number of stresses with varying number of syllables. His attitudes were tough-minded, his insights shrewd and penetrating. He could be aligned with no poetic party and had at this time almost no following.

A FEW MINOR POETS

Some poets, young and old, illustrate that idealistic and genteel sentiment in Victorian styles could still constitute the accepted idea of poetry. John Galsworthy wrote verses occasionally throughout his career, though they were not finally collected as a volume until 1934. They show nothing of a novelist's sense for character, episode, or even for particular fact. Instead they are abstract, utterly insipid verses on "Love," "Beauty," and the like, and might have been composed by Soames Forsyte. That Galsworthy put little effort into them may explain their conventional character; but because they exemplify one mode of the poetically conventional in his generation they have some historical interest.

With Galsworthy we may place Eden Phillpotts (1862–1960), the regional novelist of Dartmoor. This amazingly prolific writer published over two hundred and fifty books, including, besides much poetry, detective stories, essays, fairy tales, travel books, and books on gardening. Since his first book of poems was published in 1905 he is, like Galsworthy, of an older generation than other poets in this chapter, but he is included because most of his poetry came out in the 1920s and 1930s. His early productions were newspaper verse. *Wild Fruit* (1911), the first collection that could be called a serious effort, contained poems in different conventions—genteel sonnets, eighteenth-century descriptive poems, music-hall songs in dialect—and the best of them had nicely swinging rhythms. The thoughts and language, however, were routine. Phillpotts usually must have taken the first epithet that came to his mind. Although his descriptive poems are his best, there is little freshness even in these. His work did not change much in later years. Some of his volumes are on the light or humorous side. Some of them are philosophic argument in verse, Phillpotts advocating rationalism, evolution,

good tone
Peaking!

and determined hopefulness. His verses improved in the 1920s, though they were still quite conventional and wholly lacked what he called "The Great Lines":

> How rare the master lines that soar and sing
> To challenge every conscious heart and ear . . .

If we ask why he wrote "conscious," the only pertinent answer is, "why not?" The writing is not sufficiently functional or intense to demand one word more than another.

Hugh I'Anson Fausset (1895–1965) was a reviewer and man of letters. He wrote critical studies of Donne, Cowper, Coleridge, Tennyson, Keats, Tolstoy, Whitman, and Wordsworth. He sometimes did as many as four hundred reviews in one year for the *Times Literary Supplement* and other journals. At the age of twenty-two he asserted in the Preface to *The Lady Alcuin and Other Poems* (1918) that "poetry, as I see it, must be a holding up of all the passions and emotions of men in their ideal aspect." He felt that "though this poetry may not add to the knowledge of men, it may add to their happiness" and held to this view of poetry thereafter, although he much refined it. His poetry is of the kind variously exemplified by Bridges, Sturge Moore, and Mary Coleridge. Nineteenth-century styles were still completely viable in his eyes, as were nineteenth-century opinions. Fausset might have said with Charles Lamb, "Damn the age; I will write for Antiquity!" He did not handle the old-fashioned mode with much success, however. When a sonnet begins,

> And if I die, what is it I should fear?
> A little tremor on the face of time . . .

one is not tempted to read further.

L. A. G. Strong (1896–1958) was known mainly for his novels, though he worked in several genres. His first book of poems, *Dublin Days* (1921), featured short monologues in Irish dialect. *The Lowery Road* (1924) contained similar poems in Devon speech. *Difficult Love* (1927) had lyrics of a wholly conventional kind, and in *Northern Light* (1930) the setting was Scotland. His poems were collected in *The Body's Imperfection* (1957). John Middleton Murry (1889–1957) went to Christ's Hospital and Oxford. In 1919 he became editor of the *Athenaeum*. The magazine ceased to publish in 1920, but Murry remained a familiar and important figure in the literary life of England. His talent was for criticism and earnest reflection rather than for poetry, but he published one volume of verse, *Poems, 1916–1920* (1921). Though a critical foe of the Georgians, Murry himself practiced for a while in Romantic and Victorian styles. He also composed free verse and attempted to emulate the Metaphysical poets. But however his style changed, it remained prosy.

Besides the prose fiction for which she is famous, Katherine Mansfield (1889–1923) wrote poems from time to time. These make one small volume, posthumously published in 1923. Most of them were not published during her lifetime because magazine editors did not want them, so they could appear only in journals edited by her husband, John Middleton Murry, and herself. There was, however, no reason why they should have been refused, except that they were mostly in free verse. Her talents as a writer of fiction are evident in these poems. Sensitively selected details are presented in a straightforward, factual way; they build up an impression or recollect an episode from childhood. The poems have carefully designed "plots," whether we mean by "plot" a narrative structure, a shaping of myth through interwoven metaphor, or a transition of feeling. Each poem is purposeful in the sense that it embodies an organized, imaginative conception. Each is precise in the sense that it embodies this without waste or spillage. Of the other poets writing in England in the 1920s she most resembles D. H. Lawrence, though the resemblance is remote. The two poets employ somewhat similar novelistic skills to express quite different personalities. She is sensitive, nostalgic, melancholy, gentle, and often slides to the edge of sentimentality, rescuing herself with a touch of humor.

THE SITWELLS

In 1916, though the World War was two years old, the important war poetry, realistic and denunciatory, had not yet been written. Imagism was intriguing poets in America but had made less impression in England. The poems of T. S. Eliot were still confined to obscure journals; his first book would not appear for another year. Keeping such facts in mind, it is easier to understand why Edith Sitwell's *Wheels* caused some excitement. *Wheels* was an annual anthology of verse, founded in 1916 by Miss Sitwell and edited by her. Her purpose was to challenge the Georgian anthologies by exhibiting a newer, more contemporary type of poetry.

Wheels was, therefore, the first manifestation in England of a reaction against the Georgian hegemony, the first at least that originated with English poets and caught the attention of the literary public. In fact it was, so far as Miss Sitwell's intentions are concerned, the first attempt of an English poet to create a distinctively Modernist movement. (Imagism might be called the first Modernist movement in English poetry, but although English poets participated in it, it was essentially the creation of Pound.) *Wheels* appeared annually between 1916 and 1921, but Miss Sitwell's intentions were not fulfilled, partly because her own premises about poetry were not clearly formulated and focused but chiefly because she did not capture for *Wheels* the more daringly or powerfully Modernist poems written in England. They were scattered through other journals and anthologies. In her own poems in *Wheels* Miss Sitwell's style was not yet fully mature; and the other poets she included were mostly either too young or too unenterprising to make a definite contribution. As a result, *Wheels* makes rather tame reading, but sixty years ago some reviewers found it radically modern or avantgarde. The reasons they mentioned were chiefly that the *Wheels* poets did not write about country things and were often despairing. The major reason was probably the reputation for rebellious modernity that Edith and her two brothers, Osbert and Sacheverell, were already beginning to acquire. *Wheels* featured poems by the three Sitwells, Nancy Cunard, Arnold James, Iris Tree, E. W. Tennant, Aldous Huxley, and Sherard Vines and published seven poems of Wilfred Owen in 1919.

Edith Sitwell (1887–1964) came of an old, wealthy, and titled family and passed her childhood amid the splendors of the ancestral estate, Renishaw Park, in Derbyshire. If we credit the autobiographical recollections (*Taken Care Of,* 1965) she wrote out at the embittered end of her life, her childhood was unhappy. She was plagued by doctors; trying to correct a curvature of the spine, they kept her in braces. She was an ugly duckling to her parents—she was ungainly in appearance, without interest in sports, and passionately fond of music and poetry. She knew Pope's *The Rape of the Lock* by heart, delighted in Swinburne, and was deep into Rimbaud, Mallarmé, Baudelaire, and other French poets. At the age of five she had already declared her intention of becoming a "genius" when she grew up.

In her first book of poems (*The Mother and Other Poems,* 1915) the imagery and diction were studded with Romantic clichés: "love's gold argosies" and "ope your dreamy eyes" are samples. One virtue of these poems was an unusual degree of visual sensitivity, at least of unusual ingenuity in elaborating visual images. A year later she published, with her brother Osbert, a joint volume, *Twentieth Century Harlequinade and Other Poems.* The two Sitwells had temporarily put the Romantic age behind them. They gazed on the spiritual emptiness of contemporary civilization. They tried out attitudes of light and mocking cynicism. They sought new metaphors:

> Then underneath the veilèd eyes
> Of houses, darkness lies—
> Tall houses; like a hopeless prayer
> They cleave the sly dumb air.

In June 1923 an audience at the Aeolian Hall in London was subjected to a new type of theatrical entertainment. They viewed a curtain with two masks painted on it. Nobody appeared before the curtain, but from behind the masks two voices boomed through megaphones. One was Osbert Sitwell's, announcing the poems as master of ceremonies. The other was Edith Sitwell's, reading the twenty-one lyrics of her new suite, *Façade.* There was a musical accompaniment by William Walton. The poems sounded like this:

> Cried the navy-blue ghost
> Of Mr. Belaker
> The allegro Negro cocktail-shaker . . . ;

and like this:

> Old
> Sir
> Faulk,
> Tall as a stork,
> Before the honeyed fruits of dawn were ripe, would walk
> And stalk with a gun
> The reynard-colored sun . . .;

and like this:

> When
>
> > Don
>
> Pasquito arrived at the seaside
> Where the donkey's hide tide brayed, he
> Saw the banditto Jo in a black cape
> Whose slack shape waved like the sea.

Nowadays we have heard *Façade* on records, pondered the poems at leisure, read other versions of them (for Miss Sitwell often published several different versions of the same poem), and had the benefit of her own comments on them. But it is not surprising that to her first audience the poems seemed meaningless. There were some cheers, but on the whole the audience was alienated and the reviews were murderous.

The poems in *Façade* and in Miss Sitwell's other work of this period startled readers with such phrases as "allegro Negro," "donkey's hide tide," "creaking empty light," "Emily-colored primulas," "noisy cock's crow trees," "furry" fire, and so on. "Creaking light," Miss Sitwell later explained, articulates the observation that "after rain, the early light seems as if it does not run quite smoothly. Also, it has a quality of great hardness and seems to present a physical obstacle to the shadows—and this gives one the impression of a creaking sound because it is at once hard and uncertain." As for "Emily-colored primulas," we need only reflect that "Emily is a countrified old-fashioned name, and pink primulas remind one of the bright pink cheeks of country girls." And if we think this unduly subjective, Miss Sitwell adds: "Obviously I could not mean yellow primulas, since nobody is of that bright yellow color." So far as I know, "cock's crow trees" were nowhere interpreted by the author. Presumably they are trees outlined by the sun at dawn, that seem to stand up ruffling and preening like crowing cocks; Miss Sitwell might have thought also that there is something especially clear and carrying about this sight, for synesthesia was a frequent characteristic of her phrasing. As for the "allegro Negro," possibly he was nimble and quick in his motions. In the "furry" fire the tongues of flame may have looked like fur.

Façade was a gay, witty, and gallant harlequinade, gallant because the antics of the harlequin both expressed and masked a fundamental despair. But it was more important as a fascinating experiment in technique than in any other way. Juxtaposition of images and themes was swift. Metaphors seemed to grow out of each other by free association. Everything was conveyed by rhythm and image. The special success was in the versification, which departed from the usual norms and yet moved with authority. The verse of *Façade* differed from poem to poem; in general it was neither conventional free verse nor was it metrical verse of a traditional kind. These were strongly marked and varying rhythms that recalled both nursery rhymes and jazz syncopation.

In subsequent commentary Miss Sitwell discussed the versification of *Façade* at length. Her experiments were "inquiries into the effect on rhythm and on speed of the use of rhymes, assonances, and dissonances, placed at the beginning and in the middle of lines, as well as at the end, and in most elaborate patterns." She believed that a great deal of meaning is or can be conveyed by the sequence of verbal sounds considered merely as sounds and cited the opening lines of the fifth poem in *Façade:*

> Said King Pompey the emperor's ape,
> Shuddering black in his temporal cape
> Of dust, "The dust is everything—
> The heart to love and the voice to sing,
> Indianapolis,
> And the Acropolis . . .

And she commented:

In the first two lines, the sound rises. "Pompey," in sound, is a dark distorted shadow of "Emperor" and of its crouching echo, "temporal"—a shadow upside down, one might say, for in "Emperor" the sound dies down in hollow darkness, whereas in "Pompey" it begins in thick muffling animal darkness and then rises, dying away into a little thin whining air. The crazy reversed sound of "Indianapolis," "Acropolis"—"Acropolis" being a hollow darkened echo of "Indianapolis," broken down and toppling over into the abyss—this effect is deliberate.

There is much impressionistic analysis of this kind throughout her critical writings.

Most of the poems in her next volume, *Bucolic Comedies* (1923), had been written before those of *Façade*. They were similar ex-

cept that they were not conceived as experiments in versification. They are light, fanciful, brightly colored poems that render
life from a mannered distance, making it resemble fairy tale,
nursery rhyme, folktale, or legend. The tone of feeling is flat,
hard, and slightly mocking. "Aubade," for example, presents a
kitchen maid of dull sensibilities, her thoughts limited to the
kitchen and garden, to the stove, carrots, turnips, and the like.
The title is ironic, for there is no joy or love in this morning
song:

> Jane, Jane,
> Tall as a crane,
> The morning light creaks down again;

> Comb your cockscomb-ragged hair,
> Jane, Jane, come down the stair.

In the mid-1920s Miss Sitwell returned to more traditional
and Romantic types of poetry. *The Sleeping Beauty* (1924) was a
long, musical, fanciful, and agreeable poem. Some typical lines
are,

> Night passed, and in that world of leaves
> The Dawn came, rustling like corn-sheaves;

> And a small wind came like little Boy Blue
> Over the cornfield and rustling through
> The large leaves.

Troy Park (1925) contained the veiled, wistful autobiography,
"Colonel Fantock":

> I always was a little outside life—
> And so the things we touch could comfort me;
> I loved the shy dreams we could hear and see—
> For I was like one dead, like a small ghost,
> A little cold air wandering and lost.

Elegy on Dead Fashion (1926), a poem in many quatrains on the
fashions in dress of the past, was reprinted with two other
longish poems in *Rustic Elegies* (1927). None of these long poems
showed much power of construction.

In 1929 *Gold Coast Customs* was published. The Gold Coast is
that of Africa; the customs are savage and shocking; and
throughout the poem these are juxtaposed with the "customs" or

mores of contemporary London, which are equally repulsive. The poem is composed in short lines and drumming rhythms. Miss Sitwell's anger and horror are vividly present as well as her sympathy for the poor and the victimized. To convey such emotions was a striking reversal in the poet of *Bucolic Comedies* and *Façade,* and so were the biblical and Christian imagery throughout the poem and the note of social and religious hope on which it ends. These pointed to the poetry of her last phase.

But first there were more than ten years in which she wrote relatively little verse. She produced a highly sympathetic, almost sentimental, biography of *Alexander Pope* (1930); her identification with him may disclose something of the way Miss Sitwell viewed her own embattled and difficult existence. She also wrote a novel about Jonathan Swift and a biography of Queen Victoria. Her book of *The English Eccentrics* (1933) makes very pleasant reading. *Aspects of Modern Poetry* (1934) contains essays on several major and minor poets. Her criticisms are independent but erratic and show no highly trained intelligence.

With *Street Songs* (1942) she re-emerged as a poet, but a poet of a different kind. These are poems of direct personal feeling and consecutive discourse. Some, such as the mordant "Lullaby" sung by a baboon, are tough-minded, disillusioned, witty, and grim. Others, such as "Still Falls the Rain," are less successful. Here she uses a long line and a repetitive, accumulative, emotive type of statement. This loosely constructed poem was much admired, especially by readers who craved emotional directness and sincerity. It was one of many she wrote in compassionate, grieving response to the war. From now till she died Miss Sitwell published seven more volumes of poetry and in them she wrote as a prophetess. Her themes and images might be called elemental or archetypal. One hears much of the sun, earth, love, harvest, honey, lions, darkness, cold, death, Cain, Adam, and Christ. These are not presented with particularizing detail but only in general reference. She holds or attempts to hold the great opposites of life and death in one vision or perspective; she resolves to "love" despite the fact of "death," or she asserts that in or through darkness and death comes the harvest: "Love is not changed by Death, / And nothing is lost and all in the end is harvest." She was much praised for these late volumes and acquired a wider following than she had ever enjoyed before.

Some of the admirers were persons of taste and experience, and many a reader must feel that I am unjustly hurrying over these late volumes. But however impressive their ambitions and intentions, many of the poems are orotund and wordy. To move from the antic despair of *Façade* to a vague affirmation, pantheistic with Christian trappings of redemption and mercy, may be a kind of personal victory, but the poems that express this victory have more the character of fervent chants or effusions than of realized works of art.

Sir Osbert Sitwell (1892–1969) went to Eton and fought in the First World War. *Argonaut and Juggernaut* (1919) represented his abilities as a poet at the start of his career. The volume included both metrical and free verse and the poems ranged in type from the insipid and genteel "Song of the Fauns" ("Out from our bosky homes we spring") to light or savage satire. *The Winstonburg Line* (1920) was a political satire on the English intervention in Russia in 1920. Sir Osbert continued to cultivate both a satiric and a lyric vein; and beginning in the later 1920s, he also composed poetic portraits of English types. He wrote novels, short stories, and miscellaneous prose. His chief work is his five-volume autobiography, which appeared between 1945 and 1950. His brother Sacheverell, who was born in 1897, is also more important as an author of prose than of poetry. His poetry includes pastoral verse and adaptations of Baroque or neoclassic poets; some of it seems slightly archaic in diction and imaginative habit. *Doctor Donne and Gargantua,* on which he worked intermittently for several years, is a whimsical, occasionally satiric narrative. His poetry is pleasant and sometimes charming but rather insipid. Were he not a Sitwell, he might have been thought a belated Georgian.

HUXLEY, MONRO, AND RICKWORD

The verses of Aldous Huxley (1894–1963) are often pointed presentations of human psychology or reflections upon the generally unsatisfactory relations of humanity to the universe. They are psychological or metaphysical commentaries in a continuing, ultimately religious quest. They dwell on the unpleasant sides of reality, though since they are also witty, they give an astringent pleasure. In versification they use traditional forms; their diction is not "poetic," but is in vocabulary and syntax the written English of educated persons. In his first volume, *The Burning Wheel* (1916), "The Walk" is an intellectual dialogue; "Mole" is an extended allegory; "The Garden" and "The Canal" are finely centered on symbolic images. In *The Defeat of Youth and Other Poems* (1918) the title poem is a psychologically probing sonnet sequence, competent but adjectival. *Leda* (1920) is a strange retelling of the myth in pentameter couplets. It runs the gamut from Romantic idealism and beauty in the description of Leda to a broad, satiric realism in the description of Jove's sexual itch. The poem narrates how Jove and Venus together plot the rape of Leda and how Jove, taking advantage of her pity for the swan, carries it out; Huxley's objective, impersonal presentation makes the story a cruel one. Other observations in this volume are similarly designed to shock: Saint Simeon Stylites on his pillar envies the "fetid vices" of the people below. Jonah in the whale sees "huge festoons of mottled tripes." In subsequent volumes, *Arabia Infelix and Other Poems* (1929) and *The Cicadas and Other Poems* (1931), Huxley's poetic texture was denser but he remained perspicuous, though economical. Except for their general intelligence none of his poems is really memorable. One remembers the point and the vehicle by which it is conveyed, but nothing in the phrasing and rhythm makes the lines stick in mind.

Harold Monro (1879–1932) was older than the other Modernist poets. In fact, if he can be called Modernist, the term applies only to his volumes published after 1917. In its successive phases his work reflects the general evolution of English poetry during his mature years. Until he was thirty he led a footloose life in England and Europe. Like Shelley, whom he read devotedly, he had inherited money and felt tempted to withdraw from the ordinary strifes and cares of the world in order to write poetry. But he also wished to do good to mankind in a direct, practical way. In 1911 he quit Florence, where he had been living, returned to London, and founded the *Poetry Review*. In this journal he associated himself with the Poetry Society, which proved an irritation, so in 1913 he founded a second journal,

Poetry & Drama. As an editor Monro was stubbornly honest to his own convictions, a virtue which led him to refuse "The Love Song of J. Alfred Prufrock." At about this time he felt that a new age was dawning and that men and women would henceforth "live more joyously and rationally." Perhaps Eliot's poem collided with these Shelleyan illusions. On most occasions his taste was better or luckier, and he published poems by Brooke, Colum, Pound, and James Stephens.

In 1913 Monro opened the Poetry Bookshop. At a time when most bookstores stocked little poetry this shop in Devonshire Street, Holborn, had everybody's. It became a place where poets and poetry-lovers browsed, getting acquainted with each other's books and personalities. It greatly assisted the younger poets in making themselves known. Through the Bookshop, Monro also sponsored readings. Yeats, de la Mare, Brooke, Pound, W. H. Davies, and T. S. Eliot were among those who performed. By way of introduction Monro often read Shelley's "Hymn to Intellectual Beauty." Edward Marsh published his Georgian anthologies through the Poetry Bookshop. During the war Monro was drafted and the Bookshop was carried on by Alida Klemantaski, who later became his second wife. As the years passed Monro fell into a vicious circle of depression and alcohol. His wife carried on most of the work of the Bookshop in its later years. It closed four years after Monro died.

Most of his poetry might be described as thoughtful statement in traditional stanzas and meters. Eliot remarked that from the perspective of literary history Monro belonged neither to "the 'Georgian' poets of one decade" nor to "the more 'modern' poets of another," but was *sui generis.* In fact, Monro began (in *Poems, 1906*) in typically Romantic styles. *Judas* (1908) was a long, blank-verse monologue intended to "disclose" the kinship of Judas Iscariot "with the money-victims of this and every age." *Before Dawn* (1911) was also Shelleyan in its diction, versification, and opinions. Readers were exhorted in the Dedication to "praise, worship, and obey the beautiful Future, which alone we may call God." Up to this point little in Monro's work could be called individual, though there were obvious sincerity and high-mindedness. After he had put himself at the center of the London poetry milieu, his verse began to reflect the various influences that beat upon him. *Children of Love* (1914) contains some poems that suggest he had been reading Aldington or H.D. "Milk for the Cat" illustrates Georgian taste on its sentimental side, but the cat is intensely real. "The Strange Companion" is a queer, bitter, ironic, and private utterance. "Suburb" presents a dreary city-scape. By 1922 he had joined the cry against Georgian "affectations," with which (he admitted) some of his poems had been tainted, and was writing a plainer, more direct and somber kind of poem. So far as one can judge from his poetry, the "modern" influence liberated him to use a language closer to authentic speech and to express the depressed, bitter, and disoriented states of mind to which he became increasingly subject. During the last ten years of his life his lyric utterance seemed to come immediately from his own experience and introspection, not from other people's poetry. Hence it has the distinction of confronting us with a definite personality.

Strange Meetings (1917) articulates moments of pain, mystery, delight, horror, or wonder. What typifies Monro is not only that he voices opposite states of emotion in different poems but that he keeps in mind that all these emotional states as well as the alternations between them are nugatory routines. Within all moments of life, whether painful or joyous, he was aware of death as the deeper, more essential reality.

> Oh, how reluctantly some people learn
> To hold their bones together, with what toil
> Breathe and are moved, as though they would return,
> How gladly, and be crumbled into soil!

> They knock their groping bodies on the stones,
> Blink at the light, and startle at all sound,
> With their white lips learn only a few moans,
> Then go back underground.

Real Property (1922) activates the question, what "real property" do we have. *The Earth for Sale* (1928) was his last collection of lyrics. They are even more direct and intimate than the lyrics in previous volumes in expressing his own fears and self-thwarting emotions, and they employ at times a cruder, more shocking imagery.

Between 1921 and 1931 Edgell Rickword (b. 1898) published three volumes of poetry. He also edited (1925–1927) *The Calen-*

dar of Modern Letters, and in this and other journals he published some of the more penetrating book reviews of the decade. In the 1930s, however, this brilliant man of letters devoted his energies to left-wing politics. He helped found the *Left Review* in 1934. With the exception of a satiric poem occasioned by the Civil War in Spain, he published no more verse.

Without being a follower or even an associate of Eliot, Rickword was a co-worker in establishing a new taste in poetry and a new manner in criticism. Among the many things they shared was a close appreciation of French symboliste poetry; and Rickword published a book-length study of Rimbaud (1924, revised 1963). He appears to have steeped himself in the English Metaphysical poets of the seventeenth century from an early age. He felt that the Romantic tradition in English poetry had been limiting from the start and was now utterly played out. He had a tormented perception that dim, crude routines took the place of thought and feeling in most of his fellow countrymen and felt that a responsible literary criticism was essential to the existence of whatever genuine culture might be possible in the contemporary world.

Of his three volumes of poetry, the first, *Behind the Eyes* (1921), showed an influence of the French poets Rickword had studied. Thereafter he rid his poetry of impressionistic feelings and Romantic imagery. In *Invocation to Angels* (1928) he wrote with a heightened elegance and wit, taking the Metaphysical poets for his models. *Twittingpan* (1931), his final book of verse, contained satiric poems, including one extended portrait of a fellow poet ("The Encounter"). Composed in closed, heroic couplets, the poem hit as hard, though not as imaginatively, as similar passages in Pope. Despite this development, his character as a poet remained much the same throughout the ten years of his productive career. His was a poetry of tension, ambivalence, continuously active thinking, and irony. He composed in traditional stanzaic forms, with meter and rhyme. The structures or "plots" of his lyrics are clear and purposeful. Images come thickly and carry much of the burden of meaning, and his condensed, concrete phrasing makes considerable demands on the reader. The speaker is self-conscious and introspective, analyzes his own emotions, and keeps in mind other, contrasting emotions, points of view, or truths that are or might be engaged within the same experience. But the emotional response is strong. Despite poems of physical, sexual, and intellectual joy, the emotions expressed are on the whole of painful kinds: dreariness, disillusion, repugnance, *Weltschmerz*. The title of one of his poems is, "Regret for the Passing of the Entire Scheme of Things"; as the dry irony indicates, the regret is mild.

D. H. LAWRENCE

Had D. H. Lawrence (1885–1930) written only poems, he would be remembered as one of the most important English poets of his generation. As it is, his poetry is overshadowed by his novels and short stories. His poems have the same qualities and vision as his prose, but the works of prose fiction generate more power, being longer and more detailed. Neither have Lawrence's poems any skill in the writing that is not at least equally present in the better passages of his prose. This does not make his poems redundant. There are hundreds of poems in his collected edition, each was a moment of perception and feeling, and he was under no obligation to adjust these moments to each other, as he had to do within the longer forms of a novel or short story. Hence, as with Hardy, his poetry, taken as a whole, may exhibit the range and variety of his mind and personality more fully than his prose.

In the practical struggles of writing poets are guided, however much or little they may recognize the fact, by theoretical premises, by ideas of what poetry is and how it should be written. Lawrence articulated a new idea, which his poetry exemplified. More exactly, he gathered together some thoughts about poetry that had been sporadically recurrent since the Romantic age and phrased them in a way so little qualified and so extreme that they amounted to a new approach. Precisely what his thoughts were is not easy to say, however, for although he felt them deeply, he expressed them with confusion. The most important statement of his views is found in the Preface to the American edition of his *New Poems* (1918). Here he contrasts a type of poetry which carries the mind back into the past or forward into the future with a different type, "the poetry of that which is at hand: the immediate present." The poetry of the past and future makes up the greater part of all poetry that has been written. The poetry of the present is best seen in Whitman. It does not become "of the present" by virtue of its subject matter but by having the character of present experience.

Whether Lawrence had pondered Pater's famous conclusion to his *Studies in the History of the Renaissance* I do not know, but it sounds as though he were partly echoing, partly quarreling with Pater. The present, he says, is a moment in transition. It has, however, no teleological direction. The moment is its own end and purpose. Neither does the ongoing, forever unfolding creativity of life bring forth any perfected form, ideal, or essence. At least this is true if we mean by the perfect, ideal, or essential something completed and isolated from change. And so, accordingly, with the poetry of the present; in it there can be neither perfection nor finality. "There must be mutation, swifter than irridescence, haste, not rest, come-and-go, not fixity, inconclusiveness, immediacy, the quality of life itself, without dénouement or close." As he describes a poetic form, he is also implying a method of composition. Immediate, spontaneous expression guarantees that a poem participates in a present moment of life. Such poetry will be written in free verse, for only free verse can remain fully and continually responsive to the immediate fluctuations of impulse. "The bird is on the wing in the winds, flexible to every breath, a living spark in the storm." Free verse was not for Lawrence a form that the poet manipulates, adjusting his cadences. It comes into being as the "insurgent naked throb of the instant moment." It is, or should be, "direct utterance from the instant, whole man."

The value of such a poem, in his opinion, lies in the extent to which it is authentic life; other criteria of value are either irrelevant or secondary. Immediacy is, for Lawrence, practically the same as reality, provided that the immediacy is organic and whole, synthesizing the depths as well as the surfaces. The self in the instant moment is the "quick of Time," the "quick of the universe." But the self must be the whole, "pulsating, carnal self," not some aspect of our being that we abstract from the whole and identify as the self. The poetry of the present is "life surging itself into utterance at its very well-head" in the "instant, whole man."

These ideas amounted to a rebellion against the "art-for-art's-sake" tradition, against the genteel formalism of Bridges and his school, against all that was tamed and reassuringly traditional in the Georgian anthologies, and against the restrictions of Imagism. Later they would run counter to the influence of Eliot and the New Critics. Though this particular concatenation of ideas was peculiar to Lawrence, elements of it may be found in many of his contemporaries—in the Futurists and Surrealists, in Aiken, Fletcher, and Williams, and in admirers of Whitman such as Sandburg. Although the most obvious, general tendency of English and American poetry from the 1920s through the 1940s was the cultivation of an intricately polysemous, deliberately complex manipulation of language, there was always a counter-trend or Cave of Adullam. To those in the Cave the dominant tendency seemed academic, cerebral, bloodless, and impersonal, and although they were not necessarily followers or even readers of Lawrence, they were in general sympathy with his point of view. To those of the dominant party Lawrence's Preface simply advocated throwing off the corset and sprawling in self-indulgence. It explained everything that was wrong with his poetry.

He did not always hold these ideas. He began under the influence of the Pre-Raphaelites. Up to at least 1916 Hardy was the strongest influence on his verse. Both poets present incidents and moments of feeling in a realistic way. Both are direct and even a little naive in phrasing, both a trifle awkward in gait; the lack of finish contributes to an effect of authenticity. They both wrote occasionally in dialect, and Lawrence even fell at times into Hardy's metrical habit of mixing iambs and anapests. Both locate their human figures in a rural landscape, and both have a strong sensuous and imaginative response to nature, though they do not see quite the same nature. If we set aside the powerful imaginative effects of Hardy's looming backgrounds and vistas, the best gift of the two poets was their ability to suggest the complexities of emotional relationships through minute adjustments of language. In this respect the sequence of Lawrence's poems on the death of his mother may be compared in kind, though not in achievement, with those Hardy wrote after his wife died (*Veteris vestigia flammae*).

In the realistic, quasi-narrative or novelistic character of this Hardyesque poetry, Lawrence was typical of several English poets who came to maturity just before the First World War. Like other Georgians he was often tempted to write in a weakly conventional, vaguely emotive style. His initial struggle as a poet was to rid himself of this. He hailed the first Georgian anthology, in which he was represented, as promising a "great liberation." But there were already obvious differences between Lawrence and the other Georgians. In such poems as "The Wild Common" and "Love on the Farm" he explored erotic feelings of a kind they did not touch on. Even in his early poetry he had a mythopoeic intensity the Georgians lacked. Animistic responses were already stirring, and the "dark gods" were more real to him than any deities were to the Georgians. Lawrence soon found the Georgian poets and their editor, Edward Marsh, excessively tame.

He continued to "modernize" himself, as Pound would have put it. In 1914 he read the Italian Futurists, whose work he liked for its "purging of the old forms and sentimentalities." They composed in free verse with a direct, conversational diction and word order. He steeped himself in Whitman. He appeared in Amy Lowell's Imagist anthologies and studied the work and manifestos of the Imagists, though he never agreed with them. One may see an Imagist influence in his poems on the death of his mother, for example, in the opening of "Suspense":

> The wind comes from the north
> Blowing little flocks of birds
> Like spray across the town.

By 1916 he wrote Catherine Carswell that "the essence of poetry with us in this age of stark and unlovely actualities is a stark directness, without a shadow of a lie, or a shadow of deflection anywhere. Everything can go, but this stark, bare, rocky directness of statement, this alone makes poetry, to-day." It is not a surprising statement for a poet in the vein of Hardy, but it has the ring of the modern age.

In 1917 he published *Look! We Have Come Through!* This sequence of free-verse lyrics was intended, said Lawrence, as a "story, or history, or confession, unfolding one from the other

in organic development, the whole revealing the intrinsic experience of a man during the crisis of manhood, when he marries
and comes into himself." The man of course was Lawrence, and
the poems record moments in the early years of his marriage
with Frieda von Richthofen. (The daughter of a German Baron,
she had been married to a professor in England before she ran
off with Lawrence.) In the best of these poems he conveys delicate and fugitive emotional responses and sensitivities by means
of simple statements and images. The diction and word order
are that of prose. The images and metaphors are fresh, unexpected, and specific, so that Lawrence makes one see precisely
what he himself saw. On the other hand, there is much Romantic cliché in the circumstances depicted—for example, he
associates sexual passion and a thunderstorm—and there is
much dull, inexpressive writing, some hardly above the level of
Hyde Park oratory.

Birds, Beasts, and Flowers (1923) is a collection of poems that
describes and reflects upon various types of fruits, trees, flowers,
beasts, reptiles, birds, and so forth. The animals and vegetables
become metaphors or symbols through which Lawrence voices
his insights, attitudes, and feelings. The awkward love-making
of the tortoise, for example, illustrates the humiliation to which
the "ache" of sex drives us all:

> Stiff, galant, irascible, crook-legged reptile,
> Little gentleman,
> Sorry plight,
> We ought to look the other way.

As narrator and commentator, Lawrence is continually present,
and the poems give pleasures analogous to those of good talk;
they are lively, perspicuous, informal, witty, resourcefully on-
flowing, and full of personality. They notice from fresh angles
and surprise with apt illustrations. But though the creatures are
used as illustrations and metaphors, there is a strong attempt to
describe them as they really are. Lawrence emphasizes how
other and remote from the human must be their sensations and
psychology and empathizes with them. Sometimes these poems
exemplify, as a theme or plot, the effort to overcome sentimental and projective interpretations of nature on the analogy of the

human. The well-known "Snake" expresses an especially complex knot of ambivalent feelings, which are gradually sorted out. There is the "educated" repulsion and the prudent common sense urging that poisonous snakes should be killed. Against this there is sympathy for the reptile in its snaky being. And there is the imaginative transformation of the snake into a symbol, so that the mingled fear, welcome, fascination, horror, and reverence of the speaker are directed not only toward the snake as such but toward the associations and connotations of darkness, death, the underworld, the erotic, and the divine that have been woven about it in the course of the poem.

Concentration on particular objects kept Lawrence's tendency to rant under control, relatively speaking, in *Birds, Beasts, and Flowers,* but few checks were operating in his next volume, ironically named *Pansies* (1929). The title may be derived, Lawrence explained, either from the French *pensées* (meaning both "thoughts" and "pansies") or from *panser,* "to dress or soothe a wound; these are my tender administrations to the mental and emotional wounds we suffer from." They are mostly splenetic. Some are epigrammatic in form and some are long, tooth-gnashing invectives. The objects of attack range from Oxford accents, machines, movies, the bourgeois, and "ego-bound women" to the financial system and "cerebral emotions." Occasionally there is poetry. "November by the Sea" ends in grandeur:

> The wide sea wins, and the dark
> winter, and the great day-sun, and the sun in my soul
> sinks, sinks to setting and the winter solstice
> downward, they race in decline
> my sun, and the great gold sun.

At the approach of his own death Lawrence wrote two of his finest poems, "The Ship of Death" and "Bavarian Gentians." Both speak with solemn splendor of dying as a journey into mystery and darkness and imagine the journey in concretely detailed, imaginative terms. In "Bavarian Gentians" the blue flowers are compared to torches from the underworld, spreading their "blaze of darkness" in his sickroom. "Reach me a gentian, give me a torch," for he will take the long way down into the dark, guiding himself with the "smoking blueness" of the "ribbed hellish flowers":

> Reach me a gentian, give me a torch!
> let me guide myself with the blue, forked torch of a flower
> down the darker and darker stairs, where blue is darkened
>   on blueness
> down the way Persephone goes, just now, in first-frosted
>   September.
> To the sightless realm.

PART FOUR

THE BEGINNINGS OF THE HIGH MODERNIST MODE

20

EZRA POUND: THE EARLY CAREER

THE high Modernist mode dominated English and American poetry for approximately thirty years, from the early 1920s to the 1950s. A few names and titles may call to mind the brilliance of its beginning: Eliot's *Prufrock and Other Observations* in 1917 and *Poems* in 1920; Pound's *Hugh Selwyn Mauberley,* 1920; Marianne Moore's *Poems,* 1921; Edith Sitwell's *Façade,* 1922; Eliot's *The Waste Land,* 1922; and, in 1923, Stevens' *Harmonium,* William Carlos Williams' *Spring and All,* Jean Toomer's *Cane,* E. E. Cummings' *Tulips and Chimneys,* and D. H. Lawrence's *Birds, Beasts, and Flowers.* The flow of important publications continued into the 1940s, by which time the ascendancy and grip of the mode seemed almost unshakeable. After the Second World War, however, the movement began to erode, not in academic and critical prestige (for it was soon incorporated into academic orthodoxy) but as a combination of values for practicing poets; by the later 1950s a "post-Modernist" poetry was becoming more widespread.

What is called here the "high Modernist mode" is really a synthesis of diverse types of poetry that had gradually been created and made available as resources or models in writing during the thirty years between 1890 and 1920. These included the careful and polished formalism of the London avant-garde in the 1890s,

449

the impressionism and dandyism of the same group, and the early uses of symbolism in Yeats, together with the growing awareness of French symboliste poetry. The United States had the tradition of Whitman. Also, the 1890s in America saw in Robinson an assimilation of methods and purposes usually associated with prose fiction. This assimilation resumed independent of Robinson in England and America during the 1910s. In reaction against the melodious and "poetic" diction of most poets at the end of the nineteenth century Hardy, Robinson, Frost, Yeats, and some of the Georgians cultivated a sinewy colloquialism that was subtly and dramatically expressive. And Kipling, Davidson, Masefield, and Sandburg exploited the colloquial even more boldly to render the speech of the people. The Imagists adopted a direct, spoken idiom, while emphasizing the prose values of economy and exactitude. There was also a tendency to express harsher facts and emotions; this culminated in the violence and satire of the poets of the First World War. Meanwhile, several poets discovered and eagerly responded to the fopperies and surprising verbal juxtapositions of Laforgue and the intellectual complexity and ironic "wit" of the Metaphysical poets.

To these developments within poetry we should add the impact of psychological and anthropological lore. New subjects and techniques were suggested by concepts of the streaming, irrational, associative flow of consciousness, the prevalence of mental maladjustment or neurosis, the unconscious mind, the revelation of it in dreams, the collective unconscious, archetypal imagery, and the universality and significance of myth as well as of the primitive or myth-making mentality. Also, poets were influenced by techniques developed in other arts, such as the leitmotiv in music and the collage in painting.

Although the Modernist synthesis took different forms in individual poets, Modernist poets generally shared the feeling of a breakthrough. The "movemong," as Pound called it in burlesque French, possessed an idiom that was not merely fresh and challenging but also, in their opinion, superior to that of the nineteenth century. For the new, Modernist idiom was either more intense—more packed, dense, polysemous—or else it was more exact and precise. Perhaps it was both at the same time. And the idiom permitted, in fact, had been created in order to convey a richer, more authentic rendering of reality.

The chapters that follow deal only with the years in which the high Modernist mode was becoming established; the period of its dominance will be covered in a forthcoming volume. Hence, although I take up such major poets as Eliot, Stevens, Pound, and Williams, I concentrate only on their early careers. They continued to write for another thirty to forty years, and the second volume describes their later works. During the years observed here each of these poets "Modernized" himself. For the most part they did so deliberately and with struggle. Our account of each poet traces the course and phases of his evolution into Modernism, noticing what it meant to him. In this way we come as close as is possible to the actual development of Modernist poetry as it took place.

Many Modernist poets whose careers fell roughly within the same decades as those of Eliot, Stevens, Pound, and Williams are not discussed at this point. Marianne Moore is an exception. Most of the other young poets who began to publish in the 1920s or even earlier—Robinson Jeffers, John Crowe Ransom, Archibald MacLeish, Edwin Muir, Hart Crane—are treated in the second volume, in relation to the period in which they did their best work or had their greatest influence. Since Yeats became a Modernist poet only in his last phase, I here describe his whole career. To do so is especially appropriate, since his poetry changed greatly from the 1890s to his death in 1939, and the changes correspond in some respects to the general development of poetry in his time. His work allows us to bring the long, complex history here narrated to a final focus.

POUND BEFORE IMAGISM

Pound's achievement in and for poetry was threefold: as a poet, and as a critic, and also as a befriender of genius through personal contact. The least that can be claimed of his poetry is that for over fifty years he was one of the three or four best poets writing in English. During a crucial decade in the history of modern literature, approximately 1912 to 1922, Pound was the most influential and in some ways the best critic of poetry in England or America. He had an almost unerring eye for quality. And of all that he read—whether Eliot, Joyce, Yeats, Flaubert, Voltaire, Dante, Guido Cavalcanti, Arnaut Daniel, the Anglo-

Saxon "Seafarer," Sappho, or Homer—he asked, what does it show about writing? Thus sifting, he developed principles of style which he conveyed to other poets in instructions that were intensely practical and specific. These had a large impact on style and form and still throw a spell over young poets. Finally, he spent much time and energy aiding other writers. W. C. Williams, H.D., Frost, Eliot, Joyce, Hemingway, and E. E. Cummings were indebted to him for encouragement and criticism when they were still unknown. Some of them were also helped to publication, money (of which he himself had very little), and reputation, not to mention more personal services of miscellaneous kinds. He did this for the sake of literature, for he did not always like the writers he helped. Without his harassed ingenuity, some of the brilliant literature of the early twentieth century would not have been written. Besides his labors as a poet, critic, and befriender, Pound also devoted himself to enthusiasms in art, sculpture, music, history, politics, and economics. Each of these influenced his approach to the others, and their complex interaction shaped his changing attitudes and techniques in poetry.

Pound was born in a mining town in Idaho in 1885. The family moved shortly to the suburbs of Philadelphia, where Pound grew up in middle-class circumstances. At least from his early teens he gave past and living poets the devotion some boys give to athletes. "The study of literature," he later wrote, "is hero-worship." In college and graduate school he specialized in the late medieval and Renaissance literature of the Romance languages—in, for example, the troubadours of Provence, the *Cid*, early Tuscan poetry, Dante, Rabelais, Villon—and this literature continued to fascinate him for the rest of his life.

That a chief urger of the Modernist revolution was also an avid trotter over the past, as Wyndham Lewis put it, is a fact of much meaning. Pound's awareness and use of many pasts was one of the characteristics by which he distinguished his type of modernism (and that of Eliot and Joyce) from the Georgian poets and from the "Futurists," as he called them, lumping most of the "new" poets in America with the followers of Marinetti. For him the former were uncritically continuing an outworn tradition; the latter wrote as if there were no literary past whatsoever. Both lacked the high standards of craftsmanship that a close study of past "masterwork" may inculcate and both lacked the range of different techniques and the critical and self-critical alertness a writer may develop through comparing and crossing different traditions. (To Pound most avant-garde poets of his generation in America—for example, Williams and Sand- burg—were Futurists, and he would certainly have applied the term to most poets of the present time.)

Although he held and promulgated the belief that the past must be known and used, he also held that a poet must "mod- ernize" himself and "make it new." The relation between these convictions caused him much anxiety. The point also teased Eliot, eliciting some of his especially complex critical formula- tions. No one has yet studied the extent to which Eliot's general positions as a critic were formed in a dialogue with Pound. But if one reads their writings concurrently and in chronological order, one sees that they were addressing the same problems re- markably often. And one sees also that the conceptions devel- oped in Eliot's essays must frequently have been suggested, or independently supported, or provoked in reaction, by Pound's conversation and literary journalism—just as Pound echoed and debated with Eliot. Eliot's suave and subtle criticism will be read long after Pound's remarks are forgotten, but Pound was first in the field. Many of the viewpoints he and Eliot later elaborated were originally articulated by Pound in connection with his study of early Romance literature. In this literature he observed that each poet had a strongly individual character but also ex- pressed the mind of his age. From the Provençal troubadours to Dante he saw an ongoing and international tradition of poetry, a style and a sensibility that continued and developed from one poet to another and finally culminated in Dante, who had been aware of his predecessors and built on their work, and had thus expressed what Eliot later called the "mind of Europe" in that phase of its evolution. One may add parenthetically that early Romance poetry was difficult to read and that to understand it often required special information; in these respects it was un- like the poetry written in America and England in Pound's youth but not unlike the poetry he would eventually write.

He also admired the qualities and performances of Browning ("Ueberhaupt ich stamm aus Browning," he later wrote), Ros- setti ("my father and my mother" in "my knowledge of Tuscan poetry"), Swinburne, Yeats (he was "drunk" with "Celticism"), Symons (almost a "god"), Fiona McLeod, and Ernest Dowson. All of these enthusiasms are visible in his first volume of verse, *A Lume Spento*. This was printed at his own expense in 1908 in Venice, to which city he had migrated after a brief experience of teaching at Wabash College in Indiana. In Venice he lived at first over a bakery, tried to earn money as a gondolier (his muscles were not strong enough), and enjoyed the company of a lady piano player fifteen years older than himself. He soon made his way to London, arriving in September 1908 with a few copies of *A Lume Spento* and £3 cash. He saw Ford Madox Hueffer frequently, attended Yeats's Monday evenings, Ernest Rhys's evenings, the Poets' Club, and Hulme's evenings at the Eiffel Tower restaurant.

He went to London because it was the literary capital of the English-speaking world. "London, deah old London," he wrote W. C. Williams in 1909, "is the place for poetry." In his next letter, commenting on Williams' recently published *Poems,* he wondered how many of the poems his friend would have published had he known the current poetry in London: "You are out of touch." But if London was the place to master the "complete art" and also to make one's reputation in both England and the United States, it was shrewd to arrive in London as a published poet, which may be one reason why Pound paid for *A Lume Spento* in Venice. His gift for literary salesmanship, which later boomed so many reputations, was first applied to his own.

During the next four years four volumes of his verse appeared: *A Quinzaine for this Yule* (1908), *Personae* (1909), *Exultations* (1909), and *Canzoni* (1911). These volumes contained such still-anthologized favorites as "Cino," "Na Audiart," "Sestina: Altaforte," and the "Ballad of the Goodly Fere." Collectively, these volumes show Pound before he "modernized" himself, while he was still in many respects a typical Edwardian poet. He was at this time making no special effort to be modern, unlike such otherwise diverse poets as Kipling, Masefield, and Symons. Often his poems adopted styles of the past—for example, of Bertran de Born or Villon—and whatever the many explanations for his writing such poems, the poems would not have seemed unusual to readers of Robert Bridges, Sturge Moore, or Mary Coleridge, poets who felt that the past was never out of date; what had been written long ago could be written again in the same style, for one might still feel just as those poets had felt.

Viewed in the context of Edwardian verse, Pound's early work is uncommonly excellent—energetic, crowded with thought, and varied in artistic intention. (By "early work" I mean the five volumes of poetry already mentioned and *The Spirit of Romance*, 1910, his most important piece of criticism during this period, a book-length survey of medieval poets of southern Europe.) But it is not unusual in kind, and for this reason I dwell on it less than some readers may think appropriate. The mystical and occult elements of it are discussed in the second volume with the later *Cantos*.

Some of Pound's fundamental endowments and commitments as a poet reveal themselves in this first period. Of the early poems still retained in his collected shorter poems (*Personae*), more than half render a figure or aspect of the historical past rather than the present. But his fascination with the past was not with events and characters as such; it was with states of mind and the milieus that shaped them. What he sought to present in Arnaut Daniel or Guido Cavalcanti, and later in Sigismundo Malatesta, John Adams, and his other major exemplars, was not only an individual but also the "mind" of an historical period, which may be seen in the individual and especially in his verbal style. Pound writes in sympathetic identification. The speakers are Cino, Bertran de Born, François Villon, or Peire Vidal; we encounter their temperament, experience, and style, not Pound's.

Most of the historical figures with whom Pound identified were poets; in poems without such speakers the subject usually has some connection with his own personal preoccupation with the question of what sort of poetry to write. *The Spirit of Romance* is the criticism of a poet seeking models and instructions. Thus his better poems, such as "Sestina: Altaforte" or "Villonaud for this Yule," fulfilled at least three impulses at the same time: they were history, the representation of figures or states of mind out of the past; they were acts of identification; and they were exercises in ways of writing he admired. Many of Pound's more extended efforts in the next fifteen years—*Cathay*, "Homage to Sextus Propertius," "Hugh Selwyn Mauberley," the uses of Homer and Ovid in the early *Cantos*, the Malatesta *Cantos*—were similarly shaped by this triple motivation.

Although poetry and the other arts were Pound's main concern throughout his life, he was seldom willing to make them his main subject. The fact is much to his credit, for it was a victory of conscience, but the credit belongs also to his early milieu. So far as poetry is concerned, the greatest fact of the years 1900 to 1914, if literary history ever permits such generalizations, was that Yeats was changing his style. He was dispelling the vapors and yearnings of his early verse and was thus the most distinguished and articulate exponent of a general reaction of poets against the avant-garde of the nineties. Though Yeats's opinions were as always many-sided, the direction of his thought was: a poet's experience must not be that of the artist's cell but full, varied, active, and abroad, so that he may have the intense emotions of actual life; he should write direct, "personal utterance"; his words should take their force from his life, as with a character in a play. But Yeats was mingling two doctrines, and Pound agreed with one and not the other. So far as "personal utterance" meant self-expression, Pound usually rejected it. But that poetry should reflect life, not art, he affirmed often and with fervor, for he was struggling against himself. "Art that mirrors art is unsatisfactory," he said, meditating on Camoëns, "and the great poem, 'Ignes da Castro,' was written in deeds by King Pedro. No poem can have as much force as the simplest narration of events themselves." A favorite example for Yeats (and for Synge in his influential Preface to his *Poems,* 1909) was Villon. When Pound came to Villon in *The Spirit of Romance,* he said: "Villon's verse is real, because he lived it . . . [It is] no brew of books, no distillation of sources . . . His poems treat of actualities . . . filth is filth, crime is crime, neither crime nor filth is gilded. They are not considered as strange delights and forbidden luxuries, accessible only to the adventurous few."

Pound's early verse is often of this "lived" kind, and powerfully so—though in a special way. In "Cino," "Na Audiart," "Villonaud for this Yule," "Sestina: Altaforte," and "Ballad of the Goodly Fere," the speakers are completely unlike fin-de-siècle poets; they are warriors, vagabonds, lovers, as well as poets; their strong emotions rise from their own experience. Bertran de Born, who speaks in "Sestina: Altaforte," is an example. When the battle standards are spread, he says, "Then howl I my heart nigh mad with rejoicing." And we believe him; for we hear the howl in the cluster of long and stressed syllables. With respect to Pound himself, the poem is a "brew of books," a "distillation of sources." It depicts an ideal type of poet and in the last analysis expresses the self-criticism of the modern poet, not the direct engagement in life of the medieval one. But no matter. Such poems were still in keeping with the essential Yeatsian doctrine that "art that mirrors art is unsatisfactory."

Concrete presentation was already Pound's preferred mode of expression. In his early poetry he was more or less faithful to the Pre-Raphaelite principle that poetry must not weaken its force by discussion and reflection. In *The Spirit of Romance* he let his authors speak for themselves in quotations and translations: his remarks about them are relatively scant and mostly factual. In an important series of articles and translations in 1911 ("I Gather the Limbs of Osiris") he argues for a "new method in scholarship," a method that presents and relies on the "luminous detail," on the telling fact that gives "sudden insight into circumjacent conditions, into their causes, their effects, into sequence, and law." For example, in 1422 "the Venetians refused to make war upon the Milanese because they held that any war between buyer and seller must prove profitable to neither"; the fact shows that the Middle Ages were giving way to the modern era with its commercial motivations. A "few dozen facts of this nature give us intelligence of a period." The artist, he adds, "seeks out luminous detail. He does not comment." The fragmentary, continuously concrete style of the *Cantos* had its roots in techniques and convictions that were forming between 1908 and 1911.

POUND'S MODERNIZATION: THE FIRST PHASE

The story of Pound's modernization between 1909 and 1921 would involve all that he read and wrote, saw, heard, and lived through during these years. If I stress that he met Yeats, Hueffer, Hulme, Eliot, and Wyndham Lewis and eagerly read Fenollosa and Joyce, while other happenings go unmentioned, the reason is a lack of space, not that I imagine Pound's development is to be conceived as a sequence of a few encounters and reactions. But even if we notice only some significant moments, we can articulate the main themes and chronology, showing what modernization meant in the case of Pound.

His re-education began the moment he arrived in London,

eager to find out "how Yeats did it." The new stylistic values to which his eyes gradually opened are summed up in some of the ideas pressed upon him by two friends he now made, T. E. Hulme and Ford Madox Hueffer (Hueffer subsequently dropped his Germanic surname, becoming Ford Madox Ford). "I would rather talk about poetry with Ford Madox Hueffer," said Pound in 1913, "than with any man in London." In 1937, when Harriet Monroe reprinted in her autobiography some precepts Pound had sent her in letters twenty-five years before, Pound added a footnote: "It should be realized that Ford Madox Ford had been hammering this point of view into me from the time I first met him (1908 or 1909) and that I owe him anything that I don't owe myself for having saved me from the academic influences then raging in London." The point of view Pound credited to Hueffer is that

Poetry must be *as well written as prose*. Its language must be a fine language, departing in no way from speech save by a heightened intensity (i.e. simplicity). There must be no book words, no periphrases, no inversions. It must be as simple as De Maupassant's best prose, and as hard as Stendhal's. . . . Objectivity and again objectivity, and expression: no hindside-beforeness, no straddled adjectives (as 'addled mosses dank'), no Tennysonianness of speech; nothing—nothing that you couldn't, in some circumstance, in the stress of some emotion, actually say. Every literaryism, every book word, fritters away a scrap of the reader's patience, a scrap of his sense of your sincerity.

That the language of poetry should be modeled on speech was a commonplace by this time. But Hueffer went further. Insisting on what Pound called the "prose tradition" in poetry, he praised clarity, precision, objectivity, contemporaneity, and, in Pound's phrase a "hard" or unsentimental "constatation of fact"; the doctrine was radical.

The "hammerings" of Ford must often have struck the same place as those of T. E. Hulme (1883–1917). Hulme was a huge, colorful, overbearing, "ham-faced, idle man," as Sir John Squire later remembered him, who spent much of his time arguing or monologuing among his friends. He pocketed, synthesized, and put in a catchy way some of the newer ideas running loose at the time. (His generalizations had a powerful attraction for T. S. Eliot.) Just how much Pound picked up from Hulme is a puzzle. In later years Pound resented biographers who nosed out influences on him ("cut the 'influence' cliché"—though he boasted of his own influence on others) and, in contrast to his grateful praise of Hueffer, he dismissed Hulme's talk as "a lot of crap about Bergson." Most of Pound's recent commentators, taking their cue, mention Hulme only incidentally. On the other hand, Hulme voiced his thoughts regularly at meetings of the Poets' Club in 1908, and late in 1908 or early in 1909 he lectured to the Poets' Club on modern poetry, Pound attending. In 1909 Hulme assembled an additional group of poets—F. S. Flint, Francis Tancred, Edward Storer, Florence Farr, Joseph Campbell—who used to meet weekly at the Eiffel Tower restaurant in Soho. They are the "forgotten school of 1909" to which Pound referred in 1912, when speaking of the origins of Imagism. According to F. S. Flint, writing in *Egoist* in 1915,

what brought the real nucleus of this group together was a dissatisfaction with English poetry as it was then (and is still, alas!) being written. We proposed at various times to replace it by pure *vers libre;* by the Japanese *tanka* and *haikai;* . . . In all this Hulme was ringleader. He insisted too on absolutely accurate presentation and no verbiage. . . . There was a lot of talk and practice among us . . . of what we called the Image.

Pound was present on these occasions, he undoubtedly read Hulme's articles in the *New Age* in 1909 and 1911, he heard Hulme's lectures on Bergson in 1911, and he saw Hulme informally. There is a striking similarity at some points between the views Hulme voiced in 1908 and 1909 and those Pound promulgated three years later, when he began his great campaign to reform modern poetry.

So far as they dealt with the question of how to write—the only topic Pound was listening to—Hulme's opinions were, briefly, that the poet's job is to render what he sees and feels precisely, to get "the exact curve of what he sees whether it be an object or an idea in the mind." "Wherever you get this sincerity," Hulme adds, "you get the fundamental quality of good art." It follows that its subject has no bearing on the value of a poem, which can be worth just as much whether it be on "a lady's shoe or the starry heavens." Neither does the scale or kind of emotion matter. There is no need of "dragging in infinite or serious." The questions to be asked about a poem are, "Is there any real zest in it? Did the poet have an actually realized visual object before him in which he delighted?" Did he make one "see" the object "or idea in the mind" in all its individuality and fullness?

But language is a conventional and communal medium and resists exact expression. It is constantly decaying into abstractions, which cannot render experience in its full concreteness. As ordinarily used, it instigates no imaginative process by which, as Keats once put it, the object swells into reality. To overcome all this, the poet must present images. The image (which may also be a metaphor), embodying the object or state of mind concretely, arrests the reader and sets his imagination working to grasp the thing vividly and completely. Hulme usually speaks of visual perceptions and how to convey them, these offering the simplest illustration of what he means. Poetry "always endeavours to arrest you, and to make you continuously see a physical thing, to prevent you gliding through an abstract process. . . . Visual meanings can only be transferred by . . . metaphor . . . Images in verse are not mere decoration, but the very essence . . . You could define art . . . as a passionate desire for accuracy."

With respect to meter and rhythm Hulme's argument is similar. Each emotion has its particular character or "shape." A poet can embody and make us "see" the shape through "rhythmical arrangements of words." As Pound put it in 1912, "I believe in an 'absolute rhythm,' a rhythm, that is, in poetry which corresponds exactly to the emotion or shade of emotion to be expressed." The standpoint does not necessarily imply free verse, but justifies it. "I believe," Pound continued, "in technique as the test of a man's sincerity . . . in the trampling down of every convention that impedes or obscures . . . the precise rendering of the impulse."

If we combine the views of Hueffer and Hulme, we have the essential doctrines of the new, Imagist poetic Pound was to spread abroad so effectively in 1912 and 1913. But the conversation of Hueffer, of Hulme, and of Hulme's fellow poets at the Eiffel Tower must have had a further, in some ways more fateful, meaning for Pound. His Imagist manifesto and similar utterances of 1912 and 1913 had their impact as the basis for a new poetry partly because they were united with a scornful, particularized indictment of the poetry of the recent past and of the present day. These were not Pound's opinions when he first arrived in London. He came as an enthusiast for Browning and Rossetti, Swinburne and Dowson, Symons and Yeats and, on arriving in London, reported to William Carlos Williams that even the poets of "second rank" were doing "damn good work"; he instanced Margaret Sackville, Rosamund Watson, Ernest Rhys, and Jim G. Fairfax! Hueffer and Hulme turned him around. Hulme especially made him feel that a revolution was needed. To a young poet who had come to London in an intimidated frame of mind, this was exhilarating. He was suddenly no longer there to sit at the feet of Yeats—not to mention Ernest Rhys and Margaret Sackville. He cast a colder eye on the London verse and saw imprecision, abstraction, conventionality, and Victorian decoration. There was slush all about him, and with a suddenly energized self-confidence, almost a new identity, he set about cleaning up the mess. In October 1912 Yeats gave him five poems to send to *Poetry* magazine. Before forwarding them to Harriet Monroe, Pound went through them and made some changes. Four years earlier such liberties would have been unthinkable. Yeats was irritated, but it was not long before he asked Pound to "go over all my work with me" to eliminate rhetoric and abstraction.

By 1911 Pound's own verse was beginning to change. His vocabulary was relatively stripped of poetic diction; his syntax became more direct and natural; he compressed his phrasing by excising much that he might formerly have included, so that individual lines and phrases took on a greater weight of implication; images and metaphors were more carefully poised and expressive; and his rhythms, always his strongest gift, were now those of a master. But his poems were by no means Imagist; most of them were still not particularly modern in their attitudes or feelings; the finest was, typically a version of a medieval original, the Anglo-Saxon "Seafarer":

> Waneth the watch, but the world holdeth.
> Tomb hideth trouble. The blade is layed low.
> Earthly glory ageth and seareth.
> No man at all going the earth's gait,
> But age fares against him, his face paleth,
> Grey-haired he groaneth, knows gone companions,
> Lordly men are to earth o'ergiven.

The impact of Hulme, Hueffer, and other instructors first

showed itself not so much in experiments with new kinds of poetry as in Pound's greater "efficiency" as a stylist in the kind of poem he had been composing right along.

Pound's great work of 1912 and 1913 was his disseminating of the principles of style he had learned since coming to London. Meanwhile, his own "modernization" continued. He read recent French writers at the instigation of F. S. Flint. Flint's article on "Contemporary French Poetry" in the *Poetry Review* laid out various schools and movements of Paris (Unanisme, Paroxysme, Futurisme, and so on), each marshaled by Manifestos—why not also "Les Imagistes"? From the young Richard Aldington he heard about newly found fragments of Sappho's poetry and saw how much a few, disconnected phrases can stir the imagination. He read and was delighted with the "civilized mind" of Remy de Gourmont. He met Henry James of fascinating conversation, with its "weight of so many years' careful, incessant labour of minute observation." Soon he was reading "more" of Henry James. He discovered Flaubert's "exact presentation." In March 1913 the brief statement of Imagist principles appeared in *Poetry* magazine. One month later *Poetry* printed a miscellaneous batch of his poems. They include the much interpreted haiku, "In a Station of the Metro," but also his "Pact" with Walt Whitman, whom he had been reading in his enthusiasm of hope for the "American Risorgimento." Some of his poems in this cluster combine Whitman with Imagism. "Salutation," for example, might have been written by Sandburg. All these encounters were significant in the long run, but in the short run what mattered most were the notebooks and papers of Ernest Fenollosa that Pound acquired in the latter part of 1913.

A philosopher from Massachusetts, Ernest Fenollosa (1853–1908) taught in Japan and studied the art and poetry of Japan and China. Pound worked over his manuscripts in the winter months of 1913–14, when he shared a cottage with Yeats in Sussex, read aloud evenings to spare Yeats's eyesight—

> and his hearing nearly all Wordsworth
>   for the sake of his conscience but
>   preferring Ennemosor on witches—

and turned into verse Fenollosa's translations of the Japanese Noh drama.

In Fenollosa's notebooks he also found transcriptions and translations of classical Chinese poetry, together with an "Essay on the Chinese Written Character." These characters, said Fenollosa (whose views on this subject are not now accepted), are "shorthand pictures." The character that means "man," for example, is a simplified image of a man. A line of a Chinese poem is a row of such "pictures" (Fenollosa transcribed them from left to right). Under each character Fenollosa supplied a literal translation. Line three of the poem Pound translated as "Lament of the Frontier Guard" appeared in Fenollosa's notebook as (omitting the Chinese characters),

tree   fall   autumn   grass   yellow.

This meant, as Fenollosa explained, "The tree leaves fall, and autumn grass is yellow." (Pound eventually rendered the line, "Trees fall, the grass goes yellow with autumn.")

This poetry was received into a mind already prepared for it. The Chinese written language, it appeared, was undeviatingly concrete. Every word was an image; the line was a succession of images. Pound must have wondered how he might achieve an equivalent in English. The Chinese poetic line presented images without syntactical directions. Fenollosa's manuscript "Essay on the Chinese Written Character" pointed out that nature itself is without grammar or syntax, so Chinese poetry may be said to come upon the mind as nature does. However the method might be explained, it was a succession of images without the less active, more abstract parts of language that ordinarily connect and interpret them and it afforded speed, suggestiveness, and economy. Pound had by this time composed "In a Station of the Metro":

> The apparition of these faces in the crowd;
> Petals on a wet, black bough.

The poem juxtaposes two complex images without comment and obtains its intense imaginative impact from the suggestive relation suddenly effected between them. He had also reworked some translations of Chinese poems he had found in Herbert Giles's *History of Chinese Literature,* making, for example, out of twelve lines in Giles his "Fan-Piece, for Her Imperial Lord":

> O fan of white silk
>> clear as frost on the grass-blade,
> You also are laid aside.

Here again two images, clearly and directly presented, are compared, and they have a further, more densely suggestive and active interplay as elements in the larger comparison of the woman to the fan. Other poems more or less similar were "Ts'ai Chi'h," "Liu Ch'e," "April," "Gentildonna," and "Alba."

Reading Fenollosa's "Essay on the Chinese Written Character," Pound came on something else that was strongly to influence the way he thought about poetry and the way he wrote it: the ideograph. Some Chinese characters, according to Fenollosa, are "simple, original pictures"; others are compounds. "The ideograph for a 'messmate' is a man and a fire." In another example (from Pound's Confucian "Terminology," 1945), the ideograph that combines the characters for sun and moon means, Pound says, "the total light process, the radiation, reception, and reflection of light; hence, the intelligence. Bright, brightness, shining."

Whatever the ideograph conveyed, it conveyed in and through concrete instances. The character did not merely signify the abstraction "bright"; it presented the sun and the moon as examples. This was not only an advantage for poetry; it was, in Pound's opinion, an intellectual, almost a moral virtue that ought to be present in all thinking and expression. And the ideograph rouses mental energy, an activity of mind toward clarification and realization. Fenollosa held that whenever we encounter the ideograph (sun + moon), we do not understand it as the conventional sign for a third meaning (bright) to which the mind effortlessly repairs. Instead, we educe the meaning by perceiving "some fundamental relation" between the component parts. Pound must have seen that Fenollosa's account of the ideograph—"two things added together do not produce a third thing, but suggest some fundamental relation between them"—was one way of describing the effect of such poems as "In a Station of the Metro" or "Fan-Piece, for Her Imperial Lord." It offered another way of emphasizing that these poems were not images in sequence but nodes of relationships, systems in dynamic interplay.

In 1913 and 1914 Pound made friends with Wyndham Lewis, a painter, novelist, and ideologue of harsh pictorial and verbal force, and with the youthful, rebellious sculptor Henri Gaudier-Brzeska. He collaborated with them and with other artists in a new journal, *Blast,* which came out in June 1914, announcing in huge, black letters the forming of a new movement in the arts, the Great English Vortex. Pound's statement of Imagist principles had appeared in *Poetry* magazine only fifteen months before, and he spoke of Vorticism in ways that made it seem continuous with his earlier revolution. His Vorticist pronunciamentos differed from his Imagist ones chiefly in three respects: he caught from Lewis a more strident tone of voice; he acquired a new taste in the fine arts for the kind of work represented by the paintings of Lewis and the sculpture of Gaudier-Brzeska and Epstein; and largely because of his association with modernist painters and sculptors, he articulated his views on poetry in a slightly different way. Though Vorticism had an important place in Pound's development he wrote no significant Vorticist poems, unless we identify the *Cantos* as such.

Wyndham Lewis, Gaudier-Brzeska, and the other Vorticists "awakened," Pound said, "my sense of form." Their art was aggressively new and, in the case of Gaudier-Brzeska, based itself on non-European cultures—Egypt, Africa, and Polynesia. The Vorticists held that each art should develop the resources of its own medium or "primary pigment," as Pound put it; a carved stone should look like a stone, not like a *tableau vivant;* a painting should not tell a story, nor music be written to a "program." They were foes to sentimental prettiness but did not therefore go in for realistic "analyses of the fatty degenerations of life," as Pound explained, for their work was nonrepresentational. ("You understand it will not look like you," Gaudier-Brzeska emphasized, chiseling at his bust of Pound.) Art was an expression of emotion ("certain emotions which I get from your character," as Gaudier had explained) by means of lines, planes, colors, or, in the case of poetry, images. For although Pound's Imagist doctrine still seemed valid, he now emphasized that the Image is not mimetic. It is better thought of as a form produced by an emotional energy, as iron filings shape themselves when magnetized. It has a meaning, but the meaning is not "ascribed" or "intended"; it is variable, so the Image may be compared not to arithmetical numbers but to the letters—x, y, z,—of algebra. The Image is "a radiant node or cluster; it is what I can and must perforce, call a VORTEX, from which, and through which, and into which ideas are constantly rushing." Borrowing his terminology from sculpture, Pound thought of the Imagist poem as "planes in relation." If we view the first line of "In a Station of the Metro," with all its associational, semantic, and emotional connotations, as one plane, and the second line as another plane, "planes in relation" seems a suggestive way to describe the poem.

Pound now urged more than ever that poetry is concentrated presentation as opposed to "elaboration" and "dispersedness." "The Image is . . . endowed with energy." The Vorticist poet cannot possibly "get a vortex into every poem," but when he does, his words are maximally "charged." "The general weakness," he wrote Harriet Monroe in January 1915, "of the writers of the new school"—by which he meant Aldington, H.D., Williams, Amy Lowell, Fletcher, Masters, Sandburg—"is looseness, lack of rhythmical construction and intensity; secondly, an attempt to 'apply decoration,' to use what ought to be a vortex as a sort of bill-poster, or fence-wash."

Meanwhile, on September 22, 1914, T. S. Eliot paid his first visit; a week later he brought "The Love Song of J. Alfred Prufrock." "He is," Pound immediately wrote Miss Monroe, "the only American I know of who has . . . actually trained himself *and* modernized himself *on his own*. . . . It is such a comfort to meet a man and not have to tell him to . . . remember the date (1914) on the calendar." And Pound was now in active correspondence with Joyce, of whom he had first heard from Yeats and whose short stories in *Dubliners* he had greatly admired for their "clear hard prose."

Late in 1914 Pound started redoing Fenollosa's manuscript translations of Chinese poems. The result made one of his finest volumes, *Cathay* (1915). Everything Pound knew about writing went into these versions of Fenollosa's literal translations. Pound had no idea how the Chinese characters might sound when spoken and was thus free to shape the rhythm and sound as seemed best to him. But he kept one feature of the original form as Fenollosa presented it: each line is an integral unit of meaning. For line after line he laid clear, direct, idiomatic statement next to statement, spare image next to image. "The Lament of the Frontier Guard" is spoken by a soldier on the northern marches, fought over from time immemorial by the Chinese border troops and the nomad Huns without:

> I climb the towers and towers
>   to watch out the barbarous land:
> Desolate castle, the sky, the wide desert.
> There is no wall left to this village.
> Bones white with a thousand frosts,
> High heaps, covered with trees and grass.

If we use the terms Pound learned, probably from the Vorticists, "There is no wall left to this village" and "Bones white with a thousand frosts" are "planes in relation." If we evoke the criteria of what he considered "efficient" prose, we might say that these are carefully chosen and telling items, quickly and clearly set forth. The prose of Joyce's *Dubliners,* Pound wrote in July 1914, presents "swiftly and vividly." Joyce "does not sentimentalize . . . he does not weave convolutions. He is a realist. . . . He gives the thing as it is . . . he excells . . . because of his more rigorous selection, because of his exclusion of all unnecessary detail." In *Cathay* the factual, declarative sentences, the flat statement or understatement of emotion, the lack of interpretation or generalization, the allusions to traditional Chinese heroes, customs, and localities, all suggest an alien culture and sensibility.

In 1916 *Lustra* was published. Collecting poems written in the previous four years (including *Cathay*), *Lustra* exhibited Pound modernized. For the most part the poems are brief free-verse observations on poetry and society. They include satiric contrasts ("Les Millwin"), epigrams adapted or emulated from Roman poets, fragments from Sappho, haiku, and epitaphs. They rely on the poised image, as in "The Encounter":

> All the while they were talking the new morality
> Her eyes explored me.
> And when I arose to go
> Her fingers were like the tissue
> Of a Japanese paper napkin.

With its high spirits and terse style, *Lustra* makes enjoyable browsing. But such poems are slight, and if his career had ended at this point Pound would be remembered only as a reformer of technique, a translator, and a latter-day Landor who made accomplished bits.

Pound had come a long way in the eight years since he arrived in London. He had learned to look with scorn on the "common verse" of England and America from 1890 to 1910. He had acquired principles of how to write and had, he could justly feel, modernized himself in accordance with them. His influence was felt, his poetry imitated. If such "new" poets as Masters, Sandburg, H.D., Aldington, and Fletcher, not to mention Amy Lowell, had shown themselves not up to the mark, they were dispensable. A "party of intelligence" was forming about himself, Lewis, Hueffer, Eliot, and Joyce. They were the bearers of a new civilization, the Lorenzo Vallas and Pico della Mirandolas of a second Renaissance (of the first Renaissance Pound had no high opinion). As Gaudier-Brzeska worked in 1913 at his stone bust of Pound (it was, Lewis said, "Ezra in the form of a marble phallus") and Pound sat as model in the studio under the railway arch, he felt that had he lived in the Quattrocento he could have had "no finer moment and no better craftsman to fill it."

But there was no money and there was the war, and in these two facts, of which the meaning was remorselessly enlarged and clarified in the next few years, there is a key to much of Pound's later writing. At first it must have seemed that the war (which need not last long) would temporarily slow the Vortex, with Lewis and Gaudier-Brzeska gone off to the trenches, but certainly the Vortex would not be dispersed. But in June of 1915 Gaudier-Brzeska was killed—"There died a myriad," Pound later wrote, "And of the best, among them." While he was alive, poverty had forced the young sculptor to work in a studio under Putney Viaduct, the trains passing overhead, the floor mud; he had lacked money to buy the stone he needed for his work. "It was done," Pound said of Gaudier-Brzeska's sculpture later, "against the whole social system in the sense that it was done against poverty." Eliot was soon in hardly better case. Joyce, it seemed, was poor as a churchmouse. Also, there were bitter frustrations in trying to get their work published, as Pound's efforts were defeated by the dullness, laziness, timidity, and venal-ity (in his opinion) of the literary and publishing establishment. Lewis' *Tarr* was repeatedly rejected. When *Ulysses* appeared serially in *The Little Review,* copies of the magazine were confiscated and burned by the Post Office Department; its editors were brought to trial. If one believed, as Pound did, that "serious" literature was indispensable to the healthy functioning of the mind ("I mean it maintains the precision and clarity of thought, not merely for the benefit of a few dilettantes and 'lovers of literature,' but maintains the health of thought outside literary circles and in non-literary existence, in general individual and communal life"), it was impossible to accept an economic system which impeded it, which, because it valued profits, not craftsmanship, hindered fine and serious workmanship of every kind. "With usura," he wrote in his splendid chant twenty years later (Canto 45),

> hath no man a house of good stone
> Each block cut smooth and well fitting
>
> . . . .
>
> Stone cutter is kept from his stone
> weaver is kept from his loom
> WITH USURA
> wool comes not to market
> sheep bringeth no gain with usura
> Usura is a murrain, usura
> blunteth the needle in the maid's hand
> and stoppeth the spinner's cunning.

Pound did not stop with complaint and invective; he looked about for a way to remedy the system. Not that he withheld invective. A direct line runs from his experience and rhetoric in these years to his terrible fulminations from Italy during the Second World War. His targets in the 1940s were no longer editors, publishers, and the "cultured" public; they were bankers and their political tools (in Pound's opinion), Roosevelt and Churchill. But at bottom they were the same targets. The difference was that after thirty years he thought he had spotted the more essential and underlying evils and had a cure, if only the world would listen. The hurts and angers of Pound in the years from 1914 till he left England in 1921, results of the enormous hope and energy he expended, mark the beginning of an ultimately disastrous development.

HOMAGE TO SEXTUS PROPERTIUS

Pound's next significant effort was his loose translation of portions of the Roman elegiac poet Sextus Propertius. "Homage to Sextus Propertius" was both the longest and the finest work he had yet accomplished. He composed it between 1917 and 1918. Most of the moods, poses, and styles of the poem could also have been found in *Lustra;* the all-important difference was that they now interacted in a single work. The poem has a continually varying feeling and rhythm, subject, and method of presentation. It is spoken by Propertius, who thus becomes the main object of attention, and has some narrative interest from its fragmentary, allusive presentation of the vicissitudes of Propertius' love affair with the courtesan Cynthia. Our imagination builds up a sense of imperial Rome, its culture, politics, history, and manners. The poem is not complexly organized or interwoven, but because it focuses on a character, Propertius, and because it remains within and creates a world, as opposed to moving in swift comparison from one to another, one reads it with a sustained, cumulative interest that most of the Cantos do not engage, however much we may prefer the *Cantos* in other respects.

The character of Propertius represents an ideal of civilized intelligence. With the war in its third and fourth years, Pound strongly felt the preciousness of this and exhibited it in Propertius with a consciousness that he was keeping faith with his own values and also defying the state of mind of wartime England. As he expressed it in 1931, the poem "presents certain emotions as vital to me in 1917, faced with the infinite and ineffable imbecility of the British Empire, as they were to Propertius some centuries earlier, when faced with the infinite and ineffable imbecility of the Roman Empire." His Propertius parodies with gusto the windy rhetoric of poets who flatter the crude nationalism and imperialism of the public and its officials:

> Now for a large-mouthed product.
> Thus:
> "The Euphrates denies its protection to the Parthian
>   and apologizes for Crassus,"
> And "It is, I think, India which now gives necks
>   to your triumph,"
> And so forth, Augustus.

He reveals his own "civilization" by maintaining private fidelities to his art and to his dubious Cynthia. Moreover—this is what especially matters—he maintains them with an acutely sensitive, complex, ironic awareness and self-awareness.

This ironic speaker, with his ebullience of mind, his manifold and quickly shifting feelings and points of view, is sometimes said to be a Laforguian character. Insofar as he is an intellectual in love with (though unfaithful to) an unfaithful mistress, is fully aware of the humorous sides of his fears and passions and keeps a distance between himself and his emotion by foppery and self-deprecation, Propertius has some traits in common with the stock protagonist of Laforgue's poems. But Pound's Propertius includes the Laforguian protagonist as only one element of a much more various character. He can be fantastic, high-spirited, frivolous, melancholy, joking, and directly and intensely passionate, not only in sequence but in the same breath.

Reading and translating Laforgue, Pound was fascinated by a quality of style he had not so clearly discriminated before. He called it "logopoeia," by which he meant "a play in the shading of the words themselves." It is, he said, a "dance of the intelligence among words," that is, "it employs words not only for their direct meaning, but it takes count in a special way of habits of usage, of the context we *expect* to find with the word." In addition to Laforgue, he found logopoeia exemplified in Propertius, Alexander Pope, T. S. Eliot, and Marianne Moore. It is omnipresent in "Homage to Sextus Propertius"; the repetitive or parallel syntactical constructions common in the poem afforded a special opportunity—for example,

> The Parthians shall get used to our statuary
> and acquire a Roman religion.

The "play in the shading of the words" is felt not only in the individual phrases ("get used to" suggests the boredom of imperial statuary; "acquire" is delicate irony—"the citadel of the intelligent," Pound said—by euphemism, since the "acquisition" will come not by conquest but by being conquered) but in the "play" between the phrases: moving from the native and colloquial "get used" to the Latinate "acquire," the shading of the diction wittily reflects the process of conquest and acculturation. It is through the logopoeia of his utterance that Propertius defines himself most subtly and vividly as a character.

His logopoeia reminds us of Henry James. In 1918 Pound reminiscently described James's conversation, and the peculiarities he noted significantly resemble stylistic effects in "Homage to Sextus Propertius": "the long sentences piling themselves up in elaborate phrase after phrase, the lightning incision, the pauses, the slightly shaking admonitory gesture with its 'wu-a-wait a little, wait a little, something will come.'" What comes in Pound's "Homage" as in James's conversation is the *trouvaille,* the found, unexpected epithet that sheds a new crosslight. Speaking of the boring poets who write "to Imperial order," Propertius remarks,

> Out-weariers of Apollo will, as we know, continue
> their Martian generalities.

One senses the suspenseful pause between "continue" and the next phrase, the unspoken "wu-a-wait a little" before the *trouvaille.* Or,

> May a woody and sequestered place cover me with its foliage
> Or may I inter beneath the hummock
> of some as yet ['wu-a-wait a little'] uncatalogued sand.

And so, out of James, Laforgue, the original Propertius, and many other voices, Pound builds the talk of his own Propertius. Taking him at his most ardent in section II, we have, in the opening line,

> Me happy, night, night full of brightness,

a Latinate construction of the initial phrase, followed by a lapsed grammar that is pure Pound out of Chinese. The next line begins in apostrophe to the "couch," a typical bit of Laforguian fantasticality, and ends in a Latinate and Jamesian *trouvaille,* "delectations," that beats a Laforguian retreat from emotion:

> Oh couch made happy by my long delectations.

The underlying emotion breaks through such defenses,

> Though you give all your kisses, you give but few,

and the defenses are immediately, though only partly, repaired ("shift my pains"!)—and broken again:

> Nor can I shift my pains to other,
> Hers will I be dead.

I have been speaking of the poem almost as though it were an original work by Pound, but of course it is not—or not quite. It is a translation in which Pound sometimes closely follows the original, sometimes rearranges, modernizes, makes it more graphic, and puns on it. The fact that it is a translation strongly influences responses to it, whether or not one knows the Latin original. Readers who can trace the changing relation between the original and Pound's version may find the experience not only pleasurable but indispensable for appreciating Pound's intentions and his artistry; they may, on the other hand, find it a shock. No one is likely to conclude that Pound closely rendered either Propertius' language or his general effect. Readers who do not know Latin are possibly more ready to accept some features of its style because they approach it as a translation. One wonders whether in 1917 and 1918 Pound himself would have been willing to adopt in his own person the bold, flowing rhetoric of the opening of section VI:

> When, when, and whenever death closes our eyelids,
> Moving naked over Acheron
> Upon the one raft, victor and conquered together,
> Marius and Jugurtha together,
> > one tangle of shadows.

He seems to have thought of his poem as heuristic translation, that is, a translation that would direct attention to some qualities of the original, while also rendering equivalent effects in contemporary English.

POUND'S MODERNIZATION: THE SECOND PHASE

To the older generation of readers in 1916 much of Pound's *Lustra* might have seemed condensed, unpoetic, and disagreeable. But it would not have seemed formidably difficult, and the same may be said of "Homage to Sextus Propertius." Between 1915 and 1920, however, Pound wrote his first seven Cantos and *Hugh Selwyn Mauberley*. In parts of these works he adopted for the first time the extraordinarily compressed, oblique, learned, elliptical, allusive style that still baffles most readers. In 1922 Eliot used a somewhat similar style in *The Waste Land*. Although the styles of both poets changed continually thereafter, and although many of the subsequent Cantos are not difficult, for at least two decades readers associated Pound and Eliot with "obscurity" in poetry.

From the moment he conceived them, Pound viewed the *Cantos* as his major undertaking, the poem through which he hoped to live in history as a great poet. The opening three Cantos were first printed in *Poetry* magazine in 1917. They had been worked on at least since 1915, and bits of them may date from much earlier. These so-called Ur-Cantos differ greatly from the three that now begin his long poem. They commence as a chatty monologue. Pound is the speaker, Robert Browning the hearer, and long poems—their materials, forms, styles, and how and where to begin them—the subject. As a prototype for the work he has in hand Pound refers to Browning's learnedly obscure poem on the thirteenth-century troubadour Sordello:

> Hang it all, there can be but one *Sordello!*
> But say I want to, say I take your whole bag of tricks,
> Let in your quirks and tweeks, and say the thing's an art-form,
> Your *Sordello,* and that the modern world
> Needs such a rag-bag to stuff all its thought in;
> Say that I dump my catch, shiny and silvery
> As fresh sardines flapping and slipping on the marginal
>   cobbles?

This uncompressed, talky style was totally at variance with Pound's Imagist and Vorticist principles, which at this time he felt were inappropriate for a long poem. The Ur-Cantos are not always this accessible. The conversation with Browning fades periodically into a stream of memories and associations. Rapid transitions require mental agility. Allusions to historical, geographical, literary, and autobiographical lore and phrases in foreign languages are not always explained or translated. Nevertheless, for his long poem Pound had given up the "intaglio method," as he put it, and his decision to appear in the poem as its speaker or thinker was of special importance. As in "Homage to Sextus Propertius," whatever came into the poem was going on in the mind of the protagonist, "Pound." This mode of presentation tended both to hold the diverse materials together and to justify the transitions; the heterogeneity and the discontinuity have a psychological verisimilitude, and build up our sense of the protagonist.

But to use the first person forced Pound to write passages of lesser intensity. Successive revisions of the Ur-Cantos progressively eliminated the speaker and advanced toward an objective, maximally compressed presentation, in which the principle of progression is juxtaposition, not transition. It was not in the opening three Cantos, however, but in the fourth that Pound achieved this in a way that satisfied him. He had been working on the fourth Canto since 1917; when he published it in 1919, it began:

> Palace in smoky light,
> Troy but a heap of smouldering boundary stones,
> ANAXIFORMINGES! Aurunculeia!
> Hear me. Cadmus of Golden Prows.

To a considerable extent this style was only a return to principles of writing he had previously formed and a ruthless application of them: Here the "image" was again the poet's "primary pigment," the medium in which he thinks and expresses himself, and the "meaning" was embodied in the image, not expressed discursively; the image was set before the reader with maximum economy, using "absolutely no word that did not contribute to the presentation"; nature, as Fenollosa had pointed out, is without grammar, and an elliptical or lapsed grammar, as it was variously to be studied in both Chinese and French symboliste poetry, afforded speed and intensity (for example, it promoted sudden juxtaposition); the reader was to be made to think, to go through a process of perceiving and relating, working toward earned insight or realization; poetry was not "mimetic," it conveyed reality not by "representing" it but by building a structure of parts ("planes in relation"), whose relation created an emotion and a meaning; the emotion and the meaning were not "ascribed" or "intended" but "variable," capable of changing from reader to reader.

Because these were Pound's views in 1915, when he began composing the original or Ur-Cantos, he must have been of two minds as he wrote them. On the one hand, "the FIRST requirement" of a long poem, as he remarked twenty years later of Laurence Binyon's translation of Dante, "is that the reader be able to proceed"; on the other hand, to compose verse of less than utmost intensity troubled his conscience. His dissatisfactions with the Ur-Cantos were much exacerbated because of his relationship with Joyce and Eliot. In 1917–1919 Eliot wrote his poems in quatrains and "Gerontion"; Joyce sent *Ulysses* from Zurich in manuscript installments. Because Pound recognized these as masterworks, they caused him much anxiety. He might be left behind in the very qualities of modernized style that he had himself first developed and expounded. In the grip of this fear he returned, as he worked on the fourth Canto, to the principles of his own modernization, and emphasized them in an even more uncompromising way. He also displayed techniques learnt from Joyce and Eliot.

Speaking to Joyce of the Ur-Cantos in March 1917, three months before they were published, Pound wondered "what you will make of it." Probably, he guessed, they were "too sprawling . . . to find favour." One sees how the thought of Joyce brought his doubts to a focus. Nine months later he read the first manuscript installment of *Ulysses;* he found in it "compression, intensity," and rapid juxtaposition and was doubtless further convinced that his Ur-Cantos were encumbered with transitions. He saw literary allusions, sometimes in foreign languages; suddenly inserted into the text, they opened to the imagination what Eliot called a "vista"; for example:

—God, he said quietly. Isn't the sea what Algy calls it: a grey sweet mother? The snotgreen sea. The scrotumtightening sea. *Epi oinopa ponton;*

Algernon Swinburne speaks thus of the sea in "The Triumph of Time," and next to "the scrotumtightening" comes Homer's "wine-dark sea" in swift juxtaposition and equally voweled and dentaled sonority.

Eliot was also reading *Ulysses,* and in May and June of 1918 Pound could admire in "Sweeney Among the Nightingales" and "Mr. Eliot's Sunday Morning Service" the "swift alternation of subjective beauty and external shabbiness, squalor, and sordidness" that he commented on in a review of Joyce at this time (May 1918). Pound could also note the allusions at the end, for example, of "Sweeney Among the Nightingales," allusions that suddenly drew Sweeney into relation with the myths of Orpheus and of Agamemnon. (Eliot said that the "bloody wood" refers to the death of Orpheus, though no unaided reader would catch this allusion in the poem.) These myths are telescoped. One is made to slide into and blend with another; in the fourth Canto, Pound similarly superimposes the troubadour legends of Cabestan and Peire Vidal on the classical myths of Philomela and Actaeon.

In September 1918 Eliot published in *Today* a review of Joyce which briefly compared his work with Pound's *Cantos.* (Eliot was referring to a revised version of the Ur-Cantos which had appeared in the American edition of *Lustra,* October 1917.) His remarks revealed an attitude toward the Cantos which may have been further communicated in person, may in fact have been Pound's also:

Joyce . . . uses allusions suddenly and with great speed, part of the effect being the extent of the vista opened to the imagination by the very lightest touch. Pound . . . proceeds by a very different method . . . In appearance, it is a rag-bag of Mr. Pound's reading. . . . And yet the thing has . . . a positive coherence; it is an objective and reticent autobiography.

The comparison was not favorable to Pound. Where Joyce opened vistas, Pound seemed to stuff in odd rags of his reading. Joyce brought off his effects "suddenly and with great speed"; there was no mention of such virtues in Pound. "Autobiography" could hardly come as a compliment from one who insisted that poetry was or ought to be impersonal.

So Pound eliminated the first person completely from his fourth Canto. "Palace in smoky light": it begins with a sentence fragment, and one is there, present at the burning of Troy or in the mind of someone who sees or imagines it. The second line explains and elaborates with a second image: "Troy but a heap of smouldering boundary stones." The poetry is moving fast, enforcing the rigorous selection of detail Pound had praised in Joyce, rendering, as in Joyce, the flow of consciousness; suddenly, without transition, three allusions enter the field:

> ANAXIFORMINGES! Aurunculeia!
> Hear me. Cadmus of Golden Prows.

"Anaxiforminges" ("lords of the lyre") is the first word of a poem by Pindar. "Aurunculeia" has its provenience in Catullus, who writes of her marriage; a later passage in the fourth Canto associates her name with a marriage rite. In connection with the fall of Troy and the mention of Cadmus, founder of Thebes, the cluster of allusions may suggest the rise and fall of cities, love and war, heroism and marriage, public order and rhetoric (dubiously hollow rhetoric, given Pound's view of Pindar) versus private rites and lyric sincerities of feeling; and it may compare or alternatively blend together Troy, Thebes, and Rome; Homer, Pindar (poet of Thebes), and Catullus; Helen and Vinia Aurunculeia. In short, the method is amazingly oblique and the sudden vistas open in too many directions at once. One understands more or less why Pound wrote this way, but the passage remains quirky, without imaginative effect. It is not merely that there are too many possible implications but also that the allusions have no adequately sustaining context. The passage is composed out of parts or fragments too briefly presented to create much effect by themselves. Hence the passage emphasizes and throws all the work on the relations between the parts, but these relations are not coherent.

yes!

If the fourth Canto was not always successful poetry, there was much in it from which other writers might learn. We may take for just one illustration a passage that comes slightly further on and renders the suicide of Marguerite, wife of the lord of Chateau Roussillon in the twelfth century. Pound does not write that "she threw herself out of the window" but presents the scene from the point of view of a watcher. The action is broken into sequential phases and the narration arrests itself in details of seemingly secondary significance. These convey the transfixed attention of the watcher and obliquely create the scene in vivid, shadowless clarity. The versification embodies the rhythm of the action and emotion:

> And she went toward the window,
> > the slim white stone bar
> Making a double arch;
> Firm even fingers held to the firm pale stone;
> Swung for a moment,
> > and the wind out of Rhodez
> Caught in the full of her sleeve.
> > . . . the swallows crying.

If this resembles *mutatis mutandis* the style by which Ernest Hemingway made himself famous in the 1920s it is partly because Hemingway learned from the same masters as Pound and partly because Pound was his master. Throughout the fourth Canto there are fine, local successes of perception, phrasing, and rhythm:

> Like a fish-scale roof,
>> Like the church roof in Poictiers;
>
> . . . .
>
> Smoke hangs on the stream,
> The peach-trees shed bright leaves in the water,
> Sound drifts in the evening haze,
>> The bark scrapes at the ford,
> Gilt rafters above black water,
>> Three steps in an open field,
> Gray stone-posts leading.

When the revision of Canto II was finally accomplished, one could read:

> Olive grey in the near,
>> far, smoke grey of the rock-slide,
> Salmon-pink wings of the fish-hawk
>> cast grey shadows in water,
> The tower like a one-eyed great goose
>> cranes up out of the olive-grove;

and, of the water off Chios in the Aegean,

> There is a wine-red glow in the shallows,
>> a tin flash in the sun-dazzle;

which, for what they are, could not be bettered.

During these years Pound was getting through an incredible amount of work. He seized all opportunities to tout for Joyce, Eliot, Lewis, Epstein, and Gaudier-Brzeska. "Les jeunes," as he called them, sent him their poems, and he took pains to reply sensitively. Forced by lack of money into literary journalism, he served as both art and music critic for the *New Age,* reviewing art shows under the name of B. H. Dias, concerts as William Atheling. He reviewed books in batches. He wrote miscellaneous essays—including five articles on "Elizabethan Classicists," three on Henry James, a sixty-one-page discussion of modern French poets—some of which cut seriously into his time. He spent the better part of two months reading for his "Elizabethan Classicists" in the British Museum. Over two hundred and fifty prose items appeared in magazines between 1917 and 1919; during the same period he also published five books.

Meanwhile he was absorbing the economic theories of Major H. C. Douglas, whom he met in 1918 and whose important writings started to appear in articles in the *New Age* in 1919. Douglas taught him what he was very ready to learn, that a relatively simple expedient, the State Dividend, could eliminate many of the irrationalities of the economic system and provide a richer and more secure life for all mankind. Douglas argued that the value of a product (Pound thought, among other things, of his own products and of those of Eliot, Joyce, and Lewis) was not to be measured by what it cost to produce or by the demand for it but by the degree to which it ministered to a "definite, healthy, and sane human requirement." From now on Pound's arguments stressed how "art of maximum intensity" was preeminently valuable by this criterion. But though he adopted many of Douglas' views, the particular ideas were less important than the general fact that Douglas helped substantiate Pound's dawning conviction of the fundamental, omnipresent influence of the economic system. Henceforth a just and rational system seemed to him the indispensable basis for any hope of a "civilization" or Vortex. Bankers and financiers increasingly figured as archvillains in the theater of his imagination. A bank can promote the real wealth of the people, for example, the Bank of Siena, founded in 1624 to lend money "to whomso can best use it USE it," but for the most part bankers and financiers manipulated for their own gain. They brought about depressions in order to be able to collect loans in deflated currency. They plotted wars for profits. Bank interest added an artificial cost to production. For the next forty years Pound read and wrote often on economic history and theory, and the subject was never far from his mind.

HUGH SELWYN MAUBERLEY

In 1920 Pound composed and published *Hugh Selwyn Mauberley*. These two sequences of poems in quatrains explore the life, character, times, and works of a poet in London around 1920. The relation between Mauberley and Pound is complex, for in Mauberley, Pound projected and confronted what Erik Erikson calls a "negative identity." He saw himself in Mauberley, but a self he wanted to reject. Given the psychological dynamics of this situation, it is easy to understand that the poem might be difficult to interpret. Pound's attitude toward Mauberley could be influenced by such defense mechanisms as censorship, projection, and overcompensation. It is ambivalent and unstable, swinging between wide extremes. In the opening poem one cannot be sure whose career, Pound's or Mauberley's, is characterized; nor can one finally determine whether the characterization is made from Pound's point of view or from that of the age. The poem seems to attack the age that has no praise for chiseled and delicate workmanship such as Mauberley's but it also seems to maintain an ironic reserve of judgment toward such workmanship. In the end, the introductory poem establishes no attitude whatever toward a career such as Mauberley's.

As the first sequence progresses, however, we are no longer much concerned with Pound's attitude to Mauberley, for he writes mainly a satiric attack on the age. He portrays venal writers and la-di-da patronesses; makes allusive, invidious juxtapositions of twentieth-century culture with that of the ancient world—

> The pianola "replaces"
> Sappho's barbitos;

and cries straightforward invective against war and usury. But through most of the second sequence the object of Pound's repulsion is Mauberley himself, and this artist of the poetic medallion (shall I "give up th'intaglio method?" Pound had asked in his Ur-Cantos) is presented as sexually timid, helpless before the age (he lacks Pound's aggressive, reforming energies), and in retreat from life:

> Firmness,
> Not the full smile,
> His art, but an art
> In profile.

Eventually he becomes capable only of escapist reveries.

In a letter to Felix Schelling, his old teacher at the University

of Pennsylvania, Pound dismissed the Mauberley sequences as
"mere surface . . . a study in form . . . Meliora speramus."
But he had handled the form and texture effectively. The sequence begins:

> For three years out of key with his time,
> He strove to resuscitate the dead art
> Of poetry; to maintain "the sublime"
> In the old sense. Wrong from the start—
>
> No, hardly, but seeing he had been born
> In a half savage country, out of date;
> Bent resolutely on wringing lilies from the acorn;
> Capaneus; trout for factitious bait.

Here again are the sudden allusions and juxtapositions he had
developed in the fourth Canto. Capaneus implies the hubris and
inevitable defeat of Mauberley's aspiration. "Trout for factitious
bait," a fish attracted to an artificial fly, presents the same aspiration in a different light as it compares Mauberley to a blindly instinctive, gullible, and hooked fish and the art he emulates to the
delicately contrived, unnatural fly. The lapsed grammar brings
these quite different "planes" or perspectives into relationship
with utmost speed. The Mauberley sequence also exploits the
verbal play and irony Pound had mastered in "Homage to
Sextus Propertius" but had not yet ventured to employ in the
Cantos. In 1920, *The Waste Land* not yet written, the Mauberley
sequences were the most ample exhibition available of modernized style in poetry.

Pound wrote in quatrains because he was disgusted with the
"floppiness" of contemporary free verse. As he later told the
story, he and Eliot agreed in 1917 that the "dilution" had proceeded too far, and "some countercurrent must be set going."
Pound recommended a study of Gautier's terse and polished
quatrains in *Émaux et Camées,* whereupon Eliot wrote "The Hip-
popotamus" and, later, his other poems in quatrains. Pound followed with the Mauberley poems. These examples might have
had some effect against free verse, but Eliot's *The Waste Land*
soon had far greater importance in leading poets back to meters.
The deepest influence of Pound's trim, rigorous quatrains on
other poets was probably in the high standards of workmanship
he set for stanzaic verse. And in some parts he grafted into the

meter a syncopation based, he said, on the Greek poet Bion. In general the versification of the Mauberley poems reflects not only his disgust with the free versifiers but also, as he explained, his "distaste for the slushiness and swishiness of the post-Swinburnian British line."

In other ways also Pound could justly feel that the Mauberley sequences marked new and important advances in his own modernization. While Eliot and Joyce had been inspecting the "mess" of the twentieth-century mind, Pound had hitherto been bustling about in the past, resurrecting Rome, China, the Italian Renaissance, medieval Provence, and medieval Japan. He had to be sure included sketches of contemporary social types and manners in *Ripostes, Blast,* and *Lustra,* but the Mauberley sequences made up his first long poem dealing with the modern world directly. (He told Schelling that the Mauberley sequences were an "attempt to condense the James novel.") In Monsieur Verog, Brennbaum, Mr. Nixon, and Lady Valentine, not to mention Mauberley himself, he assembled a gallery of contemporary portraits, as Eliot had in Prufrock, Aunt Helen, Mr. Apollinax, Burbank, and Sweeney. In transcribing what he called "moeurs contemporaines," the nuances of contemporary social behavior, he had used an objective and impersonal method, as opposed to the "autobiographical" method Eliot had adverted to in discussing the Ur-Cantos. While expressing his feelings about the economic system, social mores, and literary world of England, he had kept, as Eliot did, an ironic distance and control.

THE CANTOS

Pound's *Cantos* were composed over roughly fifty-five years, and the poem was finally left unfinished. Because most of the Cantos were composed after the 1920s, the notice of them here is preliminary to a fuller discussion in the second volume. The 109 completed Cantos and "drafts and fragments" of eight additional ones have a total of roughly 23,000 lines. The figure may be compared with the 10,465 lines of *Paradise Lost* or, perhaps more relevantly, with the 433 lines of *The Waste Land,* which Pound in 1921 had thought "the longest poem in the English

langwidge." Since the style of much of the *Cantos* is not less difficult than that of *The Waste Land,* the poem requires a formidable
commitment of attention and time.

Perhaps the most striking feature of the *Cantos* is the presentation of many different historical cultures: ancient China,
eighteenth-century America, the Renaissance, Homeric Greece,
twentieth-century Europe and America, the Middle Ages. These
times and places are exhibited in concrete samples. There are
passages from the letters of John Adams, laws from ancient
China ("In doubt, no condemnation, rule out irrelevant evidence"), translations or adaptations of poems from diverse
times and cultures, extracts from the accounts of medieval
Venice ("3 lire 15 groats to stone for making a lion"), and there
are anecdotes of what such figures as Sigismundo Malatesta,
Confucius, Yeats, Baldy Bacon, So-Gioku, and Corporal Casey
did or said. Such concrete cases embody values, and Pound
believed that from so large and varied an accumulation his
readers would gradually and tacitly form a sense of what is
permanently valuable. Because these values were concretely
presented, they would be formative and productive in a way that
abstract argument can never be. Viewed in this light, the *Cantos*
are the most ambitious educative effort that any poet has
undertaken in the twentieth century.

The values highlighted in Pound's multiplied and recurrent
examples might be generalized as sincerity and productivity.
The ideal of sincerity reflects, as he handles it, a Confucian ambience, though the *Cantos* do not associate it only with China.
The sincere man has clarified his intellect and will. He is imbued
with persisting truths of nature and human nature and judges
and acts properly in relation to them. His way of life has sanity,
order, and continuity with human tradition. Pound puts special
emphasis on sincerity in relation to language. He interprets the
Confucian ideogram of sincerity as, "the precise definition of
the word, pictorially the sun's lance coming to rest on the precise
spot verbally. The righthand half of this compound means: to
perfect, bring to focus." Another ideogram is interpreted: "fidelity to the given word. The man here standing by his word." As
for productivity, Pound's heroes get work done. By work he
means especially clearing out the deadwood and promoting new
growth. He praises the Chinese emperor who wrote MAKE IT

NEW on his bathtub, and he endows the ideographs with driving energy as he translates them:

Day by day make it new
cut underbrush,
pile the logs
keep it growing.

His creative figures such as Malatesta and Adams are, like himself, phenomenally busy, carrying on multiple projects at the same time. He gave a natural sanction to productive work. For to his imagination (as to Dante's) there was a deep, mysterious connection, which he expressed in juxtaposed images, between founding a state, like the first Chinese emperors, building a Tempio, like Sigismundo Malatesta, or writing a poem and the fundamental creativity of nature, which he thought of as a generalized sexuality and symbolized in the goddess Aphrodite and in other myths or mythical embodiments of sexuality.

The Ur-Cantos dwelt on the problem of organizing a long poem in the modern world. When Pound saw Eliot's completed *The Waste Land* he reflected ruefully on his own inability to create similarly integrated wholes: "Complimenti, you bitch. I am wracked by the seven jealousies, and cogitating an excuse for always exuding my deformative secretions in my own stuff, and never getting an outline. I go into nacre and objets d'art." Whether or not the *Cantos* have an overall form, as contrasted with formless ongoingness, like a railroad train, has been much debated. Those who find a governing form disagree in describing it. Those who do not, may or may not think it matters. Speaking of W. C. Williams in 1928, Pound argued that "Major form is not a non-literary component. But it can do us no harm to stop an hour or so and consider the number of very important chunks of world-literature in which form, major form, is remarkable mainly for absence"; and he goes on to cite the *Iliad*, Aeschylus' *Prometheus*, Montaigne, and Rabelais. If there is no "major form" in the *Cantos*, there is certainly an incremental recurrence of phrases, allusions, persons, historical events, and myths, and as these references accumulate they tend gradually to become both clearer and more weighted with implications. Thus, any part of the poem is richer and more meaningful if it is read in the context of the whole.

The method of presentation is for the most part that of "planes in relation," the juxtaposition of concrete particulars. The method prevails on the large scale—Cantos and sequences of Cantos are juxtaposed with each other—and also within individual Cantos. For example, Cantos 8-11 present the Renaissance condottiere Malatesta, whom we see amid the welter of his activities as soldier, ruler, man of culture, and patron of writers and artists. He is creating his Tempio, the church of San Francesco at Rimini, which he redid in Renaissance style as a monument to himself and his mistress. The Tempio was an ambitious work of art, carried out over a period of years despite enemies, hardships, distractions, and the age—which Pound considered a florid period unpropitious for art. Nevertheless, the Tempio—

> in the style "Past ruin'd Latium"
> The filagree hiding the gothic,
>   with a touch of rhetoric in the whole—

was, though unfinished, a magnificent achievement. Against Sigismundo Malatesta, Pound juxtaposed (Canto 12) a modern soldier of fortune, Baldy Bacon. The contrast highlights the degeneration of the type in the modern world, for although Baldy Bacon has an engaging picaresque unscrupulousness, he is a financial manipulator, building nothing:

> Baldy's interest
> Was in money business.
>   "No interest in any other kind uv busnis,"
> Said Baldy.

Then Canto 13 presents Confucius. There is no attempt to articulate Confucian ideas systematically; instead, Pound relates in simple, factual style the sage's sayings and doings. As in reading the gospels, one must infer the whole ethos from the fragments given. Immediately after this come Cantos that picture the modern world as a filthy and obscene hell through which the narrator makes his difficult way. These so-called Hell Cantos are thematically comparable in some ways to the Malatesta Cantos; in both groups one sees a man struggling against the pulluating resistances of a corrupt age and society—the good man amid the muck, as Pound might have put it. The situation corresponds to Pound's view of his own activities at this time.

Similarly, within particular Cantos, Pound juxtaposes successive passages, lines, or parts of lines. As the years passed, he increasingly tended to describe these structures of concrete, heterogeneous materials as "ideograms." For example (from Canto 74):

> rain also is of the process.
> What you depart from is not the way
> and olive tree blown white in the wind
> washed in the Kiang and Han
> what whiteness will you add to this whiteness,
> what candor?

Reading this ideogram, one must keep in mind that the parts are discontinuous, that there need be no narrative or logical transition from one line to the next. Obviously we are not to think of olive trees washed in rivers of China. The images of the olive leaves blown by the wind, making the whitish undersides gleam and ripple, and of being washed in the sacred rivers of China, are two separate suggestions of cleansing or purification. In *Confucius,* Pound quotes Mencius: "After Confucius' death, when there was talk of regrouping, Tsang declined, saying: 'Washed in the Keang and Han, bleached in the autumn's sun's-slope, what whiteness can you add to that whiteness, what candour?'" What the whole, complex ideogram implies is impossible to paraphrase, but it speaks of a spiritual quality which is natural to man, yet at the same time is achieved only gradually. The process of this achieving is the path or way, and the process includes the purification that comes with the natural undergoings and sufferings of life. The spiritual quality or nature that thus realizes itself is suggested in such terms as rectitude or sincerity, in the form in which such virtues are contemplated in the ideals of Athens and republican Rome (olive tree, candor) and of ancient China.

LATER LIFE

Pound's later career belongs to the period covered in the second volume of this history. But a few words may be said about it here. After living in Paris from 1921 to 1924, he then moved to Rapallo, Italy, where he made his home until the close of the Second World War. He continued to aid avant-garde magazines and writers—for example, E. E. Cummings, Basil Bunting, and Louis Zukofsky; he studied music, organized concerts, tried to learn Chinese, and took all occasions to propagate his ideas on economics and currency reform. He was favorably impressed with Italy's Fascist government, though he did not necessarily think fascism the right path for other countries, and developed an attitude of hero-worship toward Mussolini. The "Boss" had found his *Cantos* "entertaining" (the Boss remarked at their one interview), which was more than could be said for most *soi-disant* literati. Besides, "I don't believe any estimate of Mussolini will be valid unless it *starts* from his passion for construction. Treat him as *artifex* and all the details fall into place." One of the things he felt "Muss" would construct was a currency system along the lines Pound advocated. By the mid-1930s the greater bulk of his writing was on political and economic topics, though Cantos were still accumulating. Toward the end of the thirities he was taking a keen interest in American politics and was trying to influence it through his articles and correspondence. He felt that the drift toward war resulted from criminal ignorance and profiteering. His own ideas, if adopted, would bring peace and economic well-being. He worked desperately to put them across.

In 1939 Pound visited the United States for the purpose of educating Roosevelt (whom he did not see) and members of Congress. When the war broke out he was back in Italy and he strove through letters and other writings to keep the United States from entering the war. He regarded himself as an American patriot and Roosevelt as an unscrupulous misleader of the people. From 1941 to the end of the war he broadcast regularly over the Rome radio, his talks conveying for the most part his economic message, though he also quoted poetry, engaged in literary reminiscence, and fulminated against America's part in the war. At the end of the war he was taken into custody by the United States Army and kept for six months in a prison camp near Pisa. At first he was in a cage, without shelter from rain, heat, or dust. After his health broke down, he was transferred to the prison hospital. Here, with his world in ruins, and (so far as his mental condition allowed him to appreciate his actual position) in fear of hanging, he wrote his eleven Pisan Cantos, the finest section of the whole poem. They are poems of memory, extending back to his early years in London and they are a final affirmation of his ideas and ideals. They reach their climax at the end of Canto 81, where Pound speaks with a new profundity out of his own immediate experience:

> What thou lovest well remains,
>   the rest is dross
> What thou lov'st well shall not be reft from thee
> What thou lov'st well is thy true heritage.

From Italy, Pound was brought to the United States to stand trial for treason. The examining psychiatrists reported, however, that he was legally insane, and he was not brought to trial. Instead, he was committed to a mental institution, where he spent the next thirteen years. He translated the Confucian *Analects* (1951), *The Classic Anthology Defined by Confucius* (1954), and Sophocles' *Women in Trachis* (1956) and composed more Cantos. Friends had long been working for his release, and finally the United States government agreed to dismiss the indictment against him. He returned to Italy in 1958, where he lived another fifteen years, dying in Venice in 1972 at the age of eighty-seven. He was the last of the major poets who had brought about the Modernist revolution.

21

T. S. ELIOT: THE EARLY CAREER

THOMAS Stearns Eliot (1888–1965) was born in St. Louis. On both sides of his family he descended from old New England. His grandfather, the Reverend William Green-leaf Eliot, founded the first Unitarian church in St. Louis and also Washington University. The ancestral sense of election and of mission still lingered in such genteel families of New England background, though the sense of election was transposed from the religious to the moral, social, and cultural spheres. A shy, bookish, bird-watching child, Eliot went to Smith Academy in St. Louis and Milton Academy in Massachusetts and spent summers on the Massachusetts coast near Gloucester. In 1906 he entered Harvard University; in 1911 he became a graduate student in philosophy. Not to name the teachers "of men illustrious for lit-erature," as Samuel Johnson remarked in his life of Addison, "is a kind of historical fraud, by which honest fame is injuriously di-minished." Among Eliot's teachers were George Santayana, whose course in the "History of Modern Philosophy" began his deep immersion in that field, and Irving Babbitt, whose lectures on nineteenth-century French critics extolled "classical" reason and balance while bombarding "modern" liberalism, Romanti-cism, democracy, and emotional spontaneity. (Babbitt inciden-tally dazzled students with his one-upmanship in learned allusions, an art Eliot subsequently mastered.) Bertrand Russell, briefly a guest professor at Harvard, recorded his impression of Eliot in letters to Lady Ottoline Morrell: "very well dressed and polished with manners of the finest Etonian type . . . ultracivilized, knows his classics very well, is familiar with all the French literature from Villon to Vildrach, and is altogether impeccable in his taste but has no vigour of life—or enthusiasm." The date was 1914. Eliot, a twenty-six-year-old graduate student in philosophy, was about to leave on a Sheldon Fellowship for study in Germany and England. In another fifteen years he would conquer literary London, but this future was utterly undreamed-of, for he intended to become a university professor of philosophy.

Eliot's demeanor, which he had achieved by this time, was not the least of his works of art and had much to do with his subsequent authority in the literary world. It changed somewhat as the years went by; in younger days he was relatively more elegant and occasionally waspish (some of his college friends called him "tsetse" alluding both to his initials and to the celebrated biting fly), and in later years he was more owlish, clerical, and benevolent. But till the end of his life one encountered on meeting him the sober three-piece suit, the "necktie rich and modest" like that of Prufrock, the black hair plastered down, the precise conversation in complete sentences, the unbending reserve, propriety, and courtesy. He amused some persons as an eccentric but he overawed more, arousing their insecurities. In short, he was formidable, though he could not have been so through his bearing alone. It was rather the combination of this with intellectual acuteness, force of character, disinterested purpose, moral intensity, and dangerousness—for one could be ambushed by a snub or a sneer—that gave him his personal ascendancy.

He had been reading and writing verse since his schooldays. (His first literary ventures were in childhood: compositions for the family to which the six-year-old signed his name "T. S. Eliot.") His earliest taste in poetry was for Macaulay's "Horatius," Tennyson's "Revenge," Burns's "Bannockburn," and the like. With adolescence came the *Rubaiyat* and then Byron, Shelley, Keats, Rossetti, and Swinburne. Early in his college career he read Dante, puzzling out the Italian with the aid of a prose translation and memorizing long passages that especially delighted him. He was permanently impressed by the precision, economy, concreteness, and austerity of Dante's style. What he then thought of his religious view of life we do not know, except that he preferred the *Inferno* to the *Paradiso,* for he associated the latter with Pre-Raphaelite verse and with "cheerfulness, optimism, and hopefulness; and these words stood for a great deal of what one hated in the nineteenth century." Poetry, he then felt, could "find its material only *in* suffering." The poems he composed before 1909 are derivative exercises in various styles, especially the late-Victorian styles of England. In 1910 he wrote the college class ode, which is no better than most commencement odes. Yet at the same time he was working on "The Love Song of J. Alfred Prufrock."

THE ENCOUNTER WITH LAFORGUE

In December 1908 a fateful moment occurred in the history of modern poetry. Reading Arthur Symons' *The Symbolist Movement in Literature* (discussed in Chapter 3), Eliot was introduced to the writings of Jules Laforgue. He soon purchased the complete works of Laforgue, and the impact on his own poetry was radical. He acquired an ironic attitude and a new subject matter and style. Within a year he reached a much higher level of achievement. The momentum lasted for three years, as Eliot continued in this first period of creative breakthrough to develop along new lines the resources he had discovered. In 1909 he wrote "Nocturne," "Humoresque," "Spleen," and "Conversation Galante," four poems that are similar in some ways to Laforgue's; only the last was retained in his *Collected Poems.* In 1910 and 1911 came "Portrait of a Lady," "Rhapsody on a Windy Night," and "The Love Song of J. Alfred Prufrock." They effected a total departure from the Victorian and Genteel tradition of English and American poetry; in fact, no other poet in England or the United States had written anything so arrestingly "modern." They were the finest poems written in the twentieth century up to that point by an American. These facts are the more remarkable when we remind ourselves that Eliot was only twenty-three in 1911 and that he had matured his talent in an independence hardly less than that of Robinson in Gardiner, Maine, or Robert Frost on his chicken farm. No one in his milieu could have suggested to Eliot this way of writing.

A literary departure of this rapidity and completeness cannot have been altogether unprepared. Eliot must have found in Laforgue a writer who, as he later put it, helped him to become aware of what he wanted to say himself. The poetry of Laforgue was—in one of its aspects—a rebellion against the late-Romantic style, the style Eliot had been practicing in his own early work. Laforgue's poetry was, in other words, not a completely new way of writing, for it was partly a negation of a familiar one. (Had it been merely new, perhaps Eliot would have found it neither so intriguing nor so easy to assimilate.) Laforgue exploited stock themes, images, attitudes, and emotions of late-Romantic poetry, but with the all-important difference that he exploited them with disbelief, that is, ironically. He conveyed his ironic vision through deliberate incongruities. If the lady in a moonlit scene waits for the tender, conventional vows, the Laforguean lover overflows with repartee; or, uttering the sentimental declaration, he falls into a too-brisk rhythm or a vocabulary strangely abstract and philosophical. As a consequence, where the late-Romantic lyric presented through the course of the poem an undeviating unity or gradual transition of mood, point of view, and style, Laforgue jolted readers with unpredictable alternation. Eliot was struck by Laforgue's use of the conversational, including social banality and slang. He "taught me," Eliot later said, "the poetic possibilities of my own idiom of speech." Laforgue also mixed in technical and abstruse terms in a continually surprising and witty way. Partly for these reasons he seemed the last word in the contemporary or modern, as Symons had pointed out: "The old cadences, the old eloquence, the ingenuous seriousness of poetry, are all banished. . . . Here, if ever, is modern verse." Where the late-Romantic lyric had been, at least by convention, an utterance of personal emotion, Laforgue occasionally constructed his lyrics as short, objectively dramatic scenes.

In later, usually oblique, recollections Eliot tried to explain what happened in his encounter with Laforgue, psychologically speaking. He suddenly acquired a coherent poetic identity, was "changed, metamorphosed almost, within a few weeks even, from a bundle of second-hand sentiments into a person." In other words, he integrated his own personality on the basis of Laforgue's. (Such identifications are liberating precisely because they evoke and organize only some elements of the personality, while inhibiting others; they suppress conflicts and ambivalences. For the same reason such identifications may quickly give way to others, perhaps of a quite different tendency.) Moreover, Eliot suddenly felt himself to be the bearer of a tradition. The tradition would be not only that of Laforgue but of French symbolist and post-symbolist poetry in general. As the bearer of this alien tradition in an English-speaking context, Eliot might feel that possibilities of a new development were especially open to him. How clearly he saw this at the time cannot be known, but he modified Laforgue's methods from the start. He kept the conversational but dropped the medley diction; he created quasi-dramatic scenes far more effectively; and he combined the stylistic resources and emotions of Laforgue with those of other French poets, with the Jacobean dramatists of England, and with a wide range of other writers, including Browning, Symons, and Henry James. In "The Love Song of J. Alfred Prufrock," at the close of this three-year period, one can isolate aspects of characterization, imagery, and theme which might have come from Laforgue. The ensemble of the whole, however, is not only unlike Laforgue (or any other French or English poet) but is finer and more mature than anything Laforgue wrote.

If we ask why this liberating identification crystallized around Laforgue rather than some other poet, Eliot suggests that he read the "dead author" with a "feeling of profound kinship, or rather of a peculiar personal intimacy." Since Laforgue had been, by his own classification, a "lunar Pierrot," a sad clown from a dead world, the feeling of "personal intimacy" was remarkable in a poet of puritan-Unitarian background, with his bedrock seriousness and essentialism of character and his childhood inculcation in high-minded, conscientiously hopeful views of man and the universe. According to the literary categories of the time, Laforgue was a Decadent. Having read deeply in Schopenhauer and Hartmann, he felt the nothingness of existence. Behind the Pierrot mask he suffered the inevitable pain, which he met with an impeccable demeanor. "He has invented," Symons emphasized, "a new manner of being René or Werther: an inflexible politeness towards man, woman, and destiny." We cannot know just which aspects of Laforgue evoked Eliot's sense of "profound kinship," but perhaps his evasion of emotional commitment and his self-protective, intellectual irony should be stressed. And even without a sense of personal kinship Eliot might have regarded the character portrayed in Laforgue's poetry as a case worth study; he reveals, Symons had pointed out, "the possibilities for art which come from the sickly modern being, with his clothes, his nerves: the mere fact that he flowers from the soil of his epoch."

ENGLAND AND MARRIAGE

For the next four years philosophy, strongly backed by prudence and the family, overcame Eliot's inclination to verse. He wrote his Ph.D. thesis on F. H. Bradley; it was mainly completed by the end of his year at Oxford in 1914–15. Meanwhile, in September 1914, he had called on Ezra Pound in London, Conrad Aiken, a college friend, having provided him with an introduction. "I think he has some sense," was Pound's impression, and after reading "Prufrock," added: "He has actually trained himself *and* modernized himself *on his own*." By the spring of 1915 Eliot was grumbling about an academic career. Roused perhaps by Pound's enthusiasm, he resumed writing poetry and composed "The *Boston Evening Transcript*," "Aunt Helen," and "Hysteria." The laughing lady in the last of these may have been Vivien Haigh-Wood, whom he married in June 1915. It was an impetuous step, for he had not known her long and he had no money.

Though Eliot could sometimes act recklessly, he could not do so heedlessly, that is, without knowing what the act might imply. To marry an Englishwoman under these circumstances meant that he was choosing poetry rather than philosophy and literary life in London rather than university teaching in the United States. What it may have further implied can only be guessed, but since in the inner landscape of Eliot's imagination "life" and "death" were dominant symbols, he probably perceived Vivien, marriage, poetry, loss of financial security, and the total risk involved in a literary career as a choice of "life," as opposed to the "death" of abstract philosophizing in a university niche. If "life" through the next year was in some respects "the most awful nightmare of anxiety that the mind of man could conceive," it was still better than the type of existence he had been expecting.

Strang
Comment:

Seven months after marriage he wrote Aiken, "I have *lived* through material for a score of long poems in the last six months. An entirely different life from that I looked forward to two years ago. Cambridge [Massachusetts] seems to me a dull nightmare now."

The marriage that released him in so many ways also brought immense troubles. Vivien Eliot was vivacious and acutely sensitive, particularly in the arts. She was among the first and strongest appreciators of Eliot's poetry. In times of serious financial difficulty, when their problem was to get together enough money to live on, she encouraged him to go on writing. But she proved to be physically and psychologically unstable. She was afflicted with colitis, insomnia, depression, and hysteria and sometimes fell into rages. Aspects of their relationship may have been incorporated in *The Waste Land*. The passage, for example, that begins,

> My nerves are bad to-night. Yes, bad. Stay with me.
> Speak to me,

and ends,

> And we shall play a game of chess,
> Pressing lidless eyes and waiting for a knock upon the door,

probably reflects her desperation and hysteria and also Eliot's apprehension and growing hopelessness in their life together. (Yet in the manuscript of the poem Vivien Eliot wrote beside these lines, "WONDERFUL. Yes, & wonderful. wonderful.") At times she required almost constant medical attention (Pound remarked in his coarse way that Eliot had to turn his home into a "madhouse"), and Eliot, honorable, responsible, and tender, looked after her as best he could. But her condition steadily worsened, and to the unremitting tension and emotional drain Eliot lived with were added feelings of self-accusation. Whether or not they were justified, they were inevitable in a sensitive man under the circumstances.

Meanwhile, he had to put bread on the table. In 1915 and 1916 he taught school, an occupation he remembered in later years with horror. Between 1916 and 1919 he also taught Extension Courses for the universities of Oxford and London and for the London County Council. In 1916 Eliot's subjects were Modern French Literature and Modern English Literature; in 1917, Victorian Literature. His teaching of Victorian literature may remind us that the influence of the Victorian poets on him was, ultimately, as important as that of the French symbolistes, though neither he nor his early admirers much acknowledged or, perhaps, were aware of the fact.

From 1917 to 1925 he had a job in Lloyds Bank in London, where he worked in a small office under the street. He could hear the thud of pedestrians overhead. He helped edit the *Egoist*. He rose mornings at 5 in order to spend a few hours writing before he was due at the bank at 9:15. In these circumstances he turned out the critical essays and reviews that eventually became celebrated. Occasionally he wrote poems. Four composed in 1918 may reveal something of his state of mind: "Sweeney Among the Nightingales," "Whispers of Immortality," "Dans le Restaurant," and "Mr. Eliot's Sunday Morning Service." Deliberately undercutting Romantic idealizations, these poems stare at man's emptiness, egoism, psychological fragmentation, and animality, their emotion barely controlled by ironic distance and strict form. Similar perceptions were present in earlier poems, but Eliot's revulsion is now more intensely expressed. Perhaps modern poetry can show no more devastating, though elegant, gesture of "jemenfoutisme" (to adapt Eliot's word from "Mélange adultère de tout") than the closing lines of "Sweeney Among the Nightingales," where Eliot has bird droppings fall on the corpse of the classical, tragic Agamemnon.

Eliot and his works were gradually acquiring a reputation in the literary world. His first book of poems, *Prufrock and Other Observations* (1917), was admired by a small but select circle that included E. M. Forster, John Middleton Murry, and Leonard and Virginia Woolf. It seemed at the time a collection of satiric scenes and portraits, modern, urban, and immensely clever. Two more volumes added the poems in quatrains and "Gerontion" to his oeuvre, and in 1920 *The Sacred Wood* collected many of the critical essays and reviews he had been publishing in journals since 1916. It included such now-famous pieces as "Hamlet and his Problems," with its argument that emotion cannot be expressed directly but only through a circumstance, chain of events, or "objective correlative" that evokes the emotion, and "Tradition and the Individual Talent," which sums up many of his central critical standpoints. The book quickly captured the interest of younger English critics and teachers of literature.

1. The city
poem breaks fixed association betw. verse + the agreeable

THE WASTE LAND

Eliot had *The Waste Land* in mind at least as early as 1919. But, what with other work and the turmoil of his life, he was unable to make headway with the poem until 1921. By May of that year it was "partly on paper." In late September, his health seriously threatened, he was ordered by a nerve specialist to "go away *at once* for three months quite alone." He went accordingly to Margate, then to a sanatorium in Lausanne. On this enforced vacation he finished *The Waste Land,* which he seems to have regarded at first as a sequence of poems rather than a single long work. In December he left the manuscript with Pound, who was then living in Paris, and Pound went blue-penciling through it, crossing out weaker words, phrases, lines, and sections. In the process Pound made it shorter and more continuously forceful, and he also left it even more disjunctive than it had originally been. The poem won the *Dial* award for 1922. It was published in the same year and eventually became the classic, and controversial, poem of the Modernist movement.

Several of the poems Eliot published before *The Waste Land* were minor masterpieces. Moreover, Eliot tended to perfect a style quickly and not use it again. Hence his first two volumes (in 1917 and 1920) contained a remarkable diversity of performance. The interior monologue of the timid and proper Prufrock was quite unlike the objective presentation of "Sweeny Among the Nightingales," with its strange mingling of concrete particularity and symbolist vagueness, of sordid reality, recondite allusion, and elegantly strict form. This in turn differed widely from the self-analytic cerebration of "Gerontion," who was less a character than a historical phase of the European mind. Each of these poems was arrestingly "modern" in its own way, and each was imitated. But they were not so widely imitated as one might now suppose, and the main reason was the rapidity with which Eliot developed. Their impact was lost in that of *The Waste Land.* In Pound's eyes *The Waste Land* was "the justification of our

modern experiment, since 1900." In the eyes of more conservative poets and critics it was a "mad medley." For many a "new"
poet in America it was a "piece of tripe" (the phrase is Amy
Lowell's), parasitic on past styles, uprooted, formless, academic,
anti-democratic, and defeatist. But for adolescent future poets it
possessed to an unrivaled degree the prestige of the modern.
Not that they understood it better than other readers, but they
admired its technical boldness and defiance, the more so since it
defied not only conservative taste but also the free-verse and
Imagist conventions of the school that was then loudest in protesting its own modernity.

Because *The Waste Land* had a unique influence on the development of modern poetry it must be dwelt on here. And in
order to gain the necessary space further comment on Eliot's
verse before *The Waste Land* must be omitted. The earlier poetry
was important, but *The Waste Land* immensely more so. Our purpose in discussing this much-scrutinized poem is not to offer another interpretation, commentary, or evaluation but to indicate
why it came to be viewed as the chief example of the modern in
poetry, so much so that Eliot was seen as the counterpart in
poetry to Joyce, Picasso, Stravinski, and to other major creators
of the Modernist revolution in their respective arts. One reason
was Eliot's use of the modern city as setting. Precedents could be
found in English, American, and French poetry of the last
seventy-five years, notably in Baudelaire, and in some
twentieth-century poetry, such as Sandburg's *Chicago Poems*
(1916), not to mention Eliot's *Prufrock and Other Observations*
(1917). Nevertheless, no previous poem gave so vivid an impression of the contemporary, urban metropolis. In some sequences
The Waste Land resembled an avant-garde documentary film; it
explored the city and the lives of its inhabitants by juxtaposing
images, scenes, fragments of conversation, and the like. The
technique resembled cinematic montage, which was developed
at about the same time, though Eliot did not learn his methods
from films. We are present at a session with a fortune-teller, we
are later in the boudoir of a wealthy, hysterical woman, then in a
pub at closing time, and then beside a pub in Lower Thames
Street, where we hear ·

> The pleasant whining of a mandoline
> And a clatter and a chatter from within

> Where fishmen lounge at noon: where the walls
> Of Magnus Martyr hold
> Inexplicable splendour of Ionian white and gold.

Some of these sights are not unpleasant:

> The barges drift
> With the turning tide
> Red sails
> Wide
> To leeward, swing on the heavy spar.

Others explore the literary uses of the disagreeable:

> A rat crept softly through the vegetation
> Dragging its slimy belly on the bank
> While I was fishing in the dull canal
> On a winter evening round behind the gashouse.

And some are not ugly but dolorous—for example, the half-visionary scene of the white-collar workers on their way to their jobs in the morning. They have come by train from the suburbs and walk from the railroad station across London Bridge to the financial district:

> Under the brown fog of a winter dawn,
> A crowd flowed over London Bridge, so many,
> I had not thought death had undone so many.
> Sighs, short and infrequent, were exhaled,
> And each man fixed his eyes before his feet.

Eliot's achievement was not simply to present the city but to endow such scenes with imaginative intensity and suggestion; his images fuse, as he put it, "the sordidly realistic and the phantasmagoric." (He first learned, he said, the possibility of this fusion from Baudelaire.) The crowd flowing over London Bridge is a scene in contemporary London and in Dante's Limbo. (There are even verbal echoes of Dante.) Thus generalized and potentiated, Eliot's naturalistic report and interpretation of life in the city (which was also an interpretation of the life of man per se) was the most accessible and compelling aspect of the poem for its first readers. In a favorable review written in 1922 on commission for *The Dial,* Edmund Wilson warmed especially to this aspect of the poem: "All about us we are aware of nameless millions performing barren office routines, wearing down their souls in interminable labours of which the products never bring them profit—people whose pleasures are so sordid and so feeble that they seem almost sadder than their pains."

Because Eliot endowed his material with an almost visionary intensity, his poetry might from some points of view be thought "Romantic." But no reader in 1922 would have seen it this way. To dwell on the modern city, especially on the more sordid aspects of it, was to break dramatically with the Romantic tradition in poetry. The legacy of the great Romantic poets of England had created a persisting assumption that poetry would present nature or landscape. Hence, while throughout the nineteenth century cities spread and smokestacks multiplied, and while economists, sociologists, and moralists studied and debated the new phenomena, and while novelists such as Dickens (whom Eliot loved) rendered the clanging factories, the sooty fog, the crooked slum alleys and courtyards in flickering gaslight, the dust heaps and decaying houses—charging these images with intense feeling and evocative, symbolic meaning—poetry dwelt in vales and meads, locating itself in Camelot, Sicily, or anywhere that was far away or long before Liverpool, Manchester, Birmingham, Chicago, or Pittsburgh. The Georgians had lately reconfirmed this tendency to the great pleasure of their many readers.

In addition, when the Romantic poets dwelt on evil and tragedy they used images that were not only imaginatively heightened but also agreeable. Keats's "La Belle Dame Sans Merci," for example, contains fatal sickness and anguish, but of a knight-at-arms on an enchanted hillside in late autumn, not a pajamaed patient dying amid instruments and tubes in a London hospital. Because *The Waste Land* broke the fixed association between verse and the agreeable, the beautiful, or the ideal, it seemed to many readers not merely un- but anti-poetic.

Quasi-naturalistic scenes of modern life dominate (though not exclusively) the first three of the poem's five parts. The fifth part includes, however, a long passage of a directly visionary kind, which presents the speaker walking with others, or with all mankind, amid dry and stony mountains, a wasteland. The passage recalls an earlier one in the first part of the poem, where also the speaker or speakers are gazing on the "stony rubbish" of a desert,

> where the sun beats
> And the dead tree gives no shelter, the cricket no relief,
> And the dry stone no sound of water.

When two things are given at the same time readers will associate them together if possible. It was easy to suppose, especially in view of the title, that the imagery of the city and that of the desert were intended to interpret each other, that the modern city was compared to an arid, sterile waste. By the logic of this metaphor, water became a symbol for whatever would save or rescue. If this seems obvious, it also begins to indicate why the poem perplexed almost all its early readers, including admirers: to an extraordinary degree it relied on symbols and their interrelations to convey its meanings. It was not the mere activation of symbols that puzzled. But even in the most densely symbolic works to which English and American readers were up to then accustomed—Coleridge's "Ancient Mariner" or Melville's *Moby Dick* or James' *The Golden Bowl*—symbolism had been an element in a design that one apprehended primarily through other elements, especially plot and character.

The Waste Land struck readers as aggressively modern and bewildering because of what they did not find as well as what they found. It had no plot. There was no poet speaker to be identified with, as there was when reading Wordsworth, Shelley, Whitman, Tennyson, Yeats, or almost any other familiar poet of the last hundred and fifty years. Despite a strange footnote at the end of the poem about the role of Tiresias, the poem could not be taken as a dramatic monologue. Certainly it was not verse drama, though it contained quasidramatic vignettes.

My point is not simply that the poem could not be fitted into any known genre but that there seemed to be nothing—no narrative, meditation, flow of lyric emotion, characterization—which one could follow, thus "understanding" the poem. It began in a chantlike rhythm, the speakers seeming to lament the return of life in the spring:

> Winter kept us warm, covering
> Earth in forgetful snow, feeding
> A little life with dried tubers.

This was sustained for seven lines, and seemed to be continuing in the eighth line with "Summer surprised us." But suddenly an altogether different voice was heard, that of a woman named Marie, who reminisced conversationally. After eleven lines this passage also ended suddenly, and one was, with no transition, elsewhere, listening to a completely different, faintly biblical voice; the speaker seemed to be gazing on a desert:

> What are the roots that clutch, what branches grow
> Out of this stony rubbish?

Thus in the first thirty lines of the poem there were three different, apparently unrelated blocks of poetry, with dissimilar speakers, rhythms, images, and associations; and the poem continued in the same pell-mell flow of heterogenous fragments.

If readers were familiar with French symbolist poetry or with the recent poetry of Pound or with cubist painting or with stream-of-consciousness and depth psychology or with experiments in "point of view" in the modern novel, they felt they had a clue to the procedures of the poem. Not that the poem was closely similar to any of these prototypes, but they made it seem less unfamiliar. If the poem juxtaposed discontinuous fragments, the method, one might argue, released implications with a swiftness, density, and complex interaction no traditional technique could achieve. Or perhaps the fragments were not as separable as they seemed but evoked each other by irrational and subconscious associations. In either case, one thus asserted the profound meaningfulness, conscious or not, of the fragments—and especially of their multiple interrelations.

Even if single passages and juxtapositions could be explained and enjoyed on these or analogous grounds, there remained the question of the governing form of the whole. Admirers were challenged to account for their feeling of coherence in a poem without continuity of setting, style, speaking voice, or plot. The poem, they presently said, was organized like music. Of course no literary work can much resemble a musical composition, not even a composition of the later nineteenth century. The main use of the analogy was negative: it kept readers from looking for types of form and meaning they were not going to find. "Music" did not mean in this connection the sounds and rhythms but the sequence of emotions the poem created. In the sequence was a logic, it was asserted; the different phases of emotion interrelated to make a complex whole. Since an organization of emotion could only be felt, not shown, the point could not be elaborated; but it was supported by a special feature of the poem —the repetition in separate contexts of the same or easily associated scenes, images, and allusions. Recurrent passages, for example, describe a desert. The fortune-teller warns her client to fear death by water; the poem returns three times in separate allusions to Ariel's song describing the drowned Alonso in Shakespeare's *The Tempest;* it alludes also to the death by drowning of Ophelia in *Hamlet;* the fourth section of the poem pictures a drowned Phoenician floating in the sea.

Such recurring images and symbols could easily be described as "themes"; in the context of post-Wagnerian music they could be called leitmotifs. Thus it was possible to claim that *The Waste Land* was a poetic form on a new principle and that the principle was not simply the musical sequence and interrelations of emotions but the repetition and gradual interweaving of leitmotifs. As they return in a new context, they bring with them suggestions and associations from former contexts and become progressively denser nodes of connotation and feeling. At the same time, they further link the diverse passages and parts together. The literary use of the leitmotif was not unique to *The Waste Land,* but more than any other single source the poem called the attention of English-speaking readers to it. Once it was understood that works of literature could create a "web of themes," a musical "complex of relations" through the manipulation of "symbolically allusive" formulas (the phrases are Thomas Mann's, speaking of his *The Magic Mountain*), other writers tried their hands at it. The effect was noted and studied in authors, such as Dickens and Shakespeare, who had never heard of it themselves. All this helped Eliot to conceive more clearly what he had done in *The Waste Land,* and in the *Four Quartets* he carried the use of the leitmotif to its most complex development thus far in modern English and American poetry.

As they collect associations in different contexts, the leitmotifs gradually become symbols. Generally speaking, a writer may obtain an imagery of symbolic power in two different ways. Either he uses symbols previously established in literature, myth, occult lore, liturgy, and the like; or he transforms images into symbols within the context of his own work. Both methods are usually present. Fire was associated with lust long before *The Waste*

Land; the poem cites the Buddha's Fire Sermon and Augustine's *Confessions.* The symbolism of seasonal death and rebirth is age-old. But Eliot also created symbols by the incremental return to the same or closely similar images, as we see if we follow the associations that gradually gather in the poem around the imagery of water. Water is longed for if the protagonists are in a desert, yet feared lest they drown in it, and yet also—through allusions to Ariel's song—to drown may mean to be transformed in a process that is, as Ariel speaks of it, uncanny and ominous yet also strangely reassuring. Water is associated with sexual desire, and this throws still another implication into the fortune-teller's warning, "fear death by water." Assimilating such associations, we understand the mingled longing, fascination, and fear that water excites in the protagonists throughout the poem.

Death by drowning, furthermore, is one mode of the imagery of death and burial that also recurs throughout the poem. In the context of *The Waste Land* death does not mean only the extinction of life; the aimless, anxiety-ridden life of men and women in this urban wasteland is a living death. The Sibyl of the epigraph speaks for all the protagonists when, being asked, "Sibyl, what do you want?" she replies, "I want to die." But though she does not know it, her words may refer to death in a third sense, which haunts many of the protagonists of the poem, in which to die may mean to suffer a "sea-change," to receive a new being. Fearing death by water, the men and women in *The Waste Land* may fear their only hope.

THE "MYTHICAL METHOD"

In addition to quasi-naturalistic presentation and symbolism, *The Waste Land* conveyed meaning through a third dimension, the mythical. In the footnotes he included with the first publication of *The Waste Land* as a book, Eliot called particular attention to this:

Not only the title, but the plan and a good deal of the incidental symbolism . . . were suggested by Miss Jessie L. Weston's book on the Grail legend: *From Ritual to Romance* . . . To another work of anthropology I am indebted in general, one which has influenced our generation profoundly; I mean [Sir James Frazer's] *The Golden Bough* . . . Anyone who is acquainted with these works will immediately recognize in the poem certain references to vegetation ceremonies.

In *The Golden Bough* Frazer sought to demonstrate that apparently different myths may be traced back to the same underlying and original one. The myth Eliot especially had in mind is that which Frazer calls the myth of the dying and reviving god, especially as this myth was seized by Weston to interpret the medieval romances of the quest for the Holy Grail. According to Frazer, primitive men explained the annual death and resurrection of vegetation as "effects of the waxing or waning strength of divine beings, of gods and goddesses," as effects of "the marriage, the death, and the rebirth or revival of the gods." He also argued that the king was regarded as an incarnation of the fertility of the land; if he weakens or dies, the land becomes waste and returns again to fertility only when the king is healed or resurrected, either in his own person or in a successor. The ancient fertility myths were incorporated within Christianity—the vegetation king or deity was identified with the God of Christian faith—and, according to Miss Weston, the medieval romances of the Holy Grail blended these fertility myths surviving in the folk imagination with Christian materials. She called special attention to the figure of the Fisher King in many of the Grail romances (the fish, she said, is an ancient symbol of life); his land is arid and its people and animals are sterile because the king is (in different versions) dead, ailing, or impotent. If a questing knight can make his way through dangers to the Chapel Perilous, and there pass further trials, the king will be healed or restored. It is impossible in a few words to do justice to the complexity of Frazer's or Weston's argument or of Eliot's use of these sources. The point is that the poem alludes repeatedly to primitive vegetation myths and associates them with the Grail legends and the story of Jesus. In the underlying myth of the poem the land is a dry, wintry desert because the king is impotent or dead; if he is healed or resurrected spring will return, bringing the waters of life. The myth coalesces with the quasi-naturalistic description of the modern, urban world, which is the dry, sterile land.

If we ask to what extent these myths (or this myth) are actually in Eliot's poem, and important to it, the answers vary widely from reader to reader. The poem does not tell the myths as stories but only alludes to them, and the allusions may lie inert for readers unfamiliar with Frazer and Weston. The allusions are conveyed in phrases—"that corpse you planted last year in your garden," "the king my father's death"—that convey meaning even if the reference to myth is not recognized. If readers without the anthropological lore may miss some of the nuances Eliot intended, his use of myth can also produce an opposite result in other readers. For myth, which used to be dismissed as heathen darkness, has become a concept habitually invoked in modern discussion of religion, psychology, anthropology, art, and literature. The mere fact that it is present in Eliot's poem can excite ideas and feelings which are not so much derived from the poem as imposed upon it, but which modify interpretations of it. In the modern world it is possible to think at least the following things about myth: it is both a way of thinking and the object thought and in both aspects puts us in connection with the mentality of primitive man; mythical thought is different from scientific thought but valid within its own sphere; myth integrated primitive man with his natural environment, with his fellow men, with the past and the future, and with the divine and gave to man and his acts a significance lacking in a world deprived of myth; in the depths of the mind the mythical mentality persists in historical man to the present day, but we are rarely aware of it and most of us attribute little significance to it; because myth comes out of the depths of human nature and expresses them, to lose contact with it is to be alienated from powerful sources of emotional vitality; particular myths symbolize meanings of perennial psychological, moral, and religious validity, which cannot be adequately expressed in other terms. Readers strongly influenced by such assumptions usually find that *The Waste Land* implicitly attributes contemporary alienation and angst to the divorce of modern man from myth. From this point of view, the juxtaposition of present and past, which runs through the poem, generally compares that which once was fraught with mythical significance with its debased and meaningless counterpart in the modern world. This applies to the large, persisting "themes"—sexuality, death—and also to particular episodes or images, such as the Tarot pack, which was once invested with religious meaning but is now only a fortune-teller's prop.

Eliot shared some of these ideas about myth but on the whole he did not, in my opinion, believe or intend to suggest that human beings in earlier times were spiritually in better case than ourselves or that we could now recapture a vital relation to myth or in any way find our salvation through it (although he would not have argued against such interpretations of his poem, for he did not suppose a poet knew better than anyone else all that his poem might mean). It is, however, possible to be relatively precise in identifying what advantages he hoped to obtain from the use of myth. They are, in a broad sense of the term, formal and may be summed up as multiplicity of reference, depth, and shape.

Myth is story, fable; and even though Eliot does not tell the myths, his allusions to them introduce a plot or fable into the poem. When one knows the plot, one can vaguely integrate some of the episodes of the poem with it. The fable provides a third language, besides naturalistic presentation and symbolism, in which the state of affairs can be conceived; the story of the sick king and sterile land is a concrete and imaginative way of speaking of the condition of man. This story interrelates, substantiates, and nuances suggestions that are also made in other ways. The possibility of regeneration is already implied in the symbolism of the seasons and in the symbolic pattern woven through the poem by recurrent images of drowning ("death by water" may be a "sea-change"); the myth says plainly that the king may be healed, the fertility of the land restored. And the mythical background throws an additional meaning into many a particular line or phrase. When we read,

> That corpse you planted last year in your garden,
> Has it begun to sprout? Will it bloom this year?

meaning is enriched if we recollect that at the season of planting in ancient Egypt, the priests of Osiris put effigies of the god in the earth. The effigies were made out of earth mixed with grain, and, says Frazer, "When these effigies were taken up again . . . the corn would be found to have sprouted from the body of Osiris, and this sprouting of the grain would be hailed as an omen, or rather as the cause, of the growth of the crops. The corn-god produced the corn from himself: He gave his own body to feed the people: he died that they might live."

Handwritten annotations in top margin: Is "simultaneity" the keyword in E.'s historical sense – spatialization? – Yes. He is not saying, then, that we make the past, that we can never know it as a fact, is he?

To appreciate more fully why the "mythical method," as Eliot called it, appealed so strongly to him at this time, we must keep in mind his commitment to what he called "the historical sense." He did not believe that there was a value in exhibiting the past by itself; the past could have meaning only in relation to the present. But to dwell on the present in disconnection from the past is equally to drain it of significance. Instead, the past and present were to be united in one perspective. The past was to be brought to bear on the present, but not merely to invoke the past as a contrast or parallel, though this could be valuable. One had to live in the present, yet feel its continuity with the past; one had to perceive the past in the present. As Eliot put it in "Tradition and the Individual Talent," the "historical sense" is

nearly indispensable to any one who would continue to be a poet beyond his twenty-fifth year; and the historical sense involves a perception, not only of the pastness of the past, but of its presence; the historical sense compels a man to write not merely with his own generation in his bones, but with a feeling that the whole of the literature of Europe from Homer . . . has a simultaneous existence and composes a simultaneous order. . . . He must be aware that the mind of Europe . . . is a mind which changes, and that this change is a development which abandons nothing *en route,* which does not superannuate either Shakespeare, or Homer, or the rock drawing of the Magdalenian draughtsmen.

Handwritten annotation in right margin: (corresponds to incremental repetition method)

As an artist he sought a method that would incorporate the experience of men and women in the twentieth century within a larger whole of human experience throughout time.

In this connection, three of his prose pieces are particularly revealing; in all of them he testified at greater length to the impact on him of *The Golden Bough,* and in two of them he was reviewing works—Stravinski's *The Rite of Spring* and Joyce's *Ulysses*—which also introduced the mythical dimension into contemporary art and which may have helped suggest Eliot's own experiment in *The Waste Land. The Golden Bough,* he remarked in *Vanity Fair* in 1924, is "a work of no less importance for our own time than the complementary work of Freud—throwing its light on the obscurities of the soul from a different angle." Possibly, he went on, it is a work of "greater permanence" than Freud's, because the theories of Freud are debatable, whereas *The Golden Bough* "is a statement of fact which is not involved in the mainte-

nance or fall of any theory of the author's." The great achievement of Frazer was to disclose the mind of primitive man; he
"extended the consciousness of the human mind into as dark a
backward and abysm of time as has yet been explored"; he revealed, as Eliot put it in 1921 in his review of Stravinski, "that
vanished mind of which our mind is a continuation"—"vanished" only relatively speaking, since in some sense the primitive
mind still survives in the "obscurities of the soul." To incorporate myth in a literary work was to invoke and represent important, ordinarily disregarded, dimensions of reality—and of a
reality that is impersonal in relation to the poet. And to exhibit
contemporary civilization while also descending through myth
back deep into time and down into the psyche was to secure a
context of enormous depth and imaginative power.

In a "London Letter" to the *Dial* of October 1921, Eliot reported his attendance at *The Rite of Spring*. The ballet amalga-
mated primitive vegetation or fertility rites, as they are represented in the dances, with contemporary reality, as it was heard
in the music. Eliot felt no strong enthusiasm. More exactly, he
was intrigued by the music but thought little of the dances. For
the dances were too simply a pageant of primitive culture, and
he "missed the sense of the present." The music, however, "did
seem to transform the rhythm of the steppes into the scream of
the motor horn, the rattle of machinery, the grind of wheels, the
beating of iron and steel, the roar of the underground railway,
and the other barbaric cries of modern life; and to transform
these despairing noises into music." The lesson enforced was,
again, that "in art there should be interpenetration and meta-
morphosis."

When, in November 1923, Eliot reviewed *Ulysses* for the *Dial*,
The Waste Land was already in print. Hence, as Eliot pointed out
what artists could learn from *Ulysses,* he was pointing to what
could be found in his own poem; possibly he was also suggesting
what he himself owed to Joyce. (If we wish to reflect on the influence *Ulysses* may have exercised on Eliot, we should keep in
mind that he had been reading the novel in manuscript installments since 1918.) He said the novel was "the most important
expression which the present age has found" and that its "mythical method" was a breakthrough which other artists must exploit. The "mythical method" consisted in "manipulating a con-

tinuous parallel between contemporaneity and antiquity"—in this case the "parallel" of Odysseus and his adventures with Leopold Bloom and the incidents of his day in contemporary Dublin. It was "a way of controlling, of ordering, of giving shape and significance to the immense panorama of futility and anarchy which is contemporary history." "Psychology . . . ethnology, and The Golden Bough have concurred to make possible what was impossible a few years ago. Instead of narrative method we may now use the mythical method. It is, I seriously believe, a step toward making the modern world possible in art."

ALLUSION

When *The Waste Land* was published its mythical dimension did not excite as much interest as we might suppose. Eliot's references to myth seemed only additional examples of his allusiveness, and his use of allusions in the poem caused so much controversy that little attention was paid to his use of myth as a separate method or technique. Allusions in his early poems, *Prufrock and Other Observations* (1917), had been relatively few and easy to follow: "No! I am not Prince Hamlet," says Prufrock, and no reader of Eliot was likely to be unfamiliar with Shakespeare. Typically "Eliotic" (as some critics put it) allusions appeared in the poems in quatrains he composed in 1918—"Sweeney Among the Nightingales" and "Mr. Eliot's Sunday Morning Service"—not long after he had read the first installment of *Ulysses*. In *The Waste Land* they were fully developed:

> London Bridge is falling down falling down falling down
> *Poi s'ascose nel foco che gli affina*
> *Quando fiam uti chelidon*—O swallow swallow.

A few such cruxes might have passed as tolerable eccentricities, but there were not a few. The poem of 433 lines quoted or referred to at least thirty-seven other works of art, literature, or music—and to some of them several times. They were not necessarily familiar works; they included not only the Bible and Shakespeare, Virgil, Wagner, and Ovid but Baudelaire's "Les Sept Vieillards," Middleton's *A Game of Chess* and *Women Beware Women*, Webster's *The Devil's Law Case*, the Buddha's Fire

Sermon, Day's *Parliament of Bees,* Verlaine's *Parsifal,* Nerval's "El Desdichado," and so forth—and some of these back-to-back allusions were by means of quotations in Greek, Latin, German, French, Italian, and Sanskrit. As annotations piled up (in the wake of Eliot's own), it began to seem as though most of the poem might consist of echoes or quotations from other writers. Moreover, many of these allusions were presented by indirect means. Those who disliked Eliot's poetry found in them proof that he was not only pretentious and elitist but also without creative power, capable only of inorganic pastiche. Defenders were not usually wise in the arguments to which they resorted. They pointed out that other poets had been allusive; this, though true, was not candid, for in few poems throughout history had allusions come with such frequency and indirectness or referred to such obscure works or lacked to the same degree a context which interpreted them. Enthusiasts for the poem were sometimes tempted to let it be supposed that they easily recognized the allusions; whether or not Eliot's poem was pretentious, its admirers sometimes merited this criticism. It was also claimed that the allusions had their effect whether one recognized them or not, which was true only up to a point and occasionally. Though the debate had an important substance, it was conducted in defensive ways that contributed little. The truth is that Eliot's allusions generally require that the reader study and reflect. Whether the enhanced appreciation rewards the effort, one must decide for oneself, but one cannot have an opinion without having done the work.

Before Eliot made his impact on a whole generation, poets and readers were less likely to assume that modern poetry would be difficult. Robinson, Frost, Hardy, the Imagists, Masters, Sandburg, and the war poets seemed new and contemporary in technique and vision, yet their styles were not, on the whole, indirect, compressed, or obscure. The same thing might be said of Yeats if we consider only what he wrote up to about 1918. If we ask why the changed supposition of the next thirty years, during which the idiom of modern poetry was expected to be condensed and demanding, should be attributed more to Eliot than to other major poets, the answer lies in the extent to which *The Waste Land* was seen as the prototype of the "modern" in poetry.

Juxtaposition of apparently unrelated fragments, symbolism, myth, and allusion were components of an extraordinary compression of style. Juxtaposed fragments commented on each other, suggesting manifold, complex, and diverse implications. Through symbolism multifarious associations and connotations were evoked and complexly interwoven. The "mythical method" added levels of reference at every point. By allusion Eliot, like Joyce and Pound, brought another context to bear on his own, and the parallels and contrasts might offer a rich, indefinite "vista."

THE CONDITION OF MAN

Whether the poem is actually difficult depends on what one seeks to understand. Particular cruxes of interpretation cannot be decided but the vision of human nature and life is powerfully conveyed. Meanings are ambiguous, emotions ambivalent; the fragments do not make an ordered whole. But precisely this, the poem illustrates, is the human condition, or part of it. Men and women emerge and disappear; our encounters with them are brief and wholly external, for we apprehend them only as bits of speech overheard or gestures spotlighted. But this is the mode and extent of human contact in general, as the poem represents it. The protagonists in the poem are isolated from each other or they make part of a faceless crowd. When they speak there is no dialogue, for the other person, if one is present, does not reply. Whether we assume that the poem renders the stream of consciousness within a mind or that it presents modern civilization and culture by objective methods—it does both at the same time, but in many passages not quite either—it suggests that below the conscious levels of the mind and the ways of civilized life are the subconscious and primitive and that images from these spheres abide or well up suddenly, perhaps with deep significance. The personal and historical past lingers in fragmentary memories and visible reminders, which sharpen our sense of our present condition but suggest no way out of it. The individual mind and the civilization are on the edge of crack-up. Before the impending collapse there is passive waiting but no suggestion of will or even of wish. (At most the protagonists muse vaguely on what might be wished.) At the conclusion of the poem a total disintegration is suggested in a jumble (or apparent jumble) of literary quotations.

Exhibiting what men and women see, hear, say, and feel, the poem conveys in one vignette after another the sickness of the human spirit. But also in its web of vignettes and allusions the poem involves many of the current hypotheses about the cause of this modern sickness, theories then common in intellectual circles. It did not argue about the impact of historical events or social institutions on the human psyche; it did not speculate concerning the effect of new anthropological, psychological, and scientific lore; but it was plainly relevant to such familiar generalizations that sought to explain how the human spirit had been wounded in modern times. Comparative religion and mythology, depth psychology, the World War, industrialized work, and urbanized life were concretely reflected in the poem, and so were the effects to which they were often said to have contributed—the weakening of identity and will, of religious faith and moral confidence, the feelings of apathy, loneliness, helplessness, rootlessness, and fear. Yet the panoramic range and inclusiveness of the poem, which only Eliot's fragmentary and elliptical juxtapositions could have achieved so powerfully in a brief work, held in one vision not only contemporary London and Europe but also human life stretching far back into time. The condition of man seen in the poem was felt to be contemporary and perennial, modern yet essentially the same in all times and places.

ELIOT'S CRITICISM

Eliot's reviews and critical essays—approximately a hundred of which were published between 1916 and 1925—were a shock for many of their readers. To some they were reviving. Eliot's essays portended the end of an era. They dismissed the Romantic and Victorian tradition in poetry still dominant in the Georgian milieu. Eliot's style of critical prose ostentatiously lacked enthusiasm and personal charm; it seemed low-keyed and astringent to readers accustomed to the literary essays of Symons, Chesterton, Saintsbury, Yeats, or Quiller-Couch. Nevertheless, these exercises in analysis and discrimination strove for a finer precision than was usual in criticism at this time. Praise or blame was limited to aspects which were defined. Generalizations were illustrated by particular examples of verse. Conclusions were scrutinized and qualified. This intellectual conscientiousness made one feel that criticism must be more important than one had imagined. In fact, Eliot said, which writers are appreciated and why and how much are points of enormous significance. Of George Wyndham he was compelled to make the awful judgment that, "There is no conclusive evidence that he realized all the difference, the gulf of difference between" a line of Villon, which Eliot quotes, and Ronsard or du Bellay.

Poets were reminded that "the larger part of the labour of an author in composing his work is critical labour; the labour of sifting, combining, constructing, expunging, correcting, testing: this frightful toil." Many a poet, reading these words, must have searched his troubled conscience, wondering whether his toil had been sufficiently "frightful."

Eliot gave a new style to literary criticism and he endowed critical intelligence with a greater responsibility for the health of civilization than was generally supposed, although in his high estimate of criticism, as in several other ways, his views recalled those of Matthew Arnold. Gradually his essays helped form a new taste. Poets whom neither the Edwardians and Georgians in England, nor the Genteel and New Poets in America especially admired—Villon, Donne, Dryden, Baudelaire, and Laforgue—appeared on everybody's reading list, and a type of poetry strongly influenced by Eliot and by these other exemplars became conventional and expected in the little magazines.

His essays were not polemical, but his attitudes and style as a critic were shaped to some degree by irritation with the literary milieu. Insisting on "the importance of intelligent criticism," he followed his old teacher, Irving Babbitt, in discovering little "intelligent criticism" in the English-speaking world, at least since the 1820s. Pound, to be sure, was "not to be diverted . . . from the essential literary problem" and was "always concerned with the work of art, never with incidental fancies," but he was hardly a critic of the first importance. His "brief and fugitive utterances" could not bear comparison with the sophistication, clarity, and cogency of the "French Intelligence," as exhibited, for example, in Remy de Gourmont or Julien Benda. Otherwise, as one looked about in 1918 there was very little criticism to be admired in England or America. Symons had broken down and was, in any case, undesirably impressionist. Yeats was fantastic. Saintsbury, Wyndham, and Whibley were uncritical gourmandizers. P. E. More and Irving Babbitt were moralists without aesthetic sensitivity. Academic critics approached literature as though it were "an institution" like "Church and State." (Pound classified Eliot in this category: he bestowed "granite wreaths, leaden laurels" and exemplified "the 'English Department' universitaire attitude.") As for the manifesto and review-writing Imagists, free versifiers, neo-Whitmanians, and dispensers of "all-American propaganda," they were "*esprits ordinaires*." The age was cursed with a tolerance of imprecision, a tendency to confuse (from Eliot's point of view) aesthetic emotion with morality and religion, an inability to conceive a fruitful relation to the past.

Were Eliot coming on the scene as a young writer today, there is no reason to suppose he would view it with more pleasure. Perhaps he would be irritated at different points, and therefore stress slightly different values. But however much they were shaped negatively by his age, his critical essays largely reflected his own practical dilemmas as a writer. In fact they partly owed their enormous influence to their grasp of problems of art from the artist's standpoint. Other factors were their stimulating intelligence, the fame or notoriety of Eliot's poetry, and the temptations his essays offered to weaker sides of human nature. With their allusiveness, fastidiousness, picky precision, sophistication, and tough-mindedness the essays made it possible to feel that, in joining the party of Eliot, one identified oneself with the hard, acute, erudite, complex, mature, and elite as opposed to the soft, dim, bland, callow, and vulgar. According to the then prevalent senses of the terms, Eliot's line was neither Modernist nor reactionary, for he insisted that great art was always both new and traditional; nevertheless, his essays offered a basis for scorning (with some exceptions) most other schools, parties, or important figures in the contemporary scene—"new" poets, Georgians, conservatives, Futurists, Yeats, Hardy, Frost, and so forth. The opportunity was appealing, especially to the young, who did not feel themselves under attack.

His criticism paid the closest, most serious attention to the formal qualities of poetry. As he compared and analyzed poets, he noted whether they had a "bright, hard precision," a control, balance, and proportion, a succession of concentrated, concrete images, and a "perpetual slight alteration of language, words perpetually juxtaposed in new and sudden combinations" (which evidences "a very high development of the senses"), for these were the qualities of idiom he usually admired, although he could show a surprising fondness for Kipling and Swinburne and at least once reminded himself that "our standards vary with every poet whom we consider." He gave the same scrutiny to versification, detailing how the rhythm of one poet resembled or contrasted with that of another and by what means the rhythms were created. In these respects his criticism was, for its time, unusually technical; the novelty, clarity, and pinpointing minuteness of these technical observations fascinated his readers and obtained an acceptance for his broader generalizations that was less rigorous than it otherwise might have been. Because his essays seemed to illustrate that "a patient examination of an artist's method and form . . . is exactly the surest way" to appreciate his "human value," they helped bring on the criticism by close analysis of formal qualities that became widespread in England and America.

In speaking of "form," Eliot often had in mind not so much particular formal qualities (Jonson's "natural," Milton's "artificial" syntax) as something close to the notion of a "genre." He thought of this as a system of conventions, including conventions of technique (blank verse, the soliloquy, the five-act structure), of character (the vice, the braggart soldier), of plot (the revenge tragedy), and of the interpretation of human nature and experience ("the handling of Fate and Death"). Where such a form or system of conventions exists, it will have been developed and organized through several generations and there will be an audience prepared to "respond in a predictable way" to the familiar stimuli. Eliot's chief example of such major form is the Elizabethan-Jacobean drama, though he also refers to the *Divine Comedy*, which depended, in his opinion, upon a similar orchestration of conventions in the Provençal and Tuscan poetry before Dante. In an age when such a system or form was established and available to writers as a framework, "how *little*"—this is Eliot's point—Dante, Shakespeare, or any other poet was obliged to create for himself.

Because such a form exists before the writer uses it, his relation to it has a double aspect. On the one hand, he handles it in an individual way; on the other, he suppresses his own individuality by submitting to the requirements of the form. Such a writer might be compared to a medieval stone-carver; his work would not be mistaken for that of someone else but it is not self-expressive; it reflects his own skill, intelligence, and feeling, and yet it is also composed in accordance with (one might almost say *by*) conventions that have been handed down, and which he has for the most part no thought of challenging. The requirements of the form are not the same in each generation. For since the form has an objective identity and evolves through time by its own dynamic, the artist's task is conditioned by the phase of development it has reached. A major artist is characterized by a tact or intelligence which senses precisely what can and what can no longer be done; he perceives the restrictions his age imposes, and in his hands they become opportunities. The presence or lack of such a form accounts for the greater literary achievement of some ages as compared with others; it is not that talent is sometimes more abundant, but less of it may be wasted. "No man can invent a form, create a taste for it, and perfect it too." In the "anarchy" of the modern world no major form is available to the writer, who is "obliged to consume vast energy in this pursuit of form" with no hope of achieving a "wholly satisfying result."

Eliot was plainly uttering his own complaint as a poet in the twentieth century; he was also striking out against fundamental premises of the Romantic view of poetry. He was far from sharing the Romantic reverence for the poet. Where Coleridge pondered with awe the "productive life-power of inspired genius," Eliot saw a toiling craftsman. Poetry was not individual self-expression, at least, it should not be. It was objective, impersonal construction. In its creative activity the mind of a poet, he explained in "Tradition and the Individual Talent," resembles a catalyst in a chemical process; it causes materials to combine but does not enter into or express itself in the resultant combination. "Poetry is not a turning loose of emotion, but an escape from emotion; it is not the expression of personality, but an escape from personality," and "The more perfect the artist, the more completely separate in him will be the man who suffers and the mind which creates." A poet is not to be expected to hold original and profound thoughts on "Man, on Nature, and on Human Life" (the phrase is Wordsworth's). Eliot would argue that poetry is more likely to be successful to the extent that a poet echoes the "commonplaces" of his age, if there are any. His sharp trimming of Romantic attitudes is focused most provocatively in his opinion of literary conventions.

In the early part of this century the general mass of poetry was as tamely conventional as it usually is—perhaps more so. In theory, however, the conventional was hackneyed and out of touch with reality. (A "conventional" poet within the Romantic tradition is a self-contradiction, and magazine poets at the turn of the century must have assumed that the conventional was still the neoclassical and that to sound like Shelley, Wordsworth, or Keats was a gesture of freedom.) For Eliot the conventional was a positive element, and not only because it rescued the artist from the poverty of the merely individual, while also doing much of his work for him. The conventional was the necessary distortion of reality by which art sets itself at a distance and compels us to view it as art. His attitude contained much that recalled the aesthetes of the nineties. Art advanced in worth to the degree that it was strict with itself. "Artists are constantly impelled to invent new difficulties for themselves; cubism is not license, but an attempt to establish order." Of course distortion was not falsification; the purpose was to bring out the real, or aspects of it, more sharply. But between genuinely artistic representation and realistic transcription there was a difference *toto caelo*.

From this point of view, even the Elizabethan dramatists were part of the movement of "deterioration" which "culminated in Sir Arthur Pinero and in the present regimen of Europe." For they were unwilling to "accept any limitation and abide by it"; they did not lack a system of conventions, but in their greediness "for every sort of effect together," they lacked artistic clarity and discipline; there was "no firm principle of what is to be postulated as a convention and what is not." The error grew in later centuries, but it was characteristic of Eliot to find the first symptoms of decay very far back and precisely in the period and

Shakespeare's later plays

genre of literature generally viewed as the greatest in English literary history. It was also characteristic that he postulated, as an example to be followed, a pre-Elizabethan drama. "In one play, *Everyman,* and perhaps in that one play only, we have a drama within the limitations of art; since Kyd, since *Arden of Feversham,* since *The Yorkshire Tragedy,* there has been no form to arrest, so to speak, the flow of spirit at any particular point before it expands and ends its course in the desert of exact likeness to the reality which is perceived by the most commonplace mind." Sometimes Eliot reminds one of Dr. Breisacher in Mann's *Dr. Faustus,* who thought that Hebrew religious feeling was already in decay in the time of David and Solomon.

Eliot's criticism pondered the relation that should pertain between the poetry of the present and of the past. It was a question that inevitably presented itself to a thoughtful mind at a time when the poetic milieu was divided, roughly speaking, between those who continued more or less in familiar modes and those who were seeking to write in entirely new ways, either because they felt that the traditional modes were played out or because they felt that in a new age and, in the case of American poets, a new country a vital poetry must reflect the current language and sensibility only—whatever smacked of the past thereby divorced itself from the present time and place. Eliot agreed that one could not simply continue in the conventions of the nineteenth century, as the work of the Georgians illustrated. Yet he did not think it either possible or desirable to throw off the past completely. For one thing, the notion was impractical. A poet must have models, standards, aims, and procedures. These are not innate and must be formed through contact with external influences; whatever auxiliary influences may derive from other forms of literature, from art, music, philosophy, and scientific lore, or from the audience, the main influence comes from the poems a poet reads. If he reads only contemporaries, his work will cultivate with diminishing hope the ground they have already worked over. He can go further and deeper by including the past, or by amalgamating native traditions with those of a foreign country.

There were also less immediately practical considerations. Arguing in a more or less idealist way, Eliot posited that there is a "mind" of Europe. This mind alters as time passes, yet remains essentially the same. Similarly there is a "mind" of the nation: "We suppose a mind which is not only the English mind of one period with its prejudices of politics and fashions of taste, but which is greater, finer, more positive, more comprehensive than the mind of any period." This mind appears in the "organic whole" a "national literature" makes, for a "national literature" is not merely a "collection of the writings of individuals" but a "system" of works between which there is a relation. Whether or not a work belongs within this system or "tradition," or is eccentric to it, has nothing to do with the originality or genius of the individual writer. But it has a great deal to do with our sense of the depth, relevance, and permanent value of the work itself, for it is only "in relation to" such systems that "individual works of literary art, and the works of individual artists, have their significance."

Finally, there was the enormous influence of Eliot's premise that the poetry of a diverse and complex age such as the present must itself be complex, compressed, and ironical. He said this in many different ways, but perhaps the single most influential way was in connection with the English "metaphysical" poets of the early seventeenth century. His important essays on them were published in 1921, and republished in *Homage to John Dryden* (1924). The book assured Eliot's rank, at the age of thirty-six, as one of the foremost living critics. It is incorrect to suppose that Eliot alone revived interest in these poets, for they were by no means neglected before he wrote about them; but his essays made appreciation of them an "in" attitude. Moreover, his careful and repeated attempts to define the characteristic "wit" of the "metaphysical" poets stimulated modern poets to emulate it. Because of his praise of this wit as the evidence or product of a healthy state of "sensibility," it became in the minds of some critics a criterion by which all poetry should be judged. Thus, Eliot's essays did more than anything else to spark the Metaphysical Revival of the 1920s and 1930s.

Eliot reminded readers that he was recalling older meanings of the word "wit," when it implied not so much a mode of humor as intellectual power and quickness, especially as these manifest themselves in apt, unexpected combinations. In his essays wit gradually came to mean an adequate complexity of response. For example, in a witty, or mature, person, emotion does not dislocate awareness; intelligence stays wakeful to judge or criticize feeling. The "ordinary man," Eliot explains, "falls in love, or reads Spinoza" (the affectation in this phrasing—the "ordinary man" reading Spinoza—made him wince in later years); and in the "ordinary man" these remain separate, disconnected experiences, but in a poet they interreact. Romantic and Victorian poets such as Shelley, Tennyson, and Browning resembled the "ordinary man" in this respect, for they could not, Eliot maintained, think and feel in the same moment or, as he better put it, they did "not feel their thought" immediately. A "dissociation of sensibility" was already setting in during the later seventeenth century, and from it "we have never recovered."

Trying further to define this lost wit, Eliot suggests that it was "a tough reasonableness beneath the slight lyric grace." Wit shows itself in an "alliance of levity and seriousness" by which "the seriousness is intensified"; it is not "cynicism," though it may "be confused with cynicism by the tender-minded," for it "implies a constant inspection and criticism of experience. It involves, probably, a recognition, implicit in the expression of every experience, of other kinds of experience which are possible."

Romantic and Victorian poetry was not only or always serious—far from it. Twentieth-century poetry has not always qualified its earnestness with irony or humor; and by "wit" Eliot did not mean verbal banter or joking. Nevertheless, in the "alliance of levity and seriousness" found in some mode and degree in much of our greater poetry, the element of levity has been more strongly emphasized in the twentieth century than it was in the hundred years before. One thinks of the country humor of Hardy—if Hardy was a twentieth-century poet—and of his sense for the grotesque. One thinks of the ironies of Housman, the humorous shrewdness and pathos of Robinson, the teasing evasiveness of Frost and Edward Thomas, the "Romantic" irony of de la Mare, the Georgian appreciation for the light touch, the accusing satire of the English war poets, the buffooneries, fopperies, and deliberate fantasticalities of the New York set. In this perspective Eliot's praise and emulation of "metaphysical wit" appear as part of a broader tendency.

LATER LIFE

In 1925 Eliot left Lloyds Bank and joined the publishing firm of Faber and Gwyer (later Faber and Faber), where he worked for the rest of his life. In 1932 he separated from his wife. His days were busy with editorial chores, with Church concerns, with writing and lecturing, and with the endless jobs a famous author cannot avoid. In 1948 he received the Nobel Prize for literature. In 1957 he married Valerie Fletcher, and very happily.

After 1932, when his *Selected Essays* gathered together what he considered the best of his critical pieces, he held an acknowledged authority in the literary world for which no comparison can be found in England or America unless one goes back to the later years of Samuel Johnson. Even Johnson was not so much regarded as an oracle on the literature of his own lifetime. Unless one still remembers or reads the literary discussions of twenty to forty years ago, one can now have no idea how frequently Eliot's sentences were quoted as sources of authority or points to dispute. He held this position more or less to the end of his life, conducting himself on his eminence with tact, dignity, and benevolence.

Throughout the 1920s Eliot was exploring a new world of thought and feeling in religion. At the age of twenty-one he had found himself strangely mirrored in the despairing pessimism of Laforgue. He had lived through growing emotional anxiety, depression, and guilt in his personal life during his early years in London and had sought and not found a belief or faith that would give a meaning to man's suffering. He had put his personally lived emotion into *The Waste Land.* Although the poem dwells on the meaningless and degraded life of man, it also evokes in thick allusion the religious faiths that may have given significance to life in other times and places—the pagan world, ancient Palestine and India, the centuries of Christian belief in Europe. Symbols of religious faith, even fragments of prayer, are present; they are not necessarily understood or, if understood, believed in, but they are very much in mind.

The steps of Eliot's religious conversion cannot be closely traced. As early as 1920 he was speaking appreciatively of Dante's *Paradiso,* against which he had harbored a prejudice ten years before. The *Paradiso* completes and explains, he said, the horrible and disgusting episodes in the *Inferno*. Dante's world has a definite structure, one that articulates life totally and endows human character and action with moral and religious meaning. Eliot's study of Dante (who meant more to him than any other poet throughout his life) was one of the experiences that shaped his growing change of mind. *The Hollow Men* (1925), his next major poem after *The Waste Land*, descends further into emotional despair and paralysis, yet symbols of Christian hope are present in a more explicit way, as though despair were focused on Christianity as the only alternative. In 1926 he was reading sermons and other works of Anglican clerics of the sixteenth and seventeenth centuries. In 1927 he formally became a member of the Anglican Church. His poems and plays henceforth were written from within a Christian commitment. The finest of them, *Ash-Wednesday* (1930) and the *Four Quartets* (1943), deal with the struggle for faith in a person who has made such a commitment.

The same year that he was baptized Eliot became a naturalized English subject. England had been his home for twelve years; his wife, job, and friends were there. But these were not the only grounds of his gesture. The formal acts of baptism and naturalization expressed his resolve, at the age of thirty-nine, to make fundamental, deliberate, and final commitments, determining who he was and would be in the future. *Ash-Wednesday*, composed at this time, articulates his complex, ambivalent feeling at having decided; his emotional and spiritual struggle henceforth would be to live with the choices made:

> Because I do not hope to turn again
> Let these words answer
> For what is done, not to be done again
> May the judgement not be too heavy upon us.

His new citizenship expressed Eliot's growing sympathy with English literary, historical, and religious traditions. He frequently noted that there was in English literature a succession of major poet-critics—Sydney, Dryden, Johnson, Coleridge, and Arnold—which was unique among the literatures of the world, and he derived a sense of his own possible role from these predecessors. Johnson and Coleridge had been lay champions of the church; Coleridge and Arnold had written works of social theory and criticism; Eliot was presently to emulate them. *The*

Idea of a Christian Society (1939) may be compared with Coleridge's *On the Constitution of Church and State; Notes Toward the Definition of Culture* (1948) with Arnold's *Culture and Anarchy*. For twenty years Eliot had been studying the poets and dramatists of the seventeenth century. At first he had been intrigued by their versification, then by other qualities of style; gradually the question had deepened, and he had tried to conceive and describe the sensibility and vision that formed their style. Hence as throughout the 1920s he felt his way toward a religious commitment and conversion, the particular religion or church that held his imagination was Anglican—more exactly, an Anglo-Catholicism rooted in the English Renaissance—and when he was baptized in 1927, he felt himself to have become a "bearer" of this tradition. Remembering Eliot's earlier feeling of "profound kinship" or "peculiar personal intimacy" with Jules Laforgue, one may say that he was consolidating a second identification, though it was a complex, diffused identification with several writers rather than with one. In the seventeenth-century Anglican bishop Lancelot Andrews, for example, Eliot observed a man of "decorum and devotion" in his private life, who had a "passion for order" in religion and in prose. With his "breadth of culture" Andrews transcended English provinciality and spoke with "Continental antagonists" as an equal. His sermons are "not easy reading" for they are "peppered with allusion and quotation"; moreover, they do not satisfy the Romantic taste for personality and self-expression. Andrews' emotion "is not personal" but is "wholly contained in and explained by its object"; his "voice" is not merely that of a private individual but "the voice of a man who has a formed and visible church behind him."

As the fascist and Communist dictatorships loomed abroad in the 1930s and class conflict intensified at home, Eliot wrote much on problems of social organization and politics. His position was conservative, in some statements radically so. It seemed the more conservative in the context of the 1930s, for his religious view of man's innate evil put him at a wide distance from contemporary, secular hopes of renovation through social institutions. The strictness of his moral and intellectual conscience made his politics somewhat impractical, as he himself recognized; in all parties and programs he saw inconsistency, danger, and wrong. He was, for example, against the dictators, but democracy as it existed in England and America also excited his distaste.

He continued to write criticism (*Dante*, 1929; *The Use of Poetry and the Use of Criticism*, 1933; and *On Poetry and Poets*, 1943, collecting his later essays). He edited *The Criterion*, a journal of literature and ideas which he founded in 1922 and which lasted until 1939. He attempted to develop a poetic drama that would be viable on the modern stage. *Sweeney Agonistes*, his first and most brilliant experiment, was left unfinished in the 1920s and published in 1932. It was followed by *The Rock* (1934), *Murder in the Cathedral* (1935), and *The Family Reunion* (1939). In these plays the poetry is still compelling, but when, after a ten-year interval, he returned to the form in *The Cocktail Party* (1950), it was not. Though the play had considerable commercial success, it seems unlikely to last except as a curiosity in the career of a great poet. The same thing may be said of his two subsequent plays, *The Confidential Clerk* (1954) and *The Elder Statesman* (1959).

Between the early 1930s and 1942 Eliot composed the finest sequence of long poems yet written in the twentieth century, the *Four Quartets*. The first of these, *Burnt Norton*, grew out of lines not used in *Murder in the Cathedral* (just as *The Hollow Men* crystallized around bits left over from *The Waste Land*). The final three, *East Coker, The Dry Salvages*, and *Little Gidding* developed out of the first and kept the same form. *The Four Quartets* are poetry of a widely different kind from *The Waste Land*. The dramatic vignettes of *The Waste Land* are absent, as is, for the most part, the urban scene. There is still allusion to past literature, still a fragmentary or, at least, disjunctive progression, but these features are less noticeable. It is still densely symbolic, even symbolist writing; the same or closely associated symbols—the fire, the rose—weave incrementally through the whole work. But it also employs a directly meditative and generalizing style not found in *The Waste Land*. It makes a poetic use of place as the subject or occasion of meditative reflection; in doing so it adopts a convention which has persisted in English poetry from the descriptive-meditative verse of the eighteenth century to the present day. The feeling of piety before past life and history, as they are embodied or brought to mind in the village of East Coker, for example, or in the chapel at Little Gidding, was also usual within this convention. Thus, the *Four Quartets* were a more traditional and accessible type of poetry than *The Waste Land*.

22

THE NEW YORK AVANT-GARDE
STEVENS AND WILLIAMS TO THE
EARLY 1920s AND MARIANNE MOORE

BETWEEN 1912 and 1922 poets and painters in New York City formed a thriving avant-garde. The dates are chosen to mark approximately the first phase of the Modernist movement, extending from the founding of *Poetry* magazine to the publication of *The Waste Land*. During this period there were numerous little magazines in and around New York: *Others, Rogue, Camera Work, 291, The Seven Arts, Broom, The Dial. The Little Review* moved from Chicago to New York in 1917. The New York poets were Alfred Kreymborg, Mina Loy, Maxwell Bodenheim, Orrick Johns, William Carlos Williams, Walter Conrad Arensberg, Donald Evans, Pitts Sanborn, Allen and Louise Norton, Wallace Stevens, Lola Ridge, and Marianne Moore. Thirty to forty years later, some of these New York poets were to become famous, but compared with Eliot, Pound, and H.D. in London, Amy Lowell and Robert Frost in New England, and Masters, Lindsay, and Sandburg in the Midwest, they all seemed of lesser significance in the 1910s.

Surveying the city in 1915, we may begin with nearby Grantwood in New Jersey. Here Alfred Kreymborg shared a three-room shack with two artist friends, Man Ray and Samuel Halpert. To this shack in 1913 came a parcel from London, wrapped in butcher's paper, containing the manuscript of

Pound's Imagist anthology (*Des Imagistes*). Unknown and impecunious though he was, the delighted Kreymborg managed to publish it in 1914.

In Greenwich Village, Allen and Louise Norton were editing *Rogue*. To them the mode of London twenty-five years before seemed the last word in modern daring, and *Rogue* aimed to be exquisite, dandyfied, and decadent. Allen Norton may be sampled in *Saloon Sonnets: With Sunday Flutings* (1914). Donald Evans was the best of the *Rogue* poets, unless we include Wallace Stevens among them. Poems of Stevens in *Rogue* were "Tea," "Cy Est Pourtraicte . . . ," and "Disillusionment of Ten O'Clock."

At parties for *Rogue*'s contributers Kreymborg met Walter Conrad Arensberg. The wealthy Arensberg agreed with him that Harriet Monroe's *Poetry* was much too conservative and conventional, and the two poets decided to found a rival poetry monthly, Arensberg paying the printers. *Others* thus came into being in 1915. Edited by Kreymborg, it printed in its first year poems by Mina Loy, William Carlos Williams, Wallace Stevens, Amy Lowell, Maxwell Bodenheim, T. S. Eliot, John Gould Fletcher, Richard Aldington, Ezra Pound, Marianne Moore, Padraic Colum, and Carl Sandburg—not to mention Kreymborg, Arensberg, and numerous poets now forgotten. After undergoing the crises of erratic editing and failing finances common to little magazines, *Others* folded in 1919. Its last word was a prose supplement of wild and sour "Belly Music" by William Carlos Williams.

Others was not devoted to a particular group or school. Its representation of the "new" poetry was broad, and Kreymborg was admirably eager to help unknown poets by printing their work. His magazine differed from *Poetry* mainly in that it did not also find space for the more conservative or traditional verse of the age, though this was a considerable difference. Those who helped Kreymborg edit the magazine and published frequently in it—such as Bodenheim, Williams, Orrick Johns, and Mina Loy—were said to make up an "Others group." Wallace Stevens and Marianne Moore were sometimes classified with them. As their contemporaries viewed them, the *Others* poets were the fantastics of the avant-garde.

Alfred Kreymborg (1883–1966) probably most wished to be

remembered as an experimental dramatist. His first volume of
poetry, *Mushrooms* (1916), was read with at least enough interest
to excite parody. (In Orrick Johns it excited emulation; see his
"Olives" in the first issue of *Others*.) The mushrooms are short,
free-verse utterances, and include the notoriously cute "The
Tree" ("I am four monkeys . . ."). They are fanciful, wistful,
graceful, touched with humor and resignation, and expert in
rhythm and music. "Nocturne" is typical:

> The pantaloons are dancing,
> dancing through the night,
> pure white pantaloons
> underneath the moon,
> on a jolly wash line
> skipping from my room,
> over to Miranda,
> who washed them this noon.

"Vista" may also be quoted:

> The snow,
> ah yes, ah yes, indeed,
> is white and beautiful, white and beautiful,
> verily beautiful—
> from my window.
> The sea,
> ah yes, ah yes, indeed,
> is green and alluring, green and alluring,
> verily alluring—
> from the shore.
> Love?—
> ah yes, ah yes, ah yes, indeed,
> verily yes, ah yes, indeed!

Like several of the early champions of free verse, Kreymborg
in later years took to composing in regular stanzas and meters
and even brought forth a multitude of sonnets. In 1921 and
1922 he edited a second little magazine, *Broom*. He also wrote
novels and put together an admirable anthology of American
poetry. *Our Singing Strength* (1929), a critical history of poetry in
the United States, and *Troubadour* (1925), his charming autobiography, contain a wealth of information about twentieth-century
poetry.

Kreymborg dropped in frequently at the photography and art gallaries of Alfred Stieglitz at 291 Fifth Avenue. Known for his experimental photography and for his magazine, *Camera Work,* Stieglitz decided in 1907 to exhibit drawings and paintings as well. Between 1908 and 1911 his gallery showed the work of Matisse, Toulouse-Lautrec, Henri Rousseau, Cézanne, and Picasso. Modern European painters had not been publicly exhibited in the United States up till then, not, at least, in a selection and quantity that allowed them to be intelligently studied. *Camera Work* began to publish reproductions of their paintings and drawings and it explained Cubist and abstract art in essays. Stieglitz's next journal, *291,* continued this effort and also presented some literary experiments with dream sequences and with collage techniques adapted from painting.

In 1913 the famous exhibition of Modern Art at the Armory on Lexington Avenue brought paintings by Renoir, Matisse, Picasso, Cézanne, Braque, Gauguin, and Picabia to America. The interest in modern European painting that had gradually been spreading among avant-garde writers in New York now reached new intensity. "We'd have arguments," Williams later recalled in his *Autobiography,* "over cubism which would fill an afternoon. There was a considerable whipping up of interest in the structure of the poem." In his apartment on West 67th Street, Arensberg had already begun to assemble the famous collection of modern paintings now in the Philadelphia museum. Painters and writers met at his parties. Stevens, for example, spent an evening with Arensberg and Marcel Duchamp. Looking at Duchamp's "things," he "made very little out of them," for, as he told his wife, he was "without sophistication in that direction, and with only a very rudimentary feeling about art." (Despite these intimidated disclaimers, he had a very considerable interest in paintings and later collected them to the modest extent that his purse would bear.) The intentions, values, and techniques of all the painters thus brought to the attention of poets differed widely. Moreover, they could not easily be adapted to the different art of poetry. But familiarity with Modernist painters, sculptors, and photographers was possible in the United States only in New York, a fact that helps explain why poets of the avant-garde in New York developed somewhat differently from "new" poets elsewhere.

A COMPRESSED IDIOM

Discussing Modernist style in British poetry, we dwelt on the dense, active texture of the phrasing—for example, the nimble associations of Edith Sitwell or the compressed, cerebral wit of Edgell Rickword. In England such texture developed in the 1920s, with the work of Eliot an important stimulus. The same stimulus was felt by younger poets who began publishing in the United States in the twenties. But in New York an equally active, close texture of phrase had evolved independently of Eliot during the 1910s.

Imagism was a concise, precise, elliptical way of writing, but it was seldom packed or difficult, at least as practiced by Amy Lowell, H.D., and their American followers. Neither was the poetry of Robinson, Frost, and the so-called "Chicago school" of Masters, Lindsay, and Sandburg. But in the 1910s Mina Loy was writing:

> We might have coupled
> In the bed-ridden monopoly of a moment;

and Marianne Moore, in a swift succession of witty metaphors referring to a carrot:

> with everything crammed belligerent-
>   ly inside itself, its fibres breed mon-
>   opoly—
>   a tail-like, wedge shaped engine with the
>   secret of expansion;

and Maxwell Bodenheim in "An Old Negro Asleep,"

> As spilled, dried wine that colors earth,
> The yellow-white light sinks into his rubbed brown face,
> And perhaps reaches even the seeded dreams below,
> Melting then to webbed shapes he cannot hold;

and William Carlos Williams, adapting Futurist and painterly effects in "Spring Strains":

> But—
> (Hold hard, rigid jointed trees!)
> the blinding and red-edged sun-blur—
> creeping energy, concentrated

> counterforce—welds sky, buds, trees,
> rivets them in one puckering hold!
> Sticks through!

and Wallace Stevens, at the start of "Le Monocle de Mon Oncle":

> "Mother of heaven, regina of the clouds,
> O sceptre of the sun, crown of the moon,
> There is not nothing, no, no, never nothing,
> Like the clashed edges of two words that kill."
> And so I mocked her in magnificent measure.
> Or was it that I mocked myself alone?

Pitts Sanborn occasionally experimented with eliptical juxtapositions in his "Vie de Bordeaux" poems, and even Arensberg, whose verse was often old-fashioned, is quoted in an *Others* article as having written,

> which have the butters of extra broken,

though I have not seen the poem from which this is cited. The quotations are all taken from *Others.*

Mina Loy was English and came to New York with imposing avant-garde credentials, for she had known Marinetti in Milan and Apollinaire in Paris. As a woman poet, she was regarded as a serious rival to Marianne Moore. Her best-known work was her "Love Songs." They are witty, physical, philosophical, anti-sentimental, and vigorously phrased:

> I must live in my lantern
> Trimming subliminal flicker
> Virginal to the bellows
> Of experience
>   Coloured glass;

or,

> I am the jealous store-house of the candle-ends
> That lit your adolescent learning.

Her poems were published in journals but were not collected in books. At least, the only volume of hers I have seen dates from 1923 and was printed in Paris by Robert McAlmon.

John Pitts Sanborn (1879–1941) knew Wallace Stevens from Harvard. He joined the editorial staff of *Trend* in 1914 and the journal was thereafter open to avant-garde poets. In fact, Stevens himself was first published in *Trend*—"Carnet de Voyage" in 1914. Sanborn's Vie de Bordeaux poems are sometimes fantastical in their conceptions. They have a French setting, may be influenced by Laforgue, and include nicely flowing free verse. Sanborn became a noted music critic and a radio commentator for the Philadelphia Orchestra. Walter Conrad Arensberg was also a friend of Stevens from Harvard days. His translations of French symbolistes were valuable but he soon ceased to write poetry.

Because Maxwell Bodenheim (1892–1954) ended as a derelict, selling poems for whiskey, his life has been more talked about than his writing. He has been viewed as the prototypical bohemian, free and tragic, whose existence is somehow closer to essentials than that of most of us. This is a sentimental myth. As Jack B. Moore points out, in the only book about Bodenheim, there is nothing to romanticize in the mental fears that preyed on him.

At the start of his career he seemed promising. Some poems were printed in *Poetry*. He got to know a number of writers in Chicago before moving to New York, where he stayed for a while with Kreymborg and his wife. Here he met other poets and also became acquainted with the Provincetown Players, who performed two of his plays in 1917. He was now twenty-five. The next year his first book of poems appeared, to be followed by five more in the next five years.

Many of Bodenheim's poems show the influence of Sandburg. They are warmly sympathetic, free-verse impressions of people and scenes, usually in an urban, working-class milieu ("The Vagabond in the Park," "The Rear-Porches of an Apartment Building"). They differ from Sandburg's in that they make a more frequent and surprising use of metaphor. His metaphors, typically, are vivid as images or pictures and indefinite in their implications. In "Sunday in a Certain City Suburb," for example, the lives of the dominoe-players

> are the centers of half-cloudy days,
> With now and then a noisy evening
> In which they hang the crude little japanese lanterns
>   of their thoughts
> On the ever-swaying strings of their minds.

In "Advice to a Forest" there are

> trees, to whom the darkness is a child
> Scampering in and out of your long, green beards,

and in "To Li T'Ai Po,"

> Faces where middle age
> Sits, tearing a last gardenia.

He is a relatively inward poet, whose elaborations of metaphor capture complex emotional impressions. "Images of Emotions," the title of one of his poems, indicates the intention and method to which he was increasingly attracted.

We come now to three poets who were later to acquire wide reputation—Wallace Stevens, William Carlos Williams, and Marianne Moore. Of Williams and Stevens we shall here notice only their early careers down to 1923, when Stevens published *Harmonium* and Williams *Spring and All*. Both continued publishing into the second half of the century and became major influences in modern American poetry. Hence it seems useful to postpone a full discussion of their whole career until the forthcoming volume, where they can be viewed along with the younger poets who turned to them for example. With Marianne Moore the case is different. She also continued to publish, and her reputation grew steadily. But her style was so idiosyncratic that other poets could not do much with it, and she was admired without being much emulated.

WALLACE STEVENS

Wallace Stevens (1879–1955) was born in Reading, Pennsylvania. He studied at Harvard (1897–1900), acted as president of the college literary magazine, the *Advocate,* and met other student poets such as Arthur Davison Ficke, Witter Bynner, and Walter Conrad Arensberg. He tried to make a living at journalism in New York City until, yielding to his father's arguments, he entered Law School. He was admitted to the bar in 1904, and for the next twelve years practiced law or did legal work for business firms in New York. In 1909 he married Elsie Kachel of Reading, whom he had long courted and by whom he had a daughter, Holly Stevens. In 1916 he joined the Hartford Accident and Indemnity Co. and moved to Hartford, Connecticut, where he lived for the rest of his life, working with the same firm and concealing his activity as a poet from his business colleagues. At least, he concealed it as well as he was able and until he was well established in his firm. At his office he is said to have hid his poems by writing them on small pieces of paper which he tucked inside large law books.

Through Arensberg, Stevens met the *Others* group in New York. He published in little magazines ("Peter Quince at the Clavier" and "Sunday Morning" in 1915, "Letters d'un Soldat" and "Le Monocle de Mon Oncle" in 1918, for instance) and wrote three experimental, hopelessly undramatic plays.

In 1923 *Harmonium* appeared in an edition of 1,500 copies. The book aroused little interest and was soon remaindered. For the next few years Stevens wrote very little. He devoted his energies to the insurance business and relaxed with books, music, and gardening. But his reputation as a poet continued to grow, and his sense of this helped revive his imagination or ambition. In his fifties his career entered its second phase. Beginning with *Ideas of Order* in 1935, one book followed another in rapid succession: *Owl's Clover* (1936), *The Man with the Blue Guitar and Other Poems* (1937), *Parts of a World* (1942), *Notes toward a Supreme Fiction* (1942), *Esthétique du Mal* (1945), *Transport to Summer* (1947), and *The Auroras of Autumn* (1950). *The Necessary Angel* (1951) was a collection of essays on his central theme of "Reality and the Imagination."

Until the 1950s Stevens had enjoyed only a gradually spreading *succès d'estime* as a "poet's poet" or a "critic's poet." He now discovered that graduate students were reading him with enthusiasm, and some wished to write about him. At this academic reception he was wryly ironic as well as incredulous. Honors piled on him in his sixties and early seventies, including the offer, in 1954, to serve as Charles Eliot Norton Professor of Poetry at Harvard. (He turned it down, for he was diffident about lecturing on poetry. He also feared that acceptance would entail retirement from the insurance company.) Despite his growing reputation, he had been unwilling to bring out a collected edition, fearing lest such a climax to his career might also prove a termination. But in 1954 he admitted to his publisher,

Alfred Knopf, that he would "have difficulty in putting together another volume" and authorized publication of the *Collected Poems* (1954). An *Opus Posthumous* of poetry and prose appeared in 1957.

Harmonium contains poems written between 1915 and 1923. Because all his poems from before and many from after 1915 were rejected from this first volume, and because the arrangement of those selected is not chronological, the book does not reflect the stages by which Stevens' art developed. There is no reason why it should. But this mannered and dazzling style was not achieved all at once, and before taking up the poetry of *Harmonium*, I will try to indicate by what steps it came to be what it is.

Stevens began around 1899 as both a Romantic of the period of Keats and an aesthete of the 1890s. Going back to 1896, we find him writing letters in which he exercised himself in impressionistic descriptions, for as a teenager he planned to become a writer. In 1898 he started to keep a journal; during the next few years it reveals that he aspired to sincerity, "great" feelings, and "vigor" of thought and style, qualities he believed necessary for a poet. Inspecting his own character, he criticized himself for artificiality, coldness, and excessive self-analysis. Whether the criticisms were justified or not, they imply his Romantic preference for the opposite qualities of naturalness, warmth, and enthusiasm. He took long walks, during which he conscientiously noted the look of natural things from snails to clouds. He listened to birds "ease their hearts" in song; as he lay in a field to watch a sunset, he thought "that this must have been an old, Greek day, escaped, somehow, from the past." He came home, and began to read the third book of Keats's *Endymion*: "It was intoxicating." This was in 1899, while at Harvard. His college poems are exercises in nineteenth-century styles. The best of them, the "Ballade of the Pink Parasol," was probably influenced by a poem of Austin Dobson's.

As a journalist and law student in New York Stevens continued to produce poems. A typical example is "A Window in the Slums," four trim stanzas with inverted syntax and an interjected "Ah!":

> I think I hear beyond the walls
>   The sound of late birds singing.
> Ah! what a sadness those dim calls
>   To city streets are bringing.

In 1901 he drafted a four-act play to be called "Olivia: A Romantic Comedy." He read a great deal of poetry in English and French and continued to find pleasure in long walks, on one of which the future author of "The Snow Man" beheld "every leaf and blade of grass revealing or rather betokening the Invisible."

As early as 1896 he had signed a letter to his mother, "Forever with supernal affection, thy rosy-lipped arch-angelic jeune"; in the playfulness, ironic affectation, and self-protective somersaults of this one glimpses the future author of *Harmonium*. At least until he was thirty his informal prose in letters and journals is more characteristic than his poetry. His self-analysis is minute and sometimes boring, especially when he shows himself fascinated and relentless in discriminating the nuances of his sensations. But the rendering of sensations is vivid and the play of mind often subtle and rapid. He is remarkably likely to hold diverse, opposed points of view in one perspective, or suddenly to confront one with another.

By 1906 Stevens' jotted descriptions of nature in his journal, which had previously been more or less close and Keatsian, began to reflect a Dandy's pose. One day in March the clouds "were a most fashionable shade . . . Poor, dear, silly Spring, preparing her annual surprise!"; "Clear sky," goes another notation, "the twilight subtly medieval—pre-Copernican." In 1907, writing to his future wife, he identifies himself with Pierrot. His poetry was developing along similar lines, though more slowly. He was still writing sonnets. Incidentally, he continued to say his prayers every night, though he was reading Nietzsche and prayed without belief. He was still reading a great deal of poetry and enjoying most of what he read. He mentions Campion, Binyon, Verlaine, Keats, and Bliss Carman. Santayana's sonnets struck him, in 1906, as poems that fill the mind with Life and Truth. Some of his poems of this period are of the conventional type already sampled. Others emulate the terse, sometimes elliptical "sculpture of rhyme" of the 1890s. Some also show the influence of the exotic orientalism and poetic impressionism of those days. A poem of 1909 indicates how far he had developed:

> She that winked her sandal fan
> Long ago in gray Japan—
>
> She that heard the bell intone
> Rendezvous by rolling Rhone—

> How wide the spectacle of sleep,
> Hands folded, eyes too still to weep.

Between his years in college and the outbreak of the First World War, Stevens must also have read in the French symboliste poets. Possibly he owes something to Mallarmé for his exotic images and colors and to Verlaine for his word music. But chiefly, I think, the symboliste poets accentuated tendencies of his literary personality that we already remarked in his youthful letters and journalizings—his sudden transitions and ironic reversals, his oblique modes of statement, and his foppish pose. If in connection with the French symbolistes these phrases especially recall Laforgue, Stevens suggested that he got "a great deal" from Laforgue because he felt an affinity of "attitude."

Stevens had been pursuing the affectations of the 1890s ever since his last year at college, and, by 1915, in "Cy Est Pourtraicte . . ." he was able to equal the Aesthetes in naughtiness. The poem portrays God as a decadent artist, moved to the "subtle quiver" of a suppressed snicker by the simplicity and naive goodness of Saint Ursula, who offers Him radishes. "Le Monocle de Mon Oncle" (1918) was his single most brilliant exploitation of the literary possibilities of foppery. The character of the speaker—precious, self-mocking, yet with a serious meaning amid his persiflage and a kind of heroism in his affectation—owes something to Baudelaire's presentation of the Dandy and more to Laforgue's. (The poem may also owe something to Donald Evans, who had read his Laforguian "En Monocle" at a party Stevens attended.) The *ubi-sunt* meditation on hairdos in the third stanza of "Le Monocle . . ." illustrates the point:

> Is it for nothing, then, that old Chinese
> Sat tittivating by their mountain pools
> Or in the Yangtse studied out their beards?
> I shall not play the flat historic scale.
> You know how Utamaro's beauties sought
> The end of love in their all-speaking braids.
> You know the mountainous coiffures of Bath.
> Alas! Have all the barbers lived in vain
> That not one curl in nature has survived?
> Why, without pity on these studious ghosts,
> Do you come dripping in your hair from sleep?

The lines illustrate the wit, high spirits, freshness, and fantasticality of Stevens in this period, as well as his ability to convey subtle and complex attitudes. Perhaps they also illustrate a remark of his wife: "I like Mr. Stevens' things when they are not affected; but he writes so much that is affected."

Although Stevens was never an Imagist, he read *Poetry* and was a friend of Williams, Kreymborg, and Arensberg—all "enthusiasts for Pound and the imagists," as Kreymborg phrased it. Because of the doctrine and example of the early Imagists, Stevens may have appreciated the poetic uses of spare, close, sensory particularities more than he otherwise would have. In "The Snow Man" he catches in a fresh, arresting way the look of "junipers shagged with ice" and "spruces rough in the distant glitter / Of the January sun." Imagist poetry may also have contributed something to his impersonal presentation and emotional restraint. And he was now writing free as well as stanzaic verse. But Imagism was antithetical to fundamental habits of his mind and imagination—to his abstraction and meditative onflowingness—and few passages in *Harmonium* could be called Imagist in their total effect.

Many of the poems in *Harmonium* bring the art of painting vaguely to mind. There are such titles as "Domination of Black," "Floral Decorations for Bananas," "Six Significant Landscapes," "Bantams in Pine-Woods," and "Sea Surface Full of Clouds." Stevens' bright, fresh colors are pleasing and sometimes recall a particular painter. In "Sunday Morning" the "sunny chair," oranges, and "bright, green wings" of a "cockatoo / Upon a rug" suggest Matisse to some readers. "Sea Surface Full of Clouds" resembles Impressionist painting:

> The sea-clouds whitened far below the calm
> And moved, as blooms move, in the swimming green
> And in its watery radiance.

Sometimes Stevens lays on colors in slabs. The sky in "Banal Sojourn" is a "blue gum streaked with rose. The trees are black"; in "Two Figures in Dense Violet Night" the "palms are clear in a total blue"; in "Anecdote of the Prince of the Peacocks" the plain is a "blue ground," and Beserk is a patch of "red / In this milky blue."

Stevens shared the interest of his fellow poets in Modernist technique in painting. He would have been struck by the tendency in this painting and in art theory to reject naturalism or illusionism. Transposed into literary terms, this would mean the rejection of the representation of reality as an aim. If "abstract" means nonrepresentational, art or literature of this kind is abstract, although in other respects it may be intensely sensuous, rhythmical, concrete, and expressive. If the representation of nature or reality introduces an impurity into aesthetic experience, such art may be called pure.

Whether or not Stevens sought to create something analogous to abstract or "pure" art cannot be known. In later years he recollected that "when *Harmonium* was in the making there was a time when I believed in *pure poetry*, as it was called," but on this occasion he identified the "pure" with the merely "decorative." Whatever his intention, his poems often remind readers of modern painting and are viewed as analogous works in a different medium. "Earthly Anecdote," for example, typically tells no anecdote. It speaks of "bucks" and a "firecat" who "bristled in the way" of the bucks. Because of the firecat, the bucks

> swerved
> In a swift, circular line
> To the right,

or to the left:

> The bucks clattered.
> The firecat went leaping,
> To the right, to the left,
> And
> Bristled in the way.

In this representation there is no mention of horns, hooves, rolling eyes, claws, or blood. The bucks and the firecat are rendered without naturalistic detail in a few simple, repeated images. Their encounters are perceived as shaping a system of lines in dynamic opposition—as aesthetic design.

By all these explorations and undergoings—his youthful Romanticism, his wide reading in other past and present poets, his sympathies with the aesthetic sensibility of the 1890s, with oriental art, Imagism, Symbolisme, Dandyism, and modern painting and art theory—Stevens came to the age of thirty-six, by which time he was writing such famous poems as "Peter Quince at the Clavier" and "Sunday Morning." His restless experiment continued between 1915 and 1923, when *Harmonium* was published. I shall discuss Stevens' production from his first mature work to the end of his life in the forthcoming volume. Here I will merely amplify a few points already suggested: the poems in *Harmonium* tend to be comic, abstract, and meditative, and the meditation centers on the interrelations of reality and the imagination. As the title indicates, Stevens wishes us to regard them as the poetic, quasi-musical meditations of an amateur. The "harmonium" was the small parlor organ to which one sat down in leisure hours.

Stevens' comedy ranges from high spirits, exaggeration, and play to complex irony and sophisticated wit. To sample these qualities we need only glance through the table of contents. Most of the titles are conventional enough, but "The Revolutionists Stop for Orangeade" is intriguing, "The Emperor of Ice-Cream" incongruous, "Le Monocle de Mon Oncle" a verbal game, "Floral Decorations for Bananas" spritely silliness. One title is itself a lyric: "Frogs Eat Butterflies. Snakes Eat Frogs. Hogs Eat Snakes. Men Eat Hogs." "Gubbinal" must voice a depressed inarticulate state of mind. "Tea at the Palaz of Hoon," on the other hand, suggests a special treat. Hoon may be the name of a person or a place, but if it is a place, Hoon is no home, for the name is exotic and foreign. The sound associates itself with hoot, hooey, hooray, and the like, and the vocable, *hoo*, appears elsewhere in Stevens as a cry of self-assertion. Palaz is also exotic and suggests gaudy facades and stucco work, bedizened, overdone, and blowsy. Nevertheless, a brief visit for tea must be a fine experience.

"Disillusionment of Ten O'Clock" is a bohemian sally, pointing out the prevalence of stereotyped conventionality or unimaginative dullness. It is an elaborate, foppish complaint that throughout the entire town there are only white nightgowns. No one is wearing a green gown:

> Or purple with green rings,
> Or green with yellow rings,
> Or yellow with blue rings.
> None of them are strange,
> With socks of lace

> And beaded ceintures.
> People are not going
> To dream of baboons and periwinkles.
> Only, here and there, an old sailor,
> Drunk and asleep in his boots,
> Catches tigers
> In red weather.

The poem is typical of *Others* in its fantasticality, and to select a drunken sailor as an image of vital imaginativeness is a further gesture in the convention of *épater le bourgeois*.

Steven's poetry is abstract not only in painterly senses but also in the more general, overlapping sense that it rarely dwells on the concrete case. Vivid images compose brief scenes or still lifes, but there is nothing like the rich, circumstantial representation of people and actions found in *The Waste Land*, "The Death of the Hired Man," or many of the *Cantos*. In "Peter Quince at the Clavier" the speaker desires a woman and thinks of her "blue-shadowed silk." But this bit of present actuality is noted briefly and generally and not allowed to hold attention. The speaker's desire is expressed obliquely and put at a distance by being represented in the desire of the elders for the biblical Susanna. This story, furthermore, is not told in Stevens' poem but rendered with further obliquity as an orchestral composition, which the poem suggests through metaphors. The composition is being played at the clavier by Peter Quince, the comic play director in Shakespeare's *A Midsummer-Night's Dream*.

Or there is Stevens' "The Snow Man." When we think of a snowman, most of us visualize balls of snow placed on top of each other, coals for eyes, a carrot nose, and the like. I mention these details only to point out that Stevens does not. His poem does not describe but merely invokes "The Snow Man" by mentioning him in the title; thereafter the snowman is involved in the poem only as a metaphor of a metaphor. He is a metaphor of "a mind of winter," and this, in turn, is a metaphor of something even more abstract: a mind that entertains nothingness.

> One must have a mind of winter
> To regard the frost and the boughs
> Of the pine-trees crusted with snow;

And have been cold a long time
To behold the junipers shagged with ice,
The spruces rough in the distant glitter

Of the January sun; and not to think
Of any misery in the sound of the wind,
In the sound of a few leaves,

Which is the sound of the land
Full of the same wind
That is blowing in the same bare place

For the listener, who listens in the snow,
And, nothing himself, beholds
Nothing that is not there and the nothing that is.

But it is easy to imagine that whoever speaks or thinks this poem is himself looking at a snowman. In this case the poem may be related to the descriptive-meditative tradition in English poetry that comes down to us from the eighteenth century and the Romantic period. Poems embraced within this genre would include Gray's "Elegy Written in a Country Church-yard," Wordsworth's "Lines . . . Above Tintern Abbey," and Keats's "Ode on a Grecian Urn." A convention organizing all such poems is that the poet finds himself at some place or views some prospect or object. The poem describes what is seen and, as it proceeds, enacts a train of thought and feeling occasioned immediately by the place or object and referring repeatedly to it. Stevens' "The Snow Man" presents the meditation with the description omitted. As "meditation," its form is thinking, the mind in activity, and this is also in part its subject. The poem is one sentence. It proceeds by amplification, illustrating the inherent dynamism of the mind, its fertile power to proceed on its own impulse.

Still dwelling on "The Snow Man," we may note that the poem posits two types of listener. One would hear a "misery in the sound of the wind." Through his own imaginative creativity he would project a human emotion into the scene and locate it there. Thus, he would make the landscape one with which human beings can feel sympathy. The other listener would hear nothing more than the sound of the wind. He would exert none of this spontaneous and almost inevitable creativity. The poem embodies Stevens' central theme, the relation between imagination and reality. Endless permutations of this theme were possible. Was reality the world seen without imagination? If so, was imagination the world seen without reality? That was a bitter truth, if it was a truth. But perhaps the snowman, who heard no "misery" in the wind, was projecting himself into the scene just as much as the other listener. Perhaps the snowman beheld nothing only because he was "nothing himself," since, to cite a later poem, whoever "puts a pineapple together" always sees it "in the tangent of himself." "Crow is realist," but "Oriole, also, may be realist." Perhaps imagination was not the opposite but the reordering of reality, like the "mountainous coiffures of Bath" in relation to the natural mop of hair. Coiffures express human creativity, but that does not make them less real. Was the important distinction simply that the mop of hair is always the same, while its rearrangements into coiffures vary with time and place? Perhaps religion was like a hairdo. It was a myth that humanized the facts of man's situation and fate. The facts never changed essentially, but the myth did and must. Perhaps the role of poetry now was to create a new myth. But in sketching some aspects of this central theme, we have already gone beyond *Harmonium* and drawn on poems of a later period, and further elaboration must be deferred.

WILLIAM CARLOS WILLIAMS

Since William Carlos Williams (1883–1963) is also discussed at some length in my forthcoming volume, along with the younger poets he strongly influenced, the account given here confines itself to his early career down to 1923. He belonged to the Modernist avant-garde of writers and painters and shared their point of view to an extreme degree. No poet was more imbued with the idea that the modern age required a new style "consonant" with modern sensibility. Yet in some essential respects the appeal of his poetry resembles that of the Georgians and Robert Frost. Common sources of appeal may be suggested by noting that Williams, Frost, and the Georgians were all accessible and entertaining; they possessed or cultivated poetic personalities that have much charm; and they discovered "poetry" in the familiar circumstances of contemporary life. An additional reason for their rising reputations in the 1950s was the attraction readers found at that time in the deliberately scaled down, the unassuming. Williams' emotions are not romantically intense; his profundities, if any can be claimed for him, are not insisted on. Hence he was not much recognized in the 1920s. But precisely these qualities contributed to the eager discovery of his poetry later.

He was born in Rutherford, New Jersey, and went to secondary schools there and in New York City, with a two-year interval in Europe. By the time he enrolled in medical school at the University of Pennsylvania, he hoped to become a poet as well as a doctor. At the university he became a friend of Ezra Pound, a "fine fellow . . . a brilliant talker and thinker," he wrote his mother, and through Pound met Hilda Doolittle, a "rather bony" but "bright" girl of nineteen. With Miss Doolittle, Williams took long country walks in suburban Philadelphia and "talked of the finest things: of Shakespeare, of flowers, trees, books, and pictures." Conversing with Pound, he already felt how difficult it was for him to compete. He lacked time to study literature and was doomed to an amateur role, whereas Pound was "making a life work" of it. In later years Williams struggled to overcome this sense of inferiority; parts of his theory of poetry—for example, the emphasis he placed on immediacy and spontaneity—were motivated, among other considerations, by the need of a busy doctor to justify a type of poetry he had time to write.

He received his medical degree in 1906 and became an intern in a New York City hospital. He specialized in obstetrics and pediatrics. In 1909 and 1910 he was in Europe for medical study and for travel. Returning, he married and settled for the rest of his life in Rutherford. He wrote much of his prose and some of his poetry late at night or between patients. The total number of his books amounts to more than forty titles, including fiction, drama, and essays, as well as poetry.

In London he had visited Pound, who had escorted him to the literary haunts, including a visit to Yeats's lodgings, where the famous older poet had read his own verse by candlelight. Characteristically, Williams tried not to feel intimidated by London glamour and sophistication. He was already telling himself that the "old world spirit" was "run down," while the "New World spirit," in which he naturally included himself, was "young, ignorant but . . . full of the strength of abundant resource and opportunity not unmixed with contempt for old forms."

But his early poetry did not exemplify this contempt for "old forms." In his teens Williams had admired Whitman and burst out occasionally in imitations. But he loved Keats and composed a long verse romance in what he conceived to be Keats's style. One of his starting points as a poet may be seen in a sonnet he included in a letter to his brother. It was written in 1906, after meeting "one of the most sensible and generally likeable, beautiful girls I have seen in a long time." He "came home feeling sort of funny" and sat down to write:

> Last night I sat within a blazing hall
> And drank of bliss from out a maiden's eyes.
> The jeweled guests passed by . . .

In 1909 his first book of poems was printed in Rutherford at his own expense. In 1913 a second book, *The Tempers*, was published in London, Pound having persuaded Elkin Matthews to bring it out. Pound was now the dominant influence on Williams' writing, and *The Tempers* included several poems in types Pound had favored in his early verse, such as the Browningesque monologue and the Renaissance lyric—

> Lady of dusk-wood fastnesses,
> Thou art my Lady.

Despite the stylistic and thematic emulations of Pound, Williams' characteristic humor, liveliness, unpretentiousness, ingenuous happiness, and charm are also strongly present.

By 1912 Pound was propagating, as Imagism, the principles of "efficient writing" to which he had gradually sifted during four years of conversation, experiment, and self-criticism in London. No American poet was more receptive than Williams to Pound's practical instructions for Imagists. The founding of *Poetry* had another, less traceable, impact on his career. After he had appeared in its pages, he could henceforth feel that he was himself among the "new" American poets. This feeling was enormously reinforced by his association in and around New York City with the *Others* group. He read their works in manuscript, eagerly debated their theories, and felt that he was in the thick of a new movement. Throughout his life his happiest times seem to have been of this kind, when he saw himself as a member—or even a leader—of a movement that was going to capture the future of poetry, or the poetry of the future. A favorite rhetorical device in his prose is the first-person-plural "we," which he used to identify himself with unspecified fellow writers, with the movement: "What a battle we made of it. Merely getting rid of capitals at the beginning of every line!" From 1920 to 1923 he edited *Contact I* with Robert McAlmon.

Meanwhile, he had also met the painters Marcel Duchamp and Man Ray and the photographer Alfred Stieglitz. In 1913 came the Armory Show. Moreover, between 1914 and 1919 Pound had printed some of Williams' poems in *The Egoist*, and Williams had become an attentive reader not only of the literary part of the magazine but also of the feminist and philosophical essays by Dora Marsden with which each issue began. He was both an Egoist, he said, and an Imagist.

These excitements were reflected in his volumes of poetry in the next several years: *Al Que Quiere* (1917), *Sour Grapes* (1921), and *Spring and All* (1923). There was also *Kora in Hell* (1920), a group of prose poems he wrote as spontaneous improvisations. *Kora in Hell* had a Preface attacking Pound and Eliot for aping the poetry of Europe, and *Spring and All* included swatches of theorizing about poetry. In fact, many of the poems in these volumes were intended as demonstrations or metaphors of poetry, what it should be and how it should be written. These early books contained many of the poems that were later to be reprinted in one anthology after another—"Tract," "The Young Housewife," "El Hombre," "Danse Russe," "To Waken An Old Lady," "Queen-Ann's Lace," "The Widow's Lament in Springtime," "Spring and All," "To Elsie," and "The Red Wheelbarrow"—and in them Williams' poetry was fully formed in its first phase. The attractions of this poetry are at least fourfold: the personality and attitudes of the speaker; the clarity and vividness in presenting things to the senses; the use of spoken language, in other words, Williams' liveliness, authenticity, and immediacy in imitating spontaneous, characteristically American talk; and the subtlety and many-sidedness of emotional awareness and response.

The images are close, fresh, concrete, and empathetic. In "Spring and All" he catches "the stiff curl of wildcarrot leaf" with memorable, typical exactitude. There are not only color and motion in the

> surge of the blue
> mottled clouds driven from the
> northeast—a cold wind,

but also in "surge" and "driven" there is Williams' characteristic organic participation in dynamic energies and tensions within the objects or events he renders. In the same poem the seemingly lifeless bushes of early spring are described in a string of accurate yet unexpected adjectives:

> All along the road the reddish
> purplish, forked, upstanding, twiggy
> stuff of bushes . . .

"Tract" illustrates his rendering of American speech. The poem is an address to his "townspeople," telling how a funeral should be performed. The directions are implicitly a commentary on the writing of poetry. "Knock the glass out" of the hearse, he says, for glass suggests a wish to deny reality.

> My God—glass, my townspeople!
> For what purpose? Is it for the dead
> to look out or for us to see
> how well he is housed or to see
> the flowers or the lack of them—
> or what?
> To keep the rain and snow from him?

The exclamation, the heaped-up questions, the blunt irony of "housed," the mention that there may be no flowers are all brought to a focus in the aggressive-contemptuous question, "or what?" The question would lose much of its effect if we could not recognize the typically American intonation implied. After the question there comes, as the line indicates, a deafening pause, before the speaker piles on another aggressively ironic question. The whole passage is flat, blunt, energetic, and driving and renders what Williams conceived to be a typically American voice.

The fineness of Williams' "emotional equipment," as Pound

called it, is seen in "To Waken An Old Lady." If the poem is read as a metaphor of old age, every detail expresses a delicate, complex awareness. It is winter and life is on the whole diminished to a "shrill piping." But, just as the poem is the opposite of the sentimentally wishful, it also refuses to simplify into mere pathos or pessimism. Winter is no unchanging state but a varied season that includes its times of content:

> Old age is
> a flight of small
> cheeping birds
> skimming
> bare trees
> above a snow glaze.
> Gaining and failing
> they are buffeted
> by a dark wind—
> But what?
> On harsh weedstalks
> the flock has rested,
> the snow
> is covered with broken
> seedhusks
> and the wind tempered
> by a shrill
> piping of plenty.

Though Williams was bringing out books steadily from 1909 until his death, his appeal to readers and his influence on younger poets increased greatly toward the end of his career. He himself felt that his own poetry was the polar opposite of Eliot's and that the hegemony of Eliot had delayed his recognition. *The Waste Land*, Williams said in his *Autobiography*, "wiped out our world as if an atom bomb had been dropped upon it." He felt that Eliot's poem had set back for twenty years the acceptance and spread of the poetic values for which "we" contended. Be this as it may, in the 1940s and 1950s, when younger poets began to follow his lead, the reason was partly that he was a poet of the older generation—and Pound's friend—whose work offered younger poets a way out of the cul-de-sac in which many of them felt that contemporary poetry was expiring. This is not the place to tell the history of American poetry between 1930 and 1950, but it may be noted, in a too simplified summary, that the premises and methods of the New Critics were much influenced by the poetry and critical writings of Eliot, that they trained readers especially to appreciate formally complex, compressed ways of writing and that they gradually influenced the teaching of literature in schools and colleges. Eventually this approach to literature began to seem "academic," to separate literature from life.

Rebelling against this, young writers after World War II looked about for alternative premises and styles. They found Williams. As James Dickey put it, Williams was "usable." "Many beginning writers," he suggests in praise of Williams, "were encouraged to write" because they felt, "Well, if *that's* poetry, I believe I might be able to write it, too!" The attractions of his open, natural, low-pressured idiom were further enhanced by his conceptual moilings in essays and manifestos. These formulations explained and defended his way of writing; they worked the more suggestively because they were vague. But Williams' increased appeal in the forties, fifties, and sixties did not come about only because young poets sought a new parental model. They were responding to trends in American life that shaped literature by shaping feelings, values, and life styles. In other words, many readers, especially the young, recognized in Williams attitudes with which they felt a warm sympathy.

At the center of these poems is the "I," the speaker, who presents himself as a plain, unpretentious man, a doctor, living an ordinary life with his family in Rutherford. He has and feels that he has freshness of response, humor, wholesomeness, and joie de vivre. Watching his "wife's new pink slippers,"

> I talk to them
> in my secret mind
> out of pure happiness.

His pose is nonchalant, off hand; his subject matter frank. In "The Ogre" he tells with much charm of his sexual response to a

> Sweet child,
> little girl with well-shaped legs.

Erotic feelings are diffused throughout most of his responses, not only to people but to weather, flowers, trees, and bushes, and they are presented casually, as an omnipresent, natural aspect of life.

His poetry exhibits Williams vis-à-vis the world. Sometimes it exhibits only the world, or parts of it, leaving the speaker out. In either case the situation is essentially the prototypical one of Romantic poetry, the poetic imagination alone with nature. Confronting the welter of phenomena, the imagination attempts to find or create order and meaning; especially it strives for an order or meaning that would support feelings of acceptance, or even of joy. So also with Williams.

The poetry of Williams can be read as a demonstration that here, now, and everywhere the world is always fresh, full, and vivid. More exactly, the world has this character for whoever can see it this way. We must strip away preconceptions, habitual associations, and literary and social conventions in order to see the thing as it immediately is. This fresh, authentic perception is enough, but there may also be a discovery or creation of aesthetic value in the objects seen. In Williams' well-known "The Red Wheelbarrow," composed in two minutes, the objects—a wheelbarrow, rain water, chickens—evoke no associations from poetic tradition. Neither, as Williams renders them, do they evoke any particular associations of other kinds; we do not think of rural life, for example. They are merely things perceived and they are so familiar that they would usually rouse little interest or emotion. In each pair of lines the poem notes first a color and then an object, and thus enacts a process in which a bright, pleasing quality is located in an ordinary thing. Together the things make a pattern of contrasts, an aesthetic composition. The poem says that so much depends on these objects or the composition they make. But it also means that so much depends on the eye that perceives.

> so much depends
> upon
>
> a red wheel
> barrow
>
> glazed with rain
> water
>
> beside the white
> chickens.

"The Red Wheelbarrow," like so many of Williams' poems, is about poetry, but it is also about finding and relating to reality—the themes are inseparable for Williams. The poem derives its interest solely from its character as an implicit credo or demonstration. It is remarkably easy and obvious and might almost have been written as a parody, reducing Williams' style and theme to their minimum.

But Williams' poetry is built on the paradox that less is more. Beneath this there is the paradox that all is nothing. As with most human beings, Williams' beliefs were partly shaped by subjective needs. His emphasis on making "contact" with the world was a natural expression of a personality for which some kinds of contact were difficult. And his poetic exhibitions that he, for one, could be vital, full, happy, and related to the world are not to be taken literally. They were counterattacks in a lifelong battle with disgust and despair. The prototypical situation is that in "Danse Russe," where the speaker dances alone and naked at dawn in his "north room." Who, he asks, "shall say I am not / the happy genius of my household?" But the demonstration is for himself. He is watching his dance in a mirror.

The only person Williams' poetry characterizes in depth is himself. Many poems, however, are sketches of other people. He portrays especially the unfortunate—the impoverished, old, alienated, deprived, derelict, criminal, or ill—and he makes us sympathize with their situation and feelings. His attitude toward such characters is unsentimental, tolerant, and appreciative. He admires their tough-mindedness, endurance, vitality, and stubborn assertion of identity. He sees himself in them, and them in himself, with a fellow feeling that might be called democratic. Despite this, there is an essential detachment, for his interest in such persons is primarily aesthetic. As he later explained in his *Autobiography*, he sought "poetry" in the lost, the dispossessed, the renegade, and the uneducated because such persons seemed to him to be whole and integral. They were "sure, all of a piece . . . instant and perfect."

His program for poetry—or "the poem," as he called it—may be quickly stated, at least as it was by 1923. The core of it was the idea that poetry must be "consonant" with the modern age. Despite his early fondness for Keats, Williams soon convinced himself that previous poetry was irrelevant, for the forms of ear-

lier ages could not embody contemporary states of consciousness. It is likely that in his mature years he spent more time
reading little magazines than in reading the great poets of the
past. Poetry that is alive, he told Miss Monroe (she had criticized
two poems he submitted to *Poetry*), must be, like life itself, "at
any moment subversive of life as it was the moment before.
Verse to be alive must have infused into it some tincture of dis-
establishment."

He subscribed to the ideas of Imagism as Pound had formulated them. A poem, as he then thought of it, "was an image, the
picture was the important thing." Just what was pictured mattered less. "We have discarded beauty," he said in 1914. Following the principles set forth in "A Few 'Don'ts' by an Imagiste,"
he stressed the value of swift, uncluttered, functional phrasing,
without the inversions and redundancies imposed by the effort
"to fill out a standard form." On this ground he still argued at
this time for free verse. He differed from Pound, however, in
that he put less emphasis on a compressed presentation but
spoke rather of momentum, "an unimpeded thrust through a
poem from the beginning to the end." He was highly attracted to
spontaneous composition as a method; it would guarantee that
worries about "formal arrangements" would not deflect the
"development of what you see and feel"; it would bring about
or, at least, promote "immediate contact with the world." He was
also beginning to stress that poetry must find its "primary im-
petus," as he later put it, in "local conditions." Local implies, in
his sloganizing, the opposite of classical, medieval, or similarly
remote subjects—"I was determined to use the material I knew."
And among "local conditions" Williams included the spoken
American language, its vocabulary, rhythm, and syntax.

Williams was forty years old when *Spring and All* was published. His life henceforth continued to center in his active medical practice and his career as a writer, along with the usual domestic troubles and happinesses. In the early 1920s he started to
write his important prose work, *In the American Grain*. His aim
was "to try to find out for myself what the land of my more or
less accidental birth might signify. . . . The plan was to try to
get inside the heads of some of the American founders . . . by
examining their original records." The book "fell flat" when it
was published in 1925 and was soon remaindered, though it has

since been reprinted several times. In 1924 he spent some months in Europe, where he saw much of the American expatriate colony in Paris, and he was again in Europe in 1927. He continued to found or help others found little magazines, for, he said, without them he would himself "have been early silenced." One of his enterprises in the early 1930s was the Objectivist Press, in which he was associated with Basil Bunting and Louis Zukofsky. At this time he also articulated an "Objectivist theory of the poem." About this time he also edited *Contact II* with McAlmon and Nathanael West. In the 1930s he began to be invited to read his poems at colleges. He was not yet counted among the more important poets, however, and his pay was the average fee for a "reading" in those days—twenty-five to fifty dollars. His poetry won the *Dial* award in 1926 and the *Poetry* magazine prize in 1931, then there were no more prizes until 1948. Between 1946 and his death, however, he received five honorary degrees and seven prizes or awards. From 1946 to 1958 he was working on *Paterson,* which he left unfinished. He suffered a stroke, and resigned from medical practice. Despite further paralyzing strokes, he heroically continued to write, and some of his finest poems date from his last years.

MARIANNE MOORE

Marianne Moore (1887–1972) was born in St. Louis, the daughter of John Milton Moore. Her father left the family when she was still a child, and she was brought up in the home of her maternal grandfather, John Warner, a pastor in the Presbyterian church. Her girlhood ambition was to become a painter, though she was also interested in medicine and biology. In 1894 the family moved to Carlisle, Pennsylvania, and she received her education at the Metzger Institute there and later at Bryn Mawr College (A.B., 1909). After a year at the Carlisle Commercial College, she spent four years (1911–1915) teaching stenography and bookkeeping at the United States Indian School at Carlisle. Always interested in athletics (she was a good tennis player, and in her later years became an enthusiastic baseball fan), she also coached the Indian boys in outdoor sports. In 1918 she moved to New York, taught, and then worked (1921–1925) in the Hudson Park branch of the New York Public Library.

In 1915 she began to publish verse in the *Egoist*, *Poetry*, and *Others*. In 1921 the Egoist Press, without her knowledge, brought out a volume of twenty-four of her poems. In 1920 she began to publish in the *Dial*, and received the Dial award for the first volume she herself published: *Observations* (1925). She became acting editor of the *Dial* (1925–1929) for the remainder of its publishing life. Her verse, praised by Ezra Pound for its "dance of the intelligence" (1918), continued to receive applause from distinguished poets and critics, such as T. S. Eliot, Yvor Winters, W. H. Auden, and Randall Jarrell. *Selected Poems* (1935), with a commendatory Introduction by Eliot, was followed by *The Pangolin and Other Verse* (1936), *What Are Years?* (1941), *Nevertheless* (1944), and *Collected Poems* (1951), which received the Bollingen and other prizes. By now Miss Moore's reputation was widely as well as firmly established. In 1954 her long-awaited translation of the *Fables* of La Fontaine appeared, and in 1955 a collection of essays, *Predilections*. Now almost seventy, she continued to publish prolifically: *Like a Bulwark* (1956); two lectures given at the University of California, *Idiosyncrasies and Technique* (1958); *O To be a Dragon* (1959); *The Absentee* (1962), a comedy based on Maria Edgeworth's novel of the same name; *The Arctic Ox* (1964); *Tell Me, Tell Me* (1966); and *Complete Poems* (1967).

According to her own testimony, Miss Moore met no writers before 1916 and until then was, as she said, "isolated" from contemporary poetry. The Imagists, she said, were not an important influence on her work. She had not read the French symbolistes. Perhaps she learned more from prose writers, but she was aware of no literary antecedents for her style. The statement corrects some stock notions about literary history. It suggests that modern poetic style depended rather less on Hulme, Pound, the Imagists, and the Symbolists than is usually supposed. Instead, it developed from sources and tendencies so multiple that is was in the air, so to speak, and by 1915 even a young schoolmistress fresh from Bryn Mawr College could be writing it. For stylistically her poems are Modernist. She shared with the Imagists the effort for exact presentation of the object and the use of prose rhythms. She employed with Pound and those he influenced, the techniques of the ideogram and juxta-position by excision of connecting statements. Before the Meta-physical Revival was much heard of, she was writing a poetry of irony and wit. Her diction sought the colloquial and the specifi-cally American spoken idiom. She was part of a reaction against the traditionally beautiful or poetic in favor of the authentic and functional. Hulme's opinions that poetry should be inorganic, contracted rather than expansive, impersonal, disciplined, hard, and dry found an exemplification in her work. But if her tech-nique was Modernist, her temperament was not. She seemed to have little connection with conventionally modern attitudes, unless she was felt to rebuke them. Shy, rationalist, and bristling with rectitude, her views were simple. She was untouched by ex-istential angst, and the delighted reading of her work among so many highly sophisticated writers resembles Werther's love for Charlotte.

Marianne Moore's career evolved without dramatic changes in style or attitude. The poems published in magazines between 1915–1921 and in *Poems* (1921) are often astringent comments in discursive, economical speech. They deal especially with writ-ers, other types encountered in the literary world (the steam-roller, the pedantic literalist), ideas about writing ("Ecstacy affords / the occasion and expediency determines the form"), and so on. The much-quoted "Poetry" is typical. They are in syl-labic verse, although the scansion of "To a Prize Bird" is tradi-tional and such poems as "England," "When I Buy Pictures," and "Those Various Scalpels" are in a free verse very close to prose. Only in "The Fish" does one find among these early poems a fully developed example of the several idiosyncrasies of manner especially associated with her, although she never had merely one manner. With the *Selected Poems* of 1935 the liking for animal subjects became noticeable for the first time ("The Jerboa," "The Plumet Basilisk," "The Frigate Pelican," "The Buffalo"), and only now could critics begin to speak of her "bes-tiary." (The remark became commonplace, prompting the con-spiracy of encouragement that helped elicit her translation of La Fontaine's *Fables* in 1954.) The poems written between 1921 and 1935 were on the whole more elliptical, oblique, and difficult than the earlier ones; they showed for the first time an effort of accurate observation that went almost to fantastic lengths. In the

next few years, in important poems such as "Virginia Bri-
tannia" or "The Pangolin" she reversed or at least halted these
tendencies. These poems were more spacious and accessible,
closer to the descriptive-meditative tradition.

Her approach toward a more accessible style continued.
During the Second World War some poems were in an emotional, rhetorical vein ("In Distrust of Merits," "Keeping Their
World Large"), and throughout her later work there was a
slightly more direct expression of personal feeling. The looser
manner was also present in a good many occasional poems
written either to support worthy causes or out of local Brooklyn
patriotism. The humor of her verse was also more varied. Where
it was once a tart remark or darning-needle stab, it now ranged
from broad effects to verbal play:

> The pin-swin or spine-swine
>   (the edgehog miscalled hedgehog) with all his edges out . . .

At the same time there was an occasional or partial return to traditional versification, either in poems that scan and rhyme in the
old ways or in the blending of syllabic with accentual verse, as,
for example, in "The Mind Is an Enchanting Thing." The mel-
lowing was not necessarily a good thing, for her work tended to
become rather less taut and brilliant. But neither did it go very
far. The poetry still gave the effect of "stepping as though
through / harp-strings in a scherzo." She could still say: "If tributes cannot / be implicit, / give me diatribes and the fragrance
of iodine."

Her technical or stylistic innovations were chiefly four: syllabic
verse on a new principle, light rhyme, inorganic stanza forms,
and miscellaneous quotation. By syllabic verse is meant simply
that the line is measured by counting not the number of accents
but the number of syllables. It is the ordinary scansion of French
poetry. What is novel in Marianne Moore, however, is that the
line may have any number of syllables from one to twenty, and
caesuras fall where they may. As a result, there is no way of
knowing that it is a meter until the same number of syllables are
counted in corresponding lines of each stanza. This compels, as
one reads, a primary attention to the prose rhythm. Other
rhythms are going at the same time of course, created by the di-

vision into lines and the occasional counterpointing of syllabic with accentual meter, but syllabic verse does not create a rhythm of its own. Its function in English seems primarily to negate accentual scansion and allow the prose rhythm to move forward and receive first emphasis. For the poet, syllabic meter may serve more personal needs. One easily learns to think in blank verse, for example, and to a lesser degree in other traditional meters also. Thus, for most poets the metrical aspect is partly unconscious. But syllabic meter can never become habitual. The syllabic line presents itself to the poet as an external form that must be filled consciously.

"Light rhyme" is a phrase applied by T. S. Eliot to what Miss Moore was doing. In English poetry the rhyme word normally takes a special emphasis, and among the unquestionably valid contributions of the Modernist poets is their renewed recognition that, since the rhyme word is emphasized by its position and function, it should be worthy of the attention it receives—that is, it must do more than merely rhyme. In Marianne Moore, however, there is rhyme that receives no emphasis and would be anticlimactic if it did. Eliot points out that "the effect sometimes requires giving a word a slightly more analytical pronunciation, or stressing a syllable more than ordinarily," or "the use of articles as rhyme words":

> ac-
> cident—lack
>   of cornice, dynamite grooves, burns, and
>   hatchet strokes, these things stand
>   out on it.

Similarly with stanzaic patterns. In the simpler forms of English verse the pattern of the stanza coincides with the grammatical and syntactical ordering of sense and feeling:

> Apeneck Sweeney spreads his knees
> Letting his arms hang down to laugh,
> The zebra stripes along his jaw
> Swelling to maculate giraffe.

When the sense and feeling overflow or run on beyond the verse or the stanza a counterpoint is set up, the versification maintaining one pattern while the sense and feeling set up another. But the disjunction is rarely complete; the sense and feeling

slightly coincide with the units of the verse, even while they run
on, and the partial violation of a norm is itself expressive, a further refinement of meaning. In the case of Marianne Moore,
however, the syllabic verse, the light rhyme, and the arbitrary
lengths of the line contribute to a stanzaic pattern that may be
intellectually recognized but is not much felt in reading:

> The Indian buffalo,
> led by bare-leggèd boys to a hay
> hut where they
>   stable it, need not fear comparison
>   with bison, with the twins,
>   indeed with any
>   of ox ancestry.

The separation or lack of relation between the pattern of verse
and pattern of meaning is rarely so complete as in this instance,
but separation is the norm, the expectation, with which the
reader starts, and any, even slight convergence of these patterns
becomes the more noticeable and felt. This indeed is one gain to
Miss Moore's poetry. If you begin with external, inorganic
forms, any more organic relation of pattern and meaning dramatically enhances expressiveness. More than this, however,
these arbitarary forms make the meaning more difficult to grasp
and so rouse attention. They also contribute to the air of eccentricity and self-imposed difficulty that pervades her verse,"the
love of doing hard things."

The quotations from various sources, such as the *National Geo-
graphic Magazine* or the sports pages, are a further oddity. They
are not usually memorable in themselves. Miss Moore explains
them as simple integrity: if you use someone else's words, it is
right to acknowledge the borrowing. But, then, why use someone else's words? Moreover, some of the quotations she seems to
have invented herself, and quotations are used with a frequency
that gives some readers the impression of a nervous tic. Her
quotation marks function generally in two ways: they call attention to the words and they give them an ironic cast. Quotation
may be a way of disowning the words she uses, of refusing to
take full responsibility for them. It is a mode of armor, of hiding
from the reader. Her book reviews are frequently mosaics of
quotation.

In structure her poems seem often to lack a principle of transition, whether by narrative, argument, meditation, stream of consciousness, or free association. The impression arises in part from the fact that she often prefers to speak through concrete instances rather than discursive generalization. The steps of the argument, if there is one, must be inferred through the juxtaposition of images. But there is much discursive statement in her work, although it is likely to be elliptical and fragmentary. "The Hero" is an example:

> We do not like some things, and the hero
>   doesn't; deviating headstones
> and uncertainty;
>   going where one does not wish
> to go; suffering and not
>   saying so; standing and listening where something
> is hiding.

Here the assertions, though slightly elliptical, are not difficult to follow. Immediately, however, one comes to a dense cluster of negative or positive examples, and the ellipsis is drastic:

> Jacob when a-dying, asked
> Joseph: Who are these? and blessed
> both sons, the younger most, vexing Joseph. And
> Joseph was vexing to some.
>   Cincinnatus was; Regulus; and some of our fellow
> men have been . . .

Jacob, one infers, is tricky and noncommittal, as the hero never is, and so is Joseph. But Cincinnatus and Regulus were true heroes. The poem as a whole is static. The hero is presented through instances of his attitudes, tastes, behavior, and so on, but the purpose is to give his character ("This then you may know / as the hero"), which, as in a bestiary, is known from the start, not thought out in the course of the poem. Put another way, the poem is an assemblage of images and statements around a general theme. In this it typifies many of Miss Moore's poems, such as "England," or "Marriage," a poem she footnotes with ironic modesty as "Statements that took my fancy which I tried to arrange plausibly." In other poems, however, an argument proceeds, often in ample discourse; a poem such as "Snakes, Mongoose, Snake Charmers, and the Like" enacts the seemingly casual or natural transition from apprehending the object to reflection upon it that typifies meditative verse. The tendency in her work to construct poems by aggregating rather than developing is only a tendency, not a rigid instinct.

Her idiom, like her stance generally, is low-keyed, prosaic, American, and precise. Precision is the master word. It is the effect and—because it is a moral as well as a stylistic value and effort—to some degree the meaning of her poetry. It involves not only accuracy ("certainty of touch") but also self-discipline. It is from the game of bowls or from the "Chinese lacquer carving," where "layer after layer" is

> exposed by certainty of touch and unhurried incision
> so that only so much color shall be revealed as is necessary
> > to the picture,

that Miss Moore is gratified to

> learn that we are precisionists,
> not citizens of Pompeii arrested in action
> as a cross section of one's correspondence would seem
> > to imply.

That the carving exposes layer after layer may be taken as a reminder that precision does not preclude suggestion. The suggestions are activated here by the associations and semi-puns (layers exposed–cross section–incision–precision–carving–picture–arrested in action, with a separate pun in "arrested"), but the suggestions are as controlled as everything else in the poem. The seemingly prosaic and low-keyed talk is minutely ordered and vibrant with intellectual energy. This idiom stands equally removed from romantic beauty, direct emotion, and vagueness, on the one hand, or modern tolerated opaqueness, on the other. (Miss Moore's opacities are the opposite of self-indulgence; they are excesses of excision.) The precision appears not only in the way of saying but in the selection and ordering of things said, and the precision of speech and form expresses a further precision of feeling. But precision is easiest to illustrate as a quality of the idiom.

For one thing, there is the scrupulous minuteness of description: the newt "with white pin-dots on black horizontal spaced / out bands"; "The fine hairs on the tail" of the jerboa that repeat "the other pale /   markings, lengthen until / at the tip they fill / out in a tuft—black and /   white." In the manner prescribed by T. E. Hulme, one is ordinarily compelled to visualize the thing still more exactly through comparison or metaphor. The whiskers of Peter the cat are "shadbones regularly set about the mouth / to droop or rise in unison like porcupine-quills." The things compared are ordinarily quite disparate—"the lion's ferocious chrysanthemum head"—and a special peculiarity of Miss Moore is that the thing used for illustration is at least as closely seen as the thing itself. Fledgling mockingbirds emit "the high-keyed intermittent squeak / of broken carriage springs." Camellia Sabina has a pale stripe "that looks as if on a mushroom the / sliver from a beetroot carved into a rose were laid." Even when she uses metaphor to convey something indefinite, an impression or feeling, the particular things are still very particular, as in the brilliant impression of the mind's brilliance, "The Mind Is an Enchanting Thing":

> is an enchanted thing
>   like the glaze on a
> katydid-wing
>   subdivided by sun
>   till the nettings are legion.
> Like Gieseking playing Scarlatti;
>
> like the apteryx-awl
>   as a beak, or the
> kiwi's rain-shawl
>   of haired feathers, the mind . . .

We may never have noticed the glaze on a katydid wing, or read about the apteryx (also called kiwi), or heard Gieseking playing Scarlatti, but the particularity elicits confidence that Miss Moore has remarked these things and that, if we look them up, we will find out exactly what she means.

Even when Miss Moore is not elliptical, her style is terse. She never uses more words than she needs and is always trying to use less. One result is a mode of statement that, if not quite aphorism—for it is part of a context—can at least be said to carry as much meaning in as few words as possible: "His shield was his humility"; "uncircuitous simplicity / with an expression of inquiry"; "all are / naked, none is safe"; "a spruce

tree— / vertical though a seedling—all / needles." Terseness
requires search for the exact word, and she illustrates the search
through unexpected discriminations of nuance or implication:
marriage, for example, "This institution, / perhaps one should
say enterprise"; "Henry James, 'damned by the public for decorum'; not decorum, but restraint"; her father used to say,

> "The deepest feeling always shows itself in silence;
> not in silence, but restraint."
> Nor was he insincere in saying, "Make my house your inn."
> Inns are not residences.

Terseness is related to understatement: "Discreet behavior is
not now the sum / of statesmanlike good sense"; the mind is
"not a Herod's oath that cannot change";

> The passion for setting people right is in itself an afflictive
> > disease.
> Distaste that takes no credit to itself is best.

And the juxtaposition of laconic statements almost always pro-
duces the surprise of wit:

> I have seen this swan and
> I have seen you; I have seen ambition without
> understanding in a variety of forms.

There is rarely anything in Miss Moore's verse that is not a
species of wit.

The animals which make up the subject or illustration of so
many of her poems are of either the more harmless or exotic
sort (jerboa, swan, basilisk, frigate pelican, buffalo, cat, unicorn,
snail, ostrich, reindeer, pangolin, kiwi, arctic ox, elephant). Because they are used as in fables to present moral types and states
they are not always beheld sympathetically, but even so her
poetry creates through them a simpler and more charming
world than our own. Moreover, they are usually treated not as a
mirror to the human race but a contrast, and the contrast is altogether in favor of the animals. Miss Moore admires their prudence, courage, and functional adaptation to the conditions of
their life. Above all she admires their seriousness and sensible-
ness, that they are free from affectation and romantic illusion,
how precisely they know and submit to the discipline of fact.
They are rigorists. Miss Moore would have liked us all to be

like that. "It is self-evident" that the way to "romantic" achievement is prosaic "capacity for fact":

> that one must do as one is told
> and eat rice, prunes, dates, raisins, hardtack, and tomatoes
> if one would "conquer the main peak of Mount Tacoma."

The moral realm is as plain and inexorable as the natural, and
here, too, Miss Moore would have us "rigorists." "Guns, nets,
seines, traps and explosives" are not allowed in the National Park,
for it is or should be "self-evident / that it is frightful to have
everyone afraid of one." She is committed to a copybook morality
with its definiteness and simplicity and cites the old-fashioned
heroes—"Cincinnatus was; Regulus"—of the copybook. She
sympathizes with whatever is integral, positive, self-controlled,
and self-respecting. Reticence is a virtue, and few things can be
worse than crying in someone's lap. In poetry there must be no
adventitious charm or seductiveness. It "must not wish to disarm
anything." It must be what it is and you must like it or leave it, for
that is the way superior people behave. They respect one
another's individuality and do not intrude by offering or seeking
intimacies, much less confessions. If the way they express
themselves is rather complicated and punctilious, this is partly to
effect the precise nuance and implication, partly to secure close
attention, and partly, it must be acknowledged, to keep people
off. The matter and the rind of her poetry are somewhat prickly,
like the upright spruce tree, "all needles," like the hedgehog
"with all his edges out," like the monkey puzzle tree, "this pine
tiger,"

> This porcupine-quilled, complicated starkness—
> this is beauty—"a certain proportion in the skeleton
>   which gives the best results."

23

WILLIAM BUTLER YEATS

THROUGHOUT the entire period covered in this volume Yeats was one of the major living poets. We have discussed his work in connection with the poetry of the Celtic Twilight, with the development of Symbolism in the 1890s, with the reaction against *l'art pour l'art* after the turn of the century, and in several other contexts. For this reason he can here be discussed more briefly than would otherwise be the case. He was born in Ireland in 1865, and named William Butler after his grandfather, a clergyman. His father, John Butler Yeats, married Susan Pollexfen, who was descended from a family of shipowners. J. B. Yeats was a painter. He delighted in conversation and argument, and his opinions changed like shot silk. Chesterton used to say that he never knew but one man who could talk like old Yeats, the painter, and that was young Yeats, the poet. Yeats spent his boyhood and early youth in London and in Sligo, on the west coast of Ireland, where he stayed with his maternal grandparents. Between these two homes was no very long journey, but they were different worlds.

In the 1890s Yeats's lyrics evoked a bleakly beautiful landscape of streams, lakes, hills, rocks, woods, wind, and clouds, and it was the countryside about Sligo that planted these images in his imagination. Persons and places in the vicinity came back in memory to the end of his life. In Lough Gill, three miles from Sligo, was the small, wooded island of Innisfree. On the shores of this lake, where midnight was

> all a glimmer, and noon a purple glow,
> And evening full of the linnet's wings,

he picked blackberries and daydreamed of living alone in a hut on the island. West along the coast was the hill of Knocknarea, with a cairn on the summit under which the legendary Queen Maeve of Connaught was said to lie buried. Not far off was the great country house of Lissadell. All through his later boyhood Constance Gore-Booth, who lived there, was an object of romantic interest to Yeats, though he did not then meet her. Years later he recalled his impression:

> When long ago I saw her ride
> Under Ben Bulben to the meet,
> The beauty of her country-side
> With all youth's lonely wildness stirred.

A few miles north of Sligo was the mountain of Ben Bulben, with the waterfall on its side that "childhood counted dear"; under "bare Ben Bulben's head" was Drumcliff Churchyard, which Yeats later chose for his place of burial.

For the artist's son the Sligo relatives were a romantically different type of person. In London and in Howth, near Dublin, where his family settled when he was fifteen, the adults Yeats met were artists, lawyers, professors, intellectuals—his father's friends. They talked of paintings, books, styles, politics, morals, philosophy, religion, in short, of ideas, and his father, at least, talked with irresponsible exaggeration. But in Sligo were silent, practical men of action and business, like his formidable grandfather, who had once been shipwrecked, or his horse-racing uncle, George Pollexfen. Their talk at the dinner table was of ships and cargoes. J. B. Yeats admired the Pollexfens as the opposite of himself and later speculated that his son's poetic genius derived from the union of the sociable, vocal, and imaginative Yeatses with the deep-feeling, intuitive Pollexfens: "By marriage with the Pollexfens," he said, "I have given a tongue to the sea cliffs." Yeats later remarked that this was the only compliment that ever turned his head.

Yeats's education began at home, when some of his Sligo uncles and aunts tried to teach him to read. He made so little progress that they feared he did not have all his faculties. In London he was sent to school. His teachers reported favorably on his character, but he was not a gifted scholar. "My thoughts were a great excitement, but when I tried to do anything with them, it was like trying to pack a balloon into a shed in a high wind." He had many fights, partly because his English school-mates looked down on him as Irish, while he looked down on them as English. Eventually he cultivated the friendship of an athlete, who protected him. After his family moved from London to Dublin, he attended the high school there. His formal education ended in 1883.

His family called him Willie. Gentle and dreamy, he pored in adolescence over *Alastor,* Shelley's romantic, obscurely symbol-ical, narrative poem about a world-disappointed visionary. Shelley's poet-hero saw and loved a woman in his dreams, and afterwards no mortal girl, not even a passionate Arab maiden, could win his heart. Seeking the dream, he floated down a river to his death. Yeats longed, he recalled in his *Autobiogra-phy,* "to share his melancholy, and maybe at last to disap-pear . . . drifting in a boat along some slow-moving river between great trees." Sometimes he would sleep out at night in a cliffside cave above the sea, for Shelley's sages had dwelt in cav-erns by the sea. As he climbed along the narrow ledge to the cave, he thought of Byron's romantic hero Manfred on his gla-cier. The tendency to make such indentifications did not fade away as Yeats grew older. He associated himself and the people he knew with figures in story and poetry. His imagination myth-ologized his life.

From the time he was eight or nine years old his father read poems to him; his *Autobiography* mentions Macaulay's *The Lays of Ancient Rome* and Scott's *The Lay of the Last Minstrel;* the latter made him wish to be a magician. Shelley, Byron, Wordsworth, Tennyson, Spenser, and Morris seem to have been among his favorites in adolescence. By the time he was seventeen, he was writing poetry. In fact, he never seriously imagined any other role in life. From his earliest verses on, his father took a great, encouraging interest. J. B. Yeats was brimful of ideas about poetry and daily urged them on his son, beginning at breakfast.

Since the father's opinions were the second important influence in forming Yeat's poetry (the first being the English poets of the nineteenth century), we may briefly summarize them. Some can be read in letters to his son, subsequently published. But because what J. B. Yeats may actually have said matters less than what his son took to heart, we can turn to Yeat's *Autobiography* for his recollections of his father's doctrine. The major Victorians, J. B. Yeats said, had loaded their verse with arguments and ethical teachings. These, however, had no place in poetry. This tenet was typical of the Pre-Raphaelite generation; another was less so: he cared little "for any of that most beautiful poetry which has come in modern times from the influence of painting." If we think of the Pre-Raphaelite verse J. B. Yeats had in mind, we understand that not just the pictorial, but a nexus of associated values also—contemplative mood, symbolism, quasi-religious mysticism—were under attack. In poetry J. B. Yeats relished what he called drama, by which he meant character revealing itself in a moment of intense feeling. "He did not care even for a fine lyric passage unless he felt some actual man behind its elaboration of beauty." Poetry was an "idealization of speech." These views were never accepted by Yeats without strong qualifications, and they were more or less adverse to his own tastes when his father argued them in his adolescence. But they influenced his poetry from the start. Later in his career he sought to write poetry that would be "an idealization of speech," and his father's ideal found a marvelous fulfillment in the Yeatsian talk of the son's mature style.

Yeats thought of himself as a person of religious temperament who had been deprived of religion by nineteenth-century science. A "religious temperament" in his case implied a need to sense a spiritual depth and mystery in the universe and, beyond this, an ultimate coherence and meaning. It implied also an imaginative need for concrete symbols in which the mystery could be invoked and contemplated. His religious quest was more urgently motivated by metaphysical and imaginative hungers than by moral ones. Feelings of the vanity of human life unless religion gives a purpose or of the evil of the heart unless it can be redeemed—feelings that sent Eliot on his religious quest—did not press upon Yeats so strongly or appall him so intensely as the thought of the drabness and emptiness of the universe as it was conceived in the materialistic world-view of nineteenth-century science.

Christianity was, from his point of view, impossible to believe, and his religious needs drove him to other traditions. He studied occult, hermetic, theosophical, kabalistic, Rosicrucian, alchemical, astrological, mystical, magical, and spiritualist lore with Mohini Chatterji, with the Dublin Hermetic Society, with the Order of the Golden Dawn, with the celebrated Madame Blavatsky (said to be in telepathic communication with immortal Tibetan sages), and with many other groups and persons. He worked with Edwin Ellis for four years (1889–1893) on an edition of the writings of William Blake. For this edition the two students thought out an "interpretation of the mystical philosophy of the Prophetic Books." The atmosphere of Yeats's hermetic studies is illustrated by a passage in an autobiographical manuscript published in 1972: in the Dublin Hermetic Society he was

a member of their Esoteric Section, an inner ring of the more devout students, which met weekly to study tables of oriental symbolism. Every organ of the body had its correspondence in the heavens, and the seven principles which made the human soul and body corresponded to the seven colours and the planets and the notes of the musical scale. We lived in perpetual discussion.

Yeats began to devote himself to these matters in the 1880s. His interest, which perhaps never passed over into absolute credence, lasted all his life. The casual reader of his poetry can have no idea how constant and intense this interest was. He invoked magical symbols, saw visions, consulted the stars, attended seances, and wrote out several esoteric systems of his own elaboration. This had a profound effect on his poetry. The first important effect was that it gave him a cluster of ideas and imaginative habits that might be called a theory and practice of symbolism.

His studies suggested that certain symbols can summon unknown spiritual powers—such symbols, traditional in occult lore, as the four elements, the planets, the directions of the compass, the sun, the moon, the sea, the rose, and various geometrical designs. Even if one doubted this premise of magic, it was certain, at the very least, that such symbols in poetry evoked ancient traditions and manifold, complex associations, so a poem using such symbols acquired a depth and density of implication greater than even the poet might know. "A hundred generations might write out what seemed the meaning . . . and they would write different meanings, for no symbol tells all its meanings to any generation." As Yeats put it in an essay on Shelley (1900):

It is only by ancient symbols, by symbols that have numberless meanings besides the one or two the writer lays an emphasis upon, or the half-score he knows of, that any highly subjective art can escape from the barrenness and shallowness of a too conscious arrangement, into the abundance and depth of Nature. The poet of essences and pure ideas must seek in the half-lights that glimmer from symbol to symbol as if to the ends of the earth, all that the epic and dramatic poet finds of mystery and shadow in the accidental circumstances of life.

Along with concepts of symbolism, Yeats's occult studies taught him a technique of what he called "reverie." He would fix his mind upon a symbol, and this would call up other images or symbols, provided only that he could suppress his own will and remain passive in order to receive whatever was presented. He presumed that such reveries might put him in touch with profound meanings or profound "states of the soul." His commitment to symbolism and reverie shaped his style. He thought in images; he was alert to exploit their manifold possible implications; he felt that the value of poetry lay in its power of implication or suggestion, not in anything it could state. In an essay on "The Symbolism of Poetry" (1900) he asked himself how poetic style would change if poets learned that they should evoke and contemplate symbols; his answer partly described his own style. It also revealed how much his "theory" of symbolism at this time gathered in other ideas typical of the nineties. If or when the symbolical movement comes, we shall see

a casting out of descriptions of nature for the sake of nature, or the moral law for the sake of the moral law, a casting out of all anecdotes and of that brooding over scientific opinion that so often extinguished the central flame in Tennyson . . . and we would cast out of serious poetry those energetic rhythms, as of a man running, which are the invention of the will with its eyes always on something to be done or undone; and we would seek out those wavering, meditative, organic rhythms, which are the embodiment of the imagination.

Since the contrary is still sometimes assumed, we may repeat that Yeats was a Symbolist before he encountered the French symbolistes. As he wrote to Ernest Boyd in 1915, "My interest in mystic symbolism did not come from Arthur Symons or any other contemporary writer. I have been a student of the medieval mystics since 1887 . . . Of the French symbolists I have never had any detailed or accurate knowledge."

As he prepared his edition of Blake, Yeats came more and more to feel that there was a hidden significance in his initials. Were not Blake's initials W.B., and were not his W.B.Y.? It was not surprising that Blake would appear to Yeats from time to time and dictate revisions in the poems of Blake that he was editing—revisions which Yeats faithfully incorporated in the text he published. It was also typical that Yeats found what no one else has found: that Blake had been an Irishman. Blake's grandfather had been an O'Neal, Yeats argued, and "Ireland takes a most important place" in Blake's "mystical system."

For still another factor shaping Yeats's early poetry was his Irish nationalism. These were times of boiling emotional politics in the Irish struggle for independence from England. Yeats aspired to bring into being an Irish national literature. Perhaps he would have written in Gaelic, had he known the language. As it was, he would at least be an Irish, rather than an English, poet. He would draw on Irish myth and legend, as opposed, for example, to classical or Germanic myth. His poetry would assimilate the native folklore of the peasantry. It would rid itself of "Shelley's Italian light" and dwell amid the low, wet skies, the rock and heather of Ireland. The legends and history associated with particular places and objects would be revived and made familiar. He would "bring again in[to] imaginative life the old sacred places—Slievanamon, Knocknarea—all that old reverence that hung—above all—about conspicuous hills," so that, as in classical Greece, the local features of the landscape would have imaginative resonance for the people who lived there, and, up to a point at least, a shared imaginative lore would once again unite the poet with a whole people, as it had in the heroic ages of the past. Above all, however, this national literature would be written in accordance with exacting standards of taste and style, of sensitivity and imagination. A national literature emphatically did not mean writing down. It was not to be a literature of patriotic rhetoric; although Yeats himself wrote some poems of this kind, he quarreled bitterly with nationalists for whom any criticism of patriotic verse was treason. His idea was to create through literature a national mind, which would, in turn, bring a nation into being. But the "national mind" was to be one that would support a great literature.

For his cause Yeats learned to give speeches and dominate committees. He helped form the Irish Literary Society in 1891 and the National Literary Society in 1892 and gradually engaged in more direct political activity. There used to be many a former Irish revolutionary who knew little of Yeats the poet but remembered very well Yeats the agitator. In 1896 he joined the Irish Republican Brotherhood, and a police report from 1899 speaks of him as "a literary enthusiast" and "more or less of a revolutionary." In the speeches and articles—even, to some degree, in the poems in which he elaborated his idea of what Ireland would be—he was articulating a vision that had little relation to possibility, just as his characterizations of England presented a monstrous bogey. Both images help define what he valued, however. In brief summary, England was the home of materialism and middle-class morality, of industrialism and imperialism, of power, wealth, and the coarse insensitivities these things breed. (One of his favorite symbols of all this was Carlyle's prose.) The Irish, on the other hand, would become a mainly agricultural people of delicate perceptions, imagination, and spiritual insight.

He immersed himself in nationalist politics out of conviction and also, as he said, out of "desire for a fair woman." "The great trouble of my life," as he called his love for Maud Gonne, began in 1889, when he met her in London. She was a nationalist, a revolutionary, a maker of incendiary speeches, wholly devoted to the bringing about of Irish independence. Yeats was in love with her for at least fifteen years, and during the 1890s his political activity was a kind of wooing; he hoped to draw her to him by sharing her cause. To this love Yeats brought his immense capacity for imaginative idealization. He felt a high-minded pride in Maud Gonne, in her beauty, courage, and "pilgrim soul." He compared her to Helen of Troy. He felt a tender protectiveness. He was proud also of his own passion. But she would not have him, though she would not decisively drop him either, and the years of frustration doubtless contributed to the eventual hardening and embittering of his character. For reasons of poetic style and personal discretion, the many poems he wrote to or for Maud Gonne in the 1890s—such poems as "Aedh Gives His Beloved Certain Rhymes," or "Aedh Hears the Cry of the Sedge," or "When You Are Old"—are rather abstract. Nevertheless, they make up the finest group of love lyrics that has been written in modern times and are the more moving to the extent that one knows the biographical circumstances. "The Fish" is one example:

> Although you hide in the ebb and flow
> Of the pale tide when the moon has set,
> The people of coming days will know
> About the casting out of my net,
> And how you have leaped times out of mind
> Over the little silver cords,
> And think that you were hard and unkind,
> And blame you with many bitter words.

As late as 1908 Yeats was still addressing much of his poetry to Maud Gonne. As he soliloquized in a journal of that year, she "never really understands my plans, or nature, or ideas," but "How much of the best I have done and still do is but the attempt to explain myself to her? If she understood, I should lack a reason for writing, and one never can have too many reasons for doing what is so laborious."

In London in the 1890s he knew most of the poets of that time. Henley, with whom he shared almost no opinions, he nevertheless admired for his sincerity, generosity, and "aristocratic attitudes, his hatred of the crowd and of that logical realism which is but popular oratory . . . frozen and solidified," and Yeats was one of the young writers Henley warmly encouraged and published in his *National Observer*. At an opposite pole of the literary world, Yeats also admired Oscar Wilde, whom he met before Wilde was famous, having been invited by his fellow Irishman to Christmas dinner in 1888. Wilde read from *The Decay of Lying*, and Yeats found the style flawed. "Like all of us," Wilde had learned from Pater, "but in him the cadence became over-elaborate and swelling, the diction a little lacked in exactness." But Yeats was dazzled by Wilde's audacious, self-

possessed wit, in which Yeats saw a swaggering courage, and said
of Wilde, "He is one of our eighteenth-century duellists born in
the wrong century" and "he would be a good leader in a cavalry
charge." As for Dowson, Yeats did not know him well but sensed
in him "that weakness that seems to go with certain high virtues
of sweetness and of courtesy." He "was burning to the socket, in
exquisite songs . . . full of subtle refinement." Lionel Johnson
became "for a few years my closest friend . . . He had taken
from Walter Pater certain favorite words which came to mean
much for me: 'Life should be a ritual,' and we should value it for
'magnificence,' for all that is 'hieratic.'" Arthur Symons at first
"repelled" him because he "saw nothing in literature but a series
of impressions." But Symons later became, briefly, his "most intimate friend," and the two shared lodgings for a while. "Whatever I came to know of Continental literature I learned of
him . . . He had the sympathetic intelligence of a woman and
was the best listener I have ever met." All of these writers except
Henley belonged to the Rhymers' Club, "a weekly or was it fort-
nightly meeting of poets at the Cheshire Cheese," the London
tavern associated with Samuel Johnson. At these meetings the
poets would read and discuss their verses.

When he came to write of these figures in his *Autobiography*,
Yeats called them the "tragic generation" and described them
with warm sympathy and admiration, even if he told many feline
anecdotes about them. They disdained, as he portrayed them,
the middle-class reading public, its attitudes, values, and way of
life. Their art rejected rhetoric, mechanical logic, and moral
responsibilities and embodied subtle and delicate sensitivities in
clear, firm forms. In some degree or way they all had that "noble
courage" that Yeats, thinking of Aubrey Beardsley, was tempted
to call "the greatest of human faculties." On drink, drugs,
scandal, passion, or madness their lives had shipwrecked; contemplating this, Yeats felt that self-destructiveness had been at
work in them all and that whatever brought about their personal
tragedies had also limited their art. Just what this was he could
not make completely clear to himself; more exactly, he made it
clear in several different ways. But he seems to have felt that
in the intensity of their rejection of middle-class existence they
had also—inevitably in their circumstances—rejected life itself—that is, natural, normal existence with its experiences and

passions—so that there was not enough to nourish their art. In turning away, they had not turned toward anything. Only the mystic and the saint, Yeats later believed, could reject nature and the world and still be full. For anyone else, there would be only an "unnatural emptiness." Johnson had taken to drink in order, Yeats said, to recapture "accident, the unexpected, the confusions of nature," without which "we cannot live."

What Yeats most learned from these poets was, he felt, the necessity of working as a close, fastidious craftsman. In London in 1890 he had "still the intellectual habits of a provincial, and fixed my imagination on great work to the neglect of detail." These poets taught him that we must "constantly analyze what we have done, be content even to have little life outside our work, to show, perhaps, to other men as little as the watchmender shows, his magnifying glass caught in his screwed-up eye." However clearly he saw their limitations, Yeats sympathized with their rejection of the attitudes of the Victorian middle-class, and critics whose judgment carries much weight have thought that his own values to the end of his life were ultimately aesthetic ones. Such oppositions as those between art and natural life or between imagination and moral responsibility were always, for Yeats, real and vital in a way that reflects a nine-tyish influence on his thinking. They were fought out in many poems and also in his journals and letters, where one finds such typical remarks as, "Evil comes to us men of imagination wearing as its mask all the virtues. I have known, certainly, more men destroyed by the desire to have wife and child and to keep them in comfort than I have seen destroyed by harlots and drink." But also typically, on the other hand, he wrote another journal entry only twelve days later: protesting against the time and energy he was taking away from his poetry and spending on other work, he added, "yet perhaps I must do all these things that I may set myself into a life of action, so as to express not the traditional poet but that forgotten thing, the normal active man." That Yeats did not resolve for one side or the other, but lived in tension and inner debate, was characteristic and is one of the reasons for his poetic achievement.

In a single chapter on Yeats's whole career, one can hope to characterize his poetry of this period only in a general way, and in earlier chapters I attempted this. The point to be stressed here is that all we have noticed in his early career helped form this poetry. His aims as a poet were diverse, but he struggled to unify them. In the many lyrics he wrote to the rose, for example, the "Red Rose, proud Rose, sad Rose of all my days" that he invoked as both subject and inspiration is a traditional symbol. It is perhaps the Beauty to which the London aesthetes, disciples of Pater, devoted themselves, and it is certainly the eternal and transcendent Beauty and Love of which Yeats read first in Shelley and later in Neoplatonic, Rosicrucian, and other occult books. (He may also have read Plato, for Lionel Johnson had given him a one-volume edition of Plato in 1893, saying, "I need ten years in the wilderness," and "you ten years in a library.") In all these respects the rose was an image of symbolic, even mystical, profundity, appropriately to be invoked and contemplated in wavering yet incantatory rhythms, in moods of solemn awe and religious prayer. Yet if Yeats was hearing or hoping to hear "strange things said by God," he had also heard and absorbed his father's argument that poetry lies essentially in the rendering of passion, character, and speech, and his style had somehow to reflect these premises also. Moreover, the rose is Ireland in its long history of suffering, and Yeats, writing to serve "old Eire," felt that he must write for the people, which meant, he sometimes thought, that he must forsake elaborate symbolism for "Ballad and story, rann and song." Certainly it meant that while his lyrics invoked the symbolic rose, they must also present heather and thorn trees, describing the natural landscape of Ireland. Finally, Yeats was in love; in her old age Maud Gonne, having outlived Yeats, used to say that the rose was a symbol of herself, and surely it was.

REMAKING A SELF, 1899–1914

Yeats's early style reached its finest development in *The Wind Among the Reeds,* which was published in 1899. The next fifteen years were difficult and bitter. At the end of them he had developed a new lyric style, a style of talk that could be intensely actual and personal, often with stark directness and force. In "A Coat" (1914) he referred to this change of style while exemplifying it:

I made my song a coat
Covered with embroideries
Out of old mythologies
From heel to throat;
But the fools caught it,
Wore it in the world's eyes
As though they'd wrought it.
Song, let them take it,
For there's more enterprise
In walking naked.

Gentle, dreamy Willie Yeats, with his sweet and wistful melody and his beautiful symbols, had died into a larger, more formidable poet, amazingly articulate in all his many moods, though not necessarily more attractive in personality.

If we ask why Yeats's style changed, we can again recall that from his earliest efforts as a poet he had been pulled in different directions. At one pole he had been symbolist and hieratic, to use Lionel Johnson's favorite word; at the other he had responded to his father's praise of simple, passionate speech. As early as 1888 he had written Katharine Tynan, "I have woven about me a web of thoughts. I wish to break through it, to see the world again"; after finishing his Romantic and symbolical *The Wanderings of Oisin* that year, he had "simplified" his style by filling his "imagination with country stories." He had admired folk ballads and tried to imitate their diction and rhythm. In 1899 he had read some verses written by a man returning to Ireland to die. Though they were not good verses, they had moved him, "for they contained the actual thoughts of a man at a passionate moment of life." We should, he had decided, make poems by writing out "our own thoughts in as nearly as possible the language we thought them in, as though in a letter to an intimate friend. We should not disguise them in any way; for our lives give them force as the lives of people in plays give force to their words." Twenty-four years later, in a 1913 letter to his father, he explained the new style he had now achieved in more or less the same terms:

I have tried to make my work convincing with a speech so natural and dramatic that the hearer would feel the presence of a man thinking and feeling. . . . It is in dramatic expression that English poetry is most lacking as compared with French poetry. Villon always and Ronsard at times create a marvellous drama out of their own lives.

These opposed alternatives of symbolist mystery and folk or dramatic actuality were part of a wider dialectic to which we shall come back in connection with Yeats's achievement in the 1920s and 1930s. To his mind "art" was a polar opposite to "nature," and he assumed a similar, mutually excluding opposition between such values as "intellect" and "wisdom," on the one hand, and "passion" and "life," on the other hand. His career of fifty-seven years was an ongoing attempt to conceive how such antithetical values might be reconciled and to embody such a synthesis in his poetic style. At the same time one can also view his career as a sequence of gradual shifts of emphasis, his poetry developing from one pole to the other and then moving back again. In this perspective the change of style that was consolidated by 1914, when *Responsibilities* was published, was both a reaction against his earlier style and the culmination of a tendency that had been intermittently strong in the 1880s and 1890s and gradually assumed prominence after 1900.

His changed style was a victory in the realm of technique and even more in the overcoming of psychological inhibition. In 1892 he hated what he called "generalization" and "abstraction" as much as he ever did later. But he did not know how to escape them and began a love poem,

> A pity beyond all telling,
> Is hid in the heart of love.

By 1910 he had learned how to write poetry that sounded like "the actual thoughts of a man at a passionate moment of life" and compelled himself to speak directly from his personal self, writing of the actual woman in the actual world and in his own life:

> Why should I blame her that she filled my days
> With misery, or that she would of late
> Have taught to ignorant men most violent ways,
> Or hurled the little streets upon the great?

"We see all arts and societies passing from experience to generalization," he said in 1909, "whereas the young begin with generalization and end with experience."

Yeats's stylistic development was motivated and assisted by many experiences life brought him. His immersion in Irish politics, with his work as an organizer of meetings and manipulator of committees, dealing with practical men for a practical purpose, had an effect on his character and, more important, on his idea of his character. He was proud of himself in evenings "spent with some small organizer into whose spittoon I secretly poured my third glass of whiskey."

From 1899 on Yeats was seeing his plays performed in the theater, and in 1902 what became the Abbey Theatre Company was formed. This is not the place to tell the history of this famous theater, neither can we notice the plays Yeats wrote for it, but his experience with the theater contributed strongly to the formation of his poetic style. Between 1899 and 1908 he wrote twelve plays, some of them in prose. In the discipline of composition for the stage he was forced to write dialogue, direct speech in which characters talked to each other and in which what they said could be taken in by an audience. In contrast to his symbolist poetic, which emphasized the importance of rich, suggestive words, writing for the theater drove home the importance of construction. "Poetry," he now said, "comes logically out of the fundamental action" and must not turn aside "at the lure of word or metaphor."

Two close and admired friends, Lady Gregory and John Millington Synge, had a direct influence on his style through their own writings and especially through their dramas. He met Lady Gregory in 1896 and began spending summers at her estate of Coole in the western part of Ireland. She took him collecting folktales in the cottages of the local peasants, and in the evening she wrote out in dialect what they had heard. Yeats now told George Moore "that one could learn to write" only from the peasants, "their speech being living speech, flowing out of the habits of their lives, struck out of life itself." In the comedies she composed for the Abbey Theatre, Lady Gregory used an approximation to a folk dialect; Yeats collaborated in some of these. A similar idiom was handled much more powerfully in the plays of Synge. Yeats was fascinated by the character and work of this "rooted man," who had a "hunger for harsh facts, for ugly surprising things, for all that defies our hope."

Yeats handled the affairs of the Abbey Theatre for its first ten years. "Theatre business, management of men" further developed his sense of his own character as capable and formidable and of his own life as charged with the interests and passions of the "normal active man." When their plays aroused religious, moral, or patriotic protest—Synge's *The Playboy of the Western World,* for example, caused a week of riots in the theater in 1907—Yeats fought back in letters to newspapers, in essays, and sometimes in speeches to hostile crowds. He was brave and effective, and felt himself to be so, rejoicing in this image of himself.

Meanwhile, in 1903 Maud Gonne married Major John McBride, a soldier and, in Yeats's opinion, "a drunken, vainglorious lout." Yeats received the news in a letter from her just as he was about to give a lecture and, though he managed to get through the lecture, he was afterwards unable to remember what he had said. For the next several years he wrote few lyrics. In his hurt he emphasized his ideal of "noble courage," which he increasingly thought of as "aristocratic." At the same time he fought against his tendency to imaginative idealization, for Maud Gonne's marriage suggested that he had been living in a fool's romantic dream. She had always seemed "in some sense, Ireland," and what with his disillusion at her marriage, his anger at religious or patriotic protest over the plays in the Abbey Theatre—not to mention other similar episodes in the cultural life of Dublin—and his own increasing absorption in concerns other than politics, he swung violently against his earlier political idealism. His view of things was much embittered, and he also deliberately embittered it, cultivating an unflinching realism as part of a heroic attitude.

The attitude was especially difficult to maintain in the lyrics he wrote to Maud Gonne. In 1909 he began a poem,

> All things can tempt me from this craft of verse:
> One time it was a woman's face, or worse—
> The seeming needs of my fool-driven land.

He was insulting Ireland, and doubtless enjoyed this arrogance, but he was also dismissing reductionistically, as "a woman's face," his long idealistic love of Maud Gonne.

"All art," he said, "is in the last analysis an endeavor to condense as out of the flying vapour of the world an image of human perfection." The moral ideal he now strove to embody in his style had to do with wholeness and energy of personality.

The writing of plays was "the search for more manful energy,"
he said in 1906, for "more of cheerful acceptance of whatever
arises out of the logic of events, and for clean outlines, instead of
those outlines of lyric poetry that are blurred with desire and
vague regret." He held before his mind's eye the image of medieval and Renaissance writers, as he conceived them: "those careless old writers, one imagines squabbling over a mistress, or
riding on a journey, or drinking round a tavern fire, brisk and
active men." He told Lady Gregory, with much satisfaction, "My
work has got more masculine. It has more salt in it." In his early
verse, he explained in a letter to George Russell, there had been
"an exaggeration of sentiment and sentimental beauty which I
have come to think unmanly." And he called in the world of
spirits to support him in his new ideal: "A mysterious command
has gone out," he said, "in the invisible world," and we are to
have "no emotions, however abstract, in which there is not an
athletic joy."

In accordance with this ideal he labored to express in his
poetry a greater variety of feelings, including especially feelings
excluded from his earlier lyrics, such as anger, insult, mockery,
and humor. He began "September, 1913" in scornful irony, attacking the Irish middle class, which he considered pinched,
money-grubbing, and superstitious:

> What need you, being come to sense,
> But fumble in a greasy till
> And add the halfpence to the pence
> And prayer to shivering prayer, until
> You have dried the marrow from the bone?

Although addressed to Parnell's ghost, "To a Shade" was no
mystic incantation. It opened with a line made colloquially awkward by many weak accents and a late caesura, and the paren-
thesis of the third line, conveying the witty aside of conversation,
reinforced the effect of actual talk:

> If you have revisited the town, thin Shade,
> Whether to look upon your monument
> (I wonder if the builder has been paid).

Not that Yeats always spoke in his own person, but when he
adopted other roles, they were no longer those of his earlier

poetry, such as Aedh and wandering Aengus. He was now more likely to speak in the person of

> A cursing rogue with a merry face,
> A bundle of rags upon a crutch,

and in such alter egos he also extended his repetoire of moods. "Beggar to Beggar Cried" (1914) was sardonic mockery and self-mockery. Lady Gregory and other friends had been urging unromantic, prudential advice upon him—take a vacation for his health, find a wife, settle down—and Yeats put something of this into the mouth of a beggar who talks as though he belonged to the middle class:

> "Time to put off the world and go somewhere
> And find my health again in the sea air,"
> *Beggar to beggar cried, being frenzy-struck,*
> "And make my soul before my pate is bare."

> "And get a comfortable wife and house
> To rid me of the devil in my shoes,"
> *Beggar to beggar cried, being frenzy-struck,*
> "And the worse devil that is between my thighs."

But Yeats knew that he was not the sort of man who squabbled over a mistress or drank round a tavern fire. He did not feel an "athletic joy." He was not at all instinctive, direct, or spontaneous in his emotions. On the contrary, he still usually seemed to himself dreamy, sentimental, shy, timid, and uncertain, always doubting and qualifying, and so little capable of instinctive emotion that he constantly paralyzed himself by self-analysis. Self-distrust was, he suspected, usually the main motive for whatever he did; "I even do my writing by self-distrusting reasons." So, though he argued that one should not "find one's art by the analysis of language or amid the circumstances of dreams but . . . live a passionate life, and . . . express the emotions that find one thus in simple rhythmical language," he knew that the deeper psychological truth was that his bold, direct style of speech as from the active, whole man was a deliberate pose, a stance assumed, a mask worn. It was an image he held before himself, a role he played, hoping he would become the role. "Active virtue," he said, "as distinguished from the passive acceptance of a current code," is "theatrical, consciously dramatic, the wearing of a mask."

So, real virtue is trying to be what you're not —

A NEW LEVEL OF ACHIEVEMENT, 1914–1928

After *Responsibilities* (1914) Yeats's poetry gradually consolidated a third phase in a sequence of memorable volumes, *The Wild Swans at Coole* (1919), *Michael Robartes and the Dancer* (1921), and *The Tower* (1928). In *The Tower*, which included such famous lyrics as "Sailing to Byzantium," "Leda and the Swan," "Among School Children," and the title poem, the evolution was complete. If we ask why Yeats's lyrics of these years grip readers so powerfully, we think of the intellectual excitement they generate, their depth of suggestion, human interest, emotional intensity, imaginative sweep and surprise, and vivid, supple, concentrated presentation. But these or similar generalities would be true of many great poets. Yeats's mature poetry was shaped especially by three fundamental tendencies of his mind. Symbolism is central to his art, for he assumed that symbols invoke, embody, or, perhaps, are identical with "reality." Hence he wrote poems in which the entire poem might be described as the creation and contemplation of a symbol; "The Magi" is an example. And he wrote poems in which he explored the interaction of two or more symbols. He was deeply versed in the symbolic meanings that poetic tradition and occult lore had bestowed on countless images and he exercised to the full the symbol-making power of his own imagination. Images in his poetry that seem merely descriptive or incidental may, if we ponder them, disclose depths of implication. But Yeats was also committed to the expression in poetry of what he often called "personality." His poetry is to be read as the talk of a man vigorously responding to actual experience, a humorous, unpredictable, rich-natured man in whom we take a lively interest. Finally, his poems are shaped by his tendency to think in terms of antitheses; in fact, this figure of thought corresponded, Yeats believed, to the ultimately tragic structure of reality.

Between 1914 and 1921 Yeats wrote out recollections of his life up to the age of thirty-five (later published as *Reveries over Childhood and Youth*, 1916; *The Trembling of the Veil*, 1922; and *Memoirs*, 1973). The setting down of these memories made the happenings and persons he described more fixed and vivid in his own mind and endowed them with symbolic meaning. About this time he was hammering his thoughts into a "religious system," as he called it in a letter to his father. This "prose backing to my poetry" was published in 1918 as *Per Amica Silentia Lunae*, and expounds Yeats's theory of the "mask," by which he meant a character that is the polar opposite of one's own. If mask and self could be unified, one would experience completeness of being. The mask is also the anti-self or Daemon, the "illustrious dead man" who is most unlike the living man and weaves his destiny. There is much about the *Anima Mundi,* or "great memory passing on from generation to generation" and how images from the great memory enter the individual mind. Yeats also explains the complex fate of the soul after death, the several phases it goes through before it is born again. "I find," he wrote his father, that "the setting it all in order has helped my verse, has given me a new framework and new patterns."

For three winters, 1913–1916, Ezra Pound acted as his secretary, the two poets sharing a cottage in Sussex. Pound was going through the manuscripts of Ernest Fenollosa, and Yeats was intrigued by what he learned of Japanese Noh drama. In Noh he saw a traditional and esoteric, symbolical and anti-naturalist art for the few. The plays he wrote henceforth were strongly influenced by Noh. Meanwhile, his ears full of Pound's praise of "efficient" writing, of spare, functional, concrete presentation, he asked the younger poet to go through his collected poems and cross out the abstract words and conventional metaphors. He was surprised to find there were so many. He set to work once again to clean up his style (from which he had been eliminating the nineties for more than a decade), and the results could be seen in the first play he had written in six years, *At the Hawk's Well* (1916):

> The mountain-side grows dark;
> The withered leaves of the hazel
> Half choke the dry bed of the well.

It was probably because of such verses that Eliot, watching the play (which may have influenced some passages of *The Waste Land*), concluded that at least in his stark diction Yeats was a modern.

In 1916 the Easter Rebellion against British rule in Ireland revived Yeats's dream of a heroic Ireland and he wrote one of his finest poems, "Easter, 1916," on this event. But as bloody and vicious wars raged intermittently in Ireland between 1919 and

1923—first between the Irish patriots and the English troops
with their Irish auxiliaries, and then between rival Irish factions—he again despaired of politics:

> We, who seven years ago
> Talked of honour and of truth,
> Shriek with pleasure if we show
> The weasel's twist, the weasel's tooth.

During the Easter Rebellion, Maud Gonne's husband was
killed, and Yeats again proposed to her. When she refused, he
proposed, with much hesitation, to her adopted niece, Iseult.
She also lacked "the impulse," and in October 1917 Yeats married Georgie Hyde-Lees. His way of life now became more settled, and he had much domestic happiness in his wife, his two
children, and the bustle of a thriving household. In 1915 he had
purchased a Norman tower with an attached cottage in Galway,
not far from Lady Gregory at Coole. During the next several
years the cottage and tower were gradually made livable. "I am
making," he wrote John Quinn, "a setting for my old age, a place
to influence lawless youth, with its severity and antiquity." At
this cottage and tower Yeats spent summers with his family, living within a symbol. The ancient tower recalled Shelley's towers
in which sages and visionaries had dwelt; it brought to mind the
tower in which "*Il Penseroso*'s Platonist," as Yeats called the
protagonist of Milton's poem, would outwatch the midnight
hours, poring over Hermes Trismegistus or Plato. Seen from
far, the midnight candle burning in the tower beside an open
book was an emblem of "mysterious wisdom won by toil." The
tower was also an emblem of many modes of integrity amid ad-
versity—of the "unageing intellect" with its proud, embattled
exultation amid the "wreck of body" in old age; or of the aristocratic past and those who still lived by its values against the com-
mercialized, middle-class present; or of the soul confronting
"the desolation of reality," its heroic defiance grounded in
nothing except courage. The "narrow, winding stair" of the
tower reminded Yeats of gyres or spiraling cones, symbols
which, for him, diagrammed ultimate processes of reality. Even
the rose that flowered in his "acre of stony ground" was symbolical.

During the 1920s Yeats read much philosophy, for he wished

to back up with reading and arguments the truths that came to him from esoteric sources. He traveled in Italy in 1924 and 1925 and had much pleasure in the paintings and mosaics of churches and museums. In 1922 he was named a Senator in Ireland and in 1924 received the Nobel Prize.

The most significant event of these years, however, was his composition of *A Vision,* whose first version he completed in 1925. I cannot here summarize this complex, pedantic prose work that sets forth his occult system. In *A Vision* one can read about the inexorable cycles of history that determine all that happens, each cycle starting over again every two thousand years, and how the cycles revolve from objective to subjective phases, from phases in which men abnegate themselves before some external reality to phases, such as the Renaissance, which take individual self-fulfillment as their ideal. One can study the twenty-six types of personality—twenty-six even though there are twenty-eight phases of the moon, for "there's no human life at the full or the dark." Or one can trace the labyrinth of Yeats's thought on the four faculties of the soul, the four tinctures, and the fate of the soul between death and reincarnation—a fate more complicated than it was in *Per Amica Silentia Lunae.*

To call Yeats the author of *A Vision* is to beg a question. Four days after they were married, Yeats discovered that his wife was psychic and that spirits spoke through her, at first by means of automatic writings and later by speech as she lay in a trance. After three years of such communications, he found himself with fifty notebooks of automatic writing and a much smaller number of notebooks recording what had been dictated orally through his wife. From these notes he pieced out his book.

That the communicators were actually spirits Yeats was not willing to affirm, at least publicly; perhaps there were more natural explanations for the sayings that filled the notebooks. If one asked him whether he believed in the doctrine of his *Vision,* he would have answered evasively. He believed what he had written, but sometimes more and sometimes less, sometimes literally and sometimes metaphorically. Perhaps he would have said that his "supreme fiction," to use Wallace Stevens' phrase, had as much to recommend it as any other. And if one pressed him hard enough, he would have entrenched himself within his system, saying that he was a man of the seventeenth lunar phase and the thoughts that came to men of that phase must seem true to him. When he asked the spirits why they had given him their messages, they replied, "we have come to give you metaphors for poetry," and Yeats reminds us that poets have often before nourished their imaginations in strange places. The muses, he says, are like women who creep out at night and give themselves to unknown sailors and then return to talk of Chinese porcelain or the Ninth Symphony.

As he elaborated his esoteric system in the 1910s and 1920s, the normally much-doubting, much-qualifying Yeats was occasionally confident that he had "mummy truths to tell." A new mode of address, which may be called the oracular, was sometimes heard in his poetry. One finds it in "Mohini Chatterjee," in the several poems spoken by Tom the Lunatic, in the "Supernatural Songs," and in the Crazy Jane sequence. The convention that governs our response to oracular utterance in literature is that the truths imparted are ultimate; no equal countertruth can be summoned against them. Hence the oracle, however brief and obscure, is spoken without qualification and accepted without question (unless there is the question of what it may mean): "Fair and foul are near of kin, / And fair needs foul," "Men dance on deathless feet," "All things remain in God," "All the stream that's roaring by / Came out of a needle's eye." Since originally the gods were thought to be the source of oracles, the mode of address presupposes an unchallengable, mysterious authority in the speaker. Naturally, therefore, Yeats was usually unwilling to voice oracular sayings in his own person, however much he wished to do so. He invoked, instead, the poetic conventions that put ultimate truths in the mouths of Eastern sages, fools, children, mad persons, and the like. The Crazy Jane poems differ from the others cited in that they include voices other than Jane's and much that is spoken or implied contradicts or qualifies her sayings. But no reader finds that the Bishop or any other countervoice opposes Jane's with a truth of equal authority, and the function of debate and irony in this sequence is to exhibit and enforce Jane's intuitions.

A SYSTEM OF SYMBOLS

A larger impact of Yeats's esoteric system on his poetry was on his symbolism and the ways in which it functions. This aspect of his art is probably the chief single source of the imaginative power and appeal of his poetry, and we notice what unusual, intriguing symbols he now deployed: the bird made of gold that crows on a golden bough in the starlight; the "rough beast" with a lion body and head of a man; Chinese sages that stare at the world from a carved piece of lapis lazuli; the interpenetrating gyres or spiraling cones; the moon with its twenty-eight phases and the weird sequence from hunchback to saint to fool associated with the final ones. The thinking out of *A Vision* supplied many of these symbols; it also exercised and emboldened his imagination to a heightened ingenuity and fantasticality. Even when Yeats seems most subject to hocus-pocus—

> Crazed through much child-bearing
> The moon is staggering in the sky;

or,

> He holds him from desire, all but stops his breathing lest
> Primordial Motherhood forsake his limbs;

or,

> The gyres! the gyres! Old Rocky Face, look forth—

the hocus-pocus has its own attractions for imaginative minds. Of course it is not mere hocus-pocus but has esoteric meanings.

In the lyrics Yeats composed between 1900 and 1914 symbolism had been less prominent. The larger role it now acquired in his poetry can be seen as a return, with important differences, to a poetic method he had developed in the 1890s. That the "circus animals," as Yeats called his symbols in a late poem, no longer came from Celtic myth and legend was one of the differences. Such Celtic figures or features as Cuchulain, the Sidhe, and the valley of the black pig were not filled with associations for most readers. They brought to mind only whatever suggestions Yeats first pinned to them and thus contradicted his theory of the way symbols should function. Leda and the swan, however, or Byzantium, or the Second Coming are symbols of a much richer kind, and even though Yeats charged them with esoteric and private meanings, the familiar and traditional ones are also activated.

The writing of *A Vision* gave his ideas, memories, habitual

Note: reconsidering his past material in A Vision invests it w. added density + significance and supplies new symbols for future poetry — incremental technique of working

images, and symbols place and interrelation within a comprehensive system. Thus, it tended to make even more dense and
elaborate the associative interconnections that had been important to the effect of his poetry from the 1890s on. Whoever
reads many pages of Yeats's verse finds that any particular poem
acquires greater depth of suggestion because it brings other
poems of his to mind. We encounter the same or similar images,
themes, symbols, and autobiographical references in different
poems. We associate them, and the associations thus gathered
about an image through the whole context of Yeats's writing
create overtones of feeling and suggestion in the particular context. In the opening lines of "The Wild Swans at Coole"—

Eliot + Joyce: incremental repetition

> The trees are in their autumn beauty,
> The woodland paths are dry—

the first line might have come from a typical Georgian poem of
nature appreciation. It has no special reference for habitual
readers of Yeats. The second line continues the Georgian nature
description, but in this Yeatsian context it also activates vague
but relevant associations. The stress by rhyme on dryness does
not suggest merely that the paths make pleasant going. The dry
woods where the aging man walks contrast with the water of the
lake where the swans drift, and the contrast may bring to mind
that Yeats associated water with mortal and physical life, dryness
with wisdom and death. Straight paths are symbols of abstract
intellection in Yeats, as in Blake, and the paths of imagination
and life are winding or crooked. But the dead may retrace the
winding path from their dry realm to the watery realm of generation.

The swan figures prominently in many other poems of Yeats,
such as "The Tower," "Nineteen Hundred and Nineteen,"
"Among School Children," "Leda and the Swan," and "Coole
Park and Ballylee, 1932." In one or another of these contexts the
swan is associated with such things as youth, passion, and conquest, the animal as opposed to the human, being as opposed to
knowing, and the solitary and defiant soul as opposed to nothingness. All these associations make a resonating background
for any poem in which the swan appears. Or, to take a final instance from "Leda and the Swan," when the poem refers to the

"burning roof and tower" at the fall of Troy, we may call to mind the many towers of Yeats's poetry—his home at Thoor (or "tower") Ballylee, the defensive guard towers, the phallic towers, the towers from which Babylonian astrologers observe the stars, and the towers where students seek wisdom from books. We also remember the poems in which supernatural revelation is associated with fire, so that the "burning tower" suggests the disintegration in a quasi-sexual violence of a civilization. It also suggests the sudden destruction of a traditional lore or wisdom. But it suggests further that the disintegration and destruction come in or with a moment of supernatural revelation.

After 1914 Yeats's poems typically combined the symbol-making or symbol-contemplating impulses of his imagination and his impulse to create a personal or dramatic utterance that would seem vigorously rooted in actual life. He spoke directly of himself and of objects, places, and persons he knew or had known—his children, his house, his grandfather, friends, Lady Gregory's demesne at Coole, the lake and swans there, his Japanese sword, and even the bird's nest at his window. But these now brought to his mind dense associations and were transformed into symbols. He also continued, however, to derive symbols from poetic tradition, occult lore, and his own creative fantasy, but he tended now to handle them differently. He did not simply invoke and contemplate them but also talked to them in a personal or dramatic voice. He had done this to some extent in the 1890s. The change is more in degree than in kind. The speakers of his poems celebrate or query the symbols, they accept, reject, supplement, counter or complete them by other considerations, often by turning to different symbols. In short, they interact with the symbols in ways that create a strong human interest, and the symbol becomes only one element in a drama of human reactions. The difference is approximately that between "Byzantium," where the symbol is beheld and described in a mood of intense excitement, and "Sailing to Byzantium," where the speaker, not the symbol, is the primary focus. The latter poem generates intense dramatic and human interest as the expression of an old man in a moment of emotional and intellectual crisis and choice.

combination of symbolmaking + creation of personal utterance rooted in real life

different use of symbol: only one element in a drama of human reactions

YEATSIAN TALK

Whatever else might be said of Yeats's mature poetic style, most of his poems give the impression of talk—pithy, usually excited talk that confronts us with a personality. He labored to create this impression, and the human interest it generates is one source of his appeal. Yeatsian talk had a large influence on younger poets from Masefield to Auden, although his style of poetic talk is strongly individual and does not resemble the imitations of the colloquial in Masefield, Auden, Frost, Stevens, Eliot, Pound, Williams, and Marianne Moore.

Analysis will show that in syntax and diction Yeats's lyrics can be quite remote from actual speech. He inverts normal word order, suspends syntactical constructions, and involves himself in extremely complicated grammar. How much he cared about economy and rapidity of presentation and how little, if he had to choose, about keeping close to the spoken language, is obvious, especially when he puts words in the mouths of unlettered persons. Crazy Jane deploys absolute constructions and the subjunctive mood. Yeats pursued concreteness of phrasing so eagerly in his mature verse that it became a mannerism. It is generally effective, but not as an approximation to talk. "Beyond that ridge lived Mrs. French," says the speaker in "The Tower," and the simple, direct words are colloquial English. "She was having dinner," might have been the natural next phrase, but Yeats composes a picture instead:

> and once
> When every silver candlestick or sconce
> Lit up the dark mahogany and the wine. . .

The metonymy ("mahogany" instead of "table") is typical, and the effect, as is usual with this figure, is to secure a greater particularity and concreteness in the image. His substitution of concrete for generalizing diction contributed to the compressed, polysemous language that is one of his strengths. The lines in "Leda and the Swan"—

> A shudder in the loins engenders there
> The broken wall, the burning roof and tower
> And Agamemnon dead—

imply that the rape of Leda brought in the fall of Troy and the cycle of Greek civilization, but imply this in a few, spare images.

Economy, speed, and concreteness were general stylistic aims that tended to conflict with Yeats's wish to create an illusion of talk, and yet the illusion is strongly created. If we ask how, we must think again of the ways in which his poems, or many of them, are presented as what Yeats called "personal utterance," as the words of a man speaking amid the actual circumstances of his life. He describes, to repeat, his home, children, ancestors, friends, possessions, memories, plans, and doings, and in this and other ways activates the familiar Romantic convention that the poem puts us into direct contact with the writer. The poetry of Yeats, like that of Shelley, Goethe, or other Romantics, affords a special type of pleasure, besides the pleasure we have in it as art. We take an interest in the poet as a person. A similar convention prompts us to read the poems as spontaneous utterance, as tumblings-out of thought and feeling as they come to mind. Because the poem is read as spontaneous expression our sense of its form includes an appreciation of the natural course, the germination, development, and resolution of the emotions and trains of thought it embodies. The development may include digressions, unexpected amplifications, parentheses, dramatic turns of feeling, sudden introductions of new material, and the like, so long as these do not violate our sense of psychological probability.

"Talk" seems an appropriate term for most poetry within this system of conventions. Whether or to what extent a poet's uses of language actually correspond to those of informal speech is not necessarily important. What matters is that the poetry creates in the reader the presumption or illusion of hearing or overhearing talk, and to this effect such things as a personal subject matter and an apparently unpremeditated progression of thought contribute at least as much as a colloquial idiom. If the subject of a poem is "The Stare's Nest by My Window," we assume that the mode will be talk, and it would require a considerable degree of artifice in the language to dispel the illusion that it is talk. And we should keep in mind also that although "talk" implies informal speech, it need imply no lowering of mental or emotional intensity.

In Yeats the scale of "talk" is generally excited. His phrasing has immense verve and force, expressing strong emotion. At the end of "The Tower" he does not tamely "disagree" with Plotinus or deny Plato's philosophy, but,

> I mock Plotinus' thought
> And cry in Plato's teeth.

In "Sailing to Byzantium" an old man is not merely "a coat upon a stick"; the scarecrow is provided with a "tattered" coat. The expression of emotional excitement through syntax appears especially in his interrupted or uncompleted grammatical structures, his suddenly changing modes of address, and his accumulations of words, phrases, or clauses in series of from two to eight or more. "The Tower" begins with a question—

> What shall I do with this absurdity—

which is interrupted by an apostrophe—

> O heart, O troubled heart—

and the sudden shift is typical and energizing. The sentence continues with phrases in apposition to "absurdity"—

> this caricature,
> Decrepit age that has been tied to me
> As to a dog's tail?

Yeats shares with the English Romantic poets a tendency to put the main business of his sentences in subordinate clauses or in appositional or participial constructions. The construction suggests spontaneity, the discovery of one's thought in the process of saying it. The final section of "The Tower" contains extreme examples of such syntax. Perhaps Yeats had such syntax in mind when in "A General Introduction for My Work" (1937) he spoke of his "powerful and passionate syntax." He had discovered "some twenty years ago" that in order "to make the language of poetry coincide with that of passionate, normal speech," a "natural momentum in the syntax" was more important than any qualities of diction. The unusually excited or passionate character of Yeatsian talk may account for much in it that would embarrass other modern poets, most of whom linger more in lower ranges of emotion. Yeats makes a typically Romantic use of such sweeping collectives as "all," "every," "any,"

"everything," "everywhere," and the like, as in "Everything that
man esteems / Endures a moment or a day" (from "Two Songs
from a Play") or "and everywhere / The ceremony of innocence
is drowned" (from "The Second Coming"). Similarly, there are
his rhetorical questions and his huge hyperboles—

> I need some mind that, if the cannon sound
> From every quarter of the world, can stay
> Wound in mind's pondering
> As mummies in the mummy-cloth are wound—

and extravagant gestures—

> Arise and bid me strike a match
> And strike another till time catch.

Poetry of "personal talk," as Wordsworth once called it, is felt
as talk all the more to the extent that it seems to break away
toward the colloquial from norms of poetry—norms that may
change from generation to generation. Such norms are present
in the mind of every qualified reader, but they can be activated
to a greater or less degree in different poems. If Yeats's style
seems more effectively talky than that of most other modern
poets, one reason may be that it is actually less so. The traditionally poetic is strongly present; therefore, the deviations toward a
talky style become noticeable and expressive. His versification is
the most obvious example. Without going into innumerable fine
touches for particular effects, of which he was a master, we
might describe the general impression of his versification as a
pleasing awkwardness—pleasing precisely because it expresses
personality and sounds like speech. He rejected free verse, for
he wanted a regular beat in the background as "an unvariable
possibility, an unconscious norm." But he handled his traditional meters with uncommon irregularity. Generally speaking,
the roughening is obtained through frequent spondees, pyrrhic
feet, inverted feet, hovering accents, and unusually late or early
caesuras. His diction is stylized through words and phrases that
are not apt to be part of anybody's speech nowadays: knave,
lout, dolt, aye, cosseting, twelvemonth, "rhymer" for poet, and
"day's declining beam" for sunset. In "Nineteen Hundred and
Nineteen" rhythm compels us to pronounce "wind" with the
long "i" that is traditional when the word is a rhyme word: he
mocks the "great" who toiled

> To leave some monument behind,
> Nor thought of the levelling wind.

Yeats had no reluctance about using the more artificial figures of rhetoric; in "Sailing to Byzantium" one finds oxymoron ("dying generations"), apostrophe ("O sages"), antithesis, and a very rich assonance and alliteration. Tom the Lunatic implausibly concludes his oracular utterance with a chiasmus:

> Nor shall the self-begotten fail
> Though fantastic men suppose
> Building-yard and stormy shore,
> Winding-sheet and swaddling-clothes.

It is because they interplay with such stylizations that his colloquial idioms and homely metaphors come with special force—his "maybe's," his contractions of "is" or "was" to " 's," his exploitations of "dog's day" and "go pack" in "There's not a neighbor left to say / When he finished his dog's day" and "It seems that I must bid the Muse go pack." And, finally, we may also note the fact that he did not always speak as "Yeats" amid the circumstances of his own life. Throughout his last twenty years many poems were composed in accordance with a different convention; they contrast with the poems of excited, personal talk, and each kind highlights the other. As much as he praised and wrote the Romantic poetry of personal utterance, Yeats also asserted and exemplified that a writer of lyrics must speak in some traditional role as lover, seer, madman, shepherd, or beggar. "I commit my emotions," he said near the end of his life, "to shepherds, herdsmen, camel-drivers, learned men, Milton's or Shelley's Platonist. . . . Talk to me of originality and I will turn on you with rage."

THINKING IN ANTITHESES

A further source of the human interest of Yeats's poetry is the many-sided debate with himself that runs through it. To say what the debate is about is not easy. One urgent question was what sort of person to admire, what sort of person to be. He searched for models. His poetry holds up for admiration and criticism a numerous collection, including Lady Gregory, Swift,

Berkeley, Blake, King Lear, Crazy Jane, the wild swans at Coole, and the Chinese carved in lapis lazuli. There are also the many different forms in which he represented himself—the master of occult truth, the "normal active man," the "Wild Old Wicked Man," and the like. All imaged for him one or a few virtues or ideal states. In Yeats's eyes all were admirable. But they were diverse virtues or states and could not all be reconciled. How could he possess the traditionally ordered and ceremonious way of life of the aristocratic Lady Gregory and also the total acceptance of life, even its foulness, embodied in Crazy Jane? How could he pursue both the wisdom that comes with age and the unaging "passion or conquest" of the wild, sexual swans in Coole Park? And how could a seer or Platonist in his tower aspire also to be a "normal active man" abroad in the world? The tendency of Yeats's imagination to strip these figures of natural complexities—to ignore that in actual life seers may also have children and business affairs—gave them greater impact as symbols, but it also made them more difficult to reconcile.

The values Yeats dwelt on as opposites include nature and art, youth and age, body and soul, passion and wisdom, beast and man, creative violence and order, revelation and civilization, poetry and responsibility, and time and eternity. The ultimate antithesis is that between antithesis itself, as the moral structure of human existence, and a realm or state of being in which all antitheses are annihilated. For each of the antithetical terms, moreover, he had many synonyms and symbols. "After Long Silence" concludes with the antithesis of passion and wisdom—

> Bodily decrepitude is wisdom; young
> We loved each other and were ignorant—

and this antithesis inextricably involves that of youth and age. The antithesis of passion and wisdom closely resembles that of power and knowledge in "Leda and the Swan," where in the closing lines the speaker asks whether the raped girl put on the "knowledge" of the swan

> with his power
> Before the indifferent beak could let her drop.

Each antithesis restates the others in a different frame of reference, so that in this Yeatsian context power brings to mind also the connotations of passion, nature, youth, body, beast, and so forth. Combining knowledge and power, the god in the form of a swan is a symbol of antitheses reconciled, and the antithesis Yeats poses at the end of the poem is that between the supernatural and the human. The supernatural is whole or unified being, and the question is whether even in a fleeting moment the human is capable of such completeness.

Antithetical thinking accounts for much of the complexity and intellectual excitement of Yeats's verse. It made all his attitudes ambivalent. Youth was ignorant but passionate. In old age the soul might "clap its hands, and sing," but the heart had grown cold. "The Coming of Wisdom with Time," though published in 1910, is a good example, for it is short and can be discussed as a whole:

> Though leaves are many, the root is one;
> Through all the lying days of my youth
> I swayed my leaves and flowers in the sun;
> Now I may wither into the truth.

Plato's and Yeats's antithesis of the many and the one, of concrete, natural life and the transcendent idea are here associated with the antithesis of youth and age. To grow old is to move from the many to the one, from deception to knowledge or truth. But deception is associated with motion, light, and life, and truth with darkness and death. Yeats himself sought truth in the messages "breathless mouths" brought from the grave, but in this poem the association of truth with darkness and death preserves, nevertheless, its full, ironic force as a grim reversal of what would be expected. The poem presupposes and exemplifies in a metaphor that youth and its rhyming term, "truth," are both ideal values and yet each can be realized only at the cost of the other. The typically Yeatsian premise leads to the bitter ambivalence of "wither into the truth."

YEATS'S LAST DECADE:
"THE HEROIC CRY IN THE MIDST OF DESPAIR"

During the last eleven years of his life, from the publication of *The Tower* in 1928 to his death in 1939, Yeats continued to write as much and as well as ever. Among his notable works of the period are the Crazy Jane sequence, the "Supernatural Songs," "Lapis Lazuli," eight plays, and a revised edition of *A Vision* (1937). His last poem, "The Black Tower," was written seven days before he died.

He was often very ill during these years and death sometimes seemed near. He cultivated in his poetry a heroic pose. Against the failing body and the "approaching night" he celebrated physical and sexual vitality, life in all its coarseness. Because body and soul, passion and wisdom, time and eternity were antithetical, the aging poet felt forced to choose between them and chose, with defiant incongruity, the life of bodily passion, the confusion of the desiring creature in the realm of time. The theme was elaborated in many aspects. He felt that his temptation, as an old man, was "quiet," and in "A Prayer for Old Age" his plea was

> That I may seem, though I die old,
> A foolish, passionate man.

Reincarnation was preferable to Nirvana:

> I am content to live it all again
> And yet again, if it be life to pitch
> Into the frog-spawn of a blind man's ditch,
> A blind man battering blind men.

Yeats often reviled life as he portrayed it, for the worse he painted it, the more triumphant his life-affirming cry. The many poems on sexual themes written in his later years provoked much comment from diverse points of view. His typist refused in tears to copy "Leda and the Swan"; at the other extreme, T. S. Eliot found in "The Spur" an impressive honesty. However else we can explain such poems, they expressed his defiance of old age. The same thing may be said of his many poems praising drunkenness, roaring tinkers, and every sort of turbulence up to the collapse in war and the creative revival of civilizations. They are "all praise of joyous life," as Yeats said of the Crazy Jane poems, even though "it is a dry bone on the shore that sings the praise."

Such commitment to life was heroic, he felt, precisely because it was doomed. He had seen many apparitions in his life, but the worst was himself in old age:

> Fifteen apparitions have I seen;
> The worst a coat upon a coat-hanger.

The "mystery and fright" of the inevitable end was never far from his mind. But a doomed heroism, a hopeless battle to the end, had always been the heroism that moved Yeats most deeply, that most addressed his sense of man's case.

YEATS AND THE MODERN MOVEMENTS IN POETRY

The long career of Yeats is sometimes said to reflect, in its successive phases, the development of modern poetry to the 1930s. The statement is an oversimplification, but a suggestive one. Modernism did not come about in a sudden revolution, but in a difficult, gradual transition. The starting point is the poetry of the later nineteenth century. This is true not as a vague generalization, but as a biographical fact in the lives of the poets who created the modern revolution. Eliot, Pound, Frost, Stevens, and Williams, along with most of the less important poets of their generation, started where Yeats did, as devotees in youth of the English Romantic and mid-Victorian poets and of the generation of English writers—Swinburne, Pater, Rossetti, and Morris—that had come of age in the 1860s and 1870s. Their earliest poems were composed out of feelings and styles they took over from their predecessors.

The first distinct identity Yeats imposed upon his poetry was a Celtic one, and the Celtic movement in Irish literature was a belated Romanticism. In London during the 1890s he was friendly with the avant-garde, the poets of what we have called *ars victrix,* and the attitudes of these poets collided in some ways with his Celtic Romanticism and began to transform it. In his Celtic poetry he wrote ballads of peasant life, he expressed the folk imagination, he described a natural landscape typical of Ireland, he voiced nationalist sentiment, and he spoke, although disguised as "Aedh," of his love for Maud Gonne. But so far as he was a London aesthete, he could not wholly approve of such poetry, for he believed that an artist must work only for the small audience of his peers. Art was the shaping of an impersonal beauty; it had nothing to do with the folk mind, nature, politics, or personal life. In this phase also his development was representative, for the aesthetic movement in British poetry had more influence on the Modernist poets than is usually recognized. Particularly it transmitted a sense of the importance of patient, laborious, and minute craftsmanship and helped spread the notion that the poet is inevitably alienated from his society.

Meanwhile, in his study of the occult Yeats convinced himself that supernatural realities could be invoked through symbols; when in the 1890s Arthur Symons instructed him in the poems and theories of Baudelaire, Mallarmé, Nerval, Verlaine, and other French poets, he saw a coincidence between their ideas and his own. He was convinced that he could see a new movement developing in the arts. Literature since the *Kalevala,* he said, had been descending the stairway toward ordinary reality, but the direction was now reversing itself and poets were abandoning realism for the evocation of "essences and pure ideas." Yeats called this the "symbolical movement" and explained that symbolical art would be evocative, subtle, and remote. Its rhythms would be wavering, unemphatic, and organic; its ancient symbols full of secret meaning for the adept. The self-conscious manipulation of symbols in twentieth-century literature developed from multiple sources, and Yeats was not an important, independent source for most poets. Nevertheless, his theory and practice of symbolism kept him in touch with one of the central tendencies in twentieth-century literature.

The new century was not far advanced when the praiser of unemphatic rhythms decided that "we possess nothing but the will" and must fly from the hollow land of sentiment and vague desire. He cultivated the homely phrases and the rhythms of the spoken language. He crowed in triumph when, revising an early play, he could work "creaking shoes" and "liquorice-root" into "what had been a very abstract passage." He resolved to "walk naked," to articulate experience and feeling without robing them in myth and symbol; his lyrics descended the stairway, after all, and dwelt in zest or scorn on actual existence. The transformation was not total. Yeats did not begin to praise Ibsen. He was still repelled by the "mechanical" logic of Shaw, who once appeared to him in a dream as a sewing machine, clicking and shining. He did not abate his scorn of science, newspapers, materialism, and the middle class. In his personal life, as opposed to his lyrics, he remained devoted as ever to the occult and symbolical. Nevertheless, the change that now took place in his poetry makes it possible to align him with such other figures as Frost and Hardy and to say that in these three poets a typical mode of the age—what I have called the reflective, vernacular poem of actual life—reached its finest development. Such poetry was often written by some of the Georgians also, and it has continued as a live mode in England to the present day.

Between 1912 and 1916 Yeats saw much of Ezra Pound, who included Yeatsian doctrine in the principles of "efficient" writing that he spread abroad as Imagism. Pound revealed to Yeats that his rejection of poetic diction and dreamy sentiment was "modern." He told Pound of the existence of Joyce and doubtless heard much from Pound of Eliot, Wyndham Lewis, Gaudier-Brzeska, the Image, and the Vortex. Although interested in these figures and movements, Yeats kept his humorous distance and continued to prefer the Pre-Raphaelites to the young Modernists. Nevertheless, Pound helped him to reduce still further the density of abstract terms (beauty) and conventional metaphors in his poetry. Although Yeats never shared the resolve of the Modernists to represent the contemporary, urban world, he put medieval and legendary Ireland behind him after 1900 and forced himself to articulate a wide range of "unpoetic" emotions in spare, frank language. These transformations repelled some former admirers but extorted praise from younger poets. "There is a new robustness," said Pound in reviewing *Responsibilities* (1914), and "there is the tooth of satire which is, in Mr. Yeats's case, too good a tooth to keep hidden."

In the 1920s and 1930s Yeats, now in his fifties and sixties, remained a contemporary. His work was of such kind and rank that he must be placed among the greatest writers of the twentieth century, with Joyce, Mann, Proust, Kafka, Rilke, and Eliot. He shared their ironical vision, for he contemplated human life in relation to remote, largely unknowable realities that wholly or partly determine individual fate and history. And yet, although the human so often seems dwindled and futile in his perspective, the characters and lives of men and women take on depth and significance by becoming symbolic or mythical. Sometimes in these years his poems dwell on the shocking, horrible, or grotesque, particularly in connection with his sense of the violence of history. The vision of life that dominates his poetry in this period may best be characterized as tragic irony. It is an ironic vision for the reason given: he sees that the structure of existence will inevitably defeat human wish and effort. It is also tragic because, whether his protagonists are Crazy Jane, Mohini Chatterjee, Rocky Face, Ribh, Tom the Lunatic, The Wild Old Wicked Man, or Yeats himself, we feel that they are in some sense above us, richer in insight, courage, or experience. It is the persistence and depth of his Romantic belief in the possibility of human greatness that most essentially distinguishes Yeats from the other Modernist writers we mentioned.

ACKNOWLEDGMENTS

Grateful acknowledgment is made for the use of material from the following:

Richard Aldington, *Collected Poems,* 1929; by permission of George Allen and Unwin, Ltd.

Hilaire Belloc, *Complete Verse,* 1970; "George" by permission of Duckworth and Company, Ltd. and Alfred A. Knopf, Inc.; other materials reprinted by permission of A. D. Peters and Co., Ltd.

Stephen Vincent Benét, from *Ballads and Poems* by Stephen Vincent Benét. Copyright 1931 by Stephen Vincent Benét. Copyright © 1959 by Rosemary Carr Benét. Reprinted by permission of Holt, Rinehart and Winston, Publishers, and Brandt and Brandt. From *John Brown's Body* by Stephen Vincent Benét, Holt, Rinehart and Winston, Inc.; Copyright, 1927, 1928, by Stephen Vincent Benét; Copyright renewed, 1955, 1956, by Rosemary Carr Benét. Reprinted by permission of Brandt & Brandt.

Gwendolyn Bennett, in *American Negro Poetry,* Revised Edition, ed. Arna Bontemps, Farrar, Straus & Giroux, Inc., 1974.

Laurence Binyon, *Selected Poems,* The Macmillan Co., 1922; by permission of the British Library Board.

Edmund Blunden, *Poems of Many Years,* 1957; reprinted by permission of A. D. Peters and Co., Ltd.

Maxwell Bodenheim, *Advice,* Alfred A. Knopf, 1920.

William Stanley Braithwaite, from *The Book of American Negro Poetry,* edited by James Weldon Johnson, Harcourt, Brace and Co., 1922.

Robert Bridges, *The Poetical Works of Robert Bridges,* 1953; by permission of the Oxford University Press, Oxford.

Sterling A. Brown, *Southern Road,* Harcourt Brace Jovanovich, Inc., 1932.

Joseph Campbell, *The Poems of Joseph Campbell,* 1963; by permission of S. Campbell.

Bliss Carman, "A Vagabond Song," *Poems,* 1931; by permission of Dodd, Mead & Company. Reprinted by special permission of the Bliss Carman Trust, The University of New Brunswick, Canada.

Padraic Colum, from *The Poet's Circuits,* Oxford University Press, 1960; by permission of Oxford University Press.

Countee Cullen, *On These I Stand: An Anthology of the Best Poems of Countee Cullen,* Harper & Row, 1947; by permission of Harper & Row.

W. H. Davies, *The Complete Poems of W. H. Davies,* 1934, Copyright © 1963 by Jonathan Cape Ltd; used by permission of Jonathan Cape, Ltd, Wesleyan University Press, and Mrs. H. M. Davies.

Walter de la Mare, *Winged Chariot,* 1951; by permission of The Literary Trustees of Walter de la Mare, and The Society of Authors as their representative.

Hilda Doolittle, *The Collected Poems of H. D.* Copyright 1925, 1953 by Norman Holmes Pearson; reprinted by permission of New Directions Publishing Corporation for Professor Pearson.

T. S. Eliot, from *Collected Poems, 1909–1962;* copyright, 1936, by Harcourt Brace Jovanovich, Inc.; copyright © 1963, 1964 by T. S. Eliot. Reprinted by permission of Harcourt Brace Jovanovich, Inc., and Faber and Faber, Ltd.

Hugh I'Anson Fausset, Sonnet LVI from *The Spirit of Love,* Methuen & Co., Ltd., 1921.

Arthur Davison Ficke, *Selected Poems,* 1926; copyright 1926 by George H. Doran Co., by permission of Doubleday & Company.

John Gould Fletcher, from *Selected Poems,* 1938. Copyright 1938 by John Gould Fletcher. Copyright © 1966 by Charlie May Fletcher. Reprinted by permission of Holt, Rinehart and Winston, Publishers.

John Freeman, *Collected Poems,* 1928; reprinted by permission of A. D. Peters & Co., Ltd.

Robert Frost, from *The Poetry of Robert Frost,* edited by Edward Connery Lathem. Copyright 1916, 1923, 1930, 1939, © 1969 by Holt, Rinehart and Winston. Copyright 1936, 1942, 1944, 1951, © 1958 by Robert Frost. Copyright © 1964, 1967, 1970 by Lesley Frost Ballantine. Reprinted by permission of Holt, Rinehart and Winston, Publishers, the Estate of Robert Frost, and Jonathan Cape Ltd. From *Selected Letters of Robert Frost,* edited by Lawrance Thompson. Copyright © 1964 by Lawrance Thompson and Holt, Rinehart and Winston. Reprinted by permission of Holt, Rinehart and Winston, Publishers, the Estate of Robert Frost, and Jonathan Cape, Limited.

Wilfrid Gibson, *Collected Poems,* Macmillan and Co., Ltd., 1929, and *The Golden Room: Poems, 1925–1927,* Macmillan and Co., Ltd., 1928; by permission of Mr. Michael Gibson, Macmillan, London and Basingstoke.

Gerald Gould, *Collected Poems,* Victor Gollancz, Ltd., 1929; by permission of Michael Ayrton.

Robert Graves, *Collected Poems,* Cassell and Co., 1975; by permission of Robert Graves.

Louise Imogen Guiney, *Happy Ending,* 1927; by permission of Houghton Mifflin Company.

Ivor Gurney, *Poems,* 1954, by permission of Hutchinson Publishing Group, Ltd.; *Severn & Somme,* 1917, by permission of Sidgwick & Jackson, Ltd.

Thomas Hardy, *Collected Poems,* 1928; Copyright 1925 by Macmillan Publishing Co., Inc. Reprinted by permission of the Trustees of the Hardy Estate; Macmillan, London and Basingstoke; The Macmillan Company of Canada Limited; and The Macmillan Publishing Co., Inc. *The Dynasts,* 1924, by permission of the Trustees of the Hardy Estate; Macmillan, London and Basingstoke; and Macmillan Publishing Co., Inc.

Roy Helton, from "Old Christmas," in *Lonesome Water.* Copyright 1930 by Harper and Row, Publishers, Inc., renewed 1958 by Roy Helton; reprinted by permission of the publisher.

F.R. Higgins, *The Gap of Brightness,* Macmillan & Co. Ltd., 1940; *The Dark Breed,* Macmillan & Co., Ltd., 1927; by permission of Mrs. May Higgins.

Robert Hillyer, "Night Piece," "The Scar," and "A Letter to Robert Frost," from *Collected Poems,* Alfred A. Knopf, 1961; copyright 1961 by Robert Hillyer; by permission of Alfred A. Knopf, Inc.

Ralph Hodgson, *Collected Poems,* Macmillan, 1961; copyright 1917 by Macmillan Publishing Co., Inc.; renewed 1945 by Ralph Hodgson. Reprinted by permission of Macmillan, London and Basingstoke, Macmillan Publishing Co. of Canada, and Macmillan Publishing Co., Inc.

A. E. Housman, from "A Shropshire Lad"—Authorized Edition—from *The Collected Poems of A. E. Housman.* Copyright 1939, 1940, ©1965 by Holt, Rinehart and Winston. Copyright © 1967, 1968 by Robert E. Symons. Reprinted by permission of Holt, Rinehart and Winston, Publishers, and The Society of Authors as the literary representative of the Estate of A. E. Housman and Jonathan Cape, Ltd., publishers of A. E. Housman's *Collected Poems.*

Langston Hughes, *Montage of a Dream Deferred,* 1951; copyright 1951 by Langston Hughes; reprinted by permission of Harold Ober Associates, Inc. *The Dream Keeper and Other Poems,* 1932; by permission of Alfred A. Knopf, Inc.

Orrick Johns, *Asphalt and Other Poems,* Alfred A. Knopf, Inc., 1917; *Black Branches,* Macmillan Publishing Co., Inc., 1920.

Fenton Johnson, *The Book of American Negro Poetry,* ed. James Weldon Johnson, Harcourt, Brace and Co., 1931.

James Weldon Johnson, *God's Trombones,* 1932, copyright 1927 by The Viking Press, Inc.; copyright © renewed 1955 by Grace Nail Johnson. Reprinted by permission of The Viking Press.

Thomas S. Jones, *The Rose-Jar,* George William Browning, 1906.

from *Collected Poems,* Harper & Row; copyright, 1923, 1951, by Edna St. Vincent Millay and Norma Millay Ellis. Other poems from *Collected Poems,* Harper & Row; copyright, 1928, 1955, by Edna St. Vincent Millay and Norma Millay Ellis.

Harold Monro, *Collected Poems,* 1970; by permission of Gerald Duckworth and Co., Ltd.

Marianne Moore, "Roses Only," in *Selected Poems,* 1935. Copyright 1935 by Marianne Moore, renewed 1963 by Marianne Moore and T. S. Eliot. Reprinted by permission of Macmillan Publishing Co., Inc., and Faber and Faber Ltd., London, publisher of *The Complete Poems of Marianne Moore.* Other poems: copyright 1935 by Marianne Moore, renewed 1963 by Marianne Moore and T. S. Eliot; copyright 1941 by Marianne Moore, renewed 1969 by Marianne Moore; copyright 1944 by Marianne Moore, renewed 1972 by Marianne Moore; copyright 1951 by Marianne Moore—all from *Collected Poems* and reprinted by permission of the Macmillan Publishing Co. and Faber and Faber Ltd. "Combat Cultural" and "The Indian," copyright © 1959 by Marianne Moore; reprinted by permission of The Viking Press and Faber and Faber Ltd.

T. Sturge Moore, *The Poems of T. Sturge Moore,* Macmillan, 1932; by permission of Macmillan, London and Basingstoke.

Alfred Noyes, *Collected Poems,* 1963; by permission of John Murray Ltd., J. B. Lippincot Co., and Hugh Noyes Esq.

Wilfrid Owen, *The Collected Poems of Wilfrid Owen,* ed. C. Day Lewis, 1964; copyright Chatto and Windus, Ltd. 1946, © 1963. Reprinted by permission of The Owen Estate, Chatto and Windus, and New Directions Publishing Corporation.

Eden Phillpotts, *A Hundred Sonnets,* Ernest Benn, 1929; by permission of Ernest Benn Limited.

Ezra Pound, *Collected Shorter Poems,* 1968; reprinted by permission of Faber & Faber Ltd. *Personae;* copyright 1926 by Ezra Pound; reprinted by permission of New Directions Publishing Corporation. *The Cantos,* 1956; copyright 1934, 1937, 1948 by Ezra Pound; seven lines only from early version of Canto II—copyright 1917, 1934 by Ezra Pound; reprinted by permission of New Directions Publishing Corporation and Faber & Faber Ltd. *Lustra,* 1917; by permission of New Directions Publishing Corporation and Faber & Faber Ltd.

Herbert Read, *Collected Poems,* copyright 1966; by permission of the publisher Horizon Press, New York, and Faber & Faber Ltd.

Lizette Woodworth Reese, *Wild Cherry,* The Norman, Remington Co., Baltimore, 1923.

Edwin Arlington Robinson, *Collected Poems,* 1937. "Richard Cory" and "Credo" are reprinted by permission of Charles Scribner's Sons from *The Children of the Night* by Edwin Arlington Robinson. Lines from "Miniver Cheevy" are reprinted by permission of Charles

Scribner's Sons from *The Town Down the River* by Edwin Arlington Robinson. Copyright 1907 Charles Scribner's Sons.

Isaac Rosenberg, *The Collected Poems of Isaac Rosenberg,* ed. Gordon Bottomley and Denys Harding, 1949; by permission of The Author's Literary Estate and Chatto & Windus: © Literary Executors of Mrs. A. Wynick, 1937, and Schocken Books, Inc. "August 1914," copyright 1937 by Mrs. A. Wynick.

George Russell (AE), *Collected Poems,* Macmillan, 1926; by permission of A. M. Heath & Company Ltd. as Agents for the Estate of George Russell.

Carl Sandburg, "Chicago," "Working Girls," "The Right to Grief," "Fish Crier," "The Shovel Man," "Buffalo Dusk," "Jack," "Cool Toombs," "Harrison Street Court," "Alley Rats," "Happiness," "Nocturne in a Deserted Brickyard," "Jazz Fantasia," from *Complete Poems,* 1970; by permission of Harcourt Brace Jovanovich, Inc.

George Santayana, *Poems,* 1923; by permission of Charles Scribner's Sons and Constable & Co., Ltd.

Siegfried Sassoon, *Collected Poems,* 1961, copyright 1918 by E. P. Dutton and Co.; copyright renewed 1946 by Siegfried Sassoon. All rights reserved. Reprinted by permission of The Viking Press and G. T. Sassoon.

Edith Sitwell, *Collected Poems,* 1968. Copyright © 1968 by The Vanguard Press, Inc.; copyright © 1949, 1953, 1954, 1959, 1962, 1963 by Dame Edith Sitwell. Reprinted by permission of The Vanguard Press, Inc., and David Higham Associates Ltd.

Sir Osbert Sitwell, *Argonaut and Juggernaut,* 1919; by permission of Gerald Duckworth and Co., Ltd.

James Stephens, *Collected Poems,* 1926; copyright 1912 by Macmillan Publishing Co., Inc., renewed 1940 by James Stephens. Reprinted by permission of Mrs. Iris Wise, Macmillan, London and Basingstoke, The Macmillan Company of Canada Ltd., and Macmillan Publishing Co., Inc.

Wallace Stevens, *The Collected Poems of Wallace Stevens,* 1955; copyright 1923, 1931, 1935, 1936, 1937, 1942, 1943, 1944, 1945, 1946, 1947, 1948, 1949, 1950, 1951, 1952, 1954 by Wallace Stevens; reprinted by permission of Alfred A. Knopf, Inc., and Faber and Faber Ltd. *Letters of Wallace Stevens,* ed. Holly Stevens, 1972; by permission of Alfred A. Knopf, Inc. "Carnet de Voyage," IV, originally published in Robert Buttel, *Wallace Stevens: The Making of Harmonium,* Princeton University Press, 1967; reprinted by permission of Miss Holly Stevens.

Jesse Stuart, "Back Where I Belong," published in *The Progressive Farmer,* May 1956, and republished in *Hold April,* 1962. Reprinted by permission of Jesse Stuart and *The Progressive Farmer.*

Arthur Symons, Poems, 2 Vols., 1916, by permission of William Heinemann, Ltd., and Dodd, Mead & Company.

Sara Teasdale, "I Shall Not Care," Copyright 1915 by Macmillan Publishing Co., Inc.; renewed 1943 by Mamie T. Wheless, "Let It Be Forgotten" and "The Long Hill," Copyright 1920 by Macmillan Publishing Co., Inc.; renewed 1948 by Mamie T. Wheless, "Arcturus in Autumn," Copyright 1926 by Macmillan Publishing Co., Inc.; renewed 1954 by Mamie T. Wheless—all from *The Collected Poems of Sara Teasdale,* 1937; reprinted by permission of The Macmillan Publishing Co., Inc.

Jean Toomer, *Cane,* University Place Press, New York; Copyright 1951 by Liveright Publishing Corp.; reprinted by permission of Liveright, Publishers, N.Y.

Ridgely Torrence, "The Son," from *Poems,* 1941, Copyright 1925 by Macmillan Publishing Co., Inc., renewed 1952 by Olivia H. D. Torrence; by permission of Macmillan Publishing Co., Inc.

W. J. Turner, *Selected Poems* (*1916–1936*), Oxford University Press, 1939.

Sir William Watson, *Selected Poems,* Thornton Butterworth Ltd., 1928.

William Carlos Williams, *Collected Earlier Poems,* copyright 1938 by New Directions Publishing Corporation; reprinted by permission of New Directions Publishing Corporation. *The Selected Letters of William Carlos Williams,* copyright © 1957 by William Carlos Williams; Reprinted by permission of New Directions Publishing Corporation, for Mrs. W. C. Williams.

Theodore Wratislaw, *Aesthetes and Decadents of the* 1890's: *An Anthology,* ed. Karl Beckson, Random House, 1966.

Elinor Wylie, *Collected Poems of Elinor Wylie,* Knopf, 1933; by permission of Alfred A. Knopf, Inc.

W. B. Yeats, *The Variorum Edition of the Poems of W. B. Yeats,* ed. by Peter Allt and Russell K. Alspach, Macmillan Co., New York, 1957. Copyrights 1906 by Macmillan Publishing Co., Inc., renewed 1934 by William Butler Yeats; 1912 by Macmillan Publishing Co., Inc., renewed 1940 by Bertha Georgie Yeats; 1916 by Macmillan Publishing Co., Inc., renewed 1944 by Bertha Georgie Yeats; 1919 by Macmillan Publishing Co., Inc., renewed 1947 by Bertha Georgie Yeats; 1924 by Macmillan Publishing Co., Inc., renewed 1952 by Bertha Georgie Yeats; 1928 by Macmillan Publishing Co., Inc., renewed 1956 by Georgie Yeats; 1933 by Macmillan Publishing Co., Inc., renewed 1961 by Bertha Georgie Yeats; 1934 by Macmillan Publishing Co., Inc., renewed 1962 by Bertha Georgie Yeats; 1940 by Georgie Yeats, renewed 1968 by Bertha Georgie Yeats, Michael Butler Yeats, and Anne Yeats. Reprinted by permission of Macmillan Publishing Co., Inc., M. B. Yeats, Miss Anne Yeats, and The Macmillan Company, London and Basingstoke.

Andrew Young, *Complete Poems,* ed. Leonard Clark; by permission of Martin Secker & Warburg Limited.

INDEX

Abercrombie, Lascelles, 139, 191, *194–96,* 197, 206, 209, 213, 229
Adams, Henry, 84
Adams, John, 455, 484, 485
Aeschylus, 485
Aesthetic movement, 7, 10–11, 25, 32, *33–37,* 300; reactions against, 60–62, 64, 75, 76, 77, 79, 100, 138, 139–40, 194, 258
"Agreeable," the, in poetry, 4–5, 170, 177–78
Aiken, Conrad, 85, 104, 336, *378–80,* 441, 495, 496
Aldington, Richard, 272, 311, 327, 330–35, *338–39,* 344, 346, 374, 420, 437, 462, 466, 468, 528
Aldrich, Thomas Bailey, 107
Allen, Hervey, 376, 387
Altgeld, John P., 351, 357
American poetry, 1890–1912: isolation of poets, 85–89; innocence of approach, 87–90; preoccupation with England, 90–94; search for identity of, 92–94; recoil of from contemporary America, 94–96
Anderson, Sherwood, 355, 356
Andrews, Lancelot, 525
Anthologies, 108; effect of reading on American poets, 86–87; Binyon's

The Golden Treasury of Modern Lyrics (1925), 170; *Georgian Poetry,* 203–06; *Des Imagistes,* 331; *Some Imagist Poets,* 331; *The New Poetry* (1917), ed. Monroe and Corbin, 369; *Modern American Poetry* and *Modern British Poetry,* ed. Untermeyer, 369–70; *Caroling Dusk,* ed. Cullen, 407; *Wheels,* ed. E. Sitwell, 428
Arensberg, Walter Conrad, 527–28, 530, 532–34
Armstrong, Martin, 420, 421
Arnold, Sir Edwin, 8, 20
Arnold, Matthew, 15, 16, 24, 25, 41, 95, 173, 300, 310, 340, 515, 524–25
Art for art's sake. *See* Aesthetic movement
Atlantic Monthly, 97, 98, 320, 332
Auden, W. H., 7, 8, 128, 163, 233; on Frost, 238; 278, 279, 285, 346, 418, 420, 555, 591
Audience for poetry: in 1890s, 12–14; Masefield on, 79–81; and Modernist idiom, 129–30; expansion of in England after 1911, 141; expansion of in America after 1912, 317–24
Augustine, Saint, 505

Edwardians

Yeats
Hardy

Kipling
Chesterton
Masefield
A. Noyes

Beautiful + agreeable:

Robert Bridges
Laurence Binyon
Walter de la Mare

Georgians

Rupert Brooke
Gibson
Davies
Hodgson
David Thomas
Blunden
etc.

W. Owen   }
Isaac Rosenberg } War
Siegfried Sassoon } poets
                  (+ Brooke)